The Devil and Demonism in

This original book examines the c … veen the Reformation and the end of the … ks at the ways in which beliefs about the … n affairs changed as a consequence of the Reformation, … s, literary and political culture. He moves away from the established … ology as a component of the belief in witchcraft and examines a wide range of religious and political milieux, such as practical divinity, the interiority of Puritan godliness, anti-popery, polemic and propaganda, and popular culture. The concept of the Devil which emerged from the Reformation had a profound impact on the beliefs and practices of committed Protestants, but it also influenced both the political debates of the reigns of Elizabeth I, James I and Charles I, and popular culture more widely.

NATHAN JOHNSTONE teaches history at Canterbury Christ Church University.

Cambridge Studies in Early Modern British History

Series editors

ANTHONY FLETCHER

Emeritus Professor of English Social History, University of London

JOHN GUY

Fellow, Clare College, Cambridge

JOHN MORRILL

Professor of British and Irish History, University of Cambridge, and Vice-Master of Selwyn College

This is a series of monographs and studies covering many aspects of the history of the British Isles between the late fifteenth century and the early eighteenth century. It includes the work of established scholars and pioneering work by a new generation of scholars. It includes both reviews and revisions of major topics and books which open up new historical terrain or which reveal startling new perspectives on familiar subjects. All the volumes set detailed research into our broader perspectives and the books are intended for the use of students as well as of their teachers.

For a list of titles in the series, see end of book.

THE DEVIL AND DEMONISM IN EARLY MODERN ENGLAND

NATHAN JOHNSTONE
Canterbury Christ Church University

CAMBRIDGE
UNIVERSITY PRESS

CAMBRIDGE UNIVERSITY PRESS
Cambridge, New York, Melbourne, Madrid, Cape Town, Singapore, São Paulo, Delhi

Cambridge University Press
The Edinburgh Building, Cambridge CB2 8RU, UK

Published in the United States of America by Cambridge University Press, New York

www.cambridge.org
Information on this title: www.cambridge.org/9780521120548

First published 2006
This digitally printed version 2009

A catalogue record for this publication is available from the British Library

ISBN 978-0-521-80236-9 hardback
ISBN 978-0-521-12054-8 paperback

For Pat and Ian Johnstone

CONTENTS

Acknowledgements *page* ix

1 Introduction 1
The English Reformation and the Protestant Devil 1
The historiography of the Devil 8
The Devil and 'the persecuting society': witches, Puritanism and despair 12

2 The synagogue of Satan: anti-Catholicism, false doctrine and the construction of contrariety 27
The Devil as fact: the Protestant perception of diabolic power 28
The Devil's church: the construction of contrariety 41

3 Temptation: the Protestant dynamic of diabolic agency and the resurgence of clerical mediation 60
Liturgy, theology and conduct literature 62
Resisting Satan: prayer and dialogue 83
The Protestant ministry and the mediation of resistance 95

4 Satan and the godly in early modern England 107
The context of demonism and models of temptation 108
Cyclical affliction and spiritual progression: the experience and rationalisation of temptation 118
Diabolic affliction and godly community 135

5 Incarnate devils: crime narratives, demonisation and audience empathy 142
Reporting Satan's agency: crime and the pulp press 144
Components of the Devil's kingdom 150
Devilish humans and audience empathy 153
Temptation and the physical Devil 170

6 'What concord hath Christ with Belial?': de facto satanism and the temptation of the body politic, 1570–1640 175
The Elizabethan religious controversies and the concept of de facto satanism 177
The divine monarch and the Devil: Elizabeth I, James I and Catholic treachery 184
The divine Charles and the Devil: diabolic subversion and the language of political opposition 196

7 'Grand Pluto's Progress through Great Britaine': the Civil War and the zenith of satanic politics 213
'Sworne Sword-men of the devill': diabolic service in parliamentary propaganda 217
'Hell's Black Parliament': demonism, rebellion and diabolic government in royalist propaganda 236

8 'The Devil's Alpha and Omega': temptation at the cutting edge of faith in the Civil War and the Interregnum 250
The synagogue of Satan revisited: the Devil turned Independent 253
The interpretation of sectarianism in the 1650s 265

Conclusion 286

Bibliography 294
Index 326

ACKNOWLEDGEMENTS

I have been fortunate to be able to test out my ideas on a number of scholars who have, without exception, been generous both with their enthusiasm and critical judgement. Thanks go to Peter Lake, Anthony Fletcher, Marion Gibson, Nick Vincent, Stephen Hipkin, Grayson Ditchfield, Steven Rowlstone, Tim Ling, Mark Arvanigian, Andrew Palmer and Peter Davie. My greatest scholarly debt by far is to Jackie Eales, who as my doctoral supervisor, and later colleague, has been a mentor in the truest sense of the word. This book is undoubtedly much the better for our many discussions of its subject and her careful reading of numerous drafts, and I am deeply grateful. Whilst I feel certain that I am not the first author to have tried the patience of his editors, that of mine at Cambridge – William Davies and then Michael Watson, and the series panel – is apparently boundless, and I should like to express my thanks.

The long gestation of this book would have been made far more onerous without the presence of friends, family and colleagues who provided both practical help and professional advice, and vital distractions as required. I must especially thank Zafer Djabri, Steve Westlake, Brett Mills, Matt Walter, Trevor Grimshaw, Wayne Veck, Tom Hennessy, Nigel Harwood, Tim and Ruth Ling, Andrew and Elizabeth Bartlett, Philip Hastie, Cecilio Lopez, Brian Capper, Ge Jin, Matthew Johnstone, Sarah and Mark Ratcliff, Mike Chandler, Sean Greenwood, Tony McCulloch, Roger Wells and Alfred Smyth. My deep gratitude goes also to Ning Qiuhong, without whose support the Ph.D. on which this book is based could not have been completed.

My earliest and greatest debts are to my parents, who from the first expressions of my aspiration to be an historian were unceasingly supportive, and who never once told me to 'get a proper job'. Its subject matter may not be the most convenient for such a purpose, but it is to them, with love and gratitude, that this book is dedicated. Finally, I must express my deepest appreciation to Esther Snell, whose love and encouragement sustained me through the preparation of the book, and who made finishing it possible.

1

Introduction

THE ENGLISH REFORMATION AND THE PROTESTANT DEVIL

Baudelaire's famous comment – that the Devil's best trick was to convince mankind that he did not exist – was written in the hindsight of the scientific revolution and the Enlightenment that were believed to have rendered Satan a rather unworthy hangover from a more primitive age.[1] Yet for all its contemporary novelty and wit, it gave expression to a far older concern over Satan's effective agency. Take away the connotations of his non-existence (made possible by the late seventeenth-century fashion for scepticism) and the same concern can be found underlining much of the religious and moral polemic produced during the English Reformation and its aftermath. Sixteenth- and seventeenth-century Protestants in particular were afraid, not that the Devil might convince man that he did not exist, but that he would persuade them that he was absent from their everyday lives.

In England the concept of the Devil underwent a very subtle process of cultural change in the hands of the Protestant reforming clergy. They were convinced that Satan offered an intimate threat to every Christian, especially when his agency was hidden from perception by the physical senses. This conviction was driven equally by a sense of personal danger in the face of demonic power, and by a belief that diabolism lay concealed behind the superficial piety of the Catholic church. The reformers did not wish to overturn traditional belief in the Devil as they did more high-profile aspects of Catholic religion such as eucharistic piety or the doctrine of good works, and hence there was no explicit reform of demonological theology. Instead a characteristically Protestant demonism emerged from a subtle realignment of

[1] 'Mes chers frères, n'oubliez jamais, quand vous entendrez vanter le progrès des lumières, que la plus belle ruse du diable est de vous persuader qu'il n'existe pas' ('My dear brothers never forget, when you hear the progress of the Enlightenment praised, that the Devil's cleverest ploy is to persuade you that he does not exist'): 'Le joueur généreux', in *Le Spleen de Paris*, quoted in J. B. Russell, *Mephistopheles: The Devil in the Modern World* (Ithaca and London, 1986), p. 206.

emphasis rather than an open attack upon tradition. The central focus of this change was to emphasise the Devil's power of temptation, especially his ability to enter directly into the mind and plant thoughts within it that led people to sin. As a result of the fall of Adam, everyone was born spiritually corrupted. This stock of inbred evil was supremely malleable under the Devil's influence, and the effect of temptation was akin, in the words of the Cambridge theologian William Perkins, to putting a match to gunpowder.[2] Such power had long been part of the Devil's remit,[3] but Protestant theologians now elevated internal temptation into the most important and dangerous aspect of his agency. Subversion was now the Devil's greatest threat – of the pious aspirations of the individual Christian, and of the godly nation as a whole.

This change of emphasis had profound consequences for reformed liturgical and devotional practice. Most striking was the reform of the baptism ceremony that took place between 1549 and 1552.[4] By the publication of the second Edwardian prayer book the rite had been stripped of the exorcism that had assumed that all children were born possessed by Satan. Christian initiation, which in the Sarum rite had been assumed to involve a tangible victory over the Devil, was now understood to draw the individual into a life of perpetual struggle with the demonic.[5] Liturgical reform did not seek to deprive Satan of his power by implying that clerical mediation was unnecessary; rather it was informed by a belief that Catholic ceremonial diverted attention from the real site of conflict with the diabolic. The Sarum baptism, and ceremonies such as Candlemas and Rogationtide, concentrated on the external protection offered by the priest's mediation of divine power, and by holy artefacts and saintly intercession.[6] Protestants instead advocated a personal engagement with the demonic within the conscience, and they stressed that every individual was ultimately responsible for resisting Satan's influence.

[2] William Perkins, *The Combat between Christ and the Divell displayed*, in *The Works of … William Perkins* (London, 3 vols., 1616–18) vol. III, p. 376.

[3] Norman Cohn, *Europe's Inner Demons: An Enquiry Inspired by the Great Witch-Hunt* (London, 1975), p. 73; Fernando Cervantes, 'The Devil's Encounter with America', in J. Barry, M. Hester and G. Roberts (eds.), *Witchcraft in Early Modern Europe: Studies in Culture and Belief* (Cambridge, 1996), p. 128.

[4] *The booke of the common prayer, and administration of the sacramentes* (London, 1549), fols. 135–52v; and *The Boke of common praier, and administracion of the sacramentes* (London, 1552), sigs. P4–Q2; on the reform of baptism see Keith Thomas, *Religion and the Decline of Magic: Studies in Popular Beliefs in Sixteenth- and Seventeenth-Century England* (London, 1971; reprinted, 1991), pp. 62–4; Eamon Duffy, *The Stripping of the Altars: Traditional Religion in England 1400–1580* (New Haven and London, 1992), pp. 280–1, 473.

[5] The Sarum ritual is available in English in J. D. C. Fisher, *Christian Initiation: Baptism in the Medieval West. A Study in the Disintegration of the Primitive Rite of Initiation* (London, 1965), pp. 158–79.

[6] Duffy, *The Stripping of the Altars*, pp. 280–3.

The Protestant ministry took on a central role as adepts able to aid men in warding off the Devil. The Reformation encompassed a fundamental challenge to the spiritual power of the clergy, who were stripped of their ability to mediate between God and humanity in the Mass.[7] But in one sense the reformation of the clergy turned full circle as the Protestant ministry shaped a role for themselves as the mediators, not of preternatural power, but of support for the individual in his personal battle with Satan. Emphasis on struggle and resistance imbued demonic temptation with a soteriological significance. Increasingly it was understood to be an internal dialogue in which Satan sought to undermine pious instincts by appealing to man's natural corruption, and, most threateningly, by introducing doubts as to election.[8] Protestant divines recognised how profoundly disturbing temptation might be, and they set parameters on the experience in their sermons and conduct books. God permitted temptation as a test of faith but would never allow a godly man to be tempted beyond his endurance. In effect temptation provided an opportunity for the practice, and the display, of trust in God above normal piety. Thus, for the self-conscious godly, Satan's attention to drawing them away from their proper devotions might indicate that they were among his special targets, whilst their response could be measured for its godliness against that set out in devotional literature. Prayer, faith and a sound understanding of the meaning of temptation became the most important weapons an individual could deploy against the Devil. In ideal at least, an educated Protestant ministry was the natural repository of these assets. Their sermons and conduct books rehearsed the arguments that could be employed against the Devil when he tempted men to sin or to despair. Ministers became personally involved in mediating the correct understanding of temptation to their parishioners, encouraging them to see their doubts as a demonic intrusion within their consciousness and providing them with doctrinal tenets and scriptural authorities to counter the Devil's assaults. This ideal found wide expression in accounts of death-bed sufferings and possession, in which struggle with the demonic was increasingly presented as a literal debate over soteriological truth carried out between the Devil and an expert minister. By the later seventeenth century, when Samuel Clarke

[7] For a discussion of the spiritual power of the medieval clergy and the effect of the Reformation, see Thomas, *Religion and the Decline of Magic*, chapters 2 and 3, and especially the conclusions on pp. 87–9.

[8] On religious despair more generally, see John Stackniewski, *The Persecutory Imagination: English Puritanism and the Literature of Religious Despair* (Oxford, 1991); Paul S. Seaver, *Wallington's World: A Puritan Artisan in Seventeenth-Century London* (Stanford, Calif., 1985), pp. 14–44; Michael Macdonald, *Mystical Bedlam: Madness, Anxiety, and Healing in Seventeenth-Century England* (Cambridge, 1981), pp. 220–2.

was collecting his 'godly lives', the minister as disputant with Satan had become an important part of the imagery of the Puritan 'hero'.[9]

More widely, temptation provided a dynamic by which to define the character, motivations and mentality of identifiable groups of satanic agents who were believed to act out of a shared interest with the Devil and his aims. Satan's kingdom was more a demographic than a physical reality, and every individual who allowed temptation to conflate his own natural corruption was considered to be one of its components. The term 'synagogue of Satan' – derived from the denunciation of the Jewish church in the Book of Revelation – was applied to the Catholic church by generations of Protestant polemicists. It expressed the insidious subversion Protestants believed to lie behind Catholic false doctrine and empty piety – a church that appeared Christian was in fact its opposite. More loosely the term was applied to other demonic agencies that were assumed to act in the same way. For instance, corrupting popular pastimes, such as the theatre or dancing, were believed to proffer seemingly harmless entertainment as a cover for the demonic idolatry they in fact encouraged.[10] The notion that a fragile subjectivity might be prey to demonic invasion pervaded the depiction of sin and violent crime in both the pulp press and on the stage. Criminals were believed to fall progressively under the sway of the Devil as he tempted them into ever greater evils. Narratives of murder and violent crime drove home the message that the difference between the temptation to mundane sins such as laziness or greed, and the temptation to criminality, was a difference in scale only. A universal vulnerability to demonic temptation imbued all men with the potential to descend into the most terrible sin, and so to themselves become components of the Devil's kingdom.[11]

Thus the threat posed by temptation to the individual could be extended to the commonwealth as a whole. A concept of the temptation of the body politic developed in parallel to that of the human body. The Devil's human servants were commonly represented as a de facto demonic potential within the commonwealth, analogous with the inherent spiritual corruption which

9 See, for instance, the biographies of Richard Rothwell and Robert Balsom in Samuel Clarke, *The Lives of Thirty-two English Divines, famous in their generations for Learning and Piety, and most of them suffered in the cause of Christ* (London, 1677), pp. 72–3, 181–2.

10 John Northbrooke, *A Treatise wherein Dicing, Dauncing, Vaine playes or Enterludes . . . are reproued* (London, 1577); Stephen Gosson, *Playes confuted in five Actions, Prouing that they are not to be suffred in a Christian common weale* (London, 1584); William Prynne, *Histrio-mastix. The Players Scovrge* (London, 1633).

11 For only a handful of examples, see Anthony Munday, *Sundry Strange and Inhumaine Murthers* (London, 1591); Gilbert Dugdale, *A True Discourse of the Practices of Elizabeth Caldwell* (London, 1604); John Reynolds, *The Triumphs of Gods Revenge against the crying and Execrable sinne of (willing and premeditated) Murther* (London, 1657; first edn, 1621); William Rowley, Thomas Dekker and John Ford, *The Witch of Edmonton: A known true Story Composed into a Tragi-comedy* (1621), in Thomas Dekker, *The Dramatic Works of Thomas Dekker*, ed. F. Bowers (Cambridge, 4 vols., 1953–61), vol. III.

man inherited as a legacy of the fall of Adam, and which was so susceptible to the Devil's influence. This emerged most forcefully out of a dissatisfaction with the Elizabethan religious settlement which saw elements such as the episcopacy, or Catholic recusancy, as diabolic intrusions into the commonwealth. Their very existence constituted a potential for diabolic activity which might be activated, again as a spark might be put to gunpowder. Indeed the Catholic plot to blow up parliament in 1605 was widely understood to be just such an activation of demonic potential. The split loyalties recusants were understood to experience between their duties to the monarch and to the Pope constituted a catalyst for potentially lethal Catholic militancy.

This provocative political analogy undermined the Elizabethan and Stuart rhetoric of consensus that emphasised unity under theocratic rule.[12] For many the ideal of consensus could not be allowed to overshadow the importance of establishing and maintaining the purity of the Christian commonwealth. The language of 2 Corinthians 6: 14–15 – 'What concord hath Christ with Belial?' – was widely used to denounce tolerance and compromise, be it of crypto-Catholicism, or religious radicalism. The phrase in 2 Corinthians 11: 14 – 'for Satan himself is transformed into an angel of light' – emphasised the need for constant vigilance lest the Devil hide himself in the most seemingly benign political and religious activities. The possibility of the temptation of the body politic stressed the importance of identifying those diabolic triggers that Satan had introduced into the nation to activate its corrupt potential and seduce it into apostasy. Where those triggers might lie was a heavily contested issue. It was defined by an individual sense of tangibility rather than an allegiance to an abstract ideal. Thus conformists and nonconformists, Puritans and Arminians, royalists and parliamentarians employed the language of diabolic subversion in turn against each other.

But, perhaps most significantly, the concept of the diabolic temptation of the body politic helped to strengthen and reinforce resistance theory in England. The notion that the government might, wittingly or unwittingly, be tolerating de facto demonic subversion equated resistance with exorcism. Throughout the reigns of Elizabeth I and James I the notion was (with one notable exception) kept well away from the person of the monarch.[13] But

[12] On consensual politics see J. P. Kenyon, *The Stuart Constitution* (second edn, Cambridge, 1986), p. 9; Glenn Burgess, *The Politics of the Ancient Constitution: An Introduction to English Political Thought, 1603–1642* (University Park, Penn., 1992), chapters 5–7; for a challenge see Johann Sommerville, *Politics and Ideology in England 1603–1640* (London, 1986), pp. 3–4; Linda Levy Peck, *Court Patronage and Corruption in Early Stuart England* (London, 1990), pp. 185–221.

[13] The exception was Peter Wentworth who, in 1576, made a speech in parliament in which he accused Elizabeth of turning a blind eye to the use of diabolic tactics to enforce her prerogative over the discussion of religion and the succession. See *Proceedings in the Parliaments of Elizabeth I*, ed. T. E. Hartley (Leicester, 3 vols., 1981–95), vol. I, pp. 426–7.

increasingly in Charles I's reign disaffection with 'new councels' and the influence at court of perceived crypto-papists encouraged the regime's critics to see diabolic subversion closer to the throne. The Puritan lawyer William Prynne, for instance, accused Charles of encouraging diabolic apostasy in his promotion of the theatre, a charge that was quite accurately highlighted by his prosecutors in Star Chamber in 1634.[14] In 1639 John Lilburne, imprisoned for his involvement in clandestine Puritan publishing, had visions of proving in the presence of the king that Archbishop Laud was a servant of Satan. Lilburne's belief in the diabolism of his adversaries was the organising principle of his resistance to his prosecutors.[15] In many respects the printed propaganda of the Civil War and its aftermath represented the zenith of the political use of the concept of diabolic subversion. As the war progressed, accusations of diabolism became increasingly sharply focused on Charles, firstly as a victim enveloped in a web of diabolic temptation woven by Laud, the Earl of Strafford and Henrietta Maria, and finally, to justify his execution, as a witting agent of Satan, whose inflated claims to divine right focused idolatry upon himself. Historians have argued that resistance theory was only adopted in retrospect after 1642 to explain actions already taken.[16] But the perception of Arminianism as crypto-Catholicism in the minds of its enemies associated criticism of the regime's religious policies with an identified source of de facto satanic subversion with a very long pedigree. The polemical manoeuvring of 1640–2 may not immediately have called for parliament to take up arms against the king, but it certainly argued that the government was rife with diabolic subversion and this implied that the body politic was in need of exorcism.[17]

Whilst this theologically driven picture of the Devil's invisible subversive agency was increasingly dominant in shaping cultural expressions of demonism in sixteenth- and seventeenth-century England, popular ideas of the Devil persisted alongside it. Satan was still widely believed to appear in physical

[14] *Documents relating to the proceedings against William Prynne, in 1634 and 1637*, ed. S. R. Gardiner, Camden Society, new series, 18 (1877), pp. 5, 11–13, 19, 20, 23.

[15] John Lilburne, *Come out of her my people: or An Answer to the questions of a Gentleman (a professor in the Antichristian Church of England) about Hearing the Publicke Ministers* (London, 1639), pp. 13, 25.

[16] John Morrill, 'Introduction', in J. Morrill (ed.), *Reactions to the English Civil War, 1642–1649* (Houndmills, 1982), pp. 5–7; Conrad Russell, *The Causes of the English Civil War: The Ford Lectures Delivered in the University of Oxford 1987–1988* (Oxford, 1990), pp. 23–4, 132–6; for a challenge to the argument see Sommerville, *Politics and Ideology in England*, pp. 71–7.

[17] *News from Hell, Rome, and the Innes of Court, wherein is set forth the copy of a letter written from the Devil to the Pope* (London, 1641); W. F. X. B., *Camilton's Discovery of the Devilish Designs, and Killing Projects, Of the Society of Jesuits . . . intended, but graciously prevented, in England. Translated out of the Latin Copy. Dedicated to the High-court of Parliament* (London, 1641), in *The Harleian Miscellany* (London, 12 vols., 1810), vol. V, pp. 103–17.

shape to trick or tempt men out of their souls, or to exercise God's providential judgements. The physical Satan retained an absolute hold in narratives of witchcraft, in which he appeared in a variety of human and animal guises to enter into a formal pact with the witch.[18] In many ballads, pamphlets and stage-plays the Devil appeared as a physical entity.[19] In some cases the invisible tempting Devil of the Protestant reformers and the physical popular Devil were antagonistic concepts. One Puritan minister was moved to complain that the populace were so conditioned by the grotesque of the traditional mystery plays that they feared no harm from Satan until he appeared before them with the requisite horns and cloven feet.[20] But Protestant demonism never denied that Satan had the power to appear in physical form; it only asserted that his practice of internal temptation was more common and more dangerous. 'God's hangman' – the physical manifestation of the Devil in which he punished sinners on behalf of God – was as comfortable in Protestant culture as he had been in Catholic. He took pride of place as the dispenser of poetic justice in the Puritan Thomas Beard's hugely successful *The Theatre of God's Iudgements*, published in 1597.[21] In September 1621 the Puritan lawyer and future member of the Long Parliament, Sir Simonds D'Ewes, recorded in his diary that all the ships docked at Plymouth had been destroyed by a storm that followed the appearance of the Devil in the form of a black dog.[22] Indeed the Protestant emphasis on internal temptation was quite capable of interacting with more

[18] See, for example, *The Examination and Confession of certaine Wytches at Chensforde in the Countie of Essex* (London, 1566); *The Apprehension and confession of three notorious Witches. Arreigned and by Justice condemned at Chelmes-forde in the Countye of Essex* (London, 1589); Thomas Potts, *The Wonderfull Discoverie of Witches in the Covntie of Lancaster* (London, 1613); Henry Goodcole, *The Wonderfull Discouerie of Elizabeth Sawyer* (London, 1621).

[19] See, for example, the ballads, *A Pleasant new Ballad you may here behold, how the Deuill, though subtle, was guld by a Scold* (no date), in *Ancient Songs and ballads ... Chiefly collected by Robert Earl of Oxford* (London, 4 vols., arranged and bound 1774, hereafter Roxburghe Collection), vol. I, pp. 286–7, 340–1; *The Wretched Miser: or, A brief Account of a covetous Farmer, who bringing a Load of Corn to market, swore the Devil should have it before he should take the honest market price; which accordingly came to pass* (no date); *Dirty Dolls Farewel. Being an account of a certain Woman ... who was in her Life-time so notorious for several misdemeanours, that it is said, the Devil about the 17th, or 18th of August 1684, appeared to her, between whom there hapened a terrible Combat* (1684?), in *The Pepys Ballads: Facsimile*, ed. W. G. Day (Cambridge, 5 vols., 1987), vol. IV, p. 331; vol. V, p. 47.

[20] The opinion was that of Thomas Pierson, the rector of Brampton Bryan, and editor of some of William Perkins' works. See his preface to Perkins', *The Combat between Christ and the Divell displayed*, sigs. Kkk6–Kkk6v.

[21] Thomas Beard, *The Theatre of God's Iudgements: reuised and augmented* (London, 1631; first edn, 1597).

[22] Simonds D'Ewes, *The Diary of Sir Simonds D'Ewes 1622–1624*, ed. Elizabeth Bourcier (Paris, 1977), pp. 95–6.

popular notions of the physical Devil. In ballads and on the stage, physical appearances by the Devil could be used to provide a tangible demonstration of his ability to conflate man's natural corruption. In *A new Ballad, shewing the great misery sustained by a poore man in essex*, conversation with the Devil in human guise is sufficient to drive the pauper into a violent rage without the subject of murder being openly mentioned. In the play *The Witch of Edmonton* (1621) a single touch from the Devil in the shape of a dog drives a bigamous husband to murder.[23]

Thus the concepts of an internal (invasive) and external Devil were in no way mutually exclusive, within or outside Protestant culture. But the emphasis on internal temptation was increasingly dominant. Devotional, literary and even visual culture either presented the Devil as an entirely spiritual presence, or blurred the dynamic of temptation when he was presented physically. Only witchcraft narratives continued to maintain a purely physical conception of diabolic temptation, and it must be recognised that this made them increasingly unusual in early modern English demonism.

THE HISTORIOGRAPHY OF THE DEVIL

This is a significantly different picture of the Devil to that which has emerged in early modern social and cultural history, in which Satan tends to be presented stereotypically as a functionalist symbol of evil and a tool of persecution. There are remarkably few historical studies of the Devil (given his importance to western culture), and they have tended to be informed by the perception of continuities in belief which span vast periods of western history. The basic concept of the Devil has remained fundamentally unchanged since its establishment in Christian orthodoxy, around the fifth century AD, and historians have generally passed over what can appear to be a generalised demonism in a culture dominated by religious language.

Other continuities have been more explicitly constructed. Evil, argued to be one of the most fundamental of human experiences, has been particularly problematised in Christian theodicy.[24] According to J. B. Russell, the author of the only dedicated treatment of the Devil's entire history, Satan has

23 *A new Ballad, shewing the great misery sustained by a poore man in essex, his wife and children, with other strange things done by the Devill*, in Roxburghe Collection, vol. II, pp. 222–8; Rowley, Dekker and Ford, *The Witch of Edmonton*, Act III, scene iii, 7–40.

24 Richard Cavendish, *The Powers of Evil in Western Religion, Magic and Folk Belief* (London, 1975); Hans Schwarz, *Evil: An Historical and Theological Perspective* (Minneapolis, 1995), p. 1; Paul Ricoeur, 'Evil, a Challenge to Philosophy and Theology', *Journal of the American Academy of Religion*, 53 (3) (1985); Marilyn McCord Adams and Robert Merrihew Adams (eds.), *The Problem of Evil* (Oxford, 1990), p. 1; Charles Journet, *The Meaning of Evil* (London, 1963), p. 13.

consistently been used by theologians to divert responsibility for evil away from God. Correspondingly he judges the Devil's significance largely on the basis of how much theoretical coherence figures such as Origen or St Augustine were able to enforce upon the concept in this role. The result is largely a history of abstract theology which sees theodicy in essentialist terms, influenced by, but largely separate from, social and cultural change.[25]

A history of the Devil's role in persecution has developed in the light of the twentieth-century phenomenon of genocide, as historians have sought to trace the origins of society's willingness to scapegoat minorities. There is argued to have emerged in medieval Europe a persecutory mentality which actively classified minorities and produced convoluted myths of anti-human activity to justify their persecution.[26] In its earliest stages it was aimed at Jews, heretics and lepers, and imagined them to be diabolic servants working to destroy Christendom.[27] A stereotype of the Devil's servant developed into a complex and lethal mythology of a clandestine society marked out by pacts with Satan and diabolic rituals carried out at witches' Sabbats.[28] Once established, the persecutory mentality pervaded the history of western Europe, and eventually became secularised. Yet popular stereotypes, most notably those of demonic Jews, retained the essential characteristics that the medieval world had given them. The persecution of Jews as servants of Satan in medieval Europe and the genocidal anti-Semitism of the twentieth-century, are taken to be variants of

[25] The term theodicy was coined in 1697 by Gottfried Leibniz, but has been applied retrospectively to the whole history of Christian theology's problem with evil. Jeffrey Burton Russell, *The Devil: Perceptions of Evil from Antiquity to Primitive Christianity* (Ithaca and London, 1977); *Satan: The Early Christian Tradition* (Ithaca and London, 1981); *Lucifer: the Devil in the Middle Ages* (Ithaca and London, 1984); *Mephistopheles: The Devil in the Modern World* (Ithaca and London, 1986); Neil Forsyth, *The Old Enemy: Satan and the Combat Myth* (Princeton, N.J., 1987). Henry Angsar Kelly is more polemical, tracing a series of interpretative mistakes he claims have allowed the Devil to occupy a place within Christian orthodoxy that he never deserved; see *The Devil, Demonology and Witchcraft* (Garden City, N.Y., 1974).

[26] R. I. Moore, *The Formation of a Persecuting Society: Power and Deviance in Western Europe, 950–1250* (Oxford, 1987), pp. 35, 64–5, 89–91, 123.

[27] Joshua Trachtenburg, *The Devil and the Jews: The Medieval Conception of the Jew and its Relation to Modern Anti-Semitism* (Philadelphia and Jerusalem, 1943; reprinted 1993); Carlo Ginzburg, *Ecstasies: Deciphering the Witches' Sabbath*, trans. R. Rosenthal (London, 1991); Elaine Pagels has also found similar processes prevalent in the development of early Christian identity. See *The Origin of Satan* (London, 1995).

[28] Cohn, *Europe's Inner Demons*; Ginzberg, *Ecstasies*; Robert Muchembled, 'Satanic Myths and Cultural Reality'; Robert Rowland, '"Fantasticall and Devilishe Persons": European Witch-Beliefs in Comparative Perspective'; Gustav Henningsen, '"The Ladies from Outside": An Archaic Pattern of the Witches' Sabbath', all in *Early Modern European Witchcraft: Centres and Peripheries*, ed. B. Ankarloo and G. Henningsen (Oxford, 1990), pp. 139–215; Robin Briggs, *Witches and Neighbours: The Social and Cultural Context of European Witchcraft* (London, 1996), pp. 25–59; Stuart Clark, *Thinking with Demons: The Idea of Witchcraft in Early Modern Europe* (Oxford, 1997), pp. 80–93, 161–78, 321–34.

the same process.[29] Thus, as an interpretative model, willingness to act on a belief in the Devil has to a large extent been equated with persecuting zeal and fanaticism, unchanged in nature for nearly a thousand years.

These continuities are bisected by one enormous cultural change. Between the sixteenth and eighteenth centuries Europe underwent what Max Weber termed 'disenchantment'.[30] A traditional world view which saw man at the centre of an ordered cosmos in which macrocosm and microcosm constantly interacted was increasingly challenged. The Protestant rejection of magic favoured belief in human agency under subjection to God. Whilst the existence of preternature was not denied, it was increasingly considered a sphere of activity reserved only for the deity.[31] In the later seventeenth and eighteenth centuries the scientific revolution undermined the basic rationale of magic, as mechanical philosophy emphasised the orderly and regular functioning of the universe, upon which spirits and demons were incapable of acting.[32] As Robin Briggs has noted, the reason for this 'conceptual revolution' has defied adequate historical explanation.[33] But it had profound consequences for the educated perception of the Devil. The question of evil was central to the thinking of *philosophes* such as Liebniz, Hume and Voltaire. But they found the Devil to be little more than a telling example of the absurdity of traditional Christian belief. Natural disasters and other evils were to be attributed instead to the inevitable action of the laws of nature. Similarly, liberal Christians who sought to reconcile their faith with rationalism found the Devil to be cumbersome baggage. In response, alternative theodicies gained prevalence, for example the belief that evil had no existence and was merely a relative declension from good. In eighteenth-century England, so J. B. Russell argues, only the theology of John Wesley continued to be influenced by a profound sense of the demonic.[34]

[29] This continuity has been relied on in works dealing with the holocaust. Recent examples include Richard L. Rubenstein and John K. Roth, *Approaches to Auschwitz: The Holocaust and its Legacy* (Atlanta, 1987), chapter 2; Daniel Jonah Goldhagen, *Hitler's Willing Executioners: Ordinary Germans and the Holocaust* (London, 1996), pp. 39–43, 52–3; Joel Carmichael, *The Satanizing of the Jews: Origin and Development of Mystical Anti-Semitism* (New York, 1992). But this view has been convincingly challenged by David Nirenburg, who argues that in all periods persecution, and anti-Semitism in particular, must be understood in its immediate context, and that assumptions about the long-term continuity of anti-Semitism are ahistorical. See *Communities of Violence: Persecution of Minorities in the Middle Ages* (Princeton, N.J., 1996), pp. 3–17.

[30] Alan Macfarlane, 'The Root of All Evil', in D. Parkin (ed.), *The Anthropology of Evil* (Oxford, 1985), pp. 57–76; R. W. Scribner, 'The Reformation, Popular Magic, and the "Disenchantment of the World"', *Journal of Interdisciplinary History*, 23 (3) (Winter, 1993), pp. 475–94.

[31] Briggs, *Witches and Neighbours*, pp. 378–81.

[32] Brian P. Levack, *The Witch-Hunt in Early Modern Europe* (London, 1987), pp. 217–24.

[33] Briggs, *Witches and Neighbours*, p. 377.

[34] Russell, *Mephistopheles*, pp. 130–2.

The hindsight of the effect of the Enlightenment on the preternatural has greatly coloured the cultural history of the Devil in sixteenth- and seventeenth-century Europe. For Professor Russell the period saw 'the Devil between two worlds' as Europe witnessed 'a profound shift in the centre of gravity of perceptions of evil, from the world of spirits to the world of humanity'.[35] The Protestant Reformation, he argues, marked the last chapter in the Devil's unassailed dominance in theodicy, and Protestantism itself was infused by contradictory impulses over the Devil. Its leaders, such as Martin Luther and John Calvin, were deeply concerned with the profound personal experience of evil, and the principle of *sola scriptura* instilled in them a regard for the synoptic conception of the Devil. According to Russell, they 'uncritically accepted virtually the entire tradition of medieval diabology'.[36] At the same time Protestant concern over clerical abuses encouraged a rejection of the preternatural agencies which had provided a barrier between man and the demonic.[37] Satan's victims, Russell notes, found themselves alone with no solace other than their faith and their bibles.[38] Yet, he continues, even as this more pessimistic demonism was taking hold, an undercurrent was emerging to challenge the Devil's dominance in the question of evil. In the period's tragic literary characters – such as Faustus or Iago – could be seen the earliest expressions of evil embodied entirely in man. But whilst they were human, the evil of these characters bore the hallmarks of Satan's wanton and self-fulfilling malice. Thus, for Professor Russell, the sixteenth and seventeenth centuries constitute a half-way house between the cosmic evil of the medieval Devil and the purely human evil of the post-Enlightenment. As a precursor to the Enlightenment, early modern culture began to find cosmic evil in a human form.[39]

The enormous scope of such a history naturally brings with it problems of simplification and distortion. Whilst the Devil has undoubtedly been central to Christian approaches to theodicy, the latter should not be assumed to define the concept at all levels of society at all times. Russell's methodology shapes his history into a single linear narrative in which a variety of disparate writers are made to correspond in their theodician purpose. The terms of reference for the interpretation of the early modern Devil – how far the

[35] Ibid., p. 25.

[36] Ibid., p. 36; H. R. Trevor-Roper, *The European Witch-Craze of the Sixteenth and Seventeenth Centuries* (London, 1969), p. 72; John Hick, *Evil and the God of Love* (London, 1968), pp. 121–3.

[37] Russell, *Mephistopheles*, pp. 31–3; Thomas, *Religion and the Decline of Magic*, pp. 60–5.

[38] For a discussion of the traditional protectives offered by pre-Reformation Catholicism, see Duffy, *The Stripping of the Altars*, pp. 266–82; Thomas, *Religion and the Decline of Magic*, pp. 31–52; R. N. Swanson, *Religion and Devotion in Europe, c.1215–c.1515* (Cambridge, 1995), pp. 142–7, 158–61, 162–5.

[39] Russell, *Mephistopheles*, pp. 66–76.

concept constituted a medieval remnant, and how far it was challenged by the precursors of the Enlightenment – prevent it being examined as a discrete cultural phenomenon, influenced by and expressive of the religious and political concerns of the sixteenth and seventeenth centuries. The literature of the period, from its high theology to its popular ephemera, eloquently testifies to the cultural importance of the Devil, but relatively little of it was concerned with questions of cosmic theodicy. Considerations as to the nature of evil were, of course, implicit in all representations of diabolic agency. But these were far more deeply grounded in the specific contexts of the period than the intellectual history of theodicy can reveal, and they can only be fully understood in those terms. Whilst, therefore, Russell's history provides a broad framework for the study of the Devil, a deeper contextualisation reveals a significantly different picture of his place in early modern culture. The force of the concept, it becomes apparent, was not dependent on its usefulness in theodicy, nor was it a leftover from the medieval world, increasingly beset by humanistic willingness to bear the responsibility for evil. The post-Reformation Devil was a powerful figure not because the reformers neglected to clip his wings, but because they were adamant he should remain so. When set in its religious, social and political contexts, early modern diabology appears not simply as an uncritical inheritance from the medieval world, but as a powerful and reflective belief, subtly but importantly different from its predecessor, and one that, in both its continuities and changes, expressed what was a profound experiential reality for its adherents.

THE DEVIL AND 'THE PERSECUTING SOCIETY': WITCHES, PURITANISM AND DESPAIR

Historians of the early modern period itself are perhaps more familiar with the Devil as an aspect of the history of persecution, in which he has emerged most forcefully as a symptom of society gone awry.[40] Implicit in this history is an index of significance for belief in the Devil. The more extreme the conceptualisation, and the more discernible its consequences, the more significance it is allowed. Hence the seemingly pathological fantasies of the Sabbat are seen as inherently more significant than more commonplace demonological beliefs. A picture has emerged which stereotypes the Devil as a tool for creating victims. No phenomenon illustrates this persecuting mentality more clearly than the prosecution of witchcraft in Europe between 1500 and 1750. When popular notions of witchcraft were intertwined with ideas about the Devil, *maleficium* became assimilated into belief in a broad

[40] Trevor-Roper, *The European Witch-Craze*, pp. 11–23.

demonic assault on Christendom, which shifted the emphasis from individual witches to a collectivity of apostates.[41] The diabolic pact thus became central to what Robin Briggs has described as 'the myth of the perfect witch' – the old hag who, trading her soul for *malefic* power, entered the anti-world of the Sabbat in which obscene rituals parodied and inverted Christian and human norms.[42] This victimisation approach is consciously adopted in the work of Norman Cohn, whose history of the witch-hunt was written under the auspices of the Columbus Centre, a group interested in the study of 'collective psychopathology' and the 'dynamics of persecution and extermination'. For Cohn, the significance of the witch-hunt was its utter dependence on the scapegoating myth of a clandestine and subversive society, addicted to anti-human practices. Such myths are almost universal, but, Cohn argues, unlike the demonisation of medieval heretics or the Knights Templar, the search for a collectivity of witches had no pre-existing momentum. Only because 'the minds of the authorities were obsessed by the central fantasy itself', did the witch-hunt reach such lethal proportions.[43]

Unfortunately, the Devil responds well to the index of significance implicit in this argument, and this marginalises the concept at the extremes of early modern culture. Even within the contemporary remit of diabolic agency, the narratives of the Sabbat orgies were extreme. Moreover, the willingness of women to confess to 'impossible' crimes demands an explanation.[44] Perhaps most importantly, the difficulties in proving witchcraft were, until the later seventeenth century, no deterrent to its prosecution. Instead a whole judicial system was manipulated and reshaped – incorporating diabolic elements

[41] Cohn, *Europe's Inner Demons*, pp. 226–8, 232–9, 252–3; R. Kieckhefer, *European Witch-Trials: Their Foundation in Popular and Learned Culture, 1300–1500* (London, 1976), pp. 73–92; V. Flint, *The Rise of Magic in Early Medieval Europe* (Oxford, 1991), pp. 101–8, 146–57; B. Easlea, *Witch-Hunting, Magic and the New Philosophy: An Introduction to Debates of the Scientific Revolution, 1450–1750* (Brighton, 1980), pp. 6–7.

[42] Briggs, *Witches and Neighbours*, pp. 25–59. The origins of the concept lay possibly in ancient Persia, and it was incorporated into Christianity by the Church Fathers. The narrative developed and gained wide currency in legends such as that of St Theophilis and eventually Dr Faustus. See Rudwin, *The Devil in Legend and Literature* (La Salle, Ill., 1931), pp. 167–85; Levack, *The Witch-Hunt*, p. 32; Russell, *Lucifer*, pp. 80–4; Christopher Marlowe, *The Tragical History of Doctor Faustus* (*c.* 1589), in *The Complete Plays*, ed. J. B. Stearne (London, 1969), Act I, scene v; *The Historie of the damnable Life, and deserved Death of Doctor Iohn Faustus* (London, 1592), pp. 2–9, 78–82; Lucy de Bruyn, *Woman and the Devil in Sixteenth-Century Literature* (Tisbury, 1979), pp. 3–19. For a discussion of the anti-world of the Sabbat see Rowland, '"Fantasticall and Devilishe Persons"', pp. 161–8; and for an account of the development of the pact, and a cautious assessment of its influence in England, see Thomas, *Religion and the Decline of Magic*, pp. 521–34.

[43] Cohn, *Europe's Inner Demons*, chapters 2, 3 and 5; Levack, *The Witch-Hunt*, p. 36.

[44] Of course it was entirely possible for woman and men to believe that they were witches, and the practice of folk magic, and magic employing the aid of spirits, was widespread throughout early modern Europe. But historians agree that witchcraft was probably not practised in covens, and that the murder and cannibalism of the Sabbat were fictions.

such as the witch's mark and the swimming test – to overcome the lack of direct evidence left by the secret crime.[45] The acceptance of this index of significance has especially marginalised the Devil within early modern English culture. Keith Thomas argued that English witch beliefs – driven primarily by a desire to redress *maleficium* – remained remarkably impervious to elite attempts to focus attention on the diabolism of the crime, and hence remained more moderate. Despite the emerging definition of felonious apostasy in statutes between 1542 and 1604, trials for diabolism alone were extremely rare.[46]

More recent studies of witchcraft have, of course, made this picture of the Devil much more sophisticated. Within the elite/popular dichotomy established by Professor Thomas, more nuanced pictures of the interaction between concerns over *maleficium* and diabolism have emerged. Clive Holmes has examined the ways in which concerns as to the nature of evidence in *maleficium* cases drove magistrates and divines to reinterpret aspects such as the familiar and witch's mark in line with expectations drawn from continental demonology.[47] Deborah Willis has argued that the Devil was used to rewrite a popular narrative of witchcraft that centred on the notion of 'malevolent nurture'. The witch's relationship with her spirit familiars, by which she gained her power, represented an inversion of nurturing; the witch herself was thus an anti-mother. In the learned discourse which emerged in England, the Devil was used to rewrite this essentially popular narrative of female power in order to deprive the witch of her autonomy and place her in subjection to a male master.[48] Other historians have challenged the Thomas orthodoxy itself. James Sharpe and Robin Briggs have both noted the overtly diabolic characteristics of the familiar spirit in English witch narratives.[49] The familiar, almost unique to English witch beliefs, was a demon in the shape of an animal, most usually a cat or other small mammal.[50] Found in the first pamphlet accounts of witchcraft in England in the 1560s, the concept developed in complexity until it encompassed both the bizarre familiars of the Hopkins' witch-hunt

[45] Cohn, *Europe's Inner Demons*, p. 255; C. Holmes, 'Women, Witnesses and Witches', *Past and Present*, 140 (1993), pp. 65–75; Levack, *The Witch-Hunt*, chapter 3; J. A. Sharpe, *Instruments of Darkness: Witchcraft in England 1550–1750* (London, 1996), pp. 88–94; Briggs, *Witches and Neighbours*, pp. 187–208.

[46] Thomas, *Religion and the Decline of Magic*, pp. 525–9.

[47] See Holmes' important article, 'Women, Witnesses and Witches', pp. 51–9; Thomas, *Religion and the Decline of Magic*, p. 534.

[48] D. Willis, *Malevolent Nurture: Witch-Hunting and Maternal Power in Early Modern England* (Ithaca and London, 1995), pp. 52–5, 89–91; Purkiss, *The Witch in History*, p. 134; similarly, see Laura Levine's discussion of the use of the Devil to rewrite narratives of sympathetic magic in witch trials in Scotland, *Men in Women's Clothes: Anti-Theatricality and Effeminisation 1579–1642* (Cambridge, 1996), pp. 108–33.

[49] Sharpe, *Instruments of Darkness*, pp. 71–5; Briggs, *Witches and Neighbours*, pp. 25–31.

[50] For the only other appearance of the familiar in Basque witch trials, see Gustav Henningsen, *The Witches' Advocate: Basque Witchcraft and the Spanish Inquisition* (Reno, 1980), p. 94.

and the presence of the Devil in human form who personally donated to witches his demon minions in the shape of animals.[51] Professor Sharpe argues that the familiar may be part, not of a popular notion of witchcraft, but of a popular concept of the Devil.[52] Robin Briggs points out that familiars quite clearly perform the Devil's role as tempter in English witchcraft narratives, whilst the witches' suckling of the spirit accords to the European blood sacrifice.[53]

The most important re-examination of the concept of the Devil within witchcraft has been provided in Stuart Clark's highly impressive and ground-breaking book, *Thinking with Demons*. Professor Clark argues that the Devil had essentially a 'contingent reality', expressed in the discursive conventions of the period, most notably that of inversion.[54] Satan was not understood positively in terms of what he was, but only in terms of what he was not. Inversion was central to the 'common stock of familiar ideas' which pervaded European culture of the period.[55] Universal order was shaped by a conception of 'substantive contrariety' in all natural, intellectual, moral and social phenomena. For instance traditional medicine relied on the notion of opposed elements, qualities and humours in the constitution. Most discussions of morality, psychology and good conduct employed simple dichotomies, between the spirit and the flesh, or reason and passion.[56] The challenge offered by the Devil to the perfection of government and order represented just such a contrariety. In Clark's words, 'the devil's regimen was a compendium of the paradoxes of misrule; a hierarchy governed from the lowest point of excellence, a society in which dishonour was a badge of status, and a speculum imitable only by the politically vicious'.[57] Inversion was not simply a policy by which Satan undermined Christendom; it was what he was. He could only be understood as an inversionary rebel, whose parodic rituals, embodied by the Sabbat baptism, were expressions of his defining characteristic. All contemporary demonologists reinforced the point by asserting that the Devil's inversion represented a counterfeit, a dissembling mockery of the nature of God.[58] It was by understanding the nature of God, of the true church, and of the ordained political and social order that Satan's shallow impersonation could be comprehended.

[51] *The Examination and Confession of certaine Wytches at Chensforde in the Countie of Essex*; Potts, *The Wonderfvll Discoverie of Witches in the Covntie of Lancaster*, sigs. B2v–C2; *The Witches of Northamptonshire* (London, 1612), sigs. C3–C3v; Matthew Hopkins, *The Discovery of Witches* (London, 1647).

[52] Sharpe, *Instruments of Darkness*, p. 75. [53] Briggs, *Witches and Neighbours*, pp. 25–31.

[54] Clark, *Thinking with Demons*, p. 9; the term 'contingent reality' is borrowed from Forsyth, *The Old Enemy*, p. 4.

[55] D. Underdown, *A Freeborn People: Politics and the Nation in Seventeenth-Century England* (Oxford, 1996), p. 12.

[56] Clark, *Thinking with Demons*, pp. 46–53, 61–8. [57] Ibid., p. 87. [58] Ibid., p. 82.

This emphasis on contrariety has taken the study of demonology more firmly into the history of early modern political culture, and has broadly supported the claims of revisionist historians that the English political nation possessed no language of opposition. Political rhetoric was dominated by an emphasis on consensus. Thus conflict, culminating in the breakdown of government in the Civil War, originated in disagreements over the practical operation of the constitution.[59] Within this framework an equation between witchcraft and rebellion provided, in Peter Elmer's words, a 'normative system of discourse which fostered unity and concord in the body politic'.[60] The ideas and the practice of divine kingship were bound up with a perceived opposition between what Professor Clark has called 'marvellous monarchy' and witchcraft as anti-government. The position was expressed by consistent reference to 1 Samuel 15: 23 – 'For Rebellion is as the sin of witchcraft'.[61] This rhetoric of consensual politics was employed widely through early modern Europe to demonstrate the mirror kingly authority provided to its divine origin. Challenges to that authority must by definition be an expression of the contrariety practised by God's ape. Theocracy, like so many early modern political, religious and social tenets, was best understood through an exploration of its antithesis. If the witch's pact with Satan represented spiritual apostasy, it also embodied a literal resistance to secular authority. Through their acts of *maleficium* witches brought disorder and a symbolic threat to the commonwealth, perhaps nowhere better expressed than in their well-known ability to undermine marital hierarchy through the infliction of impotence.

The work of Clark and Elmer has opened up many new avenues in the study of demonology, recognising the importance of language and discourse, the complex relationship between demonology and natural science, and the importance of the perception of demonic power to the practice of theocracy. Demonology, they reveal, was a vastly more complex area of early modern culture than historians have credited, and one that provides vital insights into the contemporary mind more generally. However, by arguing that, through the linguistic conventions of demonology, the Devil had only a contingent reality, their studies implicitly downplay the possibility of a 'positive' experience of demonic agency. Satan appears to have been more *understood* than he was actually *felt*.[62] But whilst it is undeniable that contrariety and inversion

[59] Kenyon, *The Stuart Constitution*, p. 9; Burgess, *The Politics of the Ancient Constitution*, chapters 5–7.

[60] Peter Elmer, '"Saints or Sorcerers": Quakerism, Demonology and the Decline of Witchcraft in Seventeenth-Century England', in Barry, Hester and Roberts, *Witchcraft in Early Modern Europe*, p. 174.

[61] Clark, *Thinking with Demons*, pp. 610–12; Elmer, '"Saints or Sorcerers"', pp. 164–5.

[62] For an explicit statement of this argument with relevance to visual depictions of the Devil in medieval and Renaissance art, see Luther Link, *The Devil: A Mask without a Face* (London, 1995), esp. pp. 183–93.

were of great importance to the concept of the Devil, they did not define it. As this study will seek to show, demonism maintained a hold in early modern culture because its identification of diabolic agency within religious, social and political commonplaces allowed people to engage with an experience of the Devil which was positively felt. This in itself militated against easy otherisation in those who felt his presence most keenly. Protestants emphasised diabolic agency as a ubiquitous phenomenon, understood through an empathy with the experience of its victims (however culpable they might be) and recognised as a condition that might be overcome and see its sufferers returned to the Christian fold. As a result, diabolism was as much a language of negotiation as it was one of separation: one which, as we shall see, was fully exploited in the religious and political conflicts of the period.

Whilst the work of Clark and Elmer has fixed witchcraft more certainly at the centre of early modern political culture, the wider interpretation of demonic belief has been influenced by its more traditional marginalisation, most significantly in terms of its place in Protestant religious culture. For Keith Thomas, Protestantism's deep sense of human sin and vulnerability to the forces of evil left it largely hostage to the concept of the Devil, despite its emphasis on single divine sovereignty.[63] In this context, the language of the Devil was most notably the language of religious despair for a minority of the (over-)zealous godly; in Blair Worden's phrase, Satan was part of 'the darkness of Puritanism'.[64] The theme has been expanded upon in the work of Paul Seaver, Michael MacDonald and John Stachniewski.[65] 'Afflicted consciences' emerged from a dislocation between the individual's religious convictions and his belief that he was unworthy of salvation. The Protestant emphasis on double predestination could translate into experiences of 'spectacular despair' for those individuals who felt they did not meet the criteria of the elect.[66] Satan loomed large in the experiences of these despairing Christians. As Richard Godbeer has noted, 'it was when Puritans sought to account for their spiritual deficiencies that Satan figured most prominently in their thoughts'.[67] Some,

[63] Ibid., pp. 560–6.

[64] Blair Worden's review of Seaver's *Wallington's World*, in *London Review of Books* (23 Jan.–6 Feb., 1986), quoted in Stachniewski, *The Persecutory Imagination*, p. 1.

[65] Seaver, *Wallington's World*; MacDonald, *Mystical Bedlam*, pp. 220–2; Stackniewski, *The Persecutory Imagination*, pp. 37–61.

[66] Michael MacDonald, '*The Fearful Estate of Francis Spira*: Narrative, Identity, and Emotion in Early Modern England', *Journal of British Studies* 31(1992), pp. 32–3; Stachniewski, *The Persecutory Imagination*, pp. 19–20, 37–9; Beard, *The Theatre of Gods Ivdgements*, pp. 62–4; Robert Bolton, *Instructions for the Right comforting afflicted consciences* (London, 1631), pp. 18–19.

[67] Richard Godbeer, *The Devil's Dominion: Magic and Religion in Early Modern New England* (Cambridge, 1992), p. 97.

such as Richard Norwood or John Bunyan, believed they encountered the Devil as a physical manifestation, and many cases of suicide were attributed to Satan, who deluded men into thinking there was no point in putting off their inevitable damnation.[68]

Within this scheme, then, the Devil appears as another tool of victimisation: a means certainly of stigmatising the ungodly, but also, more insidiously, as a device employed within the Puritan community itself. Zealous Protestant clergy used the concept to browbeat their parishioners with the threat of hell, and were the apex of a broader emphasis on sin that was an effective form of social control.[69] The process was extended by the laity in the strict regime of the Puritan family, and in the ironic self-sabotage of godly individuals themselves. These became obsessed with fathoming the depth of their own sin, and lived in constant expectation of the Devil. At best, personal relationships suffered from this self-obsession; at worst victims became completely incapable of meaningful interaction.[70] According to Dr Stachniewski, Puritan obsession with Satan was passed through generations in the brutalisation of children in some families. Childish wilfulness was commonly viewed as a manifestation of satanic influence, needing to be strictly controlled, whilst the victims of such abuse were often unable in adulthood to escape the force of their conditioning, finding and punishing the Devil in their own children.[71]

I do not seek in this book to challenge the historical interpretations of the Devil's role within witchcraft, but to question the extent to which they can be taken as representative of demonological beliefs more widely. The broad function played by the Devil in witchcraft narratives has been accurately analysed, if debate is still prevalent as to its idioms and nuances. Instead, I want here to shift the focus away from witchcraft, which, I would argue, did not in fact define demonic belief more widely in the period. The Devil pervaded the written culture of early modern England, in tracts, sermons, devotional and conduct literature, plays and ballads, as well as in diaries and

[68] Seaver, *Wallington's World*, p. 23; John Bunyan, *Grace abounding to the chief of sinners*, ed. R. Sharrock (Oxford, 1962), p. 34. John Rogers, *Ohel or Bethshemesh A tabernacle for the sun, or Irenicum evangelicum: an idea of church-discipline in the theorick and practick parts* (London, 1653), pp. 419–20; Richard Norwood, *The Journal of Richard Norwood* (New York, 1945), p. 93; Hannah Allen, *Satan his Methods and Malice baffled* (London, 1683), pp. 31–3, 36; Stachniewski, *The Persecutory Imagination*, pp. 46–52; Michael MacDonald and Terrence Murphy, *Sleepless Souls: Suicide in Early Modern England* (Oxford, 1990), pp. 34–41, 50–60.

[69] See Stachniewski's account of the fire-and-brimstone preaching of 'sons of thunder' like William Perkins and John Rogers in *The Persecutory Imagination*, pp. 86–87; Thomas, *Religion and the Decline of Magic*, pp. 561–2; C. Hill, *The World Turned Upside Down* (London, 1972), pp. 151–83; for a challenge to Hill's argument see J. C. Davis, *Fear, Myth and History: The Ranters and the Historians* (Cambridge, 1986), pp. 132–4.

[70] Seaver, *Wallington's World*, pp. 23–4, 26–30.

[71] Stachniewski, *The Persecutory Imagination*, pp. 96–9.

conduct books. Recent work focusing on these sources has begun to redress the imbalance, arguing for the importance of alternative schemes of demonological belief in devotional and popular culture. Publications by Frank Luttmer and Darren Oldridge, and the doctoral thesis that formed the basis for this book, all identified independently the existence of a characteristically Protestant conception of the Devil that centred around the notion of temptation.[72] Temptation had, of course, been central to the concept of the Devil throughout Christian history. Protestant demonic belief thus involved a change of emphasis rather than of theology, but the change was highly significant. Whereas the medieval remit of the Devil had included temptation as one of a variety of activities with which he might afflict mankind, Protestants elevated it into the single most important aspect of his agency, which virtually eclipsed all others.

What is remarkable about this broad spread of contemporary Protestant literature is that throughout there was a consistent emphasis on notions of demonic agency that were essentially separate from those associated with witchcraft. Indeed, with its emphasis on the physical manifestation of the Devil, I would argue that witchcraft became increasingly idiosyncratic in demonological beliefs through the period. It may, therefore, be useful to distinguish between the 'academic' *demonology* of witch texts and pamphlets and a broader *demonism*. The first intensively sought to delineate diabolic activity in one sphere. It was arguably constrained within the parameters set by explaining the nature and significance of witchcraft, and required that the Devil's physical presence be demonstrated as a mechanism of the witch's fall into apostasy. The second was a more nebulous belief that, starting from an a priori acceptance of the reality of pervasive satanic activity, compiled and described the wider experience of diabolic agency around a small number of central emphases, of which temptation was the most prominent. Demonology and this more general demonism were, of course, closely interrelated. As Stuart Clark has noted, Protestant witch texts were written by the pastorate, within the broader context of the reformation of manners.[73] But whilst the depiction of satanic agency was fully consistent between them,

[72] Nathan Johnstone, 'The Protestant Devil: The Experience of Temptation in Early Modern England', *Journal of British Studies*, 43 (2) (April 2004), pp. 173–205; Nathan Johnstone, 'The Early Modern Concept of the Devil: Diabolic Agency in Elizabethan and Stuart Anti-Stage Polemic', paper given at the Institute of Historical Research, University of London, January 1997; Nathan Johnstone, 'The Devil in English Culture, c. 1549–c. 1660', Ph.D. thesis, University of Kent (2000); Frank Luttmer, 'Persecutors, Tempters and Vassals of the Devil: The Unregenerate in Puritan Practical Divinity', *Journal of Ecclesiastical History*, 51 (1) (2000), esp. pp. 43–56; Darren Oldridge, *The Devil in Early Modern England* (Stroud, 2000).

[73] Stuart Clark, 'Protestant Demonology: Sin, Superstition and Society (c. 1520–c. 1630)', in B. Ankarloo and G. Henningsen (eds.), *Early Modern European Witchcraft: Centres and Peripheries* (Oxford, 1990), pp. 54, 58–62.

they represented very different aspects of the Protestant agenda. The Devil's work in tempting witches might be a striking demonstration of the iniquity of the Last Days.[74] As such, however, witchcraft was an extreme example of Protestant pastoral concerns. For the most part these identified the norm of diabolic agency in less extraordinary occurrences such as everyday temptation.

Once we no longer look at the Devil only through the lens provided by the study of witchcraft, we find the concept to be of importance throughout early modern culture, at least in England. Here, only his place in Puritan thinking has received any dedicated attention from historians, and here also the interpretation of the evidence is problematic. Again, I do not seek to dismiss the reality of a 'darkness of Puritanism' per se or the extremity of the symptoms it induced in some individuals. But the picture of Puritan despair presents an over-functionalised interpretation of the Devil, in which the concept is taken to have operated largely as a symbol for guilt and unacknowledged desires. For example, Richard Godbeer's study of demonology in Puritan New England interprets the Devil as a barometer of the godly conscience, rather than a discrete experience in itself. Samual Parris, at the centre of the Salem witch trials, presented his congregation with an image of Satan's all-pervasive power and malice, which tended to downplay individual responsibility for sin. By contrast, those with more self-confidence, like Samuel Willard and Michael Wigglesworth, were adamant that men must accept the blame for their lapses from godliness, and had relatively little sense of diabolic power. The norm, Godbeer argues, was to divide responsibility for sin on 'a continuum of blame from self to Satan'.[75]

The work of Frank Luttmer and Darren Oldridge has provided a much more sophisticated and nuanced picture of Protestant demonism, but it also has a number of significant limitations for understanding the position of the concept of the Devil in early modern English culture. Luttmer is interested in the insights the Devil provides into the issue of the Protestant conception of the reprobate and their separation from the godly. He argues that Protestant divines posited a 'vast' distinction between the regenerate and unregenerate in their relationship with the Devil, which was central to the definition of spiritual 'contrariety' by which they formed their identity.[76] The unregenerate were conceived as the vassals of Satan, governed by the influence of temptation (of which they were usually unaware) on the corrupt flesh. They were thus the Devil's peaceful subjects, as opposed to the regenerate soldiers perpetually waging war on the diabolic kingdom. But the consequences of this position were, Luttmer argues, problematic for practical divinity.

[74] Clark, *Thinking with Demons*, pp. 369–71.
[75] Godbeer, *The Devil's Dominion*, pp. 93–106, quote at p. 97.
[76] Luttmer, 'Persecutors, Tempters and Vassals of the Devil', esp. p. 55.

Whatever the theory, Puritans could not argue that all reprobates were overtly wicked, and indeed many were honourable and moral.[77] Moreover, in emphasising the inherent relationship between reprobates and the Devil, Puritan divines necessarily heightened lay sensitivity to the spiritual ramifications of the occurrence of temptation amongst the godly themselves.[78] In response, Puritans emphasised the power of God's providence in the apparent good conduct of reprobates, whilst the experience of temptation among the godly served to reinforce vigilance, with the ultimate proviso that those whose backsliding proved permanent could be assumed to have never been effectively called. Ultimately, Luttmer concludes, such a position must have contributed to the darkness of Puritanism, but divines attempted to alleviate its resultant anxieties with reference to the virtue of struggle. The scheme, he argues, with all its inherent difficulties, was effective in allowing the godly to separate themselves from the mass of devilish reprobates.[79]

Luttmer's analysis is subtle, identifying many complexities in the Puritan understanding of the Devil's agency, but there are problems in his approach, which sees the interest in diabolic agency as essentially consequential of other theological and devotional concerns. The desire for an effective practical divinity, predicated on a didactic understanding of the situation of the reprobate, drove the emphasis on Satan's power, expressed in print and from the pulpit. The examination and definition of the godly's relationship to the diabolic followed in its wake as the unfortunate corollary of this emphasis on Satan's power in the world. But such an analysis tends to emphasise the Devil's conceptual importance over his experiential force for Protestants. Self-definition by opposition to the unregenerate surely did appeal to many of the godly, but their sense of the Devil's tangibility was arguably not determined or dependent upon this. Again, Protestantism was not hostage to the concept because of its functional utility; rather Satan's agency was a reality that pervaded the experiences of the self-consciously pious. Divines suffered as much, and sometimes more, than their parishioners, and the demonism which informed their practical divinity was born of a perception of the intimate tangibility of the demonic. Indeed the experience of diabolic temptation amongst the godly was possibly too widespread, its disruption of their devotions too profound, for it to be an effective measure of reprobation. Protestant writers set no absolute theoretical or practical distinctions between the demonic experiences of the elect and the reprobate. Their ultimate conclusion, that the response to temptation, rather than the experience itself, might be an indicator of election was not simply a functional mechanism for assurance, but a testament to their understanding of the depth and apparent perversity of the experience amongst the godly.

[77] Ibid., pp. 49–50. [78] Ibid., pp. 59–68. [79] Ibid., pp. 66–7.

Darren Oldridge's book on the Devil has a necessarily broader scope than Luttmer's article, addressing not only Protestant devotional culture, but also areas such as popular culture, possession, witchcraft and gender. But again the interpretation offered is largely functional. Dr Oldridge identifies the development of a Protestant concern with the Devil in a combination of the pessimistic theology highlighted by Thomas and Russell, and the experience of failing to reform the religious convictions of a majority of layfolk. This, Oldridge argues, led to the development within Protestantism of a confrontational world view in which the godly identified themselves as an embattled minority, beset on all sides by the adversaries of reform, who could only be the servants of Satan.[80] Thus the Devil was elevated in Protestant thinking to become the leader of a vast army of reprobates, whose existence provided both an explanation for the frustrations experienced by would-be reformers, and a rationale for the perpetuation of the conflict, since the identification of diabolism allowed opposition to reform to be assimilated within a narrative of the continuing battle between God and Satan which ultimately guaranteed the latter's defeat. Here temptation is accorded a significant place in the culture of the godly, but continues to be seen as largely a function of the Protestant emphasis on introspection and of the Puritan culture of despair. Oldridge extends Godbeer's interpretation, agreeing that the notion that Satan could invade the mind meant that individuals could absolve themselves of the responsibility for ideas that might be a challenge to their faith. But he goes further, in according temptation a communal function. The language of diabolic invasion, he argues, not only allowed Protestants personally to come to terms with their concerns, but also to give them public expression. 'Devout Protestants', Oldridge notes, 'could safely give voice to any fears and anxieties they harboured about their faith, and express any hidden desires, in a context which acquitted them of responsibility and guilt.'[81] Thus the diabolic was not simply a private recourse for those of a weak faith, it was an important and familiar mode of expression that, to an extent, ensured a sympathetic hearing. Oldridge emphasises the psychological importance of this projection of unwanted thoughts onto the Devil, and although he does not define it in detail, he seems to imply that the Devil could be used by the godly as a mechanism for alleviating the cognitive dissonance inherent in the rigours of their faith. The later chapters of the book then deal with a number of discrete aspects of early modern diabolism, such as the role of the Devil in popular culture, witchcraft or possession. Here Oldridge examines the survival of traditional concepts of diabolic agency (often associated with the Devil's physical manifestations) and their uncomfortable relationship to the

[80] Oldridge, *The Devil*, pp. 35–9. [81] Ibid., pp. 46–7, quote at p. 46.

Protestant emphasis on temptation. His findings are broadly conversant with the arguments of Peter Lake and Alexandra Walsham that Protestantism was forced into an uneasy accommodation with a popular culture that it could not override and which it increasingly found useful to appropriate for its own ends.

Whilst Dr Oldridge's analysis provides many broad insights into the place of the Devil in early modern culture, it is over-schematised, simplifying, and thus misrepresenting, a number of the fundamental characteristics of early modern demonism. As we will see, the experience of the Reformation produced a very different response amongst early Protestants than a simplistic othering of their enemies. Whilst Protestant writers produced numerous works detailing their differences from Catholic persecutors, these were not transparent statements of fact so much as testaments to the painful experience of separation from the church they had once embraced. They reflected the need to explain why Catholicism was such a convincing fake, why it appeared to satisfy the devotional needs of men whose piety and intelligence could not be denied. It was this experience, rather than simply a dual perception of the ubiquity of sin and the prevalence of apathy amongst the laity, that produced the Protestant emphasis on the hidden agency of the Devil. The consequences of the process were profound. The notion of the potential hidden diabolism of the apparently benign and even pious helped to shape Protestant devotional experience, cultivated a suspicion of the most commonplace activities, and problematised both in learned and popular culture the notion of the physical appearances of the Devil. Ultimately, as noted above, it would produce a viable language of both political opposition and negotiation based on the analogies of the temptation of the body and of the body politic that was dependent for its force on the sophisticated understanding of the mechanisms of hidden diabolic agency.

Moreover, there are problems with the approach to the experience of internal temptation adopted by Godbeer and Oldridge. Whilst psychological processes of projection must, of course, have been open to the inhabitants of early modern England, we must be careful not to overlay a predetermined scheme onto a range of experiences that were, a close reading of the accounts reveals, more various and nuanced. In functionalising diabolic assault by rationalising it as a palliative for something else – vulnerability of conscience and devotional weakness – there is a tendency to present the experience of the demonic as largely a retrospective process of narrative creation. This implicitly assumes a linear progression in the mind of the sufferer from discrete experience to interpretation in which the identification of diabolic agency provided a resolution to an uncomfortable experience. The resulting historical picture of demonic temptation tends not to credit the depth of *engagement* with the continuing experience to which contemporary writings testify. Whilst the demonic certainly did provide a language by which spiritual experiences might be articulated, it was not understood to absolve individuals of responsibility for their evil thoughts. Rather it problematised the origin of the individual's innermost thoughts – whether they were to be attributed to oneself or to the Devil. Moreover, Protestant writings reveal that it was not only obviously sinful thoughts that might be suspect, but also those which, although ostensibly pious, might hold within them the seeds of heresy or antinomianism. Indeed, it was often the very subtlety of the thoughts Satan was understood to introduce into the conscience that made their threat so profound and insidious. Such an understanding brought with it the responsibility of continually keeping watch over one's own thoughts and encouraged a necessary engagement with the experience of diabolic intrusion, the manifestation of which might be far from obvious. Thus the functional use of the demonic to project responsibility away from the self was neither advocated in Protestant devotional writing, nor easily accomplished by those godly who felt Satan's presence deeply. As we will see, the identification of the Devil's presence instead refocused attention back on the individual and offered relief only through the rigorous examination of the conscience.

The aim of this book, then, is to provide a detailed analysis of early modern *demonism* rather than *demonology*. It examines a wide body of source material, drawn from all areas of contemporary literary culture in which the Devil can be found to be a significant figure. The majority of sources are printed material intended for public consumption, for it was in the liturgy, in sermons, conduct books and pulp press pamphlets that the fullest descriptions and narratives of demonic agency were recorded and transmitted to a wider audience. More private sources, such as diaries and commonplace books, are examined in order to trace everyday lay demonological beliefs and experiences. Often these provide evidence of a keen awareness of conventional demonism filtered through personal experience to make it meaningful. Spiritual autobiographies and godly lives are similarly of central importance. These narratives of spiritual progress and conversion often depicted intense periods of struggle with the Devil. A broad sweep of political culture illustrates further the influence of demonism in the period. For the Devil's presence in the minds of many individuals of the governing elite was pronounced (if not actually pervasive), and a conception of demonic subversive agency was fully congruous with the political rhetoric of the times.

None of these sources are without problems. The difficulty presented by the absence of evidence from the illiterate or semi-literate mass of the population is perennial in cultural history, and the study of demonism is no exception.[82] The vast majority of the population of sixteenth- and

[82] Tim Harris, 'Problematising Popular Culture', in T. Harris, (ed.), *Popular Culture in England, c.1500–1850* (Houndmills, 1995), pp. 6–9.

seventeenth-century England have left no record at all of their demonological beliefs. It is simply impossible to say with any certainty to what extent the Devil played a significant role in the lives of those who either lacked the education or the inclination to record their experiences. Such judgements as have been attempted have largely been based on absences in court and parish records, the forum in which the voice of the illiterate majority might be heard, even if it was mediated by the process of recording. But they point eloquently to the problems of such an approach. Alan Macfarlane has suggested that an absence of words such as 'devil' and 'evil' in the records of the Essex parish of Earls Colne indicates that the prosaic nature of ordinary parishioners in the seventeenth century found little place for notions of the agency of the Devil.[83] And yet such an absence is only significant if those records can be accepted to fully encompass all other important aspects of early modern culture. If we are not to argue from absences we must engage with the sheer number of literate sources which give ample testimony to the importance of the Devil. Of course, it is difficult to gauge precisely their influence. Theological discussion of the Devil was academic, whilst the *practical* influence of prescriptive conduct literature is difficult to judge. On very rare occasions we can trace the influence of a specific book on a specific individual, but invariably the individuals concerned were self-consciously godly, and we cannot be confident that theology had a wider lay audience. Yet to look for such definite chains of influence is unrealistic, and seeks to impose a hierarchical structure onto early modern culture which did not exist. The influence of demonism was more fluid and more opaque, based as it was on a subtle realignment of emphases rather than a fundamental change to the concept.

The fullest demonological narratives were those left by the literate, whose education and reading must have allowed them a far more sophisticated articulation of demonological experience than the uneducated. And, amongst this group, those who wrote about the Devil were, by definition, those zealous Protestants and Puritans who felt his presence most keenly. These spiritual autobiographies themselves were influenced by the conventional narrative cycle of struggle, conversion and assurance. Even these sources, then, are not necessarily a fully reliable testament as to 'real' demonological experience in early modern England. Yet they are by no means too jaded to be useful or important. The very nuances of narrative, prescription, selectivity and fiction provide in themselves vital insights into the culture of demonism and the ways in which it might be expressed. Within the social context which defined emotional norms – illustrated by prescriptive and imaginative literature – sense of self and self-evaluation could be constructed

[83] Thomas, *Religion and the Decline of Magic*, p. 627; Macfarlane, 'The Root of all Evil', pp. 62–5.

in terms of narrative.[84] The narrativity of experience was at least as meaningful (and probably far more so) to the contemporaries who constructed it as any historically imposed picture of the 'reality' that underlay it.

Nor is it acceptable to dismiss literate sources as 'elite' and thus unrepresentative. Cultural historians have increasingly challenged the simplistic separation of elite and popular culture, emphasising the extent to which people were exposed to written material by reading aloud, oral transmission and illustration. The Devil featured prominently in the 'populist' literature of the pulp press and the early modern stage. Whilst such works were produced (in part at least) 'for', as opposed to 'by' the populace, they were influenced by the financial pragmatism of the market place. The consistency with which the Devil was presented in these sources suggests – if it does not prove – that prevalent religious concepts of diabolic agency appealed to the popular imagination. Moreover, narratives of diabolic agency consistently relied on the reader's sense of identification with the internal experience of temptation in order to make them comprehensible and engaging. Indeed this study has found no real basis on which to delineate differences between popular and elite conceptions of the Devil so far as they are represented in the written sources. Perception of satanic agency was broadly shared at all levels of early modern society. Equally scepticism might be found amongst the highest and lowest, but at all levels it was attributable to personal conviction rather than class culture.

Thus what follows concentrates on the aspects of demonism that were most prominent across the various genres of early modern culture. As a consequence the model of demonism it describes cannot be entirely comprehensive. As a familiar and complex belief, demonism was employed in widely differing areas of contemporary culture, and the extensive remit the Devil had adopted by the sixteenth century – from pseudo-deity to providential hangman, trickster and tempter – provided a rich source for religious and political manipulation. Whilst this study argues that an emphasis on the Devil's role as tempter came to dominate contemporary demonism, no aspect of his traditional agency was dismissed and all aspects continued to find expression after the Reformation. Thus the study does not seek to argue that there was a single demonism in early modern England to which all subscribed. Rather, it suggests that emphasis on certain aspects of demonological belief changed as a result of the Reformation, and that the change was highly influential within a demonism that maintained the central tenets of the Devil's established conception.

[84] MacDonald, 'The Fearefull Estate of Francis Spira', pp. 35–7.

2

The synagogue of Satan: anti-Catholicism, false doctrine and the construction of contrariety

The study of the Devil in early modern English culture begins with the Reformation, or, more precisely, with the understanding of satanism that emerged out of Protestant attempts to comprehend the corruption of traditional Catholicism. As the will to reform in England gathered pace, Protestant polemicists targeted not only specific clerical abuses but the Roman faith as a whole. They adopted a long-established heretical association of the Pope with Antichrist, and behind Antichrist lay the Devil, the guiding hand of apocalyptic subversion.[1] In describing how Satan came to exact such a profound influence over generations of ostensibly pious men and women, Protestants articulated a demonic agency which placed the Devil's power firmly in the human consciousness and in the manipulation of man's instincts, both godly and ungodly. In effect Catholicism might be a parody, a contradiction of everything sacred to the true faith.[2] But this was hidden behind a pious gloss which had hoodwinked millions into their own eternal destruction. Nor were its victims naive or ignorant; many learned and zealous Christians continued to believe in the veracity of the Roman church. It fell then to the reformers to explain why Catholicism was such a convincing fake, and in so doing reveal its contrariety with Christianity. Paradoxically, this very process forced Protestants to engage with the spiritual and emotional experience which bound men to Catholicism, and to find a congruous place for the Devil within it. As a consequence Protestantism emphasised the Devil's presence in the everyday religious instincts of the average Christian and, as this emphasis pervaded

1 R. Bauckham, *Tudor Apocalypse: Sixteenth-Century Apocalypticism, Millenarianism and the English Reformation from John Bale to John Foxe and Thomas Brightman* (Abingdon, Oxon., 1978); K. R. Firth, *The Apocalyptic Tradition in Reformation Britain, 1530–1645* (Oxford, 1979); C. Hill, *Antichrist in Seventeenth-Century England* (Oxford, 1971; rev. edn, London, 1990), pp. 1–25; Clark, *Thinking with Demons*, pp. 346–53.

2 P. Lake, 'Anti-Popery: The Structure of a Prejudice', in R. Cust and A. Hughes (eds.), *Conflict in Stuart England: Studies in Religion and Politics, 1603–1660* (London, 1989), pp. 72–4; Clark, *Thinking with Demons*, pp. 349–51.

its more general devotional considerations, the Devil's greatest threat seemed to be his power to invade the consciousness disguised as the most commonplace thoughts and desires. We will see in the next chapter that this emphasis crystallised in the elevation of internal temptation as the most significant aspect of Satan's agency, and that it was enormously influential in shaping demonism in the century to 1660. This chapter examines how the concerns and conflicts of the English Reformation shaped the perception of the Devil's agency as an intimate everyday experience with profound consequences within a wider apocalyptic cosmic scheme that saw the world divided between the powers of light and darkness.

THE DEVIL AS FACT: THE PROTESTANT PERCEPTION OF DIABOLIC POWER

Peter Lake has described anti-Catholicism in seventeenth-century England as 'the most obvious and important example of that process of binary opposition, inversion or the argument from contraries which, we are increasingly being told, played so central a part in both the learned and popular culture of early modern Europe'. Anti-Catholicism, Professor Lake argues, was a form of inverted self-advocacy. By highlighting the diabolism of hated aspects of Catholic worship, Protestants implied an ideal of faith in practice to which they believed they conformed. Balanced against superstitious popery was the purity of the Protestant faith, which asserted by implication the values of *sola scriptura*, clerical humility and iconophobia.[3] Anti-Catholic inversions might also be the result of wider social tensions. David Underdown argues that a widespread adherence to millenarianism in the seventeenth century made the identification of Catholics as agents of Satan 'natural'. Scapegoats were necessary at all levels of a society facing, or so it believed, a combination of crises of order, and in the fears of many Catholics and witches became fused into a single diabolic threat to society.[4]

This was the culmination of a process begun in the English Reformation, in which the success of the identification of Catholicism as a diabolic church was far less certain. Protestant reformers became convinced that Catholicism embodied a complete inversion of true religion, substituting an empty and diabolic piety based only on the authority of man for faith

[3] Lake, 'Anti-Popery', p. 73; on the concept of contrariety and inversion see Stuart Clark, 'Inversion, Misrule and the Meaning of Witchcraft', *Past and Present*, 87 (1980); Clark, *Thinking with Demons*, pp. 3–93; Peter Burke, *Popular Culture in Early Modern Europe* (London, 1978), pp. 185–91.

[4] David Underdown notes that it was no coincidence that a number of Protestant writers, James I among them, noted that women were especially susceptible to both witchcraft and recusancy. See Underdown, *A Freeborn People*, p. 17.

in the word of God. In thus corrupting the church, Catholicism was the 'synagogue of Satan'. The term was coined in the Book of Revelation to describe the apostasy of the Jewish church, but, whilst St Augustine introduced the division of the world into rival camps of light and darkness into orthodoxy, the language of the 'two churches' came into its own only when it offered medieval heretics a needed critique of the established faith.[5] In England it was Lollardy that had most recently attacked the papacy with accusations of diabolism.[6] But whilst the rhetoric of the synagogue of Satan associated the reformers with a long tradition of attacking the Roman church, its use in sixteenth-century England emerged out of the specific interaction of an experiential approach to the forces of evil and a concern that the satanic corruption of the papacy was not being recognised. In reforming polemic, then, 'the synagogue of Satan' described a very specific process whereby piety was distracted from its true course by the Devil, and it required Protestants to claim a monopoly of insight into the workings of the demonic.

In England, demonism was not reformed in the sense that eucharistic theology or the cult of the saints were reformed. There was no attempt to alter the fundamentals of belief in the Devil or to deny him the power he had previously been accorded. Indeed the major writers of the early Reformation produced no dedicated works of demonology, and, with the exception of discussions of witchcraft, such works remained rare throughout the sixteenth and seventeenth centuries.[7] But mainstream Protestant writing was pervaded by a profound sense of the Devil's power. The Lutheran William Tyndale's works are littered with references to Satan's relationship with man. His first known book, *A Pathway into the Holy Scripture* (1525), contains a passionate account of man's fall from grace into diabolic slavery. During his long career, Thomas Becon turned his attention to a wide variety of religious

[5] Bauckham, *Tudor Apocalypse*, pp. 56–7.

[6] In 1406 William Taylor described the clergy as the 'mynystris of antecrist' and the limbs of Satan, in *Two Wycliffite Texts*, ed. A. Hudson (Oxford, Early English Text Society, 1993), pp. 10–11. The Lollard text of 1409–10, *The Lantern of lyght* (which was printed in 1530) noted that there was a 'church empropered to the devil, the which is the number of them that be encumbered to serve him after his tising against God's hests', *Here begynnethe the Lantern of lyght*, ed. L. M. Swinburn (Oxford, Early English Text Society, 1971), p. 127.

[7] Whilst continental witchcraft texts seem to have been widely known in England, English versions began to be produced only after 1584. Early examples include George Gifford, *A discourse of the subtill practices of devilles by witches and sorcerers* (London, 1587); *A Dialogue Concerning Witches and Witchcraftes* (London, 1593); James VI, *Daemonologie* (Edinburgh, 1597); William Perkins, *A discourse of the damned art of witchcraft*, pub. Thomas Pickering (Cambridge, 1610). Stuart Clark suggests that witchcraft drew the attention of Protestant theologians because it had an 'unforced relevance' to their programme of establishing doctrinal purity and eradicating superstition. See Clark, 'Protestant Demonology', pp. 80–1.

subjects, and Satan is rarely absent from his thirty-three identifiable works. Whether he was turning out anti-Catholic polemic, devotional prayer books or instructions for children, Becon found the Devil to be a pertinent, if not fundamental subject.[8]

This powerful sense of the Devil's presence was combined with a pragmatic focus on scriptural authority in questions of doctrine. The result was a 'de facto' approach to Satan's reality in which his agency was to be experienced rather than speculated about. The emphasis is clearly seen with regards to the question of the Devil's fall from heaven. Lucifer's rebellion had, in all probability, introduced evil into the cosmos, but the truth remained obscure. 'Some murmur', John Calvin noted in his *Institutes of Christian Religion*, 'because the Scripture does not in various passages give a distinct and regular exposition of Satan's fall, its cause, mode, date and nature.' But this only indicated that the information was 'of no consequence to us'.[9] The same approach was implicit in virtually all English reformed discussion of the Devil from the early Lutheran-inspired texts to the Protestant writings of the Elizabethan 'orthodoxy'. In his *A Pathway into Scripture*, William Tyndale did not mention the Devil's fall, whilst in *The Image of God* (1550) Roger Hutchinson argued that belief in the Devil was fundamental, but offered only proofs from Job, and in the writings of St Paul and St Peter.[10]

Thus English reforming theologians were relatively unconcerned with what might be termed 'fundamental' theodicy – the cosmic origin of evil. But in stark contrast to this reticence was their concern over Satan's earthly activity. The Devil's agency was not a theological puzzle to be pondered on, but a demonstrable certainty to be recognised and reckoned with, and the havoc he wreaked on earth was only too apparent. Preaching to Convocation in 1537, Hugh Latimer expressed this experiential approach to demonism. Man's only experience of the Devil was of his agency, and hence his agency was *all* that could be known of him:

> I cannot wholly express him, I wot not what to call him, but a certain thing altogther made of the hatred of God, of mistrust in God, of lyings, deceits, perjuries, discords,

[8] Thomas Becon, *Early Works*, ed. J. Ayre (Cambridge, Parker Society, 1844); *The Catechism of Thomas Becon, with other pieces*, ed. J. Ayre (Cambridge, Parker Society, 1844); *Prayers and Other Pieces of Thomas Becon*, ed. J. Ayre (Cambridge, Parker Society, 1844).

[9] John Calvin, *The Institutes of Christian Religion*, Bk I, chapter xiv, trans. H. Beveridge (Grand Rapids, Mich., 2 vols., 1989), vol. I, pp. 152–3; similarly, see Heinrich Bullinger, *The Decades of Henry Bullinger*, ed. T. Harding (Cambridge, Parker Society, 5 vols., 1849–52), vol. IV, pp. 348–9.

[10] William Tyndale, *A Pathway into the Holy Scripture* (1525), in *Doctrinal treatises and introductions to different portions of the Holy Scripture*, ed. H. Walter (Cambridge, Parker Society, 1848), pp. 7–28; Roger Hutchinson, *The Image of God, or the laie mans booke*, in *The Works of Roger Hutchinson*, ed. J. Bruce (Cambridge, Parker Society, 1842), pp. 140–1.

manslaughters; and to say at one word, a thing concrete, heaped up and made of all kind of mischief. But what the devil mean I to go about to describe particularly the devil's nature, when no reason, no power of man's mind can comprehend it? This alonely can I say grossly, and as in a sum, of which all we (our hurt is the more) have experience, the devil to be a stinking sentine of all vices; a foul filthy channel of all mischiefs; and that this world, his son, even like a child meet to have such a parent, is not much unlike his father.[11]

Satan's 'evils no man can number nor rehearse', observed Thomas Cranmer in 1548. But he made a fair attempt notwithstanding, listing among the afflictions suffered at the Devil's hands, 'sadness, sorrow, trouble of conscience, faintness of heart, sickness of the body, poverty, slanders, despising, reproaches, persecutions, battle, sedition, hunger, pestilence and all plagues'.[12] If scripture revealed little of the Devil's origins, it provided him with a powerful didactic nomenclature which expressed well this intimate power over man. 'The tendency of all that scripture teaches us concerning devils is to put us on our guard against their wiles and machinations', explained John Calvin; 'the object of these descriptions is to make us more cautious and vigilant, and more prepared for the contest'.[13] The Greek and Hebrew names, 'Devil' and 'Satan', were derived from expressions of his agency, the first meaning a slanderer, the second an opposer.[14] In England the traditional lists of the individual demonic powers were all but abandoned in favour of a concentration on man's relationship with the Devil himself.[15]

The experience of persecution lent an even greater tangibility to the notion of a demonic assault on the faithful, as individual impulses to bible-based piety came into conflict with the government's determination to stamp out Lutheranism and vernacular translation. Historians have noted that 'fiery clerical reformers' were largely absent from England's political and factional Reformation. Enthusiasts for bible-based piety, like William Tyndale and Robert Barnes, were more or less thrown into the arms of Lutheranism by

11 Hugh Latimer, *Sermons by Hugh Latimer*, ed. G.E. Corrie (Cambridge, Parker Society, 1844), p. 42.

12 Thomas Cranmer, *Catechismvs, that is to say, a shorte Instruction into Christian Religion* (London, 1548), fols. 151v–2.

13 Calvin, *Institutes*, Bk I, chapter xiv, p. 150. 14 Bullinger, *Decades*, vol. IV, p. 355.

15 Whilst demonologists in continental Europe, such as Johan Weyer, devoted great energy to calculating the exact number of individual demonic 'powers', figures such as Agares, Amon, Bathin, Eligor, Bileth, Gamigin and Balam were almost entirely absent from English demonology in the sixteenth and seventeenth centuries. There was no attempt among English theologians to investigate the infernal hierarchy or to produce lists and breakdowns of the identifiable demonic generals. Indeed the most important English work which provided any such hierarchical picture did so in order to dispute its reality. This was Reginald Scot's much vaunted sceptical tract *The Discoverie of Witchcraft* (London, 1584), see the edition of Montague Summers (New York, 1972), pp. 217–25.

clerical intransigence, and much flirtation with heresy came from individual crises of faith.[16] In the 1530s, the needs of Henry VIII's divorce catapulted cautious figures such as Thomas Cranmer and Nicholas Ridley into prominence, tensely balanced with more radical men like John Hooper.[17] But whether on trial for heresy, or defending the king himself against the papal supremacy, the Devil's persecution provided a powerful sense of identity to reformers in England. For the London merchant-tailor, Richard Hunne, the Pope was 'Satan'.[18] John Stilman, tried before the bishop of London in 1518 noted that the College of Cardinals was the limb of Antichrist whilst 'all other inferior prelates and priests are the synagogue of Satan'.[19] As William Tyndale's writing became increasingly polemical, so too did his demonism. His exposés of clerical abuse, *The Practyse of Prelates* (1530), The *Exposition of the Fyrste Epistle of Seynt Jhon* (1531), and *An Exposition uppon the V. VI. VII. Chapters of Mathew* (*c.* 1532), focused the sense of vulnerability to Satan that he had expressed in *The Pathway into Holy Scripture* more clearly on the Catholic church.[20] In *The Practyse of Prelates* Tyndale described how the Pope had 'put down the kingdom of Christ, and hath set up the ministers of Satan'.[21]

At his trial for heresy in 1532, Thomas Bennet, an Exeter schoolmaster and protégé of Thomas Bilney, denied the church's jurisdiction since it was based on papal authority. 'The church that is built upon a man', he told his examiners, 'is the devil's church or congregation, and not God's.'[22] One of Bennet's protagonists was a relapsed heretic named Gregory Basset. In John Foxe's polemical account of the trial, Basset became representative of the prosecution as a whole, and thus when Bennet declared that Basset's arguments contained nothing 'but what maintaineth the Devil', he implied an accusation of betrayal by apostasy.[23] Such self-conception imbued the Protestant cause with a palpable sense of urgency. 'Mark out the people of God from the synagogue of

[16] C. Haigh, *English Reformations: Religion, Politics, and Society under the Tudors* (Oxford, 1993), pp. 57–60, 67–8; Diarmaid MacCulloch, 'England', in A. Pettegree (ed.), *The Early Reformation in Europe* (Cambridge, 1992), p. 166.

[17] MacCulloch, 'England', pp. 166–9.

[18] John Foxe, *Acts and Monuments of these latter and perilous dayes, touching matters of the Church*, ed. S. R. Cattley (London, 8 vols., 1841–89, hereafter *A & M*), vol. IV, p. 186; S. Brigden, *London and the Reformation* (corrected edition, Oxford, 1991), pp. 98–103.

[19] *A & M*, vol. IV, p. 208. See also the heretical views of Patrick Hamilton (Scotland, 1528), in *A & M*, vol. IV, pp. 559–61; James Bainham (1532), pp. 699, 705; Thomas Bennet of Exeter (1532), in *A & M*, vol. V, p. 23; Alexander Seton, in *A & M*, vol. V, pp. 449–51.

[20] William Tyndale, *The Practise of Prelates* (1530), *The Exposition of the Fyrste Epistle of Seynt Jhon* (1531), and *An Exposition uppon the V. VI. VII. Chapters of Mathew* (*c.* 1532) in *Expositions and notes on sundry portions of the Holy Scripture*, ed. H. Walter (Cambridge, Parker Society, 1849).

[21] Tyndale, *The Practise of Prelates*, pp. 273–5. [22] *A & M*, vol. V, p. 23. [23] Ibid.

Satan', the ex-Carmelite monk, John Bale, exhorted in 1548, 'and delay not to nourish them with the sweet fruits of the Spirit.'[24]

Henry VIII's government was itself willing to perceive diabolic persecution in its conflicts with the Pope over the royal divorce. In the wake of Henry's excommunication in 1533, churchmen such as Stephen Gardiner and Cuthbert Tunstall defended the royal supremacy in print and from the pulpit. Tunstall, the bishop of Durham, preached a sermon before the king on Palm Sunday in 1534 in which he characterised the Pope's claims to supremacy as Luciferian. 'The bishops of Rome', he apparently preached, 'following the pride of Lucifer their father, make themselves fellows to God ... and will be like to Almighty God.'[25] Demonism demonstrated just what was a stake in the disputes with Rome. Tunstall and John Stokesley, the bishop of London, warned Cardinal Pole in a letter of 1534, that if they heeded 'the bishop of Rome' over the nation's monarch they risked becoming 'but the ministers of Satan'.[26]

Schooled in a tradition of attacks on heresy, conservatives were equally prepared to see diabolism in the reformer's schismatic tendencies. Reforming doctrine carried *too* far became an upstart satanism, and Protestants were the deluded instruments of the Devil's latest assault upon the true faith. The curate of Harwich, Thomas Corthorp, appalled at the headway made by 'new-fangled' preaching in London, complained that 'the Devil reigneth over us now'.[27] The bishop of Winchester, Stephen Gardiner, denounced the violent Lutheran, John Barnes, in a sermon at Paul's Cross on 14 February 1540. Satan sought to subvert the reform of clerical abuse, he noted, for if it were no longer possible to buy salvation, 'the deuyll hath excogitate to offre heaven without works for it'. Thus new-styled 'ministers' were but the latest diabolic agents. 'If the Kinges Majestie', he noted, 'as he hath banyshed freres by the Frenche name, wolde also baysh these that call themselves bretheren in Englishe, the deuyll shulde be greatly discomforted.'[28] In a broadside describing Barnes' execution, the refusal of the 'vicar of Hell' to recant was said to be at Satan's instigation.[29] Thomas Becon did recant his Protestantism in 1541 and declared that in all his preaching he had 'continuallye laboured in the service of the Dyvell'.[30] Around the controversy over transubstantiation Gardiner published *A Detection of the Deuils*

[24] John Bale, *The Image of Bothe Churches*, in *Select works: containing the examinations of Lord Cobham, William Thorpe and Anne Askewe, and the Image of both churches*, ed. H. Christmas (Cambridge, Parker Society, 1849), p. 384.
[25] *A & M*, vol. V, pp. 84–5. [26] *A & M*, vol. V, p. 90.
[27] Quoted in Brigden, *London and the Reformation*, pp. 256–7.
[28] Stephen Gardiner, *The Letters of Stephen Gardiner*, ed. J. A. Muller (Cambridge, 1933), pp. 168–70; Brigden, *London and the Reformation*, pp. 309–10.
[29] Quoted in Brigden, *London and the Reformation*, pp. 323–4.
[30] *A & M*, vol. V, p. 448, appendix XII.

Sophistrie in 1546, in which he argued that through the 'carnal' arguments of the reformers the Devil was poised to lead men 'captive and thralde from the true Catholique byleefe in this moost holye sacramente'.[31]

The very indeterminacy of England's Reformation encouraged Protestants to develop a diabolic rhetoric which incorporated the elasticity of progress and reversal. Tunstall, preaching against the Pope's supremacy, characterised the desertion of Reginald Pole as a diabolic subversion of a subject's natural loyalty.[32] William Turner, writing against Gardiner in *The huntyng and findyng out of the Romish Fox* in 1543, saw the central experience of Reformation as a tug-of-war between the anti-papal policies of Henry VIII and the backsliding of a demonic episcopate. The Pope had been driven from England, and Gardiner had been one of those appointed to institute the king's policy. But rather than lose his entire hold in the nation, the Devil had persuaded the bishop to subvert the Reformation and protect Catholic doctrine, particularly clerical celibacy, in exchange for land and riches.[33] Satan also sought to subvert committed reformers' own progress towards doctrinal purity. 'A more sincere and pure feeling of religion has begun to flourish with success', John Burcher commented of England's religious progress in 1548, 'but Satan, through his hatred of this, has been endeavouring to throw every thing into confusion by means of dissension.' In particular Burcher referred to Cranmer's defence of the real presence in the Eucharist.[34] To continental reformers England could appear a frontier of Reformation in which all progress was countered by diabolic action. Peter Martyr perceived satanic reprisals in the response to his attack on transubstantiation at Oxford in May 1549. 'If you knew what numerous and powerful enemies the devil has stirred up against me on this account, you would be surprised', he told Heinrich Bullinger in a letter of January 1550.[35] But the international network of Protestants provided a means of mutual support by which strength could be gained in the face of Satan's most concerted activity. In 1552 Calvin wrote to

[31] Stephen Gardiner, *A Detection of the Deuils Sophistrie, wherewith he robbeth the unlearned people, of the true byleef, in the most blessed sacrament of the aulter* (London, 1546), fol. 5v.

[32] *A & M*, vol. V, p. 88.

[33] William Turner, *The huntyng and findyng out of the Romish Fox: which more than seven yeares hath bene hyd among the Byshoppes of England, after the Kynges Hyghnes, Henry VIII, had commanded hym to be dryven out of his Realme* (reprinted Cambridge, 1851; First edn, 1543), p. 37; Gardiner answered Turner in *The Examination of a Prowd Præsumptuous hunter* (1544?, no longer extant in print), attributing his arguments to the malice of the Devil; see Gardiner, *Letters*, p. 480.

[34] John Burcher to Heinrich Bullinger, 29 October 1548, in *Original Letters Relative to the English Reformation*, ed. H. Robinson (Cambridge, Parker Society, 1846–7), pp. 642–3. Also his letter of 21 January 1551, concerning satanic accusations of heresy against John Hooper, pp. 676–7.

[35] Ibid., p. 478; see also the comments of Martin Micronius to Bullinger on the troubles experienced by the stranger churches, 7 November 1551, pp. 577–8.

both Edward VI and Thomas Cranmer exhorting them to remain faithful in the face of the Devil. He sought to consolidate Edward's sense of the importance of his own Protestantism, noting 'I doubt not, sire, but that Satan is placing many hinderances in the way, to retard and cool your zeal. A great portion of your subjects are not aware of the good you are procuring them.' To Cranmer he observed that diabolic activity was a central experience of Reformation, and that England could never have too many champions 'well qualified to confute the lies of Satan'.[36]

A sensitivity to the political fortunes of those who were sympathetic to their cause infused the reformers' perception of the struggles around Edward VI's minority with an awareness of diabolism. Peter Martyr wrote to Martin Bucer in January 1549 of the arrest of Thomas Seymour, brother to the Protector, and 'a great friend to religion'. 'The devil is using every endeavour to drive away Christ', he concluded.[37] A letter written by Calvin to Somerset following his release from the Tower (February 1550) is striking. It cautioned the duke to resist the temptation to take revenge on those who had deposed him, and instead to concentrate on the spiritual significance of events in England. 'Let us not . . . wait trifling with men', he commented, 'but rather turn our attention to Satan . . . as there is not doubt but that he has been the author of the mischief that has been devised against you, to the end that by this means the progress of the gospel might be hindered.' In pardoning his enemies Somerset might 'repel the malice of him who has made use of them'.[38]

By the 1550s the nomenclature by which the Devil was commonly known fully reflected the prevalence of these concerns. Two scriptural terms in particular became central to the Protestant expression of Satan's reality and power. 'Baal', the name of the ancient Persian deity, described his role in ? idolatry. In the prophesy of Jeremiah it was used to characterise the idolatry of the pagan Chaldeans, whilst in Judges it expressed the faithlessness of the Hebrews who 'forsook the Lord, and served Baal and Astaroth'.[39] Even more commonly employed was the description of 1 Peter 5: 8 in which Satan was 'a roaring lion', who roamed constantly about 'seeking whom he may destroy'. This image haunted the Protestant imagination, embodying their conviction that true faith survived on a knife-edge over complete destruction. Peter 'compareth him to a lion', commented Roger Hutchinson in *The Image of God*; 'he walketh, he seeketh'. 'The deuyl seking like a roryng Lyon, whom he may deuoure', noted Thomas Lever in 1550, 'nyghte and day, winter and sommer, wyth a wonderful sorte of wicked spirites, doth euer besyge

[36] Ibid., pp. 708, 712; see also Thomas Lever, *A Sermon preached . . . in Lent before the Kynges Maiestie*, in *Sermons 1550* ed. E. Arber (London, 1870), pp. 61–2, 68.

[37] *Original Letters Relative to the English Reformation*, p. 475. [38] Ibid., pp. 704–5.

[39] Book of Jeremiah 33: 29; Book of Judges 2: 13.

byshoprykes, shyres, townes and parishes'.[40] Other descriptions were plainly derivative. 'How doth Satan spread his nets in every forest and park, that no deer may escape his devouring teeth and ravening paws', was one of Thomas Becon's slants.[41]

Having made headway with reform under Edward VI, Protestant perception of diabolic activity was sharpened even further by the setbacks of the Marian regime.[42] English Protestants had to come to terms with a stark reversal of fortune. They were removed from the ascendancy in the church which Northumberland's regency had afforded them, and forced into exile or persecuted at home.[43] Two distraught letters by Heinrich Bullinger, written as events were unfolding in August and October 1553, give a sense of the shocking palpability which Mary's accession lent to the Devil's agency. 'Where is our Martyr?', he wrote in August to Theadore Beza, 'Where John à Lasco? Where is Hooper, bishop of Worcester? Where is Cranmer, archbishop of Canterbury? ... Lord, have mercy upon them! I cannot easily express how greatly these things distress me.'[44] To Calvin in October he wrote of his fear that John Hooper was already dead, and of the execution of Northumberland, noting 'let us pray the Lord to preserve his people in these sad commotions, and to beat down Satan under his feet'.[45] The enormity of the sense of betrayal felt towards those who deserted the Protestant cause is demonstrated by a scathing letter written in 1554 by Lady Jane Grey to Thomas Harding, the one-time Protestant divine who became chaplain to

[40] Hutchinson, *The Works of Roger Hutchinson*, p. 141; Lever, *A Sermon preached at Paules Crosse*, in *Sermons*, p. 98; Becon, *The New Years Gift*, in *Early Works*, p. 323; *A Fruitful Treatise of Fasting*, in *The Catechism*, p. 543; John Bradford, *The Writings of John Bradford*, ed. A Townsend (Cambridge, 2 vols., Parker Society, 1848), vol. I, p. 136; Latimer, *Sermons*, pp. 492–3; see also 'An exhortation against the fear of death', 'An homily against gluttony and drunkenness' and 'An homily against idleness', in *Certain Sermons or Homilies appointed to be read in Churches in the time of Queen Elizabeth*, ed. J. Griffiths (London, 1864; reprinted 1908), pp. 107, 311, 555; Edwin Sandys, *The Sermons of Edwin Sandys ... to which are added some miscellaneous pieces*, ed. J. Ayre (Cambridge, Parker Society, 1842), pp. 175, 181, 263; William Perkins, *Foure Godly Treatises; very necessary to be considered of all Christians* (London, 1587), p. 1; Thomas Pierson, 'Epistle Dedicatory', in Perkins' *The Combat between Christ and the Divell displayed*, sig. Kkk6; Lewis Bayly, *The Practice of Pietie: Directing a Christian how to walke that he may please god* (Edinburgh, 1635; First edn, 1615), p. 475.

[41] Becon, *Early Works*, p. 125; 'An homily concerning the coming down of the Holy Ghost and the manifold gifts of the same', in *Certain Sermons or Homilies*, pp. 498–500.

[42] The role of demonism in the Protestant reforms under Edward VI will be discussed with particular reference to the liturgy and baptism in chapter 3, pp. 62–7.

[43] Joy Shakespeare, 'Plague and Punishment', in P. Lake and M. Dowling (eds.), *Protestantism and the National Church in Sixteenth Century England* (London, 1987), pp. 103–4; Hill, *Antichrist in Seventeenth-Century England*, p. 11; Bauckham, *Tudor Apocalypse*, pp. 46–7, 64.

[44] Heinrich Bullinger to Theadore Beza, 30 August 1553, in *Original Letters Relative to the English Reformation*, p. 741.

[45] Ibid., pp. 742–3.

Gardiner. 'I cannot but marvel at thee, and lament thy case', she said, 'who seemed sometime to be the lively member of Christ, but now are the deformed imp of the devil; sometime the beautiful temple of God, but now the stinking and filthy kennel of Satan.'[46] According to the martyr Richard Woodman in 1557, the renewed Catholic parish church was a 'church of Satan' where man went to 'hear the detestable doctrine, that they spit and spew out of their churches and pulpits, to the great dishonour of God'.[47]

For many Protestants the explanation for the crisis lay in biblical precedent – God was punishing the nation for its sins. The people, offered the gospel, had refused to take the opportunity to live according to the word. 'We set nought by the ministration of the holy and blessed communion of the body and blood of Christ', Thomas Becon explained in 1554, 'therefore this plague is worthy to come upon us, that in stead of the Lord's supper we have the most wicked and abominable masses set up, invented by the devil, brought in by antichrist.'[48] The return of popery was a plague in the biblical style, not solely punitive, but also intended to open the eyes of the nation,[49] and the Devil allowed Protestants to comprehend and engage with the extent of the setback.

Only Satan could persuade an entire nation to recant, and Protestant polemic exaggerated England's relapse by exaggerating the success of its pre-Marian Reformation. 'Of late in every congregation throughout all England was made prayer and petition unto God, to be delivered from the tyranny of the bishop of Rome', wrote Nicholas Ridley from his cell in Oxford, 'and now alas! Satan hath persuaded England, by his falsehood and craft, to revoke her old godly prayer.'[50] Ridley's prison writings found their emotional drive in a powerful sense of being engaged with the forces of Satan, and it was an understanding that must have bolstered many of the Marian heretics. He wrote a letter to be circulated amongst Protestant prisoners throughout the country in which he made clear that imprisonment was the agency of the roaring lion, 'that goeth about by all manner of subtle means to beguile the world, and also busily laboureth to restore and set up his kingdom again, that of late began to decay and fall to ruin'.[51] In this atmosphere dissensions among the exiles on the continent also appeared to be a

[46] *A & M*, vol. VI, pp. 418–19. [47] *A & M*, vol. VIII, p. 369.

[48] Becon, *A Comfortable Epistle to the afflicted people of God* (1554), in *Prayers and Other Pieces*, p. 207.

[49] Shakespeare, 'Plague and Punishment', pp. 107, 109.

[50] Nicholas Ridley, *A Piteous Lamentation of the Miserable Estate of the Church in England in the time of the late Revolt from the Gospel*, in *The Works of Nicholas Ridley*, ed. H. Christmas (Cambridge, Parker Society, 1843), pp. 49–50.

[51] Ibid., pp. 342–5, quote at p. 342; see also pp. 349–52, 366–8, 369, 374, 385, 404, 410, 415–16; Becon, *A Comfortable Epistle*, p. 211.

symptom of Satan's malice. Thomas Sampson described to Calvin disagreements in Strasbourg over the English prayer book, noting that 'Satan is permitted both at home and abroad to rage against the English.'[52]

The return to an official Protestantism in 1559 did appear to be the deliverance from Satan promised by the reassuring polemic of the Marian persecution, even if the Elizabethan religious settlement left large numbers of zealous Protestants disaffected with the state of England's Reformation.[53] For Edwin Sandys, newly made archbishop of York in 1576, Elizabeth's accession was a providence that paralleled Christ's passion. 'As Christ hath delivered all his out of the captivity of Satan and sin', he preached, 'so hath he also us . . . out of that prison of Romish servitude, out of the bloody claws of that cruel and proud antichrist.' 'Let us serve no more him that serveth Satan', he concluded.[54] But balanced against such optimism was a continued perception that Elizabeth's England struggled against the satanical synagogue. The apologist for the English church, John Jewel, wrote to Heinrich Bullinger in 1566 of his dispute with Thomas Harding.[55] It was his 'lot', Jewel bemoaned, 'to be always battling with these monsters. May the Lord give me strength and courage, and beat down Satan under our feet!'[56] In 1577, the perceived spread of recusancy around Southampton caused the bishop of Winchester, Robert Horne, to write of the 'fearful deceivers Satan has heretofore raised up, and daily continues to do, that he may throw all things into confusion, and especially destroy the peace of the church'.[57] The arrival of the first of the Jesuit missionaries in 1580 provided a new focus for fears of Catholic subversion. According to Sir Walter Mildmay, addressing parliament in January 1581, the Jesuits sought to 'corrupt the realme with false doctrine, [and] also under that pretence to stirr sedition to the perill of

52 Thomas Sampson to John Calvin, 12 February 1555, in *Original Letters Relative to the English Reformation*, pp. 170–1. See also Sampson's letter to Heinrich Bullinger of 6 April 1556, p. 174.

53 Hierome Zanchius wrote to Edmund Grindal in 1563 comparing England's 'peace and Agreement in pure doctrine' with satanic persecution being suffered by the church in Strasbourg, *The Zurich Letters (second series) comprising the correspondence of several English Bishops and other with some of the Helvetian Reformers*, ed. H. Robinson (Cambridge, Parker Society, 1842), pp. 81–2. The controversies over the 'half-reformed' state of the church after 1559 themselves incorporated a contested perception of diabolic subversion inherent in the maintenance of popish remnants such as the episcopate. A provocative parallel between the temptation of the body and the temptation of the body politic increasingly found a place within political rhetoric. These issues are discussed in full in chapters 6 and 7.

54 Sandys, *The Sermons of Edwin Sandys*, pp. 180–1.

55 Harding retired to Louvain during Elizabeth's reign, and his *A Confutation of a booke, Intituled An Apologie of the Church of England* was published in Antwerp in 1565.

56 'Bishop Jewel to Henry Bullinger and Lewis Lavater', 8 February 1566, in *The Zurich Letters*, pp. 147–8.

57 'Bishop Horn to [certain brethren]', 16 January 1577, in ibid., pp. 321–3.

her Majestie.'[58] Thus the words of the former playwright turned Puritan minister, Stephen Gosson, summed up England's predicament. The Devil, he noted, 'feeling such a terrible push, given to his breast by the change of religion, and by the happy entraunce of her maiestie to the crown, hath played wily beguilie ever since'.[59]

So central had diabolic persecution become to the Protestant identity that it provided a framework for a much wider social critique. Whilst Catholicism had been ejected from England, the popularity of 'sinful' pastimes such as the theatre, the alehouse and dancing appeared to many Protestants to reintroduce the synagogue of Satan by the back door. The minister Henry Roberts noted in 1572 that although England had been freed from 'the filthy corruptions of the popes decrees', yet the general abuse of the sabbath remained, 'whiche might make us muche to marvell, were it not that the gospell doth manifestly testifie, that Sathan our Auncient Enemye, is now busie wt us, as he was in tempting of our first parents Adam & Eve'. It was manifest ingratitude for God's Reformation that 'Sathan so much prevaileth in this our time wherein raigneth coveitousness & usery, whoredom and fornication, pride and vainglorie, swearyng & forswearyng, fraude and deceit, almoste amongst all sorts of people.'[60] If the Catholic 'throne' of Satan had been ejected, William Perkins noted, others remained. 'All dicing', he declared, 'and all brothell houses, wherein abhominable wickednesse is freely committed, are Satans thrones.'[61] The theatre and Catholicism were so closely linked that they were almost interchangeable. Anthony Munday noted in 1580 that if the stage was tolerated England would fall 'into the handes, if not of foraine enemies, which I feare; yet of our spiritual adversarie, the Pope or Diuel, which I am sure of'.[62] Such associations continued to haunt the Protestant imagination in the seventeenth century. In 1609 the Puritan William Crashaw, prebend at Ripon, noted that England was beset by the machinations of a triumvirate of the Devil, the Catholics and the

58 *Proceedings in the Parliaments of Elizabeth I*, vol. I: *1558–1581*, p. 504; James Aske, *Elizabetha Trivmphans. Contayning the Damned Practices, that the diuelish Popes of Rome haue used sithence her Highnesse first coming to the Crowne* (London, 1588), pp. 10–11; Anthony Marten, *An Exhortation To stir vp the mindes of all her Maiesties faithful Subiects* (London, 1588), sig. Bv.

59 Gosson, *Playes confuted in five actions*, sig. B6–B6v. According to Gosson the Devil's first ploy was to import into England a great number of wanton Italian books to poison the nation's manners with an appetite for sinful 'foreign delights', but Satan had overlooked the fact that England was largely illiterate. See also Aske, *Elizabetha Trivmphans*, pp. 2–3.

60 Henry Roberts, *An earnest complaint of divers vain, wicked and abused exercises, practiced on the saboth day* (London, 1572), p. 2.

61 William Perkins, *A Godly and learned Exposition ... of the Revelation*, in *Works*, vol. III, pp. 292–3.

62 Anthony Munday, *A Second and third blast of retrait from plaies and theatres* (London, 1580), sigs. A3v–A4.

players. 'I would gladly separate them', he noted, 'but they will not: for who but the Diuell, and Papists, and Players do mocke at religion, and abuse the holie Scriptures.'[63]

Without an heir, Elizabeth herself appeared a precarious guarantor of Protestantism in England. Satan's hand was discerned behind the plethora of conspiracies to replace her with Mary, Queen of Scots, who herself was styled as a devil incarnate.[64] Similarly the Spanish threat of 1588 was the work of 'the beast from the bottomless pit'.[65] In the face of the Armada, Anthony Marten exhorted his countrymen to 'strengthen yourselves against that horrible beast who hath received power from the dragon'.[66] Spanish propaganda declaring that Francis Drake had been captured and that Elizabeth's army had mutinied was denounced in England as a diabolic plot to bolster a discredited assault on a godly nation. The pamphlet *A Packe of Spanish Lyes* sought to expose the desperation of such strategies carried out by the 'intelligencers for the deuill'.[67] Events in Europe provided a chilling example of what would happen if the Devil ever regained his presidency in England. For the layman John Norden, writing in 1596, the St Bartholomew's Day massacre had seen the Parisian Huguenots 'swallowed up in [a] devilish fury'. 'Who doth not see how manifestly it appeareth', Norden asked 'that our church is that church which resembleth our head Christ Jesus in suffering, and the other to be the church resembling their father the devil by massacring and killing'.[68] Thus he was able to sum up of the experience of being a Protestant in Elizabeth's England: 'How hath the rage of Satan appeared against us with bitter threats from Spain, with excommunications and condemnations from Rome!'[69]

Fears of diabolic Catholic aggression continued throughout the early Stuart period, but they became far more certainly focused on the threat of internal subversion.[70] We must now consider in detail how these perceptions of persecution shaped the Protestant conception of the dynamic of diabolic Catholicism.

[63] William Crashaw, *A Sermon Preached in London before the right honourable the Lord Lawarre, Lord Governour and Captaine Generall of Virginea* (London, 1610), sig. Hv.

[64] *Proceedings in the Parliaments of Elizabeth I*, vol. I, p. 312; vol. II, p. 228; Aske, *Elizabetha Trivmphans*, pp. 12–13; the perceived connection between Mary Stuart, the Devil and treason is discussed below, see pp. 189–96.

[65] Marten, *An Exhortation*, sig. A3v; William S. Maltby, *The Black Legend in England: The Development of Anti-Spanish Sentiment 1558–1660* (Durham, N.C., 1971), pp. 76–87.

[66] Marten, *An Exhortation*, sig. A2v.

[67] *A Packe of Spanish Lyes, sent Abroad in the world* (London, 1588), sigs. A2, A4, B4.

[68] John Norden, *A Progress of Piety, whose jesses lead into the Harbour of Heavenly Heart's Ease* (1596; reprinted Cambridge, Parker Society, 1847), p. 93.

[69] Ibid., pp. 93–5; Philip Stubbes, *The Second part of the Anatomie of Abuses* (London, 1583), sigs. B5–B6.

[70] This is discussed fully below, pp. 189–96.

THE DEVIL'S CHURCH: THE CONSTRUCTION OF CONTRARIETY

Oppositional rhetoric was central to both the elite and the popular culture of early modern Europe, and notions of contrariety and parody fed common fears over the destructive potential of disorder and the horror of 'the world turned upside down'.[71] Everybody, it seems, understood the notion of contrariety, and fantasies such as the witches' Sabbat embodied fears of the inversion of the ordered world.[72] As Peter Lake has argued, it was into this framework that attacks on Catholicism as an 'anti-religion' fitted. But despite its prevalence, contrariety was not an uncontested rhetoric. Whilst the reformers became convinced that popery embodied a direct inversion of Christianity, their conception of diabolic Catholicism was shaped by the need to persuade others, for whom its contrariety was far from obvious. As a consequence Protestant polemic aimed to reveal the hidden contrariety of Catholicism by emphasising the insidious demonic subversion of faith inherent in its practice. It was this focus which produced Protestant demonism's wider emphasis on the hidden dynamic of diabolic agency.

Maintaining the Protestant inverted self-presentation was extremely demanding. A close reading of reformers' demonism reveals that their self-confidence was belied by a deeper fear of the Devil's power to disguise himself within Christian piety. Catholics were often reasonable men, rather than vicious malcontents, and Protestants had to assume that they had been brought to apostasy by a desire to express a genuine, if misconstrued, Christian faith. After all, the first generation of reformers were by definition lapsed Catholics, and their construction of contrariety must have mirrored a very real experience of progressive disillusionment. Protestant writers had to admit that Catholicism was a very convincing fake. It answered most of the requirements that were placed on it by ordinary parishioners and laymen. It gave comfort and security, made the world more comprehensible and offered extensive protection against the vagaries of providence. The concerns that popery inspired might be worldly, but worldly or not they answered to much of the human condition. For the reformers, therefore, Catholicism was pernicious precisely because it could appear altogether reasonable, comforting and just.

The Cambridge theologian and martyr Robert Barnes made a typical show of confidence in his contention that the Catholic church 'did no more agree with the manners of holy church, then darkness and light, then God and the

[71] Burke, *Popular Culture*, pp. 185–91; Clark, *Thinking with Demons*, chapters 3–6; Davis, *Fear, Myth and History*, pp. 96–107; Underdown, *A Freeborn People*, pp. 17–18.

[72] Clark, *Thinking with Demons*, chapter 6; Rowland, '"Fantasticall and Devilishe Persons"', pp. 166–9.

devil'.[73] Whilst the papacy was Satan's synagogue, Protestants, noted John Rogers, the one-time prebend of St Paul's, 'are by Gods grace assuredly certified in our own consciences – that we are no heretics, but members of the true catholic church'. But such sentiments were often accompanied by wary qualifications admitting that these convictions needed some justification. From his prison cell in 1555 Rogers recognised how far the message still had to spread. 'If I might have life and books', he enthused, 'I would so set forth, that all the world should see it: that our adversaries, with their antichristian head, are the members of the devil's church, as they undoubtedly are.'[74] In his earlier conflict with Sir Thomas More, William Tyndale showed himself sensitive to the possibility that the widely held assumption that the Catholic church was the sum of the Christian faith was in danger of perpetuating the satanic hold over the world.[75] In his translation of the New Testament, he chose to employ 'congregation', instead of 'church', as a translation of *ecclesia* in order to highlight the contrariety of the Catholics with the godly. 'For wheresoever I may say a congregation', he noted, 'there may I say a church also; as the church of the Devil, the church of Satan, the church of wretches, the church of wicked men, the church of liars, and a church of Turks thereto.'[76]

A number of reformers drew up lists of antitheses to demonstrate more clearly the opposition of the two churches. In 1529 the martyr John Frith composed *Antithesis, wherein are compared together Christes actes and the Popes*. The tract listed seventy-eight differences, concentrating on the contrast between the humility of Christ and the arrogant ostentation of the Pope.[77] A similar device was used repeatedly by Thomas Becon who, writing during Mary's reign, listed fifty ways in which the church of Satan differed from that of God. Later he would enumerate 126 oppositions in the acts of Christ and Antichrist, and 100 more in points of doctrine.[78] These texts drove home the contrariety between satanic Catholic and godly Protestant

[73] Robert Barnes, *What the Church is: and who bee thereof: and whereby men may know her*, in *The whole workes of W. Tyndall, Iohn Frith, and Doct. Barnes*, ed. John Foxe (London, 1572), p. 242; William Tyndale, *An answer to Sir Thomas More's dialogue*, ed. J. Walter (Cambridge, Parker Society, 1850), p. 104; Bale, *The Image of both churches*, p. 252; Hooper, *A godly Confession and protestation of the Christian Faith* (1550), in *Later Writings of Bishop Hooper*, ed. C. Nevinson (Cambridge, Parker Society, 1852), p. 71.

[74] *A & M*, vol. VI, p. 607.

[75] Tyndale, *An Answer to Sir Thomas More's dialogue*, pp. 11–15; John Hooper, *A Declaration of the Ten Commandments* (1548), in *Early Writings of John Hooper*, ed. S. Carr (Cambridge, Parker Society, 1843), pp. 276–7.

[76] Tyndale, *An Answer to Sir Thomas More's dialogue*, p. 15.

[77] John Frith, *Antithesis, wherein are compared together Christes actes and the Popes* (1529), in *The whole workes of W. Tyndall, Iohn Frith, and Doct. Barnes*, pp. 97–106.

[78] Becon, *A Comfortable Epistle to the afflicted people of God* and *The Actes of Christe & of Antichrist concerning both their life and doctrine*, both in *Prayers and Other Pieces*.

with all the subtlety of a sledgehammer. 'What concord hath Christ with Belial?', Becon asked, taking his cue from 2 Corinthians. The answer was simple – 'there is not one thing in the world that is so contrary to another thing, as the synagogue of Satan is contrary to the church of Christ, both in doctrine and life'.[79] Christ's church honoured God 'in spirit and truth', Becon noted in a typical passage; 'the synagogue of Satan honoureth God with surplices, copes, vestments, bells, organs, censers, candlesticks, fire, palms, ashes, bread, water, oil cream, building of monasteries, free chaples, chanteries, &c.'[80] Other observations included that the Catholic church forbade clerical marriage, bred superstition in reliance on the saints, and was obsessed with worldly riches. 'Who seeth not now', the reformer asked, 'what great diversity there is between these two churches?'[81] Again the implication was that many people did not appear to see at all.

The contrariety of 'God's ape' and the witches' Sabbat was of little use in persuading people of the diabolism of Catholicism.[82] Located on a distant mountain-top, the anti-world of the Sabbat drew its force from the imagination of people who never witnessed it, and it could have little persuasive power over their familiarity with Catholic worship.[83] Even the most imaginative anti-Catholic had difficulty in arguing that the mass was *open* Devil-worship, even if he thought (and many of them did) that such acts took place hidden in Rome.[84] The reformers had to concede that disguise was perhaps the greatest of Satan's talents. Rather than inverted religion, English Protestants concluded that the dynamic of Devil-worship was false doctrine. As 2 Corinthians 11: 14 predicted, 'Satan himself is transformed into an angel of light.'[85] Whilst the rituals and paraphernalia of Catholic worship might debase Christianity, and ultimately replaced faith with idolatry, their effects were largely hidden from the perception of the ordinary parishioner.

79 Becon, *A Comfortable Epistle*, p. 195; *The whole workes of W. Tyndale, Iohn Frith, and Doct. Barnes*, pp. 242–3; 'An homily of the right use of the church', 'An homily against the peril of idolatry', in *Certain Sermons or Homilies*, pp. 172–3, 192–3.

80 Becon, *A Comfortable Epistle*, pp. 195–6; Sandys, *Sermons*, p. 12.

81 Becon, *A Comfortable Epistle*, p. 201; *The whole workes of W. Tyndale, Iohn Frith, and Doct. Barnes*, pp. 242–3.

82 On 'God's ape' see Clark, *Thinking with Demons*, pp. 81–2.

83 Cohn, *Europe's Inner Demons*, pp. 100–2; Clark, *Thinking with Demons*, pp. 80–6; Muchembled, 'Satanic Myths and Cultural Reality'; Rowland, '"Fantasticall and Devilishe Persons"', pp. 161–9.

84 See, for example, the German anti-Jesuit pamphlet of 1607, reprinted in England in 1641 as *Camilton's Discovery of the Devillish Designs, and Killing Projects, Of the Society of Jesuits … intended, but graciously prevented in England*, which described in detail the diabolic ceremonies and initiation rituals carried out in chthonian vaults hidden in the major cities of Europe. The pamphlet is reprinted in *The Harleian Miscellany* (London, 12 vols. 1810), vol. V, pp. 103–17.

85 James Calfhill, *An Answer to John Martiall's Treatise of the Cross* (Cambridge, Parker Society, 1846; first edn, 1565), p. 12.

Satan's impersonation of God, rather than his parody, was his greatest threat. 'The subtilties of the Devil must be taken heed of', wrote Bishop John Hooper in 1548, 'lest he shew us God in another form than he sheweth himself in his word.'[86] It was a theme that pervaded anti-Catholic polemic into the seventeenth century. 'Into what shape cannot he transform himself?', asked John Jewel, 'in whose name will not he craftily set forth his errors, which dareth falsley to set himself in the place of God?'[87] According to James Calfhill in 1565, the Devil 'compasseth by all means to win himself some credit with us' and to destroy the knowledge of God. But 'he hath of himself too ill a name to be esteemed so; and therefore, under visor of that that he is not, he wins men to yield to that they should not'.[88] Oliver Ormerod sought in his tract of 1606, *The Picture of a Papist*, to demonstrate that this disguise was 'the very cunningest strategeme the deuill hath ... he being a fiend of darkenesse'.[89] Thus John Boys summed up a fully established polemical tradition when in 1615 he warned that the Devil was 'the most diligent preacher in the whole world'.[90]

This emphasis on subversion rather than inversion required Protestants to conceive a dynamic of satanic agency which explained why man's perception was so woefully inadequate in discerning his strategy. In Calvinist terms the fall of man had resulted in an alienation from God, which was conceived as the loss of spiritual gifts, such as faith and the study of holiness, but also as a weakening of the physical senses. Indeed the physical and spiritual senses were inseparable, and Adam's apostasy had removed the spiritual insight that brought him close to God. 'Gentiles walk in the vanity of their mind', Calvin commented, 'having the understanding darkened, being alienated from the life of God through the ignorance that is in them, because of the blindness of their heart'.[91] 'We threw away the love of God's eternal truth', noted Edwin Sandys, 'and, according to the blindness of our hearts, hungerly fed upon all poisoned error, and plunged ourselves into all wickedness.'[92] For Protestants this spiritual blindness became the first principle of the Devil's agency. No longer able to

86 Hooper, *A Declaration of the ten holy commandmentes*, in *Early Writings*, p. 294.

87 John Jewel, *An Exposition upon the Two Epistles to the Thessalonians*, in *The Works of John Jewel, Bishop of Salisbury, The Second Portion*, ed. J. Ayre (Cambridge, Parker Society, 4 vols., 1848), vol. II, p. 894.

88 Calfhill, *An Answer to the Treatise of the Cross*, p. 12; 'An homily against the peril of idolatry', in *Certain Sermons or Homilies*, pp. 192–3, 240–1.

89 Oliver Ormerod, *The Pictvre of a Papist: or, A Relation of the damnable heresies, detestable qualities, and diabolicall practices of sundry hereticks in former ages, and of the papists in this age* (London, 1606), sig. A2.

90 John Boys, *An Exposition of the festivall Epistles and Gospels vsed in our English Liturgie* (London, 1615), p. 82; Issac Bargrave, *A Sermon Preached before the Honourable Assembly ... of the lower House of Parliament* (London, 1624), p. 24.

91 Calvin, *Institutes*, Bk II, chapter iii, pp. 249–50.

92 Sandys, *Sermons*, pp. 178–9.

perceive godliness, man floundered about helplessly, easily falling prey to Satan's hidden suggestions. In 1538 John Lambert, another of Bilney's protégés, accused his examiner, Archbishop William Warham, of naivety. 'Be ye not children in wit and understanding; but concerning maliciousness, be you children', he quoted from 1 Corinthians. St Paul's words articulated mankind's lack of 'discretian to judge the good from the ill, and the ill from the good', and Catholicism exemplified this failure.[93] Similarly, John Jewel paraphrased 2 Thessalonians. 'The devil is subtile', he noted; 'you are weak and simple: he will soon deceive you.' Such weakness was general to man's condition, as Jewel continued: 'when I say man may be deceived, I mean not boys, or children, or fools, or the simpler sort of men; but the learned, the wise, the politic'.[94]

It was spiritual blindness, then, that explained Satan's ability to corrupt Christendom through the Catholic church. Whilst man had been degraded by the fall of Adam, he remained a creature of God, imbued with an instinctive need to worship his creator. This, and man's spiritual blindness, was a potent mix for Satan to prey upon. The understanding was central to the reformers' conception of the dynamic of Catholic idolatry. Idolatry was an expression of helplessness, as the mind, unguided by spiritual insight, was simply unable to escape the limitations of its own imagination. As John Hooper noted:

> the mind of man, when it is not illuminated by the scripture, it imagineth and feigneth God to be like unto the imagination and conceit of his mind, and not as the scripture teacheth. When this vanity or fond imagination is concieved in the mind, there followeth a further success of the ill. He purposeth to express by some figure or image God in the same form and similitude that his imagination hath first printed in his mind; so that the mind conceiverth an idol, and afterward the hand worketh and representeth the same unto the senses.[95]

Unguided expressions of faith were channelled through an image considered a reasonable embodiment of God, and taken to be 'a testimony of his presence'. Hooper continued: 'the original cause why they [idols] are made, is, that man thinketh God would not be present to help him, except he be presented someways unto their carnal eyes'.[96] Thomas Pickering, prefacing William Perkins' posthumous tract on witchcraft, showed how the Devil made use of man's confusion:

> First he knowes that man naturally out of the light of grace hath but a meere soule, indued onely with some generall and confused notions; and as for matters of deeper apprehension touching God and heavenly things, there is a vaile of ignorance and

93 *A & M*, vol. V, p. 185. Lambert was saved by the death of Archbishop Warham in August 1532, but was burned in 1538 as a convenient demonstration of Henry VIII's orthodoxy; Haigh, *English Reformations*, pp. 136–7.

94 Jewel, *An Exposition upon the Two Epistles to the Thessalonians*, p. 891.

95 Hooper, *A Declaration of the ten holy comandmentes*, p. 318. 96 Ibid., p. 319.

> blindnesse drawne over the eyes of his minde. Whereupon, though he be apt to knowe and worship a God, and learn his will, yet for want of information by the word, he is prone to erre in the practice of his notion. Here Satan applyes himself to mans measure and at his own will, drawes the minde into errour, by his delusions and impostures.[97]

Catholic false doctrine provided the superficial piety and immediacy of God's presence which man's degraded soul yearned for. As William Grey, a member of Thomas Cromwell's household, described it in a ballad of around 1538 (written to promote the royal injunctions against shrines), idolatry promoted a 'fantasie' of religion. 'We poore soules', he noted, are 'Begyled with idolles, / With fayned myracles and lyes, / By the devyll and his doctors, / The pope and his proctors: / That with such have blerid our eyes.'[98] 'The papists', preached Hugh Latimer in 1552, 'which are the very enemies of Christ, make him to be a Saviour after their own fantasy, and not after the word of God.'[99]

From this understanding the entire Catholic clergy might readily be demonised as diabolic servants in Christian camouflage. 'Judas was an apostle, and taken as so of all his company, but yet our master Christ calleth hym a deuil', remarked Robert Barnes, identifying the archetype for disguised diabolism.[100] For Tyndale, Catholicism had trampled down Christ's teachers and 'set up the ministers of Satan, disguised yet in names of and garments like unto the angels of light and ministers of righteousness'.[101] John Frith noted that if the Devil was accustomed to presenting himself as a godly servant it should be considered 'no great thyng, if his ministers do take upon them a similitude, as though they were the ministers of Iustice'. Although men might be known by their works, Frith had to concede that the papists put on a convincing show of godliness, and to the unwary could be successfully 'transfigured into Christ's apostles'.[102] Thomas Becon

[97] Thomas Pickering, 'Dedication', in William Perkins, *The Damned Art of Witchcraft*, in *Works*, vol. III, sig. Kkkk5v.

[98] William Gray, 'The Fantassie of Idolatrie', in *A & M*, vol. V, pp. 404–9, quote at p. 409; Duffy, *The Stripping of the Altars*, pp. 408–10.

[99] Latimer, *Sermons*, p. 146; 'An homily against the peril of idolatry', in *Certain Sermons or Homilies*, p. 280.

[100] Robert Barnes, *What the Church is*, and *Another declaration of the Church, wherein he answereth to Maister More*, in *The whole workes of W. Tyndall, Iohn Frith, and Doct. Barnes*, pp. 243, 251–3, quote at p. 253; Calfhill, *An Answer to the Treatise of the Crosse*, pp. 100–1.

[101] Tyndale, *The Practice of Prelates*, p. 273; see also William Fulke, *A Discoverie of the Davngerous Rock of the Popish Church* ed. R. Gibbings (Cambridge, Parker Society, 1848), p. 378.

[102] Frith, *Antithesis*, p. 97; Calfhill, *An Answer to the Treatise of the Cross*, p. 15; Thomas James, *A Manuduction, or Introduction unto divinitie: Containing a confutation of Papists* (Oxford, 1625), p. 51.

employed the same scriptural reference to denounce the 'false prophets' of the Catholic church who were and remain 'deceitful workers [that] fashion themselves like unto the apostles of Christ'.[103] Satan's servants were instructed to use the scriptures in their deceits. 'Because his lying chaplains should the better fight against Christ', bishop Miles Coverdale noted, 'he teacheth them to go craftily to work, to lie and spare not, to call the disciples of Christ new fellows ... and not only this, but also to wrest and wring the scripture from the manifest understanding of it.'[104] The text of Matthew 7: 15 was the most prevalent of a number of scriptural warnings that provided a basis for the demonisation of the Catholic clergy. 'Beware of false prophets', it read, 'which come to you in sheep's clothing, but inwardly they are ravening wolves.'[105]

Catholic false piety made a direct appeal to man's tendency to look for religion in simplistic and unconsidered displays of commitment. Rome's image worship was of course little more than idolatry, the institutionalised betrayal of the second commandment. It was the 'suggestion of the Serpent that lurketh within' that made men believe they were devout when they honoured material objects.[106] Idolatry was meaningless because it allowed for no covenant between man and God. Robert Barnes took the temptation of Christ as an exemplar, noting, 'the deuil required that hee should fall downe and honour him, hee required no faith nor any hope on him, nor yet that hee should make any prayers, or desire any petition of him ... but alonely to fall downe, and so with exteriour service to honour him'.[107] Overblown Catholic ceremonial cheapened God's ordinances by an excess of such empty piety. James Calfhill noted with disgust that the baptism of bells was afforded more 'majesty' than the baptism of children. 'Papists', he declared, 'by the spirit of the Devil, ordained that a bishop must needs christen a Bell; whereas every poor Priest may christen a Child.'[108] Satan used the seductive excitement of intense devotion to disguise the emptiness of the gesture. 'When they come before her image, all, yea the greatest persons in the basest manner that may be humble themselves before her', William

103 Thomas Becon, *Articles of Christian Religion*, in *Prayers and Other Pieces*, p. 405; see also John Terry, *The Trial of Truth: containing a plaine and short Discouery of the greatest pointes of the Doctrine of the Great Antichrist* (Oxford, 1600), p. 145.

104 Miles Coverdale, *The Order of the Church of Christ in Denmark and other countries for the Lord's Supper, Baptism and Holy Wedlock*, in *Writings and Translations of Miles Coverdale*, ed. G. Pearson (Cambridge, Parker Society, 1844), pp. 484–5; Terry, *The Triall of Truth*, p. 145.

105 Tyndale, *An Exposition uppon the V. VI. VII. chapters of Mathew*, pp. 121–8.

106 Robert Barnes, *That it is against the Holy Scripture to honore Images, and to pray to saintes*, in *The whole workes of W. Tyndall, Iohn Frith, and Doct. Barnes*, p. 346.

107 Ibid., p. 352; Turner, *The huntyng and fyndyng out of the Romish Fox*, p. 21.

108 Calfhill, *An Answer to the Treatise of the Crosse*, p. 15.

Perkins noted of the worship of the Virgin in Lauretto, but 'the thing worshipped vnder the name of the Ladie of Lauretto is indeed neither God nor Saint, but the diuell himselfe'.[109] False piety was so dangerous because it was self-perpetuating. It encouraged further empty gesturing by persuading men that godly intent only was paramount. Thomas Becon noted: 'Antichrist affirmeth that it is lawful to worship God in any manner of way, so it commeth of a good intent, good mind, good zeal, good devotion, &c.'[110] God would not cast away the sincere devotion of any man. For James Calfhill this was exposed in Catholicism's compromise with paganism, in which it took the 'superstitious and detestable rites of the heathen folk', and covered them with the 'manners' of Christianity.[111]

False piety bolstered the position of the Catholic clergy by convincing men that they embodied godliness above and beyond the capabilities of ordinary men. In this process clerical celibacy was a particularly diabolical device. According to William Turner in his attack on Stephen Gardiner, *The huntyng and fynding out of the Romish Fox* (1543), the God-given need to procreate imbued man with an appetite that few could deny, but which was legitimised through the ordination of marriage. 'The devil gat many a prey' by subverting this through a mixture of corrupted doctrine and papal authority which moved 'all men to think that marriage was sin, and that the estate of marriage was a sinful estate'.[112] 'Who would think there were any evil forcing of virginity, chastity, or single life?', asked John Jewel. Such committed abstinence from the world and the flesh must, by its very nature, be pious – 'he that is unmarried careth for the things of the Lord, how he may please the Lord, that he may be holy both in body and spirit'. Moreover, who could seriously object if the papacy attempted to save the world from itself by enforcing celibacy on the clergy and degrading sex as a sin in the laity.[113] 'Strange attire, difference of meats, refusal of marriage, rising at midnight, shutting up in a cloister, erecting of images, worshipping of Saints, service in Latin, gadding on pilgrimage', were, according to Calfhill, ordinances by which the Devil marked out his servants in contrast to the unpretentious faith

109 Perkins, *A warning Against the Idolatry of the Last Times. And an instruction touching religious or divine worship*, in *Works*, vol. I, pp. 678–9.

110 Becon, *The Acts of Christ and Antichrist*, in *Prayers and Other Pieces*, p. 522; 'An homily of good works: and the first of fasting', in *Certain Sermons or Homilies*, p. 297.

111 Calfhill, *An Answer to the Treatise of the Cross*, p. 13.

112 Turner, *The huntyng and fyndyng out of the Romish Fox*, pp. 36–7; Coverdale, *A confutation of that treatise which one John Standish made agaynst the protestacion of D. Barnes* in *Remains of Myles Coverdale of Exeter*, ed. G. Pearson (Cambridge, Parker Society, 1844), p. 400; Sandys, *Sermons*, pp. 51, 321–2.

113 Jewel, *An exposition upon . . . Thessalonians*, p. 911; *The whole workes of W. Tyndall, Iohn Frith, and Doct. Barnes*, p. 242.

required by God. But 'the simple have been so deluded, that they thought God's service consist herein'.[114]

If the contrariety of Catholicism could not be readily seen, means had to be found to make it apparent, and Protestant writers developed a scheme by which hidden satanic agency might be discerned. The assumed principles of uncluttered 'primitive' Christianity formed the basis of the Protestant's monopoly on interpretation which privileged their own judgement of contrariety. 'All doctrine that withdraweth thyne hope and trust from holy Christ', noted Tyndale, 'is of the deuill and the doctrine of antichrist.' 'Examine ye Pope by this rule', he advised, and the reader would soon discover the demonic reality of Catholic doctrine, dressed up in a perversion of the scriptures.[115] James Calfhill was more cautious, arguing that human reason alone was incapable of penetrating Satan's deceit. In disguising himself as an angel of light, the Devil had 'handled himself so workmanly, that he looks very narrowly that can discern the difference'. 'The eyes of [man] must be better cleared than by the light of reason', Calfhill believed, 'or else he shall be blinded in the mist.'[116] The Protestant attempt to monopolise the interpretation of diabolic subversion is well illustrated by the inclusion in John Day's 1572 edition of the works of Tyndale, Frith and Barnes of a compendium, *A General Collection out of Doctour Barnes Woorkes*, in which he identified valid scriptural and traditional sources, quoting from the work of renowned theologians such as St Augustine and St Chrysostom. In the preface 'T.G.' noted how the book might be put to use to determine whether the writings and laws of the papacy originated in God. If they did not accord with Barnes' sources, he noted, 'then mayest thou suspect, that they have gone astray, and that the Deuill hath transformed him selfe into an Aungel of light, and that they are his ministers'.[117] In filtering the writings of the established church, Barnes' work had thus provided a guide by which the deceptive papist gloss might be stripped away.

It was partly as a means to discern false doctrine that the apocalyptic prophesies of Revelation assumed such a prominent place in Protestant thinking. As John Bale explained in the preface to his exposition on the subject:

herein is the true christian church, which is the meek spouse of the Lamb without spot, in her right-fashioned colours described. So is the proud church of hypocrites, the rose-coloured whore, the paramour of antichrist, and the sinful synagogue of Satan,

114 Calfhill, *An Answer to the Treatise of the Cross*, pp. 17–18.
115 Tyndale, *An Exposition upon the first Epistle of S. Iohn*, pp. 196–7.
116 Calfhill, *An Answer to the Treatise of the Cross*, pp. 12, 316–18.
117 [?T.G.], *A Generall Collection out of Doctour Barnes Woorkes*, in *The whole workes of W. Tyndall, Iohn Frith, and Doct. Barnes*, p. 368.

in her just proportion depainted, to the merciful forwarning of god's elect. And this is why I have entitled this book, The Image of both Churches.[118]

Encompassing a symbolic depiction of the entirety of Christian history – conceived as a constant struggle with the synagogue of Satan – Revelation contained all the knowledge necessary to meet his assaults. 'He that will be strong when adversity shall come', Bale continued, 'and avoid all the assaults of antichrist and the devil; let him give himself wholly to the study of this prophecy.'[119] Revelation itself contained an allegorical illustration of the Christian's 'diligent' search for the false church. In the thirteenth chapter the prophet is given a rod with which to measure the temple of God – the congregation and doctrine of the faith. 'Prove all beliefs', the scripture demonstrated; 'examine their works, whether they spring from God's commandments or men's traditions'. Even the altar, which represents Christ, must be measured (tested), since 'many false Christs are abroad in the world to seduce his people'.[120]

From the study of Revelation an influential picture of the Church's history developed which provided a scheme for discerning the hidden diabolism of the Roman faith. For Bale the form of the dragon of Revelation, with its seven heads, presented a chronological picture of Satan's attempts to corrupt mankind.[121] Although the form of the seven heads was not made explicit in the text, 'very easy it is to conjecture what matter of heads they were, marking other places in scripture'. The first head was that of a serpent, indicating the corruption of Eden; the second, a calf, symbolised the idolatry that had become rife after the great flood. Other heads denoted the cruelty of historically specific oppressors of the godly such as the Assyrians and the Persians. The fifth, 'a leopard's head of many colours' symbolised fickleness and the 'inconstant reign of the Greeks', whilst the sixth, 'the head of a beast unlike all other beasts', denoted Rome and its persecutions. The seventh head expressed contemporaneous concerns. Shaped like that of a man it expressed carnal wisdom and false religion, and symbolised 'the very papacy here in Europe'.[122]

Although they differed on details, Protestant eschatologists agreed that post-incarnation ecclesiastical history followed a progression defined by the status of the Devil – *free on the earth – chained in hell – free on the earth*. The Apocalypse predicted that an angel (commonly identified as Christ by the reformers) would descend from heaven carrying a great chain with which he would bind up the Devil and cast him into hell for a thousand years, at the end of which, in preparation for the Last Judgement, Satan would be set free

[118] Bale, *Image of both churches*, p. 251. [119] Ibid., p. 252. [120] Ibid., pp. 383–5.
[121] Book of Revelation, 12. [122] Bale, *Image of both churches*, p. 407.

once more to torment the godly 'for a little season'.[123] Thus, if correctly filtered through Protestant polemical interpretation, the history of the church might point to the distinguishing features of unfettered diabolic activity that could be seen beneath the gloss of false doctrine.[124] The binding and loosing of Satan imposed a cycle on ecclesiastical history which saw the Devil's agency as timeless, unchanging and recorded. The primitive church was persecuted by a satanical synagogue that was openly pagan, and parallels with the aggression of the Roman church illustrated the latter's hidden contrariety. This redefinition of the demonological parameters of church history was necessarily proactive. As John Foxe noted, 'the opinion of many is deceived by ignorance of histories, and the state of things done in the church'.[125]

Within the interpretative cycle a linear progression of successive manifestations of the Devil's church might be discerned. 'He hath his kingdome in this world', wrote William Perkins in 1595, 'and for the establishment thereof, he must have his thrones where wickedness and idolatrie is maintained without controlment . . . in all ages it hath been thus, and will continue so to the ende.' History could be made to embody a linear progression through the successive manifestations of the Devil's church:

> in the olde world he had his thrones among Caius posteritie: in the church of the Iews, euen in the dayes of the Kings of Israel, the high places and groues, wher the people sacrificed to their idols, were the devils throns: the oracles of the gentiles where the deuils gaue answer vnto men, were his chiefe throns . . . in the daies of poperie, every church and chapel were the throns of Sathan, wherein were erected images and holy roods for the worship of saints.[126]

The history of the Devil's contrariety was an exercise in hindsight, which placed the origin of his agency not with the temptation of Adam and Eve, but at the point at which he was first able to divide human society between the faithful and the reprobate. Satan did not simply impose his synagogue on the world; it emerged only when man actively received his word over that of God, and contrariety began with the corruption of Cain. As God had built his church in the righteousness of Abel, so the Devil had responded with the corruption of Cain, introducing murder into the world.[127] From this starting point, all those who had opposed the Hebrew or Christian faith might be

[123] Revelation, 20; Bale, *The Image of both churches*, p. 558; *A & M*, vol. II, p. 725.
[124] Hugh Broughton, *A Concent of Scripture* (London, 1590), sig. G2.
[125] Ibid., p. 724.
[126] Perkins, *A Godly and Learned Exposition . . . of the Revelation*, in *Works*, p. 292.
[127] Becon, *Certain articles of Christian Religion*, p. 400; Miles Coverdale, *The old faith, an evident probation out of the holy scripture, that the christen fayth which is the right, true, old and undoubted fayth hath endured sens the beginning of the worlde*, in *Writings and Translations*, pp. 27–31; James Calfhill, *An Answer to the Treatise of the Crosse*, p. 12.

characterised as members of Satan's synagogue. The godly Lot and his house had to live among the 'stinking Sodomites and filthy Gomorrians' who maintained the Devil's religion with their 'corrupt lives'. Abraham, Isaac and Jacob had lived as a manifestation of God's church, 'so likewise did the devil build his chapel in the Egyptians . . . and in such other ungodly people'. Of course the incarnation itself had been opposed by a diabolical monarch in the shape of Herod, who led the Jews 'hurly-burly against the Lord and his Anointed'.[128] The dichotomy was easily extended into the history of the primitive church. Ignatious, Polycarp and Justin Martyr succeeded scriptural figures as the embodiment of God's church; their enemies, pagans and heretics, did very well for the Devil.[129]

In the apostasy of the Old Testament churches the reformers found a tangible example of the fickleness that prompted men to seek out any effortlessly satisfying religious practice. Here were the seeds of the idolatry that would be the foundation of diabolic Catholicism. According to John Hooper the decalogue was given to the Hebrews that they might be redeemed through a 'confederacy' with the divine but, through spiritual blindness and laziness, they 'believed and trusted better the devil' and rejected God's covenant.[130] Similarly, in his paraphrase on Revelation, James I described God's many attempts to save the Hebrews from themselves. Notwithstanding they were given prophets, miracles and holy laws to protect them from their 'weakness and incredulitie', 'there crept in such a generall corruption amongst them, that scarce one might be found that bowed not his knee to Baal'.[131] For John Jewel the ingrate Hebrews delivered out of Egyptian bondage provided a striking illustration of man's fickleness. Israel, 'the apple of the Lord's eye', had been led through the Red Sea, but the Hebrews' subsequent behaviour could scarce be credited. 'Who would think', Jewel asked, 'so great mercies would ever be forgotten? or that such a people, so well instructed in the knowledge of God, and so often put in mind of their duty, should either the most part, or all of them turn from God?' But no sooner was Moses absent than fickleness drove the Hebrews to idolatry, and into the arms of 'Baal and Astaroth'.[132]

The Jewish deicide was a watershed in the history of demonic contrariety. According to Bale, Satan could 'not shew him self in his own likenesse, that is

128 Becon, *Certain Articles of the Christian Religion*, p. 400; Perkins, *A Godly and Learned Exposition . . . of the Revelation*, p. 293.
129 Becon, *Certain Articles of the Christian Religion*, p. 401; Henry Lawrence, *Of Our Communion and Warre with Angels* (?London, 1646), p. 86.
130 Hooper, *A Declaration of the ten holy commandmentes*, p. 256.
131 James I, *A Paraphrase Vpon the Revelation of the Apostle S. Iohn*, in *The Workes of the most High and Mightie Prince, James* (London, 1616), pp. 4–5.
132 Jewel, *An Exposition upon the Two Epistles to the Thessalonians*, pp. 891–2.

to saye, Christes open adversary, tyll Christe came in the flesh'. The incarnation allowed the Devil to drive Herod and his people into open rebellion in seeking the messiah's death.[133] 'Never could Satan have put Christ unto death', Bale wrote in *The Image of Bothe Churches*, 'had he not entered into Judas, and so betrayed him; had he not entered into the bishops and lawyers, and so condemned him'.[134] The crucifixion was not a victory for Satan – no suggestion of the sort could ever be countenanced – but it did represent a final consolidation of the diabolic agency which had beset the Hebrew church. It had ever been the Devil's policy to prepare for the incarnation by undermining belief among the Jews in the prophesies of the messiah. The reaction of the onlookers as Christ was crucified demonstrated the strength of the hold the Devil exercised over their minds. Christ was reviled on the cross by those, Miles Coverdale noted, who 'should have bewailed their own great sins: but there is no compassion of mercy in them; their hearts are stopped, Satan hath the leading of them'. At the time when the meaning of Christ's sacrifice should have been apparent, as a fulfilment of their prophesies, the Jews were utterly blinded by the Devil.[135] If in the end the redemptive power of the crucifixion overturned Satan's triumph, it was only because a minority of Christian converts replaced the apostate Jews as God's chosen people.[136]

Yet, when discussing the Jewish apostasy, Protestants never lost sight of their primary target. This greatest apostasy of all was polemically significant largely because the crimes of the Catholic church could be made all the more comprehensible by comparison. 'I may well compare you unto the wicked Jewes that crouched & kneeled unto Christ', Robert Barnes berated his Catholic opponents; 'they did it neyther of loue, nor favour, but of mockage, as you doe honour your sayntes and images'.[137] The 'example of the Iewes', argued William Perkins, 'must be set before our eies continually' since 'now for their unbeleefe they are cast off from God, and are become a synagogue of the Devil'. 'And so', he continued significantly, 'we must say of the church of Rome.'[138] Perkins treated the idea at length in his commentary on the first three chapters of Revelation. The Devil had played on the Jews' conception of themselves as the chosen people of God, persuading them that they were pious by simple virtue of their birth. Such complacency led them to maintain

133 Bale, *The Actes of English Votaries* (London, 1560), p. 32.
134 Bale, *The Image of both churches*, p. 422.
135 Miles Coverdale, *Fruitfull Lessons vpon the Passion, Bvrial, Resvrrection, Assention, and of the sending of the holy Ghost*, in *Writings and Translations*, pp. 300–1; 'An homily or sermon concerning the nativity', in *Certain Sermons or Homilies*, pp. 430–1.
136 Lawrence, *Of Our Communion and Warre with Angels*, pp. 84–5.
137 *The whole workes of W. Tyndale, Iohn Frith, and Doct. Barnes*, p. 353.
138 Perkins, *A Godly and Learned Exposition . . . of the Revelation*, p. 286.

only the outward appearance of Judaism, allowing Satan's false doctrine to permeate beneath the surface. Thus the contrariety that had been open in paganism found a hiding place in a Jewish faith emptied of all meaning. 'A company of men that seemed to serue God after the Iewish manner', ran Perkins' description, 'but did indeede worshippe the Deuill'.[139] 'Hence we may learne', Perkins concluded, 'what we are to think and iudge of the church of the Papists.' 'Though they holde the Bookes of the Olde and Newe testament, with the Creede of the Apostles', he elaborated, 'yet the truth is, that indeede they hold them not. The Christ of the Papists is but a fained Christ.'[140]

Perkins could even downplay the importance of the deicide in order to emphasise the continuity of contrariety from the Jewish to the Roman faith. The Jews did not become a satanical synagogue at the moment at which they began to hold a heresy 'against the foundation of religion' – i.e. at the point when they first denied Christ's divinity – but when they used the church's authority to persecute the early Christians. In effect it was the rejection of the apostles, rather than the actual crucifixion, that marked Judaism's irredeemable descent into diabolism. This functioned entirely as a prelude to the persecutory practices of the Catholic church which, according to Revelation, were the hallmarks of the synagogue of Satan, and the very essence of contrariety. John Terry perceived a similar continuity. 'The Deuil in the primitive Church made his chiefe battery against the doctrine of the most glorious Trinity', he noted in 1600, 'but that his repulse therein was not such, as caused him altogether to giue ouer that enterprise.' 'He hath in some countryes renewed the same assault', Terry continued, noting that the Roman Antichrist would usurp divine authority to enforce apostasy whilst posing as God's lieutenant.[141]

Rewritten, the history of the corruption of the Pope encompassed an inversion of the story of Christ. In *The Practice of Prelates* William Tyndale described the Pope's seduction into diabolism as a sequel to Satan's temptation of Christ in the desert. 'The kingdoms of the earth and the glory of them, which Christ refused', Tyndale recounted, 'did the devil proffer unto the pope; and he immediately fell from Christ, and worshipped the devil, and received them.' The deal struck, the Pope adopted his role as 'Satan's vicar', offering the same avaricious temptation by proxy, to the corruption of religion. The Pope 'took up in the like manner all Christendom on high, and brought them from the meekness of the Christ unto the high hill of the pride of Lucifer'.[142] The image

139 Ibid., p. 285; Bale, *Image of both churches*, pp. 276–7.
140 Perkins, *A Godly and Learned Exposition . . . of the Revelation*, p. 286.
141 Terry, *The Triall of Truth*, pp. 145–6.
142 Tyndale, *The Practice of Prelates*, pp. 274–5; Broughton, *A Concent of Scripture*, sig. G2; William Turner, *The huntyng and fyndyng out of the Romish Fox*, pp. 36–7; 'An homily concerning the coming down of the Holy Ghost', in *Certain Sermons or Homiles*, pp. 498–9.

became increasingly focused as an overt diabolic pact entered into by a number of identified popes.[143]

It was in the construction of contrariety that the figure of the papal Antichrist became the exemplar of the Devil's procurator. The thirteenth chapter of Revelation described the beast rising out of the sea, which Protestant eschatologists identified as the Antichrist in the Pope. The symbolic differences between the beast and the dragon expressed the persecutory power of the Catholic church which, by the example of the Jewish apostasy, marked it out as the second of the principal synagogues of Satan. Whereas the dragon had seven crowns upon seven heads, the beast wore ten crowns upon his ten horns. 'In this only point', noted Bale, 'differeth the dragon from the beast, the devil from his members, or Satan from his carnal synagogue'. The extra crowns of the beast represented the Pope's primacy over the terrestrial world. Whereas Satan attempted to seduce or 'dallyingly persuade' men to apostasy, the papacy had the power to compel. 'When he hath proponed an error', Bale continued, 'they may by their power establish it for an infallible truth, and make of it a necessary article of the christian belief.' 'Much more mischief may they do, they being his spiritual instruments', Bale concluded, 'than he can do alone.'[144]

The second Book of Thessalonians described the coming of Antichrist as 'the mystery of iniquity'. For Protestant writers like John Jewel the phrase expressed the slow and careful process by which the Devil introduced Antichrist into the world, a process calculated to hide his pernicious nature from the view of man. When St John commented 'even now there are many antichrists come already', he referred to the way being prepared for the emergence of the papal Antichrist, who would not appear suddenly 'as a robber by the highways, or like a murderer'. Antichrist would not announce his presence; rather he would 'cast himself in the colour of holiness', adopting the empty trappings of false piety – 'he shall fast, he shall pray, he shall give alms and shew mercy: he shall walk as if he were a disciple of Christ: he shall counterfeit an angel of light'.[145] He would be adept at perverting the word of God whilst maintaining its basic integrity. 'He shall walk in craftiness and handle the word of God deceitfully', Jewel continued; 'he shall mingle his lies

143 Bale, *Actes of English Votaries*, sigs. B3–B4; John Foxe, *Actes and monuments of these latter and perilous dayes* (London, 1563), p. 11; Barnabe Barnes, *The Divils Charter* (1607), prologue; James, *A Manuduction, or Introduction unto divinitie*, pp. 52–3.

144 Bale, *Image of both churches*, p. 422; *A Gagge for the Pope, and the Iesuits: or, the arraignment and execution of Antichrist* (London, 1624), p. 1.

145 Jewel, *An Exposition upon the Two Espistles to the Thessalonians*, p. 909; Fulke, *A Discovery of the Dangerous Rock of the Popish Church*, pp. 366–73; George Hakewill, *An Apologie of the Power and Providence of God in the Government of the World* (Oxford, 1627), p. 434.

with the truth of God: he shall mingle his poison with the wholesome fruit of our souls, so closely and subtilly it shall hardly be espied'.[146] Such a policy of slow progression was deliberately instigated to bewilder the degraded senses of man, who would be unable to perceive the slow corruption of his faith. Jewel (subscribing presumably to a contemporary notion) described the progression of an earthquake, brought about by the movement of air in the 'hollow places' below the ground, which, finally grown strong and violent, 'teareth the earth'. Antichrist's progression was comparable: 'so great and mighty at the end, so little and simple at the first'. 'At the beggining he shall be like a little wind', Jewel commented, 'and shall enter into the hollowness and darkness of the church; but after he shall shake the whole world.'[147]

This emphasis on hidden diabolism and false doctrine shaped much of the Protestant demonological approach. For having given an urgency to revealing satanic power hidden within Catholicism, the resulting model of diabolic agency provided a means of interpreting other troubling phenomena Protestants encountered. One example will suffice here. As we have seen, the Puritan attack on popular pastimes, which was carried out in earnest after the 1570s, was predicated on the belief that Satan used the theatre, the alehouse and the maypole to reintroduce the popish synagogue of Satan into England under a new guise. The establishment of the permanent playhouses in London around 1575–7 gave satanic subversion a special palpability. For Puritans like John Northbrooke, writing in 1577, these buildings were constructed with no other purpose than to promote immorality and undermine reformation. Satan, he noted, 'hath not a more speedie way, and fitter school to work and teach his desire, to bring men and women into his snare of filthy lusts of wicked whoredom, than those ... plays, and theatres'.[148] In the words of the playwright turned Puritan minister, Stephen Gosson, 'the carpenter rayseth not his frame without tools, nor the Devil his work without instruments'.[149] It soon became a cliché that the multitude preferred the alehouse and the theatre to the observance of the sabbath. Henry Roberts noted, 'a man may find the churches empty, savyng the minister & iii. or iiii. lame and old folke: for ye rest are gon to follow the Devils dance'. Similarly John Stockwood, preaching at Paul's Cross in 1578: 'wyll not a fylthye play with the blast of a trumpette, sonner call thyther a thousand, that an hours tolling of a Bell, bring to the Sermon a hundred'.[150]

146 Jewel, *An Exposition upon the Two Epistles to the Thessalonians*, p. 910.
147 Ibid., p. 911. 148 Northbrooke, *Treatise*, pp. 59–60.
149 Stephen Gosson, *The Schoole of Abuse, Containing a plesaunt inuective against Poets, pipers, plaiers, Iesters, and such like Caterpillers of a Commonwelth* (London, 1579), sigs. C3v–C4.
150 Roberts, *An earnest complaint*, p. 41; John Stockwood, *A Sermon preached at Paules Crosse on Bathelmew day* (London, 1578), p. 23.

But this dichotomy was not simply an expression of ministerial frustration at the apathy of their parishioners. Rather the Protestant understanding of diabolic agency bred a suspicion that popular culture hid a more sinister didacticism. The alehouse or the theatre might offer an escape from the rigours of the sabbath, but their greatest threat lay in their ability to usurp the place of the church within the individual's cultural and moral life. As Catholicism offered a quick and painless piety to appeal to man's corrupted and fickle religiosity, so through popular culture the Devil distracted the individual from introspection by offering an empty equation between physical and spiritual comfort. For Anthony Munday 'the drifts of Satan' in the theatre threatened to 'beguile vs, & drawe vs from the consideration of our estate'.[151] But diabolic subversion was seen to be even more proactive, and complaint literature was infused with a perception that the subjective experience of attendance at the tavern/theatre and the church shared a basic, but opposing, didacticism. The fleshpots might delude men into thinking that they offered a rival model of life as meaningful as any put forward in the pulpit. The character of 'Youth' in Northbrooke's dialogue epitomised the naivety of those who believed they could be godly without the edification of the pulpit. Could one not, Northbrooke had his character ask, find Christ as easily in the tavern as the temple?[152] The vehemence with which the complaint writers descended on such a belief did not indicate self-confidence over the issue. Philip Stubbes denounced as 'blasphemie intollerable' the opinions he heard that as many good examples might be gained from a play as a sermon.[153] But, like the protestations of Frith, Becon or Rogers concerning the obviousness of the contrariety of Catholicism, such assertions suggest that the complaint writers genuinely feared that the playhouse did indeed offer a mirror of human life which rivalled that held up in the pulpit. The danger was particularly acute since the Reformation had removed popery, but had yet to redress man's lazy religiosity. 'There are the most in number', the Essex minister, George Gifford, noted, 'who having Poperie taken from them and not taught thoroughly and sufficiently the gospel, doe stand as men indifferent, so that they may quietly inioye the world, they care not what religion come.'[154] Plays dealt with human issues, with the emotions and the motivations by which men acted, and they presented a picture of humanity in which the audience might recognise themselves. Moreover, as Patrick Collinson has illustrated, the attack on the theatre marked a watershed when Protestants abandoned a tradition of making polemical

151 Anthony Munday, *A second and third blast of retrait from plaies*, pp. 86–7.
152 Northbrooke, *Treatise*, p. 2. 153 Stubbes, *The Anatomie of Abuses*, sig. L7v.
154 George Gifford, *A Breife Discourse of Certaine Points of the Religion* (London, 1582), sig. A4.

use of plays – a tradition which had recognised and respected their didactic value.[155] Complaint writers could not be confident that the exaggerated didacticism of tragedy and revenge plays might not indeed be more immediately digestible than that of a sermon.[156]

Anthony Munday described the theatre as 'the Schoole-house of Satan, and the chappel of il counsel', seeking not merely to point to the corrupting influence of the immoral sights presented on the stage, but more specifically to identify the origin of a competing didactic scheme which challenged the church's monopoly.[157] 'God hath ordained his blessed word, and made it the ordenarie mean of our Salvation', Stubbes declared in response to claims for the moral didacticism of the stage; 'the devill hath inferred the other, as, the ordenarie meane of our destruction, and will they yet compare the one with ye other'.[158] But again contrariety was being carefully constructed in response to the belief that Satan was subverting man's corrupted insight through an hidden agency. As John Bale had used the dragon and the beast of Revelation to model a means of discerning the hidden contrariety of Catholicism, the complaint writers employed similar analogies to reveal the diabolism of the stage. According to William Rankins, author of a heated attack, *The Mirror of Monsters* (1587), in the playhouse could be seen the Devil's inverted equivalent to the Christian body politic. The players themselves were 'the limbs, proportion, and members of Satan'. The playwrights were the Devil's head; they studied to produce 'enticing shows' to seduce the audience. In the performance of the songs they represented the Devil's tongue, whilst the snare that was the playhouse constituted his arms.[159]

Thus when Thomas Becon noted that 'wheresoever God buildeth his church, there the Devil also buildeth his chapel', he referred not to an uncontentious commonplace of oppositional language, but to a painstakingly

[155] Patrick Collinson, *The Birthpangs of Protestant England: Religious and Cultural Change in the Sixteenth and Seventeenth Centuries* (Houndmills, 1988), pp. 102–6, 112–15.

[156] Taking his cue from Keith Thomas's argument that widespread occultism substituted for the metaphysical aids that had vanished with the Catholic church, Louis Montrose has recently suggested that the Elizabethan theatre did indeed offer Londoners another such alternative to the austerity of the Protestant sermon. The plays of Shakespeare and his contemporaries were grounded in fundamental cultural categories such as ethnicity, gender or political faction, and they had an affinity with common rites of passage. He notes, 'we need to remind ourselves that the Elizabethan drama-in-performance . . . had the capacity to work as a cognitive and therapeutic instrument – that is, to function *ideologically*, in the most general and most enabling senses of that term'. Louis Montrose, *The Purpose of Playing: Shakespeare and the Cultural Politics of the Elizabethan Theatre* (Chicago and London, 1996), pp. 30–4, quote at p. 40.

[157] Munday, *A second and third blast of retrait from plaies*, p. 92.

[158] Stubbes, *Anatomy of Abuses*, sig. L7v.

[159] William Rankins, *The Mirror of Monsters* (London, 1587).

reconstructed polemical history.[160] If, as Peter Lake has argued, anti-Catholicism was the most important inversionary rhetoric of seventeenth-century English political and religious culture, it was testimony to the success of the reformer's active construction of contrariety that Catholicism could so readily be perceived as the inversion of true Christianity. It was by no means as apparent in the mid-sixteenth century. But beyond the sphere of anti-Catholicism itself, the most significant effect of the construction of contrariety was to focus attention on the Devil's intimate and hidden influence over the individual consciousness. The Protestants' sensitivity to the possibilities of diabolic subversion defined their understanding of demonic agency more widely. The dynamic of false doctrine forced an engagement with diabolic agency which posited an extreme vulnerability of man's corrupted and fragile subjectivity to manipulation by Satan. The reformers' experiential sense of the Devil told them that this was the most common and most profound expression of satanic agency, and in the reform of the liturgy and in their devotional works they sought to transmit the experience as a fundamental part of the everyday life of the Christian. It is this dynamic of Protestant demonism to which we must now turn.

160 Becon, *Certain articles of Christian Religion*, p. 400.

3

Temptation: the Protestant dynamic of diabolic agency and the resurgence of clerical mediation

A child brought to be baptised in 1548 underwent a lengthy ritual of exorcism in which the Devil was driven out by the mediation of the priest and the efficacy of the holy artefacts used in the rite. Through baptism the child entered the church; Satan was denied ownership of his soul, and was publicly forbidden to trouble the infant further.[1] Four years later, a child baptised under the second of the reformed Edwardian prayer books took part in a very different ceremony. There was no longer an exorcism to provide a tangible victory over the demonic. Instead the signing of the cross and the promise to renounce the Devil were taken as an indication that the new Christian's life was to be characterised by a constant struggle with the demonic.[2] This was a fundamental shift in the demonological rationale of Christian initiation, and one which reflected the Protestant belief that Satan constantly afflicted mankind on earth, and that the pursuit of godliness depended on a rigorous defence against his attempts to lure or drive men from their faith.

Traditionally the Devil's assaults were a frightening possibility, but one which might never be realised. Catholic theology laid a quasi-dualist emphasis on Satan's power, and saw humankind as the trophies of his cosmic battle with Christ.[3] The church invested in a great number of rituals and artefacts by which the Devil might be fought off at any stage of life, from his automatic possession of the unbaptised child, through the vagaries of weather, health and fortune, to the death-bed's final struggle to determine the destination of the soul.[4] But it was by no means certain that a person would experience diabolic affliction, and if he or she did, its assimilation into the culture of

1 The Sarum ritual is available in English in Fisher, *Christian Initiation*, pp. 158–79.

2 The baptism ceremony was reformed in *The booke of the common prayer*, fols. 135–52v; and *The Boke of common praier*, sigs. P4–Q2; see also *Liturgical services: Liturgies and occasional forms of prayer set forth in the reign of Queen Elizabeth*, ed. W. K. Clay (Cambridge, Parker Society, 1847), pp. 199–209.

3 C. W. Marx, *The Devil's Rights and the Redemption in the Literature of Medieval England* (Cambridge, 1995).

4 Duffy, *The Stripping of the Altars*, pp. 313–27.

intercession provided a scheme by which it might readily be brought to an end by the mediation of a higher power, who ultimately accepted responsibility for protecting the individual. The Protestant de facto approach to demonism saw satanic affliction as a near certainty within the life of the average Christian. Man's corrupted state was a result of the Devil's temptation of Adam and Eve, and Satan continued to define his earthly experience. His loss of spiritual insight left him vulnerable to the Devil's machinations until his dissolution reunited him with his redeemer. But if the roaring lion was hungry for all human souls, the Protestants' sense of election told them that his malice would naturally be concentrated on the godly. Thus a picture of unremitting diabolic assault – combined with a focused belief in the special responsibility of the godly to resist it – developed in parallel to that of the seduction of corrupted man in the synagogue of Satan polemic. Protestant devotional works aimed to transmit the experiential certainty of the Devil that they felt so keenly. As their anti-Catholic writings sought to convince men of the diabolism hidden in the familiar and comforting rituals of the traditional church, their liturgical approach, their sermons and their conduct books persuaded them to feel the Devil's presence by discerning his agency within their most commonplace experiences.

The medieval remit of the Devil had included temptation as one of a variety of activities with which he might afflict mankind. He was equally likely to manifest himself in storms and blights, or to appear as God's hangman to tear sinners limb from limb or drag them screaming to hell. Protestant theologians, however, elevated temptation into the single most important aspect of satanic agency. They thereby focused the site of diabolic conflict very firmly within the individual soul, and the archetype of temptation became the Devil's power to enter directly into the consciousness and introduce thoughts that were barely distinguishable from man's own. Temptation encapsulated Satan's all-pervasive malice, and allowed his agency to be potentially felt within the life of every Christian. In the face of the Devil's certain agency, Protestants stripped the faith of its 'magical' protectives, but they did so in order that a more rigorous method of resistance might force men to engage with the diabolic and understand its significance. Strength against the Devil was to come from an understanding of the meaning of his agency. Allowed by God as a test of faith, diabolic affliction could indicate election, and enable people to express their trust by relying completely on him to ultimately constrain the Devil, but not to intercede directly. If faith was to be discerned in the correct response to temptation, temptation had to be experienced in full. These emphases allowed Protestant ministers to adopt a new role as adepts able to mediate the correct response to temptation to their parishioners and, through their published writings, to society more widely. In so doing they re-established remarkably quickly part at least of the clerical role as mediators between man and the divine which had been stripped away by the Reformation.

LITURGY, THEOLOGY AND CONDUCT LITERATURE

The most obvious place to look for evidence of a distinctive Protestant approach to a devotional experience of the Devil is in the reformed liturgies which were produced between 1549 and 1552. In the redrafted ceremonies of the Edwardian prayer books can be seen what reformers intended to be the basic demonological experience of the average parishioner. Personal piety, and hence demonological awareness, had always differed as a result of individual commitment, and Protestantism invested much in the value of study outside the church. Thus the parishioner who relied only on attendance at service for his spiritual needs would not be exposed to the full complexities of the Protestant conception of demonic activity. But the changes in liturgical demonism were so striking that he would have found the reformed emphasis difficult to escape.

Eamon Duffy has described the Edwardian prayer books, first of 1549 and later of 1552, as an attempt to transform the lay experience of the Mass, sweeping away many of the central elements of eucharistic piety and most of the liturgical year.[5] They also encompassed a transformation of the lay experience of the diabolic which was no less dramatic. For the reformers, the traditional rites and ceremonies of the Sarum Missal failed to correctly express or engage with satanic agency as an intimate experience. They dealt largely with externals and superstitions, promising an easy victory over the Devil through the mediation of the Virgin, the saints and the quasi-magical paraphernalia of the sacraments. Highlighting the ever-present threat from Satan, the reformed liturgy drove home the message that only God could be relied upon to free man from his assaults. In the 1552 litany and suffrages, for instance, radically different to the kyries of the Sarum Missal, God was asked to spare man 'from all evyl and mischiefe, from synne, from the craftes and assaultes of the deuyll, from thy wrath, and from euerlastinge damnation'. The details of these assaults implied temptation, being 'fornication, and all other deadly synnes, and ... all the deceites of the world, the flesh and the deuyll'.[6] Indeed, the litany subverted its own rationale, emphasising not so much its tradition of intercession but rather the ultimate responsibility of each Christian to wage his own war with the demonic. The congregation of Christian soldiers requested 'that it maye please thee to strengthen suche as dooe stand, and to comfort and helpe the weake hearted, and to rayse up them that fall, and finallye to beat downe Satan under our feete'.[7]

[5] Ibid., p. 464. [6] *The Boke of common praier* (1552), sig. B4v. [7] Ibid., sig. B5v.

Most significant in this transformation of diabolic experience was the reform of the baptismal rite. The Sarum rite centred around the formal exorcism of every initiate, a ceremony that was downplayed and finally abolished by 1552. This is well documented, but the reasons for the demonological changes to the baptism have never been fully explored.[8] Martin Bucer, asked to comment on the 1549 prayer book, set out common objections to the Sarum rite in his *Censura* of 1551. Although the practice was ancient it was not endorsed by scripture, and in it the clergy claimed for themselves a power over the Devil which belonged only to God. Implicit was the assumption that all unbaptised children must be possessed by Satan, which was simply untrue and robbed the exorcisms performed by Christ and the apostles of their significance.[9] The issue could be highly emotive. Thomas Becon, writing from exile in 1554 after the second prayer book had been overturned, described how 'Baal's priest … conjureth the Devil out of the poor young infant [and] bespueth the child with his vile spittle and stinking slavering.'[10]

Behind the changes lay a fundamental shift in the demonological rationale of Christian initiation. In 1548 baptism constituted a very real victory over Satan, who was literally cast out of the infant and denied further access to his soul. In stark contrast, by 1552 it was understood to initiate the new Christian into a life that would be characterised by a perpetual struggle with the Devil. The traditional assumption that all infants were demoniacs was offensive, but exorcism's real superstition lay in its unrealistic promises of freedom from Satan, rather than its emphasis on diabolic power.

The triumphalist stance of the Sarum rite was unmistakable. Throughout the series of exorcisms that began at the church door the 'accursed Devil' was commanded to remember his sentence of damnation and that Christian initiation put men beyond his reach. Through baptism the initiate's thoughts were elevated above the carnal, and hence beyond the Devil's sphere of influence. 'With thy envy thou has been conquered', the exorcism declared; 'trembling and groaning depart: let there be nothing in common to thee and to this servant of God'.[11] The Sarum rite emphasised the passivity of the initiate. He would be given the opportunity to voluntarily renounce the Devil (through the

8 On the reform of baptism see Thomas, *Religion and the Decline of Magic*, pp. 62–4; Duffy, *The Stripping of the Altars*, pp. 280–1, 473; for more general discussion of the association of Catholic ceremony with superstition and witchcraft, see Clark, *Thinking with Demons*, pp. 533–5.

9 The complete text of the *Censura* is reproduced Martin Bucer, *Martin Bucer and the Book of Common Prayer*, ed. E. C. Whitacker (Great Wakering, 1974), see p. 92; the belief that the continuing use of exorcism undermined Christ's miracles became a mainstay of the Protestant attack on the practice. See, for example, Samuel Harsnett, *A Discovery of the Fravdvlent practices of Iohn Darrel* (London, 1599), pp. 43–5.

10 Becon, *An humble supplication unto God*, in *Prayers and Other Pieces*, p. 231.

11 Fisher, *Christian Initiation*, p. 162.

godparents) only after he had been freed from the possession into which he was born. As the baptism prayers made clear, God had 'called' him to take the first steps in the faith, and it was God who would 'drive' blindness from him and 'break all the bonds of Satan'.[12] In the second of two adjurations Satan was commanded to make way for the Holy Spirit, who was at that moment 'descending from the highest arch of heaven' to cleanse the infant's soul.[13] Thus baptism was individualised as a victory in which the Devil was robbed of one of his victims. In practice the victory was equivocal. Entire genres of saints' lives, folklore and *ars moriendi* demonstrated how Satan could, and did, renew his attentions to the initiated Christian.[14] But as a self-contained piece of liturgical theatre the baptism conquest of Satan was taken to be final.

The exorcism of the 1549 prayer book was far less imposing than its predecessor, but it still evidenced a very real victory over Satan, and assumed he was present in the church.[15] In 1552, however, there was no attempt to maintain even this belief. The ceremony simply bypassed the exorcism, implicitly denying that it was necessary, and that the minister had power of command over the Devil. After a prayer asking God to receive the initiate (written for the 1549 service), the ceremony moved straight to a reading from the gospel of Mark. Only the godparents' promise and the signing of the cross remained to indicate baptism's demonological significance.[16] The abandonment of exorcism implied its inefficacy, whilst the change in rationale was made explicit in what was added (or rewritten) in the Edwardian service. In particular the signing of the cross, which the Sarum rite understood to have its own efficacy in protecting the infant, became a declaration of the acceptance of life-long conflict with Satan.[17] The 1549 ceremony was transitional. It kept the signing of the cross at the church door (where it may have maintained an implication of exorcism) whilst redrafting its wording to deny its efficacy.[18] In 1552 it was moved to the end of the ceremony with the godparents' promise, allowing the conclusion of the baptism to centre

[12] Ibid., p. 159. [13] Ibid., p. 162.

[14] Jacobus de Voragine, *The Golden Legend: Readings on the Saints*, trans. W. G. Ryan (Princeton, N. J., 2 vols. 1993), vol. I, pp. 192, 238, 369–70, 223, vol. II, pp. 4, 69, 86, 193–5, 224; *Here begyneth a lityll treatise shorte and abridged spekynge of the arte & crafte to know well to dye* (Westminster, 1490); Richarde Rolle, *Remedy against the troubles of temptacyons* (London, 1519); Duffy, *The Stripping of the Altars*, pp. 266–80, 313–27.

[15] *The booke of the common prayer* (1549), fols. 136v, 137v–8.

[16] *The Boke of common praier* (1552), sigs. P5, P6, P6v.

[17] On the efficacy of the signing of the cross, see Thomas, *Religion and the Decline of Magic*, p. 34; Duffy, *The Stripping of the Altars*, pp. 273–83.

[18] If, as Eamon Duffy implies, the signing of the cross retained its implication of exorcism in the 1549 ceremony, it could do so only because the congregation remembered its traditional meaning. This was perhaps part of the expedient compromise which some historians have seen as informing the 1549 prayer book. See Duffy, *The Stripping of the Altars*, p. 473; on the 1549 prayer book as compromise see Haigh, *English Reformations*, p. 179.

around the understanding of the diabolic struggle. The cross was now to be a symbol only of the public profession of faith, a 'token' that the child should never be ashamed to proclaim himself a Christian. As Bucer described it in 1551, it was 'an admirably simple reminder of the cross of Christ'.[19] But, more significantly, with this open proclamation of faith the initiate declared also his intention 'manfully to fight under [Christ's] banner against synne, the worlde and the deuill, and to contynue his faythfull soldiour and servaunt unto [his] lyfes ende'.[20] The Edwardian Book of Homilies noted that it was not 'our office, after that we be once made Christ's members, to live contrary to the same, making ourselves members of the devil'.[21]

Such statements were more likely to draw Satan's attention than dispel his threat. As Edwin Sandys noted of the Devil in 1574, 'so soon as we profess to be Christ's soldiers, as a malicious and fierce enemy he invadeth us'.[22] After all, if Christ was tempted immediately after his baptism, how did ordinary men expect to escape?[23] Conflict with Satan was no longer to be sited at the baptismal font, or in any other ceremonial, but within the individual conscience. The baptism prayer asked that God grant the initiate the power to vanquish the Devil himself, implying that the mediation of the priest and the ritual was unnecessary. In the final exhortation explaining the godparents' promises on behalf of the child, the nature of the expected diabolic assault was made explicit. Forsaking the Devil involved 'continually mortifying all our evil and corrupt affections', an understanding which focused attention very sharply on the Devil's supposed ability to be able to enter the mind, and

19 Bucer, *Censura*, pp. 90, 91. Bucer did not actually approve of the words which accompanied the signing of the cross. Although they expressed a 'holy aspiration', they constituted more of a 'theatrical diversion' when addressed to an infant who could not understand them. Bucer therefore argued that the same sentiments should be contained in a prayer expressing the hope that the child might become a soldier of Christ.

20 *The booke of the common prayer* (1549), fol. 136. Thus in 1549 the signing of the cross directly contradicted the rationale of the exorcism which would follow, and which claimed that the Devil could no longer 'exercise any tyranny' against the baptised.

21 'A sermon of the salvation of mankind', 'A short declaration of the true, lively and Christian faith', 'A sermon against contention and brawling', 'An homily or sermon concerning the nativity', 'An homily for Good Friday', in *Certain Sermons or Homilies*, pp. 30, 43, 154, 436–7, 440.

22 Sandys, *Sermons*, p. 166; William Gurnall, *The Christian in Compleat Armour. Or a Treatise Of the Saints War against the Deuil* (London, 1654), p. 94.

23 Thomas Becon, *The Christen Knighte, teaching the Warriors of God ... how they may preuaile against Satan* (n.d.), in *The Catechism of Thomas Becon*, p. 623; Miles Coverdale, *An Exhortation to the carienge of Chrystes crosse with a true and brefe confutation of false and papisticall doctryne* (1554), in *Remains of Bishop Coverdale*, pp. 233–5; writing in 1664, Richard Baxter described the belief that external baptism only washed away sin as a temptation from Satan, by which he drew men from the pursuit of a godly life and into complacency, see *A Christian Directory: Or, a summ of Practical Theology, and cases of conscience* (1673), in *Practical Works*, (London, 4 vols., 1707), vol. I, p. 22.

which made temptation the most common form of diabolic assault.[24] When, nearly a century later, the Westminster assembly compiled the *Directory for the Publique Worship of God* (1645), the baptism was further reformed and both the signing of the cross and the godparents' promise were removed. However, the new rationale of Christian initiation remained, as the renunciation of the Devil was now declared to be implicit within the ceremony itself, and a final prayer asked that God 'make [the infant's] baptism effectuall . . . that by faith he may prevail against the Devil'.[25]

The reaction of parishioners to this change is irrecoverable. The 1549 prayer book met with widespread opposition, and action had to be taken against ministers who continued to use ceremonies that were not explicitly banned, and approximated those that were.[26] It is likely that a powerful experience of confrontation with the diabolic was lost after 1549. Even if they could not understand the Latin of the Sarum rite, the congregation were well aware that the Devil was present in the church, hidden within the body of the child. They were witness to Satan being put to flight, as the contemptuous tone of the exorcism invited them to believe that they saw a palpable victory being played out. Protected in a consecrated building by the 'magical' paraphernalia of the rite, and by the power of the priest's mediation, they could share in the derision being meted out to a Devil they imagined skulking away, forbidden ever to return. In 1549 removing the adjurations and prayers on either side of the formal exorcism took away the focus of attention from the rite itself. Robbed of a significant period of expectation the exorcism must have lost much of its impact. The Devil was now dispatched with such speed and ease that it is likely the exorcism was no longer satisfying to those onlookers who retained a profound sense of its spiritual and emotive importance. Those used to the triumphalist harangues of the Sarum rite probably found the expedition of the 1549 exorcism confusing and unsettling and its absence in 1552 must have profoundly altered the experience of baptism. It was surely this theatre which imbued the liturgical artefacts with the quasi-magical properties which Eamon Duffy has identified. Baptismal water was commonly considered so powerful a protective that the clergy found it necessary to lock it away to prevent its misuse, and the chrisom had also to be returned by the parents for destruction.[27]

But it was precisely this kind of demonological experience, mediated through the church, and experienced with the bravery of being out of

[24] *The book of the common prayer* (1549), fol. 139; *The Boke of common praier* (1552), sig. P6v.

[25] *A Directory for the Publique Worship of God, Throughout the Three Kingdoms of England, Scotland and Ireland* (London, 1645), pp. 39–47, esp. pp. 42, 47.

[26] Haigh, *English Reformations*, pp. 173–6.

[27] Duffy, *The Stripping of the Altars*, p. 280.

range, that aroused Protestant suspicion. In their view it clouded parishioners' perception with a smoke-screen of empty ceremonies and victories, substituting a fake demonic experience to distract attention from the real site of diabolic conflict. In discounting such easy victories, Protestantism demanded a more rigorous engagement with the experience of diabolic agency, a subject we will return to later in this chapter.

Protestant demonism was laid out for parishioners in more detail in the catechisms, sermons and expositions that sought to transmit the Protestant message. The message that Satan would be a constant and vigilant enemy was constructed around a number of scriptural archetypes. The significance of the fall of Adam lay not so much in the historical event, but in the spiritual condition it bequeathed to humankind. Thus the story demonstrated that humans were born to be Satan's quarry. Christ's temptation in the desert further demonstrated that diabolic affliction was inescapable, and provided a dynamic of satanic agency which focused firmly on the individual rather than the corporate. Finally the Lord's Prayer, which encompassed man's ongoing relationship with God, emphasised his weakness in the face of demonic affliction.

A very large number of catechisms were published in English in the sixteenth and seventeenth centuries whose purpose was to instil a knowledge of the fundamentals of Christianity, often to an audience considered unwilling or unable to benefit from sermons.[28] These catechisms varied enormously in length, content and style and, as Ian Green has demonstrated, there was no uniform, centrally imposed pattern of catechising.[29] Those with a liturgical use were short and to the point, requiring only a cursory knowledge of the basics. The confirmation catechism, which involved a brief rehearsal of the significance of the Creed, the decalogue and the Lord's Prayer, sought to reinforce the demonology of baptism. It required the child to demonstrate that he understood and considered himself bound by the promise to forsake the Devil which had been made on his behalf.[30] Other catechisms were designed to be worked through at a more leisurely pace and provided more detailed expositions. If they could vary widely in style and content, most dealt with demonism by a rehearsal of the story of Adam and Eve and an exposition of the Lord's Prayer.[31] Consistent with Protestant

[28] See the 'Finding list of English Catechisms', in Ian Green, *The Christian's ABC: Catechisms and Catechising in England c. 1530–1740* (Oxford, 1996), pp. 580–751; Patrick Collinson, *The Religion of Protestants: The Church in English Society 1559–1625* (Oxford, 1982), pp. 232–4.

[29] Green, *The Christian's ABC*, p. 5.

[30] *The booke of the common prayer* (1549), fols. 143v–4; *The Boke of common praier* (1552), sigs. Q2v–Q5v.

[31] On the subtleties of catechists' readings of the fifth and sixth petition of the Lord's Prayer, see Green, *The Christian's ABC*, pp. 497–504.

emphases, reference to fundamental theodicy and the fall of the Devil was conspicuous by its absence. Of the most influential catechists, only Alexander Nowell mentioned the fall of Lucifer when using free will to dismiss the notion that God might have abandoned the care of any of his creatures.[32] Thomas Cranmer's *Catechism* of 1548, based on the *Nuremberg Catechism* of Justus Jonas, provided a number of short sermons rather than the more familiar series of questions and answers. Satan's role in the fall of man featured in the second of three sermons on the creation, redemption and sanctification. A separate sermon dealt with each petition of the Lord's Prayer in turn, giving a concise but detailed description of the Devil's agency under the sixth and seventh petitions.[33] The most mainstream of the catechisms followed this general pattern. John Ponet's influential *A Short Catechism* (1553) had less to say on the subject of demonism, but dealt with the same issues, as did Alexander Nowell's famous catechism, printed in English in 1570.[34] Thomas Becon's *A New Catechism set forth Dialogue-wise in familar talk between the Father and the Son* (1563) belied its title, providing a longer, more detailed and more scripturally conversant exposition of Christian fundamentals than was likely to have been of use to a child. Here Becon was more interested in the end of redemption than the beginning, and the book touches only briefly on the fall of man. But an exhaustive description of the Devil's agency makes up the exposition of the sixth petition of the Lord's Prayer.[35]

Satan pervaded the enormous number of sermons that found their way into print, and it is reasonable to assume that he had a similar influence on the parish preaching which left no record. The programme of sermonising contained in the *Book of Homilies*, first published in 1547, contained no dedicated treatment of the Devil, but an awareness of his agency was central to the subjects intended to comprise a basic religious understanding. Of the thirty-three sermons that made up the book in its Elizabethan format, only ten made no mention at all of Satan. Moreover, the book may reflect an increase in the perceived importance of the Devil. Of the twelve homilies of the 1547 edition, five made no mention of diabolism, whilst of those added in

[32] God, Nowell noted, did not create evil angels; instead they 'by their own evilness, fell from their first creation, without hope of recovery, and so are become evil, not by creation and nature, but by corruption of nature'. See Alexander Nowell, *A Catechism written in Latin by Alexander Nowell* (1570), ed. J. Bruce (Cambridge, Parker Society, 1842), p. 147.

[33] Cranmer, *Catechismvs*, fols. 123–4v, 147–60v.

[34] John Ponet, A short Catechisme, or playne instruction (1553), in *The Two Liturgies, A.D. 1549 and A.D. 1552*, ed. J. Ketley (Cambridge, Parker Society, 1844), pp. 502–5, 522–3; Nowell, *Catechism*, pp. 148–50, 201–2.

[35] Thomas Becon, *A New Catechism set forth Dialogue-wise in familiar talk between the Father and the Son* (1563), in *The Catechism of Thomas Becon, with other pieces*, pp. 184–98.

1562, the figure was five out of twenty-one.[36] The *Homilies* offered an uncompromising picture of the antithesis of Christ and the Devil, and of their human servants.[37] Discussions of the fall of man, the reign of the Devil and Christ's victory through the passion were accompanied by detailed treatments of individual sins, which sought to highlight the role of diabolic temptation.[38] At the same time the *Homilies* attempted to broaden parishioners' political understanding of demonism. The lengthy sermons against idolatry exposed the Devil's role in Catholic image worship, the discussion of fasting revealed the diabolism of an empty faith in good works, a sermon on the Holy Ghost (to be read on Whit Sunday) listed the tyrannical acts of a variety of popes as evidence of 'the spirit of the Devil', and the sermon against rebellion drew direct comparisons with the revolt of Lucifer.[39] Whilst it is debatable to what extent any audience might have assimilated the entirety of the *Homilies*' demonism (the message being dispersed over the liturgical year), it is a testament to their authors' intent that demonological knowledge should have a wide devotional, social and political base.

Christ's temptation in the desert provided a scriptural exemplar of man's duty to follow him in resisting the Devil.[40] William Perkins produced a detailed description of the nature of diabolic temptation in his *The Combat between Christ and the Divell displayed*. In doing so he provided one of the most detailed descriptions of the dynamic of temptation of all the Protestant theologians. Demonic agency continued to be a popular subject into the later seventeenth century. Henry Lawrence, forced into retirement by the Civil War, found time to pen *Of Our Communion and Warre with Angels* in 1646. The book was mainly a lengthy exposition on Ephesians 6: 12–19, a very commonly cited source for scriptural proof of Protestant demonism. Perhaps the most detailed description of temptation to be produced in England was contained in Richard Baxter's *Christian Directory*. This massive conduct book was written around 1664, but was not published

36 The majority of the homilies were divided into two or more parts and it is not the case that the Devil would be discussed every week, but demonism was thought pertinent to the majority of subjects. Similarly the Henrican Primer of 1545 contained relatively few references to the Devil in its collection of prayers, in contrast to that of 1553. See *The Primer, and Catchechisme, sette furthe by the Kynges highness and his clergie* (London, 1552; first edn 1545), sigs. P4v, S, T3v, T6v–T7.

37 'A sermon of Christian love and charity', 'A sermon against whoredom' and 'An homily of the right use of the church', in *Certain Sermons or Homilies*, pp. 69, 130, 170.

38 'A sermon of the misery of all mankind', 'A sermon of good works annexed unto faith', 'An homily of the resurrection', 'An homily against gluttony and drunkenness' and 'An homily of the place and time of prayer', in ibid., pp. 17, 51–2, 311, 362, 463.

39 'An homily against the peril of idolatry', 'An homily of good works: and first of fasting' and 'An homily against disobedience and wilful rebellion', in ibid., pp. 240–1, 249, 280, 297, 588, 606, 610, 617–18, 626.

40 'An homily against the peril of idolatry', in ibid., pp. 193–4.

until 1673. It reproduced in great depth the dynamic of demonic affliction that had been expressed by Protestant theologians over a hundred years earlier, isolating each aspect of temptation and revealing how it might be resisted.

Satan's powerful hold over man was understood to be a consequence of the fall of Adam. Unlike the fall of Lucifer, the question of how evil was introduced to the terrestrial world was not limited by scriptural obscurity. Satan's corruption of Eden was a historical fact. According to Thomas Becon, the Devil, desiring man's perdition, 'like a wily serpent attempted the woman "as the more frail vessel", and ready to be devict and overcome so that at the last, through his subtle and crafty persuasions, she gave place to that wily serpent, the father of lying, and wickedly transgressed God's most holy commandment'.[41] Some put it more simply, like John Ponet, who noted only, 'Eve [was] deceived by the devil counterfeiting the shape of a serpent.'[42] Henry King, preaching a sermon on Lent in March 1625, provided one of the most elaborate pictures, highlighting the speed of man's fall into a Faustian bargain. 'In the morning of the sixt day was Man made', he commented, 'and before the evening of that same day had he, upon the Devil's short parley, surrendered up his innocence & libertie, quite sold away his Patent, the privileges of his birth, and at that scornefull rate wherewith we purchase the love of children, for an Apple.'[43] For John Cosin the rebellion of Adam was 'a story delivered to us in Scripture and made good by experience'. Even if the bible had been silent, the 'universal irregularity of our whole nature' and daily exposure 'to continual afflictions and sorrow' must assure people that they had not been created so by God. Logic then demanded that some common father must have infected him and his posterity with sin, and the bible filled in the blanks. 'That poison, to go now by the Scriptures', Cosin noted, 'was brought him by the devil, and down it went.'[44]

The Devil had enticed man into sin, but he also played the role of God's executioner, into whose hands mankind was delivered as punishment. 'The fall of Adam', Tyndale noted, 'hath made us heirs to the vengeance and wrath of God, and heirs of eternal damnation; and hath brought us into captivity and bondage under the Devil.' Thomas Becon highlighted the

[41] Becon, *News from Heaven*, in *Early Works*, p. 46; 'A sermon of good works annexed unto faith', 'An homily or sermon concerning the nativity and the birth of our Saviour Jesus Christ', in *Certain Sermons or Homilies*, pp. 51, 426.

[42] Ponet, *Short Catechisme*, in *Two Liturgies*, p. 502; Nowell, *Catechism*, pp. 148–9.

[43] Henry King, *Two sermons preached at Whitehall in Lent* (1626), in *The Sermons of Henry King (1592–1669)*, ed. M. Hobbs (Rutherford, 1992), p. 116.

[44] John Cosin, *The Works of the Right Reverend father in God, John Cosin* (Oxford, 4 vols, 1843–51), vol. I, p. 209.

change in man's nature, passing from the 'glorious state in which he stood' to become the 'servile, thrall, captive, and a very bond-slave of Satan'.[45] 'We are all become dirt by the fall of the first Adam' was Roger Hutchinson's succinct comment in his *The Image of God*. Man's rebellion, according to Alexander Nowell, left him 'holden bond, and fast tied with impiety and wickedness, and wrapped in the snares of eternal death, and holden thrall in foul bondage of the serpent the devil'.[46] Henry King described man's punishment in line with his conception of the fall as a fateful transaction that got its just rewards. 'The first man sold himselfe to sin', he noted, '& in that luckles bargaine concluded us, his wretched posteritie – passed us away into the power of the Devil, who bought him from all Obedience.'[47]

But when Protestants spoke of slavery they had something very specific in mind. Mankind's degradation actually made his nature similar to that of the corrupted angels. The rebellious angels had become hideous monsters, but man's debasement manifested itself in physical weakness and loss of spiritual insight. For John Hooper, fallen man exchanged his 'original perfection' for 'the image of the devil'.[48] Adam, argued Alexander Nowell, had been endued with all the best 'ornaments' of mankind, to keep or to lose as his free will determined. In rebelling against God he forfeited them for himself and his descendants, leaving mankind with 'short ... and uncertain race of life', 'infirmity of our flesh', 'feebleness of our bodies' and 'horrible blindness of our minds and perverseness of our hearts'.[49] Positing a common nature between corrupted men and devils enabled Protestant theologians to push the issue of human complicity in sin. For Tyndale the Devil might have become man's 'prince' or 'god' after Eden, but man was zealous in his complicity. 'Unto the devil's will consent we all our hearts', he noted, 'so that

45 William Tyndale, *Pathway into Holy Scripture*, in *Doctrinal treatises and introductions to different portions of the Holy Scripture*, ed. H. Walter (Cambridge, Parker Society, 1848), p. 17; Becon, *David's Harp*, in *Early Works*, p. 292; Coverdale, *The old faith, an evident probacion out of scripture, that the christen fayth ... hath endured sens the beginnyng of the worlde* (1547); *A Spiritual and most precious perle, teachinge all men to love and imbrace ye crosse as a most swete and necessarye thing unto the soule*, in *Writings and Translations*, pp. 3–4, 100; Jeremy Taylor, *Holy Living and Holy Dying*, ed. P. G. Stanwood (Oxford, 2 vols., 1989), vol. I, pp. 42–3.

46 Hutchinson, *The Image of God*, in *Works*, p. 59; Nowell, *Catechism*, p. 151; Miles Coverdale, *The Old Faith, an evident probacion out of scripture* (London, 1547), p. 18; Sandys, *Sermons*, p. 178. Whilst Protestants tended to emphasise the desperate state of mankind, diabolic punishment and divine mercy were understood to exist in balance.

47 Henry King, *A Sermon of Deliverance. Preached at the Spittle on Easter Monday* (1626), in *Sermons*, p. 100.

48 John Hooper, *A Declaration of Christe and of his offyce compylyd by Johan Hoper* (1547), in *Early Writings*, p. 87; 'An homily or sermon concerning the nativity', in *Certain Sermons or Homilies*, pp. 426–7; Baxter, *A Christian Directory*, p. 7;

49 Nowell, *Catechisme*, p. 149; Taylor, *Holy Living*, pp. 42–3.

the law and will of the devil is written as well in our hearts as in our members, and we run headlong after the devil with full zeal.' That fallen men and devils would suffer equally at Judgement Day was the final proof that their nature was essentially the same. When Tyndale described Adam's posterity as 'heirs' to God's vengeance, he implied that humans now shared in the divine wrath which predated the corruption of Eden. Mankind simply swelled the ranks of those angels that were already damned eternally, as the widely cited judgement in Matthew 25: 41 made clear – 'depart from me, ye cursed, into the everlasting fire, prepared for the Devil and his angels'.[50] For Hooper no creature was as great a rebel to his maker as man, 'saving the devil'.[51] In spiritual blindness Protestant writers were able to express the fine balance they saw between the condition of man sent by God, and man's own responsibility for overcoming it. The second Book of Thessalonians put it succinctly – 'God shall send them strong delusions, that they believe lies; that all they might be damned which believed not the truth but had pleasure in unrighteousness.'[52] John Jewel connected the text with 1 Corinthians 2: 14 – 'the natural man perceiveth not the things of the Spirit of God; for they are foolishness unto him'.[53]

Increasingly Satan's ability to intrude directly into the consciousness dominated this understanding of man's relationship with the diabolic.[54] He could enter the mind and place sinful thoughts within it, producing, according to Thomas Cranmer, 'sodein and vehement motions to do euel'. 'For the Deuel is a spirit, whom we can neither feal nor see', he continued, 'wherefore he can set our hartes a fyer so sodenly, that we shall not knowe from whence such soden fire and sparkes do come.'[55] 'The deuill in tempting a man to sinne', Perkins commented in *The Combat between Christ and the Divell displayed*, 'conueyes into his mind, either by inward suggestion or outward obiect, the motion or cognition of that sinne which he would

[50] Tyndale, *Pathway into Holy Scripture*, pp. 14–18; Bullinger, *Decades*, pp. 352–3; Bayly, *Practice of Pietie*, p. 63.

[51] Hooper, *Declaration of Christe*, p. 90; *Confession and Protestation of Faith*, in *Later Writings*, pp. 70–2; 'The second homily concerning the death and passion of our Saviour Christ', in *Certain Sermons or Homilies*, pp. 448–9, 455–6; Lewis Bayly, *The Practice of Pietie*, p. 41.

[52] 2 Thessalonians 2: 11–12; See Jewel, *An Exposition upon the Two Epistles to the Thessalonians*, p. 924; 'A sermon of the salvation', in *Certain Sermons or Homilies*, p. 30; Alexander Cooke, *Pope Ioane. A Dialogue between a Protestant and a Papist* (London, 1625), sigs. A2–A2v.

[53] Jewel, *An Exposition upon the Two Epistles to the Thessalonians*, p. 924; The later King James version of the New Testament translated this passage differently, replacing 'perceiveth' with 'receiveth'.

[54] For a different interpretation see Oldridge, *The Devil*, pp. 48–9.

[55] Cranmer, *Catechismvs*, fols. 147v–8.

have him to commit'.[56] This conception of satanic agency continued to dominate into the seventeenth century. To Henry King, preaching on deliverance at Spitalfields in 1626, man was a 'beleagured Citie', the five senses 'ports' by which the Devil gained entrance. 'Hee bribes the Eye to wound the Heart', he noted, 'and by those windows of our bodies, He throwes in Lust like wild-fire.'[57] Satan was the 'internall cause' of sin, observed the demonologist Henry Lawrence in 1646, 'for hee mingles himself with our most intimate corruptions, and because the seate of his warfare is the inward man'.[58]

The notion of internal temptation was not, of course, an invention of Protestantism. On the contrary, it was central to the traditional remit of satanic agency. The exact dynamic of temptation was traditionally an open question, complicated, as William Perkins himself pointed out, by different possible readings of the temptation of Eve and that of Christ.[59] Theologians from the Church Fathers to Thomas Aquinas argued that temptation (both internal and external) was the truest manifestation of the Devil's policy of opposing God.[60] In the work of writers such as St Augustine or Gregory the Great, the dynamic and experience of internal temptation were described in terms that would be repeated by Protestants in the sixteenth century.[61] Moreover, the 'saints' lives' embodied numerous tales of the Devil disguised as a beautiful woman, or as the physical tormentor who tempted men to impatience. Temptation as an internal working of the mind also found a place in devotional works. The fourteenth-century *Contemplations of the Dread and Love of God* predicted a 'war of temptacions' for the Christian in which Satan 'putteth in oure mende diuerse ymaginations, as worldiche and fleschliche thoghts, [and sumtime other thoghts] whiche be ful greuous and perlous, eyther to make us to haue a gret lust and liking in hem that be worldliche and fleshliche, or els to bring ous in gret heuynes or drede thoru tho thoghts wiche be greuous and perlous'.[62] Of the five temptations

56 Perkins, *The Combat between Christ and the Divell displayed*, p. 376.
57 King, *A Sermon of Deliverance*, p. 106.
58 Lawrence, *Of Our Communion and Warre with Angels*, p. 1.
59 Perkins highlighted the difficulty presented by the two scriptural archetypes for temptation. In biblical phraseology the '"tempter came unto" Christ, by which phrase it is probable, though not certaine that the deuill tooke upon him the forme of some creature'. It was certain that he had appeared to Eve as a serpent, but in the temptation of Christ the case was less clear cut. 'Some indeed think', Perkins continued, 'that these temptations were in the mind onely, and by vision'. William Perkins, *The Combat between Christ and the Divell displayed*, p. 382.
60 Russell, *Lucifer*, pp. 36–7, 100–1, 202, 205–6.
61 Russell, *Satan*, pp. 40, 97, 115, 135, 172–3, and *Lucifer*, pp. 100–1; see also Michael E. Goodich, *Violence and the Miracle in the Fourteenth Century: Private Grief and Public Salvation* (Chicago and London, 1995), pp. 64–9, 74–85.
62 *Contemplations of the Dread and Love of God*, ed. M. Connolly (Oxford, Early English Text Society, 1993), p. 33.

depicted in the fifteenth-century *ars moriendi*, four were presented unambiguously as diabolic intrusions into the mind.[63] Temptation was also described in the homily on the Lord's Prayer contained in the *Festial* of John Mirk, but here diabolic intrusion was presented more as a direct control over the physical senses rather than the injection of thoughts into the mind. In tempting man, the Devil 'makyth hym cacche a delyte' in an object in his physical sight and so kindle lust in his heart.[64]

But whilst temptation exemplified the Devil's malice, it was never elevated to such a degree that it eclipsed the wider remit of satanic agency. Instead, historians have charted a developing concern with diabolic power among medieval Catholics that focused on the Devil's physicality, and that was maintained in the face of the Reformation. Julio Caro Baroja identifies a progressive, two-stage definition of satanic power in orthodox Christian theology. In the Middle Ages this sought to deny the reality of acts of witchcraft as illusions of the Devil, who worked primarily to deceive the senses.[65] As the persecution of heresy developed, the reality of the deeds ascribed to servants of Satan were affirmed by scholastic teaching and judicial practice, so that absolute doctrine, expressed by theologians such as Aquinas, asserted the physical reality of demonic power. By the end of the sixteenth century, Baroja notes, 'there was a positive obsession with the Devil's physical presence in the world'.[66] Similarly, Robin Briggs argues that post-Reformation Catholics avidly embraced opportunities to show that the Devil was an active corporeal presence as a means of resisting Protestant attempts to separate the physical and the divine.[67] The importance of the physical Devil was widely reflected in devotional culture. Traditional religious corporatism provided a powerful communal experience of warding off physical (if largely invisible) demons through intercession and ceremonies such as Candlemas and Rogationtide. The Candlemas ceremony predicted that 'wherever [the candle] be lit or set up, the devil may flee away in fear', whilst Rogationtide re-established parish boundaries each year by literally driving the demons who were believed to infest the air into a neighbouring parish.[68] Homiletic literature and the stage provided a central place for the Devil as God's hangman, and as the tormentor of the saints. The devils of the mystery plays were imaginatively grotesque and always presented as physical manifestations, as were those of the church misericord carvings, doom paintings and stained

63 *The Doctrinal of Death* (London, 1498), sigs. A4, A6.
64 John Mirk, *Mirk's Festial: A Collection of Homilies, by Johannes Mirkus (John Mirk)*, ed. T. Erbe (London, Early English Text Society, 1905), p. 286.
65 Julio Caro Baroja, 'Witchcraft and Catholic Theology', in B. Ankarloo and G. Henningsen (eds.), *Early Modern European Witchcraft* (Oxford, 1990), pp. 24–7.
66 Ibid., pp. 27–38, quote at p. 38. 67 Robin Briggs, *Witches and Neighbours*, p. 385.
68 Duffy, *The Stripping of the Altars*, pp. 16–17, 279.

glass.[69] Moreover, traditional devotional works could even be ambiguous over the question of whether the Devil was most dangerous in the mind or in the outside world. *The Dietary of Ghostly Health*, published in 1520 by Wynkyn de Worde, assured its readers that a mind constantly remembering Christ's passion was impervious to diabolic intrusion, but that Satan was an inevitable presence in 'the material cloister', and 'ye shall have of him more force and stronger battle there'.[70] Aron Gurevich has noted that the depiction of demons in medieval exemplars and art reflected an inherent tendency to 'translate the spiritual into the concretely sensible and material'. Thus stories abounded of demons interacting physically with humans – riding on the backs or clothes of sinners, or crowding around the death-bed – present but unseen by the majority of the protagonists. These Gurevich describes as instances of 'double vision', which erased the border between abstract and object.[71] The fascination with the grotesque physical demons probably ensured that an exclusive emphasis on a spiritual Devil could not gain ascendancy in traditional devotional culture.

In contrast, for Protestant theologians, it was precisely at the point of physicality that the nature of diabolic experience became a grey area. Their reticence over physicality is explained by their desire to give diabolism the widest possible transmission as a palpable experience. Recent work on witchcraft and on providence has shown that belief in the physical manifestation of Satan was difficult for Protestants to resist because it was both deeply entrenched in popular culture and could be attuned to reformist agendas. So the emphasis on the role of familiars in English witchcraft represented the accommodation of a popular notion of demons with a

[69] For the characterisation of the physical Devil in medieval exemplar tales see Frederich C. Tubach, *Index Exemplorum: A Handbook of Medieval Religious Tales* (Helsinki, F.F. Communications No. CCIV, 1969), tale types 1527–1665, pp. 125–37; Katherine Briggs, *A Dictionary of British Folklore in the English Language*, Part B: *Folk Legends* (London, 2 vols., 1971), vol. I, pp. 43–155, gives an indication of the types of traditional stories that were told of the Devil, although their dating is uncertain since the dictionary often relies on the collections of local nineteenth-century folklorists; the presentation of the Devil in the English mystery plays is discussed in L. W. Cushman, *The Devil and the Vice in English Dramatic Literature before Shakespeare* (London, 1900; reprinted 1970), pp. 1–53; for only a handful of examples of the presentation of the physical Devil in illuminated manuscripts see N. Morgan (ed.), *A Survey of Manuscripts Illuminated in the British Isles*, vol. IV (I): *Early Gothic Manuscripts 1190–1250* (Oxford, 1982), illustrations 72, 73, 129, 201, 237, 238; for the Devil in medieval church decoration, see G. L. Remnant, *Catalogue of Misericords in Great Britain* (Oxford, 1969); Kathleen M. Openshaw, 'Weapons in the Daily Battle: Images of the Conquest of Evil in the Early Medieval Psalter', *Art Bulletin*, 75 (1) (March 1993), pp. 17–38.

[70] *The Dietary of Ghostly Health* (London, 1520), sigs. A4–A4v; *The Profitable book for Man's Soul* (London, 1493), sig. A6v.

[71] Aron Gurevich, *Medieval Popular Culture: Problems of Belief and Perception*, trans. J. M. Bak and P. A. Hollingsworth (Cambridge, 1988), pp. 184–95.

clerical and judicial need to discover evidence of apostasy.[72] Similarly, the appearances of God's hangman – who visited dire punishments on reprobates – could, interpreted correctly, provide valuable ammunition for the critique of clerical and congregational intransigence in the face of the continuing Reformation.[73] But the Devil who was hidden in thunderstorms was an irregular and uncertain visitor, as was the Devil who took the shape of a black dog, or came in the night as an incubus. Protestants might be ready to appropriate stories of visitations, but they made no attempt to argue that such experiences were among the norms of satanic activity. Instead they sought to reveal the diabolic nature of the commonplace. Anger, envy, the desire to eat, to rest, to have sex, to give church a miss in favour of the alehouse – these were within the experience of all men and women. If a blanket interpretation of diabolism could be placed upon them, Satan could be brought convincingly into the most intimate aspects of people's lives, and the norm of his agency could be made insidious through the sheer banality of the sinful thoughts he was credited with introducing into the mind. 'Like as an artificer that is cunning and expert in his craft', Hugh Latimer remarked in a sermon on the Lord's Prayer, 'the devil knoweth all ways how to tempt us . . . insomuch that we can begin nor do nothing, but that he is at our heels and worketh some mischief, whether we be in prosperity or adversity, whether we be in health or sickness, life or death; he knoweth how to use the same to his purpose.'[74] This, of course, had a moralising agenda, but it was also a response to a genuine concern that the traditional focus on physical demons had lulled Christians into a false sense of security. Thomas Pierson noted in 1605: 'The naturall man doth not percieue that working of Satan which doth procure his woe, it may be that he hath seene the plaiers and the painters diuels, some black horned monster with broad eies, crooked clawes or clouen feet; and till such thing appeare vnto him, he neuer feareth hurt by Satan.'[75] Thus whilst Protestant writers fully accepted the possibility of 'satanical molestation' they were careful to incorporate it into a wider scheme of temptation by which man's faith was tested. William Perkins, in his *Cases of Conscience*, noted that physical encounters with devils could take place in certain locations, but this was because houses and other buildings could suffer from spiritual intrusions

72 Holmes, 'Women, Witches and Witnesses', pp. 67–71.
73 A. Walsham, *Providence in Early Modern England* (Oxford, 1999), pp. 186–94; see also David Cressy, *Travesties and Transgressions in Tudor and Stuart England: Tales of Discord and Dissension* (Oxford, 2000), p. 284.
74 Latimer, *Sermons*, pp. 429–30; Perkins, *Foure Godly Treatises*, p. 1.
75 Thomas Pierson, preface to William Perkins' *The Combat between Christ and the Divell displayed*, sigs. Kkk6–Kkk6v.

as a parallel to internal temptation.[76] Similarly, those Protestant ministers at the forefront of the attempt to strip the figure of the witch of preternatural power, and attribute *maleficium* to the Devil, were adamant that its diabolic rationale was to torment the mind and drive it to faithlessness.[77]

Moreover, Protestants often betrayed an ambivalence to stories of satanic visitations. For example, Henry Jessey's *The exceeding Riches of Grace Advanced* (1647) included the testimony of a sufferer who claimed to have inhaled a mysterious smoke that 'fluttered' inside her while 'a voice said within me, to my heart, "thou art damned, damned"'. Jessey did not dispute the story, but did add a marginal note that explained that another had had the same experience, 'but after she judged it was but a fancy'.[78] Since it was a commonplace of Puritan complaint literature that ingestion – of tobacco or alcohol – was a widespread means by which demonic spiritual intrusion was effected, the example is suggestive of highly complex attitudes to diabolic physicality.[79] In the scheme that emphasised the Devil's insidious use of the commonplace, it was the extraordinary nature of sudden visitations (in this case it was brimstone rather than tobacco) that made them problematic.

In order, then, to understand what Protestant writers meant by internal temptation, we need to deconstruct the monopoly of demonological interpretation they claimed over man's everyday experiences. This was an extension of what they claimed over the interpretation of the Catholic Mass. After the corruption of Eden, a powerful triumvirate – the 'World', the 'Flesh' and the Devil – ruled over the earth and enveloped the individual Christian.[80] Enticing him this way and that into sin, the three powers were commonly afforded animistic characteristics by theologians and moralists. Thomas

76 Perkins, *Cases of Conscience*, in *Works*, pp. 37–9. The term 'satanical molestation' was his. Similarly, see the opinion of Richard Greenham (1582) in K. Parker and E. Carlsen (eds.), *'Practical Divinity': The Works and Life of Revd Richard Greenham* (Brookfield, Vt., 1998), p. 217.

77 George Gifford, *Two Sermons . . . wherein it is shewed that the deuill is to be resisted only by steadfast faith* (London, 1597), pp. 70–1; Gifford, *A Discourse of the subtle Practices of Devils by Witches*. For a discussion of the ways in which Protestant demonologists argued that witchcraft, as a diabolic assault, was a consequence of sin, see Stuart Clark, 'Protestant Demonology', in Ankarloo and Henningsen, pp. 59–61.

78 Henry Jessey, *The exceeding Riches of Grace Advanced . . . in . . . Sarah Wight* (London, 1647), pp. 77–8.

79 *Work for Chimny-sweepers: or a warning for Tobacconists* (London, 1602), sigs. F4–G4v; Samuel Ward, *Woe to Drunkards* (London, 1622), pp. 8–14; *Schola Cordis* (London, 1647), pp. 22–7.

80 'A sermon of the salvation of mankind by only Christ our saviour from the sin and death everlasting', in *Certain Sermons or Homilies*, p. 26; Sandys, *Sermons*, p. 175; Miles Coverdale, *A Spiritual and most precious perle, teachinge all men to love and imbrace ye crosse as a most swete and necessarye thing unto the soule*, in *Writings and Translations*, pp. 95, 157, 165, 173; Symons, *The Lord Jesus his commission* (London, 1657), p. 8; Baxter, *A Christian Directory*, p. 83.

Becon described them as individual 'princes and rulers', and so associated them with the 'principalities and powers' spoken of in Ephesians.[81] The flesh enticed men to all things that were pleasurable to the carnal body, and operated in direct opposition to the influence of the Holy Ghost. It may 'prouoke us to lecherye, adulterye, dronkeness and such lyke', stated Cranmer's catechism, or provoke us 'to leaue any thinge vndone, which is paynful and greuous to the fleshe'. 'The flesh lusteth contrary to the Spirit', noted Becon in his *New Catechism*, 'and the Spirit contrary to the flesh.' He individualised the flesh by allowing that it was capable of enslaving men, and by unsubtly associating it with female promiscuity. Infinite numbers of people, he said, 'willingly offer themselves subjects, servants, and slaves to this vile strumpet, the flesh; and the flesh again as a most mighty empress ruleth in them, and carrieth them as bond-slaves whither she willeth'.[82] The world encompassed all the external influences that might drive men to sin, 'when' – in Cranmer's words – 'thorowe euel companye, we be corrupted in our awne lyuynge, and prouoked to folow noughty examples'. But sin through fear was also part of the world's remit, as when men were driven from godliness under the threat of persecution. For Becon the world was a deceiver which dazzled the individual with wealth and prosperity, whilst disguising its transience. The world makes us forget we are 'strangers and pilgrims', who bring nothing into it and can ultimately take nothing out. In the world is collected all the things which are not of God, and to be in love with the world is to be his enemy.[83] The tempting triumvirate emphasised the pervasive nature of sin upon the earth, but most importantly it demonstrated man's utter reliance on God to protect him. 'Father', ran a paraphrase of the Lord's Prayer by William Tyndale, 'seeing our corrupt nature can go but downward only, and the devil and the world driveth thereto that same way, how can we proceed further in virtue or stand therein, if thy power cease in us?'[84]

Increasingly, as emphasis was laid on Satan's intrusive power, the world and the flesh were subordinated as tools and accessories of diabolic temptation. They were the means by which he gained entry to the mind. For Cranmer, Satan was an opportunist who took advantage of people's temptation by the flesh and the world to 'enter in at the gate', thus making the combined assault so strong that it was hard to withstand.[85] In his 1551 book *A Fruitful treatise of Fasting*, Thomas Becon described them as the 'two

[81] Ephesians 2: 2; 6: 12.
[82] Cranmer, *Catechismvs*, fol. 147; Becon, *New Catechism*, in *The Catechism of Thomas Becon*, pp. 150–1 (the former quote Becon took from Galatians 5); Sandys, *Sermons*, p. 175.
[83] Cranmer, *Catechismvs*, fol. 147v; Becon, *New Catechism*, p. 150.
[84] Tyndale, *An Exposition upon the V., VI., VII. Chapters of Matthew*, p. 85.
[85] Cranmer, *Catechismvs*, fol. 148.

special servants' of Satan, 'the one being his waiting-man, the other being his hand-maid'.[86] Alexander Nowell had his catechumen expand on the 'temptation' of the Lord's Prayer as meaning the 'violence of the devil, the snares and deceits of this world, and the corruptions and enticements of our flesh'. But when discussing how God might defend men from them, he subsumed the latter two under the agency of Satan.[87]

In the hands of the Devil, the world and the flesh became supremely powerful weapons, offering him potential access to every single human consciousness. For if Satan might introduce whatever thoughts he wished into the mind, his cunning told him to discern the sins to which each individual was most susceptible. 'There is nothing either so high or low, so great or small, but the devil can use that self-same thing as a weapon to fight against us withal', concluded Latimer. 'It is true that euery man hath all sins in him', Perkins observed, but God might repress sin in some and renew grace in others. Thus Satan must find the easiest point of entry and so, like an army besieging a city, 'he goes about a man, and as it were turnes him to and fro, to spie out his weaknesse, and to what sinnes he is most inclined, and there he will be sure to trie him often, and to assault him with great violence'.[88] Satan caused rich men to value their wealth above God, and to use it to oppress others, whilst poor men were driven to steal. Men held in 'great estimation' the Devil made lofty and high minded, and filled their hearts with such ambition that they would trample down any that stood in their way. Those who fell into ignominy found 'the devil is at hand, moving and stirring [their hearts] to open irksomeness and at length to desperation'. Of course the young were tempted to lust and carelessness, whilst Satan moved the old to avarice and covetousness. The healthy man was driven to take advantage of his state to pursue lechery, and those who were sick the Devil encouraged to impatience and resentment of God.[89]

Temptation was dangerous to man because his nature was so corrupt that diabolic intrusions not properly resisted threatened to explode within the

86 Becon, *A Fruitful treatise of Fasting*, in *Catechism with other pieces*, p. 543.

87 Nowell, *Catechism*, p. 202; Sandys, *Sermons*, p. 300.

88 Latimer, *Sermons*, p. 432; Perkins, *The Combat between Christ and the Divell displayed*, p. 380; Baxter, *A Christian Directory*, p. 13. This picture had its origins in medieval allegory, where a castle or fortress could signify a sanctified soul. According to John Bromyard, faith and charity constituted the walls of a fortress to keep the Devil at bay, but the senses were doors by which he might gain entry, 'for many traitors may knock, and enemies of the Soul, desiring to capture the Castle of the soul and shut God out, and hand it over to the Devil'. Quoted in G.R. Owst, *Literature and the Pulpit in Medieval England* (Cambridge, 1933; republished Oxford, 1961), pp. 80–1.

89 Latimer, *Sermons*, pp. 430–2; 'A sermon against whoredom and uncleaness', 'An homily against excess of apparel' and 'The sermon against idleness', in *Certain Sermons or Homilies*, pp. 139, 331, 555; Bayly, *Practice of Pietie*, pp. 185–6; Baxter, *A Christian Directory*, p. 85.

soul, allowing sin to grow exponentially. 'Put a burning match to tinder or gunpowder and it will kindle presently', William Perkins observed; 'our hearts like tinder do easily suffer corruption to kindle in vs.'[90] The *Book of Homilies* described the process in its discussion of adultery. Adulterous thoughts, it argued, were the consequence of idleness, and were a form of gluttony. The adulterer was covetous and envious, constantly fearing to lose his 'prey' to others, and he was ireful every time his advances were refused. It was because adultery was 'a monster of many heads' that it was so 'pleasant to Satan'.[91]

Again this picture of diabolic agency crystallised in the Protestant attack on popular culture. Spiritual vulnerability at the theatre, the ale-house or the dance exemplified the threat of demonic intrusion. Stage-plays were instruction manuals in sin which encouraged their audiences to copy the violence and lasciviousness they observed, whilst drinking and dancing fired people's carnal appetites.[92] For the minister John Northbrooke, plays were 'Sathan's Banquets' where he gorged himself on the souls of his victims. In observing sin in the theatre, men and women opened the gateway to the Devil, who entered into their souls through their physical senses. 'Thou shalt', Northbrooke noted, 'by hearing diuelishe and filthie songs, hurte thy chaste eares, and also shalt see that which shall be greeuous vnto thine eyes; for our eyes are as windows of the mynde: as the prophete sayeth, Death entred into my windows, that is, by mine eyes.'[93] According to the playwright turned Puritan minister Stephen Gosson, the senses had been given to man that he might hear the scriptures and see the justice of God's precepts – by design they provided direct access to the soul. The senses lulled by pleasure were particularly vulnerable to diabolic invasion. The effect of poetry is to 'wonderfully tickle the hearers eares', and so Satan 'hath tyed this to most of our playes, that whatsoever he would have sticke fast to our soules, might slippe

[90] Perkins, *The Combat between Christ and the Divell displayed*, p. 376; Northbrooke, *A Treatise wherein Dicing, Dauncing, Vaine playes or Enterluds are reproued*, p. 61; Gosson, *The Schoole of Abuse*, sigs. D2v–D3. This understanding informed views on witchcraft. In Thomas Pickering's preface to Perkins' *Damned Art of Witchcraft* this explosion of sin was presented as an insatiable greed for knowledge and power that resulted from an initial curiosity into magic. The idolatry of paganism, the power-lust of the Catholic popes, and the popular recourse to cunning men were all explained as a consequence of an exponential growth of sin resulting from a weakness in the face of temptation. See Perkins, *Damned Art of Witchcraft*, in *Works*, vol. III, sigs. Kkkk5–Kkkk6.

[91] 'A sermon against whoredom', in *Certain Sermons or Homilies*, p. 131.

[92] Roberts, *An earnest complaint of divers vain, wicked and abused exercises*; Northbrooke, *A Treatise wherein Dicing, Dauncing, Vaine playes or Enterluds are reproued*; Gosson, *The Schoole of Abuse*; Gosson, *Playes confuted in five Actions, Prouing that they are not to be suffred in a Christian common weale*; Stubbes, *The Anatomie of Abuses*; more generally see 'An homily of the place and time of prayer', in *Certain Sermons or Homilies*, p. 362.

[93] Northbrooke, *Treatise*, pp. 61, 132–3.

down in sugar by this intisement, for that which delighteth never trouble to swallow'. In the evocative phrase of the minister of Southfleet in Kent, Henry Symons (1657), the effect of Satan's temptations was to 'rub our temples with his opium of poysonous suggestions'.[94] With a rhetoric of invasion and pollution an especially sinister picture could be drawn of those cultural items that were ingested, such as tobacco or alcohol. The exotic origins of tobacco allowed the anonymous author of *Work for Chimny-sweepers: or a warning for Tobacconists* (1602) to argue that smoking was 'first found out and invented by the diuell, and first vsed and practised by the diuels priests'.[95] As Catholic false piety dulled the senses with an outward show of holiness, tobacco and alcohol produced similar effects by ingestion. 'Dark and swart' tobacco fumes entered directly into the brain and augmented melancholy, 'the very seate of the Diuell in bodies possessed', and so the soul was prepared 'to receaue the prestigations and hellish illusions of the Diuell himself'.[96] Wine, preached Samuel Ward in 1622, was Satan's 'venom' which 'expelled' the spirit of grace from the heart, 'as smoake doth Bees out of the hive'. In this way alcohol 'makes the man a meere slave and prey to Satan and his snares'.[97] Ward drew an analogy between the dulled senses of the drunkard and the spiritual blindness of man abandoned by God, noting 'by this poyson [the Devil] hath put out his eyes, and spoyled him of his strength; he useth him as the Philistines did Sampson, leads him in a string wither hee pleaseth like a very drudge'.[98]

Through temptation the Devil worked his most insidious harm, for regardless of whether man acted on these thoughts, his soul was damaged by their very presence. 'In temptations vsvally be corrupt motions', was Perkins' assessment, 'for though a man doe not approue, neither entertaining with delight, the deuils temptations, yet shall he hardly keepe himselfe from the staine and taint of sinne, because the imaginations of his owne heart are natvrally evil.'[99] As Northbrooke noted of the theatre, 'David ... was sore hurt (in beholding Bersabe) and thinkest thou to escape? He did but behold an harlot, but on the top of his house ... thou beholdest them in an open theatre, a place where ye soule of the wise is snared and condemned.'[100] The author of *A second and third blast of retrait from plaies and theatres* noted

[94] Gosson, *Playes confuted in five Actions*, sig. D8v; Symons, *The Lord Jesus his commission*, p. 39.

[95] *Work for Chimny-sweepers*, sigs. F4–F4v. According to this pamphlet 'Indian' priests first used tobacco to effect prophetic trances, a well-known ploy of the Devil.

[96] Ibid., sigs. B, F4v–G4v.

[97] Ward, *Woe to Drunkards*, pp. 8–14, quotes at p. 14; *Schola Cordis*, pp. 24–7.

[98] Ward, *Woe to Drunkards*, p. 14; 'An homily against gluttony and drunkenness', in *Certain Sermons or Homilies*, p. 310.

[99] Perkins, *The Combat between Christ and the Divell displayed*, p. 376.

[100] Northbrooke, *Treatise*, p. 61.

that in the 'chappel of ill counsel', where so much iniquity could be readily observed, it was a wonder that any returned 'not either wounded in conscience, or changed in life'.[101]

Similar dynamics of internal temptation can of course be found in post-Tridentine Catholic devotional works. As we have seen, internal temptation was an important part of the traditional remit of satanic agency and the more introspective religious culture of the Counter-Reformation surely encouraged a sense of the insidious influence of the Devil. Texts such as the *Jesus Psalter* emphasised the centrality of temptation as a problem in the lives of devout Catholics. Its second petition asked Christ for help to 'ouercome all temptations to sinne: and the malice of my ghostly enemie'. The fifth petition requested 'suffer no false delight of this deceauable life, by fleshlie temptations and fraud of the fieend, for to blind mee'.[102] The equal prevalence of the Lord's Prayer in Catholic devotional exposition also accorded temptation a significant place.[103] A number of Catholic devotional works dealt specifically with temptation, such as Jean-Pierre Camus *A Spirituall Combat* (1632), John Castaniza, *The Spiritual Conflict* (no date) and the English translation of Robert Bellarmine's *The Art of Dying Well* (1622). These emphasised the insidiousness of internal temptation, particularly as a means of undermining faith. *A Spirituall Combat* described 'interiour skirmishes' as the appearance of 'hideous and horrible ideas' within the mind. *The Spiritual Conflict* identified tempting thoughts both as the motions of the flesh and as any thought which disrupted the peace of the pious conscience. 'Assoone as thou percieuest thy selfe to be drawn with any delectable obiect', the book warned, 'behold with thine vnderstanding, that vnder this delight, there lieth the infernall serpent.'[104] Unsurprisingly, Protestant heresy became a profound form of temptation. Bellarmine identified a common temptation as 'touching those things which we belieu God to haue done or stil to doe, as specifically the transmutation of bread and wine into the body and bloud of Christ'.[105]

But Catholic demonism also continued to emphasise the physical power of the Devil, even in temptation. Bellarmine, having discussed the internal

[101] Munday, *The second and third blast of retrait from plays and theatres*, p. 92. That pamphlet was a compilation including a translation of a third-century anti-stage tract by Salvian. Munday himself would write eighteen plays between 1584 and 1600.

[102] *Sixe Spiritvall Bookes; Fvll of merveilovs Pietie and Devotion, and First, Certaine Devovt and Godlie Petitions commonlie called, the Iesvs Psalter* (Douai, 1618), pp. 17–18, 35.

[103] Robert Bellarmine, *An Ample Declaration of the Christian Doctrine* (Rouen, 1604), pp. 98–101.

[104] Jean-Pierre Camus, *A Spirituall Combat* (Douai, 1632), pp. 73–5; John Castaniza, *The Spiritual Conflict* (Douai, 1603; first edn 1598), sigs. D8v, D10v–D11v.

[105] Bellarmine, *The Art of Dying Well*, p. 277; Gregory Martin, *The Love of the Soule* (Rouen, 1579), sig. A7v.

temptation that the Devil might offer to the dying, was careful also to describe his physical appearances. 'The Diuell', he noted, 'vseth oftentymes to be present & to shew himselfe in most dreadfull & vgly shape to such as are to dy, that in case he be not able to deceaue them, yet that therby at least he may hinder their alacrity and feruour of prayer.'[106] Devotional works that dealt with the experience of temptation continued to rely on the stories of the saints to provide exemplars, most notably examples such as St Anthony, St Francis and St Catherine of Siena.[107] These depicted the Devil tormenting his victims both internally and physically. Thus the story of St Anthony noted that he had been physically assaulted by a multitude of devils who tried to drive him to despair. Bellarmine noted that St Oportuna was visited by Satan as 'a Blacke-More, from whose head and beard did drop downe hoat and liquid pitch, his eyes were like burning iron that is taken out of the forge'.[108] Similarly, a printing of Raymond of Capua's life of St Catherine of Siena showed that she was tempted internally to lust, which the Devil 'fourmed in her fantasie (both waking and sleeping)'. But she was also tempted with 'corporal visions ... forming bodies in the air', and later demons 'tooke diuerse and sundrie shapes of men and women, and setting them selues ... before the eyes of the chast virgin, they exercised most filthie actes of the flesh'.[109] The corporeality of the experience of temptation was further enhanced in the asceticism of St Catherine's response, in which she flagellated herself with an iron chain. Whilst the value of the saints' lives as exemplars lay to a large extent in the extraordinary intensity of their temptations, their stories maintained the link between temptation and the Devil's physical manifestations. This was in contrast to the emerging Protestant godly lives which, as we shall see, emphasised internal temptation as a fundamental part of their conversion narratives.

RESISTING SATAN: PRAYER AND DIALOGUE

For Protestants, Catholic ceremonial was unable to provide adequate protection against Satan because, concerned only with externals, it failed to aim its counter-measures at the real site of diabolic conflict. The use of candles, bells and holy water to ward off Satan was superstitious, not because the Devil's threat was unreal, but because the items themselves could have no efficacy against a creature with the power to enter into the soul. Hugh Latimer

[106] Bellarmine, *The Art of Dying Well*, p. 274.
[107] Camus, *A Spirituall Combat*, pp. 80–1; Raymond of Capua, *The Life of the Blessed virgin, Sainct Catherine of Siena* (Douai, 1609), pp. 87–100.
[108] Bellarmine, *The Art of Dying Well*, pp. 274–5.
[109] Ibid., pp. 89–92, quotes at pp. 89 and 92.

ridiculed bell-ringing in order to drive away the Devil lurking in a 'storm or a fearful weather'. 'If the holy bells would serve against the devil, or that he might be put away through their sound', Latimer noted, 'no doubt they would banish him out of all England.' After all, if all the bells in the country were rung at the same moment, 'there would be no place, but some bells might be heard there'.[110] Traditionalists were certainly disturbed by the idea that men and women might be left defenceless against the Devil, and such glib attitudes seemed only to demonstrate the reformers' naivety and carelessness. In 1554, the Catholic Thomas Watson preached before Queen Mary and pointed to the protective power of the real presence in the communion. 'O what wonderful effectes be these', he proclaimed, 'which bi this blessed Sacrament by wrought in the worthy receiuer, agaynst the deuyll and his temptation.' The reformers' willingness to dispense with this vital weapon beggared belief. 'What meant they', Watson asked, 'that toke away this armour of Christes flesh and bloud from vs, but to leaue us naked and vnarmed against the deuyll?'[111]

If they have not always shared his sectarian position, historians have tended to agree with Watson that Protestantism was particularly bad at protecting Christians from the Devil. For some, like Keith Thomas, this was a symptom of Protestantism's moral pessimism, and he notes that the whole faith itself was infused with 'a sense of powerlessness in the face of evil'.[112] John Stachniewski understands Protestantism to have actively shaped a self-perception of reprobation among its adherents which, through imagery of damnation, encouraged an obsessive fear of Satan.[113] For Jeffery Burton Russell, Protestant conflicts with Satan had to have been intensely lonely experiences as, stripped of all intercessionary aid, the Christian was left alone to face the Devil with no other comfort than his bible.[114] Similarly the recent emphasis on the vitality and popularity of traditional religion, which argues that ceremonies such as Candlemas and Rogationtide had profound emotional significance for ordinary parishioners, tends to imply by contrast that the removal of intercession against the Devil left a significant gap in religious and communal experience.[115]

110 Latimer, *Sermons*, p. 498.
111 Thomas Watson, *Twoo notable Sermons, made the third and fyfth Fridayes in Lent last past, Before the Quenes highnes, concerninge the reall presense of Christes body and bloude in the blessed Sacrament* (London, 1554), sigs. A3v, F8v–G4, quotes at sigs. G3v–G4; similarly see Stephen Gardiner's defence of the power of holy water over the Devil in Gardiner, *Letters*, pp. 259–63, 486.
112 Thomas, *Religion and the Decline of Magic*, pp. 560–1.
113 Stachniewski, *The Persecutory Imagination*, pp. 17–26.
114 Russell, *Mephistopheles*, p. 31.
115 Duffy, *The Stripping of the Altars*, esp. pp. 15–18, and chapters 8 and 9.

Of course there is much truth in this picture. We have already seen that the reformed baptism must have been a confusing and dissatisfying experience for those used to the triumphalism of the Sarum rite. But to argue that Protestantism left its adherents unprotected against the Devil is misleading. Whilst the reformers were concerned to undermine reliance on ceremony and intercession, and to make the experience of the diabolic a constant of Christian existence rather than a formalised part of the liturgical year, they did not fail to substitute their own understanding of how the Devil might be fought off. The battle with Satan was unwinnable to all but God; and so Protestantism offered no means of victory, but instead concentrated on resistance.

Protection against Satan came not from candles, bells or holy water, but from the soteriological knowledge whereby temptation could be put into perspective. God allowed the Devil to tempt man in order to test his faith. 'It is a necessary thing to be tempted of the Devil', Hugh Latimer declared, 'for temptations minister to us the occasion to run to God and to beg his help.'[116] Satan would never be allowed to tempt a godly man beyond his endurance. Whilst Protestants tended to emphasise the desperate state of mankind, diabolic punishment and divine mercy were understood to exist in balance; as the homily on salvation noted, God 'hath so tempered his justice and mercy together, that he would neither by his justice condemn us unto the everlasting captivity of the devil and his prison of hell ... nor by his mercy deliver us clearly without payment of a just ransom'.[117] The correct response to temptation was not to attempt to be rid of affliction through magical ceremonies, but patiently to bear it, and so demonstrate a faith that the Devil would ultimately be constrained by God. Thus sound religious knowledge and the ability to discern for oneself the reality of diabolic temptation was to replace blind faith in the mediating power of the Catholic clergy. The final exhortation of the reformed baptism demanded that the godparents ensure that the child be educated in the faith. This was not mere rhetoric; the child was to learn the creed, the Lord's Prayer, the decalogue and 'all other things which a Christian man ought to know and believe to his soul's health'. By these means he might be 'continually mortifying all ... evil and corrupt affections'.[118] If spiritual blindness made the Devil's temptations so dangerous, the deficiency might be significantly made up with sound theological knowledge.

[116] Latimer, *Sermons*, p. 435; Perkins, *A crowd of Faithful Witnesses, leading to the heavenly Canaan*, in *Works*, vol. III, pp. 112–13.
[117] 'A sermon of the salvation of mankind', in *Certain Sermons or Homiles*, p. 21.
[118] *The book of the common prayer* (1549), fol. 139; *The Boke of common praier* (1552), sig. P6v; 'A sermon against whoredom', in *Certain Sermons or Homilies*, p. 139.

Even if diabolic affliction was to be expected, damage limitation demanded that the individual make it as difficult as possible for the Devil's influence to take hold. Stephen Gosson described ignorance of the flesh-pots as a 'bridle' by which the godly progression of the soul was kept from distraction. To remove the bridle was 'manifest treason to our souls, [delivering] them captive to the Devil'. Exposing the senses to the 'songs of devils' subverted their design as the means by which the soul gained access to God.[119] Such was the danger of those places where sin was practised openly, but diabolic affliction was often far less obvious. As Gosson warned in *The Schoole of Abuse* (1579), 'the Devil stands at our elbow when we see him not, speaks when we hear him not, strikes when we feel not, and woundeth sore when he raiseth no skin nor rents the flesh'.[120] Since Satan would search out the sins to which each man was most addicted, the godly should also examine their consciences deeply and discern them first. 'When we have truely found out our owne estate', William Perkins exhorted, 'we must set strong watch and guard about our hearts in respect of our infirmities, and so shall we be better able to break the neck of Satan's temptations.'[121] Vigilance was honed by practice, subverted by the lack of it. Sin, wrote Lewis Bayly, must be suppressed at the first motion, 'lest the coustome of sinning take away the conscience of sin'.[122] Henry Lawrence expressed a century of consensus as to the limits on Satan's power when he noted in 1646 that 'hee is a perfect iuggler, hee raignes not much when his tricks are discovered'.[123]

If perception was the key to warding off diabolic intrusion, those inclined to godliness were at an advantage. In them temptation produced emotional symptoms which aided in its discernment. 'As Sathan conuaies euil suggestions into mens minds', Perkins observed, 'so the same are full of trouble, sorrow, and vexation, at least to the godly.'[124] The godly man languishing under temptation experienced a profound internal conflict with the sinful thoughts which intruded upon his mind. As Perkins described with reference to one particular temptation, 'the deuill doth mightily assault some men by casting into their minds most fearefull motions of blasphemy against God', and these thoughts 'greatly astonish them and bring them to despaire',

119 Gosson, *Playes confuted in five Actions*, sig. Fv; Symons, *The Lord Jesus his commission*, p. 39.

120 Gosson, *School of Abuse*, sig. C4; Bolton, *Instrvctions for a Right comforting afflicted consciences*, pp. 94–5; *Schola Cordis*, pp. 9–11; Baxter, *A Christian Directory*, p. 11.

121 Perkins, *The Combat between Christ and the Divell displayed*, p. 381; 'An homily against idleness', in *Certain Sermons or Homiles*, pp. 554–5; Lawrence, *Communion and Warre*, p. 3.

122 Bayly, *The Practice of Pietie*, pp. 178, 183–4; Taylor, *Holy Living*, p. 84.

123 Lawrence, *Communion and Warre*, p. 1; Taylor, *Holy Living*, p. 86.

124 Perkins, *The Combat between Christ and the Divell displayed*, p. 376; Baxter, *The Christian Directory*, p. 83.

making 'a godly heart to tremble, and quake once to think upon'. But the experience should allow the victim to progress to an understanding of the nature of temptation and its consequences. At first the godly man is naturally appalled when his thoughts appear so alien to his inclinations, and taking them to be a symptom of his own corruption (a motion of the flesh), he struggles against them. But he must come to the realisation that he is experiencing a diabolic intrusion into his mind, and whilst blasphemous thoughts are 'heauie crosses indeed', they are 'the deuills sinnes wholly, and not ours'. Thus, if temptation was inevitable, Perkins offered to make resisting the Devil an equally certain and tangible experience. All temptation might be terrible, but Satan was only truly dangerous when his intrusions went unrecognised.[125]

This argument allowed theologians to pre-empt criticism from those whose experience did not conform to the picture. Such quibbles could be conveniently dismissed by declaring that a conscience free from trouble was a sure sign of reprobation. Hugh Latimer associated doubt over the accuracy of his picture of temptation with the blindness of corrupted man. It was the 'ignorant unlearned sort' who pestered preachers, demanding 'you speak much of temptations; I pray you tell us how shall we know when we are tempted'.[126] 'Most men', Perkins predicted, 'will say, that they neuer felt by experience in themselves the truth of this doctrine; for they haue not percieved any such combate in themselves, though they haue been baptised many years agone.' This was because they had not received the inner baptism of the spirit and so remained Satan's servants. 'While men liue in sinne, & submit themselves to Satans spiritual bondage, he will suffer all things to be in peace with them', Perkins explained, but if they turn to God 'then he will by all his force pursue them, and meete them with armes of temptations.' Consequently peace was the most dangerous state a man could be in and rather than address criticism head-on, Perkins could simply exhort those who never experienced 'spiritual conflict' to reform themselves immediately, when of course they would soon discover the validity of his description.[127]

For Catholics internal temptation was also a profoundly disturbing experience, but one that perhaps was more readily mediated by the Counter-Reformation emphasis on the sacrament of penance. The influence of the missions on devotional practice, John Bossy argues, saw the conflation of the sacramental relationship with that of spiritual counsel, with the Catholic

125 Perkins, *The Combat between Christ and the Divell displayed*, p. 376; Thomas Froysell, *The Beloved Disciple. A sermon preached at the funerall of the honourable Sir Robert Harley* (London, 1658), dedicatory epistle.

126 Latimer, *Sermons*, p. 437.

127 Perkins, *The Combat between Christ and the Divell displayed*, pp. 371–2; William Harrison and William Leygh, *Deaths advantage little regarded, and the soules solace against sorrow* (London, 1602), p. 72; Baxter, *A Christian Directory*, p. 12, 84.

laity exhorted by their priests to confess regularly and to engage in rigorous self-examination beforehand.[128] Catholic devotional works suggest that, whilst emphasising the individual's sin, the scheme might place limitations on the severity of spiritual intrusion. 'Certaine it is', the Jesuit Francis Arias commented in a book on the sacraments, 'that man is assaulted with daiely and divers temptations by the devill, the world and the flesh ... therefore passing necessary it is that he should alwaies haue a remedy to deliver his soule from veniall sinnes.'[129] In this way confession and penance redressed the spiritual consequences of temptation, but Catholic writings also suggest that they were understood to have an efficacy in relieving the experience itself. For Arias, confession cut short the Devil's influence by refocusing the individual's attention on his own responsibility for sin. It rehearsed the understanding that, whilst all were prey to diabolic temptation, sins were manifested in human acquiescence to the Devil's suggestions. Thus the penitent was to understand that he was in essence responsible for the severity and duration of his own affliction and to realise that 'being able against the tentations of the enemy, to haue holpen & strengthened my self with prayer, penance, works of mercy, spirituall talke, and reading of good bookes: yet did I not ... and therefore all the fault is mine owne'.[130] Such remorse was naturally a mainstay of writing on confession, and its corollary was to be the resultant experience of reconciliation with the divine. Ideally, penance should produce, in the words of the Jesuit Vincent Bruno, 'a singular great peace and tranquillity of conscience, together with an exceeding great sweetness of spirit'.[131] Such a communion was of course recognised to be temporary, as the emphasis on the importance of regular confession attested, but it necessarily implied the immediate alleviation of temptation.

A particularly full discussion of the anti-demonic role of penance was published in Castaniza's *The Spiritual Conflict*. The text identified the most dangerous effect of diabolic temptation to be the disruption of the 'peace' of the mind, and significantly identified the godly state, not as one of perpetual self-accusation, but of an equanimity of conscience. As with the Protestant scheme, tempting thoughts might be manifest as either desires, or fears of reprobation. An example of how the Devil unsettled the conscience was provided by the temptation of the sick to impatience which was couched in terms of the Catholic emphasis on good works. 'A person findeth himself

[128] J. Bossy, *The English Catholic Community, 1570–1850* (London, 1975), pp. 268–9.
[129] Francis Arias, *The Litle Memorial, concerning the Good and Frvitful Vse of the Sacraments* (Rouen, 1602), pp. 4–7, quote at p. 6.
[130] Ibid., pp. 28–9.
[131] Vincent Bruno, *A Short Treatise of the Sacrament of Penance* (London, 1605), pp. 7–8; Anon. *A Mirrovr to Confesse Well for such persons as doe frequent this sacrament* (St Omer, 1624), pp. 53–7.

sicke, and seeketh with patience to support the infirmitie', *The Spiritual Conflict* noted, 'the aduersarie seeing that if he continue thus, he shal get the habite of patience, opposeth himself, and proposeth vnto him a desire to do this or that other good deede: and suggesteth vnto him, that if he were in health he might better serue God.' Thus the maintenance of the equanimity of the conscience was a duty of the Catholic godly, since 'the diuell dooth so much feare this peace (as a place where God doth dwell for to woorke therein woonders)'.[132]

Penance was the key to maintaining this peace of the conscience since it defined the end point to the experience of temptation. Ideally, the sinner was to express his sorrow for succumbing to temptation, and his thanks to God for his release, and was then to give the experience no more thought. 'This being ended', *The Spiritual Conflict* noted, 'do not turne thee to thinke, whether God has forgiven thee or no? for to do so is pride, disquietnesse of the mind, losse of time, and a snare of the diuell.'[133] Thus to be overconcerned as to the consequences of temptation – to extend the experience beyond the end point set by the performance of penance – was itself to fall into a diabolic trap. Indeed, this understanding to an extent problematised the cycle of confession, penance and communion itself. Here, a number of works predicted, Satan would lay his greatest traps, precisely because it was here that he stood to lose his victims. 'The deuil', Fulvius Androtius noted in *Certaine Devout considerations of the Frequenting of the Blessed Sacrament* (1615), 'amongst other his subtil practises, is accustomed to put into such persons who frequent the sacrament, a certaine feare, terrifying them that either they haue not rightly made their Confession, or that they haue sinned when they haue not.' Diabolic agency manifested itself most notably in the subversion of the relationship between penitent and confessor. Satan might prevent the penitent from accepting the assurances offered by his confessor, causing him to 'wearie and molest him, sometime confessing more than we oughte, and sometime by often repeating what we haue already confessed'.[134] For Androtius, the remedy was a reassertion of the very mechanics of confession itself as the means to establish an equanimity of conscience. Whilst the penitent was to experience remorse, he was to leave all judgements as to his spiritual state after penance up to his confessor who, if mistaken, would bear the responsibility before God. This, accompanied by meditating on Christ's sacrifice and clemency, was the key to experiencing the tranquillity idealised as the result of penance.

132 Castaniza, *The Spiritual Conflict*, sigs. E3–E4. 133 Ibid., sig. D9v.
134 Fulvius Androtius, *Certaine Devout considerations of the Frequenting of the Blessed Sacrament* (Douai, 1615), pp. 56–8.

Thus, whilst their realism taught Catholic writers to perceive the difficulties of confession and penance, and to identify the agency of Satan within them, the advocacy of the equanimity of conscience, and the prescription to give no more thought to sins that had been repented of, is suggestive of a marked difference in Protestant and Catholic understandings of temptation. Protestants, as we have seen, characterised temptation as a *condition* of a godly life, whereas, by setting strict parameters on each individual instance, Catholics might present it as a series of single *events*. If an equanimity of conscience was indicative of faith, its disruption could not be considered normative (as it was effectively in Protestant thinking) in the lives of the Catholic godly. *The Spiritual Conflict* presented an example of the maintenance of this equanimity which could never have been countenanced in Protestant devotional writing. In discussing the experience of devotion, the book identified three sources of the motivation to godliness – nature, grace and the Devil. The last was characterised as faith that was only mechanical, producing no amendment in lifestyle. However, the Christian was not to sift his conscience in order to discern which motivations to devotion were the result of faith and which the Devil's influence. 'When thou shalt percieue thy mind to be sweetened with spirituall taste', the book noted, 'stand not to dispute, from whence it commeth.' Instead the Christian should turn his thoughts to 'desiring God onely and his pleasure: for by this meane, whether it be of nature, or of the diuel, it will become to thee as of grace.'[135]

For Protestant writers, having discerned affliction as diabolic, the single most important weapon in the Christian's armoury was prayer. 'When soeuer we be tempted', Thomas Cranmer advised, 'ther is no better remedy, then to cal for Gods helpe, and to say as Christ taught vs. Good Lord suffer vs not to be leade in to temptation.' 'It is the christian man's special weapon', agreed Latimer, 'wherewith to strike the devil, and vanquish his assaults.' 'If it chanceth that any man be bare, and not weaponed with prayer', noted Thomas Becon, 'then he is straightway plucked and tossed of the devils'. Prayer bred continual awareness, keeping the perception sharp against the dangers of spiritual blindness. 'What manner of sleeps doest thou look for', Becon asked, 'when thou dost not confirm, make strong, and defend thyself with prayers; but without any watch comest to sleep like a miser and wretch, ready to fall into the captivity and bondage of the most ungracious devils?' 'Satan ceaseth not to assault our faith', declared Edwin Sandys in a sermon at Spitalfields; 'let not us therefore cease to cry unto God.'[136]

[135] Castaniza, *The Spiritual Conflict*, sigs. F11v–F12.

[136] Cranmer, *Catechismvs*, fol. 146v; Latimer, *Sermons*, pp. 438–9, 507–10; Coverdale, *Remains*, pp. 141, 149; Becon, *A Pathway to Prayer*, in *Early Works*, p. 172; Sandys, *Sermons*, p. 263.

But the Protestant rationale behind prayer was very different to that of the pre-Reformation church. Eamon Duffy has demonstrated how the prayers of the *Horae* answered a desire to cultivate an 'intense relationship of affectionate, penitential intimacy with Christ and his mother'. Those which provided protection against the Devil tended to read like litanies or invocations, often blurring the line between prayer and magic as they came closer to being spells or charms.[137] Devotion to the angels, especially the archangels Michael, Gabriel and Raphael, provided a focus for prayers requesting intercession. The prayer 'Deus propicius esto' exhorted God to 'send to my aid Michael your Archangel, that he may keep, protect and defend me from all my enemies, visible and invisible'. Similarly the 'Crux Christi':

> Cross + of Christ ... be ever over me, and before me, and behind me, because the ancient enemy flees wherever he sees you ... Flee from me, a servant of God, o devil, by the sign of the holy Cross + behold the Cross of the Lord + begone you enemies, the lion of the tribe of Judah, the root of David, has conquered.[138]

The words of these prayers, like the paraphernalia and speeches of baptism, were assumed to hold inherent efficacy, offering protection and exorcism to challenge the Devil. They were integral to the quasi-magical practices that formed such an important part of lay devotion. Holy water sprinkled on the hearth fended off evil, candles blessed in the Candlemas ceremonies were lit during thunderstorms to drive away demons, and were brought near women in labour and the dying to ward off Satan in vulnerable moments. It is in this context, as Duffy argues, that the prayers/charms of the *Horae* must be read. The effect of the *Horae* prayers and the consecrated items was immediate, invested as they were with the very real power of God over the Devil. Most significantly they were intercessionary, abrogating personal responsibility for defeating the Devil to higher power. Like the Sarum baptism, intercession encouraged passivity in the victim of diabolic assault.

By contrast, Protestant prayers expressed in their language a sense of abjection before pervasive sin that was supposed to drive men to seek God's protection through faith. Their emotive qualities came not from rhetorical and imaginative flourishes, but from an attempt to impose de facto demonological awareness on the consciousness. Fear of Satan's agency was to be instilled by stripping it of all embellishment and presenting it as a statement of irrefutable fact. Thus it was the Devil in his guise as the roaring lion that provided the most common and most imposing image of the ever-present diabolic threat.[139] 'Our adversary the devil goeth about, like a

137 Duffy, *Stripping of the Altars*, chapters 7 and 8.
138 Both prayers are quoted in ibid., pp. 269–70, 273.
139 *The Primer, and Catchechisme* (1552), sigs. T6v–T7.

roaring lion, seeking whom he may devour', declared a prayer of the Elizabethan Primer, expressing man's weakness; 'he is busy and fierce, and breaketh in upon us, so that, if [God] help not, he will soon deceive us with his craft, overturn us with his might, and with his cruelness tear us in pieces'. 'I must always be at war and strife', observed one Elizabethan prayer, 'not with one sort of enemies, but with an infinite number, not only with flesh and blood, but with the devil which is the prince of darkness.' The exemplar of the temptation of Christ demonstrated the place of diabolic affliction within God's scheme. 'O Lord Jesus Christ ... didst suffer thy self to be tempted of Sathan', declared another of the *Godly Prayers*, in order 'that thou mightest likewise overthrow Sathan in thy members, as thou hadst afore done in thine own person.'[140] In the 1578 compilation *A Book of Christian Prayers* 'A Prayer to be said at our first going abroad' rendered the threshold of the house the boundary with a perilous world made up entirely of the Devil's snares:

> I must be fain to go abroad among the snares, which the devil, and his handservant the world, have laid for me: and I carry with me, besides, the stings of mine own flesh. Guide me therefore, O thou most sure guide: be thou my leader, thou God of my welfare. Defend me, O Captain, From the trains and stales that are laid for me: that whatsoever things I shall meet with, I may make no more account of them than they are worthy of, but keep on my way, with mine eyes so fast fixed and settled upon thee alone, as I may not deal with anything further forth than it hath respect unto thee. Lord, shew me thy ways, and lead me in thy paths, for thy sons sake. Amen.[141]

It is no accident that the language of these prayers reads like a rehearsal of the demonological expositions contained in the devotional writings of the reformers. For it was in an expression of demonological and spiritual truths that the efficacy of Protestant prayer was now understood to lie. By reciting the facts of demonic affliction and divine constraint the speaker demonstrated an understanding of the dynamic and place of temptation, and ultimately of his Christian duty to abandon himself to the will of God. In one sense, strength against the Devil came from a mixture of fatalism and informed hope. Final responsibility for defeating the Devil rested with God, but these prayers were not intercessionary. At the same time, awareness of the demonic threat was itself an encouraging sign that protection might be forthcoming: a belief that should inspire further resistance.

But the new role of prayer was not easily imposed on a laity used to the instant gratification of intercession. As in other areas of Protestant

[140] *Private Prayers, put forth during the Reign of Queen Elizabeth I*, ed. W.K. Clay (Cambridge, Parker Society, 1851), pp. 112–13; *The Primer set furth at large, with many godly and devoute Prayers* (1559), in *Liturgical Services*, pp. 248–9, 270; Sandys, *Sermons*, p. 263.

[141] *A Book of Christian Prayers*, in *Private Prayers*, p. 443.

demonism, striking a balance between demonology and providing comfort spawned some contradictions. One of the most striking is apparent in the 1553 Primer. A basic form of prayer against the Devil succinctly set out the progressive rehearsal of demonological and spiritual truths that were to define the individual's perception of diabolic assault. The prayer was intended to have a dual function, being employed in both general devotion and during specific periods of temptation. The first understanding the victim must come to is that current temptations are symptomatic of the Devil's wider agency, and so the specifics are subsumed within a description of the tempting triumvirate, highlighting the enveloping nature of demonic assault:

O Lord God, the devil goeth about like a roaring lion, seeking whom he may devour. The flesh lusteth against the spirit. The world persuadeth unto vanities that we forget thee our Lord God, and so for ever be damned. Thus we are miserably on every side besieged of cruel and unrestful enemies, and like at every moment to perish, if we be not defended with thy godly power against their tyranny.

The second part of the prayer moves to rehearsing the individual's weakness in the face of the Devil and acknowledging the corruption of sin. In asking for God's strength the individual recognises his abjection:

I therefore, poor and wretched sinner, despairing of my own strength, which is none, most heartily pray thee to endue me with strength from above, that I may be able to, through thy help, with strong faith resist Sathan, with fervant prayer mortify the raging lusts of the flesh, with continual meditation of thy holy law to avoid the foolish vanities and transitory pleasures of this wicked world, that I through thy grace being set at liberty from the power of mine enemies, may live and serve thee in holiness and righteousness all the days of my life. Amen.[142]

Thus this prayer exhibited the new emphases of Protestant demonism – the sense of envelopment by temptation, and the realisation of strength through abjection. But in its demonism the devotional culture of the 1553 Primer was still in transition. The prayer against the Devil was followed by another which employed the angeology of more traditional devotions. The prayer 'For the help of God's holy Angels' recalled the conflict between the 'infinite' multitude of evil angels and their unfallen brethren. 'Against this exceeding great multitude of evil spirits', it exhorted, 'send thou me the blessed and heavenly Angels, which may pitch their tents round about me, and so deliver me from their tyranny.'[143]

But, ultimately, the departure presented by Protestant anti-demonic measures is clearly seen in contrast to their Catholic counterparts. The Catholic devotional works that continued to circulate in England in the late sixteenth

[142] *The Primer: or Book of private Prayer* (1553), in *The Two Liturgies*, p. 474; see also *The Primer, and Catchechisme* (1552), sigs. T6v–T7.
[143] *The Primer* (1553), pp. 474–5.

and seventeenth centuries often contained remedies and prayers against diabolic affliction. We have already noted the important role which penance could play in mitigating against the effects of temptation, and Catholic books also advocated the Eucharist as the most significant means to 'destroy thy euil inclinations'.[144] As in Protestant demonism, prayer was fundamental in combating diabolic affliction. But whilst the sense of the Devil's power was prevalent and the conception of the individual's vulnerability to Satan was equally sophisticated, these prayers maintained the belief in the intercessionary shield provided by God, the angels and the saints. For example a bedtime prayer included in the *Paradise of Prayers* (1613) and addressed to God noted: 'I Request thee to shadow me this night under the comfortable wings of thy almighty power, defend my senses, and my thoughts, my soule and my body with al their powers from al the assaultes, tentations & illusions of the Diuel.'[145] Similarly, petitions of the *Jesus Psalter* read:

> With the assistance of the glorious angel S. Michael, deliuer me from the danger of my ghostly enemie . . .
>
> Sende me help from heaven . . . to overcome the olde serpent with all his cautels . . . The Angels of Light, deliver mee, from the Angels of Darkness, and from their great crueltie.[146]

The dependence on intercession was to be profoundly felt, as a prayer 'to the angel guardian' printed in *The Interiour Occupation of the Soule* (1618) made clear: 'How often had Satan styfled mee whilest I was drinking, eating, sleeping, walking? Especially at those times when he percived mee to be out of the grace of God: if thou O my guide, and singular benefactor, hadst not broken his strength, and dissipated his designs?'[147]

Intercession points to the fundamental contrast that was maintained in the purpose of Catholic and Protestant anti-diabolic prayers into the seventeenth century. Both addressed what was understood to be a very real and disturbing experience, and sought to bolster the individual Christian against satanic affliction. But the Catholic emphasis on temptation as an event rather than a condition of life characterised the function of these prayers, aiming them at the removal of diabolic affliction rather than at its management. Whereas Protestant demonism allowed for a soteriological significance to be attached to the sheer consistency of temptation, Catholic devotion maintained that the removal of satanic influence was an expression of God's love to the individual. Hence Catholic prayers were often framed as

144 Castaniza, *The Spiritual Conflict*, sigs. G3v–G4.

145 Edward Mayhew, *A Paradise of Prayers* (Douai, 1613), p. 139; Androtius, *Certaine Devout considerations of the Frequenting of the Blessed Sacrament*, pp. 25–6.

146 *The Jesus Psalter*, in *Sixe Spiritvall Bookes*, pp. 58, 83.

147 Piere Coton, *The Interiour Occupation of the Soule* (Douai, 1618), sig. D6v.

rhetorical questions to God highlighting the injustice of being left prey to the Devil. 'Did thou create me to cast me away?', an example in *The Paradise of Prayers* read. 'Didst thou redeeme me to damne me for ever?'[148] Thus the Catholic scheme allowed for the liberation of the individual from temptation to be experienced as a microcosm of the redemption, a tangible demonstration of the possibilities of salvation. 'Shew thy selfe a saviour unto me', the prayer continued, 'and either take away mine enemies, or grant me grace that without wound or fault, by thee and with thee, I may overcome them.'[149] Within this scheme the potential absence of an intercessionary shield against the Devil appeared to undermine the very rationale of the Passion, returning man to his vassalage under Satan. This apparent irony could be used as a rhetorical mechanism to assure the supplicant of the likelihood of divine intervention, for without intercession the work of the Passion would be undone: 'Shall I now hinder the fruit of thy pretious merits and commit sinne against thee? Suffer not this O merciful redeemer, but for thine infinite mercy and for the pretious blood which thou hast shed for me, I humbly beseeche thee, O my Lord, now to helpe me, and not to forsake me.'

This rationale could be directly applied to appeals for mediation by the Virgin and the saints. As a prayer in *The Occupation of the Soule* declared, 'Pray then for mee, merciful Mother, and in so dooing thou shalt pray also for thine own sonne: seeing that he desires in mee, that, which I ask of thee, a thousand times more, than I my self.'[150] Similarly, a prayer to St Peter identified a precedent to which appeal could be made: 'The divell desired to sift thee, but the prayer of the son of God, gave an invincible force to thy faith: wilt thou not then obtaine for me a vigour & strength, not to bee overcome by any snares, or forces of the infernall legions?'[151] Highlighting this irony was, of course, intended only to show its unacceptability, and to indicate that, whilst God might allow temptation, he would ultimately protect the faithful from the Devil. Thus, whilst Protestant and Catholic demonism sought to provide effective means of countering temptation, their divergent aims of manageability and victory arguably maintained their separation under the Counter-Reformation.

THE PROTESTANT MINISTRY AND THE MEDIATION OF RESISTANCE

The role of prayer books in aiding resistance to the Devil was supplemented by the efforts of the Protestant clergy, who to an extent recovered their role as mediators between parishioners and the divine which had been so

[148] Mayhew, *A Paradise of Prayers*, pp. 426–7. [149] Ibid.
[150] Coton, *The Interiour Occupation of the Soule*, sig. C11. [151] Ibid., sig. E9v.

undermined by the Reformation.[152] In one sense Protestant demonological reform turned full circle, increasingly re-emphasising the importance of the – now Protestant – clergy in mediating the defeat of Satan. If knowledge and understanding were the most important weapons against the demonic, then educated ministers were most likely to possess them. In ideal at least they became repositories of the scriptural learning and insight which might arm individuals, and society more widely, against temptation. As a result of 'the want of a sincere ministry', George Gifford noted in 1582, 'the Divell hath elbowe roome to spread abroad'.[153] 'You may see, what a spirit the deuill hath to hinder one sermon', the Puritan Henry Smith noted in his sermon on Luke 8: 19–21: 'Therefore . . . no maruell, though he stand against a learned ministry.'[154] Nor was the ideal an empty one. The wealth of books by ministers given over to dealing with afflicted consciences testifies to the seriousness with which they took their role as mediators of the spiritual learning by which the laity might overcome doubt as to election.[155] Similarly, ministers claimed to see everywhere the devastating consequences of Satan's intrusion into men's souls. Thomas Becon was moved to pen *The Christen Knight* after perceiving that godly men were commonly 'so turmoiled and tossed with the raging and cruel waves of desperation, that scarcely there remained any hope of salvation in their breasts'. He believed that if he could arm them with the doctrine of salvation the Devil might be 'driven to utter confusion'. 'How this victory over Satan and his soldiers may be gotten', Becon promised, 'is declared in this dialogue following.'[156]

The Christen Knight was one of a number of books by ministers which aimed to provide a mirror of the experience of temptation by presenting it as a dialogue between the conscience and the Devil. John Bradford's *Godlie meditations*, first printed in 1562, included a short example. In ten questions the Devil accused the conscience of being reprobate, each point being answered with reference to Christ's gratuitous mercy. Another simple

[152] Thomas, *Religion and the Decline of Magic*, pp. 87–9; R. O'Day, 'The Reformation of the Ministry, 1558–1642', in R. O'Day and F. Heal (eds.), *Continuity and Change: Personnel and Administration of the Church of England 1500–1642* (Leicester, 1976), pp. 55; T. Webster, *Godly Clergy in Early Stuart England: The Caroline Puritan Movement, c. 1620–1643* (Cambridge, 1997), pp. 95–6.

[153] Gifford, *A Briefe Discourse of Certain points of the Religion*, sigs. A3–A3v; Gosson, *Schoole of Abuse*, sigs. B5v–B6.

[154] Henry Smith, *Three Sermons made by Maister Henry Smith* (London, 1599), sig. E.

[155] A handful of the more prominent examples of what was an enormous body of literature are William Perkins, *A Golden Chaine* (1591) and *The whole treatise of the cases of Conscience* (1606) both in *Works*; Henry Scudder, *The Christians Daily Walke in Securitie and Peace* (London, 1627); Bolton, *Instructions for a Right comforting afflicted Consciences*; Richard Sibbes, *The Soules Conflict with it selfe, and Victory over it self by Faith* (London, 1635); Giles Firmin, *The Real Christian* (London, 1670); Baxter, *A Christian Directory*.

[156] Becon, *Christen Knight*, in *The Catechism*, pp. 622–5.

version was produced by William Perkins in his *Foure Godly Treatises* of 1587, in which the possible defences that could be used by 'a Christian', 'a strong Christian' and a 'weak Christian' were rehearsed.[157] Thomas Becon's *The Governance of Virtue*, composed in 1543, and the undated *The Christen Knight* were longer and far more complex. The first was moderately successful and went through six editions between 1547 and 1607, but the second only saw a single printing. The dialogue with the Devil also found its way into the 'mainstream' of Protestant printed culture, for example appearing, in a rather diffuse form, in Lewis Bayly's hugely successful *The Practice of Pietie*.

These dialogues were a form of inverted catechism. As the Devil was shown attempting to undermine the Christian's faith, it was to be apparent that he in fact offered him an opportunity to demonstrate his learning and godliness. Becon's *The Governance of Virtue* rehearsed the Devil's arguments as 'suggestions' and 'persuasions' appearing inside the mind. 'If Satan lay to thy charge that thou comest very late, and turnest unto God out of time', was one example of his sophistry; 'if Satan, or any of his, tempt thee to live at thy pleasure ...', ran another. In each case pertinent quotes and examples from scripture were offered to make the Devil's deceit apparent and thus dispel his threat.[158] Solid grounding in scripture was the key to bolstering assurance, and therefore the means of resisting Satan's suggestions. A similar model was employed in Bayly's *Practice of Pietie*. Specifically aiming at those experiencing temptation on the death-bed, Bayly provided a compendium of the arguments Satan would employ to encourage despair, countering each with detailed spiritual meditations intended to re-awaken assurance. A typical example ran: 'If Satan shall aggravate unto thee the greatness, the multitude, and the heinousness of thy Sinnes; meditate ...' Then followed a discussion of the redemptive power of repentance, backed up by examples of Christ's healing of the sick and the possessed.[159]

The inverted catechism was not merely a literary conceit. It was intended to reflect the real nature of temptation as a divinely sanctioned test of godliness. Like the prayers against the Devil, the scriptures and doctrinal truths to which ministers pointed their audiences were not intended to have an inherent efficacy in driving Satan away. Instead they were to encourage their readers to engage with the message of divine mercy being mediated to them, and so build up an informed resistance to what would be a regular experience. In this context the dialogues, and by implication the learning of the ministry that produced them, provided an exemplary demonstration of the

[157] Bradford, *Writings*, vol. I, pp. 210–11; Perkins, *Foure Godly Treatises*.
[158] Becon, *The Governance of Virtue* in *Early Works*, pp. 478, 482.
[159] Bayly, *Practice of Pietie*, p. 443.

confidence with which demonological knowledge could be wielded against Satan by those of strong faith. Having dedicated his preface to documenting the terrible vulnerability of man, Thomas Becon allowed the responses of the Christian Knight to Satan's words to be pervaded by the smugness that so often characterised the 'teacher' in other Protestant dialogues. Throughout the Devil is answered with declarations such as 'in this behalf I can easily set myself at liberty and dispatch thy argument'.[160]

Ministers' pastoral duties often required them to mediate demonological understanding more directly to troubled parishioners, and here we can trace some of the ways in which experiential demonism was disseminated to both the ministry and the godly laity. Research by historians such as Tom Webster has highlighted the role of informal networks in training Puritan ministers.[161] Such networks appear also to have been important in preparing ministers for their anti-demonic role. Often younger ministers' understanding of temptation developed as they were guided by their mentors through their own sufferings. The connections between preachers such as John Dod, Robert Harris and Richard Capel, and the lay sufferers they ministered to, are instructive here. Dod's ability to comfort those under affliction became legendary, but he himself had suffered a crisis which had been resolved by Richard Greenham, whose maxim, 'when affliction lieth heavy, sin lieth light', Dod then used throughout his own career.[162] Amongst those ministers known to have been aided by Dod through periods of affliction were John Preston, Thomas Peacock and Richard Capel.[163] John Cotton would apparently discuss his early temptations with his friends and cite them as a fundamental part of his preparation for the ministry.[164] Robert Harris, a former student of Dod's, was also celebrated for his ability in cases of temptation.[165] Harris himself was active in ministering to Capel who suffered a profound bout of temptation whilst resident at Harris's household seminary.[166] Capel would go on to become an acknowledged expert on temptation, producing one of the best-known books on the subject in 1633, and also aiding William Pemble

160 Becon, *The Christen Knight*, pp. 627.

161 Webster, *Godly Clergy in Early Stuart England*, pp. 15–35; for connections between ministers see also William Haller, *The Rise of Puritanism* (London, 1957; first edn, 1938), pp. 49–82.

162 Clarke, *The Lives of Thirty-two English Divines*, p. 170.

163 Ibid., p. 303; R. Bolton, *The last conflicts and death of Mr Thomas Peacock, Batchelour of Divinity, and Fellow of Brasen-nose College in Oxford* (London, 1646), pp. 30ff.

164 Clarke, *The Lives of Thirty-two English Divines*, p. 219.

165 William Durham, *The Life and Death of the judicious Divine, and accomplish'd Preacher, Robert Harris, D.D.* (London, 1660), p. 47.

166 Richard Capel, *Capel's Remains* (London, 1658), sigs. A4–A4v; Clarke, *The Lives of Thirty-two English Divines*, p. 303.

who would suffer death-bed temptation at Capel's house in Gloucester.[167] As the godly biographies of the later seventeenth century attest, the stories of the sufferings of these and other ministers clearly circulated widely amongst the communities of the zealous. Other ministers who were known to have suffered temptation included John Rogers and Edmund Staunton.[168] By the publication of Clarke's *Lives* of ministers this could be summed up in a maxim: 'meditation, prayer and temptation, make a Divine'.

The interaction between publication and word of mouth in the circulation of narratives of demonic temptation can be demonstrated by looking at the 1679 tract *Counsels and Comforts for Troubled Consciences* by Dr Henry Wilkinson, the Principle of Magdalen Hall in Oxford. His book was framed as a letter to a suffering friend, and he prefaced the book with exemplars of cases of affliction, some well known, others not. He cited the writings of Robert Bolton and referred to the celebrated cases of Katherine Brettergh and Thomas Peacock.[169] Of the case of Margaret Corbet, Wilkinson had personal knowledge, having preached her funeral sermon in 1656, and he described her death-bed struggle with Satan in the biography which accompanied it.[170] But Wilkinson also cited cases he had learned of from conversation with others. Notably he detailed the suffering of William Pemble, having been told by Robert Harris that Pemble had visited Capel in Gloucester where he had died having been violently assaulted in his last sickness by Satan.[171] Of course we might reasonably assume Capel himself had described the incident to Harris. Wilkinson also cited the instance of a schoolmaster in London, who had himself related the affliction he had experienced as a student, and the aid provided by John Dod, a story the author had confirmed from another source.[172] Thus Wilkinson's own treatise, an extension of his pastoral role to the individual sufferer, emerged from a milieu of the circulation of stories of affliction.

We can also be sure that Wilkinson's citations were by no means exhaustive. As a friend of Harris, he is likely to have known of Dod's work with other troubled ministers and laity such as John Preston and Joan Drake. But more significantly his own life is illustrative of another important arena in the development of the pastorate's anti-demonic skills. This was the way in which the ministerial network was employed to address the suffering of the clergy's own families. Wilkinson's wife, Elizabeth, herself became the subject

167 Wilkinson, *Counsels and Comforts for Troubled Consciences*, sigs A8–A8v; Richard Capel, *Tentations: their nature, danger and cure* (London, 1633).

168 Rogers, *Ohel*, p. 427; Samuel Clarke, *The Lives of sundry Eminent Persons in this Later Age* (London, 1683), p. 161.

169 Wilkinson, *Counsels and Comforts*, sigs. A6v–A7.

170 Henry Wilkinson, *The hope of Glory or Christs Indwelling in true Believers Is an Evident Demonstration of their hope of Glory* (London, 1657), pp. 74–5.

171 Ibid., sigs. A7–A7v. 172 Ibid., sigs., A7v–A8.

of one of Clarke's godly lives, which highlighted the almost constant affliction she had suffered during her life. Although no account is given of Henry's response to his wife's suffering, we must presume that he undertook efforts to minister to her. But, significantly, Robert Harris was also directly involved in Elizabeth's case. Elizabeth prepared a narrative of her spiritual experiences in order to be admitted to Harris's public assembly at Oxford, and Harris circulated the document as an exemplar, glossing it with his own commentary that indicates surely how he ministered to Elizabeth herself. 'God's power triumphs in the weakest vessels', he concluded in his assessment, 'the Lord trampling upon Satan in them, and in her very eminently.'[173] Moreover, Robert Harris's own wife experienced prolonged bouts of temptation 'so fierce, so horrid, and withall so subtle that they put the ablest men to their wits to answer'. She was visited by 'sundry eminent Preachers and Professors' and Harris sought the advice of his mentor, John Dod.[174] As Jackie Eales argues, the wives of ministers provided a focal point for the extension of clerical dynasties after the Reformation.[175] These examples show the potential for clergy wives to also act as focal points in the consolidation of Protestantism's understanding of the experience of diabolic temptation and its anti-diabolic strategies. Frank Luttmer has argued that Protestant understandings of diabolic temptation were informed by the perception that there was a 'vast' separation between the experiences of the regenerate and the reprobate.[176] Evidence of Protestant ministerial networks, and the emphasis on the collective spiritual experience of the household – which gave a significant place to the demonic – supports instead the contention that Protestant demonism emerged first from a sense of the vulnerability of the godly. Whilst Protestant ministers sought to transmit the experience of the demonic in the commonplace, their understanding of it, and of the measures by which it might be countered, was developed first in their own homes.

Thus when the Protestant clergy ministered to the afflictions of the broader laity, this was the wider application of a role developed within professional and domestic clerical circles. The relationship could, unsurprisingly, be especially intense between ministers and the zealous godly. Notably, ministers were often required to offset the temptations that sometimes intruded on the sick- or death-bed. In 1601, one Edward Aspinwall ministered to Katherine Brettergh as she was dying, and 'comforted her at all times with

173 Clarke, *The Lives of Thirty-two English Divines*, p. 425.

174 Ibid., pp. 319, 324–325; Durham, *The Life and Death of . . . Robert Harris*, pp. 46–8.

175 Jackie Eales, 'Wives and Daughters: Women in Early Modern Clerical Familes', forthcoming. I would like to thank Dr Eales for allowing me to read a version of this article in preparation, and for discussions of the subject.

176 F. Luttmer, 'Persecutors, Tempters and Vassals of the Devil: The Unregenerate in Puritan Practical Divinity', *Journal of Ecclesiastical History*, 51 (1) (2000), p. 55.

apt places of the scripture, meeting with her temptations, and so put the sword of the spirit into her hand'.[177] But whilst death-bed struggles may have been especially intense, they were representative of a broader and more consistent ministerial involvement in bolstering parishioners against temptation. The Barrington chaplain, James Harrison, exhorted Lady Barrington to develop a constant spiritual vigilance that would guard her against Satan, by remembering the tempting triumvirate and that God would always be 'heareing our prayers, [and] strengthening us against temptations'.[178]

Ministers were expected, and willing, to evaluate others' temptations in line with the Protestant soteriological scheme. In order to refute 'uncharitable speeches', William Harrison noted in his funeral sermon for Katherine Brettergh that 'the Devil most assaulteth them which be most godly, thinking to hinder all religion if he may prevaile'. Brettergh's case was later used by Robert Bolton as an exemplar in his highly successful *Instructions for a Right comforting afflicted consciences* (1631).[179] Robert Harris, reading Elizabeth Wilkinson's autobiography, was particularly impressed by the way in which Elizabeth's life seemed to exemplify the temptation of the godly. 'In Satan, thou seest his most ordinary way and method in tempting', he commented when he passed the narrative to a friend. God 'permitteth these Hellish Scullions to scour his Plate, and to fit the Vessels of Honour for their masters use'. We may assume he told Wilkinson much the same thing. Edmund Staunton, preaching Elizabeth's funeral sermon in December 1654, noted that 'the furious assaults of Satan' were her labours from which she was now at rest.[180]

Mediation of demonological knowledge was understood to be a two-way process. Whilst ministers were leaders in the struggle with Satan, successful resistance could occur only with the active engagement of the individual. Some accounts betray the irritation ministers could experience at stubborn refusals to accept their assurances that temptation did not indicate damnation. Robert Harris, unable to provide his wife with any comfort, eventually lost his patience, exclaiming 'what an idol do some make of comfort, as if their comfort were their Christ!'[181] Similarly, one of the plethora of ministers on hand to comfort the tormented divine Thomas Peacock, inflamed by his refusal to speak Christ's name, declared 'if I had your tongue in my hand, I would

177 *A brief discovrse of the Christian life and death, of Mistris Katherin Brettergh* (London, 1602), pp. 16–17.

178 *Barrington Family Letters 1628–1632*, ed. A. Searle, Camden Fourth Series, 28 (1983), pp. 74–5.

179 Harrison and Leygh, *Deaths advantage little regarded*, pp. 81–2; Bolton, *Instructions for a Right comforting afflicted consciences*, pp. 86–7.

180 Clarke, *The Lives of Thirty-two English Divines*, pp. 424–5; Edmund Staunton, *A Sermon preached at Great Milton in the County of Oxford ... at the funerall of ... Elizabeth Wilkinson* (Oxford, 1659), p. 5.

181 Durham, *The Life and Death of ... Robert Harris*, p. 47.

make you speak'.[182] The Lancashire minister Henry Newcome was involved with a number of colleagues in the successful exorcism of a local girl. When, however, their intervention could bring the girl no further out of her melancholy and idle state, Newcome began to suspect her of being a Quaker.[183]

The reformation of clerical mediation also sheds new light on the history of possession in England. The debate over exorcism was one of the most heated of the Reformation, reaching boiling point around the highly publicised activities of the minister John Darrell in the 1580s and 1590s. The 'Protestantisation' of exorcism has been characterised as a compromise born out of the continuing demands for spiritual healing being placed on ministers by their parishioners, and out of the challenge presented in this context by the exorcisms performed by Catholic priests.[184] But the enthusiasm of many Protestants for exorcism by prayer and fasting was surely more complex. Such methods were quite congruous with reformed demonism, despite the controversy they stirred up. That temptation and possession should be closely linked in Protestant demonism might seem an obvious point, but in the light of historians' concentration on the bizarre physical behaviour of demoniacs, it bears emphasising.[185] Possession was a spiritual phenomenon that produced grotesque physical symptoms; it *was* temptation, albeit in an extreme form.[186] Whilst the behaviour of demoniacs fascinated observers, it was the state of their souls which most interested the Protestant clergy.

182 Bolton, *The Last Conflicts and Death of Mr Thomas Peacock*, pp. 26–7.

183 Henry Newcome, *The Autobiography of Henry Newcome*, ed. R. Parkinson, Chetham Society, old series, 26 (1852), p. 107.

184 Catholic priests carried out exorcisms in Buckinghamshire and Middlesex in 1585–6 (to the concern of the Privy Council). They may have been involved in the Lancashire witch scare of 1612, and they certainly took a part in the 'Boy of Bilson' possession case of 1622; see D. P. Walker, *Unclean Spirits: Possession and Exorcism in France and England in the Late Sixteenth and Early Seventeenth Centuries* (London, 1981), pp. 43–9; Sharpe, *Instruments of Darkness*, pp. 194–5; Thomas, *Religion and the Decline of Magic*, pp. 576–80, 582–4, 586–8; M. MacDonald (ed.), *Witchcraft and Hysteria in Elizabethan London: Edward Jorden and the Mary Glover Case* (London, 1991), pp. xix–xxvi; Clark, *Thinking with Demons*, pp. 417–18.

185 Thomas, *Religion and the Decline of Magic*, pp. 569–70; MacDonald, *Witchcraft and Hysteria*, pp. vii–lv, especially pp. xxxiv–xxxix; Sharpe, *Instruments of Darkness*, pp. 195–210. Whilst they have been justifiably reticent as to suggestions about what 'really' happened in possession cases, historians have tended to be interested in how its physical symptoms, such as swellings and convulsions, might be explained, and in the cultural and sociological meaning of possession as a phenomenon that disrupted household and community. As a result relatively little attention has been given to the spiritual meaning of possession as an example of the Devil's agency. J. A. Sharpe, calling for a dedicated book on possession, notes himself that future research will need to examine how the phenomenon connected with the theological concerns of Protestant intellectuals and the Church of England. See ibid., p. 209.

186 Bishop Parkurst to Henrich Bullinger, 29 June, 1574, in *Zurich Letters*, p. 303; *A Relation of a Yovng Woman possest with the Devill* (London, 1646), p. 2; Clarke, *The Lives of Thirty-two English Divines*, p. 181.

Satan's intrusion into the body commonly effected a profound disruption of the victim's spiritual equilibrium, distracting him from religious observance and encouraging the conviction of damnation. Clerical commentators were unequivocal in their belief that these were the most dangerous consequences of possession. In 1574 the bishop of Norwich, John Parkhurst, described a local case of possession to Heinrich Bullinger, noting with relief of the victim that 'in all her temptations, however, and dilacerations, she continued steadfast in the faith, and withstood the adversary with more than manly fortitude'.[187]

In this context, exorcism by prayer and fasting was an extension of the prescribed methods of resisting Satan. John Darrell denied that he was an exorcist at all, claiming 'he tooke uppon him no greater power ... then was incident to any godlie minister ... which only was to intreat the Lord ... to dispossess the wicked spirit'.[188] Whilst his distinction was contentious, and became associated with Puritanism in the minds of men like Whitgift and Bancroft, it was congruous with a Protestant understanding which seems to have been widely held among both clergy and laity. The earliest pamphlet account of a possession case, Edward Nyndge's *A Trve and Fearfvll Vexation of one Alexander Nyndge* (1573), described how Edward and a local curate led the prayers of a group of over twenty that delivered Alexander.[189] A particularly full account of the use of prayer and fasting was given by John Swan in his pamphlet on the Mary Glover case of 1602. On 16 December a group of twenty-four godly, led by six ministers, successfully exorcised Glover through fasting and prayer.[190] In Swan's narrative the exorcism was a textbook example of clerical mediation, in which the ministers provided the example of resistance, inspiring Glover to follow their lead. The exercise began at eight in the morning, and the ministers took turns to lead the proceedings with prayers and sermons until seven in the evening. Glover was given a bible that she might look up the scriptures they referred to, and a woman was on hand to help her if her concentration lapsed. The texts selected advocated an utter reliance on God for deliverance; for instance Mr Lewis preached on Psalm 50: 15 ('call upon me in the day of trouble, so will I deliver thee') followed by Mr Evans on Matthew 11: 28 ('come unto me

[187] *Zurich Letters*, p. 303.

[188] *A Breife Narration of the possession, dispossession, and, repossession of William Somers* (?Amsterdam, 1598), p. 7.

[189] Edward Nyndge, *A Trve and Fearefvll Vexation of one Alexander Nyndge* (London, 1616; first edn, 1573), sigs A3–B3, esp. sig. A4v; similarly a counterfeited case of possession in London in 1574 was exorcised by prayer and fasting. See *The disclosing of a late counterfeyted possession by the devyl in two maydens within the Cittie of London* (London, 1574), sigs. A5, A5v.

[190] John Swan, *A Trve and Breife Report, of Mary Glovers Vexation, and of her deliuerance by the meanes of fasting and prayer* (London, 1603), pp. 8ff.

all yee that are weary and laden, and I will ease you').[191] After several hours Glover began herself to pray, her voice becoming progressively louder until she spoke over the minister. This was taken to be the decisive moment in the proceedings, when Glover took upon herself the responsibility for procuring her own deliverance.[192] Her prayers asked God to strengthen her and expressed trust in his mercy. Satan's discomfort was manifested by her falling into a fit after her prayers. The cycle was repeated twice until she was delivered after a final hour of frantic conflict between the ministers and the Devil.[193]

Thus, when its spiritual aspects were highlighted, the scenario of possession and dispossession afforded the Protestant scheme of temptation and resistance a remarkable tangibility. Ministers and demoniacs who faced down the Devil provided dynamic examples of the courageous faith which could be produced by an intense internalisation of godly rhetoric. In this way anti-demonic activity contributed to the rebuilding of the kudos of the ministry on Protestantism's own terms, rather than simply as a reaction to the challenge of Catholic exorcism. Darrell's ministerial reputation, which earned him a position as preacher in Nottingham, was based upon his success with demoniacs, and, according to his supporters, his services were sought precisely because he used prayer and fasting in cases of possession.[194] In an atmosphere of enormous controversy in the wake of contested diagnoses presented at the witch trial of Elizabeth Jackson, the family of Mary Glover seemingly specifically requested ministers to organise a day of fasting in order to pray for her deliverance.[195] Swan and his colleagues feared greatly for their careers if their identities became known, but Bancroft's concern to tar these Puritans with the brush of popery surely reflected a fear of the Protestant support they might be expected to attract.[196]

The ideal of interaction between minister and victim was consistently paralleled by a personal struggle between the clergy and the Devil. Possession narratives often included elaborate debates between the minister and the Devil which dramatised the inverted catechism presented in devotional works such as Becon's *Christen Knight*. Edward Nyndge, not a minister but an M.A., debated with Satan over the possibilities of salvation through

[191] Ibid., pp. 11–14.
[192] Ibid., pp. 22–3; similarly, see Nyndge, *A Trve and Fearefvll Vexation*, sigs. Bv–B2v.
[193] Swan, *A Trve and Breife Report*, pp. 28–47.
[194] *A Breife Narration of the possession . . . of William Somers*, p. 7.
[195] The trial was extraordinary in its use and rejection of the medical evidence of Edward Jorden and John Argent, who argued that Glover's symptoms had a natural origin. See MacDonald, *Witchcraft and Hysteria*, pp. xiv–xviii.
[196] According to Swan the assembled ministers entered into an agreement to protect the identities of each other should any be examined: Swan, *A Trve and Breife Report*, pp. 53, 56; on Bancroft's campaign, see MacDonald, *Witchcraft and Hysteria*, pp. xxii–xxvi.

repentance, and a similar debate attended the exorcism of a law student by John Foxe in 1574.[197] One such story, included in Samuel Clarke's *Lives*, concerned the minister Robert Balsom (d. 1647), who, during the Civil War, encountered a steward in Berwick who was 'very much weakened and worn out by the violence of temptation'.[198] Balsom diagnosed possession when his usual ministrations were unable to provide any comfort, and presently the Devil's voice sounded out of the steward's neck, challenging the minister's attempt to offer assurance. 'What dost thou talking to him of Promises, and free Grace?', Satan demanded; 'he is mine'. The two then debated the possibility of salvation for 'a notorious wicked wretch' like the steward, concentrating on whether sin in life could be taken as an indication of reprobation. Balsom never denied the possibility that the steward was damned, but since God's mercy might spare the greatest sinners, it was presumptuous of the Devil to lay claim to his soul. The didacticism of the confrontation for the observers (and readers) became more focused over the question of God's constraint of the Devil:

Satan: If God would let me loose upon you, I should find enough in the best of you, to make you all mine.

Balsom: But thou art bound Satan. And so turning himself to the people, with a smiling countenance, he said, what a gracious God have we, that suffers not Satan to have his will upon us?

Thus a learned minister might coax the Devil into admitting his fundamental impotency, providing a striking example to observers and readers of the veracity of the Protestant demonological scheme.[199]

By the time Samual Clarke collected his *Lives*, resistance to the Devil had become an important part of the image of a heroic Puritan ministry, proactively engaged in forcing Satan from the darkest corners of the land. One such figure included in Clarke's 'hagiography' was the Lancashire minister Richard Rothwell, who, like Balsom, debated the finer points of salvation with the Devil hidden in the body of a demoniac.[200] A more edifying Puritan hero it seems it would have been hard to find. When Rothwell became minister at Barnard Castle, Lady Bowes expressed a fear that he might be troubled by the locals, who were of a 'fierce disposition ... having never heard the gospell'. Rothwell was unfazed, replying, 'madam, if I thought I should never meet the

197 Nyndge, *A Trve and Fearefvll Vexation*, sigs. A4–A4v; Thomas, *Religion and the Decline of Magic*, pp. 574–5.
198 Clarke, *The Lives of Thirty-two English Divines*, p. 181. 199 Ibid., p. 182.
200 Ibid., pp. 72–3.

Devil there, I would never come there; he and I have been at odds in other places, and I hope we shall not agree there.'[201]

Thus Protestant demonism emerged out of a subtle realigning of emphasis, rather than an overt process of reform. Their experiential sense of the Devil's power told Protestants that satanic agency was a constant of a Christian life, and they understood man's relationship with Satan to be defined by the fall of Adam. Hence considerations of soteriology were inherent in the Protestant understanding of demonism, which in turn conceived the Devil's agency as an attempt to subvert man's attempts to achieve a communion with God. It was not in storm-raising or physical appearances that this agency was most keenly felt, but in the apparent intrusion into the conscience of thoughts which contradicted the will to godliness. Hence temptation, which had long been enshrined as part of the Devil's remit, was elevated by Protestant theologians to the single most important aspect of his agency. Whilst they did not deny the Devil's power to manifest physically, it is striking that they virtually ignored the possibility in their theological and devotional works. Moreover, they denounced the Catholic church's emphasis on conflicts with the Devil through artefacts and intercession as a distraction which drew attention from the real internal site of diabolic conflict. Protestant demonism aimed at a rigorous introspective engagement with the Devil in which his intrusions would be managed, through prayer and a sound soteriological understanding, as a defining experience of a Christian life. This rationale lay behind the reform of the demonological aspects of the liturgy, and it offered the emerging professionalised ministry the opportunity to redefine a role for themselves as the mediators of resistance to Satan. This, at least, was the theory. We must now examine the influence of the reform of demonism within the religious, social and political culture of sixteenth- and seventeenth-century England.

[201] Ibid., p. 70; apart from Rothwell's life (1563–1627), Clarke gives no dates for the events he describes.

4

Satan and the godly in early modern England

How influential was this Protestant reworking of demonism? Did it effectively transcend the boundaries of academic theology to more broadly affect conceptions of the Devil and his agency? The following two chapters examine areas of culture which provide insights into the common experience of satanic agency in England after the Reformation. This chapter examines the place of the Devil in the lives of the self-conscious godly in the sixteenth and seventeenth centuries.

It was Protestantism's aspiring godly who left the most detailed first-hand accounts of diabolic experience, and it was the Puritan sub-culture of introspection and spiritual autobiography that proved the most fertile ground for the distinctive emphasis on internal temptation. Records of the experience of temptation amongst the godly are relatively plentiful because sin and despair occupied such a central place in the discourse of spiritual autobiography.[1] The enormity of early sins served to contrast with post-conversion piety and to emphasise the escape from damnation provided by God's calling.[2] But this does not mean that narratives of temptation are stereotyped and cannot be read as 'real' accounts of diabolic affliction. Whilst the demands of spiritual autobiography shaped many accounts, individual voices emerge within the framework provided by the language of conduct literature. For the godly were not merely, as John Stachniewski implies, the unreflective recipients of someone else's demonism, prone to become victims to 'the darkness of Puritanism' when they were unable to measure up to the exaggerated demands of Calvinist devotion.[3] Whilst reading and sermon-gadding provided them with the language to express their demonological beliefs,

[1] Owen Watkins, *The Puritan Experience* (London, 1972), esp. pp. 12–14; Stachniewski, *The Persecutory Imagination*, pp. 27–84; Paul Delany, *British Autobiography in the Seventeenth Century* (London, 1969), pp. 58–63, 89–93.

[2] Bunyan, *Grace abounding to the chief of sinners* (1666); Sarah Davy, *Heaven realiz'd* (London, 1670); Hannah Allen, [*Satan his Methods and Malice baffled*] (London, 1683).

[3] Stachniewski, *The Persecutory Imagination*, pp. 44–5.

individual experience provided the emotional engagement which shaped their views of diabolic agency.

This chapter will examine the place of the Devil in the experiences of the godly, both in their private meditations, and in public, where shared experiences and clerical mediation contributed to the accommodation and interpretation of demonic activity within daily life. It will look in detail at a number of representative case studies of demonological experience provided in both the printed and unprinted writings of the godly. This experience of the Devil was far more widely differentiated than the historical emphasis on the darker psychological implications of predestinarian theology suggests. It might as readily provoke a determination to conquer Satan, or a resignation to patiently bear his assaults, as a suicidal despair. Whilst zealous Protestantism was a minority culture, it is our best illustration of the ways in which the Devil might find a place in people's everyday lives.

THE CONTEXT OF DEMONISM AND MODELS OF TEMPTATION

The Devil was part of the everyday culture of the godly (broadly defined). Through reading and attending sermons they assimilated the language of diabolic affliction and of temptation. Both the sources from which they gained demonological knowledge, and the way in which they assimilated it, varied widely. Interest in the Devil was not symptomatic of obsession or mental instability, and one person's Devil was not the same as another's. Sermons naturally provided much information. A surviving notebook kept between January 1601/2 and April 1603, by the Middle Temple law student, John Manningham, testifies to the regularity with which sermon-gadders could expect to be instructed with some form of demonological exposition.[4] Religious books could also have a profound influence on individuals. The Puritan gentlewoman Brilliana Harley derived her knowledge of the Devil from John Calvin's *Institutes of Christian Religion*, and from William Perkins' *Cases of Conscience*.[5] Elizabeth Wilkinson recorded a spiritual progression that was punctuated by the discovery of individual books which profoundly shaped her conception of herself. In her childhood she was thrown into a terrible fear of the Devil after reading Lewis Bayly's *Practice of Pietie*, but she developed a more sophisticated understanding of her relationship to Satan through encountering Calvin's *Institutes* and Henry

[4] John Manningham, *The Diary of John Manningham of the Middle Temple 1602–1603*, ed. R. P. Sorlien (Hanover, N.H., 1976).

[5] Brilliana Harley, 'Commonplace book of Brilliana Conway, 1622', Nottingham University Library, Portand Mss., London Collection, fol. 170r. I should like to thank Jackie Eales for providing me with a copy of this manuscript. See also John Bunyan's encounter with Dent's *Plaine mans Pathway*, and Bayly's *Practice of Pietie in Grace abounding*, p. 8.

Scudder's *The Christians Daily Walke in Securitie and Peace*.[6] We have seen the role ministers adopted in mediating demonological knowledge to their parishioners. For many of the godly this became a vital point of contact for the interpretation of their demonological experiences. If Robert Harris's comments after Wilkinson's death reflect the nature of their relationship, it was primarily concerned with her experience of temptation and despair, and his ability to help her assimilate her troubles within a framework of election.[7]

Godly writings give evidence of an in-depth knowledge of the conventions of Protestant demonism, particularly the defining nature of man's corruption through the fall of Adam for his constant persecution by the Devil, and his reliance on God for protection. 'Sin and corruption conceived in the heart of man is the spawn of the devil', the Elizabethan gentlewoman Lady Grace Mildmay recorded in her meditations, noting that there was 'a seed of Satan by his suggestions unto man in all opportunities as wherin he findeth his weakness, he doth most willingly and diligently apply the same'.[8] 'God by his Wisedome, / and all seeing Pow'r / ordained Man vnto Eternitie', wrote Alice Sutcliffe, the wife of an attendant to James I. 'Sathan through malice / turnes that sweet to sowre.'[9] The gentlewoman Anne Wheathill wrote her own book of prayers in which she included those to be said during temptation. Their language was reminiscent of that which filled the reformed primers. 'O Lord preserue me, that I fall not into temptation', one example read; 'neither let me be as one of them that conteme thy word, falling from thee; but arme me with an inuincible strength and constancie'.[10] The godly also assimilated the Devil's nomenclature of power and understood its significance. 'He is termed the Prince of the Are [air], and God of this world', Brilliana Harley noted in her commonplace book (1622); 'his power reacheth even to the spirit and soule of man, whereby he worketh in the children of disobedience'.[11] The Warwickshire Puritan Katherine Clarke described Satan thus: 'The Adversary who always stands at watch to insinuate and frame his Temptations answerable to our Conditions, and like a Roaring Lyon walks about continually, seeking to devour poor, yet precious Souls.'[12]

[6] Clarke, *The Lives of Thirty-two English Divines*, pp. 420–1. [7] Ibid., pp. 424–5.

[8] Grace Mildmay, 'Lady Mildmay's Meditations', in L. Pollock (ed.), *With Faith and Physic: The Life of a Tudor Gentlewoman* (London, 1993), p. 81; Mary Sidney Herbert, *A Discourse of Life and Death. Written in French by Ph. Mornay* (London, 1592), sigs. B–Bv, Cv; Alice Sutcliffe, *Meditations of mans Mortalitie. Or, a way to trve Blessednesse* (London, 1634), pp. 161–3.

[9] Ibid., p. 141.

[10] Anne Wheathill, *A handfull of holesome (though homelie) herbs, gathered out of the goodlie garden of Gods most holie word* (London, 1584), fols. 9v–10, 13v–14; Pollock, *With Faith and Physic*, p. 83; Richard Kilby, *The Bvrthen of a Loaded Conscience: or the miserie of sinne: set forth by the confession of a miserable sinner* (Cambridge, 1608), pp. 23–5, 53–4.

[11] Harley, 'Commonplace book', fol. 170r.

[12] Clarke, *The Lives of sundry Eminent Persons*, p. 161.

But individual demonological knowledge and experience was also shaped by the interaction of personal spiritual imperatives and the context in which demonism was encountered or used. Whilst the godly accepted the role of the clergy and devotional works as mediators of demonological knowledge, they shaped what they heard and read in line with their own concerns. Thus there was enormous variation in the way in which the Devil found a significant place in individuals' contemplation, and in what shape he took within it. It is undeniable that, as the history of religious despair has shown, some of the godly could become obsessed with 'the dark side of Puritanism', and felt a paralysing fear of the Devil. But there was no inextricable link between the experience of temptation and such obsession. Many who felt Satan's presence profoundly assimilated the experience within the sense of themselves as (potential) members of the elect. They understood the role of sound soteriological knowledge in warding off temptation, and they found it as appropriate and powerful a weapon as those of the pre-reformed faith had found the intercession of the saints and angels. Their diaries and autobiographies attest to the desire to find edification in temptation, and we should not doubt that this was possible, or assume that Protestant demonism did not answer to a very real and meaningful experience of the godly. Without diminishing the distress caused by temptation, many were prepared to recognise a value in the experience, and accepted that it afforded them some measure of spiritual insight, into their own condition and God's intentions for humanity. Moreover, differentiation in the experience of temptation cannot simply be functionalised, as it is in Richard Godbeer's interpretation, as a barometer of godly self-confidence, with those of the strongest assurance least likely to abrogate the responsibility for sin onto the Devil.[13] For the experience of temptation differed qualitatively as well as in intensity. As the godly measured their own experiences against the descriptions of temptation they read in devotional works, they found their own emphases, which enabled them to see the Devil, not as an inchoate generalisation onto which to project their sins, but as a tangible force which they had really encountered.

Protestant demonism bred the expectation of temptation, and consequently temptation came to dominate the demonological understanding of the godly, but within the scheme there was scope for a wide fluidity of expression and an eclectic personal demonism. Examples of this eclecticism are provided by two diaries written by Middle Temple law students in the early decades of the seventeenth century – Manningham's notebook of 1602–3 and the diary of Sir Simonds D'Ewes the future member of the Long Parliament. Manningham recorded conversations and anecdotes,

[13] Godbeer, *The Devil's Dominion*, pp. 93–106.

reports of contemporary events, his reading and his impressions of people he met, and described in detail the sermons he heard. On numerous occasions he made copious notes when a preacher gave a detailed exposition on some subject related to the Devil. Sometimes he was interested in a detailed demonological exposition,[14] but it was the moral aphorisms with which many preachers sought to enliven their sermons that seem to have particularly appealed to him. In early 1602 he recorded from Thomas Mountford, the prebend of Westminster, 'libellers are the Divels herauldes' and 'drunkennes is the divells birding synne; the drunkard like the stale that allures other to be taken like it selfe'. The same folio includes 'the love of the world is the Divels eldest sonne', a phrase heard from the Regius Professor of Greek at Cambridge, Andrew Downs.[15] A reference to the Devil might also catch Manningham's eye in any number of books or ballads. In August 1602 he copied, with no attempt to retain the sense of the original, a number of statements from 'a letter written by way of dedication of Charles the 5th his instructions to his sonne Phillip'. They included a description of the deceitfulness of Satan – 'the divel, like those painteres which are skilfull in the art of perspective, taketh pleasure, by false colours and decietful shadowes, to make those things seeme farthest of which are nerest hand (as death), and to abuse our nature with vayne hopes'.[16] In part Manningham's interest was clearly literary. He was acquainted with the London literati and he knew well their culture of wit and repartee. Like others in his age, he enjoyed clever anecdotes and Rabelaisian humour, and his notes are full of stories and quips found in books and ballads, and in conversation. The Devil was one source of such entertainment, as in October 1602 when Manningham enjoyed the description in a ballad called 'It is merry when Gossips meet' of 'the devils picture on your husbands browes'.[17] Some jokes were far more pointed, and at the height of the controversy over the Puritan dispossession of Mary Glover he recorded a jest which ridiculed the pretensions of those spectators who hankered after combat with the Devil. A gentlewoman lost her purse whilst she joined those assembled in prayer. 'Not unlikely', observed another of the onlookers, 'for you forgott halfe your lesson: Christ bad you watch and pray, and you prayed onely; but if you had watched as you prayed, you might have kept your purse still.'[18]

But for all their pith and wit these aphorisms seem to have provided Manningham with a satisfyingly succinct expression of a Protestant morality to which he subscribed, and indeed consolidated a sense of the possibilities

[14] As for instance at Paul's Cross in October 1602, when a Dr King, preacher at St Andrews in Holborn, repudiated Origen's opinion that Satan might eventually be saved. Manningham, *Diary*, pp. 103–4.

[15] Ibid., pp. 36–7. [16] Ibid., p. 79. [17] Ibid., p. 99; see also p. 122. [18] Ibid., p. 120.

of temptation. At a sermon by an unnamed minister he heard, 'the divel puts synn in our thoughts as a theife thrustes a boy in at a windowe, to open the dore for the great ones', and from Dr Thomas Holland, Regius Professor of Divinity at Oxford, he had this image: 'covetousnes is an Hydra with 7 heads; i.[e.], the Divel is the author of it; he tempted Christ with riches, when he shewed him ... the glory of the world. The divel could make shewes; he is a cunning Juggler.'[19] Whilst Manningham recorded no personal experience of diabolic affliction during his time at the Middle Temple, he was constantly aware of its potential, and found an appetite for demonological discussion well satisfied by his sermon-gadding and reading. London around 1602–3 may have encouraged a particularly fluid attitude to demonic power, for Manningham recorded, presumably with approval, both descriptions of the Devil's power of temptation, and sermons which disputed the reality of possession and exorcism by prayer in the wake of the Glover case.[20]

An eclectic demonism is also evident in Sir Simonds D'Ewes' Middle Temple diary, kept in the early 1620s. The diary, which records both political events and his experiences as a student, contains four references to the Devil, each of a completely different nature. The first reference, dated 7 January 1621, is seemingly trivial, recording news of social events at court, related to D'Ewes by a friend. Surrounded by a group of courtiers including his son, Rutland, and Buckingham, James I had apparently observed that 'the divell on me if I know which I love best'. D'Ewes seems to have enjoyed the insight into court and saw nothing remarkable or threatening in his monarch swearing by the Devil, a sin which providential ballads and pamphlets would have their readers believe was likely to see the perpetrator torn apart by Satan himself.[21] In September of the same year, however, D'Ewes recorded just such a providential appearance. A story was seemingly circulating to explain the storms that had wrecked most of the ships then docked at Plymouth. When a sailor had not been allowed to leave his ship he had threatened the crew that they would suffer for it, 'crying out "looke see you not the divell where he standeth?"' After being tied up below decks he suddenly reappeared, and, telling them they would have been better to let him go, jumped overboard. He was followed by the Devil in his common guise as a black dog. Immediately the storm blew up which destroyed the ships and killed the best part of their crews. Again D'Ewes recorded the story without comment.[22]

19 Ibid., p. 198, see also pp. 40, 66, 68.
20 See the sermons of Henoch Clapham, Thomas Holland and Giles Thompson, dean of Windsor, in ibid., pp. 185, 198, 211; on the organisation of this sermonising programme, see MacDonald, *Witchcraft and Hysteria in Elizabethan London*, p. xxiii.
21 D'Ewes, *Diary*, p. 57. 22 Ibid., pp. 95–6.

But again interest in wider demonological experience was balanced with a personal awareness and experience of temptation. Like many of the godly D'Ewes engaged in self-examination as a preparation to receive the sacrament, sometimes extending the process over a period of days. In May 1623 his conscience was troubled by thoughts he attributed to the Devil. His earliest exercise on the morning of the 11th was to examine his conscience, but 'alas, such was my weaknes and soe powerfull my roving thoughts, through Sathans suggestion that I could not receave the due comforte I hoped for'. The experience does not seem to have troubled him overmuch (in the end he could only hope that God would accept his good intentions) and, significantly, no indication is given that he considered this invasion of the Devil unusual.[23]

In some cases the demonological knowledge derived from sermons and devotional literature, mixed with the experience, or the expectation of temptation, allowed the godly to draw up a personal blueprint of diabolic operation and how it might be countered. The writings of three women demonstrate the ways in which the demonological content of sermons, books and conversations could be assimilated into an individual picture of diabolic activity. Dorothy Leigh and Elizabeth Joscelin both wrote godly instructions to be passed on to their children, and Brilliana Harley kept a commonplace book before she was married in which she described theoretically the Devil's assaults. All three were writing around the same time (*c.*1616–22), and each considered herself a representative member of the godly. But each produced a subtly different picture of Satan's agency.

In 1616 Dorothy Leigh penned *The Mothers Blessing*, spiritual advice, gleaned from experience, left for the edification of her children. For Leigh the Devil was a profoundly powerful agent, who enveloped men in a web of temptation. But her writing also expressed a deep sense of the power offered by the experience, if it could be turned against the Devil. In her scheme, introspection was not a symptom of masochistic self-accusation, but a pragmatic response to a known threat. She had internalised the assumption that, whilst all men were vulnerable to all sins, Satan honed his temptations to the particular corruption of the individual. Thus she employed the familiar image of the soul besieged by a tempting army. To each individual one sin was the 'captain' which, if admitted, 'will let in a great number of enemies'.[24] By extension, the defeat of the 'captain' would leave the tempting army impotent. Every individual then must fathom out his own chief sin, and

23 Ibid., p. 135.

24 Dorothy Leigh, *The Mothers Blessing. Or, the . . . Counsell of a Gentlewoman, . . . left behind for her children* (London, 1663; first edn, 1616), p. 135.

focus his resistance to temptation upon it. Once this spiritual watershed had been passed 'the Devil will have no cause to laugh in his face'.[25]

This pragmatism coloured Leigh's whole demonological outlook, providing a qualification to both easy assurance and despair. She attempted to instil in her children a cautious distrust of spiritual peace, since it was preferable to be beset by great temptations than to be led 'quietly to hell'. At the same time her pragmatism sought to ensure that the sense of the Devil's power was not overwhelming. Inherent in temptation was the opportunity to vanquish the Devil, which only the godly were in a position to exploit.[26] 'The Devil is a cunning Fowler', she noted; 'he will never lay a great bait, where he knows a little one will serue the turn', and so long as people's attention is distracted from God, he will leave them in relative peace.[27] But far stronger means were needed to overcome the godly, and soteriological knowledge showed up the paradox in the Devil's strategy. By focusing great temptations on individuals he allowed them an implicit acknowledgement of their election. Furthermore, by accentuating the experience of temptation, he made individual chief sins more readily discernible, and so gave the people most able to resist his power the means by which they might do so. Thus, for Leigh, temptation offered the godly a means by which they might forge their own discernible spiritual progression, but only if they engaged fully with the experience.

Elizabeth Joscelin, who died in childbirth in 1622, left behind a similar set of instructions for her child, which were published two years later. *The Mother's Legacy to her vnborn Childe* predicted that conflict with Satan would form an integral part of the child's life. Elizabeth knew how enormously powerful the Devil was, and that temptation might constantly beset the most godly.[28] Like Leigh, Joscelin saw soteriological awareness as the means to resistance, but in contrast her scheme allowed for no watershed victory over Satan; instead she sought to instil an introspective discipline that might make his assaults manageable.

Elizabeth wished to ensure that her child's life was characterised by a confidence in the mercy of God, and this relied on an assimilation of a sense of human weakness into a meditative cycle which allowed the experience of temptation to be interpreted. The first thoughts of the godly every day should concern the malice of the Devil and 'thine owne weakness'. But, unusually, Elizabeth defined weakness very specifically as the inability to constantly maintain the vigilance necessary to guard against Satan, not the spiritual

[25] Ibid., pp. 135–7.
[26] Ibid., pp. 138–40; this was of course a conventional understanding of the relationship between the Devil and the godly.
[27] Ibid., pp. 138–40.
[28] Elizabeth Joscelin, *The Mothers Legacie, To her vnborne Childe* (London, 1622), pp. 16–20, 61–2, 83–6.

corruption brought about by the fall. 'Thine owne weaknesse is apparent to thee', she told her child, for when he was asleep 'thine eies were closed, thou couldst not see to defend thy selfe, thy strength was gone'.[29] Insensibility, therefore, equalled weakness, and the sleeping man was unable to resist an attack by the smallest insect. The mind that was not turned to God left itself open to the influence of the Devil, unavoidable in sleep, but not to be endured whilst awake. 'Be assured', Elizabeth warned, 'if thou once yeeld to neglect praying to God, but one halfe houre, when [temptation] comes thou shalt be far more vnapt, and thy heart more dull to pray than before.'[30]

When the mind was thus vulnerable the Devil would introduce sinful thoughts and temptations, most commonly attempting to accentuate weakness by enticing men to abandon their observances. 'The deuils malice is easily percieued', Elizabeth noted, 'for euen now he lies lurking ready to catch euery good motion from thy heart, suggesting things more delightful to thy fancy, and perswading thee to deferre thy seruice of God though but for a little while'.[31] So dangerous was this vulnerability to the well-being of the soul, that the first task of the godly upon waking should be to examine their minds and flush out any thoughts that the Devil had placed there whilst they slept. This assault of the Devil upon the insensible mind was to teach a vital lesson, for it should be clear that the individual emerged unscathed against the odds. 'How do you thinke you were preserued from his snares while you slept?', Elizabeth asked, 'or doe you thinke that he onely besets you when you are awake?' Satan was not 'so faire an enemy', and would take advantage of sleep to 'teare your body and drag your soul to hell' if he could. Only the power of God constrained him, and it was vital that the individual acknowledged this fact. 'Now you must needs confesse who it is that is only able to preserue you', Elizabeth instructed her child, 'that it is God.'[32]

By the time she had finished describing the diabolic assault on the mind, Elizabeth had effectively sidelined the emphasis on weakness that had been central to her argument. In spite of his weakness, every morning her child awoke free of temptation was a testament to the care of God, and he could not help but understand that, as long as he maintained his faith, the odds were stacked in his favour. Elizabeth hoped that this understanding would instil in her child the gratitude that would inspire his godliness. Recognising how much he owed to God, he should 'gather to yourselfe a strong resolution with all your force to serue him all the day, and to resist all the tentations of the deuill'.[33]

The personal aspects of these demonological models are apparent and significant. For if both Leigh and Joscelin believed that preparing their

[29] Ibid., pp. 16–17. [30] Ibid., pp. 17–18. [31] Ibid., p. 17.
[32] Ibid., p. 19–20. [33] Ibid., p. 20.

children for the experience of temptation was fundamental to their upbringing, neither accepted the stark disciplinarian conventions of the Puritan household manual. In Puritan families soteriological concerns were supposed to shape much of the severe code of household discipline, which sought to overcome the handicap presented by the fact that children were conceived in sin. Household manuals stressed the evil wilfulness inherent in children and the importance of rigorous parental discipline in, literally, exorcising it.[34] John Stachniewski has highlighted the way in which such codes might encourage the brutalisation of children, who were subjected to beatings in order to drive out Satan.[35] But Elizabeth Joscelin clearly found the notion that her new-born infant might be infused with sin difficult to countenance, however closely the well-being of his soul might bear watching in future. Children, she accepted, were as likely as adults to become the servants of the Devil, but this was not because they were inherently corrupt, but because they were vessels waiting to be filled, either with godliness or diabolism. Thus Elizabeth saw the early years of life not as an attempt to rein in the sinful nature with which the child was born, but as a race between godliness and the Devil to occupy the central place in the child's development. So she advised her unborn child to 'beginnest to remember to serue God when thou art young, before the world, the flesh, and the deuill take hold on thee'.[36] Whilst Leigh was more prepared to accept the notion of natural corruption and pervasive sin, she implicitly rejected the logic of Puritan disciplinarianism. Sin must be defeated, and progress could only take place by encountering temptation, engaging with it and understanding it. Hers was not an indulgent attitude to childhood temptation, but it challenged the validity of using harsh punishments to simply stifle the Devil's influence.

Other models were produced, not from the experience of temptation, but from the expectation of it. The commonplace book (1622) kept by the gentlewoman Lady Brilliana Harley before she was married revolved almost entirely around the question of predestination and how the elect might discern the symptoms of their grace. In line with this agenda she drew up a blueprint of temptation, made up of selected quotations and heavily influenced by William Perkins' *Cases of Conscience*, that would allow her to judge whether her reaction to demonic assault was consistent with election. Her commonplace book was put together as a reference work, with subject headings organising the transcriptions and observations for easy access,

[34] John Morgan, *Godly Learning: Puritan Attitudes towards Reason, Learning and Education 1560–1640* (Cambridge, 1988), pp. 144–5.

[35] See Stachniewski, *The Persecutory Imagination*, pp. 96–9.

[36] Joscelin, *The Mothers Legacie*, pp. 12–13. It seems reasonable to suspect also, that in allowing a natural sentimentality to overturn the stark moral rhetoric of the household manuals, Joscelin may have been far from unique.

and amongst 'of the knowledge of God', 'of the decrees of God', 'of the soul' and 'of repentence' are pages dedicated to 'of the power of Satan' and 'of affliction'.[37] Here she collected extracts and observations that would help her discern the symptoms of temptation and the godliness of her response.

As we have seen, Brilliana employed the standard Protestant rhetorical device of the Devil's nomenclature of power to emphasise his strength. But this was of more personal than cosmic significance to the godly, who were incredibly weak in the face of a being whose 'power is above the might of any Man or creature that is not of an evengellicall natur as himself'.[38] This understanding should define the godly response to temptation. Mankind had no 'warrant' to attempt to overcome the Devil, since unaided 'no defense or strength of man was abel to withstand him'. It was arrogant folly to put oneself in 'needless danger', believing one's faith to be 'so strong the diuell can not touch [you]'.[39] 'Wher houses is anoyed with Evill Spirits', Brilliana quoted from Perkins, 'man must not consort together and abide there, where it is certainly known that the Lord has giuen the diuell Power and Liberty.'[40]

For Brilliana, the godly response to temptation was characterised by understanding the subtle balance in which diabolic power was held. Despite his power, God would never allow the Devil 'inlarged to the destruction of his children'. Those who sought conflict with Satan demonstrated a recklessness with their souls and a faithlessness in God. The correct response to affliction was to 'flee', but flight in this context is metaphorical. The afflicted must 'fly to God by prayer' – again from Perkins – abdicating their responsibility for overcoming Satan to God, who will either deliver them from temptation or give them the patience to bear it.[41] Thus Brilliana's emphasis advocated passivity in response to temptation; there was none of the talk of 'struggling' with the Devil that filled so many accounts of affliction. But here passivity in the face of the Devil was not a last resort, a final reliance on blind hope. Rather it was an indication that the individual had assimilated and correctly interpreted the realities of the position of man in relation to God and the Devil. For Brilliana the godly reaction to the Devil was the *informed* reaction to the Devil, and such a grasp of the finer points of faith was likely to be an indication of election.

[37] Harley, 'Commonplace book', fols. 1r–2r, 6r, 94v, 150r, 170r, 157r; on Brilliana's use of her commonplace book to put together a guide to the signs of election, see Jackie Eales, *Puritans and Roundheads: The Harleys of Brampton Bryan and the Outbreak of the English Civil War* (Cambridge, 1990), pp. 49–52.

[38] Harley, 'Commonplace book', fol. 170r. [39] Ibid., fols. 170r, 157r.

[40] Ibid., fol. 170r; Perkins, *The Whole Treatise of the Cases of Conscience, in Works*, vol. II, pp. 38–9.

[41] Harley, 'Commonplace book', fol. 170r; Perkins, *Cases of Conscience*, p. 39; Richard Norwood also assimilated this reading of Perkins into his own experiences of temptation, see his *The Journal of Richard Norwood* (New York, 1945), p. 94.

The writings of these women share two important features. Firstly, although their demonism did not step outside the conventions of Protestant theology and rhetoric, it is obvious that it was the result of reading and deliberation. None accepted the entirety of the conduct literature's picture of Satan. Instead they were selective, choosing to highlight aspects that they found especially relevant or plausible. Each assigned the Devil a significant and discrete role in their lives, rather than simply assimilating the concept into a generalised piety. Brilliana Harley expected to be tempted, and more important than the need to overcome temptation was that her response to it should be consistent with election. For Elizabeth Joscelin temptation was a constant presence, which she felt invigorated her piety by ensuring that it did not become staid and complacent. Dorothy Leigh saw temptation as a means to a discernible spiritual progression by which weakness might be overcome by self-knowledge. Secondly, it is notable that, for all the power they ascribed to Satan, none expected to be overwhelmed by him. All would have accepted that in theory this was possible (were God to allow it), but their writings were entirely lacking in any sense that temptation constituted a final battle in which the fate of their souls would be decided. Correspondingly, they did not expect to gain an outright victory, and so their concern was to make temptation manageable.

CYCLICAL AFFLICTION AND SPIRITUAL PROGRESSION: THE EXPERIENCE AND RATIONALISATION OF TEMPTATION

If this was the context in which the godly developed their understanding of temptation, what do their writings tell us about the experience itself? Temptation could potentially strike at any age, but some of the godly claimed that their first encounters with the Devil had come in childhood. Richard Kilby noted that through his childhood ignorance of the faith 'the Devill had leisure to take full possession of my heart'. He 'deepely seasoned me with sinne, that I have continued sinnefull ever since'.[42] The Puritan Elizabeth Wilkinson was tormented by a diabolic temptation to doubt her election when, at the age of twelve, she read Lewis Bayly's *The Practice of Pietie*.[43] The Baptist Sarah Davy was around the same age when she was tempted by the Devil, first into security and then to doubt her election.[44] John Bunyan was even younger when he had a similar experience. His earliest memories were of a life characterised by a struggle between an inherently sinful nature and a profound fear of damnation, and this pattern was well established

[42] Kilby, *The Burthen of a Loaded Conscience*, p. 1.

[43] Clarke, *The Lives of Thirty-two English Divines*, p. 420. Similarly, see William Cowper, *The Life and Death of the Reverend Father ... William Cowper* (London, 1619), sig. A4.

[44] Davy, *Heaven realiz'd*, pp. 8–11.

before he had reached his tenth year.[45] How far children understood the theological niceties of temptation is difficult to assess. Some may have been genuinely precocious, aware of the spiritual test provided by the Devil's agency, or at least able to convince adults that they were. The minister's daughter Mary Walker apparently 'told one of the Maids that the Devil tempted her to Play at Prayers; but she had pray'd against him, and that he did not trouble her so much since'.[46] But if it was more common for the Devil's influence to be identified later through hindsight, the experience of conflict with spiritual demands made on children, and perhaps also made by the children on themselves, was genuine.

It was more typical for significant periods of temptation to take hold in later adolescence or early adulthood. The Puritan Katherine Clarke, whose life provided an exemplar in her husband's *Lives*, encountered the Devil at fifteen, who 'assaulted her with many, and various temptations'. Another of Samuel Clarke's subjects, Mary Gunter, was in 'her young and tender years' when she was tempted by Satan to commit suicide.[47] Nehemiah Wallington was twenty when he began a protracted period of despair, in which, he later remembered, he was assaulted with 'eleven sore temptations of Satan'.[48] The future Quaker leader, George Fox, was the same age when, in 1644, he was first tempted to despair, and 'when Satan could not effect his design upon me that way, then he laid some snares for me and baits to draw me to commit some sin'.[49] It is, of course, unsurprising that many of the godly should have experienced their first temptations at the point at which they presumably became aware of the attractions of sex, drink or dancing – those activities so often damned from the pulpit as the embodiment of youthful sin and reprobation.[50] Certainly Wallington's experience of despair was particularly intense when he considered how far he was given over to lust.[51] But adolescent temptation was accentuated by a tendency to become obsessed with the absolutes of Protestant soteriology. Reading the promises to the elect, and convincing themselves they were not among them, many of the aspiring godly felt a profound sense of exclusion when they considered the blessings that were given to other members of their communities, but not to them. So the Devil did not merely appear to tempt them into sin. He found his most powerful characterisation as a jeering tormentor, who constantly

45 Bunyan, *Grace abounding*, pp. 5–6.
46 Quoted in Patricia Crawford, *Women and Religion in England 1500–1720* (London, 1996), p. 76.
47 Clarke, *The Lives of sundry Eminent Persons*, pp. 136; see also Norwood, *Journal*, p. 68.
48 Seaver, *Wallington's World*, p. 15.
49 George Fox, *The Journal of George Fox*, ed. J. L. Nickalls (Cambridge, 1952), p. 4.
50 Collinson, *The Religion of Protestants*, pp. 224–6.
51 Seaver, *Wallington's World*, pp. 21, 23, 25–6.

reminded them of their reprobation and undermined by his sophistry any assurance they might find.

The long-term continuance of affliction is highly significant and has not been addressed by historians, who have generally been interested in pre-conversion despair.[52] Adulthood tended to see the continuance of temptations which began much earlier. Again, Nehemiah Wallington, whose afflictions extended well into his forties, provides a good example. Richard Norwood could identify a specific temptation as haunting him for some twenty-four years.[53] Hannah Allen remembered in 1683 that she had been tempted in her childhood, but her greatest troubles came when she became melancholy at the long absence, and eventually the death, of her husband, when 'the Devil had the more advantage' of her condition.[54] As we have already seen, even those who had gained assurance expected to be consistently tested by post-conversion temptation. The blueprints left by Brilliana Harley, Elizabeth Joscelin and Dorothy Leigh provide an insight into a regular diabolic assault that, once assimilated into a regime of godly observance, somewhat fell from view in the conversion narratives and godly lives.

What was the subjective experience of temptation? In the twentieth century we have come to understand it as a short, sharp desire for something forbidden. The early modern godly recognised that experience too, but they understood it to be a symptom of a fundamental long-term condition of life. For them, temptation's defining characteristic was a lack of control over mind and will. Thus rather than desire per se it was the impulse to any attitude or action which was spiritually damaging. Convictions of damnation and salvation might equally be temptations of the Devil, and in godly accounts they were perhaps more prevalent than desire. For many, temptation was a chronic condition, lasting months or even years. A childhood infraction apparently plunged Sarah Wight into despair for four years.[55] If at certain moments the godly found themselves tempted to specific sins, these were peaks in a more generalised temptation, rather than discrete experiences in themselves.

Forces beyond the individual's control might sometimes manifest themselves externally. In 1579 the Windsor gentleman Richard Galis described his sufferings under 'diabolicall tiranny' at the hands of a local coven of witches.[56] Whilst not recognisable as spiritual autobiography, Galis's narrative subsumed its details of witchcraft within a Protestant framework which made his personal conflict with the Devil its overriding concern. Wracked

[52] Watkins, *The Puritan Experience*, pp. 9–15.
[53] Seaver, *Wallington's World*, p. 30; Norwood, *Journal*, p. 106.
[54] Allen, [*Satan his Methods and Malice Baffled*], pp. 7–8.
[55] Stachniewski, *The Persecutory Imagination*, pp. 99.
[56] Richard Galis, *A Brief Treatise conteyning the most strange and horrible crueltye of Elizabeth Stile alias Bockingham and hir confederates executed at Abingdon upon Richard Galis*

with illness, and believing the Devil had visited him in the night disguised as a cat, Galis resorted to his prayer book and bible in the first of his many attempts to take control of his situation. His sense of identity as a member of the beleaguered godly provided a rationale for his suffering and a focus for his resistance, as in prayer he found himself 'utterly from the bottome of my hart detesting and hauing in defiaunce all the crue of deuilish Enchaunters, whereof England at thus day dooth abounde'.[57] Yet having established an immunity from bewitchment by a sheer act of pious will, Galis found that the Devil and his witches 'stirred up others to be their cruel ministers'. His efforts to apprehend the witches were frustrated rather than supported by the mayor and the magistracy, and he was at one point chained in prison.[58] Whilst he maintained a conceptual framework of providence and Job-like endurance, his efforts to assert control grew increasingly violent, culminating in the attempted murder of one witch, and a physical confrontation with Satan in which he 'let flye with my sword, saying auoide Sathan auoyde'.[59] The notion of envelopment by affliction found a focus in Protestant conceptions of the antithesis between ministry and satanic obstruction, especially in disputes over conformity. Thomas Gataker noted of William Bradshaw that in the 1590s Satan had moved jealous ministers to denounce him to the bishop of Rochester as a nonconformist.[60] Similarly it was remembered of Herbert Palmer, lecturer at Canterbury from 1626 to 1629, that he considered his failure to attain a prebendary at the cathedral a deliverance from the 'many temptations and dangers' that would envelop the post in its subsequent responsibility for seeing through Archbishop Laud's innovations.[61] Samuel Clarke, who collected a number of these stories, was keenly aware of Satan's attempts to undermine his own ministry. From his earliest preaching, as assistant to the parson of Thornton in Cheshire in the early 1620s, his Puritanism caused him to be denounced to one authority after

(London, 1579), sig. A3. I would like to thank Marion Gibson for bringing the survival of this unusual pamphlet to my attention (it is commonly recorded as lost in bibliographies of witch texts), and for numerous discussions of it. The pamphlet was a response to the publication of *A Rehearsall both strange and true, of hainous and horrible actes committed by Elizabeth Stile, alias Rockingham* ... (London, 1579).

[57] Galis, *A Brief Treatise*, sig. A4–B.

[58] Ibid., sigs. B3–B3v. The reasons for Galis's imprisonment are not clear, but this and other episodes suggest that his mental state was considered dangerous, and with justification. In the wake of magisterial intransigence, he decided to burn one of the witches, Mother Dutton, alive in her house. When the house would not catch fire, Galis hit upon a cunning plan in which he attempted to set fire to the house next door in the hope that it would spread. Whilst Galis's mental state might be suspect, it, like that of Nehemiah Wallington, does not automatically cast doubt on the veracity of his assimilation of his conflicts with Satan with his self-identification as a zealous Protestant. See ibid., sig. D.

[59] Ibid., sig. C4v; see also recollections of M. H. in Vavasor Powell's *Spiritual Experiences, of sundry beleevers Held forth by them* (London, 1653), pp. 217–18.

[60] Clarke, *The Lives of Thirty-two English Divines*, p. 36. [61] Ibid., p. 187.

another. This he interpreted as being 'dogg'd by Sathan', who 'raised up instruments' throughout his career to obstruct him, and kept other godly ministers silent to complete his isolation.[62]

Whilst external affliction fed, and was fed by, the godly's sense of persecution, temptation as a lack of control was most commonly recognised as an internal experience. In 1584, the Protestant gentlewoman Anne Wheathill published a collection of forty-nine prayers, entitled *A handfull of holesome (though homelie) herbs*. The emphasis on internal affliction was paramount, as she asked that she 'fall not into temptation' and be given 'faith to fight against the diuell, and all his false suggestions'.[63] But it is the relative lack of direct references to Satan that reveal what the experience of temptation was for Wheathill. For she preferred to focus on the consequences of temptation for her relationship with God, experiencing the Devil as an inchoate, but very real, barrier to spiritual communion. 'My heart is . . . variable, and separated from thee', she prayed against Satan; 'joine my soule and bodie to thee O God'.[64] In her autobiography sent to Robert Harris at Oxford, Elizabeth Wilkinson described the experience of temptation as the sheer uncontrollability of thoughts introduced into her mind. 'I was sensible that it was a fearefull sinn to have any such thoughts to lodge in my brest', she noted. 'I desired my soul to be freed from them, and had continual reasonings within me against them, and yet still for a long time I was troubled.'[65] As one 'J. M.' described in a collection of godly experiences published by Samuel Petto (1654):

> I would have beleeved but could not; I would have put away thoughts of temptation but could not: the temptation grew stronger and stronger, my heart was broken by reason of sorrow; yet for a time, marvellously kept up to strive; I saw I could not hold out, and was ready to yeeld, and give over the combat.[66]

'Satan had the power to overwhelm all, as it were in a thick dark cloud', Richard Norwood remembered, 'and to captivate me in all the powers and faculties of mind and body.'[67] In Katherine Clarke the Devil raised up 'fears, doubts, and terrors of Conscience in me . . . and by reason herof I had no Peace, nor rest in my Soul, Night nor Day'.[68] John Bunyan described evocatively the

[62] Clarke, *The Lives Of sundry Eminent Persons*, pp. 3–4, 5, 6, 7; Rogers, *Ohel or Beth-shemesh*, p. 432.
[63] Wheathill, *A handfull of holesome (though homelie) herbs*, fols. 9v–10, 12v–13.
[64] Ibid., fols. 10v–11; Kilby, *The Bvrthen of a Loaded Conscience*, pp. 17–23.
[65] Clarke, *The Lives of Thirty-two English Divines*, p. 421.
[66] 'Experiences of J. M.', in Samuel Petto, *Roses from Sharon. Or sweet experiences gathered up by some precious hearts* (London, 1654), p. 24.
[67] Norwood, *Journal*, p. 100; see also the experiences of E. C. and M. W. in Powell, *Spirituall Experiences*, pp. 82–3, 143–6.
[68] Clarke, *The Lives Of sundry Eminent Persons*, p. 153; Jane Turner, *Choice Experiences of the Kind Dealings of God* (London, 1653), pp. 25, 117–18.

coaxing voice within his conscience that urged him to 'Sell Christ for this, or sell Christ for that', 'not so little as hundred times together' and 'as fast as a man could speak'. The sheer effort of holding back this wave of sinful thoughts could be overwhelming:

> For whole hours together I have been forced to stand as continually leaning and forcing my spirit against it . . . that by the very force of my mind in labouring to gainsay and resist this wickedness my very Body also would be put into action or motion, by way of pushing or thrusting with my hands or elbows, still answering, as fast as the destroyer said, Sell him; I will not, I will not, I will not.[69]

Similarly, Sarah Wight had experienced uncontrollable urges to blaspheme, and was only prevented from sinning by a providential loss of her voice at the moment at which she could no longer resist.[70]

With so much at stake and so little time, Satan's barrier to communion could intrude most viciously on the death-bed. Dying in 1601, Katherine Brettergh was thrown into panic by the Devil's interruption of her devotions. She believed Satan's intrusion had produced a dislocation in her mind between what she might objectively desire and what she could subjectively believe. When asked if she believed the promises of God she replied, 'O that I could, I would willingly, but he will not let me.'[71]

Whilst the godly were prone to temptations to carnal sin,[72] it was intrusive thoughts concerning their spiritual state which most exercised their introspection.[73] The Protestant introspective scheme surely did encourage what Dr Stachniewski has described as masochistic 'one-downsmanship', in which the godly vied with each other to be the most damned.[74] Yet this, and less indulgent self-criticism, was born out of a very real experience which gave temptation an especial tangibility. Despite the time and energy devoted to discovering the signs of grace, discerning whether they were present, and regulating all behaviour to be consistent with election, doubts still commonly intruded on the minds of those who genuinely felt an affinity with the word of God. The sheer perversity of the experience lent force to the contention that the conscience was being subverted from the inside. Whilst many came

69 Bunyan, *Grace abounding*, p. 42–3; Powell, *Spirituall Experiences*, pp. 237–8.

70 Jessey, *The Exceeding Riches of Grace Advanced*, p. 59; Norwood, *Journal*, p. 92.

71 *A Briefe discovrse of the Christian life and death, of Mistris Katherin Brettergh*, pp. 13–15; *The Christian Life and Death of Mistris Katherin Brettergh* (London, 1612), sig. B.

72 For example, see Lady Grace Mildmay's meditations in Pollock, *With Faith and Physic*, p. 81; Kilby, *The Bvrthen of a Loaded Conscience*, pp. 31, 35, 61, 74; Richard Baxter, *Reliquiae Baxterianae: or, Mr Richard Baxters narrative of the most memorable passages of his life and times* (London, 1696), p. 7; Alan Macfarlane, *The Family Life of Ralph Josselin, a Seventeenth-Century Clergyman* (Cambridge, 1970), p. 178.

73 Powell, *Spirituall Experiences*, pp. 47, 82, 135, 143, 237, 251, 254, 272, 278–9, 290, 321, 330, 353.

74 Stachniewski, *The Persecutory Imagination*, pp. 40–1.

to recognise their temptations as diabolic in retrospect, we should not doubt the reality of the experience of dislocation between pious desire and accusing conscience, and that its effect could be profound.[75]

Thus the convert, Mary Gunter, found her early Protestant aspirations undermined by an inescapable belief that in her Catholicism she had sinned against the Holy Ghost, and 'so incessantly, and violently did [Satan] pursue her in this Temptation, that she was brought to believe that it was impossible that this sin should, or could be pardoned'.[76] Satan persuaded Katherine Clarke that 'all the threatenings contained in the Book of God against the Wicked and ungodly men did belong unto me . . . Insomuch as when I took up the Bible to read therein, it was accompanied with much fear and trembling; Yet being convinced that it was my Duty frequently to read Gods Word, I durst not omit, or neglect it.'[77] Even those most prepared to meet the Devil's assaults could be taken aback by the inescapability of convictions of reprobation. Robert Bolton reported of the suffering divine Thomas Peacock that, 'his tender conscience was goared with the fiery darts of the Deuil'. 'As through a false glasse', he noted, 'the dazled eye of his astonished and amazed soul, could see nothing but hideously appearing sinne, and the terrible image of death and damnation'.[78] Richard Baxter expressed the imposing sense of perversity inherent in the experience of doubt/temptation: 'in the storm of . . . Temptation, I questioned a while whether I were indeed a Christian or an Infidel, and whether faith could consist of such doubts as I was conscious of: For I had read in many Papists and Protestants, that Faith had Certainty, and was more than an opinion'.[79]

Worse thoughts still might intrude on the conscience, perhaps the most disturbing of all being thoughts of atheism. The Devil attempted to confound Mary Gunter by 'injecting multitudes of blasphemous thoughts into her head. For now she must believe that there is no God: That the sacred Scriptures are not the Word of God, but a humane policy to keep men in order.'[80] It was a source of 'terrour' to Elizabeth Wilkinson that she found herself entertaining atheism. Preaching her funeral sermon, Edmund Staunton encouraged the congregation to take comfort in the fact that she would no longer suffer the 'injection of Atheisticall, or Blasphemous thoughts'.[81] The clergy themselves were perhaps the most vulnerable, since their learning provided a more insidious cover for Satan's perversity. The

[75] Bolton, *Instructions for a Right comforting afflicted consciences*, pp. 81–3.
[76] Clarke, *The Lives Of sundry Eminent Persons*, p. 136. [77] Ibid., p. 153.
[78] Bolton, *The last conflicts and death of Mr Thomas Peacock*, pp. 7–9, quote at p. 8.
[79] Baxter, *Reliquiae Baxterianae*, p. 22.
[80] Clarke, *The Lives Of sundry Eminent Persons*, pp. 136–7.
[81] Clarke, *The Lives of Thirty-two English Divines*, p. 421; Staunton, *A sermon preached at Great Milton . . . at the funeral of . . . Elizabeth Wilkinson* (Oxford, 1659), p. 5.

ministry held new dangers for Richard Baxter as he was 'now assaulted with more pernicious temptations; especially to question the certain truth of the sacred scriptures; and also the life to come, and the Immortality of the Soul'. Their most frightening aspect, however, was that they did not assault him 'with horrid vexing Importunity; but by Pretence of sober Reason'.[82]

Experience of the physical Devil, or the fear of his appearance, was widespread amongst sufferers of temptation. But it was invariably a symptom of temptation *in extremis*. Nehemiah Wallington's belief that Satan had disguised himself as his father's maid was a rare example of the physical Devil being conceived of as a tempter. Sometimes temptation could be so forceful that it was a near-physical experience. The mathematician and geographer Richard Norwood described Satan's assaults thus:

> sometimes he seemed to lean on my back or arms or shoulder, sometimes hanging on my cloak or gown. Sometimes it seemed in my feeling as if he had stricked me in sundry places, sometimes as it were handling my heart and working withal a wonderful hardness therein ... Also in bed somtimes pressing, sometimes creeping to and fro, sometimes ready to take away my breath, sometimes lifting up the bed, sometimes the pillow, sometimes pulling the clothes or striking on the bed or on the pillow.[83]

'In prayer', John Bunyan wrote in *Grace abounding*, 'I have thought I should see the Devil, nay, thought I have felt him behind me pull my cloaths.'[84] But for the most part it was the fear of his appearance as God's hangman that dominated the Protestant sense of his physicality. 'M. K.', contributing to the 1652 collection *Spirituall Experiences of Sundry Beleevers*, described how she believed Satan had come to take her when her dog startled her by jumping on her bed.[85] On several occasions Hannah Allen believed she had encountered God's hangman, who taunted her with her reprobation. 'I heard like the voice of two young men singing in the yard, over against my chamber', she remembered of one encounter, 'which I said were devils in the likeness of men, singing for joy that they had overcome me.'[86] Thus fear of the physical Devil was bred by the supposed certainty of reprobation.[87] But it is striking that, as these reminiscences were assimilated into a progressive narrative for spiritual autobiography, the reality of Satan's physical manifestation was often challenged implicitly. Whilst the reality of his intrusion into the mind was accepted absolutely, the perception of his physical presence was taken to be a symptom of the effect of his persuasions on the conscience. His sophistry

82 Baxter, *Reliquiae Baxterianae*, p. 21.
83 Richard Norwood, *Journal*, p. 93; see also the experience of E. C. in Powell, *Spirituall Experiences*, pp. 82–3.
84 Bunyan, *Grace abounding*, p. 34. 85 Powell, *Spirituall Experiences*, p. 175.
86 Allen, [*Satan his Methods and Malice baffled*], p. 22.
87 Powell, *Spirituall Experiences*, pp. 175, 235, 272, 330; Laurence Clarkson, *The Lost sheep Found: or, The Prodigal returned to his Fathers house* (London, 1660), pp. 6–7.

had convinced his victims of their impending damnation and so they waited for him to carry them to hell. But the end of spiritual autobiography was assurance of election, a position that made any appearance of God's hangman impossible, and which in turn may have cast doubt over the likelihood of his appearance as a physical tempter. Thus Bunyan described how in his distraction he 'thought' he felt the Devil.[88] 'M. K.' screamed in terror, but then 'perceived it was a dog and not the Devill'. Similarly, all of Hannah Allen's encounters were cases of mistaken identity, being men talking in the street or the lights of a neighbour's house.[89] Richard Norwood, unusually, remained convinced that he had been physically assaulted by Satan, but understood these intense experiences to be an aspect of chronic spiritual temptation. He was also careful to point out that his 'sensible annoyance' by Satan involved 'no visible appearance'.[90] Indeed, Norwood accepted the interpretation he found in Perkins' *Cases of Conscience* that his physical sufferings stemmed from a demonic possession of his bedchamber rather than himself. When he took to sleeping elsewhere he was no longer troubled physically, but his internal temptations remained constant.[91] Thus the logic of Protestant soteriology supported the perception of the internal temptation, but tended to undermine sufferers' confidence in the reality of his physical manifestations.

An insight into the uncertainty that surrounded the notion of the physical manifestation of the Devil is provided by John Rogers in his account of his temptation to witchcraft. Rogers was ostracised as a result of his willingness to associate with Roundheads, and he was 'turned out of doors . . . with three shillings and six pence, or thereabouts . . . to travell up and down in strange countries'. Forced to beg as he travelled to Cambridge, his near-starvation in the depths of winter drove him to eat grass and leather. 'I met with temptations in this wildernesse', Rogers explained, 'to turn stones into bread, and the Devill did often tempt me to study Necromancy & Nigromancy, and to make use of Magick, and to make a league with him, and then I should never want'.[92] The narrative is familiar in the light of the stories told by convicted witches of the ways in which the Devil approached them to persuade them to trade their souls for power and subsistence. But if it is familiar, it is unusual in that there is no suggestion of the Devil's physical presence, the defining element of the witch's pact narrative. Rogers' story was in fact an amalgam of this with the story of Christ's temptation in the desert – the Devil also

88 See also John Rogers' account of his 'frights', in *Ohel or Beth-Shemesh*, pp. 426–7, and the testimony of Edward Wayman that he had been terrified by a dream of the Devil appearing as a black dog, p. 409.

89 See also the case of A. H. in Powell, *Spirituall Experiences*, pp. 272–3, in which he connects an apparition of Satan with being 'distempered in my mind'.

90 Norwood, *Journal*, p. 93. 91 Ibid., pp. 102–3, 104–5.

92 Rogers, *Ohel or Beth-shemesh*, pp. 432–3.

offered Rogers 'the glory of the world' if he would fall down and worship him. Thus Rogers appealed to a very well-understood mechanism of apostasy, whilst at the same time incorporating it within the spiritual discourse that, for Protestants, defined experiential demonism. That this was so is even more striking given that Rogers emphasised earlier in the same account the regularity with which he had believed he had seen the Devil as a symptom of the extremity of his suffering.[93]

However, whilst experiences of temptation could be profound, we should be wary of automatically interpreting them as a symptom of the lonely obsession that characterised the lives of sufferers like Nehemiah Wallington. Temptation was cyclical, oscillating in strength and threat, and assimilated as one discernible, discrete experience in the canvas of a godly life. The diary of Lady Margaret Hoby demonstrates how routine temptation could be. Margaret wished to set down her adherence to a personal godly regime, and her diary is an uncluttered record of her daily observances. As she attended church or examined her conscience, so sometimes she found herself afflicted by diabolic temptations, as her entries for the early summer of 1602 reveal. On 6 May she recorded that she was thankful that God kept her in good health but that he had 'suffered satan to afflicte my mind'. The Devil did not find her unprepared, since she knew God offered her an opportunity to demonstrate her faith by placing all her hopes of deliverance in Him. Her next entry on the 20th summarised events since the 6th, and seemingly God had provided 'comfort euerie way' and Satan was not mentioned. Only three entries were made for June, and in the final entry, dated Sunday 27th, she summarised the past week. Satan had 'not ceased to cast his malice' upon her health, although she was well. But the Devil had also afflicted her mind. 'Temptations hath exercised me', she recorded, 'and it hath pleased my god to deliuer me from all.' An obscure entry of two weeks later – 'this day ... I was provoked to be disquiated' – hinted at some form of temptation, and in her next entry, after a further week, Satan was uppermost in her thoughts. Notably, whilst at church, Margaret suspected that she felt the early signs of a coming diabolic assault, and her diary offered her an opportunity to prepare for it. 'This day I hard the exercises and now, as though Satan would returne, I felte his buffets: but I know God will make them profitable to me.' By the end of the month temptation had certainly come upon her and she recorded on Sunday 1 August that she had to 'suffer satans buffetts so that I hard not the morninge excercise so frutfully as I ought'.[94]

[93] Ibid., pp. 426–7.

[94] Margaret Hoby, *The Diary of Lady Margaret Hoby 1599–1605*, ed. D. M. Meads (London, 1930), pp. 197–9.

Often Lady Hoby made a conscious effort to point out the routine nature of these temptations. On 26 August 1599 she felt Satan attempting to distract her in church, but, although the experience merited attention, it reflected only how constantly she was in the Devil's sights. She noted, 'this day, *as euer*, the diuell laboreth to hinder the profittable hearing of the word and callinge vpon god'.[95] She also felt her experience of temptation was sufficiently wide that she might know it at a moment, as when, in a seemingly commonplace occurrence, she recognised Satan tempting her to anger – 'after priuat prairs I went about, and had occasion to chide, which I ever take to be a buffitt of satans Malice'.[96] When discussing her experiences she was characteristically taciturn, only occasionally revealing what form these temptations might have taken. Even in these instances, the nature of the temptation was of less significance than the fact that, by God's help, it was overcome. A representative example is recorded in the margin next to the entry for 19 February 1601. She wrote: 'this day the diuell would have brought me in to question the truth of gods word which by the certefecate of godes spiritt in my hart wch had heretofore wrought in the same was soon vanquished'. The entries dealing with the temptations of the summer of 1602 were not so much records of the onset of temptation, but records of the fact of deliverance. Margaret made an entry when she was able to thank God for having delivered her, and only once did she write in the midst of a temptation. After August the Devil fell from view and Margaret did not mention temptation again. But having been released from a period of intermittent temptation of at least three months, there is no indication that she viewed the period as a watershed, or felt she had received any extraordinary assurance or insight as a result of having overcome the Devil. It was simply part of the experience of godliness: useful in providing a chance to experience God's benign providence, but no more than that.

When writing their books on afflicted consciences, Protestant divines like Thomas Becon, William Perkins and Lewis Bayly had recognised the experience of competing thoughts, and characterised it as a dialogue with Satan within the soul. The godly assimilated the notion, not simply because it was part of Protestant rhetoric, but because it accorded with their real experiences. Thus many perceived very forcefully a dialogue within their conscience as they attempted to stifle unwelcome thoughts. Understanding the origins of the thoughts that appeared in their consciences allowed the godly to identify Satan's voice 'tangibly' within them.[97] The Baptist Sarah Davy described temptation thus: 'the Devil would be ready to tell me that it was not my part, I was too apt to catch at children's bread and think that my own

95 Ibid., p. 66, my emphasis. 96 Ibid., 27 October 1601, p. 190.
97 Powell, *Spirituall Experiences*, p. 143.

[salvation] which did not belong to me', and 'he would often persuade me I was a hypocrite, and that I was fallen from grace'.[98] Similarly, Hannah Allen described Satan's intrusions to her aunt, noting, 'I am just as if two were fighting within me.'[99] The Kendal man John Gilpin produced a remarkable description of his experience of the Devil speaking within him in an account of his bewitchment into Quakerism in 1653.[100] This voice persuaded Gilpin that he was elect, but he was constantly beset with doubts as to 'whether it was really good, or I were under Satans delusions'.[101]

Of course, the identification of the satanic voice suggests that the godly were projecting their unwelcome thoughts onto an external force. Darren Oldridge has interpreted internal temptation in this way, and Richard Godbeer has suggested that a correlation can be seen between individual spiritual self-confidence and willingness to take responsibility for sin, rather than projecting it onto the Devil.[102] Such a psychological explanation must to some extent account for the experience of temptation, but it is ultimately unsatisfactory. For diabolic intrusion did not separate subversive thoughts from the conscience and so relieve cognitive dissonance by externalisation. Protestant writers never intended that it should, but rather that it should do the reverse, forcing a self-conscious and often sustained engagement with the experience of sin, guilt and the demonic. As Richard Capel noted, 'most times our temptations are mixt, [the Devil] and we concur and make one act of tempting; the sin finished is his and ours too'.[103]

Godly testimonies reveal the assimilation of this impetus to engagement. At the point at which the Devil's voice was identified the godly felt impelled to meet and attempt to answer it. Thus godly testimonies commonly rationalised temptation into a dialogue. This offered the possibility of dispelling the confusion wrought on the conscience by intrusive thoughts, and was in line with the conventions of afflicted conscience literature. The characterisations given to the satanic voice, therefore, reflected the nature of the temptations godly individuals were experiencing. For example, Richard Norwood characterised the 'inward whispering of Satan' as the voice of a gloating tormentor, and his sense of envelopment by diabolic power is transparent:

> And for thyself, thou art as surely in my hands and power as ever was any man. Well I may give thee leave to wriggle a while this or that way; better were it for thee to be quiet. Thou shalt no whit avail, but rather increase my rage so much the more to sweep thee away suddenly and torment thee so much more grievously when thou art

[98] Davy, *Heaven realiz'd*, pp. 8, 9. [99] Allen, [*Satan his Methods and Malice baffled*], p. 8.
[100] John Gilpin, *The Qvakers Shaken: or, A Fire-brand snatch'd out of the Fire* (Gateside, 1653).
[101] Ibid., pp. 11, 12, 14.
[102] Oldridge, *The Devil*, pp. 46–7; Godbeer, *The Devil's Dominion*, pp. 96–103.
[103] Capel, *Tentations*, p. 30.

in hell. And indeed thy time is even at hand. Thou needs not provoke me to make it shorter than it is. Thou shalt speedily see what shall become of thee.[104]

Sarah Davy characterised the Devil as an evil guardian angel, who constantly pestered her with questions to undermine her assurance. His suggestions made her 'soul walk heavily under much dispute a long time', and he was always on hand to 'rob' her of the benefit of 'many a sermon'.[105] Similarly, Hannah Allen perceived her temptations as a contest over the bible, in which Satan laboured to destroy any comfort she might gain from scripture. In response she kept a record of her afflictions, allowing her dialogue with Satan to take place on paper. On the 12 May 1664 she wrote: 'the Devil tempts me woefully to hard and strange thoughts of my dear Lord which, through his mercy, I dread and abhor the assenting to', and she composed an 'earnest prayer' imploring God to strengthen her. 'This I write to see what God will do with me', she concluded.[106] When her writings became the focal point of her temptations, the Devil attempted to undermine them. 'I never intended any eye should see them', she explained when she showed them to her aunt, 'but the Devil suggesteth dreadful things to me against God, and that I am a hypocrite.'[107] On occasion Hannah and her relatives played out the dialogue themselves, with Hannah, unsurprisingly, taking the Devil's part. Her aunt challenged her identification of the 'devils' singing outside her room, explaining that God never sent a miracle to show damnation. Allen simply appropriated a favoured argument of the Devil and declared that her reprobation was unparalleled.[108]

But in contrast to the picture of victimisation offered by the historians of afflicted conscience, the sense of the dialogue with the Devil might also be a source of strength for the tempted and those who watched over them. For it could dispel the tyranny intrusive thoughts exercised over the conscience by identifying lines of defence and counter-argument. Thrown into a panic by the demonic obstruction of her death-bed devotions, Katherine Brettergh's sense of dialogue provided her with something to cling to since it allowed her to exercise some control over her thoughts by *publicly* withdrawing from the conflict. It was remembered 'she said: Satan reason not with me, I am but a weake woman, if thou haue anything to say, say it to my Christ, he is my aduocate, my strength, and my redeemer, and he shall pleade for mee'.[109] Hannah Allen's mother was far less sympathetic to her troubles than her aunt, but even she found it politic to enter into the logic of her spiritual debate. Once, when Hannah was 'wearying' her mother with claims that she was dying, the

[104] Norwood, *Journal*, p. 99. [105] Davy, *Heaven realiz'd*, p. 8.
[106] Allen, [*Satan his Methods and Malice baffled*], pp. 17–18.
[107] Ibid., p. 9. [108] Ibid., pp. 22–3.
[109] *A brief discovrse of the Christian life and death, of Mistris Katherin Brettergh*, pp. 13–15.

two made an agreement that if she died during the night her mother would believe that she had been damned. As they watched through the early hours they heard a loud knock on the chamber door, which Hannah took to be the arrival of Satan, saying, 'You see, mother, though I died not tonight, the Devil came to let you know that I am damned.' But her mother beat her at her own game, replying, 'but you see he had no power to come into the chamber'.[110]

Philip Stubbes' account of his wife Katherine's dying combat with the Devil is suggestive of the theatre which could surround such public expressions of the dialogue. The Devil was on hand to obstruct her final devotions, and the onlookers knew of his approach by the change on Katherine's face. Suddenly she 'bent the browes, shee frowned, and looking (as it were) with an angry, sterne, and fierce counternaunce, as though she sawe some filthy, ugglesome and displeasant thing'. She then burst into a lengthy tirade in which she tormented the Devil, turning the dialogue on its head. She repeated the temptations he offered, for the benefit of those watching, prefacing them with 'How now Satan?' and 'What sayest thou more, Satan?', before demolishing them by claiming her assurance of election had made her 'bold' enough to treat him with disdain. Understanding that sin was a trial that beset the godly only in the world, she pursued the logic and took the unusual step of bequeathing to Satan the sins which she no longer needed since her dissolution was near. Since it was Satan who had first provided her with sin, its return was to effect a dramatic public severance of any relationship with the Devil, who was left with no alternative but to 'runne away like a beaten cocke', as she told the onlookers.[111]

In spiritual autobiographies, temptation, and victories over it, demarcated discrete stages in the subject's progression towards assurance. The dialogue with the Devil served to rehearse the arguments for salvation, and with each temptation overcome Satan had to employ more complex sophistries to meet his victim's growing soteriological sophistication. Thus Elizabeth Wilkinson characterised her afflictions as a progressive battle between intrusive thoughts of reprobation and a progressive discovery of comforting scriptures. Lewis Bayly's *The Practice of Pietie* produced in twelve-year-old Wilkinson an intense fear of damnation, unsurprising given that it opens with a vivid description of the 'fullnesse of cursednesse' experienced by the reprobate after death.[112] Her fear of hell defined her entire early response to religion, which

[110] Allen, [*Satan his Method and Malice baffled*], pp. 29–30.

[111] Philip Stubbes, *A Christal Glasse for Christian Women containing, A most Excellent Discourse, of the godly life and Christian death of Mistresse Katherine Stubbes* (London, 1592), sigs. C2v–C3v.

[112] Damnation was to be spent as an eternity in 'the bottomlesse lake of utter darknesse' in which the condemned would 'always weepe for the paine of the fire, and yet gnash [their] teeth for the extremity of the cold'; Bayly, *The Practice of Pietie*, pp. 64–5.

she characterised as a simplistic desire for safety intruding on her mind to tempt her selfishness.[113] At the height of these troubles Wilkinson encountered Calvin's *Institutes of Christian Religion*, or rather, as she later interpreted it, she was providentially guided to the book by God. His reassurance that even fallen man retained enough of God's image to redress his more general corruption provided 'such satisfaction' to Wilkinson, that her original temptations never returned.[114] But now she began to believe that in originally discounting God's mercy she had committed the one sin of faithlessness that would guarentee her damnation. Again the source of this ironic self-sabotage was located in an internal intrusion, and again providence provided a book in which she might find assurance, this time Henry Scudder's *The Christian's Daily Walke in Holy Securitie and Peace*. In the book she found a systematic description of atheism and was able to satisfy her mind that she exhibited none of 'the marks of that sin'.[115] Although she experienced no final assurance, this progressive cycle of despair and comfort continued throughout Wilkinson's life.[116]

Similarly, Sarah Davy's spiritual progression was embodied in the changing nature of her temptations, and her responses to them. She overcame her initial troubles by familiarising herself with the promises of scripture, and the assurances of afflicted conscience literature, finding convincing retorts to all the Devil's arguments that she must be damned. In doing so she ceased to be a bewildered novice, and was now armed against Satan with the insight of her reading. Immediately Satan altered his tactics and tried to deceive her into complacency. 'How had the Devil changed his note', she recollected, 'and told my proud heart my state was now good and my graces were much increased, for which I ought to be much esteemed.' So for a while Davy was content only to exhibit the outward signs of election, anything that would win her the praise of the godly. The change in the Devil's tone was noteworthy in itself, but more significant was the way in which Davy's succumbing to it reflected on her spiritual development. The insight she had gained by her

113 Clarke, *The Lives of Thirty-two English Divines*, pp. 420–1; similarly, see Laurence Clarkson's exposure to *The Practise of Pietie*, in *The Lost sheep Found*, p. 5; and John Bunyan's early wish that he could be a devil so that he 'might be rather a tormentor, then tormented', in *Grace abounding*, pp. 5–6.

114 Clarke, *The Lives of Thirty-two English Divines*, p. 421.

115 Stachniewski describes Scudder's *The Christians Daily Walke in Securitie and Peace* as 'deceptively titled', noting that Michael Wigglesworth recorded in his diary that by reading the book he became convinced that he had sinned against the Holy Ghost. But Wilkinson's reaction demonstrates how different individuals' readings of the same godly text could be, and that lengthy descriptions of the symptoms of sin were as likely to convince the aspiring godly of their innocence as their guilt. Again we should be wary of presenting the lay response to conduct literature as monolithic. See *The Persecutory Imagination*, p. 91.

116 Similarly, see the autobiography of E. R. in Powell's *Spirituall Experiences*, pp. 357–68.

reading had been demonstrably wasted, and whilst falling prey to Satan's suggestions might be understandable in a novice, it was a serious failing in one who had already experienced God's deliverance. 'Oh wicked wretch', Davy chastised herself, 'that after so much love should dare to be so careless as to let Satan steal away my heart.'[117]

Perhaps no text exhibits a more profound sense of temptation as a progressive dialogue than John Bunyan's *Grace abounding to the chief of sinners.* Hindsight in the text was not simply a literary technique, it was the exercise of a godly understanding that, in its ability to reassess past experiences, demonstrated its sophistication and maturity. Bunyan characterised his troubles as a constant renewal of temptation every time he was able to progress spiritually. In *Grace abounding* the Devil is afforded far greater characterisation than is common in spiritual autobiographies. The voice of Satan in Bunyan's mind was gloating and arrogant, attempting to intimidate with past triumphs:

> the Tempter hath come upon me also with such discouragements as these: You are very hot for mercy, but I will cool you; this frame shall not last alwayes; many have been as hot as you for a spirt, but I have quench'd their Zeal (and with this such and such who were fallen off, would be set before mine eyes) then I should be afraid that I should do so too: but, thought I, I am glad this comes into my minde; well, I will watch and take heed what I can: Though you do, said Satan, I shall be too hard for you, I will cool you insensibly, by degrees, by little and little; what care I, saith he, though I be seven years in chilling your heart, if I can do it at last; continual rocking will lull a crying Child asleep; I will ply it close, but I will have my end accomplished: though you be burning hot at present, yet, if I can pull you from this fire, I shall have you cold before long.[118]

The Devil's character changed to overcome any progression in Bunyan's spiritual sophistication. Thus it was a Satan as realist who tempted Bunyan to accept Ranter doctrine as a means to make his reprobation more bearable. Since Bunyan was damned anyway he might as well believe with the Ranters that there was no Judgement Day:

> For if these things should indeed be true, yet to believe otherwise, would yield you ease for the present. If you must perish, never torment yourself so much beforehand, drive the thoughts of damning out of your mind, by possessing your mind some such conclusions that Atheists and Ranters use to help themselves withal.[119]

This greater characterisation allowed Bunyan's debates with the Devil to be made more dynamic, and they argued, not only over the general question of election, but also over the finer points of scripture. The centrality of the

[117] Davy, *Heaven realiz'd*, p. 11; similarly, see the cyclical experience of affliction in the testimonies of Thomas Huggins, John Bywater, John Hewson and Rapheal Swinford in John Rogers' *Ohel or Beth-shemesh*, pp. 393–7. Rogers himself gave a full account of the consistent renewal of his temptations, pp. 420–1, 422, 426–7, 429, 432–5.

[118] Bunyan, *Grace abounding*, p. 35. [119] Ibid., p. 49.

bible in providing the soteriological truths by which the Devil might be countered also made it the most dangerous site of conflict. For if providence might guide a sufferer to a comforting scripture, Satan might lead him to a promise of damnation. In *Grace abounding* the Devil commonly transforms himself into an angel of light, forcing Bunyan to remember or pay special attention to specific texts which could undermine assurance. One such text that gave Bunyan trouble was Romans 9: 16 – 'it is neither in him that willeth, nor in him that runneth, but in God that sheweth mercy' – which he noted 'did seem to me to trample upon all my desires' by showing that the mere practice of godliness could not guarantee salvation. The Devil was on hand to encourage his despair:

O Lord, thought I, what if I should not [be saved] indeed? It may be you are not, said the Tempter: it may be so indeed, thought I. Why then, said Satan, you had as good leave off, and strive no further; for if indeed you should not be Elected and chosen of God, there is no talke of your being saved: For it is neither in him that willeth, nor in him that runneth, but in God that sheweth mercy.[120]

The effect of this scripture was to drive Bunyan to his 'wits end', and his torment was accentuated by the fact that he did not at that time realise it was the Devil who assaulted him. 'I little thought that Satan had thus assaulted me', he noted, 'but rather that it was my own prudence thus to start the question.'[121]

Once Bunyan was able to discern the Devil's temptations the struggle over scripture became less one-sided. He recalled John 6: 37. – 'and him that cometh to me I will in no wise cast out' – as one of the most enduringly comforting scriptures he encountered, but described the great efforts Satan went to to undermine it. The words 'in no wise', Bunyan took to mean that no sin was unpardonable, but he noted: 'Satan would greatly labour to pull this promise from me, telling of me, that Christ did not mean me, and such as I, but sinners of a lower rank.'[122] 'If ever Satan and I did strive for any word of God in all my life', Bunyan remembered, 'it was for this good word of Christ; he at one end and I at the other. Oh, what work we did make! It was for this in John, I say, that we did so tug and strive: he pull'd and I pull'd but, God be praised, I got the better of him, I got some sweetness from it.'[123] His developed spiritual awareness allowed him to see in retrospect the fundamental weakness of the Devil's case:

And this I well remember still, that of all the sleights that Satan used to take this Scripture from me, yet never did so much as put this Question, But do you come aright? And I have thought the reason was, because he thought I knew full well what comming a-right was; for I saw that to come aright was to come as I was, a vile and ungodly sinner, and to cast myself at the feet of Mercy, condemning myself for sin.

[120] Ibid., pp. 20–1. [121] Ibid., p. 21. [122] Ibid., p. 67. [123] Ibid., pp. 67–8.

Satan, who had once seemed an omniscient biblical scholar, able to devastate assurance with a few well-chosen quotes, was now revealed as only a talented disputant, selectively employing those scriptures which most readily supported his case and skirting around those he knew to confound his arguments.[124]

DIABOLIC AFFLICTION AND GODLY COMMUNITY

If experiences of diabolic intrusion were intensely personal, how did they affect the wider community of the godly? John Stachniewski has argued that Puritan self-victimisation left sufferers marginalised within a community which emphasised the restricted nature of election, and the absolute applicability of reprobation. Indeed many of the struggling godly did experience an intense isolation among those whose assurance they were unable to share. Often the belief that temptation equalled reprobation produced a fear that the godly would ostracise them should their condition become known. Elizabeth Wilkinson remembered that in her earliest temptations she could not bring herself to reveal her condition to others because 'I did not think that it was so with any other as it was with me.' Although Katherine Clarke was a member of a godly congregation, and gained some comfort from sermons during her adolescent afflictions, there were no others that she felt she could consult as to her temptations. Sarah Davy, who would become a Baptist, was isolated outside her godly community, noting, 'there was few I was aquainted with whom I could in the least have any converse with in the whole town, thus did I labour to keep my troubles to myself'.[125] Moreover, Stachniewski argues, godly ministers and laity were more likely to be on hand to confirm self-accusations of reprobation than dispute them. Sons of thunder like William Perkins and Richard Rogers could apparently inspire terror in their audiences when they preached of the terrible fate awaiting the damned.[126]

But whilst such fears were real, they may have been overpessimistic and other evidence provides a balance to the picture of isolation. Richard Norwood came to believe that a lack of godly company had actually accentuated his sufferings.[127] Sir Simonds D'Ewes recorded in his Middle Temple diary that he had spent one evening in January 1624 in the company of a Dr Haltern, 'an ancient lawyer'. 'Wee had much good discourse about the

[124] Ibid., p. 67.

[125] Clarke, *The Lives of Thirty-two English Divines*, p. 420; Clarke, *The Lives of sundry Eminent Persons*, p. 152; Davy, *Heaven realiz'd*, pp. 8–9, quote at p. 9.

[126] Stachniewski, *The Persecutory Imagination*, p. 86.

[127] Norwood, *Journal*, pp. 98, 100, 103.

temptations of the devil', D'Ewes recorded, 'and how stranglie a gentleman of the Middle Temple had been afflicted.' Whilst D'Ewes goes into no further detail, the conversation took place several months after he had recorded that he had been assaulted by Satan, and we might speculate that he discussed his own experiences.[128] M. K., in Powell's *Spirituall Experiences*, described how in her early despair friends and ministers had sought to assure her that she was simply too young to have had time to commit all the sins she believed herself guilty of. Similarly, another of Powell's contributors, F. P., described being delivered from temptation after 'many comfortable discourses from friends'.[129] Moreover, temptation might be seen by others to grant its sufferers an esoteric insight into the workings of the spirit. John Bunyan's conversion was the result of overhearing a conversation between 'three or four poor women' who expressed a faith which he was simply unable to comprehend. In fact the woman discussed their deliverance from temptation:

> they talked how God had visited their souls with his love in the Lord Jesus, and with what words and promises they had been refreshed, comforted, and supported against the temptations of the Devil; moreover, they reasoned of the suggestions and temptation of Satan in particular, and told each other by which they had been afflicted, and how they were borne up under his assaults.

Here is a picture of a group of people with a common understanding of diabolic activity, able to differentiate between specific temptations, and sharing their experiences under the assumption of mutual identification. It was Bunyan who felt isolated, not at this point by temptation, but by the belief he had not been afflicted.[130]

The belief that temptation had rewards in esoteric insight provides a significant challenge to Stachniewski's picture of the suffering godly's isolation. We have seen that Protestant ministers re-established their spiritual authority in part by mediating the resistance to the Devil to their parishioners. But the experiences of the victims themselves might equally influence ministers and help shape their understanding of the soteriological significance of temptation. Robert Harris was particularly affected by his encounter with Elizabeth Wilkinson, whose struggles he believed embodied progressive temptation and its soteriological importance. Forwarding her spiritual autobiography to a friend he explained how it illustrated Satan's changing temptations:

> His first attempt is to blow out all the light of the soul, and to quell all thoughts of a deity if possibly he can ... if that cannot be, but the Conscience will be sometimes talking; then his next work is to question and argue the case, whether indeed there be such a person as God, such a thing as the soul ... and if he cannot gain such a

[128] D'Ewes, *Diary*, p. 178.
[129] Powell, *Spirituall Experiences*, pp. 165–6; 238, see also p. 135.
[130] Bunyan, *Grace abounding*, pp. 14–15.

conclusion from the soul, then in the third place his question is, what manner a one this supposed God is? And first, whilst thou art under mercy, all of vengence and fury; there was no place for fear, and here is none for hope: there sin was an inconsiderable thing, and beneath Gods conscience; here sin is unpardonable, and beyond Gods mercy: In both estates he labours the destruction of faith; now in threats, then in promises.[131]

To arm themselves with a foreknowledge of Satan's temptations the aspiring godly could do little better than consult Wilkinson's narrative, for 'though sometimes he shifts his hands and findes out new wayes yet here lies his road for the most part'.[132] In some cases godly individuals could themselves take on the role of spiritual counsellors by virtue of the intensity of their temptations. Thus Sarah Wight was regularly resorted to by tempted godly, even though she herself was recognised to be suffering profoundly. Whilst, as Dr Stachniewski points out, this could often lead to a competition over who could claim the deepest reprobation, Wight was perceived by those who sought her out, and by those who observed and reported her conversations, to be possessed of an especial insight into both the experience of temptation, and the wider truths of the faith.[133]

Robert Harris also noted of Elizabeth Wilkinson's long-term illness that she 'was yearly dying before she dyed her last'. Her sickness had allowed her to prepare for a godly death which would be an active victory over Satan.[134] This points to another area in which deeply personal struggles with the Devil could have a profound effect on the wider godly community. Accounts of death-bed experiences were produced in large numbers, with the edifying words of dying saints avidly recorded. Indeed the transitional stage between life and death seems to have been viewed as a period of special insight in which impending dissolution brought the dying closer to the knowledge of God.[135] It might also give force to the experience of diabolic conflict. Ralph Houlbrooke has suggested that spiritual crises during last sickness were relatively rare, but the medieval *ars moriendi* tradition predicted that the dying would be assaulted by Satan, a prediction that was maintained in the guides written by Thomas Becon and William Perkins.[136] Protestantism had

[131] Clarke, *The Lives of Thirty-two English Divines*, pp. 424–5. [132] Ibid., p. 425.

[133] Jessey, *The exceeding Riches of Grace Advanced*, pp. 45–125.

[134] Ibid., p. 426. Similarly, see *The Christian Life and Death of Mistris Katherin Brettergh*, sig. B3.

[135] R. Houlbrooke, 'The Puritan Death-Bed, c. 1560–c. 1660', in C. Durston and J. Eales (eds.), *The Culture of English Puritanism* (Houndmills, 1996), pp. 139–40; A similar assumption lent force to the didactic moralising of penitent criminals as they spoke from the scaffold and warned of the consequences of sin, whilst in witchcraft accounts the identification of the witch by a dying victim was accorded special weight. See J. A. Sharpe, '"Last Dying Speeches": Religion, Ideology and Public Execution in Seventeenth Century England', *Past and Present*, 107 (1985), pp. 150–4.

[136] Houlbrooke, 'The Puritan Death-Bed', pp. 124–5, 135; William Perkins, *Salve for a Sicke Man. Or, a treatise containing the nature, differences and kindes of death*, in *Works*, vol. I, pp. 492–3.

done away with the common *ars moriendi* image of the death-bed conflict as a battle between demons and angels with the dying looking passively on.[137] The responsibility for overcoming the last temptation was shifted onto the individual and the heightened spiritual insight of the death-bed scene gave struggles with Satan a greater significance for the wider community.

The physical intensity of death-bed temptations imbued diabolic struggle with a tangibility for the observers that may have reinforced the soteriological significance of affliction in their own minds. The reformer John Knox lay for several hours 'very often giving great sighes, sobbes, and groans, so as the standers by well perceived that he was troubled with some grievous temptation'. He explained to those present that, as a final twist in their progressive life-long battle, the 'wily serpent' had tempted him to assurance, in order to overcome his vigilance at the last minute. Recalling appropriate scriptures had allowed him to resist the Devil, a deliverance he abjectly attributed to God's providence.[138] In 1644, Julines Herring was assaulted by Satan the night before he died: 'as was perceived by those who were then with him; for rising upon his knees, with his hands lifted up, he spake these words: He is ouercome, ouercome, through the strength of my Lord.' Similarly John Dod spent his last days expounding scripture to those who attended on him, and 'spake to one that watched with him all night, about two of the Clock in the morning, that he had been wrestling with Satan all that night, who accused him that he neither preached, nor prayed, nor performed any duty as he should have done, for manner or for end, but he said, I haue answered him from the example of the prodigal and the publican.'[139] As we have already seen in the cases of Katherine Stubbes and Katherine Brettergh, the edification derived from public death-bed conflicts with Satan was not confined to the ministry.

Thus whilst Protestant demonism in general emphasised the commonplace nature of demonic temptation, the introspective culture of the godly allowed it to be seen as a rarefied experience for those of tender conscience, which carried with it an inherent sophistication of spiritual insight. Richard Baxter described how, as his spiritual sophistication increased, he was able to make use of the opportunities offered by temptation. 'Though formerly I was wont', he remembered, 'when any such Temptation came, to cast it aside, as fitter to be abhorred than considered of, yet now . . . I was fain to dig to the very Foundations, and seriously Examine the reasons of Christianity, and give hearing to all that could be said against it, that so my Faith might indeed be my own.'[140] It was surely this understanding that motivated the godly to

[137] Duffy, *The Stripping of the Altars*, pp. 313–27. [138] Perkins, *Salve for a Sicke Man*, p. 514.
[139] Clarke, *The Lives of Thirty-two English Divines*, pp. 168, 178.
[140] Baxter, *Reliquiae Baxterianae*, p. 22.

record their experiences of the Devil in diaries and private (unpublished) autobiographies. As Dr Stachniewski himself has shown in his identification of Puritan 'one-downsmanship', even the intense perception of reprobation was understood to be a rarefied spiritual experience by those who suffered it.[141] Many of the godly saw their deliverance from temptation as setting them apart from those who had experienced no such special grace. Margaret Corbet apparently used to declare that, 'I was in the Deuils claws, but Jesus Christ, the sweet Bridegroom of my soul ... hath deliuered me.' Even during periods of affliction some sufferers showed an awareness of the esoteric nature of temptation in their dealings with other godly, and it could arm them against others' assessments of their reprobation. In pointing to the lack of sympathy among the assured godly, Stachniewski cites the experience of Bunyan who, when he plucked up the courage to tell 'an ancient Christian' that he believed he had sinned against the Holy Ghost, received the answer that 'he thought so too'.[142] But Stachniewski ignores Bunyan's final verdict on the ancient Christian, who he concluded was 'though a good man, a stranger to much Combate with the Devil'. However they might have liked to present themselves, those who were untroubled by Satan were not necessarily believed to have a monopoly of insight into election, and Bunyan finally decided to discount a judgement not based on experience.[143]

Finally, another of Bunyan's experiences provides a significant sidelight on the place of demonic experience within the culture of the godly community. Perhaps uniquely, Bunyan hinted at the potential dangers of the vigilance that was so often argued to be the best defence against temptation. Resisting temptation involved cultivating a profound sense of distrust in the origins of one's own thoughts that could, according to Bunyan, be disastrously misplaced on occasion. Once, he remembered, when 'ready to sink with fear, suddenly there was as there had rushed in at the window, the noise of Wind upon me'. In this wind he heard a voice, with which he conversed in exactly the same way as he had debated with the Devil. The voice questioned him,

> *Didst ever refuse to be justified by the Blood of Christ*? and withal my whole life of profession past, was in a moment opened to me, wherein I was made to see, that designedly I had not; so my heart answered groaningly No. Then fell with power that word of God upon me, *See that ye refuse not him that speaketh*, Heb. 12. 25. This made strange seisure upon my spirit; it brought light with it, and commanded a silence in my heart of all those tumultuous thoughts that before did use, like hell-hounds, to roar and bellow, and make a hideous noise within me.[144]

[141] Stachniewski, *The Persecutory Imagination*, pp. 40–1.
[142] Stachniewski gives a detailed, but over-played, description of isolation in Bunyan's *Grace abounding*. See ibid., pp. 133–6.
[143] Bunyan, *Grace abounding*, p. 55; Stachniewski, *The Persecutory Imagination*, pp. 134–5.
[144] Bunyan, *Grace abounding*, p. 53.

But although Bunyan experienced comfort as a result of this voice, he could not accept it at face value. 'As to my determining about this strange dispensation', he recalls, 'what it was I knew not; from whence it came, I knew not. I have not in twenty years time been able to make a Judgement of it.' Bunyan's implication, however, was that he believed the experience to be another deceit of the Devil, and he noted 'I thought then what here I should be loath to speak.' He was reluctant to recall his thoughts because he had since decided the voice was a message from God. But he concluded with an equivocation, 'that rushing Wind, was as if an Angel had come upon me; but both it and the Salvation I will leave until the Day of Judgement'.[145] Thus over-vigilance might lead to the sin of faithlessness, but the paradox was born out of the relatively uncontentious nature of demonic experience within godly culture. When looking for signs of election and rarefied spiritual experience, the perception of the Devil's agency was unproblematic compared with the dangerous extremist or antinomian potential of providence. When recording his demonic experiences, Bunyan dealt in matters of fact, assuming his readership's acceptance of the normality of such occurrences, even perhaps their identification with them. But he was far more uneasy recalling contact with a seemingly divine or angelic messenger. In the godly search for signs of election, the experience of a extraordinary personal communion was far more contentious than the notion that salvation might be discerned in the special attention of the Devil.[146]

Thus, far from being a marginal aspect of their culture, demonism was central to many of the godly's conception of the world, and to the observances by which they organised their lives. In line with Protestant convention, cosmic theodicy found little place in the godly's contemplation. Instead they were concerned with the nature of man's intimate relationship with Satan, defined by the fall and revolving around the experience of internal temptation. If the very expectation of temptation was self-fulfilling, this does not diminish the reality of the experience for those who felt themselves to be afflicted. But affliction, and responses to it, varied enormously. Some, like Simonds D'Ewes, seem to have been able to assimilate rare experiences with relative ease. Others, like Margaret Hoby, were afflicted more consistently, but placed temptation within a cyclical scheme which made it manageable. The extent and depth of affliction was, unsurprisingly, a result of individual personality. There is no evidence to suggest that extreme affliction was an inherent consequence of Protestant theology, only that it was produced by an individual susceptibility to the belief in reprobation. But whilst there are

145 Ibid.

146 See also Abiezer Coppe, *A Fiery Flying Roll: A Word from the Lord to all the Great Ones* (London, 1649), p. 8.

marked variations in the nature of individuals' demonological beliefs and experiences in early modern England, a picture of what the Devil *was* to the godly emerges strongly. The experience of dislocation, of an insidious barrier to communion with God, manifesting itself in an uncontrollable subversion of the conscience from within, was how the godly commonly *felt* the Devil's presence. In the twenty-first century the experience would be understood as a relatively uncomplicated form of cognitive dissonance, produced by unrealistic expectations of personal piety and discipline. To many of the godly in Reformation England, it represented a very palpable intrusion of the demonic into their minds.

5

Incarnate devils: crime narratives, demonisation and audience empathy

Temptation provided the godly with intense personal experiences of Satan's agency, but what of those, probably the majority, whose religious and moral observance was too unreflective to incorporate the rigorous introspective scheme, which for the godly identified temptation and encouraged an engagement with the experience? Were complex experiences of temptation largely confined to zealous Protestants with the inclination to indulge in in-depth self-examination and, consequently, was the influence of the Protestant emphasis on the Devil's internal agency limited? Whilst the majority of the population of sixteenth- and seventeenth-century England have left no record of their demonological beliefs, those areas of culture which sought to appeal to a sense of the demonic provide insight into the potential for a far wider influence of the concept of internal temptation. Any study of demonism must take account of demonisation, identified by historians as prevalent from the medieval period to the present. The practice of stigmatisation by associating subjects with the Devil has been interpreted as a simplistic form of projection, in which groups and individuals were marginalised in a functionalist one-way exchange of meaning. Jews, heretics, criminals, witches and subversives might be made to appear alien and 'anti-human' by association with Satan, justifying their persecution.[1] Yet a very different picture is revealed by an examination of demonisation in early modern England – particularly the 'populist' demonisation of criminals which became a prevalent part of the developing pulp press. Cheap and accessible pamphlet narratives commonly depicted crime to be the result of a diabolic seduction into sin, and this chapter will suggest that such stories could only be fully understood through an empathy with the emotional experiences of the criminal as he succumbed to temptation.[2] These narratives qualitatively

[1] Cohn, *Europe's Inner Demons*, pp. 16–59; Moore, *The Formation of a Persecuting Society*, pp. 35, 64–5, 89–91, 123.

[2] Peter Lake, 'Deeds against Nature: Cheap Print, Protestantism and Murder in Seventeenth-Century England', in K. Sharpe and P. Lake (eds.), *Culture and Politics in Early Stuart England* (Houndmills, 1994), pp. 268–9; Lincoln B. Faller, *Turned to Account: The Forms and*

associated mundane and criminal temptations and opened up the possibility that the Devil could be experienced vicariously in populist and semi-literate culture. In drawing the reader into a mental world infused with diabolic agency the pulp press gave far wider transmission to the dominance of internal temptation in demonism, and the result was a radical shift in the role of demonisation. As Lincoln Faller has noted, it was not the 'otherness' of criminals that mattered in early modern culture, but their ordinariness.[3] Similarly, an emphasis on diabolic temptation placed at the heart of commonplace experience the mechanism by which men descended into the most heinous crimes. As a result, demonisation actually discouraged the belief that intimate demonic experience was an aberration which clearly identified society's marginalised enemies. Every man and woman had experienced the same temptations that led some to murder and witchcraft; thus the gap that separated them from these 'incarnate devils' was very small.

Indeed witchcraft narratives, which emphasised the physical presence of Satan and the otherness of witches, were, in this respect, unusual in pulp press demonism. The Devil who appeared as an animal to bargain for the witch's soul has long been considered an elite interpolation which sat uncomfortably with populist non-diabolic witch beliefs.[4] J. A. Sharpe has convincingly challenged this view, arguing that the folkloric elements of the animal familiar suggest the existence of a popular conception of the Devil.[5] But the place of the Devil in pulp press narratives of witchcraft was more complex – the result of an amalgam of different influences and agendas. Legal records and the populist stories contained within them were shaped by pamphleteers' desire to place narratives within a more sharply drawn Christian scheme, and so, whilst the common reciprocal trade between witch and Devil was prevalent (incorporating popular notions of blood culture and anti-motherhood), the Devil was also depicted as the tempter who took hold of the witch's malice and conflated it into murderous desires. Thus witchcraft narratives both maintained a scheme of temptation and 'othered' witches, and the explanation seems to lie in the contested nature of the crime. The physical presence of Satan and the marginalised character of the witch were explicitly used to attest to the reality of the invisible crime, and physical

Functions of Criminal Biography in Late Seventeenth- and Early Eighteenth-Century England (Cambridge, 1987), pp. 22–31. Sources containing narrative and fiction, once considered unreliable and unrepresentative as a basis for history, are being employed with increasing confidence by historians as a means of gaining insight into the cultural processes by which identity and experience were shaped. For examples of this approach see MacDonald, 'The Fearefull Estate of Francis Spira', pp. 35–7; David Lindley, *The Trials of Frances Howard: Fact and Fiction at the Court of King James* (London and New York, 1993).

3 Faller, *Turned to Account*, pp. 52–4.

4 Thomas, *Religion and the Decline of Magic*, p. 627.

5 Sharpe, *Instruments of Darkness*, pp. 75–8.

evidence of diabolism (such as the witch's mark) became increasingly important in proving the crime in court.[6] It was the crime itself, not the Devil's involvement in it, that was uncertain. By contrast, demonic involvement in murder seems to have been relatively uncontentious, and was enshrined in the standard indictment wording. Thus, whilst witchcraft shared many elements of the scheme of temptation which became prevalent in pulp press crime narratives, its specialised agendas ensured it remained a separate, if overlapping genre, which was characterised by its interest in the physical Devil.

REPORTING SATAN'S AGENCY: CRIME AND THE PULP PRESS

Stories of murder and witchcraft were a staple of the pulp press which burgeoned in England in the late sixteenth century.[7] From the 1560s onwards they became an increasingly prevalent part of the popular literature produced in London. Before 1600 ballads were slightly more common in depicting murder than pamphlet accounts (roughly 60 per cent of the output), possibly due to the speed and ease with which they could be produced, cashing in quickly on the scandal well-known cases evoked.[8] It was common for two or three ballads to be produced on a single murder case. For instance, the murder in 1589 of one Master Page in Plymouth, by the wife who had been forced to marry him, seems to have been a notorious crime. The story was incorporated into a pamphlet written by the hack Anthony Munday, and was recounted in at least four ballads, one by Thomas Deloney.[9] Other cases, such as the murder of a goldsmith called John Brewen, and of George Saunders (both by their wives), and the attempt of a Yorkshireman called Calverley to do away with his family, occasioned similar numbers of publications.[10] As the genre developed, the publication of pamphlets increased, eventually equalling the number of ballads.

[6] Holmes, 'Women: Witnesses and Witches', pp. 45–78.

[7] Sandra Clark, *The Elizabethan Pamphleteers: Popular Moralistic Pamphlets 1580–1640* (London, 1983), chapter 2.

[8] This discussion is based on the bibliography by Joseph Marshburn, *Murder and Witchcraft in England* (Norman, Okla., 1974), as the best introduction. Marshburn's book has various problems in that it is not comprehensive and describes some works as lost when they do actually survive.

[9] Munday, *Sundry Strange and Inhumaine Murthers*; *The Lamentation of Master Pages wife of Plimmouth* (no date), in *Pepys Ballads*, vol. I, pp. 126–7; Thomas Deloney, *The lamentation of Mr Pages wife of Plimouth* (no date), in *The Works of Thomas Deloney*, ed. F. O. Mann (Oxford, 1912), pp. 482–5.

[10] *Two Most unnatural and bloodie Murthers: the One by Maister Caverly, A Yorkshire Gentleman, practised upon his wife, and committed upon his two children, the tree and twentie of Aprill 1605* (London, 1605).

The pulp press narrative of how murder occurred was very much at odds with the real incidence and nature of the crime. Social historians have shown that if the level of interpersonal violence in the period was relatively high, the number of premeditated murders was low. The majority of murders were crimes of passion made fatal by the inability of the medical profession to competently treat the wounded.[11] Yet the writers of the murder accounts insisted that the crime was never spontaneous; it always occurred as the culmination of a protracted conflict or was the end of a long-term descent into sin.[12] Murder in the pamphlets was almost always premeditated. A widower named Lincoln from Warborne, near Ashford in Kent, was motivated to murder his children by the barrier they presented to his plans to re-marry. Envy at the success of his neighbour, Robert Greenoll, caused a mercer called Thomas Smith to lure his victim with a pretence of friendship, beat him to death and hide the body in his cellar.[13] Many narratives were built around what historians have identified as 'familiar murder', an inversionary challenge offered by petty treason and uxoricide to the familial and patriarchal picture of earthly authority.[14] One such case was the murder of Page in 1589. A similar plot was hatched by the wife of Thomas Beast and her lover Christopher Tomson, whom she persuaded to poison her husband. As we shall see in the case of the petty traitor Elizabeth Caldwell, the desire to subvert patriarchal household authority by murder was often presented as diabolic temptation.[15]

11 J. A. Sharpe, *Crime in Seventeenth-Century England. A County Study* (Cambridge, 1983), pp. 123–38; Lawrence Stone, 'Interpersonal Violence in English Society 1300–1980', *Past and Present*, 101 (1983), pp. 23–33; see also the debate between J. A. Sharpe and L. Stone, 'The History of Violence in England: Some Observations', in *Past and Present*, 108 (1985), pp. 207–24.

12 Beard, *The Theatre of God's Ivdgements: reuised and augmented*, sig. A7; John Taylor, *The Vnnatural Father: Or, the Cruell Murder committed by Iohn Rowse of the towne of Ewell* (London, 1621), sigs. A3–Bv; *The life and death of M. Geo: Sands, who after many enormous crimes by him committed ... was executed at Tyburn* (1626), in *Pepys Ballads*, vol. I, pp. 128–9; see Lake, 'Deeds against Nature', pp. 268–9.

13 Munday, *Sundry Strange and Inhumaine Murthers*, sig. A3; *A Briefe discourse of two most cruell and bloudie Murthers* (London, 1583), sigs. A5–B2.

14 Faller, *Turned to Account*, chapter 2; Frances Dolan, *Dangerous Familiars: Representations of Domestic Crime in England 1550–1700* (Ithaca and London, 1994); Underdown, *A Freeborn People*, pp. 12–18.

15 Munday, *Sundry Strange and Inhumaine Murthers*, sigs. B2–B3v. The Beast conspiracy is described in *A Briefe discourse of two most cruell and bloudie Murthers*, sigs. B2v–B4; for a similar story see Arthur Golding, *A brief discourse of the late murder of master George Saunders* (London, 1573); on the case of Elizabeth Cauldwell see Dugdale, *A True Discourse of the Practices of Elizabeth Cauldwell*; numerous ballad accounts were produced about petty traitors who were burned to death: see *A warning for all desperate Women By the example of Alice Davis* (1628), *The unnatural Wife Or, the lamentable Murther of one goodman Dauis* (1628), *Anne Wallens Lamentation For the Murthering of her Husband* (1616), all in *Pepys Ballads*, vol. I, pp. 120–5.

There was a good deal of variation in the extent to which the Devil appeared in these murder narratives. Although more often present than not, some accounts gave a detailed description of his involvement, whilst others relied on simple statements or solely on woodcut images to express a deeper implication of the diabolic which was not made explicit. In the pamphlet of 1591, *The Araignment, Examination, Confession and Iudgement of Arnold Cosbie*, a very detached account of the court proceedings against the murderer, diabolism was more a concern of the courtroom than the pamphleteer. The only reference to the Devil came in a verbatim reproduction of the indictment which declared that Cosbie had committed the crime 'not having the feare of God before his eies' and 'upon a diuellish and most malicious intent'. *A cruell murther committed lately upon the body of Abraham Gearsy*, a ballad of 1635, prefaced its tale with a moral aphorism which intimated the diabolism of the crime – 'This money was the cause of manies death, / As 'twas the cause that one late lost his breath; / The devill and the money workes together, / As by my subject you may well consider.' In concentrating on the way two brothers, Robert and Richard Reeve, had lured Gearsy to his death rather than pay him the money he was owed, the ballad commented simply: 'Abraham Gearsie was his name that was kil'd / By those two brothers, as the devill wil'd.'[16] In many narratives, however, the point at which the Devil's role was made explicit, as much as the rhetoric used, could express an awareness of a certain dynamic of temptation. The early seventeenth-century ballad *A Warning for all Murderers* described how a number of relatives were disappointed of the inheritance they had expected from their uncle, whose death they had all eagerly awaited. When his fortune was left entirely to his son, who soon married and conceived a child, the cousins began to plot against him. The Devil could have been presented as the driving force behind their avarice and covetousness, but instead he enters at the point at which they search for a solution to their problem. 'Then did the Divell intice them straight / to murther, death and blood', the ballad runs, 'Thereby to purchase to themselves / their long-desirèd good.' As a result of Satan's input they devised 'a hundred waies' to kill the son.[17]

Yet, whilst the use of the Devil was prey to the most sensationalist tendencies of the printers of ephemeral literature, his role in the murder pamphlets represented something more fundamental. In his discussion of the Protestant appropriation of the murder pamphlet form, Peter Lake has

[16] *The Araignment, Examination, Confession and Iudgement of Arnold Cosbie*, sig. A2v; *A cruell murther committed lately upon the body of Abraham Gearsy, who liv'd in the Parish of Westmill, in the County of Harford, by one Robert Reeve and Richard Reeve, both of the same Parish* (London, 1635), in Roxburghe Collection, vol. I, pp. 488–9.

[17] *A Warning for all Murderers* (no date), in Roxburghe Collection, vol. I, pp. 484–5.

noted the frequency with which the Devil was used by moralising authors to instil a perception of an external 'all-pervasive malice' which preyed on the human propensity for sin.[18] Murder was to be understood as the culmination of a progression by which Satan swept men from one sin to another, hastening them to perdition. Such sins increased in scale until the reprobate could do little but descend finally into murder, the sin which (as the opening words of virtually every murder pamphlet and Protestant commentary would attest) was especially hated of God.[19] A notion of cumulative sin, and the role of Satan as the driving force behind it, allowed pamphleteers to trace by hindsight the course that the individual criminal had followed in his descent into murder and damnation. Getting the greatest didactic mileage out of the moral history of a murderer involved highlighting the common ground between his early activities and those of the readership. Thus the 'formative' years of the murderer were commonly characterised with those same sins (idleness, drunkenness, fornication and swearing) that informed so many a Protestant harangue at the 'ungodly', particularly the young.[20] From such fruitful beginnings it was a relatively simple task to isolate the one sin among so many that, Satan having caught hold of it, provided the impetus to murder. Thus the murder pamphlets, and the conduct literature from which much of their rhetoric was drawn, provided an explanatory gloss for the crime.

Witchcraft cases were similarly well publicised, becoming notorious both among believers and sceptics, but the genre was far less clearly defined. Whilst the reporting, stage depiction and academic discussion of murder tended to be fairly consistent, there was a very wide variation in focus, tone, seriousness and style amongst accounts of witchcraft.[21] Reportage was carried out almost entirely in pamphlets, and, for the most part, cases tended not to generate multiple accounts. Only a handful of ballads were

18 Lake, 'Deeds against Nature', pp. 268–9; and 'Popular Form, Puritan Content? Two Puritan Appropriations of the Murder Pamphlet from Mid-Seventeenth-Century London', in A. J. Fletcher and P. R. Roberts (eds.), *Religion, Culture and Society in Early Modern Britain* (Cambridge, 1994), pp. 313–34; Cynthia B. Herrup, 'Law and Morality in Seventeenth-Century England', *Past and Present*, 106 (1985), pp. 109–12. A treatment of crime as sin in the Augustan period is provided in Faller's *Turned to Account*, whilst a more generalised examination of the literary reaction to deviance is given in Ian A. Bell, *Literature and Crime in Augustan England* (London, 1991). Frances Dolan interprets murder narratives, including pamphlets, in terms of gender in *Dangerous Familiars*. The best general description of Protestant notions of the Devil and his part in human sin has been with reference to New England: see Godbeer,*The Devil's Dominion*, chapter 3.

19 Beard, *The Theatre of Gods Ivdgements*; John Reynolds, *The Triumphs of Gods Revenge against the crying and Execrable sinne of (willing and premeditated) Murther* (London, 1657; first edn, 1621).

20 Patrick Collinson, *The Religion of Protestants*, pp. 224–30.

21 For a detailed discussion of this issue, see Marion Gibson, *Reading Witchcraft: Stories of Early English Witches* (London, 1999).

produced on the subject,[22] and whilst the witch play became a sub-genre of the contemporary stage there was possibly only one overt attempt to dramatise an actual case.[23] The variety of contexts and agendas in which witchcraft was discussed seem also to have produced a wide variation in notions of the Devil within the genre, but he was always depicted as physically present. This seems to have been because both the authorities and the populace shared general assumptions as to how witchcraft was effected through a (normally) overt pact with Satan.[24] As J. A. Sharpe has argued, witchcraft narratives offer insights into a popular conception of the Devil which incorporated a number of folkloric elements.[25] In the earliest known pamphlet account, *The Examination and Confession of certaine Wytches at Chensforde* (1566), a cat called 'Sathan' was passed down the matrilineal line. Similarly, the network of witches apparently uncovered by Brian Darcy was based around the giving and receiving of familiars. The spirits were passed from one witch to another much in the way a useful domestic implement might be lent or given away.[26] Prosecutors and ministers were prepared to accept evidence of these spirits as a useful confirmation of the involvement of the diabolic, but equally prevalent was a notion of overt demonic seduction which accorded more closely to their expectations of the crime. In 1589, for instance, *The Apprehension and confession of three notorious Witches* printed the description, by an Essex woman Joan Prentice, of her encounter in an almshouse with the Devil disguised as a ferret, who said to her, 'I am satan, feare me not my comming vnto thee is to doo thee no hurt but to abtaine thy soule, which I must and wil haue.'[27] Satan's identification became increasingly certain as the pamphlet genre developed. In 1613, in one of the best-known accounts, Thomas Potts' *The Wonderfvll Discoverie of Witches in the Covntie of*

22 The publisher John Barnes of Christ Church produced both a pamphlet and a ballad on the case of the Flower family, who were accused of bewitching the Earl of Rutland's children in 1619. Seemingly both formats were published in parallel to catch the attention of different if overlapping audiences. See *Damnable Practices Of three Lincolne-shire Witches* (1619), in *Pepys Ballads*, vol. I, pp. 26–7. For another, much later, example of a witchcraft ballad see *Witchcraft discovered and punished* (1682), in Roxburghe Collection, vol. II, p. 531.

23 In 1621 William Rowley, Thomas Dekker and John Ford collaborated on a play based on the case of Elizabeth Sawyer, which took its details from a pamphlet written by Henry Goodcole. See *The Witch of Edmonton: A known true Story, Composed into a Tragi-comedy* (1621).

24 Perkins, *A Discourse of the Damned Art of Witchcraft* (1608), in *Works*, vol. III, pp. 614–16; James I, *Daemonologie*, in *Workes*, pp. 103–5; Robert Filmer, *An Advertisement to the Jurymen of England, Touching Witches* (London, 1653), pp. 3–9.

25 Sharpe, *Instruments of Darkness*, pp. 75–8.

26 *The Examination and Confession of certaine Wytches at Chensforde in the Countie of Essex*; W. W., *A true and just Recorde, of the Information, Examination and Confession of all the Witches, taken at S. Oses in the county of Essex* (London, 1582), sigs. A3v, A5v–A6; similarly, see *A Rehearsall both strange and true, of the hainous and horrible actes committed by Elizabeth Stile*, sigs. A5v–A8v.

27 *The Apprehension and confession of three notorious Witches*, sigs. B–Bv.

Lancaster, the Devil appeared in human shape for the first time. Elizabeth Southern of Pendle Forest confessed that some twenty years previously, returning home from begging, she had encountered a boy 'one halfe of his Coate blacke, the other browne', who bargained for her soul. Similarly, Anne Whittle was plagued for four years by a devil in the shape of 'a Christian man', and eventually succumbed to his pressure to enter into a pact.[28]

Unlike murder narratives, which highlighted the unseen demonic hold over the will, witchcraft accounts sought to expose the witting apostasy committed in a conscious and informed decision to follow the Devil.[29] Thus apostasy was the scheme into which temptation was fitted, rather than vice versa. As a consequence, temptation was presented in witchcraft narratives as a relatively straightforward reciprocal trade. The Devil commonly approached the witch and offered to perform *maleficium* on her behalf in return for her soul. Thus the temptation of the witch provided a religious gloss to the demonisation of spirit magic that had increasingly taken hold in the fourteenth and fifteenth centuries.[30] But the emphasis on the witch's malice – a conception shared between popular and elite stereotypes, and in no way confined to Protestantism – did provide an opening for some later witchcraft narratives to express more complex notions of the role of temptation. Whereas many early pamphlets tended to describe the pact with the Devil as taking place before the witch came into conflict with those she would eventually harm, some seventeenth-century examples adopted the understanding of cumulative sin, and argued that the witch's malice acted, like the murderer's anger or jealousy, as an invitation for Satan. In 1619 Joan Flower and her two daughters came into conflict with their benefactor, the earl of Rutland, becoming consumed with 'hate and rancor'. 'When the Divell perceived the inficious disposition of this wretch, and that she and her daughters might easily bee made instruments to enlarge his Kingdome', a pamphlet account of the case attested, 'he came neerer unto them, and in plaine tearmes to come quickly to the purpose, offered them his service.'[31]

[28] Potts, *The Wonderfvll discoverie of Witches*, sigs. B2v–B4v, D3–D3v. The most bizarre confessions of interaction with demons were produced during the Essex witch scare of 1645–7; see Hopkins, *The Discovery of Witches*, pp. 2–3; John Stearne, *A Confirmation And Discovery of Witchcraft* (London, 1648), pp. 13–18.

[29] *Examination and Confession of certaine Wytches*, A7–A8; *The Apprehension and confession of three notorious Witches*, sigs. B–Bv; Potts, *The Wonderfvll Discoverie of Witches*, sigs. B2v–B4v; Goodcole, *The Wonderful Discouerie of Elizabeth Sawyer*, p. 12; James I, *Daemonologie*, pp. 103–5; Perkins, *Damned Art of Witchcraft*, in *Works*, vol. III, pp. 614–16; Sharpe, *Instruments of Darkness*, pp. 74–5, 82–5, 134–7; Briggs, *Witches and Neighbours*, pp. 25–38.

[30] Cohn, *Europe's Inner Demons*, pp. 188–97.

[31] *The Wonderful Discoverie of the Witchcrafts of Margaret and Philip Flower, daughters of Ioan Flower* (London, 1619), sig. C4v.

Similarly, the ordinary of Newgate, Henry Goodcole, recorded that Elizabeth Sawyer was approached by the Devil as a result of her cursing. 'Never before ... did I see him, or he me', she apparently confessed to Goodcole in prison, 'and when he, namely the divel, came to me, the first words that he spake unto me were these: Oh! Have I now found you cursing, swearing and blaspheming? Now you are mine.'[32]

Thus, whilst both murder and witchcraft narratives sought to put across a sense of the Devil's central role in criminality as a manifestation of his earthly power, they presented very distinct pictures of the dynamic of temptation. One, with its emphasis on the fine line between sin and criminality, and on the power of unseen satanic influence, reduced the empathic gap between the reader and the criminal. The other, based entirely around physical interaction with the Devil, had the opposite effect, marginalising a single incident of temptation (but not, of course, the more general sins that led up to it) in an encounter recognised to be real, but beyond the experience of most.

COMPONENTS OF THE DEVIL'S KINGDOM

The depiction of diabolic crime was bound up with questions of perception and interpretation. The 'strange news' advertised on the frontispiece never remained so to the last page of the pamphlet. Even the most bizarre occurrences, and the most bloody crimes, could be assimilated into a scheme which deprived them of their uniqueness, and this, to a large extent, was the self-conscious purpose of the pulp press pamphlet. Acts of murder and *maleficium* might occur in isolation, but their perpetrators constituted component parts of Satan's earthly kingdom, a kingdom not here defined geographically, but as a de facto composite of human sin. Criminals became mediators of the Devil's agency, their victims the channels through which the diabolic assault on the whole Christian commonwealth was effected. A ballad of 1615, *The Araignment of John Flodder and his wife, at Norwidge*, described the punishment of two supposed papists for setting fire to the town of Wymondham in Norfolk. These 'rogues and beggars' went from town to town, until they decided on arson. The ballad was unconcerned with their motives, commenting instead that: 'sure the Diuell, or else some Feend of his, / Persuaded them vnto this foule amiss, / With Fire to wast so braue a Market Towne, / That flourisht faire, with riches and renowne.' That the criminals were merely mediating Satan's agency was further demonstrated by the seemingly preternatural nature of the fire: 'A Fier that was deuised of the Diuell, / A Fier of all the worst, and worse than euill: / Wilde fier it was, that could not

[32] Goodcole, *The Wonderfull Discouerie of Elizabeth Sawyer*, p. 12; the scene was faithfully dramatised in Rowley, Dekker and Ford's *The Witch of Edmonton*, Act II, scene i, 94–175.

quenched bee, / A ball thereof lay kindling secretly.'[33] With every crime Satan's hold over the earth was maintained and reinforced, and he ever threatened to tighten his stranglehold around the beleaguered godly, who found themselves surrounded by his human servants.

Sensational crimes emerged as the most palpable form of sin, be they attributable to man's corruption or the Devil's influence. That they be interpreted correctly was of paramount importance precisely because they forced themselves into people's line of sight. Arthur Golding, in his pamphlet *A brief discourse of the late murder of master George Saunders* (1573), bemoaned the fact that murder was the cause of so much talk and speculation, but so little introspection. God did not exhibit murder so that 'men should gaze and wonder at the persons as byrds do at an Owle', he explained, but that it 'should by the terror of the outward sight of the example, drive us to the inward consideration of ourselves'.[34] Superficial perception posed a different threat for the Exeter merchant John Reynolds, compiling throughout the 1620s his collection, *The triumphs of Gods revenge against the crying and execrable sinne of (wilfull and premeditated) murther*. The danger was that 'the crying and scarlet sin of Murther makes so ample, and bloody a progression', that man might think God had abandoned the world entirely to the Devil.[35] The perception of murder might even tempt man to atheism: 'to believe, there were no heaven, towards the righteous: or hell, to punish the ungodly'. But as with all temptations perception was also the solution, and the correct interpretation of murder was akin to regaining part of the spiritual insight men and women had lost. 'If we will divert our hearts from earth to heaven', Reynolds noted, 'we shall then not onely see what engendereth this diabolical passion in us, but also find means to detest and root it out from amongst us.'[36]

This equation was explicit in some pamphlets, and implicit in most. *A Detection of damnable driftes practiced by three Witches arraigned at Chelmisforde* (1579) promised:

on thone side the cleare sight maie espie the ambushments, which Sathan the secret workmaster of wicked driftes, hath placed in most partes of this realme, either by craftye conueighaunces, to creep into the conceipts of the simple, or by apparaunt

[33] *The Araignment of John Flodder and his wife . . . for the burning of the Towne of Windham in Norfolke* (1615), in *Pepys Ballads*, vol. I, pp. 130–1, quotes at p. 130.

[34] Golding, *A brief discourse of the late murder of master George Saunders*, sigs. A2–A2v, C3–D2, quote at sigs. C3v–C4; *A true reporte or description of an horrible, wofull, and most lamentable murther, doen in the cittie of Bristoew by one John Kynnester, a Sherman by his occupation* (London, 1573), sig., A3; *The Examination and Confession of certaine Wytches*, sigs. A4v–A5; *The Apprehension and confession of three notorious Witches*, sigs. A2–A2v.

[35] Reynolds, *Triumph of Gods Revenge*, sig. A2; see also *A Briefe discourse of two most cruell and bloudie Murthers*, sigs. A2–A3.

[36] Reynolds, *Triumph of Gods Revenge*, sig. A2.

treacherie to undermine and spoile the states of such as God permitteth him to haue power ouer. And on the other side the eye that is wimpled may hereby be advertised of the darkenesse, wherwith his understanding is ouercast, and puttyng of the viele of vanitie, maie reclaime his concept, and esteeme of the impietie of the offendours and the vilanie of their actes.[37]

The more moralistic pamphlets sought to make the wider consequences of murder and witchcraft as palpable an experience as the crimes themselves. In 1604 Gilbert Dugdale published an account of an attempted petty treason of which he had personal knowledge. Attempting to transmit to his audience the experience of a godly man coming to terms with murder, he described the progression of his thoughts – a progression followed in turn by the narrative of the pamphlet. He noted:

After my long being at Chester, in the time of this reported trouble, I in my melancholie walkes bethought me of the strange invasion of Satan, lately on the person of Elizabeth Caldwell, and her bloody louer Ieffrie Bownd . . . how that vglie fiende (euer mans fatall opposite) had made practice, but I hope not purchase, of their corruptable liues, & brought them to the last steppe of mortall miserie.

Before thoughts of the enormity of satanic power could overwhelm him he, 'revolving with myself', remembered the mercy of God in calling sinners to repentance, whereby even the most heinous criminal might find redemption.[38] The story of Caldwell's moral collapse was a depressing example of the potential extent of demonic power, but her celebrated repentance and godly end cut short the Devil's reign. As Dugdale told it, hundreds flocked to be edified by the saint in prison, and communal acknowledgement of her repentance demarcated the limits of Satan's intrusion. By the end of the pamphlet the reader was not only to have entered the narrative world of temptation and murder, but also to have experienced some identification with the cyclical progression from shock and pessimism to optimism and faith, by which Dugdale claimed to have assimilated the case himself.

Exposés of the Devil's agency were often also exposés of society's negligence in opposing it. For one author, a case of witchcraft in Windsor in 1579 was indicative of the way in which Satan 'hath of late yeares, greatly multiplied the broude of them, and muche encreased their malice'. This 'he hath more easily performed for that wholesome remedies provided for the curing of such cankers are either a whit, or not applied'. In his description of the 1582 St Osyth witch trial, Brian Darcy demanded that witches be made examples of as a demonstration, as much to God as to man, of the will to engage with diabolic 'detestable abuses'. It was a symptom of indulgence, he

[37] *A Detection of the damnable driftes practiced by three witches at Chemisforde* (London, 1579), sigs. A2–A2v.
[38] Dugdale, *A True Discourse of the Practices of Elizabeth Caldwell*, sig. B4.

noted, that these 'apparent' apostates suffered no greater punishment than other felons.[39] Satan was never at rest, making it necessary to constantly provide such exposés of his agency. The author of *A brief Discovrse of two most cruell and blooudie Murthers* (1583) reminded his readers that, concerning the stories he was about to relate, 'albeit they carrye terrour sufficient, to forwarne the unnatural children of this worlde: yet daylie doo fresh enormities spring up, able (had nature so agreed) to urge the very bowells of the earth, to heepe foorth fearefull acclamations agaynst us'. *A Most Wicked worke of a wretched Witch* (1592), saw the threat of Satan's composite kingdom to lie in his ability constantly to replenish it, remarking that, though God might 'weed' out witches, 'but Satan still doth hatch / Fresh imps, whereby of all sorts he may catch.' These pamphleteers made generalisations to argue for the wider significance of the cases they related, but concern over the issue of perception could be very specific. The fullest example was itself a response to the Windsor witch case. The local gentleman, Richard Galis, produced an autobiographical prequel to the pamphlet, in which he charted his constantly frustrated attempts to get the authorities to take his accusations against Rockingham and her accomplices seriously. Believing himself to be the principal target of their malice, he first argued that their witchcraft had turned his community against him (he was imprisoned at one point, although on what grounds is not clear), and later that the authorities' blindness was a providential test, which, Job-like, he had to endure.[40]

DEVILISH HUMANS AND AUDIENCE EMPATHY

The perception into demonic agency these publications advocated, and sought to provide for, was vicarious, seeking to transmit to the reader the experience of diabolic temptation. It demanded, not a distanced observation of the exposé, but an engagement and empathy with its protagonists. Lincoln Faller has described how early modern 'criminology' was innocent of the modern tendency to see criminality as reassuringly aberrant. It referred instead to man's inherited corruption to develop a Christian aetiology of crime that embraced the possibility of a general potential for criminality.[41] Correspondingly, narratives were written in the understanding that readers *could* empathise with the psychological/spiritual experience of criminals. The notion of cumulative sin allowed authors to force an identification

[39] *A Rehearsal both strange and true, of the hainous and horrible actes committed by Elizabeth Stile*, sigs. A2–A2v; W. W., *A true and just Recorde*, sigs. A3v–A4.

[40] Galis, *A Briefe Treatise conteyning the most strange and horrible crueltye of Elizabeth Stile*, see above pp. 120–1.

[41] Faller, *Turned to Account*, pp. 52–4.

with the commonplace emotions and drives which were the prelude to crime. As the Protestant scheme of temptation predicted, the Devil entered the conscience and took hold of the corruption already present, blowing it up until it exploded into violence or murder. The audience's recognition of the anger, greed or jealousy that Satan inflated into murder allowed them to experience diabolic agency vicariously.

Thus perception into the Devil's agency required a special insight, which could only be gained by accepting the interpretative monopoly of the pamphlets. The demonisation of 'others' in medieval Europe had relied on no such special insight.[42] Instead the allegiance to the Devil practised by Jews, Muslims and heretics was embodied in physical transformation or expressed in inversionary activity as the Devil lent his recognisable physical characteristics to his servants. Jews were commonly pictured with horns, a tail, a goat's beard and a disgusting odour.[43] Heretics in turn were demonised by their acts. Groups such as the Bogomiles, the Waldensians and the Cathars were believed to take part in an inverted diabolic baptism and to engage in unimaginable sins such as infanticide, cannibalism and incest.[44] Demonisation in such cases rested on the dehumanisation of the subject, to present him as more devil than human.

Whilst the 'otherness' of witches might be highlighted in pulp press accounts, there was no real attempt to 'other' murderers, who maintained their humanity. The symptoms of violent madness could imply the demonic, but generally murder narratives avoided physical descriptions of their protagonists. Instead early modern crime narratives were concerned with the criminal's state of mind, firstly the state by which the Devil's notice was attracted, and secondly the havoc he wreaked on the moral faculties once he gained entrance. Criminals were exposed to a conflation of two methods of diabolic temptation, both assumed to be intuitively comprehensible to the audience if the guidelines provided in the narrative were followed. It has been argued above that men's consciences were understood to exist as a balance of good and evil motions, as a consequence of the fall.[45] The godliest of men and women only maintained the most fragile equilibrium of these competing impulses by constant vigilance. In luring people into crime, a favoured policy

[42] An early example of the argument that the Devil was lord of a satanic host comprising the 'other' (although without the terminology) is to be found in Rudwin, *The Devil in Legend and Literature*, chapter 14; its best expressions remain Cohn, *Europe's Inner Demons*, chapters 1–3; and Moore, *The Formation of a Persecuting Society*, pp. 88–91; whilst Pagels, *The Origin of Satan*, chapter 5; Link, *The Devil*, pp. 183–4; and G. Messadié, *The History of the Devil*, trans. M. Romano (London, 1996), chapters 14–16, are the most recent studies to put forward this argument.

[43] Trachtenburg, *The Devil and the Jews*, pp. 44–50; Leon Poliakov, *The History of Anti-Semitism* (London, 1965), vol. I, pp. 141–4.

[44] Cohn, *Europe's Inner Demons*, chapters 2 and 3.

[45] See above, chapter 3.

of the Devil was to swamp the conscience with evil influences, not only tempting them to sin, but at the same time stifling their impulses to godliness. By these means he sought to destroy the equilibrium of the conscience that kept behaviour moderate, allowing him to take a firmer hold over the will. This hold was again understood to involve a very real intrusion of the demonic into the mind, but in narratives of crime, and especially murder, the picture of diabolic invasion was more tightly focused than in the general theological and conduct book discussions of temptation. Crimes of intent were turned into real actions by a process of amplification by which Satan took hold of sinful thoughts and blew them up into irresistible desires to commit violence or witchcraft. This picture of diabolic agency was explicit in many pamphlet accounts and implicit in all.

In populating his diabolic terrestrial kingdom the Devil of the pulp press most commonly appeared as an opportunist. Time and time again the authors of murder and witchcraft narratives bewailed the fact that in pursuing a life of sin men laid themselves open to the assaults of the Devil, should they come into his path. John Reynolds provided a detailed picture of the holistic diabolic assault assumed to be experienced by all criminals, expressed in the tempting triumvirate of the world the flesh and the Devil. For Reynolds the Devil was utterly singleminded and was 'indifferent to him, either how or in what manner we enlarge and fill the empty rooms of his vast and internal [sic] Kingdom'.[46] If the temptations of the world and the waywardness of the flesh were not sufficient to bring a man to perdition, Satan would make himself known in his usual guise as an angel of light.[47] Should insinuation still fail, Satan 'hath yet reserved troops and forces', and, 'exchanging his smiles into frowns', he would afflict man with 'Grief of mind and body ... indignation, despair, revenge and the like'. It was by this final 'string to his Bow' that the Devil brought people to murder, for he would 'watch us at every turn, and wait on us at every occasion: for are we bent to revenge, he will blow the coals to our cholar'. All men and women should expect the test of diabolic affliction, which might manifest itself in murderous passion, but temptation could be resisted by reason. To cast off religion when it was needed was akin to letting go of the helm in a storm. So when our 'cholar so far prevaileth with us (or rather the Devil with our cholar) that we ... lift up our hands against our Christian brother', man and women should consider that to do so is to be 'not of God' and to 'walketh in darkness', knowing 'not whither [we] goeth'. The latter quotes Reynolds took from 1 John and they intimate the alienation and confusion so often taken to characterise those who have thrown in their lot with the Devil.[48]

46 Reynolds, *Triumph of Gods Revenge*, sig. A2v. 47 Ibid. 48 I John 2: 2.

This holistic assault was characterised by an atmosphere of chaos and licence enveloping the lives of protagonists in pulp press narratives. As individuals were increasingly swamped by temptation, crime became more likely, and Satan was sometimes credited with arranging situations in which the bonds of a godly conscience might be loosed. In Anthony Munday's pamphlet account, the murder of Master Page stemmed from a forced marriage, attributable directly to Satan. George Strangwich, an apprentice to a shopkeeper in Testock, became involved with the shopkeeper's daughter, incurring the resentment of his master. At this point the Devil intruded on the narrative to set the scene for tragedy. 'Satan', the story continued, 'crept so far into the dealings of these persons that he procured the parents to mislike of Strangwich, and to persuade their daughter to refraine his companye, shewing her that they had found out a more meeter match for her'. By the Devil's instigation the daughter was forced to marry Page, a widower in Plymouth, but continued an affair with Strangwich that eventually led to the hire of an assassin to deal with the unwanted husband. The witchcraft practised by Joan Flower and her daughters in Lincolnshire in 1619 was the result of a protracted conflict with Sir Francis Manners, the earl of Rutland who had dismissed the daughters from his service. The pamphleteer who described the case could only explain how the malicious Flowers could ever have held the favour of the earl and his wife by attributing it to the work of Satan. 'Such was the subtlety of the Devil to bring his purposes to pass', the author noted, 'that all things were carried away in the smooth channel of liking and good entertainment on every side'.[49] In John Taylor's *The Unnatural Father* of 1621, the match made by a fishmonger, John Rowse, to a 'very honest and comely woman', presented a barrier to the Devil's influence which had to be removed. Rowse lived quietly with his wife, 'till the devil sent an instrument of his to disturb their matrimonial happiness'. The couple employed a maidservant, Jane Blundell, whose subsequent affair with Rowse was the death of his wife.[50] Freed from all constraint, Rowse embarked on a dissolute life which eventually led him to be cheated out of his land by a 'false friend', and culminated in the murder of his children in an act of despair.

[49] Munday, *Sundry Strange and Inhumaine Murthers*, sig. B2; *A Briefe discourse of two most cruell and bloudie Murthers*, sig. B2v; *The Wonderful Discoverie of the Witchcrafts of Margaret and Philip Flower*, sig. C4.

[50] Taylor, *The Vnnatural Father*, sig. A3v. A similar case was described in the murder of one Thomas Beast, killed by his wife and her lover. He 'kept a handsome Young man to his servant, called Christopher Tomason, to whome (by the wicked instigation and prouacation of the deuill) the good wife of he house used far better affection than to her owne husband'. Finally 'lust had gotten so much power of the woman', that she began to plan the murder. See *A Briefe discourse of two most cruell and bloudie Murthers*, sigs. B2–B2v.

A number of narratives used readily identifiable human tempters – such as prostitutes, lovers and Catholics – to make diabolic envelopment more palpable to the reader. These satanic agents took on diabolic characteristics, not physically, but in the means they used to further tempt their target into sin. Elizabeth Caldwell, whose absentee husband left her 'without such means as was fitting for her', fell under the seduction of one Jeffrey Bownd. Throughout Gilbert Dugdale's pamphlet account temptation was embodied in the figure of Bownd, who used all the devices commonly attributed to the Devil. He was persistent and persuasive and took advantage of the unhappy state of Caldwell's marriage to prey on her vulnerability. The words Dugdale used to describe Bownd's temptations were those commonly employed when discussing Satan – they were 'allurements', and 'assaults and incouragements'. Finally, when his own efforts were insufficient to completely stifle Caldwell's godly conscience, Bownd himself employed his own diabolic agent to envelop her. A widow, Isabel Hall, was 'prefered as *an instrument* to work her to an unlawfull reformation'.[51] Her exact role in the seduction of Caldwell was not made clear, but in echoing Bownd's arguments and enticements, her position seems to have given them some 'matronly' acceptability. Hall as sophist provided another human embodiment of a method of temptation particularly associated with the Devil, whose arguments were at their most dangerous when they appeared most reasonable. It was only with her aid that Bownd was able to entice Caldwell into committing murder.

In the pamphlet of 1616 *A pittilesse Mother*, Catholics were the incarnate devils that brought the gentlewoman Margaret Vincent to murder two of her children. 'Consider with thy self', the author advised his readers, 'how strangely the divell her set his foote and what cunning instruments hee used in his assaylements.' Vincent had the misfortune (in a woman) of 'being witty and of a Ripe understanding', and resorted frequently to divines to discuss matters of religion. Whereas in many woman such godly zeal might be praised within limits, in Vincent's case it simply left her exposed to the wiles of devilish papists, who in turn transformed her into a diabolic instrument:

> at last there were such trappes and engins set, that her quiet was caught, and her discontent set at liberty; her opinion of the true faith (by the subtil sophistry of some close Papists) was converted into a blinde belief of betwitching heresie, for they have such charming perswasions that hardly the female kind can escape their inticements, of which the weake sex they continually make prise of and by them lay plots to ensnare others, as they did by this deceived Gentlewoman, for she, good soul, being

[51] Dugdale, *A True Discourse of the Practices of Elizabeth Caldwell*, sig. A4v, my emphasis.

> made a bird of their owne feather, desired to beget more of the same kinde, and from time to time made perswasive arguments to win her husband to the same opinion.

Vincent's fall into Catholicism had dire consequences, as she eventually became convinced that the only means to save her children's souls from the pernicious influence of Protestantism was to kill them.[52]

Murder, once initiated, was believed to snowball to catch a number of seemingly innocent souls who might never have come to their respective sticky ends but for their lack of vigilance as to the Devil's wiles. Often the murderer himself was presented as the diabolic tempter, who, having had violent thoughts implanted in his mind by Satan, became the medium for their wider transmission. The story of Lincoln of Warborne was one such example. Finding himself in hardship he desired to make an advantageous match, but was refused by a widow of 'reasonable wealth' on account of his 'great charge of children'. At the point of his being presented with this dilemma 'the deuill entered so farre into his minde, that he cast many wayes in his thoughts how to make them awaie'.[53] Lincoln became the mediator of the Devil's temptations when, discussing the problem with a man who was living in his house, he hit upon his diabolic plan. He would pay the man to commit the act whilst he was out of town, and would refuse to allow him to be pursued when the hue and cry was raised. Little attention was paid in the pamphlet to the motives of the assassin – the thought of murder was passed on with a simple appeal to his greed – what was significant was that, in committing his own crime, Lincoln simultaneously acted as a diabolic agent, laying traps to catch others.

The mediation of the diabolic was at its most sinister when it intruded on the household, using familial relations to give it credibility. In such circumstances it could have a terrible ability to undermine even the most godly conscience. The pamphlet *News from Perrin* [Penryn] was constructed around the temptation of a woman to kill for money, and the protracted sophistry by which she mediated it to her husband, finally persuading him to murder his unrecognised son.[54] In the narrative a wayward son returns home a reformed man after a career as a pirate and a galley-slave. He reveals his identity only to his sister and his unsuspecting father takes him in as a lodger. The prodigal's absence has previously led to the death of his mother, and his

52 *A pittilesse Mother. That most vnnaturally at one time, murthered two of her owne Children at Acton* (London, 1616), sigs. A2–A2v. For a discussion of the depiction of motherhood and infanticide in this pamphlet, see Dolan, *Dangerous Familiars*, pp. 145–50.

53 Munday, *Sundry Strange and Inhumaine Murthers*, sig. A3.

54 *Newes from Perin in Cornwall: Of a most Bloody and vn-exampled Murther very lately committed by a Father on his owne Sonne ... at the Instigation of a mercilesse Step-mother* (London, 1618); Lake, 'Deeds against Nature', p. 265; Marshburn, *Murder and Witchcraft in England*, pp. 179–82.

good-natured but weak father has married again. The stepmother, seeing that the traveller has returned to England a wealthy man, hatches a plot to murder him and steal his money. Only after considerable effort does she manage to coax and shame her husband into committing the deed, and thus the scene is set for tragedy. The son, in his dying agony, recognises his murderer but is unable to speak, and when the father learns from his daughter the stranger's identity, he kills himself. The stepmother follows his example and the tragedy is complete. She lives long enough, however, to take the entire responsibility for the crime upon herself.

The narrative first described how Satan achieved a direct influence over the stepmother. The ease with which the weak woman gives in to Satan contrasts with her husband's resistance. But the threat lies not only in womankind's susceptibility to the Devil, but in that, as his instruments, they might hide his temptations within the everyday negotiations and compromises made between married couples. To persuade her husband to carry out the killing, the stepmother mediated the 'divellish arguments to approve the lawfullness of it' – his financial problems may be solved at a stroke and the crime may be accomplished safely since the sailor arrived late and unseen into their house.[55] Twice 'by her deuillish inticements' he attempted the deed but was unable to do it. True to form, the Devil was merely goaded by these setbacks into renewed effort, 'for the more valiantly he is resisted [he] growes the more malitious'.[56] When even the sight of the money failed to rouse her husband, the stepmother taunted him with accusations of cowardice, giving him the knife with which he finally killed his son, by which act 'the Divell and she prevailed'.[57]

What happened to the criminals themselves as they fell under the influence of the Devil and his human instruments? Most pulp press writers shared with Protestant theologians a belief in the Devil's ability to intrude directly into the mind, pushing endemic, 'normal' sin to extremes. The implication was that the consciousness, however sinful, was incapable of conceiving of murder without Satan's influence. Cumulative sin was not a seamless progression, but a series of watersheds, each confirming a further descent into sin until the mind was ready to entertain thoughts of unquestionably diabolic

55 *Newes from Perin*, sig. B5. 56 Ibid., sig. B4v.

57 Ibid., sig. B5. Hugh Latimer summed up the Devil's flexibility succinctly in his seventh sermon on the Lord's Prayer, with particular reference to the Devil, noting 'when we be in health, the devil moveth us to all wickedness and naughtiness, to whoredom, lechery, theft, and other horrible faults; putting out of our mind the remembrance of God and his judgements, insomuch that we forget that we shall die. Again, when we be in sickness, he goeth about like a lion to move and stir us up to impatiency and murmuring against God; or else he maketh our sins so horrible before us that we fall into desperation', in *Sermons*, pp. 429–32, quote at p. 432.

crimes such as murder and witchcraft. In the pamphlet account of the witchcraft of the Flower family, the conflict with the earl of Rutland (which as we have already seen was contrived by Satan), was merely a preliminary to make the women susceptible to the Devil's temptations:

> When the Diuell percieued the inficious disposition of this wretch [Joan Flower], and that she and her daughters might easily bee made instruments to enlarge his Kingdome, and bee as it were the executioners of his vengeance; not caring whether it lighted vpon innocents or no, he came more neerer vnto them, and in plaine tearmes to come quickly to the purpose, offered them his seruice.[58]

When the scope of their desired revenge widened beyond those with which they had a grievance, the Flowers passed a watershed and descended to a new depth of sin, making them vulnerable to exploitation by Satan.[59] Similarly, it was the envy of Thomas Smith at the success of his neighbour, Robert Greenoll, that provided an open invitation to Satan. 'The Deuill so farre ruled the course of his envious intent', noted the author of *A briefe Discovrse of two most cruell and blooudie Murthers*, 'as nothing would surfice the desire thereof, but onely the making away of Greenoll by death, which though he had no reason for, yet such was the persuasion of the evill spirite with him'.[60] In the Penryn narrative, the sight of the prodigal's gold ignited the stepmother's covetousness and, 'thinking of her present wants', she 'cast

[58] *The Wonderful Discoverie of the Witchcrafts of Margaret and Philip Flower*, sig., C4v. The description was closely followed by the ballad account produced by the same publisher,

> Wherat the old malitious feend,
> with these her darlings thought:
> The Earle and Countesse them disgrac't,
> and their discredits wrought:
> In turning thus despightfully,
> her daughter out of dores,
> For which reuengement in her mind
> she many a mischiefe stores.
>
> Heereat the Diuell made entraunce in,
> his Kingdome to inlarge.
> And puts his executing wrath,
> vnto these womens charge:
> Not caring whom it lighted on,
> the Innocent or no,
> And offered them his diligence,
> to flye, to run, to goe.

See *Damnable Practices Of three Lincoln-shire Witches, Joane Flower, and her two Daughters ... against Henry Lord Ross* ... (London, 1619), stanzas 9–12.

[59] The pamphlet was an example of a shift in witchcraft narratives, which increasingly played down the notion that the grievances held by witches might be justified. See Gibson, *Reading Witchcraft*, pp. 101–9.

[60] *A Briefe discourse of two most cruell and bloudie Murthers*, sig. A5.

about twenty wayes, how to enjoy it'. She was engrossed in her covetous contemplation when,

> presently the deuill, that is alwayes ready to take holde of the least advantage that may be to increase his kingdome, whispered this comfort in her eare, shewing her the golden temptation: saying, all this will I give thee, if thou wilt but make away with a poore stranger that sleeps under thy mercy.[61]

One of the stories recounted by John Reynolds in *The triumphs of Gods revenge* concerned the Italian uxoricide, Alibius, who poisoned his wife, Merilla. He was given to debauchery and abandoned her several times. He resolved to reform and try to make his fortune in Venice, but, whilst sojourning in the town of Brescia, his profligacy caught up with him, and, as the sights of the local fleshpots rekindled his old desires, Satan encouraged a new loathing of his wife, who Alibius believed had lost her beauty. As 'his eyes (the Lustfull sentynalls of his heart) espie so many beauties', Reynolds tells us, 'he began to loath his owne Merilla, and to wish her in another world, that he might have another wife in this'. But this was nothing less than the Devil amplifying his lust into thoughts of murder, as Reynolds explains: 'loe, here the divell beginnes with him anew to persuade him to hate his wife'. Through his talent for flattery Alibius became a favourite of the town oligarchy, and Satan, for his part, made sure that preferment stoked rather than dampened his murderous intent. 'The devill was so busie with him, or hee with the devill, that in hope of a higher and fayrer wife, hee resolves to poyson her according as hee heretofore had many times thought and premeditated', and his reaction to meeting the young, rich and fair Philatea confirms the Devil's hold: 'so strongly hath the devill possessed him with these hellish designes and bloody resolutions, as his love to Philatea, defacing his respect to Merilla, hee sees her a blocke in his way, and a stop to his preferment and so concludes that she must bee remooved and dispatched'.[62] Lust, greed, anger, jealousy and disappointment might all be taken hold of by the Devil and amplified into murderous intentions.

Almost invariably, premeditation was depicted as diabolic in the pulp press accounts, and Satan the adviser who provided the schemes by which evil intent might be carried out. Criminal intentions had their origins in the demonic amplification of commonplace sinful thoughts every man was prone to; but the singlemindedness necessary to carry them out was the satanic contribution which marked murderers, rapists and witches as beyond the pale of endemic, 'ordinary' human sin. One pamphlet recounted the story of a tailor called Thomas Cash who had the misfortune to marry a 'troublesome' wife, and conspired with a maidservant to do away with her. Having

[61] *Newes from Perin*, sig. B4. [62] Reynolds, *Triumph of Gods Revenge*, pp. 66–7.

decided on the act, he began to consider 'what course he were best to take, to rid himself of her', at which point 'the Divell failed not to fitte him with a Divelish devise'. He would suffocate her and attribute her death to her long and well-known illness.[63] Having instilled murderous envy in the mind of Thomas Smith, Satan also provided a plan of how the act might be committed. 'A thousand Devises were canvazed over by this lewde man', so the narrator tells us: 'at last, as the deuill wanteth no occasions to helpe man forward to his own destruction, so he presenteth Smith with a fit opportunity whereby he might execute the sum of his bloody will'.[64] The 'deuilish deuise' provided to Smith – to suffocate his wife by forcing a cloth down her throat – was so heinous that even those confirmed diabolic humans, Jews and Turks, would be shocked by it.[65]

But appealing to the commonplace emotions in which crime originated was not always sufficient to convincingly place the experience of criminals within the scope of the audience's empathy. Cumulative sin might present the didactic model of the descent into crime, but such moralising warned only of what was to come; it did not directly appeal to the reader's experience. The balancing act between the motivations of self-indulgence and social responsibility was likely to have been within the experience of the majority of the audience, and many of the narratives recognised the need to incorporate the cycles of conscience that were symptomatic of the competition between good and evil motions within the mind.

Such was the emphasis on the diabolic mental/spiritual state of murderers that, for all the pamphlets lovingly retold the bloodiest aspects of the crime, the acts themselves tended not to be directly demonised. There was no sense that the act of stabbing, bludgeoning or poisoning characterised the diabolic, even if the acts of murderers could be excessively violent. Master Page was strangled in his bed, evidence of the desperate struggle seen in the self-inflicted wounds left when he tore at his throat to try to free himself, 'even in the anguish of death'. By contrast, the wife of Thomas Cash, weakened by illness, in 'no way was able to make resistance against his barbarous crueltie'. But again it was the 'psychological' state in which these acts were carried out which confirmed the Devil's hold over the murderer, not the acts themselves. Like premeditation, such cruelty required a degree of will-power and single-mindedness that could only originate with Satan. It was the savagery with

[63] *Two Horrible and inhumane murthers. Done in Linconeshire by two husbands* (London, 1607), pp. 37–8.

[64] *A Briefe discourse of two most cruell and bloudie Murthers*, sig. A5.

[65] Ibid., sig. A5v; similarly see *A Blazing Starre seene in the West at Totnets in Devonshire . . ., Wherein is manifested how Master Ralph Ashley, a devout Cavalier, attempted to ravish a young Virgin, the daughter of Mr. Adam Fisher, inhabiting neare the said towne* (London, 1642), sig. A3.

which the Bristol man, John Kynnester, stabbed his wife to which attention was drawn. 'A wound or twoo had bene enow / If it had been no more', yet every spark of life in the injured woman had merely driven Kynnester further into a frenzy. Unaware of his murderous intent, Thomas Cash's wife had 'spoke in kind and loving manner unto him', which should have placated him, but, 'the divell growing great within him, and pricking him forwardes to the pretended murther', he abandoned all constraint of conscience and husbandly feeling.[66] In the case of John Reynolds' Alibius, when an initial attempt to poison his wife failed he remained focused – 'the deuill had bewitched his understanding and judgement: for he could see by no other eyes, but those of revenge and bloud'.[67] Sometimes the Devil's influence rendered murderers so bloodthirsty that the deaths of their victims were not enough. In 1605, the nobleman Sir John Fitz killed an innkeeper in Twickenham. The killing might have been expected to assuage his violent madness, 'yet was the Devil so strong in him, as that not contented therewith, he prickes him on vnto further mischiefe: he will not be satisfied vnlesse he shed his own blood likewise'. Fitz inserted his sword into a mud wall, enabling him to run himself through.[68]

Perhaps the best example of the Devil's work on the criminal's mental state is contained in the pamphlet produced by a number of nonconformist divines to tell the story of Thomas Savage. Savage, a profligate who went from sabbath-breaking to consorting with prostitutes, was persuaded by one 'vile strumpet' to steal money from his master, a vintner to whom he was apprenticed. His initial resistance stemmed not from morality but from practicality – to rob his master he would first have to kill the housemaid. On the day he finally committed the killing he returned to his master's house having been with his prostitute. Even though she had 'again perswaded him to knock the Maid on the head', there is no indication in the narrative that he actually intended to do so. Rather than premeditation proper, his violence seems to have been the result of an argument he had with the maid. She berated him for consorting with prostitutes, and, as he grew angry, the Devil took hold of his thoughts. 'While he was at Dinner', the pamphlet relates, 'the Devil entered so strong into him, that nothing would satisfie but he must kill her, and no other way but with a hammer.' Throwing a hammer at the maid he knocked her down, but having committed the initial assault he was paralysed, and although he attempted three times to bludgeon her, he could not complete the killing. It was only through Satan's influence that the frenzy

[66] *Two Horrible and inhumane murthers*, p. 38.
[67] Reynolds, *Triumph of Gods Revenge*, p. 68.
[68] *The Bloudy Book, or the tragicall and desperate end of Sir Iohn Fites (alias) Fitz* (London, 1605), sigs. D3–E3.

was renewed, as the pamphlet describes: 'at last the Divel was so great with him, that he taketh the hammer and striketh her many blows with all the force he could and even rejoyced that he had got the victory over her'.[69]

It has been noted that demonised criminals in the period did not exhibit the devillish physical characteristics – such as horns or tails – that had been applied to marginalised groups in medieval Europe. But there was a diabolic physicality that was symptomatic of the Devil's hold on the mind in the same way as the convulsions and ravings of demoniacs were. Rather than in aberrant (preternatural) characteristics, demonic physicality was embodied as a human grotesque, exhibiting an hysterical, murderous frenzy and unnatural strength. John Fitz provides one of the most explicit examples. Suffering from a hysterical fear of being pursued for a previous killing, Fitz had appeared: 'his eyes looking as if they hadde sparked frorth fire; his countenaunce so terrible and ghastly, as that it was of the power to have scarred a mann out of his wittes; and his strength so forceable . . . it was bootles for one or two to withstand him, (for needs must he go whom the divell drives)'.[70] But more striking was the way diabolic intrusion turned its victims into 'emotional grotesques'. Criminals mediated Satan's agency because his influence had wrought within their consciousness some fundamental confusion of morality and judgement. As empathy demanded that the reader recognise the motivating emotions of the murderer, it could also bring into focus the satanic disruption visited upon moral reasoning. Accompanying diabolic intrusion was a progressive moral degeneration, another potential vicarious experience for the reader, by which he could 'feel' the Devil turn the criminal into a human grotesque. Rather than being the unthinking servants of Satan, criminals were seen to share a basic interest with him, expressed in a corrupted moral logic. This perverse reasoning marked the crime out as far beyond the pale of endemic human sin, but the workings of the criminal's mind were still assumed to be intuitively comprehensible to the audience.

In the narrative of the Penryn murder, diabolically induced confusion was expressed in the stepmother's careless assumption that her crime might go unpunished. The author equates her with Eve when he notes that: 'she like her first Grandam, seeing the golde fare to look too, and the taske easily and without much danger to be affected, tooke the Deuill at his worde, and tyed her self to him with an oath, that if she might peaceably inioy the gold, the true owner of it should never wake'.[71] In resisting temptation, the father concentrated on the inevitable 'strange iudgements of God' worked on those

[69] Robert Franklin, Thomas Vincent, Thomas Doolitel, James Janeway and Hugh Baker, *A Murderer Punished and Pardoned: Or, a True Relation of the Wicked Life, and Shameful-Happy death of Thomas Savage* (London, 1668), p. 4.

[70] *The Bloudy Book*, sig. D4. [71] *Newes from Perin*, sig. B5.

guilty of murder, demonstrating a concern for his spiritual state in stark contrast to her carelessness. 'He concluded his speech with that part of scripture; What will it avayle a man or woman to get the whole world, and lose his owne soule', the pamphlet noted, implying his potential for godliness.[72] But Satan's control over the stepmother's mind was total: 'for such a deepe impression of gaine, and palpable reasons of safety, had the Deuill granted in her thoughts, twas impossible to rub them out'.[73] If presumption and despair represented the poles of spiritual experience, each potentially indicating reprobation, Protestant soteriology was clear as to which was the most dangerous. In *The Practise of Pietie* Lewis Bayly wrote 'despaire is nothing so dangerous as presumption; for we read not in all the scriptures of above three or foure whom roaring despaire ouerthrew; but secure presumption hath sent millions to Perdition without any noise'.[74] Presumption here expressed not a misreading of the Protestant ideal of assurance, but rather a careless assumption of a more general and less demanding election than that predicted by strict predestination. The stepmother's arguments did not stem from antinomianism, but from a spiritual carelessness instilled by Satan, 'whose advocate she was'.[75] In her words and conduct, spiritual and physical safety were equated, and her condition for carrying out the killing – that she should be allowed to enjoy her gold 'peaceably' – was to be read as a reference to both conscience and liberty. Her husband, even as he committed the act, was achingly aware that a difference must be drawn between man's earthly estate and that in which he will spend eternity. Even the former is so precarious that the latter can never be ignored; God's providence might be visited on a man at a moment if it is exercised by such a sin as murder. The confusion of the stepmother's moral reasoning was Satan's triumph. As William Perkins eloquently expressed it, in a treatise on the flesh and the spirit, the Devil was 'painting out the eye of the mind with the deceitfull profits and pleasures of poisonous sin'.[76] In the Penryn narrative the father's method of murdering his son, slitting his throat, was to be seen in all its unnatural horror, evidenced by the prodigy that accompanied it: the beating and crying of a screech-owl at the window 'as if she had said, Awake young man awake'.[77] But again it was not so much the act that was diabolic as the stepmother's spiritually careless belief that it could go unpunished. The audience was to recognise that such emotions were incongruous with the act being carried out; moral reasoning had been lost.

[72] Ibid. [73] Ibid. [74] Bayly, *The Practice of Pietie*, p. 133. [75] *News from Perin*, sig. B5.
[76] William Perkins, *Two Treatises: I. Of the Nature and Practice of Repentance. II. Of the Combate of the Flesh and the Spirit*, in his *Works*, vol. I, p. 463.
[77] *News from Perin*, sig. C.

Nor was it the act of poisoning that was diabolic in Gilbert Dugdale's account of Elizabeth Caldwell, but instead her inability to bring herself to prevent it. The satanic assault on Caldwell produced in her a kind of moral degradation, in which the moral reasoning, whilst remaining intact, was unable to assert itself over the evil that surrounded it. Throughout her seduction by Jeffrey Bownd and Isobel Hall, her developed godly conscience struggled to regain its moral equilibrium, an experience internalised as a diabolically induced psychomachia, and externally expressed as an attempt to persuade Bownd from his course:

> shee often times entring into consideration with herselfe, what a damnable part it was, first to abuse her husbands bed, and then in seeming to deprive him of his life, was greatly tormented in her conscience, and divers times, earnestlie intreated them to surcease in this practice, laying before them the great and heavy punishments, provided for such offenders in the world to come.[78]

When Caldwell finally acquiesced to the murder, and gave her husband poisoned oatcakes, her conscience was struggling to assert itself to the last. 'So soone as he was departed the chamber with the cakes', Dugdale noted, 'feare drove such a terror to her hart as she lay in bed, as she even trembled with remorse of conscience, yet wanted the power to call to him to refraine them.' Poisoning, as a secret crime, was reserved special condemnation in contemporary jurisprudence, yet Dugdale's pamphlet made no attempt to suggest that this method was unusually diabolic when practised by Caldwell and her tempters.[79] Instead it was this inability to warn her husband that confirmed her moral degradation. It was true that she committed a diabolic act in acceding to the poisoning, but more significant was that she failed to commit a godly act in preventing the crime when the opportunity was presented to her. Through the employment of his instruments, Bownd and Hall, the Devil laid, not a single snare, but a web to catch Caldwell's soul, and envelopment allowed her godly instincts to be almost completely stifled. This seems to have been how Caldwell herself came to view her crime. In her execution speech she reportedly stated that her sin stemmed from 'her owne filthy flesh, the illutions of the deuill, and those hellish instruments which he set on worke: yet notwithstanding, she ever had a detestation to those sinnes that she lived in, but she affirmed that she wanted the grace to avoid them'.[80]

Perhaps the most developed expression of the diabolic confusion of moral reasoning is to be found in those murders which betrayed patriarchal

[78] Dugdale, *A True Discourse of the Practices of Elizabeth Caldwell*, sig. B.
[79] For a useful discussion of the cultural resonance of poisoning and its manipulation in the court process, see Lindley, *The Trials of Frances Howard*, pp. 164–7.
[80] Dugdale, *A True Discourse of the Practices of Elizabeth Caldwell*, sig. D.

obligations to protect and maternal obligations to nurture – uxoricide and infanticide. The response to petty treason has often been seen to express particular fears over the fragility of patriarchy; the crime was, after all specifically defined in law, whereas uxoricide was not. But in uxoricide a man abandoned the ideal of reasoned government over his wife and embraced a form of domestic oppression which Frances Dolan has usefully termed 'petty tyranny'.[81] In such cases the illogicality of destroying one's own household was presented as chaotically demonic. In 1573, John Kynnester confessed to murdering his wife as the result of a demonic voice which intruded on his mind urging him to do it. But the act brought none of the hysterical guilt with which the more moralising of the pamphleteers liked to characterise their killers;[82] instead he experienced a bizarre satisfaction. Had he been sure of his escape, he commented, he would have called his neighbours 'to see what had between us fall', and eventually the urge to exhibit his work proved irresistible:

> For then my wife on ground laie dedde,
> Before a slepe she was on bedde,
> And yet my minde was awaies ledde,
> Against her for to be,
> For I no sorrowe yet did taste,
> Rose up againe in all the hast,
> Out at a windowe I her cast,
> Cause people should her see.[83]

Confirmed in sin, Kynnester embraced chaos for its own sake – there was no inversion or perverted logic behind his violence and his pride in meaningless, chaotic destruction was a demonstration of the indelible change the Devil had wrought on his moral faculties. As readers were able to recognise the commonplace emotions that led to murder, they might also identify the

[81] Dolan, *Dangerous Familiars*, pp. 106–9.

[82] Anthony Munday succinctly expressed a common view: 'horrour and feare alwayes accompanieth the murtherer, his owne conscience is to him a thousand witnesses, hee standeth in dreade of every bush, beast and birde, he imagineth that every thing discouereth his euill, and many times it falleth out, that the silly creatures of the earth detecteth him', *Sundry Strange and Inhumaine Murthers*, sig. A2.

[83] *A true reporte or description of . . . John Kynnester*, sig. A5. The importance of an assessment of the murderer's emotional state after the fact, and the utility of the Devil in providing one, is hinted at by other pamphlets. The bawd and petty traitor Margaret Ferneseede seems to have been convicted on purely circumstantial evidence, and the account lays a great stress on her inability to even feign sorrow over the death of her husband – 'she whome the Deuill now would not suffer to dissemble, (though his greatest art be in dissimulation)'. The implication was that Ferneseede was either unaware of the nature of her crime or utterly careless of its consequent punishment. The Devil's hold was so strong that she could not/would not even approximate the emotions of innocence in order to hide her guilt. *The Araignment & Burning of Margaret Ferne-seede, for the Murther of her late husband Anthony Ferne-seede, found dead in Peckham Field neere Lambeth* (London, 1608), sig. A4.

fundamental dislocation of morality, emotion and context which diabolic temptation produced. Satisfaction was utterly incongruous with the act Kynnester had carried out, whilst other emotions which should have been present, such as pity and remorse, were conspicuously absent. The implication was that Satan had stifled the workings of the murderer's humanity. In another example, John Reynolds endowed his narrative of Alibius' murder of his wife with overtones of suicide, equating wife murder with an abandonment of the natural human instinct of self-preservation which could only be diabolic. 'To kill those who love us', he noted, 'and to deprive those of life, who (did occasion present) are ready to sacrifice theirs for the preservation of ours, it must needs proceed rather from a monster then a man, or rather from a devill then a monster.'[84]

Child murder in early modern England was most commonly infanticide, a crime of desperation carried out by women in order to escape the consequences of bearing an illegitimate child.[85] But again pamphlet narratives could be starkly at odds with the real nature of crime, and in some cases another diabolic perversion of familial logic accounted for the murder of children. Parents were shown murdering their offspring in a confused effort to protect them. Such was the case with Margaret Vincent in 1616, whose Catholicism drove her to kill two of her children. At first her husband had indulged her religion and attempted to persuade her from it, but eventually he grew tired of debating with her, 'many times snubbing her with some few unkinde speeches which bred in her heart a purpose of most extremity'. Vincent became convinced that murder was the only way to save her children from Protestantism:

> For having learned this maxim of their Religion, that it was merritorious, yea and pardonable, to take away the lives of any opposing Protestants, were it of any degree whatsoever, in which resolution of bloody purpose she long stood vpon and at last onley by the Diuels temptation resolued the ruine of her owne children, affirming to her conscience these reasons, that they were brought up in blindnes and darksome errours, hoodwinked (by her husbands instructions) from the true light, and therefore to save their soule (as she vainly thought) she purposed to become a Tygerous Mother and so wolvishly to commit the murder of her owne flesh and blood, in which opinion she steadfastly continued, never relenting according to nature, but casting about to find time and place for so wicked a deed.[86]

'By the fury and assistance of the Devil', Vincent strangled two of her children with a garter, and was only prevented from dispatching a third

[84] Reynolds, *Triumph of Gods Revenge*, p. 63.

[85] Cynthia Herrup, *The Common Peace: Participation and the Criminal Law in Seventeenth-Century England* (Cambridge, 1987), p. 173; Sharpe, *Crime in Early Modern England*, pp. 109–110.

[86] *A pittilesse Mother*, sig. A3.

because it was with a nurse. The author drew attention again and again to her diabolically corrupted logic. Vincent 'by nature should have cherished [her children] with her owne body, as the Pelican which pecks her owne breast to feede her young ones with her own bloode'. The Catholicism that drove Vincent's 'inhumane devotion' put her actions beyond the pale, as she became a 'creature not deserving Mother's name'. But rather than an expression of the anti-motherhood which recent witchcraft studies have shown to express a pervasive threat to contemporaries, Vincent's perverted logic was a hollow mask, hiding the Devil's influence.[87] As in the case of Sir John Fitz, the emptiness of the act became clear when its commission failed to satisfy her and she was driven in a murderous frenzy to attempt suicide. 'She began to grow desperate and still desire more blood', the pamphlet noted, describing how she tried first to hang and then to drown herself.[88]

In other cases the murder of children was an expression of diabolically induced despair, akin to that by which the Devil drove men to suicide.[89] In John Taylor's account of the crimes of John Rowse, symptoms of diabolically corrupted reasoning allowed the author to explain how this most female of crimes had been taken up by a man. Necessity had driven Rowse to return to his second wife and children, but his poverty and misery made him easy prey to diabolic temptation. 'The Diuell still tempting him to mischiefe and despaire', Taylor observed, 'putting him in mind of his former better estate, comparing pleasures past with present miseries'.[90] In a state of utter despair Rowse decided to end his children's misery by working 'some meanes to take away their languishing liues by a speedy & vntimely death'.[91] He drowned them in a water spring in the cellar of his house, but was so 'weary of his life' that he made no attempt to escape.[92] Taylor's mawkish commentary sought to highlight again the incongruity between the emotional drive and the action, which were symptomatic of the Devil's influence. 'It is too manifestly knowne what a number of Step mothers and Strumpets haue most inhumanely murdred their Children', he commented,

> but in the memory of man (nor scarcely in any history) is it not to be found, that a Father did euer take two Inocent Children out of their beds, and with weeping tears of pitilesse pitie, and vnmercifull mercy, to drowne them, showing such compassionate cruelty and sorrowfull sighing, remourselesse remorce in that most vnfatherly and vnnatural deede.

[87] Willis, *Malevolent Nurture*, pp. 29–65; D. Purkiss, *The Witch in History: Early Modern and Twentieth-Century Representations* (London, 1996), pp. 129–39.

[88] *A pittilesse Mother*, sig. A4v; for a discussion of the fluid cultural associations of maternal infanticide with both self-destruction and self-preservation, with reference to *A pittlilesse Mother*, see Dolan, *Dangerous Familiars*, pp. 142–50.

[89] MacDonald and Murphy, *Sleepless Souls*, pp. 34–60.

[90] Taylor, *The Vnnatural Father*, sig. B. [91] Ibid., sig. Bv. [92] Ibid., sig. B2.

'All of which', Taylor concluded, 'may be attributed to the malice of the Diuell.'[93]

TEMPTATION AND THE PHYSICAL DEVIL

Whilst physical interaction with the Devil maintained its hold in witchcraft narratives, the notion of internal intrusion did reshape the physical depiction of Satan in some plays and ballads. For obvious reasons theatrical representations of Satan were physical,[94] but it is significant that they could be used to dramatise the diabolic intrusion into the mind inherent in temptation. The representations by which demonic activity was 'signposted' to the audience could be appropriated to intimate the invisible workings of the Devil on the conscience.

In Rowley, Dekker and Ford's play *The Witch of Edmonton* (1621), diabolic intrusion is represented in a sub-plot concerning the bigamy and then murder committed by Frank Thorney. Duped into secretly marrying Winnifride, he is then pressured into marrying Susan Carter as an advantageous match. He resolves to run away with Winnifride, but the clinging Susan, unaware of his intentions, angers him by trying to hold him back. The Devil has already appeared in the play in the shape of a black dog called Tom, and has forced the old crone, Elizabeth Sawyer, to compact with him and become a witch. Now he appears to drive Thorney to a murder he had not previously contemplated. For the Devil it is just one more malicious act, but in declaring his intention he notes how Thorney's anger has made him susceptible to murderous temptation. 'Now for an early mischief and a sudden', Dog declares, 'The mind's about it now. One touche from me / Soon sets the body forward.'[95] As Thorney and Susan argue, Dog approaches and 'rubs' him, a representation of his power over the mind, after which Thorney becomes immediately set on murder:

Frank Thorney: Why, you almost anger me. Pray you, be gone.
You have no company, and 'tis very early;
Some hurt may betide you homewards.
Susan: Tush! I fear none.
To leave you is the greatest hurt I can suffer.

[93] Ibid., sig. C.

[94] See, for example, Christopher Marlowe, *The Tragical History of Doctor Faustus* (1589) in *The Complete Plays*; Robert Greene, *The Honourable Friar Bacon and Friar Bungay* (London, 1594); *The Birth of Merlin: or, The Childe hath found his Father* (Elizabethan, printed London, 1662); *The Merry Devill of Edmonton* (London, 1608); Thomas Dekker, *If This be not a Good Play, the Diuell is in It* (1612), in Dekker, *Dramatic Works*, vol. III.

[95] Rowley, Dekker and Ford, *The Witch of Edmonton*, Act III, scene iii, 1–3.

Besides, I expect your father and mine own
To meet me back, or overtake me with you.
They began to stir when I came after you;
I know they'll not be long.

Frank Thorney: [*Aside*] So. I shall have more trouble.
DOG *rubs him.*
Thank you for that. Then I'll ease all at once.
'Tis done now, what I ne're thought on. [*To her*]
You shall not go back.

Susan: Why? Shall I go along with thee? Sweet music!

Frank Thorney: No, to a better place.

Susan: Any place, I.
I'm there at home where thou pleasest to have me.

Frank Thorney: At home? I'll leave you in your last lodging.
I must kill you.

Susan: O, fine! You'd fright me from you.

Frank Thorney: You see I had no purpose, I'm unarmed.
'Tis this minute's decree, and it must be.
Look, this will serve your turn.
[*Draws a knife*]

. . .

Your marriage was my theft,
For I espoused your dowry, and I have it.
I did not purpose to have added murder;
The devil did not prompt me. Till this minute
You might have safe returned; now you cannot.
You have dogged your own death.
Stabs her.[96]

Through the physical action of Dog, the audience – who are invited to use the same special insight as the readers of the murder pamphlets – perceive the Devil take hold of Thorney's will, which he himself does not. Thus the scene dramatised the ease with which the Devil might place thoughts of murder in a mind already given over to sin, and how those thoughts could appear to originate within the individual.[97]

[96] Ibid., Act III, scene iii, 7–25 and 34–40.

[97] For other examples in which the physicality of the stage expressed a dynamic of satanic envelopment and intrusion, unseen to the protagonists but shown to the insight of the audience, see William Shakespeare, *Othello*, esp. Act II, scene iii, 315–329; *Macbeth*, Act I, scene iii, 133–141, Act I, scene v, 48–52; *A Yorkshire Tragedy* (London, 1608), Act V, scene 43, 57–62; *The Life of Mother Shipton: A New Comedy* (London, 1660), Act I, scene i.

Similarly, the early seventeenth-century ballad, *A new Ballad, shewing the great misery sustained by a poore man in Essex, his wife and children, with other strange things done by the Devil* demonstrates how comfortably these pictures of the diabolic corruption of moral reasoning could sit with the more folkloric elements of popular narratives. The ballad may loosely be based on a real event, but is an amalgam of folklore, contemporary views on social responsibility and the motivation for entering into a diabolic pact, and the role of the Devil in driving men to murder, all glossed with a Protestant rhetoric of temptation. It does not dwell on the crime itself – indeed murder only becomes likely towards the end of the story – and is averted by the last-minute return of a local gentleman. Instead it concentrates on how the poor man is propelled by his desperate circumstances into the path of the Devil.[98]

The narrative tells of the terrible pressure on the poor man to find food for his starving family. His wife is lying in after the birth of another child, and his other children beg him 'pittiously' to provide for them. The poor man resolves to go to a wood to find acorns to roast, and on the way meets several farmers from whom he begs food. In a parallel of the witch's fall, charity is refused by these 'churlish sort', who reject his offer to work in return, claiming they have already given him too much. The poor man is now in a suitable mental state to encounter the Devil, who appears in human form: 'behold! / a tall man did him meet, / And cole-black were his garments all / from his head to his feet.' When the Devil asks him why he is so wretched, the poor man, without knowing who it is, asks to borrow some money. In other folktales in which humans made pacts with the Devil, they did so with seemingly little threat to their eternal souls once Satan's immediate machinations were thwarted. In *A new Ballad*, however, the heinousness of his unwitting apostasy is made clear, associating the narrative with more self-consciously Protestant concerns over the dangers of hidden diabolism within the 'quick-fix' culture of cunning men and folk magic.[99] 'Hereby', the ballad declares, 'this wretched man / committed wondrous evill, / He begd an almes, and did not know / he askt it of the Devill.' The Protestant emphasis becomes more apparent when Satan, adopting his familiar tempting guise as sophister, attempts to undermine the poor man's godly self-conception. He taunts him with questions such as 'an odious sinner art thou then, / that dost such want sustain?' and 'if thou so faithfull be, / why goest thou begging then?' The poor man is able to overcome these questions with reference to Job, and explicitly places himself among the 'godly'. The narrative re-adopts

[98] *A new Ballad, shewing the great misery sustained by a poore man in Essex, his wife and children, with other strange things done by the Devil* (*c.* 1620–30), pp. 286–7.

[99] Stuart Clark, 'The Rational Witchfinder: Conscience, Demonological Naturalism and Popular Superstitions', in S. Pumfrey, P. L. Rossi and M. Slawinski (eds.), *Science, Culture and Popular Belief in Renaissance Europe* (Manchester, 1991), pp. 227–35.

its folkloric style when finally the Devil gives him 'the fairest purse in sight / That ever mortall eye beheld', with a promise that he should have more if he wants it.

The poor man has fallen foul of a classic trick of the Devil, for when he gets home to his family he finds the money in the purse has turned to oak leaves. Returning to the wood to try to find the money, he encounters the Devil again, who tells him to look inside his shirt, where he had kept the purse. When the poor man finds no money, but his shirt full of toads, he is finally overcome by the Devil's arguments that his troubles are a sign of his reprobation, allowing the Devil to introduce thoughts of suicide and murder into his mind:

> 'See', quoth the Devill, 'vengeance doth
> pursue thee every houre!'
> 'Goe, cursed wretch!', quoth he,
> 'and rid away thy life;
> But murther first thy children yong
> and miserable wife.'

The poor man, 'raging mad', heads home to commit the deed, but the Devil's plan is thwarted by the providential return of 'the chiefest man / that in that parish dwelt', bringing food and money which he, in contrast to the 'churlish' farmers, deals out liberally. He has the poor man bound to his bed until, after a long sickness, he is cured of his murderous thoughts. The ballad ends with a plea to God to similarly protect others 'from all temptations'.

Thus, whilst a distinction between physical and internal temptation persisted, it only remained sharply drawn in witchcraft narratives. In other areas of culture the conception of temptation was more fluid, and more susceptible to the influence of the Protestant emphasis on internal intrusion. Through the use of 'unseen' characters on stage, or the depiction of sudden changes in character after physical contact with Satan, audiences could be expected to understand the insidious nature of the diabolic subversion of the will. Perhaps, as with the murder pamphlets, they might also be expected to enter into the scheme of special insight into satanic agency, and experience an empathy with the victim of temptation.

Is this, then, what the Devil was to the reader of the narrative of diabolically inspired crime? It is at least what their authors hoped he would be. The responses of the readers themselves are irrecoverable, but the depiction of diabolically inspired crime was consistent enough, throughout the seventeenth century and into the eighteenth, to suggest that it found favour with the readership. We cannot assume that readers responded to a narrative as a whole, and we must recognise their ability to enjoy a story without accepting, or even listening to, any of the moralising or demonisation contained within it. But I would suggest that the depiction of the Devil in these narratives is so bound up with the appeal to the audience's emotional empathy, and vice versa, and the emotions the Devil is assumed to manipulate so commonplace, that the stories become incomprehensible without to some degree entering into the dynamic of diabolic temptation depicted in them. Diabolism in criminal narratives, it is being argued, allowed the threat of demonic temptation and its consequences to be made insidious by interpreting it as the amplification of corrupt human traits and drives, recognised and identified with by the reader. This picture of diabolic agency corresponded to that being produced in theological and conduct literature, and was essentially Protestant. Even if the audience did not fully internalise the *consequences* of the dynamic of diabolic temptation, these narratives were an effective method of delineating a Satanic agency contained by the re-focused Protestant remit of his activity. The apostate stepmother took the Devil at his word when he appealed to her spiritual carelessness, and he set up his kingdom, piece by piece, in opposition to that of Christ. Caldwell's sin was spiritual weakness and the Devil was the stifling enveloper, blocking out the godly influence she so badly needed. The very emphasis on the havoc Satan wreaked on moral judgement provided further evidence of the consequences of temptation, to be understood vicariously by the reader.

The art historian Luther Link, describing the difficulty artists and iconographers had depicting Satan, notes that he was essentially an abstraction, and that 'not convincingly felt as a "person", he could not be shown as an evil force'.[100] The use of the Devil in the crime narratives would not lead us to such a conclusion. Satan was an empathic expression of the potential for evil found within men, but he was not a symbolic projection. The conception of the Devil's temptation as an internal working of the mind was not a half-way house on the way to an acceptance of the potential for purely human evil. Rather it was a sophisticated appeal to the imagination that did not transplant evil to the removed safety of the monstrous. Murderers and witches, accepting the Devil's terms and being morally/spiritually transformed by them, were, in a very literal sense, 'incarnate devils'. As such they embodied and expressed Satan's agency for those with the required insight to see. Perception did not involve a distanced observation, it required an engagement with the world of the diabolic, and incarnate devils facilitated that engagement. Rather than marginalising his influence around a criminal element, demonisation through temptation affected to bring ordinary people closer to the Devil. No reassurance was offered by asking the audience to empathise with the emotional experience of insidious temptation. Through guided empathy the Devil might indeed be 'felt'. It seems that, potentially, in the empathic expression of diabolic influence, rather than its animistic representation, the Devil might be experienced vicariously as never before.

[100] Link, *The Devil*, p. 183.

6

'What concord hath Christ with Belial?': de facto satanism and the temptation of the body politic, 1570–1640

As internal temptation allowed the godly, and the not so godly, to engage with the experience of the demonic subversion of the conscience, so a concept of the temptation of the body politic provided a parallel political analogy which gave a focus to the perception of the subversion of the commonwealth. The final part of this study examines the development of this discourse within England's internal politics, from its definition in Elizabethan conflicts over religious subversion and treason, to the Caroline regime's increasing inability to maintain a theocratic opposition between kingship and diabolism, and ultimately to the reactions to the breakdown of government in the 1640s, in which the perception of diabolism pervaded the polemic of both the royalist and the parliamentarian parties.

It has been argued by a number of historians of the early modern period that the English political nation possessed no language of opposition. Political rhetoric was dominated by an emphasis on consensus, and thus conflict originated in disagreements over the practical operation of the constitution.[1] This picture has been supported by recent work on witchcraft, which has highlighted the way in which an equation between witchcraft and rebellion provided, in Peter Elmer's words, a 'normative system of discourse which fostered unity and concord in the body politic'.[2] Moreover, this discourse could only survive as an instrument of consensus. Its factionalisation during the Civil War, Dr Elmer argues, entirely destroyed witchcraft's

[1] Kenyon, *The Stuart Constitution*, p. 9; Glenn Burgess, *The Politics of the Ancient Constitution*, chapters 5–7; Conrad Russell, 'Divine Rights in the Early Seventeenth Century', in J. Morrill, P. Slack and D. Woolf (eds.), *Public Duty and Private Conscience in Seventeenth-Century England: Essays Presented to G. E. Aylmer* (Oxford, 1993), pp. 101–20; in contrast see Sommerville, *Politics and Ideology in England*, pp. 3–4; Richard Cust and Ann Hughes (eds.), *Conflict in Early Stuart England: Studies in Religion and Politics 1603–1642* (London, 1989).

[2] Peter Elmer, '"Saints or Sorcerers": Quakerism, Demonology and the Decline of Witchcraft in Seventeenth-Century England', in J. Barry, M. Hester and G. Roberts (eds.), *Witchcraft in Early Modern Europe* (Cambridge, 1996), p. 174.

political vitality.[3] The ideas and the practice of divine kingship were bound up with a perceived opposition between what Stuart Clark has called 'marvellous monarchy' and witchcraft as anti-government. The position was expressed by consistent reference to 1 Samuel 15: 23 – 'For Rebellion is the sin of witchcraft.'[4] This rhetoric of consensual politics was employed widely through early modern Europe to demonstrate the mirror kingly authority provided to its divine origin. Challenges to that authority must by definition be an expression of the contrariety practised by God's ape. Theocracy, like so many early modern political, religious and social tenets, was best understood through an exploration of its antithesis, but preaching consensual politics as an ideal was not the same as practising it. Johann Sommerville has demonstrated that profoundly different views on the nature of politics underlay agreement on the principle of unity, and Linda Levy Peck has argued persuasively that the ideology of political patronage, and the perception of its abuse, provided a language in which opposition might be expressed through accusations of corruption, and which would eventually be used to justify the overthrow of a supposedly absolute monarch.[5]

The hitherto unexplored prevalence of a concept of diabolic subversion of the commonwealth provides a similar qualification. Within a decade of the Elizabethan settlement of 1559, a number of interested groups were arguing that the English body politic was as prey to temptation as the individual human body. In the established church hierarchy, and even in the operation of Elizabeth's parliaments, lay a satanic presence which threatened to seduce men into evil against the commonwealth. As we have seen, temptation was understood to involve the Devil entering the mind and exploiting the evil potential already lying within. Spiritual health involved actively resisting his influence and suppressing the insidious corruption he introduced into the conscience. The diabolic potential that lay within the commonwealth was the human population itself. Every individual was corrupted with the legacy of Adam, and his inherent sinfulness might be activated if the Devil managed to introduce the right triggers into the nation. Belief in the parallel temptation of body and body politic did not, of course, in itself constitute a language of opposition. It still maintained an ideal of consensual Christian government and presented satanic agency as driven by a desire to subvert that ideal. Yet where the Devil's triggers were to be found was an open question and one which allowed individuals to interpret those aspects of church or state to which they were opposed – and, as importantly, those in opposition

3 Ibid., pp. 174–5, 179.
4 Clark, *Thinking with Demons*, chapter 41; Elmer, 'Saints or Sorcerers', pp. 164–5.
5 Sommerville, *Politics and Ideology in England*; Peck, *Court Patronage and Corruption in early Stuart England*, pp. 185–221.

themselves – as pollutants from the Devil, who sought to seduce the nation into apostasy. For some the maintenance of the Devil's episcopacy provoked arrogance and tyranny in the bishops' government of the church. Similarly papal claims to deposing power could appear to be a trigger that could ignite regicidal fervour in once-loyal Catholic subjects. Or the justifications of divine right in the 1620s might seem to tempt the king to tyranny.

For many the ideal of consensus under theocracy could not be allowed to overshadow the importance of establishing and maintaining the purity of the Christian commonwealth. The verse 1 Samuel 15: 23 might express the diabolism of opposition/rebellion, but it was only one of a number of verses of scripture commonly cited to guide political judgement and action. Equally prevalent was 2 Corinthians 6: 14–15 – 'What concord hath Christ with Belial?' Used extensively in anti-Catholic synagogue of Satan polemic, the text demanded an absolute purity of religion and church government, and was extensively used by nonconformists and separatists to denounce the tolerance of popish remnants they perceived in the reformed church. A further reference to 2 Corinthians 11: 14 – 'for Satan himself is transformed into an angel of light' – warned against the potential dangers inherent in that which might appear most beneficial or harmless. Whilst all but the most radical separatist paid lip service to the ideal of consensus under the (more or less) divine monarch, many not only believed in the possibility of the demonic temptation of the commonwealth, but were also ready to vehemently argue divergent views as to where that corruption lay, often placing it at the heart of politics, culture or religion. Those most vocal in expressing these concerns were naturally those with an axe to grind, but there is no reason to suppose the perception of diabolic subversion was extremist in itself. It was a legacy of the confessional disputes of the Reformation which have been examined above, bound up with the popular fear of Catholics and witches, and it also fed the concerns over disorder, which historians have shown to be widely shared in the period.

THE ELIZABETHAN RELIGIOUS CONTROVERSIES AND THE CONCEPT OF DE FACTO SATANISM

The 'synagogue of Satan' was as suited to the denunciation of perceived failure of Protestant reform as it was to the stigmatisation of Catholicism. It rested, as we have seen, on a monopoly of interpretation demanding that the Devil be seen hidden in that which might not appear diabolic. Moreover, it had been extensively used to stigmatise popish ceremony and the episcopacy, elements which for many remained troublingly 'half reformed' after 1559. If the popish episcopate was by nature the Devil's hierarchy, why should the English bishops be seen any differently? Potential for further trouble inhered in the idea that the greatest threat to the true church lay, not from a frontal assault, but from demonic subversion. If the Devil had been able to corrupt so totally the primitive church from the inside, might not he be able to do the same to the fragile reformed faith, beset by foreign enemies and threatened from within by an uncertain number of recusants? Whilst they naturally adhered to a single interpretative and polemical scheme, which highlighted demonic subversion as the greatest threat facing the reformed faith, Protestant conformists and nonconformists each perceived that subversion to inhere in the divergent activities of conformity and resistance. In the hands of Protestant controversialists the synagogue of Satan exhibited demonism's potential to be a sharply politicised interpretative scheme within the English establishment a century before the outbreak of the Civil War.

Concern over the demonic subversion of the faith became increasingly prevalent after the religious settlement of 1559, as the prospect of further reformation seemed to diminish, and the Elizabethan regime demonstrated its willingness to enforce conformity. Clerical dress, the maintenance of superstitious elements in the sacraments and the precedence given to the reading of prepared homilies and injunctions over the pure preaching of the word: all were condemned as popish and anti-Christian remnants polluting the reformed faith.[6] For nonconformists toleration of these remnants constituted the reality of a de facto satanism within the church. Since these practices had been the very cornerstones of the demonic subversion of the primitive church they maintained, by definition, a satanic presence within the reformed faith. Indeed, refusing to cleanse the English church of long-term diabolic subversion was tantamount to advocacy. A manuscript dialogue, probably written by William Turner, interpreted the surplice as a diabolic symbol of the Marian persecution. 'Have you forgotten', Turner's nonconformist demanded, 'those cruel and popish butchers which not long ago burned so many Christian martyrs, *which had on their heads such woollen horns*?'[7] It was a taste of what was to come when frustration forced an accommodation of moderates and radicals around the issue of Presbyterianism. For reformers like Edward Dering and Thomas Cartwright, the church presented a bewildering mixture of Protestant self-awareness, anti-Catholicism and half-measures at reform, with the maintenance of unsanctioned popish remnants and the

[6] Thomas Wilcox and John Field, *An Admonition to the Parliament* (1572), in *Puritan Manifestos: A Study of the Origins of the Puritan Revolt*, ed. W. H. Frere and C. E. Douglas (London, 1907; reprinted 1954), pp. 5–39.

[7] Quoted in P. Collinson, *The Elizabethan Puritan Movement* (Oxford, 1967), p. 95, my emphasis; see also the letter of George Withers to Prince Frederick III, Elector Palatine, requesting him to use his influence with Elizabeth against a diabolic attempt to subvert the Reformation by introducing Lutheranism, and Hierome Zanchius' letter to Elizabeth I of 10 September 1571, in *Zurich Letters (second series)*, pp. 157, 339.

active suppression of well-intentioned moves to purify the faith. These contradictions became focused in the dichotomy of 2 Corinthians. The English church was mixing Belial with Christ.

Thomas Wilcox and John Field's Presbyterian manifesto, *An Admonition to the Parliament* (1572), explicitly turned synagogue of Satan polemic onto the English church.[8] England, it noted, was so far from reformation that 'as yet we are not come to the outward face of the same'.[9] The Devil's influence was most clearly to be seen in the survival of the episcopate, whose justification was derived unequivocally from the papacy, and hence from the Devil.[10] The prayer book ordinance for the consecration of bishops, Field noted, was 'nothing else but a thing worde for worde drawne out of the Popes pontifical, wherin he sheweth himself to be Anti-christ most lively'. Regardless of personnel, a hierarchy derived from papal precedent maintained the Devil's government in the church since 'the Canon law is Antichristian and devilishe, and contrarye to the scriptures'.[11]

The case for de facto satanism was polemically astute. It did not require nonconformists to elaborate on what the bishops had done to encourage diabolism within the English church so much as what they had not done to prevent it. Indeed the burden of proof was firmly laid on the episcopate to show that they were *not* the servants of Satan. The point was well made by the pamphlet *An Exhortation to the Bishops and the Clergie*, a satirical attack made in the wake of the *Admonition*. The pamphlet affected to beg for some clarity on the confusing issue, noting that if the *Admonition* was true, 'we ought not to hear [the bishops], although they speake a truth, more then the devill was to be suffered, althoughe he professed Christ'. If the bishops could prove their innocence men might 'cast away that peevishe and fonde book', but if they could not England faced a stark choice between two deities. 'If Baall be God: folowe him', the author advised; 'if the Lord be God, followe him'.[12] Such rhetoric baited the episcopate by making unacceptable any defence that did not incorporate an active separation of Christ and Belial. This pre-emptive strike denounced any relative or subjective judgements as to the possible necessity of maintaining some traditional structures, noting,

8 Collinson, *The Elizabethan Puritan Movement*, p. 119.
9 Wilcox and Field, *Admonition to the Parliament*, p. 9; see Patrick McGrath, *Papists and Puritans under Elizabeth I* (London, 1967), pp. 133–7.
10 Wilcox and Field, *Admonition to the Parliament*, pp. 11–12, 30.
11 Ibid., p. 30; similarly, *An Exhortation to the Bishops* rejected the bishops' claims to tradition, noting, 'antiquitie may deceive us, nay we see it hathe deceived us, it is not true to say, it is old, therfore it is good: Sathan hath bene Lord of this world a great while'. See *Puritan Manifestos*, p. 76. See also John Greenwood, *A Briefe Refutation of Mr. George Giffard his supposed consimilitude between the Donatists and us* (1591), in *The Writings of John Greenwood and Henry Barrow 1591–1593*, ed. L. H. Carlson (London, 1970), p. 27.
12 *An Exhortation to the Bishops*, p. 73.

it is a common saying of two evils it is best to chuse the least: better it is to have a gospel of Christ joined with a peece of Antichrist, then to have none at all: thus they persuade them selves, the other [nonconformists] do not so, they thinke it not lawful to joine God & Belial together: surely they have some reason, nay they have greate reason, for what societie hathe light with darknesse.

The theme was taken up by Thomas Cartwright in his *A Replye to an answere made of M. Doctor Whitgifte* published in 1573. Was the difference between true faith and false doctrine really so muddied that they could no longer be separated without destroying the whole church? 'Seeing that Christ and Belial cannot agree', he noted, 'it is strange that the pure doctrine of the one, and the corruptions of the other, should cleave so fast together, that pure doctrine cannot be, with her safety, severed from the corruptions'.[13] Since the Corinthians dichotomy remained a prevalent part of conformist attacks on Catholic idolatry, such polemic was probably especially cutting.[14]

But if the presbyterians were now prepared to openly talk of a devilish episcopacy, conformists were as willing to denounce Presbyterian diabolism. Of course they rejected the assessment of de facto satanism within the established church; instead they drew on another aspect of synagogue of Satan polemic, that of 2 Corinthians 11: 14 – 'for Satan himself is transformed into an angel of light.' They argued that the nonconformist attack was itself an orchestration by the Devil who, in the face of the success of the Reformation, had now to subvert the church anew by adopting the guise of an ardent reformer and throwing religion into chaos. For Whitgift the *Admonition* was driven not by an interest in the faith but by that most diabolic of motives – malice. It was 'not loving, but spiteful, not brotherly, but unchristian, nay no admonition indeed, but a very scolding and uncharitable railing'. As such the church was under no obligation to take notice of it, but it was potentially more sinister still. It sought to overthrow the 'lawful and convenient' practices of the church and replace them with chaos and confusion, exchanging sound government for disorder. Seen in this light the true nature of the *Admonition* was all too clear. It was 'the extreme refuge of

13 Ibid., pp. 76–7; John Whitgift, *The Defense and answere to the Admonition, against the replie of T. C.*, in *The Works of John Whitgift*, ed. J. Ayre (Cambridge, Parker Society, 3 vols., 1851–3), vol. I, p. 39; Robert Harrison and Robert Browne, *A Treatise vpon the 23. of Matthew* (1582), in *The Writings of Robert Harrison and Robert Browne*, ed. A. Peel & L.H. Carlson (London, 1953), p. 211; John Penry, *The Notebook of John Penry 1593*, ed. A. Peel, Camden Society, third series, 67 (1944), p. 33; similar remarks were made by Job Throckmorton, quoted in Richard Bancroft, *Davngerovs Positions and Proceedings* (London, 1593), p. 58.

14 See, for example, the Elizabethan contribution to the homilies, 'An homily of the right use of the church', in *Certain Sermons or Homilies*, pp. 172–3.

Satan, when by other means he cannot, then to seek the overthrow of the gospel through contention about external things'.[15]

The initial burst of agitation for Presbyterianism was short-lived and commanded only limited support, but its rhetoric continued to influence the nonconformist attitude to the established church and its government. The Marprelate controversy gave more focus to these debates, and took the bishop-baiting begun by the *Exhortation* to new heights. But behind their satire, the Marprelate pamphlets made very serious points about the political and pastoral consequences of diabolic subversion. Marprelate did not disguise his delight at having (so he believed) caught out the dean of Salisbury, John Bridges. Bridges, writing against Cartwright in 1587, had claimed that there were only bishops of God and bishops of the Devil, the latter being those whose authority relied on man rather than the word.[16] For Marprelate, Bridges' own words put him between a rock and a hard place, since in order to deny episcopal diabolism he had to deny Elizabeth's authority over the English church. 'Our bishops are the bishops of the diuel', he gloated in *Hay any worke for Cooper* (1589), 'or their callings cannot be defended lawful, without flat and plaine treason in overthrowing her Maiesties supremacie.'[17] In the light of Elizabeth's high-profile defence of her supremacy, this was far more than frivolous satire.

Similarly Marprelate claimed to have proof of the threat the Corinthians dichotomy posed to the bishops' pastoral authority, and the lengths they were prepared to go to maintain it. In 1586, he noted, members of the parish of Sedbergh had forced Archbishop Whitgift to deprive their Calvinist pastor, Giles Wiggington, by demanding that he take decisive action to separate Christ and Belial. According to the ringleader, one Atkinson,

> you are both so contrary the one from the other, that both of you cannot possibly be of God. If he be of God, it is certain you are of the deuill, and so cannot long stand: for he will be your ouerthrowe. Amen. If you are of God, then he is of the diuell, as wee thinke him to be. & so being of the deuill, will not you depriue him? Why will you suffer such a one to trouble the Church?

The consequences of failing to separate Christ and Belial were apparently made threateningly clear to Whitgift – the congregation would be forced to

[15] Whitgift, *The Defense of the answere to the Admonition*, p. 38; see also Heinrich Bullinger's comments to Edwin Sandys (10 March 1574) on the diabolism of separation, in *Zurich Letters (second series)*, p. 241.

[16] Martin Marprelate, *Certain Minerall and Metaphysicall Schoolpoints to be defended by the reuerende Bishops and the rest of my clergie masters of Conuocation house* (London, 1589), see point 15 – 'our L Bp [Lord Bishops] in England are the bishops of the diuell: the defendant in this point (I thank him) is father John O Sarum'; Bridges had made the point in, *A defence of the government established in the church of England for ecclesiastical matters* (1587).

[17] Martin Marprelate, *Hay any worke for Cooper* (London, 1589), p. 29.

draw their own conclusions, which would very likely tend away from sympathy with the Archbishop:

> Now, if he be of God, why is your course so contrary to his? and rather, why do you not follow him, that we may do so to? Truely, if you do not depriue him, we will thinke him to be of God, and go home with him, with gentler good will towardes him than we came hyther with hatred; and looke you for a fall.

In Marprelate's interpretation, Whitgift's bluff was being called and he deprived Wiggington to maintain the disguise over his diabolism.[18]

Whilst the perception of diabolic subversion was a powerful polemical device, profound emotional significance attached to the belief that the episcopate was forcing godly men into diabolism. The separatist Henry Barrow grieved that England was possessed of 'a people so redy and fit for the kingedome of Christ', yet the bishops suffered them 'to continue in this confusion, false worship, antichristian bondage, even the snare of the devil'.[19] John Penry, writing in his notebook in 1593, emphasised that the consequences of conformity were simply irreconcilable with his sense of Christian duty. 'Although wee differ ... in no one poynt of the truth established by hir maiestie', he remarked, episcopal tyranny prevented his practice of worship within the established church 'exept we wold joyne Christ and Antichrist god and Beliall together'.[20] This sense of duty bolstered Presbyterians and separatists against accusations of schism. 'Is Martin to be blamed for finding out and discouering traitors', Marprelate demanded, 'whether I be favoured or no, I will not cease in the love I owe to her Maiestie ... to write against the Diuels bishops'.[21] In December 1592 Henry Barrow and John Penry defended separatist leaders to Star Chamber by arguing that it was hardly

[18] Martin Marprelate, *Oh read over Dr. John Bridges* (London, 1588), pp. 26–7. The confrontation at Sedbergh was not the first time Giles Wiggington had come in to conflict with Whitgift. The two had been enemies at Cambridge when Wiggington was a Fellow of Trinity and Whitgift was vice-chancellor; see H. C. Porter, *Reformation and Reaction in Tudor Cambridge*, pp. 171–2; Collinson, *Elizabethan Puritan Movement*, p. 130; McGrath, *Papists and Puritans under Elizabeth I*, p. 158. Marprelate reported that Atkinson later repented of his actions and travelled to London the year after Wiggington's deprivation to beg his forgiveness.

[19] Henry Barrow, *A Brief Summe of the Causes of Our Separation*, originally part of *A Plaine Refutation of M. G. Giffardes Reprochful Booke* (1591), in *The Writings of Henry Barrow 1587–1590*, ed. Leland H. Carlson (London, 1962), p. 129; Greenwood, *A Breife Refutation of Mr. George Giffard*, p. 26.

[20] Penry, *Notebook*, p. 33; see also Penry's letter to the deprived nonconformist minister Christopher Goodman, p. 42; in his examination on 10 April 1593, Penry used similar arguments to contrast the motives of separatists with the diabolical separation of recusants, see *The Examinations of Henry Barrowe, John Greenwood, & John Penrie before The High Commissioners, and Lordes of the Counsel* (1593?), reprinted in *The Harleian Miscellany*, vol. II, pp. 40–1.

[21] Marprelate, *Hay any worke for Cooper*, p. 29.

surprising that they should appear seditious given that their beliefs 'cannot be made to accord to [the bishops'] kingdome and works of darkness', yet 'they will not be found contrarie or offensive to anie godly government'.[22]

Again the conformist response was to characterise Presbyterianism and separatism as diabolic agencies intent on destroying the progress made by the Reformation. These arguments were most forcefully expressed in Thomas Cooper's *An Admonition to the People of England*, published in response to Marprelate in 1589. Satan's resort to Presbyterian sedition demonstrated how effectively he had been ousted from the established church, since 'when Sathan seeth the doctrine of trueth to spring up amongst men ... then seeketh hee by lying and slander to discredit it and deface the messengers that God sendeth with his word as instruments that he useth to advance and sette foorth his trueth, by this meanes to worke hinderance to the truth itselfe'. Every watershed in Christian history, Cooper noted, had been met with similar attempts at sabotage.[23] He sought to turn the nonconformist use of the Corinthians dichotomy on its head. Either the bishops were God's chosen instruments of reform, or the progress made by the English church was entirely a sham perpetrated by demonic impostors. 'Christ would not suffer that the devill shoulde utter anything to the glorie of God', he continued, 'and will he suffer "devillish and antichristian" persons to bee the chiefe Preachers and restorers of the Gospell?'[24] If the fact of reformation was accepted, then the queen and the court were the shepherds, and the bishops the 'barking dogges' that protected the commonwealth, whilst Satan took the form of an angel of light to lend credence to his call to abolish episcopacy.[25] Pastoral concern was again prevalent, and Cooper reversed the anti-Catholic stance that had seen episcopacy as empty theatre. Presbyterianism/satanism targeted the bishops because they inspired godly men to a clerical career. 'The frailtie and corruption of mennes nature' (so often the first principle of the Devil's agency) dissuaded men from the clergy without some 'reward of learning'. 'If that state of the Cleargie shall be made contemptable, and the best reward of learning a mean pension: [the Devil] foreseeth that ... yong

22 Henry Barrow and John Penry, 'To the right honourable the Lords and others of her Majestie's most honourable Privy Counsell', in *The Writings of John Greenwood and Henry Barrow*, pp. 398–9. The evidence for Barrow and Penry's authorship is presented by Carlson on pp. 396–7. The supplication was delivered to a clerk but was never actually presented to the Privy Councillors in Star Chamber; see p. 395 and Penry, *Notebook*, p. 39. See also Thomas Cartwright's defence against taking the ex officio oath in 1590, in which he claimed it was a device employed by Satan to silence those who threatened to reveal the church's hidden corruption, in Thomas Cartwright, *Cartwrightiana*, ed. A. Peel and L.H. Carlson (London, 1951), p. 41.

23 Thomas Cooper, *An Admonition to the People of England* (London, 1589), pp. 22–25, quote at p. 23.

24 Ibid., p. 10. 25 Ibid., p. 29.

flourishing wittes will less easily incline themselves to godly learning.' Thus there would be 'farre fewer dogges to bark at him, and almost none that shall have teeth to bite those hell houndes'.[26]

Perceptions of diabolism in the episcopacy fluctuated in prominence with the fortunes of Puritanism, and after the quashing of Presbyterianism they became much less pronounced. But recent assertions that, through the maintenance of localised and less high-profile networks, organised Puritanism had far greater continuity than historians have assumed, suggest that there is no reason to suppose that suspicion of the bishops evaporated in the 1590s. Relatively quiet throughout the first decades of the seventeenth century, printed attacks on the diabolic episcopacy were to explode again in the 1630s, with, if anything, more violence than even Marprelate had been able to muster. As Jackie Eales has argued, whilst Laudian religious policies forced many Puritans into militancy, their desire to be rid of recent innovations such as the Book of Sports and the altar policy was an expression of more long-term objectives that were consciously associated with the Elizabethan Puritan programme.[27] As we will see, attacks on the bishops by Puritans such as William Prynne, John Bastwick and John Lilburne were pervaded by a sense that Laudianism fulfilled the potential for diabolism inherent in a half-reformed church. John Lilburne, flogged and pilloried for his involvement in clandestine publishing, believed all bishops came from the Devil and Laud was the most demonic of bishops. But if this was so he was only the latest, most evil incarnation of the same episcopal tyranny which had sent Penry, Barrow and Greenwood to Tyburn.[28]

THE DIVINE MONARCH AND THE DEVIL: ELIZABETH I, JAMES I AND CATHOLIC TREACHERY

Fear of the diabolic subversion of the secular government paralleled that of the church, particularly the belief that Satan lay behind all forms of treason. The problem of the succession, and priority afforded to notions of order and degree, made the threat of treason one of the perennial concerns of Elizabeth's reign. Her parliaments were pervaded by warnings of subversion and hidden danger, which argued that her life, and with it the Protestant faith, was under constant threat.[29] Similarly, the Stuarts' vigorous espousal

[26] Ibid., pp. 29–30.
[27] Jacqueline Eales, 'A Road to Revolution: The Continuity of Puritanism, 1559–1642', in C. Durston and J. Eales (eds.), *The Culture of English Puritanism* (Houndmills, 1996), pp. 184–5.
[28] Lilburne, *Come out of her my people*, pp. 28–9.
[29] *Proceedings in the Parliaments of Elizabeth I*, vol. I, pp. 203–4, 212–18, 283, 299; vol. II, pp. 28–9.

of divine right concentrated attention on the notion of politics as cosmic struggle, and demanded that political action be assimilated into a scheme which posited an absolute separation of light and darkness. Under Elizabeth and James fear of diabolic subversion was focused very firmly on personal threats to the monarch, most notably from disaffected Catholics. Lucifer, the author of the first, and all subsequent rebellions, was believed to personally target these Protestant rulers.

There was of course an obvious connection to be drawn between Lucifer's revolt in heaven and the actions of English rebels. As the regime of Protector Somerset faced uprisings over religion and enclosure in 1549, Thomas Cranmer instituted a programme of sermonising against rebellion. His own notes for an homily on the subject reveal how resistance to reformation was already giving diabolic subversion a specific tangibility. 'The devil can abide no right reformation in religion', he noted. Rebellion, he explained in another sermon, was driven only by a 'devilish' spirit of wanton destruction.[30] The rhetoric of temptation was also apparent and Cranmer described how Satan worked on the rebels' spiritual blindness. 'Is it not a great wonder', he noted, 'that the devil should so rob these men of their wits ... that they do forget death?'[31]

The Elizabethan regime sought to drive home the connection, including it as one of the fundamental subjects of the 1562 version of the *Book of Homilies*. 'An homily against disobedience and wilful rebellion', was a programme of exposition and thanksgiving in which parishioners were shown the diabolism of rebellion, and encouraged to thank God for the queen's deliverance.[32] It castigated rebels as 'the vile slaves of ... Satan' whom 'the devil hath so far inticed against God's word'.[33] Rebellion had to be understood in the context of the fall of Lucifer and the fall of man, which had disrupted the peace of the cosmos and were the 'principal cause both of all worldly and bodily miseries'. As a result God provided man with laws and governors 'lest all things should come unto confusion and utter ruin'. Thus

[30] Thomas Cranmer, '[Notes for a homily against rebellion]' and 'A sermon concerning the time of rebellion', in *Miscellaneous Writings and Letters of Thomas Cranmer*, ed. J.E. Cox (Cambridge, Parker Society, 1846), pp. 189, 196; Bishop Bonner followed his instructions to preach that Lucifer was the father of all rebellion, despite using the opportunity to argue for the real presence, for which he was denounced by Latimer and Hooper, see *A & M*, vol. V, pp. 745, 757, 760.

[31] Cranmer, 'A sermon concerning the time of rebellion', p. 192; see also Edward VI's answer to the Devonshire rebels, in *A & M*, vol. V, p. 732; John Hooper's letter to Heinrich Bullinger, 25 June 1549, in *Original Letters relative to the English Reformation*, p. 66.

[32] The homily consisted of six parts, each to be accompanied by a prayer asking God to protect Elizabeth and the Protestant cause: 'An homily against disobedience and wilful rebellion', in *Certain Sermons or Homilies*, pp. 587–642.

[33] Ibid., pp. 606, 610, 617–18.

all rebellion was demonic because it threatened to return the world to the chaos Satan had effected by tempting man to disobedience. But the homily implied a more specific analogy between the temptation of man and the temptation of the body politic. The order enshrined in patriarchy – king over commonwealth, husband over wife, parents over children – constrained the chaos wrought by Adam's rebellion in the same way that the individual godly conscience stifled the innate stock of corruption that threatened to lead to sin. As demonic intrusion subverted the conscience and allowed sin to explode within the individual, rebellion could be the catalyst for the exponential growth of sin within the body politic.[34] Thus the homily emphasised that rebels were 'the very figures of fiends and devils', who could expect only an eternity of perdition for their efforts.[35]

Unsurprisingly, Catholicism on the continent provided a focal point in which to find the demonic origins of dissent in England. But the Devil might also be perceived in the activities of Puritans, if less explicitly. In July 1574 the bishop of Ely, Richard Cox, wrote to Heinrich Bullinger of trouble with both Puritans and Catholics. Cox commiserated over the conflicts experienced within the faith in Zurich through the machinations of 'the enemy', and compared them with the storm caused by the English Puritans, of whom he noted 'we know not what monstrosities they are hiding in secret'. 'Certain of our nobility, pupils of the Roman pontiff', he continued, 'have taken flight, some into France, some into Spain ... with a view of plotting some mischief against the professors of Godliness. So difficult is it to keep the church of Christ in a state of defence against the ministers of Satan.'[36] In 1579 Edwin Sandys wrote more optimistically to Rudolph Gualter that despite the subversion of stubborn Puritans and secret papists, England's 'flourishing' Protestantism could 'neither be overturned nor defiled by any devices of Satan'.[37]

Mary Stuart's claim to the throne gave demonic treason a more specific tangibility. The duke of Norfolk, involved in the Ridolfi plot, was accused in January 1572 of 'not having the fear of God in his heart ... but seduced by the instigation of the Devil, contrary to that cordial affection and bounden duty that true and faithful subjects of our said lady the queen do bear'.[38] The duke's servant, Robert Hickford, was told at his trial the

[34] 'An homily against disobedience and wilful rebellion', in *Certain Sermons or Homilies*, pp. 588–9.

[35] Ibid., pp. 616–18, quote at p. 616. [36] *The Zurich Letters*, pp. 308–9.

[37] Edwin Sandys to Rudolph Gualter, 9 December 1579, in ibid., p. 332.

[38] *Complete Collection of State Trials and Proceedings for High Treason and other Crimes and Misdemeanours*, vols. I–IV, ed. W. Cobbett (London, 1809), vol. I, p. 959; for similar charges against Norfolk's fellow conspirators see p. 961. The wording was of course similar to that used in indictments for murder.

following month: 'God hath sown in you good gifts and qualities, meet to have served any prince on Christendom, but . . . the devil and his ministers, wicked seedsmen, sowed in you . . . treason and disloyalty.'[39] In the wake of the plot, parliament was called in March 1572 to consider measures for the queen's safety. A petition by a committee of both Houses, presented on the 26 May, described Mary's 'develishe and traiterous devices'.[40] For Nicholas St Leger (30 May), irritated by the Queen's unwillingness to take action against her cousin, Mary was 'the monstrous and huge dragon', and Norfolk 'the roaring lion'.[41] Similar language was used in the trial of Anthony Babington in 1586, and Sir Christopher Hatton concluded the proceedings by observing that the 'wicked and devilish youths' had hatched their plot at the instigation of 'devilish priests and seminaries'.[42] Pressure for Mary's execution increased following the Throckmorton and Babington conspiracies. Job Throckmorton, speaking in parliament on 4 November 1586, saw the satanic hordes of the last days revealed in the activities of Mary's supporters. 'Hath not the murder of her majestie', he noted, '(whom the Lorde still preserve in despight of Satan) found out an Allen, a Campion, a Bristow, a Saunders, a Gyfforde, and I knowe not who?' Of Mary he concluded, 'ye have heard the Devill himselfe, I trowe, or rather (yf ye will) the Devill herselfe to authorize yt'.[43]

In this atmosphere treason appeared to be an especially virulent form of temptation, in which the struggle between the forces of light and darkness – between Elizabeth and demonic Catholicism – was carried out in microcosm within the individual soul. In his judgement on Robert Hickford, the Chief Justice of the Kings Bench, Robert Catlin, noted that loyalty to the prince overshadowed all others. In putting loyalty to his master first Hickford had succumbed to a specific temptation of the Devil. 'If in any case, any respect shall allure a man from loyalty and truth to his prince', Catlin observed, 'they must be forsaken, they must come behind; it must be said, *Vade post me, Satana*.'[44] A pamphlet account of the activities of the double agent William Parry, who confessed to conspiring to murder the queen in 1584, described the internal battle in which the counter-influences of Elizabeth and the Devil acted on his humanity. 'The deuill enforcing this trayterous heart to execute

[39] Ibid., p. 1046.

[40] *Proceedings in the Parliaments of Elizabeth I*, vol. I, p. 278; see also Thomas Digges and Thomas Dannet's assessment of the motives of the duke of Norfolk: 'upon the back of these twoo untamed beastes, ambition and love, hell hath now placed the furie of revenge', p. 296.

[41] Ibid., p. 312.

[42] *State Trials*, vol. I, pp. 1132, 1133, 1139–40; see also Thomas Deloney, *A proper new Ballad breefely declaring the . . . Execution of fourteen most wicked traitors* (1586), in *Works*, pp. 464–8; Aske, *Elizabetha Triumphans*, pp. 12–13.

[43] *Proceedings in the Parliaments of Elizabeth I*, vol. II, p. 228.

[44] *State Trials*, vol. I, p. 1045.

his intent', the account noted, 'he was troubled looking on the Queene, and remembering her excellencies.' Only strength from Satan allowed Parry to stifle the last vestiges of his humanity. 'What more devilish intent could possesse a traytour', the pamphlet observed, 'then to labour to suppresse a final remaine of conscience abhorring to kill so excellent a personage.'[45]

But the very fact that demonism encapsulated the horror of rebellion undermined the regime's ability to monopolise the identification of diabolic subversion. The threat of satanic treason allowed some in parliament to assert its right to discuss contentious issues such as religion and the succession, arguing that not to do so was to knowingly expose the monarch to danger, and so to aid the Devil. A speech, possibly given by John Molyneux on 18 October 1566, implied that parliament would be playing the tempter's role in the body politic if it failed to draw the attention of the head (the queen) to the dangers of a contested succession.[46] For Molyneux resistance to temptation was inherent in parliament's function, since it was created by God's providence to guard against 'trayterous flattery and devillish dissimulation'.[47] 'We must either', he declared, 'in this counsell, serve God or Beliall, shew ourselves true Englishmen, or traytors.' Giving in to the fear of disfavour for speaking out was itself a demonic temptation that must be overcome. 'Whensoever any conceipt or terror shall ... draw us back from speaking', he noted, 'let us learne of Christ and say, "Away, Divell, with thy hellish conceipts".'[48] A decade later Peter Wentworth took these arguments much further. On 8 February 1576 he made an extraordinary speech in which he all but implicated the queen in the diabolic subversion of the Houses' rights. Elizabeth's sole prerogative to decide issues of religion and the succession was, he argued, enforced by rumours of disfavour and the bishops' vetting of bills concerning religion (instituted after 1572). 'I would to God', Wentworth declared, 'that these two were buryed in Hell, I mean rumours and messages, for wicked undoubtedly they are: the reason is, the Divill was the first author of them, from whome proceedeth nothing but wickedness.'[49] Whilst the queen was not guilty of witting diabolism, the use of methods invented by the Devil maintained a de facto satanic influence at the heart of government, turning parliament into an assembly of flatterers and 'soe

[45] *A True and plaine declaration of the horrible Treasons, Practised by William Parry the Traitor, against the Queenes Maiestie* (London, 1585), p. 49; for an accusation of diabolism at Parry's trial, see *State Trials*, vol. I, p. 1112; see also Aske, *Elizabetha Trivmphans*, p. 9.

[46] T.E. Hartley gives a number of suggestions for the possible authorship of this speech, including Peter and Paul Wentworth, and a Mr Lambert, and notes that it may be an undelivered draft, but suggests that references to the preparation of a bill on the succession make Molyneux the most plausible candidate. See *Proceedings in the Parliaments of Elizabeth I*, vol. I, pp. 119–20.

[47] Ibid., pp. 129–30. [48] Ibid., p. 136. [49] Ibid., pp. 426–7.

fitt a place to serve the Devill and his angells in and not to glorifye God and benefitt the commonwealth'.[50] Again the Corinthians dichotomy loomed large in Wentworth's argument. Had parliament not been called to advise on the Queen's safety in the wake of the Ridolfi plot, why then were its members being ignored? Parliament's unencumbered role must be to 'boldly reprove God's enemyes, our prince's and state's, and soe shall every one of us . . . shew ourselves haters of evill and cleavers to that that is good'.[51] Whilst many in parliament surely sympathised with Wentworth's frustration, his language was simply too strong, and the Commons took action themselves against him, sending him to the Tower on 15 March.

The language of temptation continued to characterise accusations of treason after the accession of James I. At his trial in 1603 Sir Walter Raleigh was accused by the Attorney-General, Sir Edward Coke, of pursuing 'a devilish policy' and 'the most horrible practices that ever came out of the bottomless pit of the lowest hell'.[52] But the Gunpowder Plot of November 1605 gave satanism an unprecedented tangibility, which overrode individual perception and allowed the regime a near monopoly of perception into diabolic subversion thereafter. In its wake a picture of the temptation of the body politic far more clearly focused on Catholic subversion was to define the notion to the end of James's reign. To contemporaries, the Protestant political establishment narrowly escaped an extinction that was a prelude certainly to a coup, and probably to another invasion. Who else but Satan could have been the author of such a heinous crime? A public thirst for details encouraged the authorities to throw together an official account of the affair, popularly known as *The King's Book*, which saw the plot as a potential outbreak of hell on earth.[53] 'The earth, as it were opened', the official commentary noted, 'should have sent forth out of the bottom of the Stygian lake such sulphured smoke, furious flames, and feareful thunder, as should have, by their diabolical doomsday, destroyed and defaced, in the twinkling of an eye, not only our present living princes and people, but even our insensible monuments reserved for future ages'.[54] Other commentators reiterated the demonism

[50] Ibid., p. 426. [51] Ibid., p. 433. [52] *State Trials*, vol. II, p. 9.

[53] On the compilation of the *King's Book* see M. Nicholls, *Investigating Gunpowder Plot* (Manchester, 1991), pp. 26–9.

[54] James I, *His majesty's speech in the last session of Parliament, concerning the Gunpowder-plot* (1605), in *The Harleian Miscellany*, vol. III, p. 15. The *King's Book* was reprinted, minus James's speech to parliament, in James I, *The Workes of the most High and Mightie Prince, James* (1616), see p. 224; see also the characterisation of 'devilish' treason in 'A proclamation denouncing Thomas Percy and other his adherents to be Traitors', 7 November 1605, reprinted in *Stuart Royal Proclamations*, vol. I: *Royal Proclamations of King James I 1603–1625*, ed. J. F. Larkin and P. Hughes (Oxford, 1973), p. 124; William Barlow, *The Sermon Preached at Paules Crosse, the tenth day of Nouember, being the next Sunday after the Discouerie of this late Horrible Treason* (London, 1606), sig. C3.

of the official line. William Barlow, the bishop of Rochester, preaching at Paul's Cross on 10 November, declared the plot was 'a cruell Execution, an inhumane crueltie, a brutish imanitie, a diuelish brutishnes & an Hyperbolical, yea an hyperdiabolicall diuelishnes'. 'Is this a rule of religion? Or rather of a legion?', asked the anonymous author of *The Arraignment and execution of the Late Traitors* (1606), 'where the synagogue of Satan sat in council . . . to make way to some fury to bring the most flourishing kingdom on the earth to the most desolation in the world; to kill at one blow . . . king, queen, prince and peer'.[55]

Divine right saw the plot as a battle in a continuing personal war between the king and Satan. For James, speaking in parliament on 9 November, it was a sequel to the Gowrie conspiracy of 1600, concluding 'it was the same devil that still persecuted me'.[56] For the vicar of Holy Trinity in Coventry, Thomas Cooper, writing in early 1606, it was a 'diuelish policie' for the plotters 'desperately to lay hands vppon the Lords anointed'. *The Arraignment and execution of the Late Traitors* emphasised that the conspiracy paralleled the rebellion of Adam, 'for, since the betraying of the Lord of heaven and earth, was there ever such a hellish plot practised in the world?'[57] Perhaps satanic assaults were only to be expected against God's king but, in threatening to also obliterate the entire political establishment, this plot was qualitatively more hellish.[58] It 'was a destruction not prepared for me alone', James reminded parliament, 'but for all you that were here present, and wherein no rank, age, nor sex should have been spared'. Thus 'this was not a crying sin of blood, as the former [Gowrie conspiracy], but it may well be called a roaring, nay a thundering sin of fire and brimstone'.[59] Such an interpretation was reflected in the consensus which immediately declared Guy Fawkes the most monstrous of the conspirators. It was probably William Barlow who coined the popular description of him as the 'Diuell of the Vault', a term that was expressive enough to become the title of a verse pamphlet describing the affair. But if it captured in a nutshell the extent of Fawkes's treachery, the

55 Barlow, *The Sermon Preached at Paules Crosse*, sig. C2v; *The Arraignment and execution of the Late Traitors* (1606), in *The Harleian Miscellany*, vol. III, p. 49; Nicholas Breton, *The Hate of Treason, with a touch of the late Treason* (1616), in *The Works in Verse and Prose of Nicholas Breton*, ed. A. B. Grosart (New York, 1966), p. 3.

56 James I, *His majesty's speech*, pp. 6–7, 13; James I, *Triplici nodo, triplex cuneus. Or an Apologie for the Oath of Allegiance*, in *Workes*, p. 247.

57 Thomas Cooper, *A brand taken out of the Fire. Or the Romish Spider, with his Webbe of Treason* (London, 1606), pp. 1–2; *The Arraignment and Execution of the Late Traitors*, p. 49.

58 'Kings', James noted, 'as being in the higher places like the high trees, or stayed mountains, and steepest rocks, are the most subject to the daily tempests of innumerable dangers; and I amongst all other kings have ever been subject to them.' See *His majesty's speech*, p. 6.

59 Ibid., pp. 6–7; Barlow, *Sermon preached at Paules Crosse*, sig. C4.

name also had very literal connotations. In being the conspirator who was ready to put fire to the powder, it was Fawkes who would have, quite literally, released hell on earth, making him, according to one anonymous pamphleteer, 'the great devil of all'. He was 'justly called, The Devil of the Vault; for had he not been a devil incarnate, he had never conceived so villainous a thought, nor been employed in so damnable an action'.[60]

Thus the plot seemed a clear-cut example of Satan's machinations against the English state, an attempt to recover God's most favoured nation by unleashing chaos and hellfire. In its wake a direct connection was made by polemicists between synagogue of Satan idolatry and the dynamic of Catholic resistance theory. Both relied on appealing to man's corrupted instincts – the first to fickle and lazy religiosity, the second to intemperate proaction.

It was James I himself who showed the keenest awareness that the Pope's claims might be a trigger to activate the diabolic potential within his people. Initially he relied on a separation between satanic potential and actuality to draw a more nuanced picture of recusant guilt which he hoped would spare his loyal Catholic subjects the possible excesses of an outraged parliament. James's position towards papists had always been ambiguous as a result of his desire for religious unity, and he tended to be more concerned over issues of religious authority than doctrinal differences.[61] Popery offered arguments to justify the overthrow of legitimate rulers, and in doing so, James believed, it bred an inherently diabolic subversive will amongst its adherents. This was another form of de facto satanism. But whether individual Catholics acted upon this will depended on the extent to which they had succumbed to the Devil's delusions. No other sect of heretics, James argued in his speech on 9 November, ever went as far as the papacy in making a virtue of murder in the name of religion. Although there were traitors and murderers of every faith, 'yet ever, when they came to their end and just punishment, they confessed their fault to be in their nature, and not in their profession, these Romish Catholics only excepted'. The Gunpowder Plot fulfilled the potential of Catholicism's murderous doctrine, representing the very depths of its 'mystery of iniquity', but it was a point to which the majority of English

[60] Barlow, *Sermon*, sig. C3v; *The Divell of the Vault. Or, the Vnmasking of Murther in a Briefe Declaration of the Catholike-complotted Treason, lately discouered* (London, 1606); *The Arraignment and Execution of the Late Traitors*, pp. 48–9.

[61] K. Fincham and P. Lake, 'The Ecclesiastical Policies of James I and Charles I', in K. Fincham (ed.), *The Early Stuart Church, 1603–1642* (Houndmills, 1993), p. 28. On the doctrine of the Pope's deposing power, and the variety in the extent to which it was accepted by Catholics themselves, see Sommerville, *Politics and Ideology in England*, pp. 13–14, 59–60 and esp. 197–8; John Bossy, 'The English Catholic Community 1603–1625', in Alan G. R. Smith (ed.), *The Reign of James VI and I* (London and Basingstoke, 1973), pp. 92–5.

recusants had not fallen. James followed his Elizabethan predecessors in recognising that the synagogue of Satan deluded men into thinking it better answered their spiritual needs, but regrettable as this was, it did not equate to treason and regicide. Most recusants, he assured his audience, had simply too shallow an understanding of popish doctrine to comprehend its treacherous content. If they could not comprehend it, they could not with justice be accused of believing it, and the fact that loyal and even godly men's consciences were distracted by issues such as the real presence and the number of sacraments was explicable in these terms. Thus whilst diabolic potential inhered in Catholicism's maintenance of the pope's deposing power, it was not necessarily activated in differences of devotional practice amongst loyal subjects. 'Honest men', James asserted, 'seduced with some errors of popery, may yet remain good and faithful subjects', and he emphasised that, without belittling the evil of the conspiracy, 'the mysteries of this wickedness' should be searched 'as far as may be', and that punishment should come only after 'due trial'.[62]

To what extent contemporaries may have taken their lead from James is unclear, but the king certainly felt a need to temper the language of some of his subjects. Whilst he did not doubt parliament's good intent he was fearful 'that the zeal of your hearts shall make some of you, in your speeches, rashly to blame such as might be innocent of this attempt'.[63] The pamphlet *The Arraignment and execution of the Late Traitors* suggests that James's careful separation between potential and actuality, and especially his locating of resistance theory in the extreme fringe rather than mainstream of recusancy, was for many unconvincing. In contrast to James, the author explicitly connected idolatry and resistance theory, presenting them as equally fundamental manifestations of Catholic diabolism. When the tract compared Satan's working of the plot to the corruption of Adam, it emphasised that in mediating the diabolic assault on the commonwealth the conspirators had, like Adam and Eve, and millions of idolaters after them, been deluded by the Devil into thinking piety lay in the easiest and most immediately satisfying way. 'If the Pope were not a very devil', the author commented, 'and these Jesuits or rather Jebusites and Satanical Seminaries, very spirits of wickedness, that whisper in the ears of Evahs, to bring a world of Adams to destruction, how could nature be so senseless, or reason so graceless, as to subject wit so to will, as to run headlong to confusion.'[64] As Catholics found comfort in empty ceremonies that answered their lazy religiosity, so too they were blinded by the demonic sophistry that justified regicide in the name of the faith. 'Ignorance in the simple, and idolatry in the subtle take ceremony for

[62] James I, *His majesty's speech*, pp. 9–10. [63] Ibid., p. 9.
[64] *The Arraignment and Execution of the Late Traitors*, p. 49.

certainties, superstition for religion'; these are the Masses 'the devil sings'. Similarly, assassination was justified in the mistaken belief in the efficacy of the Pope's absolution. 'Kill princes, sow seditions', the pamphlet continued, 'so it be for the Pope's profit, the church will absolve you; and, if you miss the mark to hit the mischief you shoot at, you shall be a hanging saint, till you be taken down to the devil.'[65]

Treachery thus became a hallmark of Catholicism's intemperance, to be contrasted with the faithful patience of Protestants. 'The traitorous papist will pull down princes and subvert kingdoms, murder and poison whom they cannot command', ran the commentary; 'the faithful protestant prayeth for princes, and the peace of the people; will endure banishment, but hate rebellion'. According to the pamphlet, Everard Digby's speech at the scaffold made the effectiveness of this kind of diabolic sophistry clear. 'Through the blindness of his bewitched wit', he had admitted that 'to bring the kingdom into Popish idolatry, he cared not to root out all his posterity.' Thus, acting on Catholic resistance theory was characterised by abandonment of the parallel and connected natural political and familial instincts:

> Oh the misery of these blinded people! Who forsake the true God of heaven and earth, to submit their service to the devil of the world; be traitors to their gracious princes, to serve a proud, ungracious prelate; lose their lands and goods, beggar their wives and children, lose their own lives with an open shame, and leave an infamy to their name foe ever, only to obey the command of that cunning fox, that, lying in his den, preyeth on all the geese that he can light on; and, in the proud belief to be made saints, will hazard their souls to the devil.

Where James spoke of the handful of his subjects who had plumbed the depths of Catholicism's mystery of iniquity, *The Arraignment and execution of the Late Traitors* preferred to refer to the 'millions' who had been carried away by the Pope's claims to deposing power.[66]

In 1606 James aimed to accommodate moderate Catholics within the regime by means of an oath of allegiance which all those suspected of recusancy were required to take. It sought to realise the separation James had posited between those whose Catholicism expressed only a misguided religiosity and those who embraced its deepest corruption. The oath made no mention of confessional positions, but instead demanded that Catholics affirm their allegiance to the king and 'abhorre, detest and abiure' the 'damnable doctrine' of the Pope's power to depose monarchs.[67] James's sense of his own magnanimity probably made him optimistic, for he seems to have believed that recusants might be persuaded to take the oath with a clear conscience, and may even have hoped that Rome would permit them to

[65] Ibid., p. 50. [66] Ibid., pp. 50–1. [67] James I, *Triplici nodo, triplex cuneus*, p. 251.

do so.[68] If so he was to be swiftly disillusioned, and the experience only heightened his sense that the Devil sought to drive a wedge between him and his subjects. The oath proved difficult to enforce, and when two papal breves denounced subscription, James was presented with a tangible example of the Devil's triggers being introduced into the commonwealth.[69] The second breve (10 September 1607) expressed displeasure at the numbers who had taken the oath, and provoked in turn a contest with James over the question of whether it was a diabolic act to subscribe or to abstain. Pope Paul V understood recusant weakness to come from the desire to escape persecution and he expressed disappointment that his authority should be questioned as an expedient to disobey his instruction to refuse the oath. But the explanation was clear: compliance with the oath was a result of Satan's influence. 'We doe herein perceiue the subtiltie and craft of the enemie of mans saluation', the breve read, 'and we doe attribute this your backwardnesse rather to him, then to your owne will.'[70] For James the breve promoted confusion by instructing recusants to forswear an oath they had already sworn. But, more importantly, it threatened to overturn his carefully defined distinctions between moderate and fanatical Catholics by forcing once loyal subjects to become active diabolic agents. In his defence of the Oath, *Triplici nodo, triplex cuneus* (1607), he argued that the Pope's actions were an attempt to subvert his own moderation in the face of the Gunpowder Plot. Recusants in general, he noted, were not 'worse vsed', for the crimes of the conspirators and legislative measures had been taken only with the support of parliament.[71] The oath was not so much an attempt to discover enemies as it was to establish friends, since it would allow him 'to make a separation betweene so many of my Subiects, who although they were otherwise Popishly affected, yet retained in their hearts the print of their naturall duetie to their Soueraigne; and those who being carried away with the like fanaticall zeale ... thought diuersitie of religion a safe pretext for all kindes of treasons, and rebellions'. Indeed it was a tool to be used *by* recusants, since by subscription 'all quietly minded Papists were put out of despaire'.[72] But the effect of the Pope's breves would be to destroy this cosy co-existance by activating the treasonous and implicitly diabolic potential inherent in the doctrine of papal authority. They

[68] Kenyon, *The Stuart Constitution*, p. 167.

[69] The first breve was dated 10 October 1606 and the second 10 September 1607. The texts were printed by James in his reply. See James I, *Triplici nodo, triplex cuneus*, pp. 250–2 and 258.

[70] Ibid., p. 258. [71] Ibid., p. 248.

[72] The oath was hardly as great a success as James claimed. It had to be enforced with the threat of praemunire for a second refusal, whilst some priests were prepared to die rather than subscribe to it. In provincial areas enforcement of the oath was fitful and contradictory. See Sommerville, *Politics and Ideology*, p. 197; Fincham and Lake, 'The Ecclesiastical Policies of James I and Charles I', p. 29, and n. 12.

forced English recusants to transform their blinded but essentially apolitical religious instincts into an active resistance to the king's authority. The Pope's commands were a diabolic 'trick for interrupting this so calm and clement a course'. Indeed James threw the Pope's words back in his face, commenting of the breves that he 'might iustly reflect his owne phrase vpon him, in tearming it to be The craft of the Deuill'. In driving English Catholics to a position of active resistance 'if the Deuill had studied a thousand yeeres, for to finde out a mischiefe for our Catholikes heere, hee hath found it in this'.[73]

The memory of the Gunpowder Plot, and the debates over the respective powers of king and Pope were prominent features of the rest of James's reign. In 1610 fears of regicide were reawakened by the assassination of Henri IV of France. On 4 May, Henri was murdered by a Catholic zealot, François Ravaillac, in revenge for his anti-Habsburg politicking with the Dutch Republic and the Protestant princes in Germany and England.[74] Horror at the assassination was almost universal, but in England it once more focused attention on the potential inherent in Catholic subjects for intemperate, diabolically inspired violence. On 8 May, Robert Cecil, the earl of Salisbury and Lord Treasurer, announced the news to the House of Lords, commenting that Henri had been killed 'by a villian guided by the devil'. Cecil did not at that point know what had motivated Ravaillac, but in his address he openly tried to impress on the Lords the need to see the event as a satanic assault on Christianity. Besides James I, the murder of Henri 'concerneth more the Christian world than the death of any other prince', he instructed the House, 'a king by whose death not only the veins but arteries of religion bleed'. In general he reminded his audience that, 'not to regard the care of the prince's person is to give way unto the temptations of the devil'.[75] In the wake of the assassination a more aggressive policy towards recusancy was given royal sanction, and on 14 July Archbishop Bancroft introduced a contentious bill into the Lords for the better security of the king's person, which provided for the punishment of any traitor's descendants by the forfeiture of his estates. Whilst he objected to the bill, Cecil noted that Protestants had little to fear since 'the fear of attempting so heinous and devilish a treason rests not in us, for they that are like to practice this are

[73] James I, *Triplici nodo, triplex cuneus*, pp. 248, 259.
[74] Robin Briggs, *Early Modern France 1560–1715* (Oxford, 1977), pp. 77–80.
[75] *Proceedings in Parliament 1610*, ed. E. R. Foster (New Haven and London, 2 vols., 1966), vol. I, pp. 83–4, 238–9. The proceedings contain two accounts of Cecil's speech, one by Henry Hastings, the earl of Huntingdon, and the other by the clerk of the House of Lords, Robert Bowyer. The clerk's account concentrates on the details of the assassination as they were reported and is comparatively uninterested in the gloss which Cecil might have placed on them, noting only 'God hath suffered the devil to work his will upon the person of that King'.

likely to be papists that do only make, and no other religion concurs in the same opinion, the killing of princes to be martyrdom'.[76]

As the Gunpowder Plot became legend, so too did the perception of its diabolism.[77] In *The powder Treason*, a broadsheet of 1615 by the satirist Richard Smith, parliament was depicted between the watchful eye of heaven and the seething chaos of the mouth of hell, replete with Satan and minor demons. The plot, it noted, was 'Propounded, By Sathan ... Founded in Hell, Confounded in Heaven'. Nicholas Breton's poem of 1616, *The Hate of Treason, with a Touch of the late Treason*, similarly placed James I's fate between the machinations of hell and the providential protection of God:

> For, Father, Brother, Neighbour, Friend or Foe,
> in each of these, but fewe to ruine runne;
> but, in a King, or princes overthrowe,
> how many Thousands are vndonne?
> woe woorth ye hand, yt such ill threed hath spunne:
> as, by ye woork of Sathans wickednes
> a Worlde of Christians should endure Distress.
> . . . . .
> But, God on High, that from his Seate beholdeth,
> Heaven, Earth, Sea, Hell, & what each one contayneth;
> and, every thought, of every harte vnfoldeth;
> and, for his service, all and som retayneth:
> hating ye pride, his powrefull hand disdayneth;
> hath broke ye Force of all theyr wicked frame;
> and made theyr woorke, vnto ye world a shame.

Similarly, the bishop of Chichester, George Carleton, reminded his audience in 1624 of the motives of the plotters whose 'hellish device' was aimed at the entire political establishment – king, princes, nobility and clergy. 'All these things', he noted, 'had the devil by his agents devised at one secret blow to destroy.'[78]

THE DIVINE CHARLES AND THE DEVIL: DIABOLIC SUBVERSION AND THE LANGUAGE OF POLITICAL OPPOSITION

Since Peter Wentworth's speech in parliament in 1576 no one had come close to publicly accusing the monarch of diabolism. Catholic regicide had seemed the most tangible of the demonic threats to the body politic. But the Devil's

[76] Ibid., pp. 150–1.
[77] The assimilation of the developing legend of the Gunpowder Plot into the 'national memory' has been charted by David Cressy in *Bonfires and Bells: National Memory and the Protestant Calendar in Elizabethan and Stuart England* (London, 1989), chapter 9.
[78] Cornelius Burges, *Another Sermon Preached to the Honourable House of Commons now assembled in Parliament, November the Fifth, 1641* (London, 1641), pp. 1–2, 7, 11–14, 35, 44–5.

agency was in the eye of the beholder, and for some satanism began to seem equally tangible in the absolutist claims and the religious innovations of the Caroline regime. The Devil's sophistry was now seen by many to lie in overarching claims to theocratic inviolability and in the Laudian rejection of reformed austerity in the church. Suspicion centred around those closest to the king, particularly George Villiers, the duke of Buckingham, and William Laud, archbishop of Canterbury from 1633. After the accession of Charles I, Buckingham, in David Underdown's words, 'became the focus of all the searing fears and anxieties that so violently gripped his contemporaries'.[79] He was blamed for the phenomenon of 'new councels' and for the forced loan. It was significant, Underdown argues, that through his plethora of female Catholic relatives Buckingham was seen to be particularly prey to the satanic forces of malign feminine influence, which in a number of recent court scandals had been palpable in its ability to unleash disorder and inversion. The trial of Frances Howard, for the murder of Sir Thomas Overbury, was infused with talk of diabolism and witchcraft, and the family of the Secretary of State, Sir Thomas Lake, were embroiled in accusations of incest.[80] Rumours circulated widely that Buckingham had, with the aid of his Catholic mother, poisoned James I.[81] The duke himself was accused of practising the black arts, often with the aid his servant, Dr John Lambe (one of 'the Duke's devils'), a notorious magician who was lynched on a London street in 1628.[82] On the day that Charles and Buckingham were supposed to have decided to dissolve the 1626 parliament, a thunderstorm and tornado apparently struck London. Rumours circulated that Dr Lambe had been behind it. As Underdown has pointed out, historians have tended to ignore the seriousness with which such accusations were made and so to downplay the central place of notions of supernatural intervention in seventeenth-century politics. But the perception of Buckingham's diabolism was at least as important as the more prosaic accusations of corruption and incompetence that were also levelled against him.[83]

The defence of the forced loan attempted to maintain the government's monopoly on the identification of diabolic subversion.[84] The dean of

[79] Underdown, *A Freeborn People*, p. 33.
[80] At the trial of one of Frances Howard's accomplices, Anne Turner, the atmosphere of diabolism had reached such a pitch that when some of the paraphernalia supposedly used by the astrologer and magician Simon Forman were displayed as evidence, at that moment there was a loud crack from the scaffold, and there was 'such a feare, and tumulte, confusion and crye amonge the spectators, and in the hall everye man fearynge hurt, as yf the divell had bene raysed among them indeed'; quoted in Lindley, *The Trials of Frances Howard*, p. 148.
[81] John Rous, *Diary of John Rous, incumbent of Santon Downham, Suffolk, from 1625–1642*, ed. M. A. E. Green, Camden Society, original series, 66 (1856), p. 20.
[82] Ibid., pp. 33–5. [83] Underdown, *A Freeborn People*, p. 35.
[84] On the detail of Charles's licensing and reluctant suppression of the forced loan sermons, see Sommerville, *Politics and Ideology in England*, pp. 130–1.

Canterbury, Isaac Bargrave, preached on 1 Samuel 15 before Charles I on 27 March 1627. Refusal to pay the loan, he noted, stemmed from the diabolic pride which man had inherited from the fall, and which 'ever since prooved naturally [fit] for infernall fuell'.[85] God had blessed Englishmen with a pious king in order to save them from the consequences of their demonic inheritance. Obedience was thus a 'sacrifice' which paralleled the patient abandonment to God's will advocated by Protestant devotion. Refusing the loan therefore made an idol of the individual will; as 'the Witch makes the devill his God: little better doth he that makes his owne will his God'.[86] This stock of wilfulness had consistently been used by Satan to subvert the progress of religion.[87] The rector of St Giles-in-the-Fields, Roger Mainwaring, preached twice to Charles in July 1627, using similar arguments to concentrate more specifically on the loan itself. In selfishly guarding their wealth for their own 'vanity . . . lust and luxury', Englishmen made tribute to Satan over the king. 'Where the Divell hath devoured all', Mainwaring noted, 'there, God and the King, doe loose their right.' Selfishly refusing to provide money for the well-being of the Christian commonwealth was, therefore, a very real act of apostasy.[88] Selfless obedience was the very essence of religion and 'no subject may, without hazard of his own damnation in rebelling against God, question or disobey the will and pleasure of the sovereign'.[89] Even under the persecution of Nero, Christians had accepted the duty of subjection, and never 'thought the contrary, till the Deuill, of late infused it into the heads of . . . the Roman Iesuites, and German Puritans'.[90]

Thus the defence of the forced loan was entirely congruous with the concepts of the temptation of the body politic, and it is striking therefore that the government's attempt to monopolise the perception of diabolic subversion was decisively rejected when parliament assembled in 1628. On 17 March parliament gathered to consider King Charles's requirements for war against France, and gathered 'in a growing atmosphere of constitutional alarm'.[91] Concern over the extra-legal precedents of the Five Knights case was acute, and the parliament that assembled was unique for its singlemindedness. It met with a conscious agenda, and focused on the question of whether the common law continued to adequately protect English liberty.[92]

The opening speeches expressed the ideal that theocracy, supported by political consensus, was defined by a dynamic struggle with the Catholic

85 Isaac Bargrave, *A sermon preached before King Charles* (London, 1627), p. 1.
86 Ibid., pp. 2, 4–5, 7, 13, quotes at pp. 2, 7. 87 Ibid., pp. 4–5.
88 Roger Mainwaring, *Religion and Alegiance: in two sermons* (London, 1627), p. 30.
89 Ibid., pp. 18, 19, 22, 27, quote at p. 19.
90 Ibid., second sermon (separate pagination), p. 42.
91 Conrad Russell, *Parliaments and English Politics 1621–1629* (Oxford, 1979), pp. 335–6.
92 Ibid., pp. 340–9; Burgess, *The Politics of the Ancient Constitution*, pp. 194–5.

forces of diabolic subversion. On 19 March the Speaker of the Commons, Sir John Finch, reminded Charles that it was a deliverance from Satan's grasp that allowed the king to continue to act as a guarantor of the faith. 'Your majesty passed the fiery trial in Spain', he remembered of the ill-fated marriage negotiations in 1623, 'and gave us then assurance that your faith is built on the rock against which the gates of hell shall never prevaile.' Charles's succession had since seen a tightening of the recusancy laws, whilst the Jesuit 'incendiaries' were banished 'to lurk in corners like the sons of darkness'. But Finch was also aware that many in his audience considered Arminianism, and the tolerance of crypto-papists at court, to still maintain a place for subversive Catholicism. In this light Finch included a veiled warning to Charles as to the dangers involved in ever abandoning a vigilant Protestant policy. The years 1605 and 1610 were still living memories and Protestant loyalty had to be contrasted with the practices of the Catholic regicides. Protestantism bred loyalty; indeed there was 'no cement so strong to hold your subjects' hearts together in their true obedience'. 'Our religion never bred a Clement or a Ravaillac', Finch declared, 'and that exercrable villainy, never to be forgotten here, when all of us here in an instant should have been turned to ashes, was a monster that could never be engendered but by the Devil or Jesuits.'[93] Finch was reminding Charles where his best interest lay as a divine king with satanic forces to fight. Replying on the king's behalf, the Lord Keeper, Sir Thomas Coventry, assured the House of continued good faith between Charles and his subjects and that they might rest assured he would view their deliberations without applying 'sinister interpretations'. Infused with divinity, he explained, Charles was possessed of an insight more angelic than human and so 'he strains not at gnats but will easily distinguish between a vapor and a fog, betwixt a mist of errors and a cloud of evil will'.[94]

This ideal of co-operation and mutual understanding within theocracy was not to be fulfilled and, although open confrontation did not occur until Easter,[95] some of the assembled members of the Commons immediately demonstrated a readiness to come up with sinister interpretations of their own, seeing the Devil at work in the heart of the English political nation. In local disruptions of the recent elections, some members concluded, the Devil had attempted to subvert the unity of the body politic. On 20 March evidence was presented to the House of attempts in Cornwall to prevent the election of the prominent critics of the forced loan, Sir John Eliot and William

[93] *Commons Debates 1628*, ed. R.C. Johnson, M. Jansson Cole, M. Frear Keeler and W.B. Bidwell (New Haven and London, 4 vols., 1977–8), vol. II, pp. 15–16.
[94] Ibid., p. 19. [95] Russell, *Parliaments and English Politics*, p. 360.

Coryton.[96] Many in the House viewed the sabotage as an attack on its integrity, and in this context Sir Edward Coke declared it to be inspired by Satan. 'Oh, let England be at unity with itself', he commented of this attempt to sow discord in the body politic. 'I see good faces and good men. But the devil hath put in a bone amongst us; the fountain is poisoned.'[97] When the House then turned its attention to the question of whether to petition for a public fast, the threat of diabolic agency was prevalent again in the minds of some members. 'If we respect dangers, none can tell that ever they were more apparent', Sir John Phelips commented. 'I hope by this meeting we shall discharge ourselves ... and free the country of their burdens.' The veteran Sir Thomas Hoby added to this that the country was in need of a Protestant exorcism. Agreeing to the petition he noted significantly, 'many a devil cannot be cast out but by prayer and fasting'.[98]

Compatible diagnoses of the sickness and the temptation of the body politic coloured the atmosphere of subsequent debates. 'The state is inclining to a consumption', Sir Edward Coke declared on 22 March; 'it is curable. I fear not foreign enemies. God send us peace at home.'[99] For some temptation seemed particularly relevant in the question of 'new councels'. Nathaniel Rich was surely invoking imagery of the garden of Eden when, on 26 March, he quoted the opinion of James I that 'whosoever should bid the King to go against the law is a viper'. Similarly the latest petition for the enforcement of the recusancy laws (31 March) condemned the freedom with which the 'viperous generation' of Jesuits was able to invade and pollute the commonwealth.[100] Occasionally some members were highly specific as to the identification of diabolic subversion. A Mr Brown, a lawyer, quoted the jurist Henry de Bracton to condemn as diabolic the Privy Council's imprisonment of the Five Knights, noting '*Altera est potestas juris, altera injuriae. Exercere potest rex ilam juris, quia solius vicarius Dei est; injuriae autem diaboli.*'[101] 'Does the Council Table do anything for the good of the common weal?' he continued; 'will you say it is *potestas juris* to imprison? I say it is *diaboli*. All that I speak is law.'[102]

possession as political metaphor

[96] For the details of the dispute between the loan refusers and the Deputy Lieutenants of Cornwall and its place in the 1628 parliament, see Richard Cust, *The Forced Loan and English Politics 1626–1628* (Oxford, 1987), pp. 168–70, 201–2, 312–14; Russell, *Parliaments and English Politics*, p. 17.

[97] *Commons Debates 1628*, vol. II, pp. 33–6, quotes at pp. 35, 36.

[98] Ibid., p. 34.

[99] Ibid., Sir Edward Coke, p. 64; Secretary Coke, p. 82; for the contemporary reporting of these fears of diabolism, see the letter of Mr Pory, in *The Court and Times of Charles the First*, ed. T. Birch (London, 2 vols., 1849), vol. I, p. 332.

[100] *Commons Debates 1628*, Sir Nathaniel Rich, p. 130; petition against recusants, pp. 214–16.

[101] 'The power of justice is one thing, that of injustice another. The king can exercise the power of justice he alone is God's vicar. The power of injustice, however, is of the Devil': ibid., p. 233.

[102] Ibid.

The disturbing notion that the king was languishing under a demonic temptation became far more focused when parliament considered the case of Roger Mainwaring, the most controversial of the forced loan preachers. On 5 May a Commons sub-committee denounced Mainwaring's claim that resistance was damnable as 'a plot and practice to alter and subvert the frame and fabric of the whole commonwealth'. He was a devil disguised as an angel of light, since he had used his ministry to cover the Jesuitical origins of his doctrine; as John Pym declared on the 14 May, 'he went to hell for proof'.[103] As formal charges were being considered, Pym drew attention to ways in which Mainwaring had tempted Charles. The sermons were 'spiritual poison offered to the ear of the King' which endeavoured 'to infuse into the conscience of the King an absolute power not bounded by law'. As the Devil used temptation to activate the sinful potential of human corruption, so these sermons sought to diabolically activate the tyrannical potential inherent in Charles's resentment at the loan refusers.[104] Thus the more vocal of Charles's critics were quite prepared to equate openly 'new counsels' with the demonic temptation of the monarch over a decade before the image would gain far wider currency in the 1640s.[105] Since 1 Samuel 15 has been identified by historians as central to the logic of theocracy and consensual politics, it is significant that, not only was its applicability to the forced loan rejected, but the text itself was perceived to have been perverted into an instrument of temptation.[106]

We should be careful, of course, of making too much of what were, after all, a handful of speeches in four months of debates. It could not be said that fear of diabolic subversion pervaded the 1628 parliament. But it was present, and it was clearly associated in the minds of some of the regime's most consistent critics with the fear that traditional liberties were under threat from encroaching royal power, if not absolutism. What is significant is the basic congruity with which concepts of diabolism fitted into the debates when they were used. David Underdown has noted that the parliamentary debates of the 1620s were marked by an increasing violence of language which culminated in the relative tolerance adopted by the Commons in 1628. Speeches that implied royal tyranny could get men like Sir George More sent to the Tower 'with Elizabethan promptness' in 1626; in 1628 similar words were quickly explained away and excused.[107] The use of the language of diabolic subversion to criticise the regime, however obliquely, supports this

[103] 'This man has learned of Jesuits and friars this doctrine, but they are honester than he. He has belied the devil himself': ibid., vol. III, pp. 261–2; for Pym's comments see p. 416.
[104] Ibid., pp. 419–10. [105] See below, chapter 7.
[106] Elmer, '"Saints or Sorcerors"', pp. 162, 164–8; Clark, *Thinking with Demons*, pp. 610–12.
[107] Underdown, *A Freeborn People*, p. 40.

interpretation. Even at the height of the anti-Buckingham manoeuvres of 1626 the notion of diabolism was not openly invoked in parliament, despite the widespread suspicion that the duke was deeply involved in the black arts, and had, with the help of his witch/Catholic mother, hastened the death of James I. In 1628, however, members of the Commons were prepared to talk of demonic agency with reference to the activities of men openly patronised by Buckingham and, in the case of Mainwaring, by Charles himself. Moreover, whatever their expectations, and whatever the impact of their words, they spoke without being censured. Whilst diabolic subversion did not come to embody a rhetoric of opposition in the 1620s in the same way that the language of patronage and corruption did, it did see its inherent political potential exploited when parliamentarians, convinced they faced profound threats to English liberties, were ready to see those threats originating in the Devil's temptation of the body politic.

Perhaps the reaction to the assassination of Buckingham indicates how far things had changed since 1605. As Alastair Bellany has shown, attempts to control the public's response failed markedly,[108] and this should be contrasted with the situation in 1605. The judges at the trial of the assassin John Felton attempted to invoke the connection between Catholic resistance theory and treason which had been so prominent in the first decade of James I's reign. They declared that 'it was either Popery or Atheism put that malice into his heart to commit so barbarous a murder', and they explicitly compared Felton to the Jesuit François Ravaillac.[109] At his execution Felton apparently declared that he had acted at 'the instigation of the devil'.[110] But the regime could no longer command a monopoly of perception of Satan's agency, and for a large section of the political nation, both elite and popular, Buckingham remained a far more tangible diabolic agent than his murderer. Celebratory ballads and libels circulated in large numbers to defy the official line that Buckingham's assassination had been a sin against God's government, and the authorities carried out the whole business of the duke's funeral and Felton's trial in a fear of demonstrations and riots in the assassin's favour.[111] For the many who looked to a new political future without the duke's hold over Charles, that hope must have been informed by the certain knowledge that a powerful agent of the Devil had been removed from the commonwealth.

108 Alastair Bellany, '"Raylinge Rymes and Vaunting Verse": Libellous Politics in Early Stuart England, 1603–1628', in K. Sharpe and P. Lake (eds.), *Culture and Politics in Early Stuart England* (Houndmills, 1994), pp. 306–9.

109 *The Court and Times of Charles the First*, vol. I, pp. 438, 445.

110 Ibid., p. 446.

111 Bellany, 'Raylinge Rymes and Vaunting Verse', pp. 306–9; Underdown, *A Freeborn People*, pp. 58–9.

Such hopes were to be short-lived, as the 1629 session of parliament was dissolved amid chaotic scenes. Members of the Commons held the Speaker in his chair whilst Eliot attacked 'new counsels' and Arminianism in three resolutions that were carried by acclamation.[112] After the dissolution of parliament in 1629 the Suffolk minister John Rous copied a letter 'sent from the Devill to the Pope' into his diary which provides an insight into the disillusionment which may have pervaded the perception of the political scene. The letter begins by congratulating Satan's 'most reverend and deere sonne' on his recent preparations for action 'against the Rebellious heretickes from the Roman Catholike religion, I mean the British, Irish, Danish and Flemish'. Now is the most propitious moment to strike, it continues, since the dissolution has left England in a state of chaos, unable to maintain a vigilant guard against diabolic assault. 'God hath forsaken them; theire land is impoverished, theire ships tatered; their state is weakened; theire parliament is ended and nothing amended; their nobles disquieted; their gentry discouraged; the Commons discontented; and the whole kingdome divided; and the Roman Catholikes in England gasping for your arrival.' Papal arms, the Devil declares, are an embodiment of the roaring lion and the Protestant states lambs in its claws, but even so the most important weapon is internal pollution and regicide. 'It were not amisse to practice some deadly stratagem', Satan advises, 'by poulder or poyson, by my servants the Seminaries and Jesuits, especially upon the king of greate brittaine.'[113] The letter was copied between 4 and 17 April and thus gives an indication as to the immediate reaction to the dissolution of parliament. Its implicit logic was strikingly similar to that of Sir John Finch's speech at the opening of parliament a year previously. Whilst it demonstrated an overt loyalty to Charles as the enemy of Satan, feared because he could 'doe much harme' to his cause, it also intimated the need for a strong parliament and Protestant governors to resist the diabolic corruption that inhered in *any* Catholic presence in England. Without attaching blame to either king or parliament, the letter pointed to the fundamental weakening of the body politic by the recent separation of the monarch from his people, and questioned its readiness now to fight off the internal assault of those diabolic triggers, the Jesuits.

The personal rule itself, however, aroused little open opposition, in part because the absence of parliament removed the only acceptable forum for the airing of national grievances, and because away from parliament many of the regime's fiercest critics still viewed it as their duty to loyally implement royal policy.[114] In the 1630s criticism centred around religious rather than secular issues. Growing suspicions of Catholic infiltration in church and state

112 Russell, *Parliaments and English Politics*, pp. 415–16.
113 Rous, *Diary*, pp. 38–9.
114 Underdown, *A Freeborn People*, pp. 41–2.

were expressed in resistance to Laudian liturgical innovations and the Book of Sports, whilst the 'new churchmen' defined their critics as seditious 'puritans'. But it has also been noted by historians such as Esther Cope and David Underdown that politics and religion can never be separated in the seventeenth century, and that if, in 1637, religious discontent was openly attached to politics when the personal rule ran into trouble, an underlying assumption that they were connected had endured throughout the 1630s.[115] Puritan concern over diabolic subversion in the 1630s certainly bears this out. As it had done in 1572 and 1588, the perceived failure of parliament may have led some of the more determined critics of the regime to talk more openly of the dangers of demonic agency. Again an understanding that the toleration of de facto satanism and complicity in diabolic subversion were synonymous was central to the Puritan characterisation of the Laudian regime. The attack on the episcopate was re-activated with force by polemicists such as Henry Burton, John Bastwick and John Lilburne, and at its heart lay the same identification of the demonic hierarchy which had motivated the Presbyterians and separatists in the late 1500s. In 1633 the lawyer William Prynne made the most striking attack on the regime's toleration of de facto satanic subversion when he re-opened the complaint attack on the stage and openly accused the royal family of promoting the synagogue of Satan.

In 1624 Prynne began to put together his massive attack on the stage, and in 1633, at over a thousand pages, *Histrio-mastix. The players scovrge* emerged from the press. The book was part of his continuing campaign to alert Protestant England to the papist activity that lay behind its moral decline.[116] *Histrio-mastix* itself was a compilation of just about everything that had already been said against stage-plays fifty years before, but said with a viciousness that Northbrooke or Gosson never approached. Prynne's central argument, wielded like a cudgel and repeated ad infinitum, was drawn from the translation of Salvian's attack on the stage, published as the *Third Blast* in 1580. The theatres, and also the dance, were the pomps of Satan, and he who attended them had renounced his baptism and committed apostasy. Stage-plays were triggers introduced into the commonwealth to activate the diabolic potential inherent in man to 'advance the diuels sceptre'.[117] They made idols of the sins it re-enacted to 'animate and draw on the spectators more securely, more boldly to commit those self same sinnes'.[118] Schooled in

[115] Esther S. Cope, *Politics without Parliaments 1629–1640* (London, 1987), chapter 2, esp. pp. 74–6; Underdown, *A Freeborn People*, pp. 42–3.
[116] William Lamont, *Puritanism and Historical Controversy* (London, 1996), pp. 16–17.
[117] Prynne, *Histrio-mastix. The Players Scovrge*, pp. 43–4.
[118] Ibid., pp. 88–95, quote at p. 95.

this particular form of idolatry and comfortable in its practice, stage-haunters were of course papists in the final analysis.[119]

What, then, given it had all been said before, made Prynne's book so offensive to the authorities that they fined him heavily, sentenced him to life imprisonment and cropped his ears? *Histrio-mastix* had referred to the Roman emperor Nero's patronage of the arts as being symptomatic of his degeneracy, and had detailed his deposition and assassination as the judgement of God on his sins.[120] In Star Chamber it was alleged that Prynne was making an implicit comparison between Charles I and Nero, and that he was thus inviting the king's subjects to depose him.[121] 'Thoughe not in expresse tearmes', the prosecution suggested, 'yet by examples and other implicite meanes, hee labours to infuse an opinyon into the people, that for the acteinge or beinge spectatours of playes or maskes it is just and lawfull to laye violent handes uppon kinges and princes.'[122] William Lamont is unconvinced that Prynne had any such seditious intent. *Histrio-mastix*, he notes, was too infused with a general misanthropy to be attempting anything so specific. Moreover, Prynne's collection of divine judgements against rulers who tolerated stage-plays had more in common with the popular moralising providentialism of Thomas Beard's *Theatre of Gods judgements* than with a programme of armed rebellion. It was Prynne's unsubtle insertion into an index of a description of female actors as 'notorious whores' at the same time as the queen was rehearsing her own part in a court masque that drew the authorities' attention to the seditious possibilities of his work. But if the lawyer was deliberately insulting the queen, the call to rebellion was only in the minds of his prosecutors. Perhaps this is so, but Prynne's attack on the monarch seems far more focused than Professor Lamont implies when the book is considered, not as a discrete document symptomatic of the lawyer's unique obsessiveness, but as part of the by now long-established practice of exploiting the potential for criticism inherent in the belief in the temptation of the body politic. The Presbyterians had seen the Devil in the tyranny of the episcopate; Peter Wentworth had taken the accusation too close to the queen and he ended up in the Tower. Prynne was in one sense Wentworth's successor. He took an established argument farther than anyone else was prepared to go, abandoned the buffer offered by 'evil councillors' and implicitly accused Charles not only of tolerating diabolic subversion in the stage, but actively encouraging it.

119 Ibid., p. 342. 120 Ibid., p. 852.

121 *Documents relating to the proceedings against William Prynne, in 1634 and 1637*, pp. 12–13, 19; Stephen Foster, *Notes from the Caroline Underground: Alexander Leighton, the Puritan Triumvirate, and the Laudian Reaction to Nonconformity* (Hamden, Conn., and Springfield, Ohio, 1978), pp. 41–5.

122 *Documents relating to ... William Prynne*, p. 13.

In order to understand the political consequences of Prynne's book we need to understand what it was that he thought Charles was encouraging. For Prynne it was unquestionable that the theatre was the Devil's church,[123] but he also instilled the stage and the dance with characteristics reminiscent of the witches' Sabbat. The Sabbat myth assumed that certain locations (usually distant mountain tops) were consecrated to Satan as a church is dedicated to Christ. Willing diabolic servants travelled deliberately to those locations in order to meet with Satan. At the meeting the witches swore allegiance to the Devil and renounced their Christian baptism, often performing inverted rites of demonic initiation. For Prynne stage-haunters and dancers were the Devil's parishioners whose renunciation of their baptism might be more implicit than the witch's, but was no less concrete. 'They that dance', he noted, 'breake that promise and agreement, which they have made to God at baptisme . . . for dancing is the pompe of the deuill, and he that danceth, maintaineth his pompe, and singeth his Masse.' Of course the connection with Catholic ceremony was irresistible and Prynne continued: 'the woman that singeth in the dance is the prioresse of the deuill, and those that answer are clerkes, and beholders are parishioners, and the music are the bells, and the fidlers, the ministers of the deuill'. As witches were called to gather at the Sabbat, so were the dancers called to attend on the Devil. 'For as when hogs are strayed', he observed, 'if the hogheard call one, all assemble themselves together. So the deuill causeth one woman to sing in the dance, or play on some instrument, and presently all the dancers gather together.' To enter into the dance was to both literally follow the Devil who was present, and to symbolically express a subsequent allegiance to him in life. Thus dancing was turned into an act of diabolic initiation: 'a dance . . . is the deuils procession, and he that entereth into a dance, entereth into his possession. The deuill is the guide, the middle, and the end of the dance. As many steps as a man maketh in dancing, so many paces doth he make to hell.' But dancing was also an act of consecration since Satan is 'ever-more *present and president* where such dancing is'.[124]

This, then, is what Prynne was accusing the royal family of promoting. *Histrio-mastix* was simply too repetitious, the argument that plays and dances were the Devil's weapons, and that attendance revoked baptism simply too central to make it plausible that when he criticised the regime for its laxity he did not have diabolism in mind. Of 'all Christian Princes, Cittyes, States, and Magistrates', he commented, their 'connivencye at any evill which they might supresse dothe make them deeplye guiltye'.[125]

[123] Prynne, *Histrio-mastix*, pp. 228–31. [124] Ibid., p. 229, my emphasis.
[125] Ibid., pp. 50, 787.

This commentary was extracted and presented as evidence in Star Chamber. Having charged Prynne with casting 'aspertion vppon the Kinge', the prosecution selected extracts to support their case, and in the light of the charges *all* Prynne's accusations of diabolism became pointed attacks on Charles himself. They quoted his opinion that both players and audience were the 'mynions of the devill', given over to 'infernall pleasures'. A general reference to the the betrayal of the baptism promise – 'God forbid that any whoe have beene dipped in the sacred laver of Regineration ... should prove such desperate incarnate devills, such atheisticall Judases to their lord and Master, such perjured cutt throats to their Religion' – seemed in the light of the charges to be a calculated attack on Charles's pretensions to divine right.[126] Prynne had written against the practice of entertaining players in private houses, which to the Solicitor-General, Edward Lyttleton, was little more than a veiled attack on the royal court, and so he quoted among the lawyer's aspersions 'vppon the Kinges howse': 'can you be soe besotted by the devill (as alas manye are) as to thincke to please, to honnour, courte, or entertayne Christe Jesus, to welcomme him into the world, to celebrate his natiuitye with infernall stage playes, the verye monuments and ensignes wherewith the Pagans did courte their devill godes?'[127] Another indication of how the case against Prynne was constructed is given in the Attorney-General John Banks's use of *Histrio-mastix*'s epistle dedicatory, in which the assessment of the number of Devil's synagogues was made a direct attack on the king:

> Mr. Attourneye chargeth him with the crymes and assertions against the Kinges person, videlicet, hee would make him worse than Neroe, vizt. London play houses beinge soe much augmented nowe as that all the devilles chappelees, beinge fyve in number, maye not contayne them, when as wee see a sixt nowe added to them, whereas in vitious Neroes raigne there was but three standinge theatres in pagan Rome.[128]

Thus Star Chamber was being asked to accept that he had accused the king of active diabolism. The method seems to have met with success. Sir Thomas Edmonds, regretting that Star Chamber could not impose a harsher sentence upon Prynne, noted of him that he 'taketh uppon him to forme a newe kinde of governmente and doth denounce all those that bee not of his opinyon to bee reprobates and lymbes of the devill'. Lord Richardson, finding him guilty of a 'seditious lybell against the Kinge and Queene, suche as theye of man never sawe', quoted his description of dancing as the Devil's procession that leads men to hell.[129]

[126] *Documents relating to ... William Prynne*, p. 5. [127] Ibid., p. 8. [128] Ibid., pp. 11–12.
[129] Ibid., pp. 23, 20.

Predictably, Star Chamber turned Prynne's arguments on himself and stated that it was he who was the agent of Satan. Giving his opinion of the case on 17 February, Lord Cottington noted that 'Mr. Pryn did not invent this booke alone, but was assisted by the devill himselfe, and it is not the first booke of this nature hee made, for hee made one booke against the due reverence of our Saviour, which none but a devill would doe.' 'The hartes and good opinyon of a subjecte is the Kinges best treasure', Lord Richardson observed, 'and for a man to endeavour to defraude the Kinge of this treasure is a most damnable offense.' He thus compared Prynne's motivation with the lethal intentions of the Catholic plotters in 1605 – 'this monster spittes noethinge but venome, and that att every man; the gunpowder traytors would blowe the state into the ayer, and this man will dampe them all to hell'. Lord Dorset in his turn strove to impose dependable contrariety on Prynne's actions. 'Christ sent his disciples with *Ite praedicate*', he explained, 'and they did accordinglye preache, teache, and practyze charytye and obedyence; but the devill, on the contraye part, wrought alsoe miracles, and scited Scriptures to wicked endes, and sendes out his disciples with *totum prosternite mundum*; and this man, forsakeinge Christes rule, as one of the devilles faithfull agentes, followes his instruccions.' We have seen such exchanges before, and that they can never be dismissed as simple name calling.[130] The real influence of Prynne's writings, before he became parliament's apologist for the Civil War, has been questioned by historians, and his persecution by the authorities, especially when it was repeated in 1637, has been seen as a massive over-reaction, which back-fired more because of disgust at the show trial than because people agreed with anything he had said. Whilst historians have rightly highlighted the personal animosity that drove the regime's pursuit of Prynne, and the cynicism with which they orchestrated his trials, there has been a corresponding tendency to understate how sinister his activities might seem to those who valued the regime and its religious practices. It was possible to see him as a profound enemy of Christianity, who, like the Elizabethan Puritans before him, held up an empty picture of pious reformation only in order to lure the commonwealth into confusion.[131]

The conviction of Prynne probably protected Charles from further accusations of diabolism,[132] but the same fears about his temptation that had been expressed in 1628 became focused on the Laudian episcopate. In his *Litany*

[130] Ibid., pp. 16, 20–1, 24.

[131] As William Lamont has pointed out, Laud and his followers were deeply affronted by Prynne's accusations that they were Jesuits. Lamont, *Puritanism and Historical Controversy*, p. 17.

[132] Apparently, however, a libellous sermon attacking the king was found in Prynne's study in the Tower in 1635. K. Sharpe, *The Personal Rule of Charles I* (New Haven, 1992), p. 759.

(1637), the Puritan physician John Bastwick attacked Laudian attempts to capture the beauty of holiness as a betrayal of the king's pious intentions, by which the bishops proclaimed 'the synagogue of Satan[,] Rome it self to be the true church'.[133] Charles might protest that he would 'neuer conniue at any backsliding to popery', but the Laudians had effected to separate him from his loyal Protestant subjects by presenting them as dangerous fanatics. They gleefully publicised the case of the Puritan Enoch ap Evan, who in 1633 decapitated his mother and brother with an axe, supposedly as a result of a row over kneeling at church. 'Have [Puritans] ever shewn the least disloyalty to his Maiesty, or plotted anything against his life', Bastwick asked, forcing a comparison with well-known Catholic conspiracies. Because 'one distempered man had perpetrated so foul a crime, through some deuillish temptation', must it follow that they were all raving homicides?[134] As Mainwaring and Bargrave had a decade before, the Laudians tempted Charles disguised as angels of light, and made 'the pulpit a stage' to parade the Devil's lies.[135] In so doing they brought 'a confusion both in Church and state for the better effecting of those devilish purposes, that no gunpowder plot could bring yet to passe'.[136] Again we are seeing Sir John Finch's assessment of the king's best interests, and their betrayal through diabolic subversion, being replayed.

In mid-1637 the now famous trial of the Puritan triumvirate was set in motion. Whereas Prynne's suffering in 1633 had aroused little public interest, his punishment with Burton and Bastwick seemed now to point to a tyrannical edge to the regime.[137] The punishment of the apprentice and future Leveller, John Lilburne, would lead to the production of a striking manifesto for resistance to the satanic government of the Laudian episcopate. Lilburne had befriended both Bastwick and Prynne and had acted as an amanuensis to both in prison.[138] He was involved in the publishing of Bastwick's *Litany*, spending several months of 1637 in Holland, and on his return he was arrested. After making himself as troublesome to the authorities as possible,

[133] John Bastwick, *The answer of Iohn Bastwick, Doctor of Phisicke, to the exceptions made against his Letany by A learned Gentleman* (Amsterdam, 1637), pp. 6, 8. On the Laudian attitude to religious organisation, see Peter Lake, 'The Laudian Style: Order, Uniformity and the Pursuit of the Beauty of Holiness in the 1630s', in Fincham, *The Early Stuart Church*, pp. 161–85.

[134] Bastwick, *The answer of Iohn Bastwick*, pp. 3–4; on the case of Enoch ap Evans, see Peter Lake, 'Puritanism, Arminianism and a Shropshire Axe-Murder', *Midland History*, 15 (1990), pp. 37–64.

[135] Bastwick, *The answer of Iohn Bastwick*, p. 4. [136] Ibid., p. 3.

[137] *A Brief relation of certain special . . . speeches in the Star-Chamber . . . at the censure of those worthy Gentlemen, Dr Bastwicke, Mr Burton, and Mr Prynne*, in *The Harleian Miscellany*, vol. IV, pp. 220–38; Lamont, *Puritanism and Historical Controversy*, p. 20; Sharpe, *The Personal Rule of Charles I*, pp. 762–4.

[138] John Lilburne, *A Worke of the Beast or A Relation of a most vnchristian Censure Executed vpon Iohn Lilburne* (London, 1638), p. 14.

he was fined, sentenced to be flogged and pilloried, and imprisoned in the Fleet. The day after, his sentence was added to when it was decided that he should be put in irons and denied all food but what he could get from the prison's poor box. In two triumphalist pamphlets, *A Worke of the Beast* (1638) and *Come out of her my people* (1639), he revealed that the reason for the harshness of his treatment was that on the pillory he challenged the bishops that in a dispute he would prove that their authority was derived only from Satan.[139] For the socialist historian H. N. Brailsford the significance of Lilburne's challenge was an affirmation to the death of the liberty of unlicensed printing, and he dismissed the apprentice's belief in a demonic episcopate as a 'juvenile thesis'.[140] But his denunciation of diabolic episcopacy was not some rash expression of youthful radicalism – as Brailsford would have it, an exciting but ultimately empty gesture – but an organising principle of his resistance to his prosecutors.

As so often before, the Corinthians dichotomy provided a means of characterising the authority of the episcopate which maintained a hold over church government by nothing more than Satan's false doctrine. 'I shall not dare to have any spirituall communion with them', Lilburne noted, 'either in publicke or private, for what fellowship hath righteousness with unrighteousness ... And what Concord hath Christ with Beliall?'[141] Beneath the seemingly pious words of the Anglican ministry their audience 'doth hear the devil'. Not only did this justify his rejection of episcopal authority, but Lilburne believed that his spiritual insight was a weapon against Satan. The power of Laud would evaporate at the moment its hellish origins were revealed by the scrutiny by one armed with the Word. The panic his challenge produced appeared to justify his faith in its efficacy. 'These Episcopall Rabbies', he recounted, 'who are Cheife members of the Kingdome of Darknesse, had no other Argument to convince me with, then to put a Gagg in my mouth, least I should have shaken the foundation of their Antichristian Kingdome.'[142]

For the moment Lilburne had found his cause célèbre and the day after his sufferings he sent a message from the Fleet to Laud repeating his challenge, offering now to prove episcopal diabolism on pain of death. Again brute force attempted to prevent his message being heard, and the archbishop commanded that he be quarantined 'in the basest place in the Wards of the Fleet' lest his words should prove infectious.[143] In mid-May 1638 an

[139] Lilburne, *Come out of her my people*, p. 25; for a rather effusive account of Lilburne and his sufferings see H. N. Brailsford, *The Levellers and the English Revolution* (Stanford, Calif., 1961; reprinted Nottingham, 1976), pp. 80–3.
[140] Ibid., p. 82. [141] Lilburne, *Come out of her my people*, p. 13.
[142] Ibid., p. 24. [143] Ibid., p. 26.

examination before the King's Attorney, Sir John Banks, and the Solicitor-General, Edward Lyttleton, offered Lilburne another opportunity to declare that he would prove the bishops to be servants of Satan. This time he had visions of opening the eyes of the king and requested that Charles be present to see him either demolish Laud once and for all or die in the attempt. The reaction was by now predictable, and Lilburne was returned to close imprisonment with the addition of a set of irons for his trouble. Concerned about the effect of his polemic, the authorities commanded that he be denied all writing materials, and when he wrote in spite of them, he justified their fears. In 1639 he produced an appeal to his fellow apprentices which was smuggled out by a maidservant and distributed during their Whitsun holidays. The result, although he did not intend it, was a riot.[144] *Come out of her my people* should be seen in the same light. It was his fourth challenge to Laud, made this time by way of the ordinary readership, and driven by the same belief that Satan's power could never stand up the scrutiny of the Word. The pamphlet ended with a direct invitation to contest the satanism of the episcopate, and the final page was given over to listing the points to that effect which Lilburne would prove on pain of death.

Did Lilburne seriously believe his gauntlet would be taken up, or was he simply exploiting the propagandist potential of his situation and baiting the archbishop? On the pillory in 1638 he seems to have believed his eloquence would move the crowd. His appeal to the apprentices in 1639 was to ask for a fair trial, and his prison writings reveal that to his mind a fair trial was one that would allow him to make his contentious inability to hold any kind of communion with the demonic episcopacy a cornerstone of his defence. Undoubtedly he took satisfaction in baiting Laud with a challenge that was unlikely to be taken up. But Laud's 'cowardice' reinforced Lilburne's view that his methods bore an efficacy which terrified the Devil's bishops.

Thus the perception of diabolic subversion cut across the political rhetoric of sixteenth- and seventeenth-century England. Employed by both the government and critics, it did not imply opposition in the sense that the language of corruption identified by Linda Levy Peck did. The notion that the body politic might be tempted was a logical extension of the belief that the human body might be so, and it could be part of the analogical thinking which Sommerville has warned against reading too literally.[145] But the actual perception of the Devil's subversion was born of conviction. Hence whilst there was a wide acceptance of the possibility of the temptation of the body politic, the experience and understanding of that temptation was defined by a far more individual sense of tangibility. The Gunpowder Plot

144 Brailsford, *The Levellers and the English Revolution*, p. 85.
145 Sommerville, *Politics and Ideology in England*, pp. 48–9.

gave the Devil's agency a palpability which went far beyond any other political event before the Civil War. But even here there was room for personal interpretation and difference. For William Prynne the theatre was the embodiment of Satan's subversion, and his writings were infused with a sense of frustration at others' refusal to see how the stage sparked off man's inherent sinfulness. Yet many others, Charles I among them, looked to a more benign didacticism in the theatre, and felt no demonic presence there at all. Charles felt his Devil elsewhere. If the writings of the theocrats he sponsored are assumed to reflect his personal convictions, Satan lurked in the conscience of those who sought to limit his power and deprive him of his favourite.

The rhetoric of witchcraft might, as Elmer suggests, encourage consensus, but only within a narrowly defined political outlook. The verse 1 Samuel 15: 23 was central only to theocracy, not to the more varied political understanding illustrated by Dr Sommerville. Theocracy versus witchcraft operated on a pre-existing identification of the nature of Satanic agency – rebellion against the divine ruler. It was an ideology that might discourage or react to opposition only if it was accepted that certain types of criticism *were* rebellion. As parliament's response to the Mainwaring case demonstrates, this was far from a foregone conclusion. The wider understanding of the demonic temptation of the body politic was simply too open to ever be able to breed consensus. Relying for its force on a personal sense of tangibility rather than on abstract theorising, the idea not only allowed for, but was defined by wide differences of perception. Elmer has also noted that 1 Samuel 15 did not become politicised until the outbreak of the Civil War, but we have seen that the perception of diabolic subversion was an inherently political act. No regime maintained a monopoly of the perception of diabolic subversion, although the tangibility provided by the Gunpowder Plot allowed James I greater control than Elizabeth I or Charles I. The 1640s saw an enormous increase in claims that Satan was walking through England, but, as we will see in the next chapter, what had changed was that diabolic agency had become markedly more tangible in the upheavals of the Civil War, and the breakdown of censorship, and wide recourse to propaganda had made such views far easier to express.

7

'Grand Pluto's Progress through Great Britaine': the Civil War and the zenith of satanic politics

For many of those who lived through it, 1642–60 appeared to mark the zenith of Satan's activity in England, a time in which he appeared especially free to plague the nation and bring about unprecedented upheaval and change. War was inherently diabolic, a civil war doubly so. Its chaos and bloodshed were the Devil's hallmarks, a sign that he now walked the earth unfettered. Peace, noted one pamphleteer in 1643, was a 'blessing' and he who worked to maintain peace in the commonwealth was 'a child of God'. By extension he who agitated for war to disrupt the godly nation was 'little better than a childe of the deuill'.[1] In 1644 a pamphlet entitled *The Great Eclipse of the Sun* noted how Charles I's belligerence could only be explained by his having fallen under the influence of Satan and his human agents. Even for a divine king, such a betrayal of godly duty tempted providence. 'Though the Pope and all the Deuills in hell should encourage him to this bloudy war', the author declared, 'yet it is unnatural in the sight of God and man.' 'There is a hell and domesday, and damnation, as well for Kings as poor subjects', he warned.[2]

The gamut of recognised diabolic phenomena seemed especially congruent with the times. God's hangman was unusually active, dragging sinners, hypocritical parliamentarians, and drunken Cavaliers off to hell.[3] Satan's trusted agents, the Jesuits, went about the nation in disguise, effecting the subversion of Protestantism, and hatching plots to do violence to its guardians, the king and parliament. Satan drove people to commit brutal murders, and tempted them to witchcraft. Between 1645 and 1647, East Anglia experienced England's only major witch panic, when, guided by the self-styled Witch-finder-General, Matthew Hopkins, a witch-hunt spread from Essex to Suffolk, resulting in

1 *The Miseries of War. By a louer of Trvth and Peace* (?London, 1643), p. 5.

2 *The Great Eclipse of the Sun, or Charles his waine over-clouded, by the euill influences of the moon* (?London, 1644), p. 6.

3 In 1641 the Devil appeared in a tavern on the Strand, causing 'multitudes of people' to flock there, whilst in 1642 he appeared before a drunken royalist, who soon died blaspheming against God and parliament. See *A Wonderfull and Strange Miracle, or Gods Just Vengeance Against the Cavaliers* (London, 1642), pp. 4–6.

the executions of at least 100 witches. In recent studies the disruptions of the Civil War have been re-emphasised as the background to the hunt.[4] But Satan also had new tricks to play. A particularly disturbing ploy involved the proliferation of religious sectarianism. A bewildering array of pernicious heretics seemed to burst from nowhere, espousing every offensive position from atheism to antinomianism and the abolition of sin.[5]

To ask why England became prey to the perception of increased diabolic activity in the 1640s and 1650s might seem a redundant question. The Civil War and the execution of the king were profoundly disturbing events which produced massive social and cultural dislocation. In J. C. Davis's words, they produced an 'extension of the range of uncertainty.'[6] As the work of Anthony Fletcher, John Morrill and Conrad Russell has convincingly shown, few, if any, conceived of the possibility of civil war when the Long Parliament met in November 1640.[7] Despite agitation for an engagement among some of the parliamentary party in early 1642, the reality of a civil war was perceived as a failure of government, which heralded a descent into chaos, and set countrymen against each other in a subversion of nature. The suddenness of this cataclysmic failure bewildered and frightened contemporaries, forcing them to find some way to come to terms with it. In such an environment the Devil's malice seemed as plausible an explanation as any. A civil war was especially demanding on this kind of explanatory device. Demonic caricatures of Cavaliers and Roundheads, set out in propaganda, provided useful ammunition. But they also betrayed a need to dehumanise in order to explain what made these countrymen not countrymen at all. Cherished political beliefs were eroded when, as the war progressed, it became increasingly difficult to shift blame from Charles to his advisers, and his eventual execution, and the abolition of the House of Lords symbolised (or so it seemed) a repudiation of patriarchal hierarchy and the end of the ancient constitution. Government in the hands of a revolutionary minority in 1649 appeared to many the very triumph of Satan.

The perception of diabolic activity must also have provided an emotive expression for the pervasive feeling of helplessness experienced both by those who took part in the war and those who did not. From 1642 many

[4] Sharpe, *Instruments of Darkness*, pp. 140–2; Briggs, *Witches and Neighbours*, p. 293; Elmer, '"Saints or Sorcerers"', p. 175, n. 86.

[5] Hill, *The World Turned Upside Down*; J. F. McGregor and B. Reay (eds.), *Radical Religion in the English Revolution* (Oxford, 1984); Barry Reay, *The Quakers and the English Revolution* (New York, 1985); Davis, *Fear, Myth and History*; Jerome Friedman, *Miracles and the Pulp Press during the English Revolution: The Battle of the Frogs and Fairfords' Flies* (London, 1993), chapters 5 and 6.

[6] Davis, *Fear, Myth and History*, p. 100.

[7] Anthony Fletcher, *The Outbreak of the English Civil War* (London, 1981); John Morrill, *Revolt in the Provinces: Conservatives and Radicals in the English Civil War* (London, 1980); Conrad Russell, *The Fall of the British Monarchies 1637–1642* (Oxford, 1991).

experienced the 'agony of choosing sides' in a conflict that they did not want, and choices were made on the basis of fear as well as conviction. Fear of an Irish invasion, or fear of disorder and rioting, motivated into action men who had hoped the crisis would be short enough to maintain their neutrality.[8] Moving armies, billeting, pillaging and war taxation threatened the livelihoods of those unfortunate enough to find themselves in the way, whilst the rumour of them was presumably equally terrifying to those who did not. Unsurprisingly, then, the war ushered in a national obsession with all kinds of cosmic influences and portents that became inseparable from its political and military upheavals and were equally disturbing. The pulp press reported widespread providences and signs of divine displeasure, feeding a fear that God would punish the nation for its disruption of divinely ordained kingship.[9]

The Devil was central to this cosmic environment of the Civil War. His appearances as God's hangman provided further indications of divine displeasure, but they also might be particularly adept at expressing the moral ambiguity of the times. For example, the pamphlet *Strange News from Warwick* (1642) told two very folkloric tales about the appearance of God's hangman in the aftermath of the Battle of Edgehill. The first concerned a soldier who was robbed of his booty by a husband and wife who kept an inn at Warwick; the second involved a soldier who returned from battle to find his fiancée celebrating her marriage to another man. In both instances the Devil appeared in different guises to make off with the offenders, in the first case as a defence lawyer in the trial of the victim, who was imprisoned after threatening violence to get his money back, in the second as a mysterious stranger who carried off the bride while dancing at her wedding.[10]

The stories embody moral turbulence and instability. The innkeeper is seduced by a 'modern' corruption of the common law, believing that it is

[8] Martyn Bennet, *The Civil Wars in Britain and Ireland 1638–1651* (Oxford, 1997), chapter 5.

[9] The number of pamphlets produced describing such prodigies was enormous. This is a sample of some of the better-known examples: *A Great Wonder in Heaven: shewing The Late Apparitions and prodigious noyses of War and battels, seen on Edge-Hill* (London, 1642); *A Blazing Starre seene in the West; A Strange And Lamentable accident that happened lately at Mead-Ashby in Northamptonshire* (London, 1642); *Signes and wonders from Heaven. With a true Relation of a Monster borne in Ratcliffe Highway, at the signe of the three Arrows* (?London, 1642); William Lilly, *The Starry Messenger, or, An Interpretation of Strange Aparitions* (?London, 1644); *A Declaration, Of a strange and Wonderfull Monster: Born in Kirkham Parish in Lancashire* (London, 1646); *The Most Strange and Wonderfull Apparition of Blood in a Pool at Garreton* (London, 1647). See also Friedman, *Miracles and the Pulp Press*, chapters 2 and 3.

[10] This pamphlet was probably regurgitated in the newsbook *The Faithful Scout* in December 1654. Although now set in Germany the same two tales of an innkeeper who steals money he has been entrusted to keep, and of a woman who deserts her fiancé, are given as news of that week. The text is reprinted in Joad Raymond, *Making the News: An Anthology of the Newsbooks of Revolutionary England 1641–1660* (Moreton-in-Marsh, 1993), pp. 192–3.

infinitely malleable, and anything that cannot be proved in a court to belong to someone else is rightfully his. His victim is a parliamentarian soldier – and perhaps there is a political bias in the pamphlet – but the soldier has got his booty by pillaging bodies on the battlefield, and, whilst he refuses to give the Devil his soul, he willingly enlists his help in exacting justice on the innkeepers when Satan appears to tempt him in his cell. Getting Satan to dispense his powers for free is a familiar victory in the folkloric narrative, but the soldier exhibits none of the clever trickery usually in evidence; instead his concern for the safety of his soul impresses Satan into helping him. As Darren Oldridge has suggested, this was an assimilation of Protestantism and folklore.[11] But it was one that was fraught with confusion. Whilst the soldier's concern for his spiritual state might be Protestant, Protestantism countenanced no witting interaction with the Devil. The only moral certainty exhibited in the pamphlet is that of the danger of swearing by the Devil, which both offenders do before being dragged off in the execution of poetic justice.[12]

Thus in one sense the perception of increased diabolic activity fits into the picture historians have drawn of the role of explanatory devices in the upheavals of the Civil War. As Conrad Russell has noted of anti-popery, the Devil's utility might lie in his ability 'to impose order on an otherwise unintelligible mass of events'.[13] But this is only one part of the picture. The conspiracy theories of anti-popery and anti-Puritanism studied by Anthony Fletcher, Conrad Russell and others, and the interest in cosmic disturbances and portents described by Jerome Friedman, are essentially seen as over-emotional reactions to political and social crisis. Professor Fletcher has described the 'abnegation of reason' by which John Pym skilfully imposed his 'over-dramatised' view of the functional breakdown of Stuart government on the Westminster establishment, and his readiness to entertain rumour and distrust exposing the obsessive anti-Catholicism which gave his tactical acumen its emotional drive. For Professor Russell, the prevalence of these conspiracy theories is indicative of a tendency among Charles I and his subjects to give in to the temptation to employ simplistic and all-embracing explanatory tools as a meaningful gloss for an infinitely more complex and confusing political reality.[14] But if the perception of diabolic activity could

[11] Darren Oldridge, *Religion and Society in Early Modern England* (Aldershot, 1998), pp. 12–13. Unlike Oldridge, however, I am not convinced that the Protestant elements in *Strange News from Warwick* can be described as characteristically Puritan, since they embody a view of diabolic temptation that was in no way the preserve of the hotter sort of the godly. See ibid, p. 19, n. 62.

[12] *Strange News from Warwick* (London, 1642), sigs. A2v–A3 and A4–A4v.

[13] Russell, *The Fall of the British Monarchies*, p. 527.

[14] Fletcher, *The Outbreak of the English Civil War*, pp. 408–12; Russell, *The Fall of the British Monarchies*, pp. 527–8.

play a similar role, far more prevalent was a positive and proactive engagement with satanism that allowed the political crisis of 1640–2, and the Civil War, to be seen as part of an ongoing campaign against Satan's attempt to subvert and tempt the body politic.

As we saw in the last chapter, demonism did not, as Peter Elmer suggests, become politicised only after the outbreak of hostilities; it was an inherently political belief from the accession of Elizabeth I. Both discerning Satan in their enemy's vanguard in 1642, parliamentarians and royalists accepted an established dynamic of diabolic agency which was bound up with the complexities of theocratic politics, rather than with an attempt to gloss them over. The demands of an intense propaganda war, and the removal of effective constraint over the press, left polemicists free for the first time to say just about anything about their enemies. The pulp press went into overdrive and openly churned out the kind of libels that had only been circulated surreptitiously before. Other areas of polemic, notably the parliamentary fast sermons, were equally free with their testaments to the perception of diabolism. What is striking about these sources is not a recourse to a functional demonisation and 'othering' (although of course those elements are present) but the consistency with which the dynamic of diabolic subversion, temptation of the body politic and false doctrine – which favoured a nuanced political understanding over crude stigmatisation – pervaded Civil War polemic.

'SWORNE SWORD-MEN OF THE DEVILL': DIABOLIC SERVICE IN PARLIAMENTARY PROPAGANDA

Nine days after Charles I raised his standard at Nottingham Castle, William Carter preached a fast sermon to the House of Commons in which he characterised the impending war as a divinely ordained struggle with the forces of Satan. Parliament was not warmongering; rather the present conflict was a natural consequence of being employed in reformation, since 'if any man be set on work for God, all the power and subtlety of Satan and his wicked instruments are set against him'.[15] The fast sermons, the area of propaganda over which parliament had the most direct control, have been used by historians as a barometer of its aims, intentions and reactions, and it is surprising that more attention has not been paid to Carter's sermon.[16] This

[15] William Carter, *Isreals peace with God, Beniamines Overthrow* (London, 1642), p. 19.

[16] See Hugh Trevor-Roper's study, 'The Fast Sermons of the Long Parliament', reprinted in his *Religion, Reformation and Social Change* (London, 1967), pp. 294–344; and Christopher Hill, *The English Bible and the Seventeenth-Century Revolution* (London, 1993), pp. 79–108, Hill briefly describes Carter's sermon on p. 90.

is largely because the fast sermons of 1642 are generally considered in the shadow of Stephen Marshall's *Meroz Cursed*, preached at the first of the regular fasts on 23 February. Six months before the outbreak of hostilities, this sermon denounced neutrality and those who balked at shedding blood in God's cause. It called for total war and marked a watershed, in Hugh Trevor-Roper's narrative of the fast sermons, after which the Commons employed a long series of 'incendiary' preachers who scandalised both royalists and moderates.[17] Yet even as the two sides prepared for war, William Carter's sermon was no thunderous incitement to violence. Rather it sought to instil in parliament an awareness of the demands placed on those who would take action in a theocentric conflict. Seeing the enemy as the servants of Satan complicated rather than simplified political understanding. It encouraged engagement by drawing a parallel between macro-political conflict and the personal struggles of the godly with diabolic temptation. But as Satan might subvert the piety of individual Christians, so too he might subvert any apparently godly cause. Hence, whilst demonism provided a similar emotional energy to that which Christopher Hill has identified in apocalypticism, it also demanded that parliament keep in sight the precarious boundary that separated just resistance from diabolic rebellion.

By the outbreak of hostilities the polemical battle lines had long been drawn. Parliament's Laudian enemies were described as popishly affected idolaters who wished to force a separation between the king and his people and turn back the Reformation. From their inception the fast sermons continued the critique of government tolerance of diabolic subversion that had emerged in the parliaments of the 1620s and the Puritan writings of the personal rule. Cornelius Burges, preaching the first of the fast sermons on 17 November 1640, asked why in the wake of escapes from the Spanish Armada and the Gunpowder Plot had England still not been given full deliverance from Babylon? The answer was that the spirit of division had allowed religion to sink into the 'deepest lakes of superstition and idolatry, under pretence of some extraordinary pietie of the times, and of some good work in hand'.[18] Satan had his covenant with his subjects, as evidenced by the pacts drawn up with witches. Now England needed its covenant with God to be renewed, for 'who will not do as much for him as Witches and Sorcerers will do for the Devill?'[19] But Burges was far more explicit than his predecessors as to the role of parliament in defeating the influence of false doctrine.

[17] Stephen Marshall, *Meroz Cursed, or, A Sermon Preached to the Honourable House of Commons, At their late Solemn Fast, Feb. 23. 1641* (London, 1641); Trevor-Roper, *Religion, Reformation and Social Change*, pp. 307–8.

[18] Cornelius Burges, *The First Sermon preached to the honourable House of Commons now assembled in Parliament at their Publique Fast* (London, 1641), p. 54.

[19] Ibid., p. 64.

The Gunpowder Plot proved, he argued, that parliament was the most important bulwark against satanism. 'For, albeit the ruine of the whole Kingdome was in their Eye who were the Cursed instruments of Antichrist, and of the Devill his Father, in that hellish Designe; yet, no blow could have come at us, but through Your [parliament's] sides.' Tradition had it that it was James I and his regime (of which parliament was only one part) which had been spared in 1605. The fact that Burges preferred to see the plotters' target as parliament itself should not be underplayed. It was highly significant if parliament was to define a role for itself as the vanguard against satanism. The members – many of whom, Burges pointed out, would never have been born had the plot succeeded – should be aware that they might once again stand in need of God's deliverance, since their work would inevitably invite Satan's attentions. 'You cannot be ignorant', he noted, 'of the many murmures and the more than whisperings of some desperate devilish conception suspected to be now in the womb of the Jesuiticall faction.'[20]

This defining of parliament's anti-satanic role became a consistent theme of the fast sermons of 1640–2. Stephen Marshall, preaching after Burges, reinforced his point. 'Your enemies are mighty, malicious, and cunning', he declared, 'and it may bee they are digging as deep as hell for Counsell to doe you mischiefe in this great worke that you are in.'[21] 'Let not the present troubles seem strange to you', the minister of Farnham in Essex, William Sedgwick, advised the Commons from the pulpit on 29 June 1642; 'we could not expect to finde the Dragon aslepe, and to steale away the golden fleece of Reformation.' He compared the work of parliament to the exorcisms performed by Christ in which, before being cast out, 'the Devil rent [the victim] sore'. 'So it is with us', Sedgwick continued; 'there have been some attempts to cast out the dumbe and deafe spirit of this Kingdome; but now Christ comes to doe it indeed, he raves, and teares, and foames, and blasphemes, shakes the very pillars of the Kingdome, crackes the foundation of Government'.[22] The Northamptonshire minister, Thomas Hill, preaching

20 Ibid., pp. 59–60. On 5 November 1641 Burges again preached before the Commons. This time his assessment of the Gunpowder Plot was far more conventional and he may well have been influenced by the official *King's Book* account which, like him, described the event as a potential breach in the boundaries of hell and earth. 'This is the day wherein the most prodigious rage of man that ever Sun beheld, or that Hell it selfe boyled up to an height justly execrable to all the world, was ready to break forth out of the nethermost Pit, against our Late King, Queene, the Royall Seed, the Parliament, Church, Kingdome, this Place, our selves, and all ours, all at once.' See *Another Sermon Preached to the Honourable House of Commons now assembled in Parliament*, p. 1.

21 Stephen Marshall, *A Sermon Preached before the Honourable House of Commons, Now assembled in Parliament* (London, 1641).

22 William Sedgwick, *Zions Deliverance and her Friends Dvty: or The Grounds of expecting, and Means of Procuring Jerusalems Restauration* (London, 1642), pp. 9–10. Sedgwick was referring to the the exorcism described in Mark 9.

on 27 July 1642, saw parliament's role as a guard against the demonic plot to subvert the nation by leading them into spiritual blindness. 'The Pope hath many Emissaries abroad', he noted, 'who joyne with the Devill, studying a method of Soule-deceiving ... you shall find the devill and deceiuers artificially methodizing their snares to draw us from the truth.' 'Never had any Parliament more work to do', he declared in the dedication of the printed version of his sermon; 'let your cause be [God's] cause ... then you will have more with you than against you, though the Devill and the Pope combine'.[23]

But if parliament was to be engaged in a struggle with the Devil, it was vital that it understand its position to be analogous to that of the ordinary Christian who sought daily to ward off his temptations. Whilst the preachers of the fast sermons provided the required exhortations to commitment to the reforming cause, they also appreciated their genuine pastoral role towards parliament. Preaching to the great and the good in London was rarely free of political implications, but neither was it simply a convenient political platform. As ministers further afield guided their more committed parishioners' devotions through the everyday conflicts with the diabolic, the fast sermons performed a similar pastoral function for a parliament willing to see satanic forces oppressing the nation's government. Spiritual preparation thus became central to political action, and there was a striking similarity of rhetoric between the 'political' demonism of the fast sermons and the personal demonism of Protestant conduct and devotional literature.

On 15 May 1642 Robert Harris preached to the Commons of the subject of steadfastness in prayer, highlighting the special role of parliament's fasts to 'loose the bands of wickedness'. He drew analogies between the position of the body politic and the private Christian, both of which were torn between the competing voices of God and the Devil. 'Satan will roare upon us', he noted of the various ways steadfastness might be undermined. 'Let the Devill promise safety, secrecy, any profit, or content in a sinfull way', he noted; 'we rest in his word ... All the threats and curses of the booke of God cannot dismay us.' 'Have we not reason to believe the God of Truth rather than the father of lies?', he concluded.[24] Edward Reynolds took Hosea 14: 2 – 'take with you words, and turn to the Lord: say unto him, take away all iniquity and receive us graciously' – as the text for his sermon preached on 27 July 1642. His exhortation to the nation to faith and prayer in the face of affliction again drew comparisons with the prescribed response to individual temptation. As with so many devotional works, Reynolds ran through the Devil's nomenclature of power to emphasise the varied nature of his agency.

[23] Thomas Hill, *The Trade of Truth Advanced* (London, 1642), sigs. A4–A4v, pp. 35–6.

[24] Robert Harris, *A Sermon preached to the honourable Hovse of commons* (London, 1642), p. 10, 11, 22.

'Dragon' signified malice, 'serpent' his subtlety and 'lion' his strength; but none of these, Reynolds noted, could stand before prayer.[25]

Preparation for political action was akin to the introspection required before communion. Preaching on the same day as Reynolds, Thomas Hill called for action informed by spiritual knowledge and warned of the dangers of diabolic subversion. 'The Schoole of Christ is indeed a Schoole of affection, and action', he noted, 'but first of knowledge; we must have science before we shall make conscience of our wayes.' 'This makes the God of this world, the Devill, bestirreth himselfe to blinde peoples minds', he continued; 'he well knew that darknesse of mind, betrays us to the workes of darknesse.' If parliament was to 'lay siege to the Devill or the Popes kingdome', it must reveal God's truth, and that process started with individuals. 'Have you set up Truth in your owne families?', Hill asked, appealing to common notions of patriarchal government; 'you reckon your house, your little Commonwealth; by what law is it governed?' Many would have men believe their households were like churches, but Hill was contemptuous of such complacency. 'Thy house a Church to God, and thou an uncleane sonne of Belial?', he demanded; 'what concord hath Christ with Belial?'[26] Just as individual parishioners were warned against presumption, now parliament was being encouraged to actively pursue godliness. Without unpolluted godly intent all talent and ability were simply turned over to the Devil. Everyone present, Reynolds noted, must 'seriously endeavour to take away all iniquity from his person ... for whatever other honour, wealth, wisdome, learning, interest a man hath besides, if sin hath the predominancy, they are but Satans Magazine, and that man his servant to imploy them against God that gave them'.[27]

[25] Edward Reynolds, *Israels Petition in Time of Trouble. A Sermon Preached in St. Margarets Church at Westminster, before the Honourable House of Commons now assembled in Parliament. At the Late Publicke and solemne Fast, July, 27. 1642* (London, 1642), pp. 7, 38–39; Obadiah Sedgwicke, *England's Preservation or, A Sermon discovering the onely way to prevent destroying Judgements: Preached to the Honourable House of Commons at their last solemne Fast, being on May, 25.* 1642 (London, 1642), p. 51; William Gouge, *The Saints Svpport, Set out in a Sermon Preached before the Honourable House of Commons assembled in Parliament. At a publick Fast, 29. June, 1641* (London, 1641), pp. 16–17.

[26] Hill, *The Trade of Truth Advanced*, pp. 19, 22–3, 41; William Greenhill, *The Axe at the Root, A Sermon Preached before the Honourable Hovse of Commons, at their publike Fast, April 26. 1643* (London, 1643), p. 26.

[27] Reynolds, *Israels Petition*, p. 25. Human resources were inherently transferable between Christ and Satan, and Reynolds also argued that that the talents of Satan's servants might as readily be employed for God; see p. 12. Marshall, *A Sermon Preached before the Honourable House of Commons*, pp. 18–19, 31, 36–7; *A Peace-Offering to God A Sermon Preached to the Honourable House of Commons assembled in Parliament* (London, 1641), p. 49; William Sedgwicke located the transferability of human talent more specifically in the universities, noting that, after the victory over the kingdom of darkness they 'will be filled, not with the

Thus when William Carter entered the pulpit on 31 August 1642, both his message that the forces of Satan were ranged against parliament, and that engagement required dedicated spiritual preparation, were familiar. Carter took Judges 20: 26–8 as his text, recounting the war between the tribes of Israel and Benjamin. The point was that although the sons of Israel were instructed by God to engage with their 'brothers' the sons of Benjamin, they were defeated in battle twice. This demonstrated that a just cause was not sufficient to secure victory even in a holy war. 'The Israelites were right in what they did', Carter noted; 'they were not right in themselves that went about it, they had their Idolls and false worships, still among them unrepented of; therefore God went not forth with their Armies'.[28] It was only after the Israelites had humbled themselves with fasting, sought God's forgiveness and renewed their covenant with him, that they were finally given victory over the Benjamites. Those engaged in God's work, Carter argued, faced two principal opponents – Satan and 'the sins of a mans own heart'. The minister resorted to the common text of Ephesians 6: 12 and observed 'who ever is imploy'd for God . . . shall have all the power of all the Divells in Hell against him'.[29] No matter how holy their work, only those reconciled with God would be able to withstand such opposition:

> for Satan, 'tis not every man can deale with him; ther's no resisting him without an holy heart, there is no getting that without a pardon . . . where there is no righteousness, that is, no pardon, the grace of Christ beares no sway in that soule; and then that man who is still in the bond of iniquity, however for the present he may in a manner, be ingaged for God, what ever is that way pretended, hee will be found at last to be of Satans party; and though he goe exceeding far in a good cause, he'l not be through in the work, and when it comes to the main principall, he'l faile, and that is as much as Satan wishes or desires.

But Carter was concerned that unregeneracy not only weakened God's cause, but was a source of profoundly damaging de facto diabolic subversion. 'If a man be unregenerate', he noted, 'Satan then hath something in him, nay all that's in him, is his own, and what ever the mans design is now, Satan knows the man is his, and that in time it will be seen, yea that such a man shall doe him better service than another can, and so much the more, by how much he seemed at the first to be against him.' As Julian the Apostate had damaged Christianity more than the persecuting emperors that preceded him, unregenerates in God's army constituted a diabolic potential that must inevitably

sonnes of Beliall, but with sons of the prophets', *Zions Deliverance*, p. 51; for the continued use of the notion in fast sermons after the outbreak of war, see Edmund Calamy, *The Noblemans Patterne Of true and reall Thankfulnesse* (London, 1643), pp. 33–4.

28 Carter, *Isreals peace with God, Beniamines Overthrow*, pp. 1–3.

29 Ibid., p. 18. Ephesians 6: 12 – 'For we wrestle not against flesh and blood, but against principalities, against powers, against the rulers of the darkness of this world, against spiritual wickedness in high places'.

be activated, and so damage the cause from the inside.[30] 'Doe not the work of God negligently, or to halves', was Carter's conclusion, which Christopher Hill cited as parliament being assured it was engaged in a holy war. But Carter's choice of text was far more complex, providing a salient example of the consequences of failing to be spiritually prepared for God's call, and of the importance of always keeping the Devil in sight.[31]

Thus the picture which emerges out of the demonism of the fast sermons is somewhat different to that advanced by Trevor-Roper. Whilst they expressed an opposition between parliament and the forces of Satan, the fast sermons tended to be more cautious than he has suggested, even after *Meroz Cursed.* They called for commitment and stigmatised moderates, but they also tended to demand rigorous introspection and self-awareness on the part of those who were to take up God's cause. In its effects this might appear paradoxical. Those employed to trumpet the call to engagement in reformation might at the same time be planting seeds of doubt in their auditors by highlighting the diabolic consequences of being wrong. In fact, far from simply providing an explanatory gloss, diabolism greatly complicated the issue. Every member of parliament was in effect a potential satanic agent, and was being told so. But this makes an important point about the place of religion in the political discourse of the 1640s. Historians have tended to see religion as a more or less malleable tool of political expression, and the fast sermons as an example of religion being very consciously put to work to advance the ideas of certain parliamentary leaders in the months before the outbreak of war. But religious messages were too complex and too nuanced to be the simple tool of political polemic. The rhetoric of Reformation, and of its enemy diabolic temptation and false doctrine, was simply too well established by the 1640s not to bring inherently introspective overtones to calls to a war against the Devil. The parliamentary leaders who controlled the fast sermons' content either could not, or, more likely, did not wish to separate calls for action from the spiritual demands they implicitly made on the audience. As we might expect, the populist pamphlets which spread parliament's message after the outbreak of hostilities were far less cautious, but members of parliament themselves were expected to be able to assimilate the connections being made between the everyday spiritual troubles of the godly and the preparations for macro-political conflict.

The notion of parliament's special role in combating diabolic false doctrine also had the potential for populist appeal. The campaign of demonisation began not, as is often assumed, as a reaction to the outbreak of the war, but in the polemical manoeuvring of 1640–2. A mixture of the dynamic of false doctrine, satire and the sensationalist devices of the pulp press provided a

30 Carter, *Isreals peace with God*, pp. 21–2.
31 Ibid., p. 44; Hill, *The English Bible and the Seventeenth-Century Revolution*, p. 90.

number of anonymous pamphlets with supposed exposés on the diabolism of the Laudian regime. Whilst providing satisfying propaganda, these works introduced complex ideas about human interaction with the Devil into the political crisis. Most notably the concept of diabolic patronage found a central, and subsequently consistent, place in parliament's populist campaign. Through the printing of letters from, and petitions to Satan, and articles of agreement signed by the Devil and his agents, the pope and his subjects in England were presented as diabolic clients. Rather than being the Devil's slaves, they subverted the commonwealth because their own personal interest was synonymous with their patron's. The device was by no means as trite as it might at first appear. It introduced into pamphlet propaganda both political and religious considerations which were astute and complex. The notion of diabolic patronage and reward has an obvious place in the oppositional rhetoric of corruption identified at the centre of Caroline political discourse by Linda Levy Peck.[32] A relocation of the origin of preferment from the king to the Devil provided a satirical exposé of the corruption of Caroline patronage, which, we may suspect, smarted particularly strongly with Charles's pretensions to theocracy. The accusations of corruption that had surfaced in the 1620s had centred on abuses by individuals, motivated by self-serving and avarice. But in the polemic of the early 1640s venality was given a central diabolic rationale; corruption was conceived, not as a selfish abuse of a benign system of patronage, but as an act of clientage in itself, carried out in the interest of a diabolic patron. Again we are in the realm of 'incarnate devils': humans whose inherent demonic potential was seen to be fully activated.

Fighting against the forces of satanism before August 1642, parliament was of course seeking to redress the consequences of Catholic infiltration and the propagation of false doctrine. The Catholics, and especially the Jesuits, were Satan's vanguard polluting the body politic in preparation for his rule. The satirical pamphlet, *News from Hell, Rome, and the Innes of Court* (1641), purported to provide an historical exposé of Satan's involvement in the events surrounding the war with Scotland, and his attempts in September 1640 to prevent the calling of parliament. The pamphlet opened with a letter from the Devil to the Pope, supposedly written on 1 September 1640 (or, as it is given, in the 5,661st year of Satan's reign on earth) in which he congratulated the pontiff on his use of the Laudian episcopate to effect a war between Charles and his Scottish subjects.[33] Similarly, a translation of a Latin pamphlet, printed as *Camilton's Discovery of the Devilish Designs ... of the Society of Jesuits* (1641) was dedicated to parliament. The original was produced in

[32] Peck, *Court Patronage and Corruption in Early Stuart England.*
[33] *News From Hell, Rome, and the Innes of Court. Wherein is set forth the copy of a letter written from the Devill to the Pope* (London, 1641), pp. 1–6.

Germany in 1607, and its translation sought to impress on parliament that the present English political crisis was in fact a sequel to that which had produced the Thirty Years War. 'The same wheel of mischief, that wrought all the woes of Germany', the dedication declared, 'hath for some years past been also set to work in England, Scotland, and Ireland; witness all the factions and fractions in church and state, the disturbances and discontents between prince and people ... all which received their birth and breeding from the devilish designs of those sons of division, the society of Jesuits'.[34]

According to these pamphlets false doctrine had profound political consequences. It was a central tenet of a satanic strategy of divide and rule, since in a country aspiring to reformation it bred disharmony and confusion. For *News from Hell*, Laudianism's great success lay in 'sowing discord among the English hereticks [Protestants], as also in provoking the Scotch hereticks to an apparent opposition against their king, yea so far as to an invasion of the territories of England'.[35] Camilton drew a detailed picture of how the Jesuits had played on differences in religion among the German princes. Desire for innovation in religion, he observed, had allowed the Jesuits to set the emperor against his subjects, amplifying the scope for their influence in the divided empire. Thirty-four years later the pamphlet's translator spelled out the English parallels for any who had failed to catch them:

As [in Germany] the foundation of their work was laid in working upon their diversities in opinions, and seconded by advantage, taken upon the several humours of the princes, propounding to each one some such ends, as his nature most affected; so I may truly say, they have done here also. To what other end was the pestilent doctrine of Arminius introduced, whereby to make a party, that might prove strong enough in time to oppose the Puritan faction, as they stiled it?

By the diabolic work of the Jesuits, Charles had been brought to an evil opinion of his subjects, the common people were discontented with their government and two opposing armies were present in England.[36]

Parliament's attempts at reformation could be presented as a providential attack on this policy of subversion by false doctrine. In *News from Hell* Satan congratulated the bishops for working the dissolution of the Short Parliament in May 1640, 'by which means nothing was effected for the good of hereticks, either concerning church of commonwealth; so as the success of this design of ours was in no way hindered'.[37] The Petition of the Twelve

[34] W. F. X. B., *Camilton's Discovery of the Devilish Designs, and Killing Projects, Of the Society of Jesuits ... intended, but graciously prevented, in England. Translated out of the Latin Copy. Dedicated to the High-court of Parliament* (London, 1641), reprinted in *The Harleian Miscellany*, vol. V (London, 1810), p. 104.

[35] *News from Hell*, p. 2.

[36] W. F. X. B., *Camilton's Discovery of the Devilish Designs*, pp. 116–17.

[37] *News from Hell*, p. 2.

Peers provided another focus of this polemic. On 5 September 1640 a petition drawn up by John Pym and Oliver St John was presented to the king by twelve peers at York. Prominent amongst the 'evils and dangers' it listed as threatening the kingdom were innovations in religion, the increase in popery and the employment of recusants in positions of power. Satan's letter in *News from Hell* contained a postscript in which he claimed to have just heard of this 'most scandalous petition ... which doth not a little touch our honour, and the discovery of this our present stratagem'. 'Our express will and pleasure is', the Devil continued, 'that there be some speedy course taken for the suppressing of the same, and the authors thereof severely punished.'[38] Thus the pamphlet indicated retrospectively that the summoning of the Long Parliament, which would take place on 3 November, was a significant blow to the Devil's plans to keep the nation in confusion and division. The Petition of the Twelve Peers had been met only with a promise to summon the Great Council, and Pym had in his frustration circulated the petition in print. *News from Hell* now repeated this propagandist device, reprinting the text of the petition under the Devil's letter, and in doing so re-emphasised that parliament had not been called at Charles's behest, but as the result of agitation to redress the demonic chaos of the nation's government and religion.[39] *Camiliton's Discovery* was less detailed, but it also explicitly identified the Petition of the Twelve Peers as a providential setback for the forces of Satan: an eleventh hour reprieve from chaos, by which God had shown more mercy to England than he had to Germany.[40] But equating petitioning with a divinely ordained policy of reformation had inherent problems, since it was a device open to those of any political persuasion. As with all godly efforts, petitioning was susceptible to diabolic subversion, a concern made explicit in the pamphlet of 1642, *A Discouery of the Ivglings and Deceitful Impostures of a Slanderovs Libell against the Parliament*. Describing the petition from the inhabitants of London, Westminster and Southwark it noted, 'the avthor of the libellovs paper ... like the deuill disguises himselfe in Samuels mantle, and takes vpon him the forme of

[38] Ibid., pp. 6–7.

[39] For the text of the petition see ibid., pp. 8–9. It is also reprinted in S. R. Gardiner (ed.), *The Constitutional Documents of the Puritan Revolution 1625–1660* (3rd edn, Oxford, 1906), pp. 134–6. *News from Hell* is confused as to the date on which the petition was presented to Charles. Gardiner dates the composition of the petition in London on 28 August, and its presentation at York on 5 September. *News from Hell* gives the date of its presentation as 12 September. However, a petition was prepared at York on this date, demanding a parliament, but it was from the Yorkshire gentlemen who were concerned at Charles's expectation that they maintain their own trained bands. Through the efforts of Strafford the petition was never presented. On the efforts to secure a parliament, see S. R. Gardiner, *History of England from the Accession of James I to the Outbreak of the Civil War 1603–1642*, (London, 10 vols., 1884), vol. IX, pp. 198–208.

[40] W. F. X. B., *Camilton's Discovery*, pp. 104–05.

an angell of light, pretending conscience, and falsley personating the honest inhabitants of those cities'. In citing scripture the petition followed the Devil's temptation of Christ, in which divine truth was made a lie.[41]

In *A Disputation betwixt the Deuill and the Pope* (1642), the two bemoan the state of England and the failure of the Catholic party to work its subversion. This triumphalist pamphlet, 'written by the author to content his friend', delights in the imprisonment of Laud and the execution of the earl of Strafford. The Devil's concern that 'mitres ar banisht' from England, and that all popish 'bookes and beads are accounted toys', is to be read as an indication of the progress being made by parliamentary moves toward reform. The satire is hardly sophisticated, but the pamphlet was able to give a more populist voice to the message that engagement required spiritual purity:

> The World doth know we live in dangerous times
> Let every good man then purge his owne crimes

and that diabolic subversion was inherent to the problems experienced in English politics:

> For my owne part I wish a generall health
> To our most gracious King and Common-wealth
> If each true Protestant wish thus I hope
> They'le shunne the Deuill as they slight the Pope.[42]

Another example of the genre was *The Papists Petition in England* (1642). This purported to contain the petition of the English Catholic subversives to the Pope ('Grand Pluto his ensigne bearer here upon earth'), and the pontiff's subsequent conference with Satan. Again the calling of parliament is presented as a profound blow against the Devil's work in England, and the pope bemoans the execution of Strafford 'for proceeding in our faith to the inlarging of our demonicall governement'. As the Devil's primate, the Pope excommunicates the entire Protestant population of England (perhaps a reference to the excommunication of Elizabeth I), and the pamphlet also publishes the Devil's council to the English Catholics. Again demonic Catholicism's only hope lies in destroying parliament, and so the Devil advises: 'Provide means to cut them off by some damnable plot; by your adherents amongst them, confiscate their pernicious parliament, destroy and put to the sword the principall men thereof.'

41 *A Discouery of the Ivglings and Deceitful Impostures of a Slanderovs Libell against the Parliament* (London, 1642), p. 1.

42 *A Disputation betwixt the Deuill and the Pope. Being a breife dialogue between Urbanus, 5. Pope of Rome, and Pluto Prince of Hell. Concerning the Estate of Five Kingdomes, Spaine, England, France, Ireland, and Scotland* (London, 1642), sigs. A2–A4, quotes at A3v and A4.

The satire of diabolic patronage was enhanced by the notion of reward, specifically chthonian preferment. The rewards given to Satan's conscientious clients were detailed as positions of influence in the kingdom of hell. In *A Disputation betwixt the Deuill and the Pope*, the issue arises over the Devil's literal possession of Irish Catholics:

> [*Devil*]
> Their onset did beginn tragick and black
> The English Protestant went first to Wrack.
> Women they kill'd, young infants they did smother
> As if each man forgot he had a mother
> Brave work for me though I prompt them to it
> They had almost as good as be damned as do it.
> *Pope*
> But in these spoles sharn't I a sharer bee.
> *Devil*
> Oh yes my Lord, when you are damned like me.
> But whilst this Fleshy substance thus . . .
> Your spirit, yoo can haue no share in soules
> But when the happy time comes you shall dye
> Thou Shalt be made as great a deuil as I.

In *The Papists Petition in England* the Devil's servants, Strafford and Laud, are to be honoured as the pope's chthonian emmisaries. Strafford's journey through purgatory has been cut short that he may immediately take up his position in hell; as for Laud and other prisoners, 'in respect of their dutiful labours' the Devil promises to spirit them out of prison and straight to hell, 'where their entertainment shall be according as they have deserved'.

This was a smugly satisfying depiction of the enemies of Protestantism getting their just deserts and, as we will see, the notion was to be used against Prince Rupert and, in 1660, against Cromwell. But it also rendered political corruption and diabolic subversion comprehensible by an appeal to a wide understanding of the most fundamental of hierarchical relationships. As in devotional works and crime pamphlets, political demonism was most effective when situated in the commonplace, where the audience's very identification with the subject of corruption might illustrate the insidious dynamic of diabolic activity. In highlighting the shared interest between the Devil and his human clients, the propaganda of the 1640s infused demonism with the same logic that pervaded political discourse and action. Satire was particularly adept at depicting diabolic patronage in practice, but we should not assume from this that the notion was not taken seriously. Satire did not invent diabolic patronage; it only reflected a common understanding that informed conceptions of witchcraft and murder, and applied it to the politicised print culture emerging out of the conflicts of the 1640s.

The notion that the royalist cause was ultimately directed from Hell persisted in parliament's wartime propaganda. A pamphlet of 1644, *The Deuils White Boyes*, an exposé of the wantonness of the royal court, drew a picture of a chthonian council of war:

They [English malignants] and the deuill haue been in covnsell a great while, to deuise a plot how to destroy all the honest Religiovs Protestants in England, and the Earl of Strafford, hee sits in Covnsell euery day abovt it with Plvto, Astaroth, and the other infernall covnsellors, bvt this deuillish table, cannot yet, nor neuer shall be able to worke the rvin of the Protestants.[43]

But the coming of war focused propagandist attention more specifically on the military conduct of the royalists, and on the figure of the godless Cavalier in particular. It was a novel expression of the long-established belief that the Devil was most active when threatened by reformation. Where Laudianism had been Satan's attempt to reduce the nation to idolatry by stealth, the demonic Cavaliers, mustered to counter the actions of a proactive reforming parliament, proposed to do so by force. A pamphlet of 1642, *The Debauched Cavalleer*, found Old Testament precedent to demonstrate the idolatrous agency of the royalist forces. It promised to describe 'their diabolicall, and hyperdiabolicall blasphemies, execrations, rebellions, cruelties, rapes and roberies', and illustrated their motives by comparing them to the Midianites of the Book of Judges. 'They were full of Rage and Blasphemy when the Altar of Baal was thrown downe', the author explained; 'so are the Cavalleers, what makes them rage, but that the Priests, and Altars of Baal are thrown down amongst us?'[44] The same year the separatist John Goodwin published *Anti-Cavalierisme*, arguing for 'as well the Necessity, as the Lawfulness of this present War'. The nation, he commented, suffered under a regime that acted 'after the manner of devils', seeking to turn back the advance of Christianity, overturning all progress in reformation. They sought 'to build up the walls of Jericho, to put Lucifer againe in to heaven, I meane, to advance the tyrannicall Thrones of the Heirarchie to their former height, or higher, if they know how'.[45] 'Do they know who is the Lord?', Goodwin asked of these policies, 'or doe they not

[43] *The Deuils White Boyes. Or, A mixture of malicious malignants with their much Evill, and manifold practices against Kingdom and Parliament* (London, 1644), p. 3; Francis Cheynell, *Sions Memento, and Gods Alarum* (London, 1643), p. 14.

[44] *The Debauched Cavalleer: or the English Midianite* (London, 1642), p. 4; Sedgwick, *Zions Deliverance*, p. 9; John Ellis, *The Sole Path to a Sound Peace* (London, 1643), p. 11; Matthew Newcomen, *The Craft and Crvelty of the Churches Adversaries* (London, 1643), pp. 3–9; Thomas Case, *Gods Rising His Enemies Scattering* (London, 1644), pp. 34–5.

[45] John Goodwin, *Anti-Cavalierisme, or, truth pleading As well the Necessity, as the Lawfulness of this present War* (London, 1642), p. 2. Thomas Wilson preached a sermon to the Commons using the analogy of Jericho and its worship of Baal in September 1643; see *Jerichoes Downfall, As it was Presented in a sermon preached at St. Margarets Westminster before the Honourable House of Commons* (London, 1643).

thinke rather, that Baal, or Belial is he?'[46] Thus parliamentarians could be assured they were waging war on Satan and his human servants. 'We stand up like men', Goodwin declared, 'and quit our selves with all our might, and all our strength, against those assacinates, and sworne Sword-men of the devill, who have conspired the death and ruine of all that feareth God in the Land.'[47]

The identification of Cavalierism with the Devil was in keeping with the millenarian nature of parliament's rhetoric, as exemplified in the fast sermons.[48] Apocalypticism, argues Christopher Hill, provided the emotional 'revolutionary energy' which would, at the end of the 1640s, make conceivable the unprecedented changes that would follow the execution of Charles I. The identification of the royalist army with the Dragon of the Apocalypse sharpened the perception of the conflict as a holy war. Thomas Hill, preaching to the Commons on 21 July 1643, furnished his audience with a description of the 'two potent Armies, under two Generals, Michael and the Dragon'. 'Betwixt these two parties there will be irreconciliable warres', Hill continued, associating the hostilities with the holy conflicts appointed by God, described in 1 Thessalonians 3: 3.[49]

As bringers of violence and chaos the royalists were an incarnation of the roaring lion of 1 Peter 5: 8. They were predatory and malicious, taking delight in destruction for its own sake, qualities which marked them out as servants of Satan. The Puritan divine, George Lawrence, used the image of the roaring lion to characterise the Laudian clergy as '*Dens Caninus Diaboli*, the Great Dogge tooth of the Deuill'. 'The corrupt clergy', he noted in *Laurentius Lutherans* (1642), go about 'snarling, shewing their teeth like so may dogges, and byting, yea tearing in peeces, were they able, everyone, who thwarts them in their way, and contradicts them in their unwarrantable insolencies, and illegal proceedings'.[50] When applied to the military the roaring lion was possessed of a potential duality which sat particularly comfortably with parliamentarian saintly self-conception. The image portrayed well the

[46] Goodwin, *Anti-Cavalierisme*, p. 2; John Lightfoote, *Elias Redivivus: A Sermon Preached Before the Honourable House of Commons* (London, 1643), pp. 40–1.

[47] Goodwin, *Anti-Cavalierisme*, p. 36; Thomas Temple, *Christ's Government In and over his People* (London, 1642), pp. 34–5; Cheynall, *Sions Memento, and Gods Alarum*, pp. 13–14; William Prynne, *Romes Master-peece: or, the Grand Conspiracy of the Pope and his Iesuited Instruments* (London, 1644), sig. A2.

[48] The millenarian character of the fast sermons is well recognised by historians. See Bernard Capp, 'The Political Dimension of Apocalyptic Thought', in C. A. Patrides and J. Wittrech (eds.), *The Apocalypse in English Renaissance Thought and Literature; Patterns, Antecedents and Repercussions* (Manchester, 1984), p. 109; Hill, *The English Bible and the Seventeenth-Century Revolution*, pp. 98–9.

[49] Thomas Hill, *The Militant Church Triumphant over the Dragon and his Angels* (London, 1643), pp. 5–6.

[50] George Lawrence, *Laurentius Lutherens. Or the Protestation of George Lavrence* (London, 1642), sig. A3v; Goodwin, *Anti-Cavalierisme*, p. 2.

rapacious and all-consuming nature of the Civil War armies, who exacted a heavy toll from the localities through which they passed.[51] David Underdown has demonstrated that an ability to constrain plunder paid dividends in popular support, and that although the difference should not be exaggerated, parliament's commanders showed a greater awareness of this than the king's.[52] At the same time the roaring lion had immediate 'confessional' connotations. It had been employed throughout the Reformation to portray the persecution of the saints, and it pervaded the devotional literature which encouraged more zealous Protestants to look for evidence of their salvation in the personal attention showed to them by the Devil.[53] Aimed at Charles's army, it at a stroke characterised royalist violence as an implicitly Laudian tyranny, and Laudian tyranny as explicitly diabolic.

The dynamic of temptation was central to the understanding of royalist violence. Natural evil in man, or the 'energy of Satan', might turn men against the church, the Essex minister, Matthew Newcomen, told the Commons in November 1642. 'But when both meet', he explained, 'a strong propension of nature in themselves, and a mighty energeticall power of Satan over them, needs must they with most impetuous violence be carried on by any craft or cruelty, no matter what or how to hinder all that tends to the church'.[54] A pamphlet of 1643, *The Bloody Prince*, juxtaposed temptation and the roaring lion to show how Satan moulded the individualised corruption of royalist soldiers and churchmen into a collective predatory force aimed at the destruction of the saints. The bishops and Cavaliers, it declared, 'are now gathered together into an Army, under the commmand of the grand captaine of wickednesse, the Divell'. Like its captain, this army 'goes about daily to see how many of the Saints of God he can devour'.[55] In their barbarity the Cavaliers revealed their corruption – 'wicked men doe wickedly because they loue it ... there is a suitableness between sin and their soules'. But their sin allowed the Devil to take hold of their wills, acting as a 'second' to their evil intents. 'The diuell dothe instigate and stirre them up thereunto', the pamphlet continued, 'he rules their hearts ... he carries them with all swiftenesse and violence to accomplish his owne will.'[56] Satan's

[51] On the excesses of the Civil War armies, see David Underdown, *Revel, Riot and Rebellion: Popular Politics and Culture in England 1603–1660* (Oxford, 1985), pp. 148–53.
[52] Ibid., p. 153. [53] See above, chapters 2 and 3.
[54] Newcomen, *The Craft and Crvelty of the Churches Adversaries*, pp. 17–18.
[55] *The Bloody Prince, or a declaration of the most cruell Practices of Prince Rupert, and the rest of the Cavaliers* (London, 1643), p. 18; Case, *Gods Rising, His Enemies Scattering*, pp. 3–8.
[56] Case, *Gods Rising*, p. 4; Gregory Thims, *The Protestant Informer or Information to all Protestants* (London, 1643), p. 2; John Ley, *The Fvry of Warre, and the Folly of Sinne, (As an Incentive to it) declared and applyed* (London, 1643), p. 22; for a similar point made in pre-war anti-Catholic literature, see *A Bloody Plot, Practiced by some Papists in Darbyshire* (London, 1641), sig. A2.

agency focused the evil of corrupted men, turning them into diabolic instruments of his malice against the godly commonwealth. 'Feeding the senses withe the delight of wickednesse' clouded the royalists' perception, ensuring they continued 'killing the people of God when your diuelish pawes can fasten upon them'.[57]

A number of pamphlets sought to make the point by recounting individual cases of demonic temptation amongst the Cavaliers. They appropriated the conventions of the contemporary murder pamphlet to equate Cavalier activity with diabolically inspired criminality. An example of 1642, *A Blazing Starre seene in the West*, told of how a 'devout cavalier', Ralph Ashley, had been providentially struck down after he had attempted to rape a young woman in Devonshire. This carefully constructed narrative highlighted the diabolism of the Cavaliers whose driving emotion was malice towards the servants of God. On the night of 14 November the daughter of one Adam Fisher set off home from town against the wishes of her friends who were concerned for her safety. Fisher was unfazed, claiming, 'God was aboue the deuill, and that she feared not, but that God which she trusted in, could, and would defend her from all enemies.' Thus, in setting the scene, the narrative intimated that the crime to be described would be a crime against God, practised in the face of divine providence. Ashley met the woman on the road and offered to escort her home. The author appealed to a dynamic of diabolic temptation commonly employed in murder pamphlets when he described how Ashley's lust, the symptom of his Cavalier corrupted morality, had allowed the Devil to take hold and drive him to rape.[58] 'With that he called to mind her beauty', the pamphlet related, 'the Deuill strait furnished him with a deuise to obtaine his purpose.' Ashley persuaded his intended victim to leave the road in order to avoid the soldiers that were known to be about and, when he attempted to rape her, a comet appeared stunning Fisher. When he continued swearing 'God-damne-him, alive or dead he would injoy her', a flame in the shape of a sword issued from the comet, striking him down. The narrative was intended to provide a timely warning as to the nature of the demonic Cavaliers 'which esteem murder & rapine the chiefe principalls of their religion'.[59]

The juxtaposition of images of tyranny and martyrdom provided further support to the perception of royalist diabolism. Self-sacrifice in the face of the synagogue of Satan was of course deeply ingrained in an English Protestant consciousness which encouraged identification with the martyrs of John Fox's *Acts and Monuments*. The recent 'martyrdom' of William

57 *The Bloody Prince*, p. 10; Case, *Gods Rising, His Enemies Scattering*, p. 34.
58 For a full discussion of diabolic temptation in crime narratives, see chapter 5.
59 *A Blazing Starre seene in the West*, quotes at sigs. A2v, A3 and A4v.

Prynne, Henry Burton and John Bastwick was also fresh in the memory for those who wished to see it as an example of Laudian tyranny.[60] In John Goodwin's *Anti-Cavalierisme* martyrdom was presented as one of the opportunities offered by a just war against the forces of the Devil. The enmity of the Cavaliers was an inverted barometer of personal godliness. These 'men of Belial' were 'as thornes in our eyes, and scourges in our sides, only or chiefly because we will be that in open and constant profession, which by the grace of God we are inwardly and in the truth of our soules; because we will not prostitute our consciences to the lusts of their Father the devil'. Martyrdom was active; it 'doth not consist of lying down and suffering proud and wicked men to ride over our heads'. Instead it was a stance taken against Belial where God provided no means of escape, an opportunity 'for expressing our love and faithfulnesse unto Christ and his Gospell in wayes of suffering'. Martyrdom associated the parliamentarian cause with the struggle depicted in Revelation and thus intimated victory. The opportunities for martyrdom were diminishing, Goodwin cautioned, since God 'will turne the wheele of his providence and dispensations, between his Church, and the Synagogue of Satan'.[61]

How far did this parliamentarian demonism touch Charles I himself? Throughout the war parliamentary polemic adopted the commonplace notion that the king was essentially misguided and manipulated by a number of 'evil councillors', who forced a separation between him and his subjects. Wartime demonism could allow this to be more dynamically expressed as a form of diabolic temptation by proxy. Matthew Newcomen, preaching to the Commons in 1642, noted that 'all visible enemies of the church of God, are but the Emissaries of Satan his agents: and therefore they observe his methods'. This might involve violence or subtlety, but a favoured method was 'to ingratiate themselves to Kings and Princes, with much officiousnesse and pretended care for their profit and honour, that so being potent with the Potentates of the earth, they may have the more power to doe the Church a mischiefe'. Susceptibility to flattery/temptation rendered princes subjects of the Devil, and to drive home the point Newcomen cited the example of the crucifixion, procured by the Jews through a pretended loyalty to Caesar. This age-old ploy of the Devil had been taught to the Arminians by the Jesuits, and now 'all of them have made it their master-piece'.[62] Again pastoral and devotional understanding informed the depiction of the 'tempted King'.

[60] For a contemporary description of their punishment highlighting their martyrdom, very much in the Fox tradition, see *A Brief relation of certain special and most material Passages and Speeches in the Star-Chamber*, pp. 233–8.

[61] Goodwin, *Anti-Cavalierisme*, pp. 34–6, Sedgwicke, *Zions Deliverance*, p. 16.

[62] Newcomen, *The Craft and Crvelty of the Churches Adversaries*, pp. 3 and 11–12.

For Francis Cheynell, Charles was the epitome of the beleaguered Christian, beset on all sides by the Devil's influence. 'His throne is compassed about with snares', he explained to the Commons in May 1643, 'and he is even wedded to a temptation, his very Counsellours are, too many of them, Seducers, or flatterers ... & therefore it is no marvaile if our King be misled.'[63]

Temptation of course did not make Charles's actions any less diabolic or any less culpable, and indeed this in itself could provide a meaningful justification for conflict. Cheynell noted that were parliament to attempt to avoid confrontation by flattering Charles, it would merely be adding to his temptations, and that it too would become an agent of Satan. Instead it was their duty to make a stand whilst praying for the king's deliverance from the satanic forces that surrounded him.[64] Thus demonism allowed for the expectation of a settlement. Unlike diabolic clientage, susceptibility to temptation, as the universal sin, was one for which it was possible to atone. If the consequences of the king's languishing under satanic influence were greater than ordinary men's, it did not make his sin qualitatively greater than anyone else's who had listened too readily to the Devil's voice. Thus the notion of Charles's temptation did not merely pay lip service to an opponent's continuing regard for his king. It made a meaningful equation between resistance to the monarch and the exorcism of the body politic.

But a far less forgiving attitude towards the king's diabolism was in evidence in January 1649. His intransigence after 1646, and the outbreak of the Second Civil War in 1648, produced a hardening of attitudes among the army leadership. He was executed on the will of a tiny minority of those who had taken up arms against him, his show trial a forgone conclusion by which the most radicalised of the army prepared the way for their revenge on 'the man of blood'. But if this was, as many historians have characterised it, an act of judicial murder, Patricia Crawford and Christopher Hill have demonstrated the intense commitment to a scriptural millenarianism that at least convinced the regicides that their revenge was just.[65] Similarly parliament's polemical use of demonism had paved the way to the concerted repudiation of Charles's pretensions to theocracy which his trial would represent. No longer willing to entertain the notion of temptation and the evil councillor, this radical minority was finally prepared to openly declare Charles himself to be an incarnate devil, wittingly employed in Satan's campaign against the faith. Had Charles made a plea at his trial the Solicitor-General John Cook stood ready with a lengthy speech in which he

[63] Cheynell, *Sions Memento, and Gods Alarum*, p. 37. [64] Ibid.
[65] Patricia Crawford, '"Charles Stuart, That Man of Blood"', *Journal of British Studies* (Spring 1977); Hill, *The English Bible and the Seventeenth-Century Revolution*, pp. 324–31.

compared Charles to the fallen Lucifer. The king's refusal to recognise the court's authority denied him the chance, but rather than lose this propagandist opportunity, the speech was printed ten days after Charles's execution to explain the justice of the act.[66]

It was now Charles who was directly responsible for the Civil War, and who, from the first deaths at Edgehill, had shown scant concern for the Protestant blood that had been shed. A beloved prince who might have had parliament's complete co-operation but for his intransigence, had instead resorted to bloody tyranny. Thus Charles had betrayed the trust placed in him as God's chosen one and his position was analogous with the first rebellion. 'I can say no less', Cook declared, 'but "O Lucifer, whence art thou fal'n and what hereticks are they in politicks that would have such a man to live?"'[67] Fallen from ordained kingship to tyranny Charles further approximated Satan, to whom God permitted only a temporary corrupted reign on the earth. 'For a king to rule by lust and not law is a creature that was never of Gods making, not of Gods approbation but of his permission', Cook continued, 'and though such men are said to be Gods on Earth, 'tis in no other sense then the Devil is called the God of this world.'[68] Cook's speech openly repudiated the notion of the evil councillor, noting that this had appeared to be the case when the duke of Buckingham was alive, but that Charles's conduct during the war had made it obvious that he was 'principle in all transactions'. Rather than being misled by Laud or Strafford, Charles had been at the centre of a religious policy that sought to make an idol of himself. Again the parallels with Satan were clear. 'It cannot be denyed but that he hath spent all his days in unmeasurable pride', Cook declared; 'that during his whole reign, he hath deported himself as a God, been depended on and adored as a God.'[69] In another pamphlet justifying the execution, John Milton also overturned Charles's claims to theocracy. Theocratic power was, by definition, exercised for God or for the Devil. Royal power that was not exercised to the 'terror' of evil was not of God 'but of the Devill, and by consequence to be resisted'.[70]

The effect of this demonisation cannot be judged, but, as we will see, it seems that the majority of people were more likely to see diabolism in Charles's execution than in the man himself. But this should not overshadow the fundamental congruity with which Cook's depiction of the diabolic Charles fitted into the wider parliamentary polemic of the struggle with Satan. Christopher

[66] John Cook, *King Charls, his Case, or, and Appeal To all rational men Concerning his Tryal at the High Court of Justice* (London, 1649).
[67] Ibid., p. 6. [68] Ibid., p. 8. [69] Ibid., pp. 34–8, quotes at pp. 35, 37.
[70] John Milton, *The Tenure of Kings and Magistrates: Proving that it is Lawfull, and hath been held so through all Ages, for any, who have the Power, to call to account a Tyrant, or wicked King* (London, 1649), pp. 15–16.

Hill has noted that the intense biblicism of the parliamentary party had made regicide conceivable by 1649. If the army leadership believed the bible's absolute demands justified Charles's beheading as a step towards the rule of the saints, this was an extreme form of a far more widely held belief about the need for violent reformation.[71] Similarly the willingness to perceive Charles as an incarnate devil extended belief in the royalist promotion of idolatry and demonic false doctrine to its most extreme, but logical, point.

'HELL'S BLACK PARLIAMENT': DEMONISM, REBELLION AND DIABOLIC GOVERNMENT IN ROYALIST PROPAGANDA

The royalist party was as quick as parliament to exploit the power of the press in putting its message across. Charles established printers in the main regions of the country within weeks of the outbreak of war, and some continued to operate throughout the war in London itself.[72] Indeed the royalists were the first to fully exploit the potential of the newly burgeoning newsbook genre, printing the official *Mercurius Aulicus* whilst parliament was tolerating a 'bewildering host of short-lived newspapers'.[73] But as Joyce Lee Malcolm has demonstrated, royalist propagandists paid attention only to the opinions of the gentry in the early stages of the war, and sneered at the supposedly plebeian origins of the parliamentary officers. Pamphlets, newsbooks and ballads peddled the official line that the parliamentary cause was populated by lower-class upstarts whose programme aimed only at anarchy and the levelling of all degrees, and appealed only to the ignorance of the rabble and, worse still, to women.[74]

Demonism could fit as comfortably in educated royalist polemic as it could in the more populist providentialist pamphlets of the pulp press. After all royalist propagandists could still refer to the argument of 1 Samuel 15: 23, that rebellion was the sin of witchcraft. Loyalist clergymen preached to the Oxford parliament on this text in 1644 and the royalist jurist Sir Robert Heath composed a private meditation arguing that rebellion was better understood through a clearer comprehension of the nature of witchcraft.[75] If by Charles's trial the Rump was willing to employ the imagery of Lucifer and his fall from heaven, it informed royalist perception of demonism from the earliest stages of the war. In 1643 the pamphlet *The Rebels Catechism* provided a discussion of the nature and practice of rebellion that

[71] Hill, *The English Bible and the Seventeenth-Century Revolution*, p. 329.
[72] Joyce Lee Malcolm, *Ceasar's Due: Loyalty and King Charles 1642–1646* (London, 1983), pp. 124–31.
[73] Ibid., pp. 140–1. [74] Underdown, *A Freeborn People*, pp. 71–2.
[75] Cited in Elmer, 'Saints or Sorcerers', p. 165.

incorporated general theories, historical examples and precedents, and contemporary parallels. Clearly aimed at an educated audience it cited ancient Roman authorities such as Tertullian and Cyprian, as well as respected medieval jurists such as Henry de Bracton. At the same time it aimed to engage in detail with the arguments of parliament's apologist, William Prynne, and with contentious issues such as the attempted arrest of the five members of parliament, and the meaning of the Battle of Edgehill. It was informed generally by the understanding that rebellion against an anointed monarch was damnable, and it cited on its frontispiece Romans 8: 2 – 'Whosoever resisteth the power, resisteth the ordinance of God: and they that resist, shall receive to themselves damnation.'

The pamphlet opened by considering the origins of the practice of rebellion, which of course came from Satan. 'The first author of rebellion', it noted in answer to the first question of the catechism, 'the root of all vices and the mother of all mischief (saith the book of homilies) was Lucifer.' This was more than a simple theological commonplace, since the ordering of catechisms was of course fundamental to their understanding.[76] All ordinary catechisms opened with the catechumen's rehearsal of his fundamental beliefs, in God the creator and the Holy Trinity, from which Christian understanding emanated. Similarly, in the *Rebels Catechism* all understanding of rebellion was to be informed by the central knowledge that it was fundamentally diabolic. It was a device which, by implication, pre-empted and undermined any arguments for lawful resistance. The story of Lucifer provided other useful parallels. He was, at first, 'God's most excellent creature, and most bounden subject, who, by rebelling against the majesty of God, of the brightest and most glorious angel, became the blackest and foulest fiend and devil; and, from the height of heaven, is fallen into the pit and bottom of hell'. The implication was clear in the light of royalist emphasis on divine right. The king created parliament in a quasi-deific act to be his own 'most excellent creature, and most bounden subject', and by rebellion parliament had turned itself into an incarnate devil.[77]

Royalists employed many of the same satirical devices as their parliamentarian counterparts, and laid a similar stress on the concept of diabolic patronage and hellish preferment. In 1646 parliamentary propaganda was personified in the pamphlet *Mercurious Britanicus his Welcome to Hell* which catalogued the Devil's delight at the slanderous activities of parliament's newsbook. 'I joy to think', he declared to the personified Mercurius

[76] Green, *The Christian's ABC*, pp. 280–9.

[77] *The Rebels Catechism: Composed in an easy and familiar way, to let them see the heinousness of their offence, the weakness of their strongest subterfuges, and to recall them to their duties to God and man* (1643), p. 2.

Britanicus, 'what bone-fires shall be made when thou shalt come.' The pamphlet ended with an epitaph to the newsbook, which emphasised the same reward/punishment paradox that informed parliamentarian notions of diabolic patronage:

> Here lies Britanicus, hell's barking cur,
> That son of Beliall, who kept damned stir;
> And every munday spent his stolke of spleen,
> In venemous railing on the King and Queen.
> Who, though they bothe in goodenesse may forgive him,
> Yet (for his safety) wee'l in hell receive him.[78]

As the parliamentarian press had gleefully speculated on the eternal fate of Strafford and Laud, royalists were sure of an equally fiery end for their most despised enemies. The arrested Cornish MP, Anthony Nichols, was, according to one ballad of 1647, bound 'for Pluto's court, / In inquest of his father', and it predicted he would there meet John Pym, John Hampden and William Strode. From there they would still be directing the parliamentarian cause.[79]

The vindictiveness of parliament's 'levelling' of royalists and their families appeared especially diabolic. Sequestration and the humiliating appearance of royalists before the Goldsmiths' Hall Committee after 1644 became a prominent example of Satan's tyranny enthroned in London. A ballad of 1647, *I Thank you Twice*, noted: 'The gentry are sequestered all; / Our wives you find at Goldsmith Hall, / For there they meet with the devil and all.' Thus, as a place of torment, Goldsmiths' Hall became a hell on earth, as the ballad *Prattle your Pleasure* (*under the Rose*) declared:

> there's a damn'd committe,
> Sits in hell (Goldsmith's Hall) in the midst of the City,
> Only to sequester the poor Cavaliers –
> The Devil take their souls, and the hangman their ears.[80]

A pamphlet of 1647, *Grand Pluto's Progress through Great Britaine*, reprinted the Devil's 'observations' as he gleefully surveyed the upheavals of the nation, which, he noted, had sprung from the Luciferian envy of 'dull swains'.[81] London is singled out for attention as a chaotic centre of libertinism and self-indulgence. In a cacophony of levelling and unnatural opinions,

[78] *Mercurius Britanicus His welcome to Hell: with the Devils blessing to Britanicus* (London, 1646).

[79] *The Members' Justification* (1647), reprinted in *Political Ballads of the Seventeenth and Eighteenth Centuries*, ed. W. W. Wilkins (London, 2 vols., 1860), vol. I, p. 42.

[80] *I Thank you Twice; or the city courting their own ruin, thank the parliament twice for their treble undoing* (1647); *Prattle your Pleasure (under the Rose)* (1647); both in *Political Ballads*, vol. I, pp. 55, 58.

[81] *Grand Pluto's Progress through Great Britaine And Ireland* (London, 1647), p. 2 (irregular pagination).

all law and government is denied as tyrannical, and the total freedom in avarice, whoring and murder is asserted as the means to restore the 'Golden Age'. Thus the seat of parliamentarian government is an earthly approximation of the chaos of hell, and the Devil declares that these indulgent rebels are his 'dearest sonnes'.[82]

But again there was nothing automatic or simplistic about the demonisation of parliament. Instead royalist recourse to diabolic patronage was a pointed attack on parliament's reforming pretensions. *The New Litany*, another ballad of 1647, was deliberately constructed to bait Puritan and Presbyterian hatred of established forms. It cited several of the religious hardships endured by the people under parliament's rule – such as the *Directory of Public Worship* and 'an ignoramus that writes, and a woman that teaches' – and accompanied them with the plea '*Libera nos, Domine*'. The Devil the ballad associated with parliament's policy of deceit, slander and masquerade, declaring:

> From being taken in a disguise,
> From believing of the printed lies,
> From the Devil and from the Excise,
> *Libera nos, Domine.*[83]

A similar ballad of 1647 specifically associated diabolism with the parliamentarian subversion of well-loved ceremonies:

> That the ring in marriage, the cross at the font,
> Which the Devil and the Roundheads so much affront
> May be us'd again, as before they were wont;
> *Te rogamus audi nos.*[84]

When, in 1646, the parliamentarian religious consensus fragmented, royalist polemicists delighted in hearing Satan's voice in the cacophany of divisive opinion aired in reformation's name:

> Take Prynne and his clubs, or Say and his tubs,
> Or, any sect, old or new;
> The Devil's i' th' pack, if choice you can lack,
> We're fourscore religions strong,
> Take your choice, the major voice
> Shall carry it, right or wrong.[85]

These accusations of diabolism struck at the heart of parliament's central claim to be itself taking effective action against the temptation of the body

82 Ibid., pp. 5–7. 83 *The New Litany* (1646), in *Political Ballads*, vol. I, p. 25.
84 *The Old Protestant's Litany. Against all Sectaries and their Defendants, both Presbyterians and Independants*, in *Political Ballads*, vol. I, p. 61.
85 *The Anarchie, or the Blessed Reformation since 1640*, in *Political Ballads*, vol. I, p. 34.

politic. John Cleveland in *The Parliament* (1647), noted that for such a godly cause, parliamentarian success against the forces of Satan in Ireland was conspicuous by its absence. 'Tis Strange your power and holiness', Cleveland noted. 'Can't the Irish devils dispossess.' Cleveland repudiated the careful Protestant compromise of exorcism by prayer as a Puritan sham as discredited as popery's exorcism by miracle. 'Tho' you do so often pray', he continued, 'And ev'ry month keep fasting day, / You cannot cast them out.'[86] For royalists, parliament's trumpeting of its ability to separate Christ and Belial lent a delicious irony to the pulp press exposure of their diabolic patronage. Those who liked to present themselves as God's champions against Satan were in fact dependent on satanic patronage for any victories they might achieve. Given the state of the royalist cause by 1648, this was a comforting notion, as the pamphlet *The Devill and the Parliament* makes clear. Written after the re-capture of Charles, this dialogue revealed that Satan had helped parliament as much as God would allow and that he was now abandoning them to their inevitable destruction. According to Satan, parliament had 'deluded the people with a vaine hope of Reformation, when your intentions even from the beginning, were for the ruine of the King, Church and Kingdome'. 'By me it was that you were prevalent against your Soveraigne', he continued, emphasising that parliament's success was simply part of a providential scheme by which God was temporarily afflicting the commonwealth. 'He that threw me downe from Heaven for conspiring against him', the Devil noted, 'permitted me to be the Patron and Protector of your Rebellion.'[87] This was a brand of the familiar baiting of Puritan self-reverence that had long been a popular pastime of the London stage and pulp press. Attacks on Puritan moral hypocrisy are generally understood to express a dislocation between the culture of the godly and their neighbours at the point at which they most commonly met. But, as this polemic suggests, there may also have been a place for popular resentment at Puritanism's religio-political reforming rhetoric. If so it indicates a comprehension and engagement with the dynamic of temptation and de facto satanism which formed the centre of Puritanism's attack on the established church.

The Devill and the Parliament brought together the various strands of the royalist understanding of diabolism to draw a picture of a personified parliament addicted to rebellion for its own sake. Diabolic patronage and Luciferian rebellion exposed the sham of parliament's supposed combat with Satan as the rebels in fact attempted to subvert the Devil's own place

86 John Cleveland, *The Parliament*, in *Political Ballads*, vol. I, p. 31.
87 *The Devill and the Parliament: or, the parliament and the Devill. A Contestation between them for the precedencie* (London, 1648), pp. 1–2.

as the principle of evil in the cosmos. 'I tell thee brother', 'Mr Parliament' tells the Devil, 'I am now as potent, and can without thee be as devillish, as when thy selfe wert most my friend.' 'I can out-doe thee Lucifer', he declares.[88] Thus behind the supposed policy of reformation lay rebellion as a self-perpetuating sin. Having, with the aid of Satan, rebelled from Charles, its earthly creator, parliament now rebelled against its chthonian patron. In both spheres of activity parliament's actions mirrored Lucifer's attempt to make himself equal to God. But as Lucifer's ambition was destined to fail because he was God's creation and so could never be his equal, parliament was doomed to be inherently subordinate to the monarch, and now to the principle of evil. At the end of the pamphlet the Devil castigates Mr Parliament for believing he might escape hell. 'God will no longer let the English Nation bee slave to thy Command', he warns; 'their ancient Discipline must be restored'. All Mr Parliament's sham and pretension avails him nothing as, like Dr Faustus, he is carried bodily off to perdition.[89]

Diabolism dominated the royalist press's reaction to the execution of Charles I. The cult of martyrdom that grew up was, unsurprisingly, fertile ground for the perception of demonic action. A sermon preached by the bishop of Rochester on 4 Febuary 1649 was soon in print under the title, *The Devilish Conspiracy, Hellish Treason, Heathenish Condemnation and Damnable Murder, Committed, and Executed by the Iewes; against the Anoynted of Lord Christ their King*. This detailed and unwieldy sermon drew parallels between the beheading of Charles and the crucifixion. Regicide was deicide, a reliving of Satan's empty triumph at Golgotha.[90] A less academic version clearly had wide appeal. A verse pamphlet of the same year, *The Insecuritie of Princes*, sarcastically derided parliament's claims that Charles's execution had been necessary:

> Necessitie? O Heavens! Curs'd be that need,
> That makes a sinner in his sin proceed!
> If these be saints, if this their doctrine be,
> From it and them good God deliver me!
> If saints be understood in this large sense,
> Twixt Saints and Devils what's the difference?
> If these be saints this their divinitie,
> A sinner rather than a saint for me!

88 Ibid., p. 5. Compare this to John Lilburne's similar boast to the Devil (disguised as John Penry) in *Grand Pluto's Progress through Great Britain*, p. 8.

89 *The Devil and the Parliament*, pp. 5–6.

90 John Allington, bishop of Rochester, *The devilish conspiracy, hellish treason, haethenish condemnation, and damnable murder, comitted, and Executed by the Jewes; against the anoynted of the Lord Christ their King* (London, 1649).

> This seems more like the voice of Hell or Room [sic],
> Into whose secrets let not my soul come![91]

The regicide was the final act of parliament's Luciferian transformation, after which it lost any vestige of the image of its quasi-divine creator, Charles. 'Abandoning their head', a pamphlet, *The Cuckows Nest at Westminster*, declared, they 'are no more a parliament, but the body of a parliament, without a head ... far different from the nature of a parliament (By reason of their Luciferian pride, to be flung down to hell) and to be deserted by all loyal subjects.' In the wake of the regicide, parliament's claims to be separating Christ from Belial in the body politic beggared belief. 'These instead of expelling out papacy, but one faction', the pamphlet continued, 'have brought in five hundred damnable sects, and set them all to devour episcopacy ... by which means they have advanced their hypocritical, diabolical, and pernicious treasons to this very day.'[92] In the early years of the Interregnum, before the regime finally managed to stamp out the last subversive presses, it was a more populist version of the royalist newsbooks which carried this message most forcefully.

That a royalist post-regicide appeal to a plebeian culture of conservatism might be effective has recently been demonstrated by David Underdown. Examining the short-lived royalist newsbooks which circulated in 1649 and 1650, he argues that they are illustrations of a very different mental world from that which produced the forward-thinking radical ideas of the Levellers and the sects. The men behind this propaganda, such as Marchemont Nedham and John Crouch, had learned the lesson of the Civil War, and now consciously aimed their work at a more populist audience. Whilst they were lurid, sensationalist, libellous and often pornographic, newbooks such as *Mercurius Pragmaticus*, *Mercurius Democritus*, *The Laughing Mercury* and *The Man in the Moon* railed against the revolutionary regime's overturning of a divinely ordained political order which had protected a value system in which social and sexual hierarchy were enshrined for the better preservation of order.[93] Charles's execution had plunged the nation into political and religious chaos, and only Satan could be behind such a calamity.[94] 'Hell's Black Parliament' now ruled in England, populated by 'sonnes of Night and Darkness', under the direct leadership of 'Grand

91 *The Insecuritie of Princes, Considered in an occasional meditation upon the Kings late sufferings* (1649), p. 4.

92 Mercurius Melancholicus, *The Cuckows Nest at Westminster: or, The parliament between two lady-birds, Queen Fairfax and Lady Cromwell* (1649), in *The Harleian Miscellany*, vol. VI, p. 138–9; see also in the same volume, *The British Bellman. Printed in the year of the saints fear* (1649), pp. 182–3.

93 Underdown, *A Freeborn People*, pp. 95–111. 94 Ibid., p. 106.

Pluto'.[95] The 'hell-bred vipers' of parliament looked only to their own preferment, 'never reflecting upon the dangerous consequences of their desperate Diabolicall proceedings'.[96] As Underdown demonstrates, England's satanic government in the eyes of the newsbooks was an inversion that traded order for chaos, social and political responsibility for libertinism and self-indulgence.

Yet amidst their horrified and violent reaction to the republic, the royalist press never lost sight of complexities of the theocratic political understanding of diabolic subversion. Their nightmare vision of satanic Westminster was not a simplistic recourse to knee-jerk inversion; it maintained always its pointed attack on Puritan reforming pretensions. According to Marchemont Nedham's *Mercurius Pragmaticus*, dated four weeks after the king's execution, the court which tried Charles was not so much a meeting of reformers as a 'conventicle of treason'. The 'Westminster Furies', it noted the following week, were infused with 'many hellish eroneus opinions meerely tending to the advancement of Satans kingdome, by building tabernacles for Deuills'.[97] *The Royal Diurnall* provided its readers with a genealogy of rebellion that ran through (among many others) Cromwell, Bradshaw, Marten and Fairfax. 'These are Plutoes black List of Saints', the newsbook commented, 'chosen for the tormentors of the Common-wealth.' They made 'idolls' of themselves to be worshipped before God or the Word.[98] For Richard Crouch's *The Man in the Moon* the regime inaugurated a new religious calendar given over to the observance of diabolism, and the most holy day was to be 30 January, or 'St Traytors Day', around which parliament would be given a week's recess to 'solemnize that bloody festivall, and sing infernall dirges to King Oliver'. Similarly *Mercurius Philo-monarchus* described the Devil's parliament as 'canonising' its victory against divine government.[99]

These newsbooks, and the more populist royalist pamphlets that now accompanied them, contained the fullest incorporation of the variety of concepts of demonism, and they produced some of the most striking imagery of the entire polemic of the conflict. Far from being the guardhouse of the nation's freedom, parliament was 'Plutoes Independant Kitchen', from which his greed for suffering and evil was fed. Bradshaw, Cooke and Prideaux were 'the Devils

95 *The Royal Diurnall*, no. 1, 25 Febuary 1650, sigs. A, A4; *Mercurius Pragmaticus*, no. 44, 27 Febuary – 5 March, 1649, sig. Hhhv.
96 *Mercurius Pragmaticus*, no. 45, 6–13 March 1649, sig. Iiiv.
97 Ibid., no. 44, 27 Febuary – 5 March 1649, sig. Hhhv; no. 45, 6–13 March 1649, sig. Iiiv.
98 *The Royal Diurnall*, no. 1, 25 February 1650, sig. A3v.
99 Richard Crouch, *The Man in the Moon, discovering a World of Knavery vnder the Sunne; Both in Parliament, the Counsell of State, the Army, the City, and the Country*, no. 43, 6–14 Febuary 1650, p. 330; *Mercurius Philo-monarchus*, no. 1, 10–17 April 1649, p. 2; Mercurius Melancholicus, *The Cuckows Nest at Westminster*, pp. 138–9.

scullions and turnspits', whilst Marten and Cromwell delivered hypocritical lectures in preparation for this latest take on the image of the Devil's feast. 'The seven deadly sinnes become new cook'd for the Devils breakfast', flavoured with 'Independants sauce, made of blood royall', and accompanied by a sycophantic demonic grace at the lips of Hugh Peter.[100] The paradox of diabolic reward/punishment mingled with Satan's familiar role as God's hangman to provide a satisfying explanation for the rash of tormented consciences and suicides that seemed to plague the regicides. Regicide/deicide would of course reserve for its perpetrators a special place in the hellish kingdom. Charles's holy blood was white, according to *Mercurius Pragmaticus*; it would thus make a 'check-work' on the regicides' 'black-soules' for devils to play chess on.[101] Hellish preferment was the reward for republican diabolism. 'Their almighty General Jones', noted *The Man in the Moon*, 'is gone on an Embassie to Pluto, to provide lodgings for the rest, who as soon as they have finished the Great Work of their double Damnation, are to march after him.'[102] Apparently Cromwell and Fairfax were so haunted with evil spirits that they could no longer sleep, and a drum-maker from Houndsditch named Tench, who had provided the ropes to bind Charles to the block, was tormented by devils.[103] Unable to tolerate his 'Hell upon Earth', and given a helping hand by Satan, Alderman Thomas Hoyle hanged himself on the first anniversary of Charles's execution, to the delight of *The Man in the Moon*.[104] The earl of Pembroke and Montgomery, Philip Herbert, apparently died screaming that the Devil was leading him to hell, a fit place for his traitor's soul.[105] But it was the sorry end of the executioner, Richard Brandon, that was most lovingly retold in the newsbooks and pamphlets. In the hands of the royalist press Brandon was a profligate who squandered the money he was paid for beheading Charles (significantly £30) on whoring and drinking, and contracted a variety of venereal diseases. Soon after the execution he became convinced that he was damned, and that his house was infested by devils. When his friends called on him to repent, he told them that Satan stood at the end of his bed to prevent him, and he died 'crying out the Devill, the Devill'.[106]

[100] Crouch, *The Man in the Moon*, no. 43, p. 330.

[101] *Mercurius Pragmaticus*, no. 44, 27 February – 5 March 1649, sig. Hhhv.

[102] Crouch, *The Man in the Moon*, no. 37, 2–9 January 1650, p. 296.

[103] Ibid., no. 2, 16–23 April 1649, p. 16; no. 7, 20–27 June, 1649, p. 94.

[104] Ibid., no. 44, 20–27 February, p. 350; *The Rebells Warning-Piece: being Certaine Rules and Instructions left by Alderman Hoyle* (?London, 1650), which gave a supposedly first-person account of his torment by Satan, and commented that he hanged himself 'by the help of the Devil', see pp. 4–5, 6; Underdown, *A Freeborn People*, p. 108.

[105] *The Last Will and Testament of Philip Herbert, Burgess for Bark-shire, Vulgarlie called Earl of Pembroke and Montgomery* (London, 1649), p. 4.

[106] *The Last Will and Testament of Richard Brandon esquire; Heads-man, and hang-man to the Pretended Parliament* (1649), p. 8; Crouch, *The Man in the Moon*, no. 43, p. 335.

This polemic was shaped by the opportunistic requirement of pulp press publishing, with its need to provide entertainment as much as news and comment. But, as Professor Underdown has suggested, it tapped into a widely shared value system, and demonism allowed it to make important, and all too serious points about the republican regime. Richard Crouch, in *The Man in the Moon*, encouraged his readers to laugh at Fairfax's fear of the Devil. The general was apparently so tormented with guilt that when he got into his coach standing on the spot in Whitehall where Charles's scaffold had been erected, and being approached by a parliament man who happened to be dressed in black, he mistook the man, Miles Corbet, for Satan. In a panic Fairfax abandoned his coach and ran home on foot.[107] The story told a moral tale about the consequences of an afflicted conscience, and held Fairfax's distracted state up to ridicule. But it also made a fundamental point about the religio-political state of the nation's republican government. Born of the usurpation of divine authority, the regime was prey at any moment to the providential retribution of God through his agent the Devil. Britain was now ruled on a knife-edge over damnation. Other important religio-political points might be made with equal force. When, in January 1650, parliament ordered all adult males to swear the Engagement Oath to the new Commonwealth, *The Man in the Moon* declared that to do so was to enter into a pact with Satan and sign away one's soul. It was an appeal to the familiar narrative of the diabolic seduction of witches, a favourite of the pulp press. But it succinctly introduced into popular discourse the notion that to take the Engagement was to embrace a very real diabolic apostasy.[108]

Again post-regicide pulp press polemic is suggestive of the potential for demonism to encourage an informed engagement with politics. Whilst the image of satanic Westminster appears hugely exaggerated to the modern reader, we must be careful not to dismiss it on account of its use of libel, metaphor and fiction. With, of course, the notable exception of Marchemont Nedham, it was not an allegation that was lightly made or quickly abandoned. In the wake of the defeat of Prince Charles at the Battle of Worcester in 1651, Cromwell persuaded the Rump Parliament to offer a general pardon for political offences committed up to that date. A ballad of 1652, *Upon the General Pardon pass'd by the Rump*, noted that parliament was more prepared to be forgiving with the royalist sentiments of journalists and poets, who had no money to take, than with the sequestered gentry. It specifically listed the accusation that parliament was diabolic as one which might be forgiven under the general pardon. But to accept the pardon was to accept the goodwill of that very devilish regime, and to declare oneself 'a rebel to

107 Crouch, *The Man in the Moon*, no. 2, 16–23 April 1649, p. 16.
108 Ibid., no. 37, 2–9 January 1650, p. 294.

eternity'.[109] Parliament, it seemed, was mistaken to think that the words of impoverished journalists carried any less conviction than the actions of the royalist gentry.

The events of 1553 produced further criticism of Cromwell, and not only from royalists. The broadside *A Charge of High Treason exhibited against Oliver Cromwell* criticised the establishment of the Nominated Assembly. Appealing to the language of murder indictments, it noted, 'Oliver Cromwell having not the fear of God before his eyes, and being instigated by the Deuill, did contriue ... a certain book called A Copy of Draughts of Acts of Parliament, out of which this mock parliament are to take their lessons.'[110] In June 1654 the book-dealer, George Thomason, copied out a verse libel entitled 'The Character of a Protector', which noted that Cromwell was 'an outside saint with a Diuell within'.[111] But as John Morrill has pointed out, criticism of Cromwell after 1653 came as a steady stream rather than a flood,[112] and the relative absence of accusations of diabolism against the regime in the second half of the 1650s is striking. In part this is explained by the effective suppression of all but the 'official' newsbooks after 1655, which cut off the most regular source of expressions of anti-parliament demonism. At the same time the pulp press found a new focus for fears of diabolism in the emergence of religious radicalism, and the Ranters and Quakers in particular. A myriad of agendas contributed to the publicising of the Ranter sensation and Quaker witchcraft, and royalists, the government, Presbyterians and sectarians alike used examples of diabolism to highlight the dangers of antinomian extremism.[113] Whilst the resentments harboured by those who had read *Mercurius Pragmaticus* and *The Man in the Moon* were unlikely to be easily dispelled, there is no reason to suppose they were unable to assimilate stories of radical diabolism on their own terms, as the fulfilment of the newsbooks' direst prophesies.

Political demonism resurfaced forcefully in 1660 as a means of engaging with the events which lead up to the Restoration. As the notion of the tempted king had kept open an avenue to compromise with Charles I, it was now used to persuade supporters of the regime to let go of the discredited republican experiment as an act of repentance. In *The Plotters unmasked*, John Clarke offered 'a word in season', to republicans, exhorting, 'Oh let not the Deuil thus deceiue you, by perswading you that you are Saints ... what a

[109] *Upon the General Pardon pass'd by the Rump*, in *Political Ballads*, vol. I, pp. 96–9.
[110] *Sedition Scourg'd, or a view of that Rascally & Venemous paper entitled A Charge of High Treason exhibted against Oliver Cromwell* (London, 1653), p. 10.
[111] British Library, Thomason Tracts, E. 743 (2).
[112] John Morrill, 'Cromwell and his Contemporaries', in J. Morrill (ed.), *Oliver Cromwell and the English Revolution* (London, 1990), p. 268.
[113] Davis, *Fear, Myth and History*, pp. 107–13.

snare hath the Deuil got into you?' The anonymous author of *The Army's declaration* rejected calls for the continued support of the Engagement Oath, noting, 'we cannot be so stupid and sencelessly bewitched, not to thinke it better seriously to crave the pardon of God for this our Engagement, and the nation for the wrong we have hitherto done them, then by our obstinate persisting in such Engagements, sell our selves to the Devill, and the Kingdom to ruin'.[114] In seeking to prepare the way for the return of Charles II, some authors offered the prospect of a renewed royal harrowing of the Devil's kingdom. *Policy no Policy* purported to reprint the reply from Brussels to an objective enquiry as to the Prince's character. 'In him that prophesy seems to be fulfil'd', it noted. 'The lyon shall lye down with the Lamb and the all-Ruling. Providence wil in due time make Vertue Glorious, when Machiavil and the Devil himself shall be Confuted in the politicks to the joy of all honest men.'[115]

Demonism was also used to reflect on and explain what had happened since 1642. Cromwell's post-mortem in the pulp press in the early 1660s concluded that he was a devil incarnate, the nearest human approximation to Lucifer the world had seen in modern times. A pamphlet of 1660, entitled *The English Devil: or, Cromwell and his monstrous Witch Discover'd at White-hall*, reprinted an eighty-year-old woodcut of a witch holding a winged devil to bring home the point.[116] Cromwell, it related, was 'that hellish monster, and damnable Machiavellian that first gave rise to our new-fangled Models of Government'. He was 'the Devil of later times'.[117] A five-act play, *Cromwell's Conspiracy*, also printed in 1660, again sought to undermine Puritan reforming pretensions. Cromwell was shown addressing Hugh Peter as 'my fine facetious Devil, who wear'st the Livery of the Stygian God, as the white emblem of innocence'.[118] In the final scene Cromwell on his death-bed was tormented by demons in the shape of black human figures. His last words were an anguished prediction as to his eternal fate – 'Blood-thirsty tyrants have their places in hell! / Thither go I.'[119] In 1661 another

[114] John Clarke, *The Plotters unmasked, murderers no saints* (London, 1660), pp. 1–3, quote at p. 2; *The Army's declaration: being a True Alarum in answer to a False and Fiery one made lately, by a Member of that detestable Rump* (?London, 1660), p. 6; on the diabolic hypocrisy of the Rump see also *A Word for All: or, the Rump's Funerall sermon* (?London, 1660), p. 24 (irregular pagination).

[115] *Policy no Policy, or, the Devil Himself confuted* (?London, 1660), pp. 4–5.

[116] *The English Devil: or, Cromwell and his monstrous Witch Discover'd at White-hall* (London, 1660), frontispiece. The woodcut was taken from *A Rehearsall both strange and true, of . . . Elizabeth Stile, alias Rockingham.*

[117] *The English Devil*, p. 3.

[118] *Cromwell's Conspiracy. A Tragy-comedy, relating to our latter Times* (London, 1660), Act I, scene 1; on the diabolism of Hugh Peter see also *The History of the Life and Death of Hugh Peters* (London, 1660), pp. 6, 12.

[119] *Cromwell's Conspiracy*, Act V, scene 1.

printed play, *Hells Higher Court of Justice* (which was probably too short to have actually been performed) was a detailed depiction of the hellish reward awaiting Cromwell as the Devil's most worthy client. Its centrepiece was the trial in hell of the souls of Cromwell, Gustavus Adolphus and Cardinal Mazarin, in which they bickered with each other over who had done the most to promote Satan's cause. 'Your services to Hell compared with mine', Cromwell tells the others; 'where thou hast sent one soul I have sent ten'.[120] The soul of Machiavelli presides over the debate and, whilst recognising the valiant efforts of Adolphus and Mazarin, declares that Cromwell 'in wickedness is chiefest of the three'. He predicts that 'Oliver' will become a universal name for the treacherous, murderous, anti-Christian and regicidal.[121] Each expects rewards for his faithful service, but instead suitable punishments are handed down by the infernal court. Cromwell's case, however, is so unique – 'his crimes ... are so strange and new' – that the chthonian judges are troubled to find punishments severe enough. Pluto himself worries that without the most dire torments others will be inspired by Cromwell to usurp his own infernal throne. Cromwell is eventually sentenced to be bound for ever to a red-hot throne, in burning regal dress, with a devil to perpetually recite his crimes, applying some 'fierie torment' as he names each one. This, notes Pluto as the play's conclusion, is the reality of infernal preferment. 'Fond small men' groomed in the service of hell, receive rewards, 'but such as scarce their flattering souls expect'.[122]

The Civil War, then, gave an entirely unprecedented tangibility to the workings of Satan within the commonwealth, as the concept of diabolic subversion was used to come to terms with the breakdown of government. In some respects this was a response to the sheer chaos of the situation, in which moral and social norms appeared to have been jettisoned, and God's hangman was kept especially busy. The use of demonisation in propaganda offered to make the enemy identifiable. But diabolism was never simply employed as a gloss to make manageable a baffling political reality. Like narratives of crime, demonisation during the Civil War involved far more complex processes than those of only functionalist projection. The force of the concept of diabolic subversion lay in its ability to encourage an engagement with the complexities of the conflict. The temptation of the body politic was well established in political discourse, and brought with it complex notions of 'national introspection' and the theocratic duty to separate

[120] *Hells Higher Court of Justice; or, the Trial of Three Politick Ghosts* (London, 1661), scene V, sig. C3; for a similar satire see *Cromwell's Complaint of Injustice: or, His Dispute with Pope Alexander the Sixth, for precedency in Hell* (no date), reprinted in *The Harleian Miscellany*, vol. VI, pp. 529–31.

[121] *Hells Higher Court of Justice*, scene V, sigs. C4v–D.

[122] Ibid., scene VI, sigs. D2–D2v.

Christ and Belial. It demanded that action be taken in the understanding that the balance between godly and satanic warfare was a subtle one. Implicit in the rhetoric of war against the Devil were demands for self-awareness that mitigated against a simplistic crusading zeal. Thus, whilst the political use of demonism was more widespread in the Civil War than it had ever been before, it had not changed qualitatively. The increasing willingness to recognise a need for a violent solution paved the way to see Charles eventually accused of being a Devil incarnate. But, as we saw in the last chapter, the potential had always been there.

8

'The Devil's Alpha and Omega': temptation at the cutting edge of faith in the Civil War and the Interregnum

We have seen the place the Devil occupied in the discourse of the opposing sides in the English Civil War, in which demonism provided a means of engaging with the complexities of the struggle. In this final chapter we will examine the role of demonism in the godly's attempts to reform the church after the calling of the Long Parliament. The controversies that soon punctured the anti-Laudians' reforming zeal are of course well documented, but the significance of accusations of diabolism between the godly themselves has been neglected. Historians of the Presbyterian/Independent controversies have had little to say concerning the demonic context of the dispute. Yet demonism permeated the issue precisely because the godly sought what they self-consciously identified as a reformation. Reform, understood through the history of Protestantism, was an inherently anti-demonic act. Its success would be measured, in part at least, by the eradication of demonic influence within the commonwealth, in terms of both politics and personal devotion. As an anti-demonic process, reformation could also be expected to be prey to a concerted campaign of diabolic subversion. Protestants had long taken to heart the convention that Satan reserved his greatest assaults for the most godly, and this understanding was extended to the process of reformation itself. It was precisely because a reformation might involve a break with the familiar and an exploration of new practices, and indeed new religious experiences, that this cutting edge of faith was perceived as an inherently dangerous place. Spiritual progress was an intense experience which was problematised by the potential for its sheer adrenalin to cloud the individual's perception. The Devil was at his most dangerous when he disguised himself as an angel of light and, should the commonwealth be unready or unworthy of reformation, God might allow Satan to tempt the aspiring godly.

Thus when the reformation of the Church of England became a realistic possibility in 1640, the issue of mixing Christ with Belial immediately re-emerged into the consideration of Puritans. For some, who would become separatists, it was the possibility of further enforced mixing of the godly and ungodly within single congregations that threatened to once again leave the church only 'half-reformed'. The growth of separatism in turn provoked fears in many that the reformation was being actively subverted by the Devil, who preyed on these godly's impatience for tangible spiritual progress by introducing false doctrines under the guise of piety. The optimism that characterised Puritan activism in the early 1640s gave way, following the schism around the Westminster Assembly and the religious libertarianism of the New Model Army, to disillusionment and even despair by the end of the decade. By the mid-1640s an extensive literature of mutual accusations of diabolism was developing. Congregationalists characterised Presbyterianism as an impotent reformation, subverted by the Devil's ability to maintain his old tyranny in the guise of a new national church government. Presbyterians in turn characterised congregationalists as a diabolic fifth column set on turning back the progress made in tearing down the Laudian church.

On the face of it, such views might appear an unproblematic assimilation of emergent folk devils into an established scheme of stigmatisation. Diabolic subversion was certainly a discourse that could interpret setbacks for the godly. But it was never simply this. It should not be seen as a convenient get-out clause to explain the failure of the godly revolution, but as a consequence of the central ethos of spiritual progress. As we saw in the last chapter, even the baldest of Civil War propaganda implied notions of diabolic subversion which reflected the very complexities of religio-political understanding. Whilst the conflict between the armies provided less scope for empathy, and greater scope for 'othering', the conflict between religious reformers and radicals fully exploited the potential of empathically based polemic. Puritans and Laudians had had years to define their sense of opposition; Presbyterians and Independents had to come to terms with a sudden schism that saw allies now ranged against each other. But what is striking about the Presbyterian/Independent polemic of the 1640s is the self-confidence and sophistication with which both sides engaged with the concept of diabolic subversion. They did not simply trade accusations of diabolism back and forth. Instead they both took as their starting point the understanding that spiritual progress was prey to diabolic subversion, and diagnosed the actions of their opponents in accordance, accepting the validity of each other's reforming motives. A significant mutual sense of identification was lacking in the encounter with the emergent sectarianism of the late 1640s and 1650s. Groups such as the Ranters and the Quakers appeared to embody a concerted diabolic assault on all forms of order and religion, and they were susceptible to an otherisation that had been absent from the intra-Puritan disputes of the Civil War. But even here, especially in the case of the Quakers, there existed a marked empathy with the sectarians' godly motives, which were often conceived of as genuine, if misguided and subject to demonic temptation.

This is significant in the light of emerging work on Civil War pluralism and its effect on traditional consensus-based discourse. In discussing the use of accusations of witchcraft against the Quakers, Peter Elmer has argued that the recourse to demonism was the result of the effective breakdown of traditional semiology. The unprecedented events of the 1640s shattered the ability of established demonological discourse to act as a 'universal signifier', whilst at the same time driving people to look to that very language as a familiar and comforting means of interpreting opposition and rebellion.[1] As the language of witchcraft itself became susceptible to intense factionalism, Dr Elmer argues, a 'radical reorientation' by the ruling elite concentrated on toleration and libertarianism as the main threat to social order, and the Quakers, who embodied these qualities, took on the role of 'surrogate' witches.[2] The pre-suppositions that inform this picture of linguistic breakdown and the fear of pluralism are effectively challenged, albeit with a different focus, by Peter Lake's recent work on the intra-Puritan disputes of the early Stuart period, in which he sees the fear of difference as far less absolute. Professor Lake disagrees with the interpretation, advocated by Christopher Hill and his followers, that radicalism constituted a tradition essentially separate from mainstream Puritanism. Instead, Lake argues, the radical fringe existed within a Puritan community that was characterised by a certain elasticity and tolerance of the eccentricities of those who were accepted as being among the godly.[3] It was the openness with which intra-Puritan disputes were carried out in the press, rather than being contained within the self-identified godly community, that marked the difference of the 1640s and 1650s. If Lake is correct, we would still expect to see evidence, in the disputes of the 1640s, of a complex attitude to religious difference, born of this long tradition of assimilating idiosyncratic elements among the identified godly. And this would qualify Dr Elmer's identification of the intense fear of religious pluralism. The widespread recourse to the language of diabolic subversion suggests that this was indeed the case. Whilst we should not dismiss the fear of pluralism, we should also not underestimate the realism with which contemporaries met with religious difference, or the sophistication of their means of interpreting it. Within a group who mutually identified with each other's reforming motives, difference was not seen automatically as terminal, as the emphasis on temptation illustrates. Temptation always implied the possibility that the victim might eventually be freed from diabolic assault and return to the fold. In this sense, between those with a mutual sense of identification it could constitute a discourse of negotiation rather than estrangement.

[1] Elmer, '"Saints or Sorcerers"', pp. 173–4. [2] Ibid., p. 176.
[3] Peter Lake, *The Boxmaker's Revenge: 'Orthodoxy', 'Heterodoxy' and the Politics of the Parish in Early Stuart London* (Manchester, 2001).

The disputes over the church settlement in the 1640s and 1650s revisited those that had raged over the 'synagogue of Satan' nearly a century before, and they are testimony to the continued vitality of a discourse that had always engaged with the reality of pluralism, albeit within the ideal of consensus.

THE SYNAGOGUE OF SATAN REVISITED: THE DEVIL TURNED INDEPENDENT

In 1641 the first rifts opened in a parliamentarian reforming junta that, historians agree, knew it wanted rid of Laudian episcopacy, but did not know what it wanted to replace it with.[4] Parliament's 'Protestation' of 3 May abjured popery, but equated the true reformed Protestant religion with the established Church of England.[5] For a number of reformers that equation was a contradiction in terms, since the Laudian popery that they had fought against had been defined by the imposition of liturgies, ceremonies and discipline. A number, such as Henry Burton, and established separatists such as Katherine and Daniel Chidley, argued for the liberty to establish separatist congregations.[6] Whilst aimed at parliament's Presbyterian leanings, their arguments were a restatement of those made half a century before by anti-episcopalian Puritans such as John Penry and Henry Barrow. But there were important, if subtle, differences which intimated a growing confidence of separatist expression. Whereas Penry and Barrow had stated that it was the painful duty of the godly to disassociate themselves from a half-reformed church, the separatists now argued more positively that it was their *right*. Using the Corthinians dichotomy, they argued that to compel them to associate with the reprobate in a national church was the enforced mixing of Christ and Belial.

Henry Burton's oft-quoted justification of separatism, in his response to parliament, *The protestation protested* – which noted that 'the church is properly a congregation of believers, called out from the rest of the world' – defined that body's rights in terms of the Corinthians dichotomy. 'To communicate with known evil doers', Burton declared, 'is to partake of their evil deeds.'[7] Thus, in order to protect the godly's right not to sin, 'of necessity there must be liberty granted of setting up Churches ... where none are admitted members of the congregation, but such as are approved of by the whole assembly'.[8] This right not to be forced to mix with Belial, Burton further elucidated in a calculated appeal to parliament's conception of itself

4 M. Watts, *The Dissenters* (Oxford, 2 vols., 1978), vol. I, p. 86. 5 Ibid., p. 84.

6 Henry Burton, *The protestation protested, or, A short remonstrance shewing what is principally required of all those that have or doe take the last Parliamentary protestation* (London, 1641), sigs. A4v–B.

7 Ibid., sig. B3v. 8 Ibid., sig. C.

as a collection of godly men. In his sermon at St Margaret's on 20 June 1641, he noted that the condition of man was a 'generall bondage' to Satan and sin from which few – and here the members might flatter themselves – were free. So much was uncontentious, but having played to the natural sympathies of his audience, Burton then sought to highjack them. 'I will speak of another bondage', he declared; 'the bondage of conscience . . . for there are many that are delivered from the bondage of sinne, yet still lie vnder the bondage of humane ordinances in the worship of God.' The enforcement of liturgy, ceremony and discipline was a tyranny akin to that exercised by Satan over men before their conversion. By implication, if the members identified with the desire to be loosed from the bondage of sin, they should also sympathise with Burton's request to be freed from the bondage of conscience.[9]

The Corinthians dichotomy re-emerged as a mainstay of the argument for independency. Independents repeated Burton's argument that the saints must not be forced into diabolism by being coerced into mixed congregations.[10] Moreover, the text provided powerful ammunition in the context of the search for a scriptural definition of the church.[11] For separatists like Katherine Chidley it demonstrated that the Apostles themselves had advocated congregationalism.[12] The Baptist *Confession of Faith*, published in 1644 by William Kiffin, emphasised the privilege of the godly being set apart from the reprobates who were ruled by Satan, a privilege expressed in the freedom to separate from the national church.[13]

Separatists did not depart from the established rhetoric of Protestant anti-diabolism, but they took reformist arguments a stage further by claiming that de facto Satanism was inherent in *any* national church. They were able to employ the experiential identification of temptation to discredit the fundamental rationale of an established church. The Presbyterian Thomas Edwards asserted in 1641 that, even given the work of the apostles, the evangelists and prophets, men were unable to stand alone in religion, and required the help of a national church. Katherine Chidley denounced this as a temptation designed specifically to undermine the self-confidence of the godly, noting 'this is the very suggestion of Sathan into the hearts of our first parents; for they have a desire for something more then was warranted

9 Henry Burton, *Englands Bondage and Hope of Deliverance* (London, 1641), pp. 20–1.
10 *A Short Answer to A.S.* (London, 1644), p. 22.
11 Katherine Chidley, *The Iustification of the Independent Churches of Christ* (London, 1641), 'Answer to Mr Edwards his Introduction'; John Goodwin, *Theomachia, or the Grand Imprudence of men running the hazard of fighting against God* (London, 1644), pp. 7, 10, 24; William Kiffin, *A Breife Remonstrance of the Reasons and Grounds of those People Commonly called Anabaptists, for their Separation* (London, 1645), pp. 4–5.
12 Chidley, *Iustification of the Independent Churches*, 'Answer to Mr Edwards'.
13 William Kiffin, *The Confession of Faith of those Churches which are commonly (though falsly) called Anabaptists* (London, 1644), sigs. B2–B2v, B4v–Cv.

by God'.[14] This combined with a largely pessimistic assessment of the practical possibility of a nationwide reformation. Robert Coachman, writing *The cry of a stone* in 1642, described how, despite some sixty years of 'powerfull preaching', the majority of parishioners stubbornly continued to 'serve Satan'. This could represent more than a simple complaint at the pig-headedness of the reprobate. Separatists could contrast the scope for a de facto satanic presence within the church provided by voluntary association on the one hand and coercion on the other. Henry Ainsworth's 1608 tract, *Counterpoyson*, brought into the fray in a reprint of 1642, contained a pointed argument that reform based only within a national church was constrained within a diabolic cycle of coercion and passive acquiescence which could never breed willing Christians. By definition, Ainsworth had argued, the imposition of a national church by coercion forced into congregations those who were 'the limmes of Satan, and ... children of the Diuill'. The ungodly multitude were perfectly content to accept any form of worship that might avoid persecution, and 'the magistrate', he noted, 'cannot work faith in any; seeing faith is the gift of God'.[15] This placed effective limits on the traditional Calvinist doctrine of the enforced good conduct of the reprobate. To say that some of the unregenerate affect religion, Ainsworth had declared, and live good lives, was simply not sufficient to justify the continued mixing of Christ and Belial. Regardless of their outward conduct, they were the children of the Devil, and thus they could only effect the diabolic pollution of godly congregations. Thus Ainsworth's defence of separation did not operate on a repudiation of the role of the magistracy in reforming the church and restraining the unregenerate, but in identifying its unavoidable limitations, he argued for the justice in allowing the godly to commune free from diabolic pollution.[16] In his *Theomachia* (1644), John Goodwin noted that a purely Presbyterian reformation would be 'as that whereby that Angel of Darkness, Satan is reformed'. There would be 'no reformation of desires'; instead it would see 'open lossenesse and prophanenesse reformed into Pharasaicall hypocrisie'.[17] A conference in the same year between Burton, Brown and Chidley demonstrated the extent to which the most committed Independents were prepared to see the Corinthians dichotomy as an absolute. Burton was criticised for continuing to preach in church buildings by those who remarked that Independents 'should have no spiritual fellowship at all with the unfruitful works of darkness'.[18]

14 Chidley, *The Iustification of the Independent Churches of Christ*, p. 1.
15 Henry Ainsworth, *Counterpoyson* (London, 1642), p. 74. 16 Ibid., p. 79.
17 Goodwin, *Theomachia*, pp. 23–4. For a denial of Goodwin's argument see *Faces About, or a Recrimination charged upon Mr. John Goodwin* (London, 1644), pp. 7–8.
18 *Two conferences between some of those people that are called separatists* (London, 1650), p. 4.

This positive and proactive reading of the Corinthians dichotomy also informed the position of the more conservative Congregationalists who attended the Westminster Assembly. Men such as William Bridge, Jeremiah Burroughes, Thomas Goodwin, Philip Nye and Sidrach Simpson had emigrated to the Netherlands in the 1630s rather than conform to Laudianism, but all were able to accept benefices within the national church when they returned at the calling of the Long Parliament. They did not see themselves as radical separatists in the mould of Burton or Chidley. Their moderate *Apologeticall Narration* argued for gathered congregations within the established church, and sought to overcome Presbyterian resistance by removing the spectre of Brownism. It is significant then that their appeal to the Assembly was couched in the language of the Corinthians dichotomy and of temptation, which was clearly intended to refer to a shared discourse. Their position, the apologists claimed, was the result of the profound changes of circumstance that had occurred since the calling of the Long Parliament. In the 1630s, when the church had been infused with 'corruptions in the publique worship', they had found it impossible to conform. Faced with the subversion of their faith, they had, they argued, been able only to concern themselves with the 'dark part' of religion: 'the evil of those superstitions adjoined to the worship of God'. Pressing need had led them to identify the corruptions of the faith and to withdraw from them. Now, they had 'nothing else to doe', but to examine the 'light part': 'the positive part of the church worship and government'. The apologists conceded that diabolic subversion presented a danger to those enquiring into religion, but were at pains to stress that they afforded 'noe temptation to byas us any way, but leaving us freely to be guided by that light and touch Gods spirit'.[19]

Burton's use of the Corinthians dichotomy was challenged in a number of subtly different ways. His long-term opponent, Bishop Joseph Hall, provided a detailed repudiation of the logic of the dichotomy in his *Survay of that ... Libell, The Protestation Protested* (1641). 'Cannot one Devill be cast out', Hall demanded, 'unlesse seaven enter?'[20] Hall further denied Burton's claim to a right of separation as both ineffectual and unchristian. A church constituted on the fear of pollution by the reprobate was one intensely vulnerable to subversion. 'Know you what iniquity some of your holy Sisters might have committed yesternight', Hall asked; 'if you communicate with them, do you partake of their profanation?' In order to protect such a community, it would be necessary 'to have [men's] brests made christall', so that any secret impurity might be known. Moreover, the fear of pollution was unchristian

[19] William Bridge et al., *The Apologetical Narration* (London, 1644), pp. 3–4.
[20] Joseph Hall, *A Survey of that Foolish, Seditious, Scandalous, Prophane Libell, The Protestation Protested* (London, 1641), p. 5.

because it denied the significance of Christ's sacrifice – 'if every knowne sin be every mans, where is Christs burthen?' As scripture made clear, Christ's ministry had been among the sinners and the irreligious, in contrast to the elitism of the Pharisees.[21] The Presbyterian John Geree also answered the *Protestation Protested* in a tract published on the authority of the Commons. As a reformer, Geree did not challenge the rationale of Burton's use of the Corinthians dichotomy, but he denied its appropriateness. The Protestation, he argued, denounced only those elements of popery that were against the doctrine of the Church of England. Those doctrines previously established in law by parliament might have popish elements, but they were not covered by the Protestation.[22] 'All the Reformation to be expected from this Parliament', he noted, 'is not to be expected by this Protestation, this is one degree to reforme whatever Popery or Innovation is against Law established, this done, the Parliament is proceeding further to perfect hoped for Reformation, by removing corruptions established by Law.' Thus Geree argued that the Corinthians dichotomy was misapplied – that the separation of Christ and Belial could take place within a national covenant – and that Burton's resort to separatism was precipitous.[23]

The Presbyterian response to the Independents was, of course, spearheaded by Thomas Edwards, whose *Gangraena* has become synonymous with the notion of intolerance. Indeed, Edwards immediately perceived the hand of Satan in the writings of figures like Burton, and published his response, *Reasons against the Independent Government of Particular Congregations*, in 1641. But his perception that the Independents had been deluded by the Devil was shaped by an understanding of the inherent dangers of godly progress and reformation. For Edwards, independency was a classic ruse of the Devil, who, if challenged by reformation, sought to reintroduce his false doctrine under the guise of the new faith. 'The deuill seeing he cannot effect his ends in the former wayes he went, he will now try others', Edwards declared, noting that 'Satan will be of that colour and temper just that men are of with whom he deals, and the times are of.'[24] But Edwards' understanding of the dynamics of diabolic subversion prevented him from seeing Independents as the witting agents of Satan, or support for toleration as grounds for the immediate repudiation of former allies such as Burton. The church could not be reformed in an instant, nor could it be subverted in an instant. Rather, independency was a long-term strategy by which the

[21] Ibid., pp. 34–7, quotes at p. 34.
[22] John Geree, *Vindiciae Voti*, in *Iudahs Ioy at the Oath* (London, 1641), sigs. B4–B4v.
[23] Ibid., sigs. B4v–C.
[24] Thomas Edwards, *Reasons against the Independent Government of Particular Congregations* (London, 1641), sig. A6v.

Devil planned the progressive usurpation of the church: 'Satan will *in time* bring about the same things though in another way, for Independencie will bring againe what now it would cast out, namely libertinism, prophanesse, errors, and will by some bring many men to no religion at all.'[25] Edwards conceded the attraction of such radicalism in a time of religious upheaval. Independency was calculated to appeal to the reforming motives of the anti-Laudians. It might be favoured by some of the 'unstable and wanton witted', but the majority of its supporters were godly men, led by the adrenalin of change into over-enthusiasm – and thus into vulnerability to diabolic temptation. In such men 'the dangers and evils may not so appear for the present, there being many things in most of the ministers lovely, which the more commends this way'. Thus the fact that godly ministers might support independency was, for Edwards, a tangible demonstration of the heightened danger posed by diabolic subversion in a time of rapid religious progress. It was, therefore, the responsibility of parliament to 'looke upon things and judge them not onely as they are for the present, but as they may be hereafter'.[26]

Edwards provided a far more detailed version of his argument in *Gangraena* in 1646, and his attitude to the Independents had certainly hardened. This lengthy catalogue of heresies is often characterised by historians as a rambling work of paranoia, which probably did more to disseminate radical opinion that to convince as to its threat.[27] Ann Hughes has convincingly challenged this view, arguing that Presbyterianism, and *Gangraena*, did have a populist potential in the late 1640s. Despite its length, the book deliberately appealed to the pulp press audience, and its very lack of structure allowed it to be browsed through rather than read systematically. The book's prominent sense of urgency might make it an 'involving and participatory text', giving it a timeliness that might excite and stimulate.[28] Indeed, for all its ramshackle organisation, the book did have a central coherence, and its identification of diabolic agency was consistent with mainstream Protestantism.

Edwards now contended that his predictions of 1641 had been fulfilled, and that England was reeling under a diabolic assault more intense than any since the Reformation. Toleration was now 'the grand designe of the Devil, his masterpeece and chiefe Engine he works by at this time'.[29] Satan had

25 Ibid., my emphasis. 26 Ibid., sigs. A6v–A7.

27 Christopher Hill, clearly enjoying a satirical attack on Edwards by William Walwyn, describes him as the 'great persecutor'. See *The English Bible and the Seventeenth-Century Revolution*, p. 163.

28 Ann Hughes, '"Popular" Presbyterianism in the 1640s and 1650s?: The Cases of Thomas Edwards and Thomas Hall', in N. Tyacke (ed.), *England's Long Reformation, 1500–1800* (London, 1998), pp. 241, 243–4.

29 Thomas Edwards, *Gangraena: or a Catalogue and Discovery of many of the Errours, Heresies, Blasphemies and pernicious Practices of the Sectaries of this time* (London, 1646), pp. 121–3.

indeed re-insinuated himself into the faith through a temptation of the body politic. 'Finding some men in name Christians', Edwards observed, 'he began to use them as his instruments very fit to bring about his deceitful work.'[30] 'We now see by this catalogue', he concluded, 'that the Devil hath recovered himself, and ... gained more in the matter of false Doctrine, Disorder, Deformation, Anarchy, and Libertinisme, then he lost in the Reformation by the putting down many Popish Errors, Superstitious Practices and Tyrannies.'[31] Thus the new impetus given to the very old problem of diabolic false doctrine was more disturbing than the novelty of the sectarian explosion itself. The proliferation of 'frogs out of the bottomlesse pit' threatened to reverse the progress made towards freeing the commonwealth from the chaotic confusion of Catholicism, with its appeal to man's corrupted and lazy religiosity. As Edwards read the words of the sectaries he saw a focused challenge to the tenets of Protestantism for which he and his ancestors had fought so hard. Behind the cacophony of sectarian opinion Edwards saw many instances of popery, but he was most horrified to find a repudiation of the principles of *sola scriptura* and the preaching of the Word, whilst the sectarian prophets were given a doctrinal authority akin to that of a pope. This was the 'greatest and highest' matter of popery, 'denying the perfection and sufficiency of the Scriptures, and pleading for some men to be infallible and to have infallible gifts'. False doctrine's new guise was so effective because the association of diabolic popery with Laudianism had blinded godly men to the possibility of its resurgence in sectarianism. 'I am perswaded', Edwards declared, 'that if seven yeer ago the Bishops and their Chaplains had but preached, printed, licensed, dispersed up and down in City and Country openly, a quarter of these errours ... the people would have risen up and stoned them and puld down their houses.' Indeed Edwards already looked back to anti-Laudianism as a time of a proactive godly defence of Protestantism, betrayed by the nation's intemperate regard for this new 'grosser and worse Arminianism'.[32]

The sense of disillusionment and frustration that permeates *Gangraena* cannot be easily dismissed as knee-jerk conservatism. Edwards saw himself as a reformer and, for him, bitterness was justified when the opportunity for a full reformation was in danger of being squandered on what he perceived as self-indulgence. 'Oh, many of us when we saw Sathan begin to fall like lightening', he declared of the early days of the Long Parliament; 'we made account the winter was past and the deluge of heresie and errour was over, and that the time of the singing of the Birds was come, and that the land should no more be drowned.' 'I think it may be said safely', Edwards

[30] Ibid., pp. 122–7 (irregular pagination, in fact pp. 132–3).
[31] Ibid., pp. 127–33 (in fact pp. 133–4). [32] Ibid., pp. 143–4.

concluded, 'that the Devil hath had a more plentiful harvest this last yeer in England, than ever in any one yeer since the Reformation.'[33]

This understanding of the temptation of the body politic allowed Edwards to now personalise the conflict with sectarianism, by presenting himself as the epitome of the idealised anti-diabolic minister. 'Ministers ... must not only build up, but also defend', he declared; 'in time of Peace they must teach, and in the time of War they must fight with, and resist Satan and Hereticks'.[34] He now placed himself in the vanguard of the anti-demonic campaign, and identified himself with the apostles who had suffered satanic assault for their pains in promoting the true faith. *Gangraena*, Edwards noted, 'will cause me all the hatred, envy, and danger, which the cunning malice, power or blinde zeale of sectaries in England can produce'. But, he continued, 'I doe from my heart rejoyce ... that I am hatefull to the divell and all his scales.'[35] This might appear a polemical self-positioning on the part of Edwards, but, as we have seen, the connection between Protestant devotional and pastoral culture and national politics was never empty rhetoric. In identifying himself as a national Christian soldier, Edwards was expanding the concept of a minister as the community's bulwark against diabolism that was firmly established in Protestantism. Parochial and national vigilance were parallel responsibilities for the ministry and, if Edwards was aggrandising his position, it was only in so far as the site of diabolic subversion was contested between Presbyterian and Independent.

Edwards' attitude to figures such as Henry Burton and John Goodwin hardened in line with this self-conception, and he characterised them as abnegating their own responsibilities to act as foci of anti-diabolic activity. The attack was all the more pointed since he was able to contrast their laxity with their previous fervour in opposing diabolism in its Laudian incarnation. Thus Edwards described Burton:

> a man who in the bishops dayes was so zealous against false doctrine ... that he was on fire against them, and no book that came from a Bishop or his Chaplain, though but a touch of error in it, could escape his pulpit and pen ... But now he can be silent enough against his bretheren the sectaries, and hath not in the growth and increase of all the damnable errors and heresies ... preached any sermon or printed any books against them that I ever heard of.[36]

Such cases demonstrated the insidiousness of toleration, in which the zeal of even the strongest reformers could be dissipated by a relativism that ultimately protected the most heretical sectarianism. Toleration, for Edwards, was nothing more than prevarication: an unwillingness to settle religion that gave the broadest scope for diabolic subversion. 'If a toleration

[33] Ibid., pp. 127–33 (in fact pp. 133–4). [34] Ibid., p. 154.
[35] Ibid., sigs. B4v–C. [36] Ibid., p. 62.

be granted', he concluded, 'the Devill will be too hard for us, though we preach never so much.' To drive home his point, he made it clear where the blame would ultimately lie, noting that 'many persons of quality and note, both ministers and others may see what they have done, and what they have to answer for'.[37]

Given the importance that ministers attached to their role as the community's bulwark against Satan, it is unsurprising that a number of the letters that Edwards received expressed a similarly complex engagement with separatism. Ministers, of course, constructed narratives in line with their own definition of benign intervention, but their testimonies cannot be easily characterised as those of a defensive conservatism. For example, *Gangraena* printed a self-congratulatory letter from a parliamentarian minister, 'S.F.', who was keen to share his insights into the dynamics of antinomianism. Since genuine spiritual experiences and diabolic temptation were bound together, ministers had a duty to guide weak Christians through their errors sensitively, 'avoiding all sharpnes in publique reproofs'. He gave an example of a woman he encountered who had recently become an Anabaptist and was refusing to have her new-born infant baptised. To S.F. it was clear that the woman's maternal delight, and her weakened physical state, had clouded her judgement, and he described her as having 'dreamt into Anabaptisme'. 'It is probable [she] had but lately received some extraordinary comfort', the minister conceded, 'but the Devil had his oar too in the Boat.' His concern was to separate the woman's genuinely spiritual experiences from Satan's temptations, but he refused to dispute with her until she recovered her strength and contented himself with preaching his next sermon on the Devil as an angel of light.[38] A similarly complex approach was evident in narratives concerning reclaimed heretics. There is much in these narratives to suggest that they were constructed between ministers and recanters for their mutual benefit.[39] They provided edifying stories of the dangers of sectarianism, but their emphasis on diabolic temptation also placed significant limits on the demand for penitence. An account by one of Edwards' correspondents, who had reclaimed a number of Anabaptists from 'the workings of Satan', intimates the kind of negotiations that produced an acceptable narrative of recanting sectarianism. Significantly they were grounded in understanding the potential attractions of heresy. The account showed how the sectarians were 'first caught and entangled with a liking of the novelty of Anabaptism'. But soon they discovered that there was a price for this exciting experience since 'being caught . . . they were carried on to it with the strongest violence

[37] Ibid., p. 72–85. [38] Ibid., pp. 50–2.
[39] Such narratives should be read with the same sensitivity to construction that historians now use in assessing narratives of criminality and witchcraft.

and impulse of spirit that is imaginable: they also discover the sad effects and influence which that way had upon their spirits'.[40] Such an account minimised the sin of curiosity, whilst maximising the influence of the Devil who drove his naive victims deeper and deeper into heresy. It also made for powerful propaganda, highlighting the diabolism of the sectaries, whilst providing cautionary tales about the enormous consequences of a little curiosity. But it did all this precisely because it appealed to a widespread and sympathetic understanding of the dangers of temptation.

That the exchanges between Presbyterians and separatists took place within a shared discourse of the danger of diabolic subversion is further evidenced by the responses of the Independents to their critics from 1641. They were, unsurprisingly, able to identify their opponents as victims of temptation, seduced into aiding the Devil to resist reformation. This was how Henry Burton described those who had protested against his fast sermon of 20 June.[41] Katherine Chidley explicitly connected Presbyterians with the diabolism of the Laudian hierarchy, identifying Edwards' attack on Burton as a repeat of the persecution of 1637. To oppose the godly in times of spiritual progress, she noted, 'hath beene always the practice of the instruments of Sathan'.[42] Independents also drove home the message of Presbyterian temptation by contrasting their previous zeal with their current conservatism. Thus a letter sent to John Vicars described William Prynne as a saint who had fallen under the special affliction of the Devil. 'I acknowledge that for a time he ran well', the author, Daniel Taylor, noted, 'but who hindered him? ... The Prince of Darknesse owed him for his sharpe contesting with his prime agents, and now he hath repaiud his debt.' But since his condition was one of temptation, it was curable: 'if Mr Prynn will bee ruled by the advice of his best friends, hee may rise again to his greater glory, and notwithstanding his fall, triumph over the envy and malice of the Devill'.[43]

But, more significantly, Independents did not seek to deny the threat posed by Satan to the Reformation. They were able to make regular use of John 8: 48, which showed that Christ himself had been accused of being possessed, and hence that the Word was consistently mistaken by the reprobate for diabolism.[44] But they were remarkably open in accepting that godly men engaged in rapid religious progress could be peculiarly vulnerable to temptation. Henry Burton in his autobiography, published in 1643, claimed to have experienced this himself. Describing his triumphant return to London in

[40] Edwards, *The Second Part of Gangraena*, pp. 170–1.
[41] Henry Burton, *A Narration of the Life of Mr Henry Burton* (London, 1643), p. 44.
[42] Chidley, *Iustification of the Independent Churches*, 'To the Christian Reader'.
[43] John Vicars, *To his reverend and much respected good friend Mr John Goodwin* (London, 1644), p. 6.
[44] For example see John Goodwin, *Calumny Arraignd and Cast* (London, 1644), sig. A3v, p. 9.

1640, he noted that he had begun to 'be sensible of a far greater danger, then I had been in during all the time of my imprisonment'. The warmth of his reception had tempted him to take pride in his vindication, 'for I began now to feele some stirrings within me, Satan now labouring to overthrow me (as he did Adam), in this my seeming paradise'. As a martyr, Burton had 'displayed all [his] sailes' to catch what little spiritual comfort was available to him; now, freed from tyranny and God's 'peoples affections blowing so strongly', he was in danger of being overwhelmed. Thus his perception of diabolic temptation taught him to 'take in [his] sailes', in effect recognising that the qualities that sustained the godly in times of persecution, might be used by the Devil to work their undoing when liberty was achieved.[45]

The writings of the famous preacher of Coleman Street, John Goodwin, give us the greatest insight into the Independents' ability to engage with the notion and experience of diabolic subversion. Goodwin was unusual in the extent to which he was prepared to openly accept that godly men might be led astray by Satan. But his position was in no way inconsistent with separatism more generally. Rather it expressed a self-confidence rooted in the belief that a reformation built on the liberty of conscience would ultimately survive the machinations of the Devil. For Goodwin, the Corinthians dichotomy justified his separatism and provided a rationale for toleration. The incompatibility of Christ and Belial provided a safety net in which a certain experimentation with religion could take place. For Goodwin it was axiomatic that if the Independents were not inspired by God, then their cause would fail, an argument based on Acts 5: 38 – 'if this counsel or work be of men, it will come to nought; but if it be of God, yee cannot destroy it'.[46] A reformation could, therefore, stand a little diabolic intrigue.[47] The godly should not be frightened to explore some of the more uncertain frontiers of religion, even if they had previously been associated with heresy, and through that diabolism. The cutting edge of the faith was an inherently dangerous place, since its uncertainties gave Satan greater latitude to confuse mankind. 'It is an old piece of subtiltie of the old serpent', Goodwin noted in his tract, *M.S. to A.S. with a Plea for Libertie of Conscience* (1644), 'to oppose God in his saints . . . by teaching his Prophets and Agents to make parallels between; to sort and to suit Gods servants with his, and Gods wayes or workes with his'.[48] *An Apologeticall Account*, written in support of Goodwin in 1646, saw the danger specifically in man's difficulty in coping with the adrenalin of divine revelation. 'Knowledge and abundance of revelations', the author noted, 'are

[45] Burton, *Narration*, p. 42. [46] Goodwin, *Theomachia*, pp. 6–7.
[47] See also, *A Short Answer to A.S.*, p. 33.
[48] John Goodwin, *M.S. to A.S. with a Plea for Libertie of Conscience in a Church Way* (London, 1644), p. 39.

apt through the weakness of the flesh to puff up even the best of men.'[49] But for all this the godly should have the courage to explore religion's cutting edge. As Goodwin explained, 'Paul [did not] count it any disparagement to him, to preach that Jesus Christ was the Son of God, because the Devill had preached the same doctrine before him.'[50]

Goodwin's understanding informed his response to Thomas Edwards in *Cretensis* (1646). Goodwin characterised Edwards as a diabolic agent, but, remarkably, he did so by accepting, rather than refuting the vulnerability of the saints to demonic temptation. Satan was allowed by God to tempt the saints to 'sift' them and 'try them to the uttermost', and in collecting stories of their lapses, Edwards had diligently brought together 'all that drosse and beggery of weaknesses and infirmities, which Satan within the compass of foure years ... was able to sift out of them'.[51] Thus Goodwin accepted that *Gangraena* did relate cases of the temptation of the saints, and that they were guilty of 'failings and miscarriages'. But again this merely demonstrated that the godly were at the cutting edge of religion, where temptation could be expected to be acute. Edwards was taking advantage of the vulnerability to satanic assault brought about by intense piety, and churlishly exposing the saints' lapses to give the false impression that they were not of God. *Gangaena* was, in effect, a celebration of the efficacy of diabolic agency, and Edwards' role was 'to call the world together to see the nakedness of the saints, and to rejoice with Satan in his victories and triumphs over them'.[52] This emphasis on a realistic assessment of the saints' behaviour was perhaps incorporated by Goodwin into his pastoral and preaching approach at Coleman Street. At least those parishioners who composed *An Apologetical Account* in defence of their pastor were willing to concede that he might be fallible. 'Because', they noted, 'the knowledge of the most knowing attaines not perfection in this life (errours and misprisions being mixt with their choycest and purest notions) wee confesse tis possible that the structure he hath set upon this foundation is not all of gold, silver and precious stones: Perhaps somewhat of the nature of wood, hay, and stubble will be found in it.'[53]

In 1647 Goodwin composed a preface to his translation of Jacob Acontius' *Stratagemata Sathanae* in which he took the final step of effectively turning

[49] Robert Smith et al., *An apologetical account* (London, 1646), p. 2.
[50] Goodwin, *M.S. to A.S.*, p. 39. [51] John Goodwin, *Cretensis* (London, 1646), p. 1.
[52] Ibid. Goodwin's argument was answered by Thomas Ashe in *A Brief Narration* (1646) who noted that if the heresies of the Independents were to be considered no more than infirmities, 'the author might have taken in the old serpent himself into the catalogue of such saints'. See *A Brief Narration of the truth of some particulars in Mr. Thomas Edwards his Book Called Gangraena* (London, 1646), p. 6.
[53] Smith et al., *An Apologeticall Account*, p. 6.

the rationale of the Corinthians dichotomy on its head. 'There is no question', Goodwin noted, 'but that there are many vile imaginations of men ... which their fathers and friends have baptized in the names of New Lights.' But, he argued, Independency had revealed many ancient truths that were being stifled by the wholesale attack on religious radicalism. 'Men make no scruple or Conscience', Goodwin declared, 'to binde up God and Belial, Christ and the Devil together in one and the same bundle of condemnation, because they are alike troublesom and offensive unto them.' Since Satan's false doctrine was admittedly difficult to discern, it was those who were quick to throw 'Firebals of Granado's' at what they perceived as heresy that were most likely to attack Christ as well as Belial. Thus Acontius' tract was intended to act as a guide for Christians to be able to discern Satan's temptations, not only that they might be protected from diabolism, but that they might also avoid rejecting true revelation through intemperate anti-demonic zeal.[54] The third book of *Stratagemata Sathanae* contained a detailed discussion of how the spread of false doctrine might be countered without the unjust condemnation of the godly, which clearly appealed to Goodwin's sense of the relativity of the dangers of diabolic subversion and the overly-zealous enforcement of conformity. What was once a just method in extirpating heresy, Acontious explained, might assume a dynamic of its own which crushed all individuality of thought and expression. 'Verily', he noted, 'thou wouldst rather that no heretick had ever been punished, then that such tyranny should come to use.'[55]

THE INTERPRETATION OF SECTARIANISM IN THE 1650S

By the late 1640s, then, the understanding that diabolism could be a consequence of godly intemperance was firmly established in both conformist and nonconformist thinking. This is highly significant in gauging the reaction to the emergence of new sects during the final stages of the Civil War and during the Interregnum. The emergence first of the Ranters and then of the Quakers appeared to many commentators to mark a new high point in the diabolic subversion of the commonwealth. The idiosyncrasies of these groups did, as many historians have pointed out, appear to contemporaries to embody dangerous novelties that inverted nature and challenged order and religion. Accordingly, conformists attempted to dissipate this threat by associating the new sects with old enemies, and so make them comprehensible. Parallels between sectarians and Anabaptists, and sectarians and Catholics,

54 Jacob Acontius, *Darkness Discovered. Or the Devils Secret Stratagems laid open*, trans. John Goodwin (London, 1651), 'To the Reader.'

55 Ibid., p. 92.

were repeated in print ad infinitum, and the sectarians were presented as irretrievably diabolic. But again this was not simply an 'othering' discourse aimed at those conformists who could not, or would not, understand. The events of the previous decade had been unprecedented, and, as J. C. Davis and David Underdown have shown, the resulting social dislocation produced as many attempts to re-establish old certainties as to exploit new freedoms. But conformists demonised sectarians, not because they were incomprehensible, but because the Protestant tradition of interpreting intra-confessional dispute had provided a discursive framework into which new radicalism could be readily assimilated.

Thus, by 1650, the author of the anonymous pamphlet, *A Blow at the Root*, could present a complex picture of the relationship between intemperate godliness and diabolism which characterised sectarian experience. 'An over curious questioning of some things appertaining to Religion', he noted, 'disposeth to separation.' From there it was a short step to Anabaptism, thence to Seeking, to antinomianism, to Levelling, and finally into Ranterism. But even if this last marked out a new depth of heresy, sectarianism was a *tragedy* because it saw godly intent become caught up in a diabolic cycle. The sectarians' curiosity was the product of their desire (shared by mainstream Protestants) to redress their spiritual blindness. 'Against [curiosity]', the pamphlet's author conceded, 'no cleare evidence can be given.'[56] Sectarianism itself was, however, the result of a diabolic perversion of this search for spiritual knowledge. The thirst for novelty drove sectaries ruthlessly from one heresy to the next, despising each position in turn as they adopted a new one.[57] 'Satan acts not unlike your Machiavalian Statists', the author commented, 'that abandon and resume the same things (upon several pretences) as they discerne them to impede or assist their plots and designs.'[58] Sectarians were addicted to the excitement of novelty, a condition which allowed Satan to keep them addled with ever more extreme doctrines. Thus, in searching intemperately for spiritual enlightenment, sectarians were led through a fog of false doctrine into a blindness even more profound. 'There Religion finds us', the author observed, 'and (if we suffer him to misguide our religion) thither he will be sure againe to bring us.' Spiritual blindness was 'the Devils Alpha & Omega'.[59]

[56] *A Blow at the Root Or, some observations towards a discovery of the subtilties and devices of Satan, practised against the church and truth of Christ* (London, 1650), p. 154.

[57] Ibid., p. 153. [58] Ibid.

[59] Ibid.; *The Snare of the Deuill Discouered: Or, A True and Perfect Relation of the Sad and Deplorable Condition of Lydia . . . how she wantyng money the Deuil appeared to her in the shape of a man* (London, 1658), pp. 1–2; *Strange & Terrible Newes from Cambridge* (London, 1659), pp. 5–6.

Again sectarian activity was seen to parallel that of Catholic false doctrine. Through each the Devil subverted the individual's faith in the scriptures by undermining his reliance on them.[60] Catholicism offered mechanistic ceremonies instead of rigorous introspection; sectarianism offered ecstatic revelation in place of a life-long study towards assurance. In both cases satanic false doctrine actively maintained and accentuated spiritual blindness, cutting men off from the means to their salvation. 'He draws them into heresies and sects', noted a pamphlet of 1658, *The Snare of the Devill Discovered*, 'that thereby (having their eyes blinded they might not see the way of truth, and that which tends to their everlasting peace) he might entrap them into his claws.'[61] Thus the anti-scriptural stance of many sectaries was not simply offensive to the godly, it was a policy which involved very real personal risk. It threatened profoundly the central principle by which God could be better understood, Satan warded off, and assurance gained. Fundamental to Protestant devotional and pastoral practice, it was one of the principles the anti-sectarians believed had been hard won and it would be foolhardy to abandon.

In the early years of the Interregnum, of course, the Ranters epitomised the depths of perversity that such false doctrine could reach. The pamphlets of 1649–53 were in the vein of the anti-Adamite and anti-Brownist literature of the early 1640s, more concerned with sensational descriptions of Ranter behaviour than with a deconstruction of their origins and descent into heresy. But attention was paid to their temptation. A pamphlet of 1652, *The Ranters Monster*, recounted a monstrous birth in Essex, to a Ranter who claimed that she was the Virgin Mary and had immaculately conceived the child. Before coming to her miserable end, Mary Adams had followed the progression laid out in *A Blow at the Root*. She was described as a Christian woman, 'being a great frequenter of the Church, and a most excellent pattern of true holiness'. Adams 'fell off from these divine and glorious principles' and into Anabaptism. Before long she became dissatisfied with this and became a Familist. Almost immediately she took the next step into Ranterism, conceiving that there was no God or hell, and that female sexual freedom was enshrined in nature.[62] Marchemont Nedham's parliamentary newsbook, *Mercurius Politicus*, recounted a similar story of a godly man who descended into Ranterism and murder. 'It is (sir) a black relation', the correspondent noted, 'that one should live a Professor some years, as he did, converse with Gods people and pray among them and then to despise Ordinances, and from thence go to the Adamites; and then to fly out against

60 *The Devil turn'd Quaker* (London, 1656), sigs. A2v–A4 (irregular).

61 *The Snare of the Deuill Discouered*, p. 2.

62 *The Ranters Monster. Being a true Relation of one Mary Adams* (London, 1652), pp. 3–5.

God himself, and say there was none, no heaven, no hell, fall into wickedness . . . and afterwards that he should let Satan make this advantage by him.'[63]

The depths of Ranter heresy extended to the rejection of Satan himself. Commonly Ranters were attributed blasphemous declarations in which they denied his significance or his reality altogether. One was reported as saying 'that he knew not any difference betwixt God and the Divell; and being asked what he thought of the Divell, he answered that it was an old woman stuffed with parsly'. In their orgies Ranters were believed to drink the health of both 'their Brother God, and their Brother Devill'.[64] In its levity such behaviour was clearly intended, either by the Ranters themselves or by the pulp press writers, to be shocking. The stories certainly recalled the popular accounts of blasphemers that circulated in pamphlet and ballad form. But in the milieu of concern over false doctrine, such statements also represented an assault on the Corinthians dichotomy. The certain belief in a separation between good and evil, between the divine and the diabolic, had, as we have seen, been a central building block of the Reformation. From a position that all revelation, rational thought and experience must fit into one category or the other, a scheme of interpretation developed in mainstream Protestant devotion. Ranter flippancy threatened to undermine this fundamental principle. Thus the pamphlet, *The Smoke out of the Bottomlesse Pit* (1650), noted that the Ranters 'say that the Devill is the left hand of God, or the back part of God, or the dark part of God; that the Devil could do no evil at all, if God did not give him a power to do it, and therefore the Devil is not so much in the fault as men think he is'.[65] For mainstream Protestants, striving to overcome the limitations of man's corrupted spiritual insight, the confusion wrought by such a doctrine could be acutely dangerous.

The work of Colin Davis has injected a healthy scepticism into the assessment of pulp press accounts of the Ranters, and their calculated blasphemies may more accurately reflect the fears of mainstream Protestants than the doctrines of an irreligious movement. If so, these stories demonstrate how widespread the concern over false doctrine and the diabolic subversion of the revolution had become. But those identified as Ranters who left testimonies as to their beliefs claimed similar positions for themselves. Most notable was Jacob Bauthumley, whose quasi-pantheist theology allowed Satan no material reality, but rendered him an expression for 'the corruption of nature'. It was Bauthumley who coined the description of the Devil as part of the 'dark side of God', in his tract of 1650. Satan, he noted, had no being, but was the evil

63 *Mercurius Politicus*, no. 211, 22–29 June 1654, pp. 3584–3585.
64 *The Routing of the Ranters* (London, 1650), p. 2; *The Ranters Religion* (London, 1650), p. 5.
65 *The Smoke out of the Bottomlesse Pit* (London, 1650), p. 5; *The Arraignment and Tryall with a Declaration of the Ranters* (London, 1650), p. 2.

impulse that resided in all men, and every individual sin might properly be called a devil.[66] Since God was not a single entity, but infused all creatures, all must proceed from his will. Thus men 'receive evill from the hands of God as well as good'. Whilst Bauthumley attempted to maintain a conceptual separation between the divine, in which there was only light, and the carnal, which was prey to darkness, his pantheism forced him to contradict it by accepting that sin must be ordered according to the will of God. 'Sin abounds that grace may abound much more', Bauthumley concluded, noting that 'in some respect these also tend to the glory of God'.[67] The demonism described by Laurence Clarkson in *The Lost sheep Found* was in a sense incomplete, but similarly undermined the logic of the Corinthians dichotomy. Clarkson described his early terrors over his spiritual state in which he believed Satan was 'some deformed person of a man ... in so much that every black thing I saw in the night I thought was the devil'.[68] But as he became increasingly antinomian, he came to believe that the attempt to be separated from sin was misguided. 'I affirmed', he recalled, 'that there was no sin, but as man esteemed it sin, and therefore none can be free from sin, till in purity it be acted as no sin.' The attempted categorisation and separation of actions between the good and the evil was therefore a diversion from the true goal of spiritual progress, which was to be able to perform any action in a state of grace. 'Till you can lie with all women as one woman, and not judge it sin', Clarkson declared, 'you can do nothing but sin.'[69] Clarkson did not relate how his beliefs as to the reality or role of the Devil changed in line with this doctrine, but it was certainly a fundamental attack on the doctrinal system that was built on the Corinthians dichotomy, and the programme of the guided perception of diabolism that had developed since the Reformation.

The most significant body of religious polemic in the 1650s was, of course, that surrounding the emergence of the Quakers, and their successful missionising programme. Again, mutual accusations of diabolism were to the fore. The similarities between 'quaking' behaviour and symptoms of demoniacs was immediately apparent to the sect's critics, and Quakers were regularly denounced as witches in the pulp press. Their espousal of the inner light, which they claimed drove irresistibly all their behaviour, was also relatively easily equated with demonic possession. On the other side, Quaker belligerence towards the ministry caused them to adopt the language of diabolism as a means of critique. Ministers were the 'priests of Baal', and the servants of Satan and Antichrist. This material has, however, largely been assessed by historians in line with a concentration of the socio-economic impact of the

[66] Jacob Bauthumley, *The Light and Dark sides of God* (London, 1650), pp. 28–31, quotes at pp. 28, 29.

[67] Ibid., pp. 32–3. [68] Clarkson, *The Lost sheep Found*, p. 6. [69] Ibid., p. 25.

movement. Barry Reay, whilst acknowledging that 'we need not doubt the extent of the outrage that was provoked by the Quakers' theology', privileges the social threat – to magistracy and patriarchy in the eyes of the elite, and to occupational status quo in those of the populace – as the primary reason for anti-Quaker hostility. Dr Reay follows the (until recently) conventional understanding of the separation between elite and popular views of diabolism in his assessment of the belief in Quaker witchcraft. 'All talk of diabolism was limited to the elite', he notes, arguing that the more prosaic populous concerned themselves instead with Quaker *maleficium*.[70] Peter Elmer's subtle and detailed study of anti-Quaker witchcraft accusations argues that the sect replaced witches as the embodiment of disorder in the nation. This reflected a shift in the concerns of the magistracy from social disorder in general to the execesses of unbridled liberty in particular. But if so the *language* of witchcraft was becoming increasingly ill-equipped to successfully embody the threat.[71]

Whilst the social impact of the Quakers is beyond question, accusations of satanism against them should be understood in the context of the intra-radical contest over the identification of diabolic subversion. The Quakers were aggressive in their presentation of the ministry as the priests of the Devil, but this was rooted in a sophisticated demonism that emerged out of the experience of temptation and of the ministerial response to it. Their attacks on the ministry were aimed at the heart of its anti-demonic role. The ministerial insistence that sin and temptation were inescapable on earth, and that they could only be made manageable through a devotional scheme devised by themselves, was denounced by the Quakers as a plot aimed at maintaining people in a cycle of subjection to the Devil. The Protestant ministry felt this attack where it was aimed. They presented Quaker disruptiveness and Quaker magic as an assault on those who were a community's main guardians against satanic subversion – ministers, magistrates and the godly laity. In their efforts to remove the ministry, they argued, the Quakers were attempting to clear the way for the unbridled satanic corruption of the commonwealth.

Whilst Ranter 'demonism' was largely amorphous, and may have represented only the idiosyncrasies of a handful of extreme antinomians, Quaker beliefs about the Devil were consistently articulated as part of their pointed attack on the ministry. Quaker demonism was rooted in the established Protestant scheme in so far as it provided a means of interpreting the

[70] Reay, *The Quakers and the English Revolution*, chapters 3 and 4, see especially pp. 59, 68–9.

[71] Elmer, '"Saints or Sorcerer"', p. 176; see also Anthony Fletcher, *Reform in the Provinces: The Government of Stuart England* (New Haven and London, 1986), pp. 333, 352.

activities of their enemies. But it also radically overhauled the interpretation of the personal experience of temptation. The Quaker world view was one infused with the perception of diabolic activity.[72] They used the Corinthians dichotomy in arguing for a fundamental separation of the servants of God and of the Devil. 'For light can have no fellowship with darkness', James Parnell declared in 1654. For Richard Hubberthorne in 1656, the dichotomy justified the denial of the sacrament of communion. Quakers, he noted, 'sit at the table of Christ, and cannot sit nor have fellowship with the table of devills'.[73] They also joined their radical forebears in characterising all opposition to their belief as a diabolically inspired plot to undermine their Reformation. This became especially pointed in the face of the active opposition Quakers encountered from the established ministry. 'There is a company of priests', Parnell declared, 'in all parts of the nation where the truth comes, who are the Devills greatest agents, who are daily plotting and inventing, and scheming everyway to blot the image of God out of the nation.' The accusation of diabolism was levelled forcefully at specific enemies of the Quakers. Lawrence Clarkson was denounced as 'a lying Prophet, and a Messenger of Satan', in a pamphlet of 1659. George Fox's *The Distinction between a Phanatick Spirit*, published in 1660, ascribed characteristics such as 'fury', 'rage' and 'persecution' to 'Protestants and Papists' who had lost the spirit of the apostles and now 'give heed to seducing spirits, the spirit of the Devil'.[74]

Whilst this perception of being diabolically opposed was shaped by the negative reaction of the ministry, the Quaker definition of the synagogue of Satan was born of their concern over perfectability. The ministry, Quakers argued, in denying the possibility of being freed from sin on earth, were agents in a diabolic plot that sought to dissuade people from attempting to reach a full communion with God. Through the influence of the Devil's ministers, mankind was locked in a cycle of corruption that was the result of ministerial insistence on the fallacy that sin was every man's burden throughout life.

[72] *The Trumpet of the Lord Sounded* (London, 1564), pp. 3, 14, 16; *Caines Bloudy Race Known by their Fruit* (London, 1657), sigs. A2–A2v; John Harwood, *The Lying Prophet Discovered and Reproved* (London, 1659), sigs. A2–A3v; George Fox, *Our Covenant with God* (London, 1660).

[73] James Parnell, *The Shield of Truth* (London, 1654), sig. A2; Richard Hubberthorne, *A true Separation between the power of the Spirit, and the imitation of Antichrist* (London, 1654); Richard Hubberthorne, *Antipathy betwixt the Flesh and the Spirit* (London, 1656), p. 3; *The Trumpet of the Lord Sounded*, p. 3.

[74] Parnell, *The Shield of Truth*, sig. A2v; Christopher Atkinson, *The Standard of the Lord* (London, 1653), sig. A2; Harwood, *The Lying Prophet*, sig. A2; see also James Naylor's reply to Ellis Bradshawe, *The Railer Rebuked* (London, 1654); George Fox, *The Distinction between a Phanatick Spirit* (London, 1660).

The Quaker rejection of sin must be set in the context of this demonism. Barry Reay has described Quakerism as a reaction to the 'psychological *malaise*' of Puritanism. Many Quakers had, in their earlier lives, been imbued with the Puritan sense of sin and experienced profound fears concerning damnation. Their willingness to accept the possibility of perfectability for men on earth was an effective break with the cycle of doubt and despair, and, in Christopher Hill's terms, a repudiation of the insidious doctrine of sin which had long been an effective method of social control. But Quaker perfectability never denied the pervasiveness of the experience of diabolic temptation. Where their demonism departed from that of Puritanism was in asserting that freedom from temptation could be achieved on earth. Quakerism extended the logic of the standard Protestant conversion narrative to incorporate the discovery of the inner light as a watershed after which the Devil could no longer afflict the individual saint. But Quakers absolutely accepted and empathised with the experience of pre-revelatory temptation.

The significance of temptation to Quakers is clearly shown in the journal of their leader, George Fox. Actually an autobiography begun in 1674, the journal provides insights into both how the early experiences of Quakers shaped their demonism, and the place demological beliefs had in 'mature' Quakerism. In the first chapter of the journal, Fox recounted his early spiritual experiences which included long periods of profound temptation. These were indeed firmly within the Puritan milieu, as Fox described how he was assaulted from all sides by Satan, and in which the spiritual condition indicated by the experience of temptation was of greater importance than the specific sin itself: 'temptations grew more and more and I was tempted almost to despair, and when Satan could not effect his design upon me that way, then he laid snares for me and baits to draw me to commit some sin, whereby he might take advantage to bring me to despair'.[75] In the narrative of the journal these experiences were formative to Fox's Quakerism in two important ways. First, he described how he found the ministry entirely unable to address his condition. As we have seen, the Protestant ministry capitalised on their role as the keepers of the knowledge by which temptation might be resisted and made manageable. Fox, however, claimed to have encountered only unsympathetic or incompetent ministers. His meeting with the Warwickshire minister Richard Abel was typical: 'he was ignorant of my condition; and he bid me take tobacco and sing psalms. Tobacco was a thing I did not love and psalms I was not in an estate to sing.' Abel further betrayed Fox's confidence by telling his servants of his temptations 'so that it got among the milklasses'.[76] By 1674, of course, Fox was justifying the

[75] Fox, *The Journal of George Fox*, p. 4. [76] Ibid., pp. 5–6.

Quakers' long-established antipathy to the Protestant ministry, but it is significant that an inability to deal with temptation featured so prominently in his critique. There is no reason to doubt that Fox had indeed been unable to find comfort from the ministers he approached and that this influenced his thinking on the fundamental role of the ministry in the light of the revelatory experiences he was soon to have.

Temptation had a second, and connected, formative influence on Fox's acceptance of the possibility of perfectability for the saints on earth. His conviction that the individual's mystical understanding of God superseded the interpretive role of the clergy emerged as a direct consequence of his struggle with temptation. Fox found assurance, not through the devotional guidance of the ministry, but through direct revelation. In the depths of his suffering, 'Christ opened to me how he was tempted by the same Devil, and had overcome him and bruised his head, and that through him and his power, light, grace and spirit, I should overcome also.'[77] The exemplar of Christ's temptation had long been central to Protestant demonism, but as a scriptural proof that even the most faithful must expect diabolic assault. Fox's use of the exemplar was, therefore, a pointed departure from the mainstream Protestant script, since he also encouraged an emulation of Christ's victory over the Devil. Traditionally this was impossible since it was Christ's unique lack of sin that had enabled him to triumph. However, Fox overturned the established emphasis on the weakness of man to instead highlight the potential for a direct communion with Christ that would empower him over the Devil: 'Christ, the Word of God, that bruised the head of the Serpent the destroyer, preserved me, my inward mind being joined with his good Seed that bruised the head of this Serpent the destroyer.'[78] This reference to Genesis 3: 15 deliberately emphasised the strength rather than the weakness of man and woman in the face of the Devil. The scripture, in which God addresses the serpent/Devil who has tempted Adam and Eve describes the perpetual conflict that will ensue as a result – 'And I will put emnity between thee and the woman, and between thy seed and her seed; it shall bruise thy head, and thou shalt bruise his heel.' It was often used by Quakers to defend perfectability by claiming the possibility of a human victory over Satan, and indeed their quotations tended to omit that last part, in which the contest was evened out.[79]

Fox's revelation that the Devil might be conquered if man entered a purified state as a result of his communion with Christ contrasted sharply

[77] Ibid., p. 12. [78] Ibid., p. 13.

[79] See, for example, George Fox and James Naylor, *Severall Papers* (London, 1653), pp. 17, 22; James Naylor, *A Few Words occasioned by a Paper lately Printed, Stiled, A Discourse concerning the Quakers* (London, 1653), p. 3; Hubberthorne, *A true Separation*, p. 1; Parnell, *The Shield of Truth*, p. 29.

with his experience of ministerial instruction. His descriptions of his earliest experiences of the inner light centred on the understanding of the place of temptation that it revealed. Since the Reformation, Protestants had argued that man's spiritual insight had been wholly corrupted by the fall, and it was this that left him so vulnerable to Satan. Fox's revelation of perfectability told him that spiritual insight was re-established by the inner light, allowing a saint to clearly perceive the agency of the Devil. This accentuated the experience of temptation in the short term, but also provided the key to its defeat. Thus Fox noted of, experiencing the inner light: 'oh then did I see my troubles, trials, and temptations more than I had ever done. As the Light appeared, all appeared that is out of the Light, darkness, death, temptations, the unrighteous, the ungodly; all was manifest in the Light.'[80] In this revelatory communion, Christ entered into Fox as a 'refiner's fire and as the fuller's soap', bringing 'spiritual discerning ... by which I was able to discern my own thoughts, groans and sighs, and what it was that did veil me, and what it was that did open me'. Thus the spiritual confusion wrought by the Devil's influence on the conscience and the flesh, the very danger of temptation in the Protestant scheme, was dissipated by an internal divine intercession. Through the inner light Fox was able to see which parts of his conscience resisted godliness and which effected a communion with God. This second constituted 'the perfect principle of God in everyone', which now could be clearly contrasted with the 'false sighings and groanings' and the 'false asking and praying' that were manipulated by Satan. These corrupt aspects of man were not obliterated by the inner light; rather this state of 'perfection' was one in which full spiritual discernment allowed them to be kept in suppression by 'the perfect law'.[81] Perfectibility was, however, conditional. The faith provided by the inner light would free men from the 'law of sin and bondage', but only as long as they actively followed it. 'If ye look out from the faith', Fox warned, 'and from that which would keep you in victory ... ye will be brought into bondage to the flesh again.'[82] Thus, rather than an outright repudiation of the Puritan emphasis on sin and the power of Satan, Fox's devotional scheme accepted the virulence of temptation and its dangers, but offered the possibility of neutralising Satan's power over the corrupted conscience.

Differences over the possibility of neutralising Satan were, then, central to the Quakers' conflicts with the Protestant ministry. Fox immediately began to missionise following his revelations, in an overt campaign to spread his doctrine of perfectability as a means of freeing people from bondage to the Devil. Thus Fox described his converts as turning 'from darkness to light, and

[80] Fox, *Journal*, p. 14. [81] Ibid., pp. 14–16, quotes at p. 15. [82] Ibid., p. 17.

from the power of Satan unto God'. In response, he noted, 'the professors were in a rage, all pleading for sin and imperfection, and could not endure to hear talk of perfection, and of an holy and sinless life'.[83]

This picture of ministerial diabolism became an important aspect of Quaker polemic. James Parnell, in his pamphlet *A Shield of Truth* (1654), gave a full account of the demonic plot which centred around the ministerial emphasis on sin. For Parnell, it was axiomatic that man must be cleansed of sin before entering the kingdom of God. The failure to recognise this fact left men imprisoned on a treadmill, constantly seeking spiritual progress, but unable to understand its most basic prerequisite. 'Your Teacher', Parnell noted, 'which tels you, you can never get out of sin, nor be cleansed from sin, erres, not knowing the Scripture nor the power of God, but denies the end of Christs coming, and brings another doctrine which they have of their Father the Devil.' For James Naylor the purpose of the denial of perfectability was to 'darken the appearence of Christ in Spirit, that none may looke for it nor believe it, for the Devill knows that faith breaks his covenant'.[84] Parnell identified ministers as the deceivers of 2 Timothy 3: 6–7, who 'creep into Steeple-houses, and lead silly people captive'.[85] According to James Naylor, 'in the Temple of God [the Devil] sits in the hearts of the people', and 'he sets his ministers to preach Christ without, in literall tradition, that so he may keepe his house in peace'.[86] Thus the denial of perfectability was an effective denial of the power of Christ's sacrifice. Either Christ died to completely wash men free of sin, or he died for nothing. 'I shall put this querie', Parnell declared, 'whether Christ is but part of a Redeemer, or a perfect and full Redeemer, and which the place betwixt heaven and earth where man shall be more free or cleansed of sin, if it be not upon the earth, seeing that no unholy, nor unclean thing can enter the Kingdom of God.'[87]

The mainstream Protestant response to the Quakers is well documented. For the ministry the concerted missionising of the sect, and its unprecedented success in recruiting members, made it profoundly dangerous. They interpreted it as a millennial plague, in which the appearence of the false prophets predicted in Revelation demonstrated the extreme sinfulness of the times. The Quakers' willingness to openly challenge the ministry, appearing in churches and haranguing ministers in their own pulpits, was a highly disturbing break with the stereotype of the lurking sectary. Zachary Crofton, in the preface to a pamphlet entitled *Quakers Principles Quaking*, noted that

[83] Ibid., pp. 18–19.

[84] Parnell, *The Shield of Truth*, pp. 6, 29–32, quote at p. 32; James Naylor, *Satan's design discovered* (London, 1655), p. 16.

[85] Parnell, *The Shield of Truth*, p. 32.

[86] Naylor, *Satan's design Discovered*, pp. 4–5.

[87] Parnell, *The Shield of Truth*, p. 29.

the Quakers set 'aside [the Devil's] usual subtilities in down and direct terms, to damn all Sacred Order and Ordinances of God, under no pretence taking with a rational man, much les an understanding Christian'.[88] The extremities of Quaker behaviour was, of course, also a cause of great concern. The parallels between the group's ecstatic fits and the symptoms shown by demoniacs were obvious and were immediately made a mainstay of the attack on the Friends. And the social consequences of Quaker doctrine – which were manifested in the refusal to express deference to their betters – threatened to further undermine the ordered structure of society which had been dealt such a serious blow by the Civil War.

Whilst the diabolism of the Quakers was beyond question, the interpretive scheme of diabolic temptation and false doctrine demanded a certain empathy even with these extremist sectaries. 'We cannot but grieve', noted the authors of *A Faithfvl Discovery of a treacherous Design of Mystical Antichrist*, 'that many simple-hearted should listen to the voice of Strangers, who come in the Semblence of Christ, remembring that we our selves have been tempted, and some of our feet had almost slipped.'[89] Effectively the revolution had provided a new scheme of interpretation based on the assessment of the translation of reforming motive into godly innovation. 'We do confess', the authors, Christopher Feak, John Simpson, George Cokayn and Lawrence Wise continued, 'that there are many words of Truth, and some of precious concernment, that come from some of them, and sundry things which have an aim, as it were, and guesse, at the state of the Church, when the New Jerusalem comes down from Heaven.' But the godly exhortations of the Quakers were 'mingled with deceits' that were a symptom of diabolic subversion and which the Corinthians dichotomy prevented them from ignoring.[90] These considerations became central to the case of James Naylor who, in 1656, was brought before parliament following his triumphal entry into Bristol on a donkey. In assessing whether Naylor was guilty of 'horrid blasphemy', a number of prominent members of the Commons argued against a capital sentence on the grounds that the Quaker was languishing under an extreme temptation. Naylor, they argued, was a godly man who had been led astray by Satan. Thus, according to Thomas Burton, the parliamentary diarist, Lambert had on 5 December declared himself baffled by Naylor's conduct since, when he had served as his quartermaster, he had been a pious man. 'This may be a warning to us all', Lambert cautioned, 'to

[88] Ralph Hall, *Qvakers Principles Quaking, or, Pretended light proved darkness* (London, 1656), sig. A1v.

[89] Christopher Feak et al., *A Faithfvl Discovery of a treacherous Design of Mystical Antichrist displaying Christs Banners* (London, 1653), p. 1.

[90] Ibid., p. 2.

work out our salvation with fear and trembling.'[91] On 8 December, Major Audley declared that 'I think there is no man so possessed with the devil as this person is.' Lord Strickland agreed that Naylor was 'under the saddest temptation of Satan that ever was', and declared that he could not be considered a blasphemer because he had shown no malice towards God. 'I believe he is one of those that would sit at the right hand of God', Strickland continued; 'he has no evil spirit or malice in him against God; but he is under the sad delusion of the devil'. Because he was a victim of diabolic subversion, Naylor should be treated as a seducer of the godly, rather than a blasphemer.[92] Even those polemicists who rejected the notion that the Quakers had anything of value to contribute to the reformation could also see them as the victims of temptation. Zachary Crofton, writing a preface to the pamphlet, *Qvakers Principles Quaking* (1656), questioned utterly the sanity of the Friends, but noted 'they are to be pittied, not hated; they are to be prayed for, not preached unto, for the Devil which possesseth them, is such as can be cast out by no other means save fasting and prayer'.[93]

Quaker doctrine was a far more tangible threat than the amorphous beliefs of the Ranters, and polemicists were able to dissect it far more effectively to show its diabolism and identify the method of temptation that lay behind it and which ensnared the Friends' converts. Feak et al. laid out the conditions that had made godly men peculiarly vulnerable to the temptation to Quakerism. First, 'the badnesse and ignorance of many of the Ministery' provided a barrier to the desired communion with God, so that honest men listen 'to these who come as it were with the presence and power of God'. Further, as a consequence of the revolution, men 'are persuaded that God is doing some great and wonderful thing ... [and] come be perswaded there is some Divine thing among them'. Thus in a time of reformation 'the mind is put forward to meet the Temptation half-way'. Significantly they also noted that real advances in personal piety might accompany sectarian temptation. Those who had previously struggled with their godly discipline might, as Quakers, become personally more pious, appearing to affirm the truth of the sect's doctrines. 'Why may not Satan help on mortification', they noted, 'and a righteousness of works, for such an end as to take away the death of Christ as for us without us, and the hearing of the Faith?' Finally sectarian temptation could permanently damage men's spiritual reasoning. 'Once the mind is blazed', the writers declared, 'he shal read the Scriptures with such spectacles, that he'l think all the Scriptures confirm his way.'[94]

91 Thomas Burton, *Diary of Thomas Burton, esq., Member of the Parliaments of Oliver and Richard Cromwell*, ed. J. Towill Rutt (London, 1828), p. 33.
92 Ibid., pp. 54–6. 93 Hall, *Qvakers Principles Quaking*, sig. A2.
94 Feak et al., *A Faithfvl Discovery*, pp. 56–7.

These themes recurred in the anti-Quaker polemic. The recanting Quaker, John Toldervy, noted that in hearing ministers he had found 'nothing sufficient to edifie or learn me with knowledge, for in hearing I could not understand, in seeing I could not perceive, that any thing I ever saw or heard did proceed from a right understanding of the mind of God'.[95] The promise of freedom from sin attracted Toldervy to the Quakers; thus he welcomed his estatic fits as a palpable experience of absolution and victory over Satan. 'I was moved by the power of that Spirit in me, to shake', he noted, 'which manner of shaking I had long waited for; believing they were Effects, in order to the rooting out and perfect destroying of that being in me, which was of the Devil.'[96] Zachary Crofton agreed that the acceptance of the inner light could only result from the habitualised corruption of reason that resulted from the years of religious confusion. This, he noted, 'is no other than the enlightenings of the Prince of Darkness, darting out Scripture words without either sense or reason, and suited to the seducement of a people to whom by providence Scripture-language is grown natural, that no delusion will down with them that favours not of it'.[97] Seemingly miraculous feats of piety performed by the Friends, which did much to boost their kudos, might also be dismissed as diabolic. Thus Christopher Wade noted that their ability to fast should not seem strange 'for it is evident the Devil did feed a great many of witches, being the Quakers neigbours, in Lancashire, with inchanted dainty food, not substantial'.[98]

The picture of the Quakers as the mediators of the Devil's temptations was fleshed out in a handful of narratives of individual cases such as that of Toldervy. By far the most important and influential was the case of John Gilpin of Kendal, who published an account of his bewitchment into Quakerism, *The Qvakers Shaken: or A Fire-brand snatch'd out of the Fire*, in 1653. His story of how he experienced the inner light as a voice within him that prompted him to antinomianism, and eventually persuaded him to attempt suicide, became a cause célèbre for the anti-Quakers, being widely reproduced and referred to, and being sufficiently damaging to occasion several Quaker responses.[99] The background to the case is complex and

[95] John Toldervy, *The Foot out of the Snare* (London, 1655), p. 2. [96] Ibid., p. 28.
[97] Hall, *Qvakers Principles Quaking*, sig. A3.
[98] Christopher Wade, *Quakery slain irrecoverably by the principal Quakers themselves* (London, 1657), p. 8.
[99] Gilpin, *The Quakers Shaken*; Thomas Weld et al., *The Perfect Pharisee under Monkish Holiness* (Gateside, 1653), pp. 26, 41–3; *Quakers are Inchanters and Dangerovs Seducers. Appearing in their Inchantment of one Mary White* (London, 1655), p. 8; Wade, *Quakery slain irrecoverably*, pp. 7–8, 31–2, Richard Blome, *The Fanatick History, or An Exact Relation of the Old Anabaptists and New Quakers* (London, 1660), pp. 71–87; B. Nightingale, *The Ejected of 1662 in Cumberland and Westmorland* (Manchester, 1911), reprints the 'Explication' of the association of Cumberland and Westmorland, which makes

obscure. At some time previously Gilpin had been arraigned for drunkenness, and the pamphlet, which was published expressly for sale in Newcastle, may have been his attempt to re-ingratiate himself with his community. The veracity of his account was attested to by a number of prominent local men, including the mayor of Kendal, the local pastor and the master of the free school. Kendal in Westmorland was an important area in the early development of Quakerism, providing a number of its prominent writers and preachers, and was something of a centre of separatist activity for those in surrounding areas in Yorkshire, and Lancashire.[100] Thus Gilpin's narrative was perhaps a construction by which his spiritual autobiography was accommodated with the needs of a community feeling threatened by intensive local sectarian activity.

The account was a crystallisation of the emergent narrative of godly descent into sectarianism through temptation shaped by the disputes between revolutionaries. Gilpin's story was to illustrate that tiring of 'old truths' and desiring religious novelty made men 'very prone to close with the suggestions of the grand adversary of his soule'.[101] Curiosity motivated Gilpin to approach local Quakers and attend their meetings, at the first of which he heard Christopher Atkinson deny all ministerial preaching and ordinances, together with all notional knowledge of religion. Atkinson's words immediately undermined Gilpin's confidence in received religion. At a second meeting he was introduced to the notion of the inner light, an experience which he was told was the voice of God speaking inside the individual. This appealed to both his religious aspirations and his curiosity and he noted, 'I resolved in my thoughts to waite for the manifestation of these things within my self.' But Gilpin had been troubled by some words of the Quakers concerning Christ's redemptive power which he had thought blasphemous. Raising his doubts at a third meeting, he was met with opportunist cynicism on the part of the Friends. He resolved to leave if they were all of the same mind, 'to which some of them (after much whispering) answered negatively, wishing me not to let it trouble me; for he that spake so to me, was not rightly called'.[102]

Thus Gilpin's account demonstrated the insidious danger of diabolic false doctrine, which undermined long-held truths in order to more easily replace them with heresies and superficial ecstatic experiences. The parallels between the experiences of the aspiring godly and those of the experimenting

reference to Gilpin in its attack on the Quakers, see p. 102; the Quaker response was headed by Atkinson in *The Standard of the Lord*; other responses included George Fox, *The Great Mystery of the Great Whore Unfolded* (London, 1659), pp. 297–9, and Gervase Benson, *An Answer to John Gilpin's Book, Published in his name, and subscribed by the Priest of Kendal* (London, 1655).

100 Reay, *The Quakers and the English Revolution*, p. 9.

101 Gilpin, *The Quakers Shaken*, p. 3. 102 Ibid., p. 5.

sectary were highlighted in the narrative. Hearing Atkinson speak further of the inner light, Gilpin began to worry that he had not experienced it, and to suspect that this signalled his reprobation. 'I earnestly desired that I might fall into quaking and trembling' he noted, 'apprehending that I should thereby attaine to the immediate discoveries of God unto me.' This indicated how corrupted Gilpin's reasoning had become, and how given the sectaries were to 'distraction' and obsession. But it also appealed to the reader's empathy in understanding the desire for tangible spiritual progress. Gilpin's obsessive need to experience quaking would have been comprehensible to those mainstream Protestants who judged their own level of assurance by comparing it to that exhibited by others.

This need provided an opening for the Devil, since it undermined the vigilance over the conscience advocated by Protestant demonism. Searching for a palpable inner divinity allowed the Devil entry disguised as an angel of light. 'I thought something entered into my body', Gilpin described as the result of an intense period of introspection over his sins, 'which I perswaded my selfe (from Satans instigation) to be the Spirit of God descending upon me like a Dove, and entering into me.'[103] Gilpin now began a lengthy period of regular conversation with a voice that sounded inside him and assured him he was saved. He began to exhibit the strange symptoms of quaking/possession, including convulsive fits, paralysis and being suddenly able to play a violin.[104] But at various stages he was thrown into doubt and 'began to recollect myself, and so to question whether that power by which I had so strangely acted, were Divine, or Diabolicall?' When the inner voice attempted to persuade him to cut his own throat, saying 'open a hole there, and I will give thee the words of eternall life', Gilpin became convinced he was languishing under a diabolic temptation.[105] He now entered a daily cycle of assurance and despair, in which every time he recognised the Devil another voice appeared telling him that Christ was now in him and he had been exorcised.[106] Like Gilpin's desire for acceptance among the saints, this narrative was familiar to the Protestant devotional focus on the cyclical struggle with temptation that was the consequence of baptism. If it said more about the conventions of Protestant spiritual autobiography than the experience of the Quaker inner light, that was the point.

Gilpin was answered in a pamphlet by Christopher Atkinson, *The Standard of the Lord* (1653), which demonstrated the level of sophistication that the debate over Quaker diabolism could reach. Rather than dismissing Gilpin's narrative, Atkinson not only accepted that he had been possessed by

[103] Ibid., p. 6. [104] Ibid., pp. 6–10. [105] Ibid., p. 10.

[106] Ibid., pp. 11–15. For a similar case of Quaker possession, including an emphasis on the voice within and an attempted suicide, see *The Devil Turned Quaker*, sig. A5–A5v.

the Devil, but also that he had genuinely been a Quaker convert. Gilpin had had some true revelatory experiences, but had fallen back and 'under darkness again, having lost his guide, the Devil whispered to him to follow his deceits'.[107] Thus Atkinson accepted Gilpin's identification of the satanic voice within him. The Quaker leader answered Gilpin point by point, accepting virtually the entire narrative, but reinterpreting each aspect to show which illustrated his conversion and which his temptation. For example, Gilpin claimed to have received from the Quakers an urge to denounce the ministry, which he interpreted as a symptom of bewitchment. Atkinson was at pains to point out that this was in fact a working of God, and proved his conversion. In reinterpreting each point of the narrative in this way, Atkinson tranformed it into a detailed description of the conflict between godliness and the Devil within one individual, displayed in very rapid changes of supremacy. Gilpin described being thrown from his chair by a mysterious power, and then compelled to write with his hand on the ground. In his account both were diabolic actions, but Atkinson separated them, noting that the first was 'of God', whilst the second was a perverse action of Gilpin's reprobate will. This allowed him to emphasise the diabolic nature of Gilpin's experiences whilst utterly denying the latter's interpretation of the inner light.[108] Thus, for Atkinson, Gilpin's account did indeed illustrate the dangers of intense spiritual progress – it was the story of the Devil's successful subversion of the convert. 'That which was pure, was raised up in thee', Atkinson declared; 'the Devils malice was great against it: who did continually labor to bring it the death, which he did'.[109] This was a remarkably self-confident position to adopt, since it accorded the Devil a great deal of power, and allowed that Quaker initates might languish under extraordinary temptation. But it enabled Atkinson to produce an extended diagnosis of Gilpin's diabolism which, he argued, continued still. 'Thou thought the Devil had been cast out', he declared, 'but he is yet ruling in thee.'[110]

To opponents of the Quakers, the sect's concerted anti-scriptural and anti-clerical campaign was as disturbing as their seduction of the curious. Few Quakers denied the validity of the bible, but they did claim that the guidance of the inner spirit was ultimately above that of the scriptures. They were, of course, not the first radicals to do this, but their position appeared unusually threatening in the light of their attacks on the ministry. Their understanding of the dynamics of satanic subversion prompted the anti-Quakers to merge these aspects of their doctrine into a single diabolic assault on what they understood to be the community's protectives against the Devil.

[107] Atkinson, *The Standard of the Lord*, p. 6. [108] Ibid., p. 14. [109] Ibid., p. 12.
[110] Ibid., p. 15.

It is in this context that many of the accusations of witchcraft against the Quakers must be understood. The reported symptoms of Quaker bewitchment were very specific, focusing on its devotional consequences rather than on *maleficium*. Thus an abhorence of scripture was a common symptom, by which Quaker witchcraft created a barrier which screened off the victim from the influence of godly words or books, and so acted as a guarantor that false doctrine might infect the victim free from impediment. John Gilpin heard Christopher Atkinson denounce ministerial teaching, and immediately he was '*afraid* to reade any good Books, or heare any Preaching Minister, or call to remembrance any thing which I had formerly learned out of Gods Word, concerning God or Christ, or mine owne estate, or any other subject contained in Scripture'.[111] Richard Blome recorded a story about a woman in London whose drink was spiked by a Quaker. She found she was suddenly driven to attend meetings and that 'her mind was much turned against the Bible'.[112] The Quakers were believed to be able to bewitch by means of a variety of artefacts – such as potions and ribbons tied around the wrist[113] – but a frequent accusation was that Quaker books themselves bewitched their readers. This was how Gilpin's intense bout of distraction began. 'I perused a Pamphlet set forth by some of the same Faction being in York Castle', he explained:

> the main scope of it was against the ministry; immediately after, walking in my Bed Chamber, I began (as I had formerly desired) to tremble and quake so extreamely, that I could not stand upon my feet, but was constrained to fall down upon my Bed, where I howled and cryed (as is usuall with them) in a terrible and hideous manner, to the great astonishment of my family.

But Gilpin welcomed the experience of bewitchment, believing it demonstrated the truth of Quaker doctrine. Significantly, it gave him the confidence to attack the ministry himself. After his quaking subsided, he noted, 'I arose up againe beginning to rejoyce, thinking with my selfe, that now I could beare witnesse against the Ministers of England, as false Prophets and Priests of Baal.'[114]

The creation of this barrier extended to bewitching those who were the promoters of the orthodox Word. Blome recorded a story about a minister in Benefield near Durham who in 1654 was bewitched when he accompanied some friends to a Quaker meeting. When the minister rose to pray he found he could barely stand for trembling, a condition that continued until he

111 Gilpin, *The Qvakers Shaken*, p. 4, my emphasis.
112 Blome, *The Fanatick History*, p. 114.
113 *Perfect Proceedings of State-Affaires*, no. 283, 22 February – 1 March 1655, pp. 4491–2; *Strange & Terrible Newes from Cambridge*, p. 7;
114 Gilpin, *The Qvakers Shaken*, pp. 5–6.

started to pray.[115] In September 1659, Quakers in Sherborne in Dorset went even further. They reportedly bewitched to death the local minister, William Lyford, and tormented his successor until they drove him out of the town.[116] The Lyford case is difficult to trace from the references made to it, but the minister may have been a prominent local opponent of the Quakers. A commemorative pamphlet, printing his last three sermons, made no reference to the Quakers, but Lyford had, in 1654, published an assize sermon in which he exhorted magistrates to be proactive against divisive sectaries.[117] In the battle of doctrines, such *maleficium* represented far more than a mechanistic attack on the Quakers' enemies. As we have seen, the Protestant ministry regained much of the mediating power of the Catholic clergy by virtue of their devotional learning. In ideal at least, they became repositories of the information and scriptural insight which armed individuals against temptation. Thus the result of Quaker witchcraft could be a quite literal removal of the Word from a parish, stripping a community of its most obvious defence against false doctrine and the Devil.

There is evidence that this focus may also have been a significant part of popular concerns about Quaker witchcraft. A pamphlet of 1655, *Quakers are Inchanters and Dangerovs Seducers*, reprinted three depositions given in Norfolk concerning the bewitchment of one Mary White. All three, taken before local magistrate Edmund Harvey, emphasise the role of Quaker books in inducing White's distractions, which led eventually to her death. The case seems to have originated in a debate between the Quaker leader, Richard Hubberthorne, and a local minister over the resurrection of the body and the Trinity. Whilst Hubberthorne's words were offensive, it was his distribution of Quaker books after the meeting that particularly disturbed the community, and White's bewitchment appeared to confirm the power of these subversive artefacts. After hearing the Quakers speak, White, the wife of a bricklayer, became ill and believed she was diabolically possessed. Throughout her sufferings she was attended by her sister-in-law, Alice White, who read to her from Hubberthorne's books. 'He verily believeth', said the pamphlet reprinted from the deposition of another local bricklayer, Bartholomew Lenald, 'that upon hearing the said Quakers speak, and hearing their Books read, by the said Alice, the said Mary became altogether distracted or inchanted.'[118]

[115] Blome, *Fanatick History*, p. 109.

[116] The story of the Sherborne Quakers was first printed in an appendix in [T. Smith], *A Gagg for the Quakers* (London, 1659); and used in Blome's *Fanatick History*, p. 118; Reay, *The Quakers and the English Revolution*, p. 68; Elmer, '"Saints or sorcerors"', pp. 151–2.

[117] William Lyford, *The Matching of the Magistrates Authority* (London, 1654), pp. 8–9.

[118] *Quakers are Inchanters and Dangerovs Seducers*, p. 4.

Both the depositions and the pamphlet itself appear shaped and negotiated into a meaningful narrative of false doctrine. Quaker books were prevalent from the beginning of the case, but their importance increased as more evidence was taken. The initial deposition (on 14 June 1655) was made by William White, Mary's husband, who was present at the first meeting in his brother's house, when the Quaker books were read. But he was absent when Mary first became bewitched, and in his account the connection between the books and Mary's sufferings was implicit, if pronounced.[119] Further detail was provided on 27 June by an eyewitness, one Susan Green. She introduced evidence of Mary's resistance to Quaker missionising, noting that at first she had refused to listen to Alice's readings. According to Green, her intransigence attracted the special attention of Hubberthorne at the next Quaker meeting, to her great disturbance. The following day 'she spent much of the time in Reading a Book set out by the Quakers, which . . . added much to her trouble and distractions'.[120] Bartholomew Lenald was not an eyewitness but his evidence, taken on 5 July, consolidated the narrative with details from hearsay. Mary not only refused to hear Alice's Quaker books, but she was so disturbed by their blasphemies that she wept openly at their missionising meetings.[121]

Thus, as the evidence was taken, a narrative emerged that provided a dynamic and reason for Mary's bewitchment. Its basic elements were present in William White's initial deposition, and there is no reason to suppose that the causal connection between Quaker words (spoken and written) and Mary's sufferings was a court interpolation and not the result of his own observation. But the rationale for her bewitchment – that, like the ministry, she was a professed enemy and barrier to Quaker false doctrine – emerged only later. Indeed White himself believed his wife had been 'seduced' by the sectarians in his absence.[122] Similarly, the role of the Quaker convert, Alice, as a mediator of witchcraft emerged only in the later depositions. Seemingly a group frightened by the appearance of the Quakers in their midst found a narrative of (the now godly) Mary's victimisation a meaningful expression of the threat they felt to their community's established religious organisation. If so, then it appears that popular fear of the Quakers was as capable of centring on diabolic false doctrine as on economic and social disruption. The case made for useful propaganda. The pamphlet published the depositions in reverse order to privilege Bartholomew Lenald's consolidated narrative of the victimisation of the prominent godly. It also provided a brief introduction which highlighted the most important points of the narrative, stressing the insidious threat posed by Quaker publishing.[123]

[119] Ibid., p. 7. [120] Ibid., pp. 5–6. [121] Ibid., p. 4. [122] Ibid., p. 7. [123] Ibid., p. 3.

Throughout this study we have seen that the concept of the Devil in early modern England was imbued with an experiential reality that ensured that he could not be reduced to an oppositional symbol or discursive tool. The Reformation placed the threat of satanic subversion at the heart of politics and the church. Experiential certainty and the emphasis on hidden demonic agency allowed a wide latitude in the identification of its individual manifestations. Thus the Devil was an inherently politicised concept long before the breakdown of the English body politic in 1640. The intra-Puritan and Presbyterian/sectarian disputes of the Civil War years and the Interregnum demonstrate how acutely sophisticated demonism could be, even in the face of the massively extended range of uncertainties. Between the opposing sides of the Civil War, the concept of diabolic subversion explained, in a way which did justice to the political and religious complexities of the conflict, how the commonwealth had come to be riven apart. As the opponents became irredeemably polarised, the language of diabolic patronage and chthonian reward expressed their estrangement. Temptation, a discourse that implied negotiation, became less prominent in royalist and parliamentarian assessments of each other after the mid-1640s. By contrast, it was the mainstay of the intra-Puritan disputes of the decade, not only because it explained the emergence of differences between reformers, but because it was a way in which difference could be understood which was long established and which held a central place in Protestant culture. Temptation implied always that its victims might be freed and thus return to the fold. But, even more significantly, it rendered difference as a *symptom* rather than a *cause*. All men were tempted, and the godly possibly more than most. Wide differences of approach and even belief need not, then, detract from the recognition that all stemmed from a godly desire for reformation. Moreover, theology, history and experience taught Puritans that Satan sought to undermine reformation by mixing his false doctrine with the true Word. This encouraged, even demanded, a subtle engagement with difference through the careful separation of truth from heresy. The approach was not limited to disputes between the self-identified godly elite. The interpretation of Quakers as godly victims of temptation demonstrates that some were willing to extend it far beyond their own circle. Thus, far from being a semiotic failure after 1640, demonism gave meaningful expression to experience of difference in the Civil War and the Interregnum. It could embody both the sense of opposition of the armies and the separation over common ground felt by Puritans. Thus, rather than seeing the recourse to demonism as a desperate and impotent attempt to paper over the semiological cracks left by the Civil War, we should perhaps see the period as one in which a potent and sophisticated language was exploited precisely because of its expressive power and its ability to engage with difference.

Conclusion

This study has sought to demonstrate that the Devil in early modern English culture was neither a leftover from the medieval world, nor a half-way house on the way to a purely human concept of evil. Rather it was an idea that embodied a very real experience of struggle within the conscience, and a fear of hidden demonic subversion. Whilst the Enlightenment would eventually challenge much of the thinking that supported belief in the Devil, the sixteenth and seventeenth centuries did not see 'the Devil between two worlds', a concept living on borrowed time as its hold on the imagination became increasingly tenuous.[1] Stuart Clark has noted that within witchcraft the concept of the Devil did contain the seeds of its own downfall, as the emphasis on his power of illusion (a rejection of the preternatural powers of witches) brought into doubt the very identification of his 'real' agency, and undermined the ability to distinguish between wonder and miracle, in consequence 'subverting' preternature itself.[2] Whilst Clark is adamant that the decline of demonology was not a foregone conclusion, he notes that 'the category of preternature was sure to become unstable in early modern conditions'.[3] But as this study has shown, witchcraft was unusual within early modern demonism. It was an area in which preternatural power came under unusually intense academic scrutiny, and was contested in a way that the Devil's wider power to influence human affairs was not. As we have seen, the broad demonism which emerged out of the Reformation was largely unconcerned with the theodician and preternatural considerations which characterised the unstable demonology identified by J. B. Russell and Keith Thomas.[4] Instead it maintained a powerful hold on early modern minds because the reformed emphasis on internal temptation provided a means of engaging with diabolic agency in the commonplace, through the interpretation

[1] Russell, *Mephistopheles*, pp. 66–95. [2] Clark, *Thinking with Demons*, pp. 172–8.
[3] Ibid., p. 177.
[4] Russell, *Mephistopheles*, chapters 2–4; Thomas, *Religion and the Decline of Magic*, pp. 681–4.

of very real personal experiences, and vicariously through an empathic understanding of the experience of others. Early modern English demonism must not, therefore, be seen as a jaded notion that survived only because rationalism had not yet exposed its fundamental weaknesses. Rather it was a powerful belief which not only answered to experiences that were felt profoundly, but drew people into an engagement with religious and political areas in which Satan's agency provided complex means of understanding.

The driving force behind the reform of demonism was this experiential sense of the Devil's power, which took precedence over abstract theories as to his cosmic significance. As Protestants felt the Devil intimately in their lives, and believed they faced a profound demonic threat in the Catholic church, they did not react by trying to come to terms with the ultimate origin of evil, but rather concentrated on discerning the earthly significance of diabolism. Thus the traditional theodicy of Lucifer's rebellion was accepted by Protestants, but largely as a background to a far less theoretical demonism that was ideally to be based on personal experience.

This experiential sense defined the emphases of Protestant demonism. The identification of the contrariety of religion embodied in the Catholic church was the result of a long process whereby Protestant polemicists addressed the question of why the Roman faith had such a profound hold over Christendom. The answer was that the Devil took advantage of the corruption of man's spiritual insight to hoodwink his half-formed instincts to piety and hold him within an apostasy disguised as Christianity. The consequence of this conclusion was to focus attention on the relationship of diabolism and human perception. The sense of the weakness of the physical senses and the mental faculties to provide adequate insight into the spiritual within the world defined by extension the nature of the Devil's most formidable agency. Man's perceptual weakness was made the first principle of diabolic activity, the surest means by which the Devil exercised his power over humanity. Thus Satan's hidden influence on the conscience came to define his relationship with men over the external manifestations of his power which had traditionally comprised his remit of activity. Inherent in the identification of Catholic contrariety, therefore, were Protestant claims to a special insight into the workings of the demonic, which in turn contributed to the inverted self-definition which Peter Lake has argued characterised seventeenth-century anti-popery.[5]

But the emphasis on hidden demonic activity was more than a polemical device with which to attack the Catholic church. For popery appeared to reformers to be only the most insidious and widespread form of the diabolic

[5] Lake, 'Anti-Popery', p. 73.

agency which they felt to affect their lives and undermine their piety. Whilst their claims to special insight allowed Protestants to separate themselves from 'deluded' Catholics, it also provided a means of understanding very real experiences which profoundly affected their sense of self. The dislocation between the desire for godliness and impulses to sin or doubts as to election was for many an experience which was striking in its perversity, and seemingly uncontrollable in its insidiousness. It was therefore unsurprising that Protestants should relate so strongly to the notion of internal diabolic temptation. But it is a testament to the importance that they placed on the experience that they not only elevated temptation to be the single most important aspect of the Devil's agency, but sought also to transmit it within the liturgy and mainstream religious culture as the norm of man's relationship with the demonic. Thus the reform of baptism between 1549 and 1552 undermined the notion that Christian initiation constituted a victory over the Devil, and replaced it with an understanding that to enter the faith was to enter into a lifelong battle with temptation. Personal engagement with the demonic not only reflected a reality of godly life, it became enshrined as part of a Christian's duty.

But Protestantism was in no way hostage to the concept of the Devil. Whilst, as historians such as Paul Seaver and John Stachniewski have illustrated, the Calvinist emphasis on double predestination, and the faith's profound sense of the Devil, could produce obsessive and masochistic reactions in some individuals, this was neither the norm of Protestant demonological experience, nor an indication that the reformers had failed to provide effective measures by which Satan might be countered.[6] Rather, the Protestant focus sought to make the experience of demonic temptation manageable, since it denied the possibility of final victory. The characterisation of the experience of dislocation as a dialogue between the Devil and the conscience found its way into English Protestant devotional literature very early in its development, and in turn provided a programme for resistance which would continue to dominate demonological awareness into the late seventeenth century.[7] The soteriological fears that accompanied, and were part of, the experience of dislocation were used as the focus of the debate with the Devil, who was conceived as attempting to undermine assurance with threats of reprobation. Hence soteriological truths, and a sound understanding of the Devil's significance to the godly, became the most significant weapons an individual could employ against him. Temptation could be taken as a sign of

[6] Seaver, *Wallington's World*, pp. 14–44; Stachniewski, *The Persecutory Imagination*, pp. 17–126.

[7] For example, Becon, *The Christen Knight* (no date), and *the Governance of Virtue* (1543); Bradford, *Godlie Meditations* (1562) in *Writings*.

election, an indication that the Christian had truly entered into the conflict with the diabolic. It was a test by which God allowed the individual to demonstrate his faith, and Satan would never be allowed to overwhelm the godly. Protestant prayer, which rehearsed these demonological truths rather than requested intercession, embodied the correct response to temptation. Whilst it was more rigorous than the traditional recourse to quasi-magical protectives had been, and held less appeal to less zealous Christians, we should not doubt that Protestant demonism answered the needs of many of those who experienced temptation most profoundly, and that it was 'effective'. In placing such a heavy emphasis on the importance of religious knowledge and insight in resisting the Devil, the reforming clergy created a role for themselves as adepts and repositories of those skills. This new form of mediation replaced the traditional 'magical' role of the priest in which much of his kudos had been contained, and which had been stripped away by the Reformation.

Thus the culture of the zealous godly provided a natural setting for the emphasis on internal temptation. But the concept's ability to bring diabolic activity into the commonplace, and to encourage engagement with its possibilities, guaranteed Protestant demonism a far wider influence. The notion that a fragile subjectivity might be prey to satanic influence, and that the Devil's agency might be hidden within the commonplace, offered the potential for the extensive identification of diabolic activity. Sixteenth- and seventeenth-century demonisation was born, not only out of the projection of alien qualities onto others, but out of the monopolisation of the interpretation of the commonplace. Its force lay in persuading that the activities of others, whilst they might appear innocuous, effected a diabolic subversion of the commonwealth. Thus popular pastimes, such as the theatre or dancing, drinking or smoking, hoodwinked the unwary into an unwitting apostasy, and consecrated the location at which they were performed as a 'school' or 'chapel' of the Devil. The effect of these activities might be catastrophic, as Satan's temptations could lead men progressively into even greater sins, culminating in murder. The stress on the commonplace encouraged an empathy with the experience of diabolic temptation which served to lessen the gap between ordinary people and 'Devil-worshippers' or the grotesque criminals of the pulp press. But for the grace of God, all men were potentially the tools of satanic agency, and the understanding encouraged an engagement with the experience of temptation and a sense of its importance.

The dynamic of internal temptation, and the notion that Satan maintained a composite kingdom, made up of all those who had succumbed to his influence, provided a powerful analogy with which to comprehend the political fortunes of the commonwealth. A concept of the temptation of the body politic emerged in parallel to that of the human body. Again it drew its authority from the monopolisation of interpretation, providing a means of expressing dissatisfaction with central aspects of the political and religious establishment. This inherently politicised notion was employed by, as well as against, the Elizabethan and Stuart regimes. It was believed, for example, that the very existence of Catholic recusancy embedded in England a potential for demonic activity that might be activated at any time, and which was seen to have been so by the Gunpowder Plot and the papal breves which proscribed subscription to the Oath of Allegiance. Equally the maintenance of popish 'remnants' within the English church constituted another such potential to those who believed the Reformation had not gone far enough. The verse 1 Samuel 15: 23 – 'For Rebellion is as the sin of witchcraft' – has been used by historians to demonstrate the way in which demonology was used to bolster theocratic notions of consensus. But as this study has shown, it was not an isolated text, but one of a number that kept theocratic ideas in balance. Most notably, 2 Corinthians 6: 14–15 – 'What concord hath Christ with Belial?' – expressed the duty incumbent on theocracy to purify church and state, and established a powerful dichotomy which placed the potential for diabolism at the centre of political thinking. It justified criticism of the government, and, eventually, the taking up of arms against the king. But, importantly, for all that demonism might constitute a language of political engagement and even opposition, the emphasis on temptation always encompassed the possibility that its sufferers might be freed from Satan's influence. After all, to discount such a possibility was to deny the absolute sovereign power of God. It might also, then, be an important language for the negotiation of heterodoxy within the religious and political debates of the period.

Thus it is apparent that demonism in sixteenth- and seventeenth-century England was not an outmoded concept. The emergence of scientific rationalism, with its consequences for Enlightenment thinking on evil, may have provided an ultimately fatal blow to the Devil's previously unassailed position in Christian thinking. But this was largely a sign that developments had overtaken the concept, rather than that it was no longer able to effectively embody people's sense of evil. For arguably the Protestant emphasis on internal temptation made demonism much more sophisticated with its demands for an engagement with demonic possibilities within the commonplace, and within the individual conscience. It brought the experience of diabolic activity more intimately into the lives of those who accepted its monopoly of interpretation. Satan's agency was no longer mediated through the alien and the 'other', where, if his power was taken to be very real, it was reassuringly easy to identify. Fears of the demonic might be focused on identifiable groups, such as Catholics, criminals or religious radicals, but (with the exception of witches) accepting their diabolism rested on the understanding that satanic temptation, an experience which *all* humanity shared, had subverted their consciences and led them into apostasy. Whilst for many such identification must have been unproblematic, the emphasis on internal temptation undermined more widely the certainty of contrariety. As this study has shown, in order to appeal to the fear of 'the world turned upside down', the contrariety of God's ape had often to be painstakingly constructed and argued for, and its identification could be highly contentious. As a result, the perception of demonic agency was highly personalised, resting not on a functionalist projection of evil onto marginalised figures, but on an informed engagement with the possibilities of diabolism within the conscience and the body politic. Hidden subversion was perhaps even more threatening than open contrariety.

If the reform of demonism was theologically driven, and involved a process of acculturation in the redrawing of liturgical, devotional and discursive norms, its success seems to have lain in the fact that it provided a demonological understanding as sophisticated as people's own experiences. For the experience of temptation was widely recognised and identified with, and it potentially provides insights into, the contentious subject of 'inwardness' in the Renaissance. Literary scholars, balancing textual evidence of self-speaking with a New Historicist suspicion of essentialist assumptions about human nature and experience, have debated whether early modern culture had a sense of the privileged inner self.[8] The criterion by which subjectivity is identified is whether evidence can be found for a discourse which privileges the interior self over outward presentation. Some, such as Francis Barker and Catherine Belsey, have been sceptical. More recently evidence has been shown for such a privileged interiority in early modern England – perhaps even that 'the sense of discrepancy between "inward disposition" and "outward appearance" seems unusually urgent and consequential for a very large number of people'.[9] But the prevalence of internal temptation is suggestive of a potential for an even more complex concern over subjectivity. Since the Devil's intrusions into the mind were effectively disguised as ordinary thoughts, the individual could be hoodwinked into sin by believing them to be an expression of his inner nature. To the godly who felt temptation most keenly, and to the moralists who used it to construct didactic narratives of human frailty, the Devil threatened to turn the inner self into the traitor to the soul. If the logic of temptation was followed, the internal self could no longer be trusted to be the true self. This was a quandary that found widespread

[8] Katherine Eisaman Maus, *Inwardness and the Theatre in the English Renaissance* (Chicago, 1995); Francis Barker, *The Tremulous Private Body* (New York, 1984); Catherine Belsey, *The Subject of Tragedy: Identity and Difference in Renaissance Drama* (New York, 1985); Richard Hillman, *Self-speaking in Medieval and Early Modern English Drama: Subjectivity, Discourse and the Stage* (Houndmills, 1997).

[9] Maus, *Inwardness and the Theatre*, p. 13.

expression in constant theological exhortations to vigilance over the conscience, in the despairing confusion of the aspiring godly struggling to decide whether their innermost thoughts indicated election or damnation, and in moralistic literature which sought to bring home the danger of the Devil's subversion by encouraging readers to empathise with the temptation of the criminals it depicted. Fear of the 'other' might be perennial in demonological beliefs, but perhaps the defining characteristic of the reformed demonism in early modern English culture was the fear of the subversion of oneself.

Thus the decline of belief in the Devil cannot be attributed to a fundamental weakness in the concept's ability to express people's sense of evil. The *philosophes* argued that Satan was a childish, animistic expression for evil, which shielded men from the need to engage with the darker potential in humanity. But this was a stereotype which barely reflected the reality of sixteenth- and seventeenth-century demonism. Such arguments were polemical rather than anthropological, but they have influenced the history of the emergence of rationalism. Whilst historians such as Russell and Thomas have been wary of taking the crusading self-presentation of the Enlightenment at face value, they have accepted that the Devil was 'the most vulnerable part of theology' which allowed an opening for the attack of the new philosophies.[10] Rather than recognising that the concept maintained a powerful hold because it allowed people a sophisticated engagement with an experience of evil which they felt profoundly, historians still prefer to imply that mankind was 'freed' from the belief in the Devil.[11] But moving beyond the areas of witchcraft and theodicy has identified important areas of demonism which should raise new questions as to the certainty of the picture of the Devil's demise. For whilst the political fortunes of witchcraft undermined its credibility, and the philosophical attack on the principle of evil forced Christian theologians onto the defensive, the Devil maintained a hold in many of the areas we have examined.[12] Far from being discredited by the Civil War, the concept of diabolic subversion was of central importance to the polemical reaction to the Popish Plot in 1678, as demonstrated by the enormous number of prints and ballads that were produced illustrating Catholic diabolism.[13] Moreover, the notion of demonic Catholicism

[10] Russell, *Mephistoheles*, pp. 128–30.

[11] Thomas, *Religion and the Decline of Magic*, pp. 681, 692–4.

[12] On the decline of witchcraft, see Ian Bostridge, 'Witchcraft Repealed', in J. Barry, M. Hester and G. Roberts (eds.), *Witchcraft in Early Modern Europe* (Cambridge, 1996), pp. 309–34.

[13] See F. G. Stephens, *Catalogue of Political and Personal Satires preserved in the Department of Prints and Drawings in the British Museum*, vol. I: *1320–1689* (London, 1978), pp. 603–22, 632–63; *Londons Drollery: or, The Love and Kindness between the Pope and the Devil* (no date), in Roxburghe Collection, vol. II, p. 292; *A View of the Popish-plot; or, A Touch of the Cunning Contrivance of the Romish Faction* (London, 1689); *The Downfall of Popery; or, the Distressed Jesuits in Flight* (no date), in *Pepys Ballads*, vol. II, pp. 281–2.

maintained a powerful hold throughout the eighteenth century, with effigies and representations of the Devil being an important part of the pope-burning demonstrations which commonly accompanied national festivities.[14] The wider danger of diabolic disguise and the satanic subversion of the commonplace continued to trouble the godly with the possibility that man's corrupted religiosity might be fatally distracted by Satan. Thus in the early decades of the eighteenth century the polemical attack on the diabolic stage was renewed with all the vigour William Prynne had been able to muster in the 1630s.[15] Finally, despite the challenge of rationalism, the notion of internal temptation continued to exercise a hold in the Protestant devotional scheme. It remained a significant aspect of the fundamentals of Christian knowledge, and continued to warn and edify from the pulpit.[16]

Similarly, the Protestant emphasis on the Devil's power to intrude into the consciousness should not be interpreted, as Jeffrey Burton Russell would see it, as evidence of a greater concern with the purely human potential for evil, forced to rely on the Devil for its expression until the Enlightenment provided a new language more capable of encompassing conflicting psychological experiences. For internal temptation in early modern culture was not used as a metaphor but as the description of a real event. We should be wary of imposing psychological explanations on a culture that would not have recognised them. Whilst the inhabitants of early modern England were as capable of diagnosing delusion as diabolism, their inclination was to accept the possibility (if not always the certainty) that the experience of internal conflict or dislocation, or the sense that the commonwealth was being subverted by a hidden agency, *was* the experience of the Devil.

[14] Colin Haydon, '"I love my King and my Country, but a Roman Catholic I Hate": Anti-Catholicism, Xenophobia and National Identity in Eighteenth-Century England', in T. Claydon and I. McBride (eds.), *Protestantism and National Identity: Britain and Ireland, c.1650–c.1850* (Cambridge, 1998), pp. 42–3.

[15] Arthur Bedford, *The Evil and danger of Stage-Plays: Shewing their Natural Tendency to Destroy Religion* (London, 1706), pp. 41–53, 195; Arthur Bedford, *A Serious Remonstrance in Behalf of the Christian Religion, against the Horrid Blasphemies and Impieties which are still used in the English Play-Houses* (London, 1719), pp. 1–98.

[16] Samuel Clarke, *An Exposition of the Church-Catechism* (London, 1730), pp. 19–24, 266–72, esp. p. 269; George Whitefield, *Satan's Devices: A Sermon Preached at Great St. Helens* (London, 1739), and George Whitefield, *The Eternity of Hell Torments. A Sermon Preached at Savannah in Georgia* (London, 1738).

BIBLIOGRAPHY

PRIMARY SOURCES

An account of the tryal and examination of Joan Buts, For being a Common Witch and Inchantress (London, 1682).

Acontius, Jacob, *Darkness Discovered. Or the Devils Secret Stratagems laid open*, trans. John Goodwin (London, 1651).

Ainsworth, Henry, *Counterpoyson* (London, 1642).

Allen, Hannah, *[Satan his Methods and Malice baffled.] A Narrative of God's gracious dealings with that choice Christian Mrs. Hannah Allen* (London, 1683).

Allington, John, *The devilish conspiracy, hellish treason, haethenish condemnation, and damnable murther, committed, and executed by the Jewes against the anoynted of the Lord Christ their King* (London, 1649).

Ancient Songs and ballads; Written on Various Subjects, and Printed between the Yeares MDLX and MDCC. Chiefly collected by Robert Earl of Oxford (London, The Roxburghe Collection, arranged and bound 1774).

Androtius, Fulvius, *Certaine Devout considerations of the Frequenting of the Blessed Sacrament* (Douai, 1615).

The Apprehension and confession of three notorious Witches. Arreigned and by Justice condemned and executed at Chelmes-forde, in the Countye of Essex (London, 1589).

The Araignment & Burning of Margaret Ferne-seede, for the Murther of her late Husband Anthony Ferne-seede, found dead in Peckham Field neere Lambeth, having once attempted to poyson him with broth, bring executed in S. Georges Field the 1st of Februarie, 1608 (London, 1608).

The Araignment, Examination, Confession and Iudgement of Arnold Cosbie: Who wilfully Murdered the Lord Burke, neere the Towne of Wandsworth, on the 14. Day of this present Month of Ianuary and was executed the 27 of the same moneth 1591 (London, 1591).

Arias, Francis, *The Litle Memorial, concerning the Good and Frvitful Vse of the Sacraments* (Rouen, 1602).

The Army's declaration: being a True Alarum in answer to a False and Fiery one made lately, by a Member of that detestable Rump (?London, 1660).

The Arraignment and execution of the Late Traitors (1606), in *The Harleian Miscellany*, vol. III.

The Arraignment and Tryall with a Declaration of the Ranters (London, 1650).

Ashe, Thomas, *A Brief Narration of the truth of some particulars in Mr. Thomas Edwards his Book Called Gangraena* (London, 1646).

Aske, James, *Elizabetha Trivmphans. Contayning the Damned Practices, that the diuelish Popes of Rome haue used euer sithence her Hignesse first coming to the Crowne* (London, 1588).

Atkinson, Christopher, *The Standard of the Lord* (London, 1653).

B., J., *Anthropometamorphosis: Man Transformed; or, the artificial Changeling. Historically presented, In the mad and cruel Gallantry ... and Loathsome Louelinesse of most nations, fashioning & altering their Bodies from the Mould intended by Nature* (London, 1650).

Bale, John, *The Actes of English Votaries, Comprehendynge their unchast practices and examples by all ages, from the worlds beginning* (London, 1560).

Select works: containing the examinations of Lord Cobham, William Thorpe and Anne Askewe, and the Image of both churches, ed. H. Christmas (Cambridge, Parker Society, 1849).

Bancroft, Richard, *Dangerovs Positions and Proceedings, published and practiced within this Iland of Brytaine, under pretence of Reformation, and for the Presbiteriall Discipline* (London, 1593).

Bargrave, Isaac, *A Sermon Preached before the Honourable Assembly; of the Knights, Cittizens, and Burgesses, of the Lower House of Parliament: February the last 1623* (London, 1624).

A Sermon Preached before King Charles, March 27, 1627, being the Anniversary of his Maiesties Inauguration (London, 1627).

Barlow, William, *The Sermon Preached at Paules Crosse, the tenth day of Nouember, being the next Sunday after the Discouerie of this late Horrible Treason* (London, 1606).

Barnes, Barnabe, *The Divils Charter* (London, 1607).

Barrington Family Letters 1628–1632, ed. A. Searle, Camden Society, fourth series, 28 (1983).

Barrow, Henry, *The Writings of Henry Barrow 1587–1590*, ed. L.H. Carlson (London, 1962).

Bastwick, John, *The answer of Iohn Bastwick, Doctor of Physicke, to the exceptions made against his Letany by A learned Gentleman* (?Amsterdam, 1637).

Bateman, Stephen, *The Crystal Glasse of the Christian Reformation* (London, 1569).

Bauthumley, Jacob, *The Light and Dark sides of God* (London, 1650).

Baxter, Richard, *Gods Goodness Vindicated for the help of such (especially the melancholy) as are tempted to deny it, and think him Cruel, because of the Present and Future Misery of Mankind; with respect to the Doctrine of Reprobation and Damnation* (London, 1671).

Reliquiae Baxterianae: or, Mr Richard Baxters narrative of the most memorable passages of his life and times (London, 1696).

A Christian Directory: Or, a summ of Practical Theology, and cases of conscience. Directing Christians, how to use their knowledge and faith; how to improve their helps and means, and to perform all duties; how to overcome temptations and to escape and mortifie every sin (1673), in *Practical Works*, 4 vols. (London, 1707), vol. I.

Bayly, Lewis, *The Practice of Pietie: Directing a Christian how to walke that he may please god. Amplified by the Author. The last and most corrected edition* (Edinburgh, 1635; first edn, 1615).

Beard, Thomas, *The Theatre of Gods jvdgements: reuised, and augmented. Wherein is represented the admirable justice of God against all notorious sinners, both great and small; but especially against the most eminent persons of the world, whose transcendent power breaketh throrow the barres of humane iustice; deduced by order of the Commandments* (London, 1631; first edn, 1597).

Becon, Thomas, *Early Works*, ed. J. Ayre (Cambridge, Parker Society, 1844).

The Catechism of Thomas Becon, with other pieces, ed. J. Ayre (Cambridge, Parker Society, 1844).

Prayers and Other Pieces of Thomas Becon, ed. J. Ayre (Cambridge, Parker Society, 1844).

Bedford, Arthur, *The Evil and danger of Stage-Plays: shewing their Natural Tendency to Destroy Religion and Introduce a general Corruption of Manners* (London, 1706).

A Serious Remonstrance in Behalf of the Christian Religion, against the Horrid Blasphemies and Impieties which are still used in the English Play-Houses (London, 1719).

Bellarmine, Robert, *An Ample Declaration of Christian Doctrine* (Rouen, 1604).

The Art of Dying Well (St Omer, 1622).

Benson, Gervase, *An Answer to John Gilpin's Book, Published in his name, and subscribed by the Priest of Kendal* (London, 1655).

Bernard, Nicholas, *The Life & Death of the most reverend and learned father of our church Dr. James Usher, late Arch-bishop of Armargh, and Primate of all Ireland. Published in a sermon at his funeral at the Abbey of Westminster, Aprill 17. 1656* (London, 1656).

Bernard, Richard, *Look beyond Luther: Or An Answer to that qvestion so often and so insultingly proposed by our adversaries, asking vs; where our Religion was before Luthers time?* (London, 1624).

Bethel, Slingsby, *The World's Mistake in Oliver Cromwell; or, A short Political Discourse, shewing, that Cromwell's Mal-administration, (during his Four Years, and Nine Moneths pretended Protectorship,) layed the Foundation of our present Condition, in the Decay of Trade* (London, 1668).

The Birth of Merlin: or, The Childe hath found his Father (London, 1662).

A Blazing Starre seene in the West at Totnets in Devonshire (London, 1642).

Blome, Richard, *The Fanatick History, or An Exact Relation of the Old Anabaptists and New Quakers* (London, 1660).

A Bloody Plot, Practiced by some Papists in Darbyshire (London, 1641).

The Bloody Prince, or a declaration of the most cruell Practices of Prince Rupert, and the rest of the Cavaliers (London, 1643).

The Bloudy Book, or the tragicall and desperate end of Sir Iohn Fites (alias) Fitz (London, 1605).

A blow at the root. Or, some observations towards a discovery of the subtilties and devices of Satan, practised against the church and truth of Christ (London, 1650).

The Boke of common praier, and adminstracion of the sacramentes, and other rites and ceremonies in the Church of Englande (London, 1552).

Bolton, Robert, *Instructions for a Right comforting afflicted consciences: with a speciall antidote against some grievous temptations: delivered for the most part in the lecture at Kettering in Northamptonshire* (London, 1631).

The last conflicts and death of Mr Thomas Peacock, Batchelour of Divinity, and fellow of Brasen-nose Colledge in Oxford (London, 1646).

The booke of the common prayer and adminstracion of the sacramentes, and other rites and ceremonies of the ... Church of Englande (London, 1549).

Boys, John, *An Exposition of the festivall Epistles and Gospels vsed in our English Liturgie. Together with a reason why the Church did chuse the same* (London, 1615).

Bradford, John, *The Writings of John Bradford ... containing sermons, meditations, examinations, & c.*, ed. A. Townsend (Cambridge, Parker Society, 2 vols., 1848–53).

Bradshaw, Ellis, *A Dialogue between the Devil & Prince Rupert, written at the Leaguer before Chester upon Ruperts coming to relieve the said City* (London, 1648).

Breton, Nicholas, *The Works in Verse and Prose of Nicholas Breton*, ed. A. B. Grosart (New York, 1966).

Bridge, William et al., *The Apologetical Narration* (London, 1644).

A Brief discovrse of the Christian life and death, of Mistris Katherin Brettergh ... with the manner of a bitter conflict she had with Satan, and blessed conquest by Christ, before her death, to the great glorie of God, and the comfort of all beholders (London, 1602).

A Briefe discourse of two most cruell and bloudie Murthers (London, 1583).

A Briefe narration of the possession, dispossession, and, repossession of William Somers: and of some proceedings against Mr John Dorrell preacher, with aunswers to such observation as are made to probe the pretended conterfieting of the said Sommers (?Amsterdam, 1598).

A Brief relation of certain special and most material Passages and Speeches in the Star-Chamber; occassioned and delivered June the fourteenth, 1637, at the censure of those three worthy Gentlemen, Dr Bastwicke, Mr Burton, and Mr Prynne (1637), in *The Harleian Miscellany*, vol. IV.

The British Bellman. Printed in the year of the saints fear (1649), reprinted in *The Harleian Miscellany*, vol. VI.

Broughton, Hugh, *A Concent of Scripture* (London, 1590).

Bruno, Vincent, *A Short Treatise of the Sacrament of Penance* (London, 1605).

Bucer, Martin, *Censura*, in *Martin Bucer and the Book of Common Prayer*, ed. E. C. Whitaker (Great Wakering, 1974).

Bullinger, Heinrich, *The Decades of Henry Bullinger, minister of the Church of Zurich*, ed. T. Harding (Cambridge, Parker Society, 5 vols., 1849–52).

Bunyan, John, *Grace abounding to the chief of sinners*, ed. R. Sharrock (Oxford, 1962).

Burges, Cornelius, *The First Sermon preached to the honourable House of Commons now assembled in Parliament at their Publique Fast* (London, 1641).

Another Sermon Preached to the Honourable House of Commons now assembled in Parliament, November the Fifth, 1641 (London, 1641).

Burton, Henry, *Englands Bondage and Hope of Deliverance* (London, 1641).

The protestation protested, or, A short remonstrance shewing what is principally required of all those that have or doe take the last Parliamentary protestation (London, 1641).

A Narration of the Life of Mr Henry Burton (London, 1643).

Burton, Thomas, *Diary of Thomas Burton, esq., Member of the Parliaments of Oliver and Richard Cromwell*, ed. J. Towill Rutt (London, 1828).

Caines Bloudy Race Known by their Fruit (London, 1657).

Calamy, Edmund, *The Noble-mans patterne of true and reall Thankfulnesse* (London, 1643).

Calfhill, James, *An Answer to John Martiall's Treatise of the Cross*, ed. R. Gibbings (Cambridge, Parker Society, 1846; first edn, 1565).
Calvin, John, *The Institutes of Christian Religion*, 2 vols., trans. H. Beveridge (Grand Rapids, Mich., 1989).
Camus, Jean-Pierre, *A Spirituall Combat* (Douai, 1632).
Capel, Richard, *Tentations: their nature, danger and cure* (London, 1633).
Capel's Remains (London, 1658).
Carmina Colloquia: Or, A Demonaicall and Damnable Dialogue; between the Devil & an Independant (London, 1649).
Carter, William, *Isreals peace with God, Beniamines Overthrow* (London, 1642).
Cartwright, Thomas, *Cartwrightiana*, ed. A. Peel and L. H. Carlson (London, 1951).
Case, Thomas, *Gods Rising His Enemies Scattering* (London, 1644).
Castaniza, John, *The Spiritual Conflict* (Douai, 1603; first edn, 1598).
Cawdrey, Daniel, *Hvmiltie, the saints liuerie; or the habit of hvmilitie, the grafe of graces: fetched out of the wardrobe of Saint Paul* (London, 1624).
Certain Sermons or Homilies appointed to be read in Churches in the time of Queen Elizabeth, ed. J. Griffiths (London, 1908).
'The Character of a Protector', verse libel recorded by George Thomason, British Library, Thomason Tracts, E. 734 (2).
Cheynell, Francis, *Sions Momento, and Gods Alarum* (London, 1643).
Chidley, Katherine, *The Iustification of the Independent Churches of Christ* (London, 1641).
The Christian Life and Death of Mistris Katherin Brettergh (London, 1612).
Clarke, John, *The Plotters unmasked, murderers no saints, or, a word in season to all those that were concerned in the late rebellion* (London, 1660).
Clarke, Samuel, *The Lives of Thirty-two English Divines, famous in their generations for Learning and Piety, and most of them suffered in the cause of Christ* (London, 1677).
The Lives Of sundry Eminent Persons in this Later Age. In Two Parts, I. Of Divines. II. Of Nobility and Gentry of both Sexes (London, 1683).
An Exposition of the Church-Catechism (London, 1730).
Clarkson, Laurence, *The Lost sheep Found: or, The Prodigal returned to his Fathers house* (London, 1660).
Clavell, John, *A Recantation Of An Ill Led Life: Or, A Discoverie of the High-way Law* (London, 1634).
Clay, W.K. (ed.), *Liturgical services: Liturgies and occasional forms of prayer set forth in the reign of Queen Elizabeth* (Cambridge, Parker Society, 1847).
Clemen, Cotton, *A large and complete concordance to the Bible in English, According to the last translation* (London, 1643).
Coachman, Robert, *The cry of a stone, or, a treatise; shewing what is the right matter, forme, and government of the visible church of Christ* (London, 1642).
Commons Debates 1628, ed. R.C. Johnson, M. Jansson Cole, M. Frear Keeler and William B. Bidwell (New Haven and London, 4 vols., 1977–8).
Complete Collection of State Trials and Proceedings for High Treason and other Crimes and Misdemeanors from the earliest period to the present time, vols. I–V, ed. W. Cobbett (London, 1809).
Contemplations of the Dread and Love of God, ed. M. Connolly (Oxford, Early English Text Society, 1993).
Cook, John, *King Charls, his Case, or, an appeal To all rational man Concerning his Tryal at the High Court of Justice* (London, 1649).

Cooke, Alexander, *Worke for a Masse-priest* (London, 1617).
The abatement of Popish Braggs, pretending scripture to be theirs (London, 1625).
Pope Ioane. A Dialogue between a Protestant and a Papist. Manifestly proving, that a woman called Ioane, was Pope of Rome (London, 1625).
Cooper, Thomas, *An Admonition to the People of England* (London, 1589).
A brand taken out of the Fire. Or the Romish Spider, with his Webbe of Treason (London, 1606).
Coppe, Abiezer, *A Fiery Flying Roll: A Word from the Lord to all the Great Ones of the Earth, whom this may concerne: Being the last Warning Piece at the dreadfull day of Judgement* (London, 1649).
Cosin, John, *The Works of the Right Reverend father in god, John Cosin, Lord Bishop of Durham* (Oxford, 4 vols., 1843–51).
Coton, Pierre, *The Interiour Occupation of the Soule* (Douai, 1618).
The Court and Times of Charles the First; containing a series of historical and confidential letters, ed. T. Birch (London, 2 vols., 1849).
Coverdale, Miles, *The old faith, an evident probacion out of scripture, that the christen fayth ... hath endured sens the beginning of the worlde* (London, 1547).
Remains of Myles Coverdale of Exeter, ed. G. Pearson (Cambridge, Parker Society, 1844).
Remains of Bishop Coverdale of Exeter, ed. G. Pearson (Cambridge, Parker Society, 1846).
Cowper, William, *The Life and Death of the Reverend Father ... William Cowper* (London, 1619).
Cranmer, Thomas, *Catechismvs, that is to say a shorte Instruction into Christian religion for the syngular commodite and profyte of childe and young people* (London, 1548).
Miscellaneous Writings and Letters of Thomas Cranmer, ed. J. E. Cox (Cambridge, Parker Society, 1846).
Crashaw, William, *A Sermon Preached in London before the right honourable the Lord Lawarre, Lord Governour and Captaine Generall of Virginea* (London, 1610).
Cromwell's Conspiracy. A Tragy comedy, relating to our latter Times. Beginning at the Death of King Charles the First, and ending with the happy restauration of King Charles the Second (London, 1660).
Crouch, Richard, *The Man in the Moon, discovering a World of Knavery vnder the Sunne; Both in Parliament, the Counsell of State, the Army, the City, and the Country*, newsbook, 1649–50.
Damnable Practices Of three Lincolne-shire Witches, Joane Flower, and her two Daughters, Margaret and Phillip Flower, against Henry Lord Rosse, with others the Children of the Right Honourable the Earle of Rutland, at Beauer Castle, who for the same were executed at Lincolne the 11. Of March Last (London, 1619).
Davenport, John, *The Witches of Huntingdon, their examinations and confessions ... whereby will appeare how craftily and dangerously the Deuil tempteth and seizeth on poore souls* (London, 1646).
Davy, Sarah, *Heaven realiz'd or The Holy pleasure of daily intimate Communion with God, Exemplified In a blessed Soul, now in Heaven, Mrs. Sarah Davy* (London, 1670).
The Debauched Cavalleer: or the English Midianite (London, 1642).
A Declaration, Of a strange and Wonderfull Monster: Born in Kirkham Parish in Lancashire (London, 1646).

A declaration of Old Nick, Prince of the Air, and all his infernal crew to the inhabitants of the whole world, but chiefly to the Quakers of Great Britaine & c (London, 1659).
Dekker, Thomas, *The Dramatic Works of Thomas Dekker*, ed. F. Bowers (Cambridge, 4 vols., 1953–61).
Non-dramatic Works, ed. A. B. Grosart (London, 5 vols., 1963).
Deloney, Thomas, *The Works of Thomas Deloney*, ed. F. O. Mann (Oxford, 1912).
A Detection of the damnable driftes practiced by three witches at Chemisforde (London, 1579).
The Deuill seen at St. Albans being a true relation of how the Deuill was seen there in a cellar, in the likenesse of a Ram (London, 1648).
The Deuils White Boyes. Or, A mixture of malicious malignants with their much Evill, and manifold practices against Kingdom and Parliament (London, 1644).
The Devil and the Strumpet: or, the Old Bawd Tormented (London, no date).
The Devill and the Parliament: or, the parliament and the Devill. A Contestation between them for the precedencie (London, 1648).
The Devil turned Quaker: or, The Damnable, Divellish, and accursed Doctrines and Designes, of these desperate, deluded, and deluding people; called Quakers (London, 1656).
The Devils Cabinet Broke Open: or a new discovery of the High-way Thieves (London, 1657).
D'Ewes, Simonds, *The Diary of Sir Simonds D'Ewes 1622–1624*, ed. E. Bourcier (Paris, 1977).
The Dietary of Ghostly Health (London, 1520).
A Directory for the Publique Worship of God, Throughout the Three Kingdoms of England, Scotland and Ireland (London, 1645).
The disclosing of a late counterfeyted possession by the devyl in two maydens within the Citie of London (London, 1574).
A discouerie of the treasons practiced and attempted against the Queenes Maiestie and the realme, by Francis Throckmorton, who was ... condemned in Guyld Hall (London, 1584).
A Discouery of the Ivglings and Deceitful Impostures of a Slanderovs Libell against the Parliament (London, 1642).
A Disputation betwixt the Deuill and the Pope. Being a briefe dialogue between Urbanus, 5. Pope of Rome, and Pluto Prince of Hell. Concerning the Estate of the Five Kingdomes, Spaine, England, France, Ireland, and Scotland (London, 1642).
The Divell of the Vault. Or, the Vnmasking of Murther in a Briefe Declaration of the Catholike-complotted Treason, lately discouered (London, 1606).
The Doctrinal of Death (London, 1498).
Documents relating to the proceedings against William Prynne, in 1634 and 1637, ed. S. R. Gardiner, Camden Society, new series, 18 (London, 1877).
Downame, John, *A Brief Concordance, or table to the Bible of the last translation, serving for the most easie fynding out of the most useful places therein contained* (London, 1659).
Dugdale, Gilbert, *A True Discourse of the Practices of Elizabeth Caldwell* (London, 1604).
Durham, William, *The Life and Death of the judicious Divine, and accomplish'd Preacher, Robert Harris, D.D.* (London, 1660).
Edwards, Thomas, *Reasons against the Independent Government of Particular Congregations* (London, 1641).

Gangraena: or a Catalogue and Discovery of many of the Errours, Heresies, Blasphemies and pernicious Practices of the Sectaries of this time (London, 1646).

Elizabeth I, *The Letters of Queen Elizabeth*, ed. G. B. Harrison (London, 1935).

The Elizabethan Underworld: A Collection of Tudor and early Stuart Tracts and Ballads Telling of the Lives and Misdoings of Vagabonds, Thieves, Rogues and Cozeners, ed. A. V. Judges (London, 1930).

Ellis, John, *The Sole Path to a Sound Peace* (London, 1643).

The English Devil: or, Cromwell and his monstrous Witch Discover'd at White-hall (London, 1660).

Epulæ Thyesteæ: or, the thanksgiving-dinner: where the Deuill finds all, meat, Cooks, Guests, & c. Together with the city Present (London, 1648).

An exact Relation of the Bloody and Barbarous Massacre at Bolton in the Moors in Lancashire, May 28. By Prince Rupert (London, 1644).

The Examination, confession, tryall, and execution, of Joane Williford, Joan Cariden and Jane Hott: who were executed at Faversham in Kent, for being witches (London, 1645).

The Examination and Confession of certaine Wytches at Chensforde in the Countie of Essex (London, 1566).

The Examination of John Walsh, before Maister Thomas Williams, Commissary to the Reverend father in God William Bishop of Excester, upon certayne Interrogations touchyng Wytchcrafte and Sorcerye (London, 1566).

The Examinations of Henry Barrowe, John Greenwood, & John Penrie, before The High Commissioners, and Lordes of the Counsel (1593), reprinted in *The Harleian Miscellany*, vol. II.

Faces About, or a Recrimination charged upon Mr. John Goodwin (London, 1644).

Feak, Christopher et al., *A Faithfvl Discovery of a treacherous Design of Mystical Antichrist displaying Christs Banners* (London, 1653).

Filmer, Robert, *An Advertisement to the Jurymen of England, Touching Witches* (London, 1653).

Firmin, Giles, *The Real Christian, or a treatise of effectual calling* (London, 1670).

Fisher, Edward, *A Christian Caveat to old and new Sabbatarians. Or, a vindication of our Gospel-Festivals* (London, 1652).

Fleming, Abraham, *A straunge and terrible Wonder wrought very late in the paris church of Bongay ... In a great tempest of violent raine, lightning, and thunder, the like whereof hath been seldom seen. With the appearence of an horrible shaped thing, sensibly percieved of the people then and there assembled* (?London, 1577).

Fox, George, *The Great Mystery of the Great Whore Unfolded* (London, 1659), pp. 297–99.

The Distinction between a Phanatick Spirit (London, 1660).

The Journal of George Fox, ed. J. N. Nickalls (Cambridge, 1952).

Our Convenant with God (London, 1660).

Fox, George and Naylor, James, *Severall Papers* (London, 1653).

Foxe, John, *Actes and Monuments of these latter and perilous dayes, touching matters of the Church* (London, 1563).

Actes and monuments of these latter and perilous dayes, touching matters of the Church, ed. S. R. Cattley (London, 8 vols., 1841–89).

Franklin, Robert, Vincent, Thomas, Doolitel, Thomas, Janeway, James and Baker, Hugh, *A Murderer Punished and Pardoned: Or, a True Relation of the Wicked*

Life, and Shameful-Happy death of Thomas Savage, Imprisoned, Justly Condemned, and Twice Executed at Ratcliff, for His Bloody Fact in Killing His Fellow-servant (London, 1668).

Frith, John, *Antithesis, wherein are compared together Christes actes and the Popes* (1529), in *The whole workes of W. Tyndall, Iohn Frith, and Doct. Barnes, ed. J. Foxe* (London, 1572).

Froysell, Thomas, *The Beloved Disciple. A sermon preached at the funerall of the honourable Sir Robert Harley, knight of the honourable order of bath; at Brampton-Brian in Herefordshire. December 10. 1656* (London, 1658).

Fulke, William, *Stapleton's Fortress Overthrown, A Rejoinder to Martiall's Reply, A Discovery of the Dangerous Rock of the Popish Church*, ed. R. Gibbings (Cambridge, Parker Society, 1848).

A Gagge for the Pope, and the Iesuits: or the arraignment and execution of Antichrist. Shewing plainly that Antichrist shall be discovered, and punished in this world: to the amazement of all obstinate papists (London, 1624).

Galis, Richard, *A Briefe Treatise conteyning the most strange and horrible crueltye of Elizabeth Stile alias Bockingham and hir confederates executed at Abington upon Richard Galis* (London, 1579).

Gardiner, Stephen, *A Detection of the Deuils Sophistrie, wherwith he robbeth the unlearned people, of the true byleef, in the most blessed sacrament of the aulter* (London, 1546).

The Letters of Stephen Gardiner, ed. J. A. Muller (Cambridge, 1933).

Gatacker, Thomas, *Of the natvre and vse of Lots: A treatise historicall and theologicall* (London, 1619).

Gee, John, *The Foot out of the Snare: with a detection of Sundry late practices and impostures of the priests and Iesuits in England* (London, 1624).

Hold Fast. A sermon Preached at Paules Crosse upon Sunday being the xxxi of October, Anno Domini 1624 (London, 1624).

Geree, John, *Iudahs Ioy at the Oath* (London, 1641).

Gifford, George, *A Briefe Discourse of Certaine Points of the Religion, which is among the common sort of Christians, which may bee termed the Countie Divintie. With a manifest confutation of the same* (London, 1582).

A Dialogue Concerning Witches and Witchcraftes (London, 1593).

A discourse of the subtill practices of Devilles by witches and sorcerers (London, 1593).

Two Sermons vpon 1. Peter 5. vers 8. and 9 Wherein it is shewed that the deuill is to be resisted only by steadfast faith (London, 1597).

Gilpin, John, *The Qvakers Shaken: or, A Fire-brand snatch'd out of the Fire. Being A briefe Relation of Gods wonderfull Mercy extended to John Gilpin of Kendale in Westmoreland. Who … was not onely deluded by the Qvakers, but also possessed by the Devill* (Gateside, 1653).

Gods Loue to Mankind. Manifested, by Dis-prouing his absolute decree for their Damnation (?London, 1633).

Golding, Arthur, *A brief discourse of the late murder of master George Saunders* (London, 1573).

Goodcole, Henry, *The Wonderfull Discouerie of Elizabeth Sawyer a Witch, late of Edmonton, her conviction and condemnation and death* (London, 1621).

Goodwin, John, *Anti-Cavalierisme, or, truth pleading As well the Necessity, as the Lawfulness of this present War* (London, 1642).

Calumny Arraignd and Cast (London, 1644).

M.S. to A.S. with a Plea for Libertie of Conscience in a Church Way (London, 1644).
Oeomaxia; or the Grand Imprudence of men running the hazard of fighting against God, In suppressing any Way, Doctrine, or Practice, concerning which they know not certainly whether it be from God or no (London, 1644).
Theomachia, or the Grand Imprudence of men running the hazard of fighting against God (London, 1644).
Cretensis (London, 1646).
Gosson, Stephen, *The Schoole of Abuse, Containing a plesaunt inuectiue against Poets, pipers, plaiers, Iesters, and such like Caterpillers of a Commonwelth* (London, 1579).
Playes confuted in five Actions, Prouing that they are not to be suffred in a Christian common weale, by the waye both the cauils of Thomas Lodge, and the Play of Playes, written in their defence, and other obiections of players frendes, are truely set downe and directlye aunsweared (London, 1584).
Gouge, William, *The Saints Svpport, Set out in a Sermon Preached before the Honourable House of Commons assembled in Parliament* (London, 1641).
Grand Plutoes Remonstrance, or the Deuill Horn-mad at Roundheads and Brownists (London, 1642).
Grand Pluto's Progress through Great Britaine and Ireland (London, 1647).
The Great Eclipse of the Sun, or Charles his waine ouer-clouded, by the euill influences of the moon (London, 1644).
A Great Wonder in Heaven: shewing The Late Apparitions and prodigious noyses of war and battels, seen on Edge-Hill (London, 1642).
Greenhill, William, *The Axe at the Root, A Sermon Preached before the Honourable Hovse of Commons* (London, 1643).
Greene, Robert, *The Honourable Friar Bacon and Friar Bungay* (London, 1594).
Greenwood, John, *The Writings of John Greenwood and Henry Barrow 1591–1593*, ed. L. H. Carlson (London, 1970).
Gurnall, William, *The Christian in Compleat Armour. Or a Treatise Of the Saints War against the Deuil, wherein a Discouery is made of that Grand enemy of God and his People, in his Policies, power, seat of his Empire, Wickednesse, and chiefe design he hath against the Saints* (London, 1654).
Hakewill, George, *An Apologie of the Power and Providence of God in the Government of the World* (Oxford, 1627).
Hall, Joseph, *A Survey of that Foolish, Seditious, Scandalous, Prophane Libell, The Protestation Protested* (London, 1641).
Hall, Ralph, *Qvakers Principles Quaking, or, Pretended light proved darkness* (London, 1656).
The Harleian Miscellany: or a Collection of scarce, curious, and entertaining Pamphlets and Tracts ... found in the late Earl of Oxford's Library, 12 vols. (London, 1808–12).
Harley, Brilliana, 'Commonplace Book of Brilliana Conway, 1622', Nottingham University Library, Portland Mss., London Collection.
Harris, Robert, *Samvels Fvneral: or, a sermon preached at the fvnerall of Sir Anthony Cope, Knight, and Baronet* (London, 1626).
A Sermon preached to the honourable Hovse of commons (London, 1642).
Harrison, Robert, *The Writings of Robert Harrison and Robert Browne*, ed. A. Peel and L. H. Carlson (London, 1953).
Harrison, William and Leygh, William, *Deaths advantage little regarded, and the soules solace against sorrow. Preached in two funeral sermons at Childwal in*

Lancashire at the buriall of Mistris Katherine Brettergh the third of Iune 1601 (London, 1602).
Harsnett, Samuel, *A Discovery of the Fravdvlent practices of Iohn Darrel Batcheler of Artes, in his proceedings Concerning the pretended possession and dispossession of William Somers at Nottingham ... detecting in some sort the deceitfull trade in thee latter dayes of casting out Deuils* (London, 1599).
Harwood, John, *The Lying Prophet Discovered and Reproved* (London, 1659).
A Health to the Gentlemanly profession of Seruingmen: or, The Seruingmans Comfort (London, 1598).
Hells Higher Court of Justice; or, the Triall of Three Politick Ghosts (London, 1661).
Herbert, Mary Sidney, *A Discourse of Life and Death. Written in French by Ph. Mornay. Antonius, A Tragædy written also in French by Ro. Garnier. Both done in English by the Countesse of Pembroke* (London, 1592).
Here begyneth a lityll treatise shorte and abridged spekynge of the arte & crafte to knowe well to dye (Westminster, 1490).
Here begynneth the Lantern of lyght, ed. L. M. Swinburn (Oxford, Early English Text Society, 1971).
Hic Mvlier: Or, the Man-Woman: Being a Medicine a cure the Coltish Disease of the staggers in the Masculine-Feminines of our times (London, 1620).
Hieron, Samuel, *The Spiritual Fishing. A sermon preached in Cambridge by that Revernd and Iudicious Divine, Mr Samvel Hieron* (London, 1618).
Hill, Thomas, *The Trade of Truth Advanced* (London, 1642).
The Militant Church Triumphant over the Dragon and his Angels (London, 1643).
The Historie of the Damnable Life, and deserved Death of Doctor Iohn Faustus (London, 1592).
The History of the Life and Death of Hugh Peters. That Arch-traytor, from his Cradell to the Gallowes (London, 1660).
Hobbes, Thomas, *Leviathan, or The Matter, Forme, & Power of a Common-wealth Ecclesiasticall and Civill*, ed. C. B. Macpherson (London, 1985).
Hoby, Margaret, *The Diary of Lady Margaret Hoby 1599–1605*, ed. D. M. Meads (London, 1930).
Hooper, John, *Early Writings of John Hooper, D.D. Lord Bishop of Gloucester and Worcester, Martyr, 1555*, ed. S. Carr (Cambridge, Parker Society, 1843).
Later Writings of Bishop Hooper, together with his letters and other pieces, ed. C. Nevinson (Cambridge, Parker Society, 1852).
Hopkins, Matthew, *The Discovery of Witches: in Answer to severall Queries lately Delivered to the Judges of Assize for the County of Norfolk* (London, 1647).
Hubberthorne, Richard, *A true Separation between the power of the Spirit, and the imitation of Antichrist* (London, 1654).
Antipathy betwixt the Flesh and the Spirit (London, 1656).
Hutchinson, Roger, *The Works of Roger Hutchinson, fellow of St John's College, Cambridge, and afterwards of Eton College, A. D. 1550*, ed. J. Bruce (Cambridge, Parker Society, 1842).
I., T., *A World of Wonders. A Masse of Murthers. A Couie of Cosonages. Containing many of the moste notable Wonders, Horrible Murthers and Destestable Cosonages that have beene within this land* (London, 1595).
The Insecuritie of Princes, Considered in an occasional meditation upon the Kings late sufferings (London, 1649).
The Iudgement of the synode holden at Dort, concerning the five Articles (London, 1619).

James VI and I, *Daemonologie* (Edinburgh, 1597).
The Workes of the most High and Mighty Prince, James (London, 1616).
His majesty's speech in the last session of Parliament, concerning the Gunpowder-plot (1605), reprinted in *The Harleian Miscellany*, vol. III.
James, Thomas, *A Manuduction, or Introduction unto divinitie: Containing a confutation of Papists by Papists, throughout their important articles of our Religion* (London, 1625).
Jessey, Henry, *The exceeding Riches of Grace Advanced ... in ... Sarah Wight* (London, 1647).
Jewel, John, *The Works of John Jewel, Bishop of Salisbury. The Second Portion ...*, ed. J. Ayre (Cambridge, Parker Society, 1847).
Jocelin, Elizabeth, *The Mothers Legacie, To her vnborn Childe* (London, 1622).
Kiffin, William, *A Breife Remonstrance of the Reasons and Grounds of those People Commonly called Anabaptists, for their Separation* (London, 1645).
The Confession of Faith of those Churches which are commonly (though falsly) called Anabaptists (London, 1644).
Kilby, Richard, *The Bvrthen of a Loaded Conscience: or the miserie of sinne: set forth by the confession of a miserable sinner* (Cambridge, 1608).
King, Henry, *The Sermons of Henry King (1592–1669), Bishop of Chicester*, ed. M. Hobbs (Rutherford, 1992).
The Last Will and Testament of Philip Herbert, Burgess for Bark-shire, Vulgarlie called Earl of Pembroke and Montgomery (London, 1649).
The Last Will and Testament of Richard Brandon esquire; Heads-man, and hang-man to the Pretended Parliament (?London, 1649).
Latimer, Hugh, *Sermons by Hugh Latimer*, ed. G. E. Corrie (Cambridge, Parker Society, 1844).
Sermons and Remains of Hugh Latimer, ed. G. E. Corrie (Cambridge, Parker Society, 1845).
Lavater, Lewis, *Of Ghosts and Spirites Walking be Night, and of strange noises, trackes, and sundry Forwarnynges, whiche commonly happen before the death of menne, great slaughter, & alterations of Kyngdomes* (London, 1572).
Lawrence, George, *Laurentius Lutherens. Or the Protestation of George Lavrence* (London, 1642).
Lawrence, Henry, *Of Our Communion and Warre with Angels. Being certain Meditations on the subject, bottom'd (though not concluded within the compasse of that scripture) on Ephes. 6. 12* (?London, 1646).
Leigh, Dorothy, *The Mothers Blessing. Or, the ... Counsell of a Gentlewoman, ... left behind for her children* (London, 1663; first edn, 1616).
Lever, Thomas, *Sermons 1550*, ed. E. Arber (London, 1870).
Ley, John, *The Fvry of Warre, and the Folly of Sinne, (As an Incentive to it) declared and applyed* (London, 1643).
Lightfoote, John, *Elias Redivivus: A Sermon Preached before the Honourable House of Commons* (London, 1643).
Lilburne, John, *A Worke of the Beast or A Relation of a most vnchristian Censure, Executed vpon Iohn Lilburne, (Now prisoner in the fleet) the 18 of Aprill 1638* (London, 1638).
Come out of her my people: or An Answer to the questions of a Gentleman (a Professor of the Antichristian Church of England) about Hearing the Publicke Ministers (London, 1639).

Lilly, William, *The Starry Messenger, or, An Interpretation of Strange Aparitions* (?London, 1644).

Liturgical Services: Liturgies and occasional forms of prayer set forth in the reign of Queen Elizabeth, ed. W. K. Clay (Cambridge, Parker Society, 1847).

Love, Christopher, *Hell's Terror: or a Treatise of the Torments of the Damned, As a presevative against security* (London, 1653).

Lovekin, Thomas, *A true Relation Of a dangerous Plot Against The Well-affected party of the Towne of Lynn* (London, 1648).

Lyford, William, *The Matching of the Magistrates Authority* (London, 1654).

Three sermons preached at Sherborne in Dorsetshire ... being his last sermons (Oxford, 1654).

A Magical Vision, Or a Perfect Discovery Of the Fallacies or Witchcraft (London, 1673).

Mainwaring, Roger, *Religion and Alegiance: in two sermons Preached before the Kings Maiestie* (London, 1627).

Manningham, John, *The Diary of John Manningham of the Middle Temple 1602–1603*, ed. R. P. Sorlien (Hanover, N. H., 1976).

Mariot, Thomas, *Rebellion Unmasked or A sermon Preached At Poplar in the Parish of Stepney ... upon the occasion of the late Rebellious Insurrection in London* (London, 1661).

Marlowe, Christopher, *The Complete Plays*, ed. J. P. Stearne (London, 1986; first edn, 1969).

The Tragical History of Doctor Faustus, in *The Complete Plays*, ed. J. B. Stearne (London, 1969).

Marprelate, Martin, *Oh read over Dr. John Bridges, for it is a worthy work* (London, 1588).

Certain Minerall and Metephysicall Schoolpoints to be defended by the reuerende Bishops and the rest of my clergie masters of Conuocation house (London, 1589).

Hay any worke for Cooper (London, 1589).

Marshall, Stephen, *A Sermon Preached before the Honourable House of Commons, Now assembled in Parliament* (London, 1641).

Meroz Cursed, or, A Sermon Preached to the Honourable House of Commons, At their late Solemne Fast, Feb. 23. 1641 (London, 1641).

Marten, Anthony, *An Exhortation To stir vp the mindes of all her Maiesties faithful subiects, to defend their Countrey, in this dangerous Time, from the Invasion of Enemies* (London, 1588).

Martin, Gregory, *The Love of the Soule* (Rouen, 1579).

Mayhew, Edward, *A Paradise of Prayers* (Douai, 1613).

Mercurius Britanicus His welcome to Hell: with the Devils blessing to Britanicus (London, 1646).

Mercurius Melancholicus, *The Cuckows Nest at Westminster: or, The parliament between two lady-birds, Queen Fairfax and Lady Cromwell* (1649), in *The Harleian Miscellany*, vol. VI.

Mercurius Philo-monarchus, newsbook, 1649.

Mercurius Pragmaticus, newsbook, 1649–50.

The Merry Devill of Edmonton (London, 1608).

Middleton, Thomas, *The Works of Thomas Middleton*, ed. A. H. Bullen (New York, 8 vols., 1964).

Mildmay, Grace, 'Lady Mildmay's Meditations', extracts reprinted in L. Pollock (ed.), *With Faith and Physic: The Life of a Tudor Gentlewoman: Lady Grace Mildmay 1552–1620* (London, 1993).

Milton, John, *The Tenure of Kings and Magistrates: proving, that it is Lawfull, and hath been held so through all Ages, for any, who have the Power, to call to account a Tyrant, or wicked King, and after due conviction, to depose, and put him to death* (London, 1649).
Mirk, John, *Mirk's Festial: A Collection of Homilies, by Johannes Mirkus (John Mirk)* ed. T. Erbe (London, Early English Text Society, 1905).
A Mirrovr to Confesse Well for such persons as doe frequent this sacrament (St Omer, 1624).
The Miseries of War. By a louer of Trvth and Peace (?London, 1643).
More, Henry, *An Antidote against Atheisme* (London, 1655).
A Most Certain, Strange, and true Discovery of a Witch. Being taken by some of the Parliament Forces, as she was standing on a small planck board and sayling on it over the River of Newbury (London, 1643).
The Most Strange and Wonderfull Apparition of Blood in a Pool at Garreton (London, 1647).
The Mowing Devil: or, strange News out of Hertfordshire (London, 1678).
Munda, Constantia, *The Worming of a mad Dogge: or, A Soppe for Cerbervs the iaylor of Hell. No confutation bvt a sharpe Redargution of the byter of Women* (London, 1617).
Munday, Anthony, *A second and third blast of retrait from plaies and theatres: the one wherof was sounded by a reuerend Byshop dead long since; the other by a worshipful and zealoys Gentleman now aliue* (London, 1580).
Sundry Strange and Inhumaine Murthers (London, 1591).
Naylor, James, *A Few Words occasioned by a Paper lately Printed, Stiled, A Discourse concerning the Quakers* (London, 1653).
The Railer Rebuked (London, 1654).
Satans design discovered: who under a pretence of worshipping Christs person in heaven, would exclude God and Christ, the spirit and light, out of the world (London, 1655).
Newcome, Henry, *The Autobiography of Henry Newcome*, ed. R. Parkinson, Chetham Society, Old Series, vol. 26 (1852).
Newcomen, Matthew, *The Craft and Crvelty of the Churches Adversaries* (London, 1643).
Newes from Perin in Cornwall: Of a most Bloody and vn-exampled Murther very lately committed by a Father on his owne Sonne ... at the Instigation of a mercilesse Step-mother (London, 1618).
News from Hell, Rome, and the Innes of Court. Wherein is set forth the copy of a letter written from the Devill to the Pope (London, 1641).
News from Pannier-Alley: or, A True Relation of Some Pranks the Devil hath lately play'd with a Plaster-Pot there (London, 1687).
Norden, John, *A Progress of Piety, whose jesses lead into the Harbour of Heavenly Heart's Ease* (1596; reprinted Cambridge, Parker Society, 1847).
Northbrooke, John, *[Spiritus vicarius Christi in terra] A Treatise wherin Dicing, Dauncing, Vaine playes or Enterluds with other idle pastimes & c. Commonly used on the Sabboth day, are reproued by the Authoritie of the word of God and auncient writers* (London, 1577).
Norwood, Richard, *The Journal of Richard Norwood* (New York, 1945).
Nowell, Alexander, *A Catechism written in Latin by Alexander Nowell* (1570), ed. J. Bruce (Cambridge, Parker Society, 1842).

A catechism written in Latin, together with the same catechism translated into English by T Norton, ed. G. E. Corrie (Cambridge, Parker Society, 1853).

Nyndge, Edward, *A Trve and Fearefvll Vexation of one Alexander Nyndge: Being most horribly tormented with the Deuill, from the 20 day of Ianuary, to the 23 of Iuly* (London, 1616; first edn, 1573).

Original Letters relative to the English Reformation, written during the reigns of King Henry VIII, King Edward VI, and Queen Mary: chiefly from the Archives of Zurich, ed. H. Robinson (Cambridge, Parker Society, 1846–7).

Ormerod, Oliver, *The Pictvre of a Papist: or, A Relation of the damnable heresies, detestable qualities and diabolicall practices of sundry hereticks in former ages, and of the papists in this age* (London, 1606).

Overton, Richard, *An Arrow against all Tyrants And Tyrany shot from the Prison of New-gate into the Prerogative Bowels of the Arbitrary House of Lords and all other Usurpers and Tyrants whatsoever* (London, 1646).

A Packe of Spanish Lyes, sent Abroad in the world: first printed in Spaine in the Spanish Tongue, and translated out of the Original (London, 1588).

The Papists Petition in England. To their diabolicall center of Impiety the Pope (London, 1642).

Parker, K. and Carlsen, E. (eds.), *'Practical Divinity': The Works and Life of Revd Richard Greenham* (Brookfield, Vt., 1998).

Parnell, James, *The Shield of Truth* (London, 1654).

Parsons, Robert, *An Answere to the fifth part of Reportes lately set forth by Syr Edward Cooke ... Concerning the ancient & moderne Municipall Lawes of England, which appertayne to spirituall power & Iurisdiction* (n.p., 1606).

A Peace-Offering to God A Sermon Preached to the Honourable House of Commons assembled in Parliament (London, 1641).

Penry, John, *The Notebook of John Penry 1593*, ed. A. Peel, Camden Society, third series, vol. 67 (1944).

The Pepys Ballads: Facsimile, ed. W. G. Day (Cambridge, 5 vols., 1987).

Perfect Proceedings of State-Affaires, no. 283, 22 February – 1 March 1655, newsbook.

Perkins, William, *A discourse of the damned art of witchcraft* (Cambridge, 1610).

Foure Godly Treatises; very necessary to be considered of all Christians (London, 1587).

The Works of that Famous and Worthy Minister of Christ in the University of Cambridge, Mr William Perkins (London, 3 vols., 1616–18).

Petto, Samuel, *Roses from Sharon. Or sweet experiences gathered up by some precious hearts* (London, 1654).

A pittilesse Mother. That most vnnaturally at one time, murthered two of her owne Children at Acton (London, 1616).

Policy no Policy, or, the Devil himself confuted. Being an Answer to a Clause of a Letter written to a person of Quality at Brussels (?London, 1660).

Political Ballads of the Seventeenth and Eighteenth Centuries, ed. W. W. Wilkins (London, 2 vols., 1860).

Potts, Thomas, *The Wonderfvll Discoverie of Witches in the Covntie of Lancaster* (London, 1613).

Powell, Vavasor, *Spirituall Experiences, of sundry beleevers Held forth by them at severall solemne meetings, and conferences to that end* (London, 1653).

Prideaux, John, *Eight sermons, Preached by John Prideaux, Doctor of Divinity* (London, 1621).

The Primer, and Catechisme, sette furthe by the Kynges highness, and his clergie (London, 1552).
Private Prayers, put forth during the Reign of Queen Elizabeth I, ed. W. K. Clay (Cambridge, Parker Society, 1851).
Proceedings in Parliament 1610, ed. Elizabeth Read Foster (New Haven and London, 2 vols., 1966).
Proceedings in the Parliaments of Elizabeth I, ed. T. E. Hartley (Leicester, 3 vols., 1981–95).
The Profitable book for Man's Soul (London, 1493).
A proper new Ballad of the dream of a Sinner, being very sore troubled with the Assaults of Satan (London, no date).
Prynne, William, *Histrio-mastix. The Players Scovrge, or Actors Tragedie ... Wherein it is largely evidenced ... That popular Stage-playes (the very Pompes of the Divell which we renounce in Baptisme, if we beleeve the Fathers) are sinfull, heathenish, lewde, ungodly Spectacles* (London, 1633).
Romes Master-peece: or, the Grand Conspiracy of the Pope and his Iesuited Instruments (London, 1644).
Puritan Manifestoes: A Study of the Origins of the Puritan Revolt, ed. W. H. Frere and C. E. Douglas (London, 1907; reprinted 1954).
Quakers are Inchanters and Dangerovs Seducers. Appearing in their Inchantment of one Mary White at Wickhamskeyth in Suffolk (London, 1655).
Rankins, William, *The Mirror of Monsters* (London, 1587).
The Ranters Declaration, with Their new Oath and Protestation ... a New and further discovery of their black Art, with the Names of those that are possest by the Devil (London, 1650).
The Ranters Monster: Being a true Relation of one Mary Adams ... who named her self the Virgin Mary, blasphemously affirming, That she was conceived with child by the Holy Ghost ... With the manner of how she was deliver'd of the ugliest ill-shapen Monster that ever eyes beheld (London, 1652).
The Ranters Religion. Or, A faithfull and infallible Narrative of their damnable and diabolical opinions, with their detestable lives & actions (London, 1650).
Raymond of Capua, *The Life of the Blessed virgin, Sainct Catherine of Siena* (Douai, 1609).
The Rebels Catechism: Composed in an easy and familiar way, to let them see the heinousness of their offence, the weakness of the strongest subterfuges, and to recall them to their duties to God and man (1643).
The Rebells Warning-Piece: being Certaine Rules and Instructions left by Alderman Hoyle (?London, 1650).
A Rehearsall both strange and true, of the hainous and horrible actes committed by Elizabeth Stile, alias Rockingham, Mother Dutten, Mother Deuell, Mother Margarte, fower notorious witches, apprehended at Winsore in the Coubtie of Barks. (London, 1579).
A Relation of a Yovng Woman possest with the Devill (London, 1646).
Reynolds, Edward, *Israels Petition in Time of Trouble. A Sermon Preached In St. Margarets Church at Westminster, before the Honourable House of Commons now assembled in Parliament* (London, 1642).
Reynolds, John, *The Triumphs of Gods Revenge against the crying and Execrable sinne of (willing and premeditated) Murther* (London, 1657; first edition, 1621).
Ridley, Nicholas, *The Works of Nicholas Ridley*, ed. H. Christmas (Cambridge, Parker Society, 1843).

Roberts, H., *An earnest complaint of divers vain, wicked and abused exercises, practiced on the saboth day: which tende to the hinderence of the Gospel, and increase of many abhominable vices. With a shorte admonishment to all popish priests and negligent ministers* (London, 1572).

Rogers, John, *Ohel or Beth-shemesh A tabernacle for the sun, or, Irenicum evangelicum: an idea of church-discipline in the theorick and practick parts* (London, 1653).

Rolle, Richard, *Remedy against the troubles of temptacyons* (London, 1519).

Roulston, Gilbert, *The Ranters Bible. Or, Seven several Religions by them maintained* (London, 1650).

Rous, John, *Diary of John Rous, Incumbent of Santon Downham, Suffolk, from 1625–1642*, ed. M.A. Everett Green, Camden Society, original series, 66 (London, 1856).

The Routing of the Ranters (London, 1650).

The Rovting of the Ranters Being a full Relation of their uncivil carriages, and blasphemous words and actions at their mad meetings (London, 1650).

The Royal Diurnall, newsbook, 1650.

Sandys, Edwin, *The Sermons of Edwin Sandys, D.D., successively Bishop of Worchester and London, and Archbishop of York; to which are added some miscellaneous pieces*, ed. J. Ayre (Cambridge, Parker Society, 1842).

Schola cordis or the Heart of it Selfe, gone away from god; brought back againe to him & instructed by him, in 47 Emblems (London, 1647).

Scot, Reginald, *The Discoverie of Witchcraft* (1584), ed. Montague Summers (New York, 1972).

The Discoverie of Witchcraft, ed. M. Summers (London, 1930; reprinted New York, 1972).

Scudder, Henry, *The Christians Daily Walke in Holy Securitie and Peace* (London, 1627).

Sedgwick, William, *Zions Deliverance and her Friends Dvty: or The Grounds of expecting, and Means of Procuring Jerusalems Restauration* (London, 1642).

Sedgwicke, Obadiah, *England's Preservation or, A Sermon discovering the onely way to prevent destroying Judgements: Preached to the Honourable House of Commons at their last solemne Fast* (London, 1642).

Sedition Scourg'd, or a view of that Rascally & Venemous paper entitled A Charge of High Treason exhibited against Oliver Cromwell (London, 1653).

A Short Answer to A. S. (London, 1644).

Sibbes, Richard, *The Soules Conflict with it selfe, and Victory over it self by Faith* (London, 1635).

Signes and wonders from Heaven. With a true Relation of a Monster borne in Ratcliffe Highway, at the signe of the three Arrows (?London, 1642).

Sixe Spiritvall Bookes; Fvll of merveilovs Pietie and Devotion, and First, Certaine Devovt and Godlie Petitions commonlie called, the Iesvs Psalter (Douai, 1618).

Smart, Peter, *The vanitie & downe-fall of superstitious Popish ceremonies: or, a sermon preached in the Cathedrall Church of Durham* (Edinburgh [London?], 1628).

Smith, Henry, *Three Sermons made by Maister Henry Smith. 1. The Benefit of Contention. 2. The Affinitie of the faithfull. 3. The lost Sheepe is found.* (London, 1599).

Smith, Robert et al., *An apologeticall account, of some brethren of the church, whereof Mr. Iohn Goodwin is pastor* (London, 1646).

[Smith, T.], *A Gagg for the Quakers* (London, 1659).

The Smoke out of the Bottomlesse Pit (London, 1650).

The Snare of the Deuill Discouered: Or, A True and Perfect Relation of the Sad and Deplorable Condition of Lydia the wife of John Rogers ... how she wantyng money the Deuil appeared to her in the shape of a man (London, 1658).

The Spiritval Conflict (no date).

Sowernam, Ester, *Ester hath hang'd Haman: or An Answere to a lewd Pamphlet, entitiled, The Arraignment of Women* (London, 1617).

Speght, Rachel, *A Movsell for Melastomvs, The Cynicall Bayter of, and foule mouthed Barker against Evahs Sex* (London, 1617).

Staunton, Edmund, *A Sermon preached at Great Milton in the County of Oxford: Decemb: 9. 1654. At the funeral of that eminent servant of Jesus Christ Mrs Elizabeth Wilkinson* (Oxford, 1659).

Stearne, John, *A Confirmation And Discovery of Witchcraft, Containing these severall particulars; That there are Witches called bad Witches, and Witches untruely called good or white Witches, and what manner of people they be* (London, 1648).

Stockwood, John, *A Sermon preached at Paules Crosse on Barthelmew day* (London, 1578).

Strange & Terrible Newes from Cambridge, being A true Relation of the Quakers bewitching of Mary Philips out of the Bed from her Husband in the Night, and transformed her into the shape of a Bay Mare, riding her from Dinton, towards the University (London, 1659).

A Strange And Lamentable accident that happened lately at Mead-Ashby in Northamptonshire (London, 1642).

A strange and true Relation of a Yovng Woman possest with the Devill. By the name of Joyce Dovey, dwelling at Bewdley neer Worcester. With a particular of her actions, and how the evill spirit speakes within her, giving fearefull answers unto those Ministers and others that come to discourse with her (London, 1646).

Strange Newes from Newgate and the Old-Baily: or, The Proofs, Examinations, Declarations, Indictments, Conviction, and Confession of I. Collins and T. Reeve, two of the Ranters taken in More-lane (London, 1650).

Strange News from Arpington near Bexly in Kent: being a True Narrative of a young Maid who was Possest with several Devils or Evil Spirits (London, 1679).

Strange News from Warwick (?London, 1642).

Stuart Royal Proclamations, vol. I: *Royal Proclamations of King James I 1603–1625*, ed. J. F. Larkin and P. Hughes (Oxford, 1973).

Stubbes, Philip, *The Anatomie of Abuses: contayning a discourse, of breife summarie of such Notable Vices and Imperfections, as now raigne in many Christian Countreyes of the worlde: But (especiallie) in the verie famous ilande calleed Ailgna* (London, 1583).

The second part of the anatomie of abuses conteining the display of corruptions, with a perfect description of such imperfections, blemishes and abuses, as now reigning in euerie degree (London, 1583).

A Christal Glasse for Christian Women containing, A most Excellent Discourse, of the godly life and Christian death of Mistresse Katherine Stubbes, who departed this liufe in Burton vpon Trent, in Staffordshire, the 14. Day of December, 1590 (London, 1592).

Sutcliffe, Alice, *Meditations of mans Mortalitie. Or, a way to trve Blessednesse* (London, 1634; first edn, 1632).

Swan, John, *A Trve and Breife Report, of Mary Glovers Vexation, and of her deliuerance by the meanes of fastinge and prayer* (London, 1603).
Symons, Henry, *Andridinases archidinases, The Lord Jesus his commission (Under the Broad Seal of his Highness the Royal & Real Lord Protector of Heavenm and Earth) as man, to be the alone Judge of Life and Death, in the Great and General Assize of the World; Proued and Improued before the Reverend Judges at the assizes holden at Maidstone, March 17. 1655* (London, 1657).
Taylor, Jeremy, *Holy Living and Holy Dying*, ed. P. G. Stanwood (Oxford, 2 vols., 1989).
Taylor, John, *The Vnnatural Father: Or, The Cruell Murther committed by Iohn Rowse of the towne of Ewell, ten miles from London, in the County of Surrey, vpon two of his owne Children* (London, 1621).
Temple, Thomas, *Christ's Government In and over his People* (London, 1642).
Terry, John, *The Trial of Truth: containing an short Discouery of the greatest pointes of the Doctrine of the Great Antichrist* (Oxford, 1600).
Thims, Gregory, *The Protestant Informer or Information to all Protestants* (London, 1643).
Toldervy, John, *The Foot out of the Snare* (London, 1655).
A true and faithful Narrative of Oliver Cromwell's compact with the Devil for seven Years, on the Day in which he gain'd the Battle of Worcester: and on which day, at the Expiration of the said Term, he afterwards died (London, 1720).
A True and plaine declaration of the horrible Treasons practised by William Parry the Traitor, against the Queenes Maiestie (London, 1585).
A true reporte or description of an horrible, wofull, and most lamentable murther, doen in the cittie of Bristoew by one John Kynnester, a Sherman by his occupation (London, 1573).
The Trumpet of the Lord Sounded (London, 1564).
Turner, Jane, *Choice Experiences of the Kind Dealings of God* (London, 1653).
Turner, William, *The huntyng and fyndyng out of the Romish Fox: which more than seven yearses hath bebe hyd among the Byshoppes of England*, ed. R. Potts (Cambridge, 1851).
Two conferences between some of those people that are called separatists (London, 1650).
Two Horrible and inhumane murthers. Done in Linconeshire by two husbands (?London, 1607).
The Two Liturgies, A. D. 1549 and A. D. 1552, ed. J. Ketley (Cambridge, Parker Society, 1844).
Two Most unnatural and bloodie Murthers: the One by Maister Caverly, A Yorkshire Gentleman, practised upon his wife, and committed upon his two children, the tree and twentie of Aprill 1605 (London, 1605).
Two Wycliffite Texts, ed. A Hudson (Oxford, Early English Text Society, 1993).
Tyndale, William, *Doctrinal treatises and introductions to different portions of the Holy Scripture*, ed. H. Walter (Cambridge, Parker Society, 1848).
Expositions and notes on sundry portions of the Holy Scriptures, together with the Practice of Prelates, ed. H. Walter (Cambridge, Parker Society, 1849).
An answer to Sir Thomas More's dialogue: The Supper of the Lord after the true meaning of John VI and I, Cor XI and Wm Tracy's testament expounded, ed. H. Walter (Cambridge, Parker Society, 1850).
Vicars, John, *To his reverend and much respected good friend Mr John Goodwin* (London, 1644).

A View of the Popish-plot; or, A Touch of the Cunning Contrivance of the Romish Faction (London, 1689).

de Voragine, Jacobus, *The Golden Legend: Readings on the Saints*, trans. W. G. Ryan (Princeton, N.J., 2 vols., 1993).

Wade, Christopher, *Quakery slain irrecoverably by the principal Quakers themselves* (London, 1657).

Ward, Samuel, *Woe to Drunkards* (London, 1622).

Watson, Thomas, *Twoo notable Sermons, made the third and fyfth Fridayes in Lent last past, Before the Quenes highnes, concerninge the reall presense of Christes body and bloude in the blessed Sacrament* (London, 1554).

Weld, Thomas et al., *The Perfect Pharisee under Monkish Holiness* (Gateside, 1653).

Wheathill, Anne, *A handfull of holesome (though homelie) herbs, gathered out of the goodlie garden of Gods most holie word; for the common benefit and comfortable exercise of all such as are deuoutlie disposed* (London, 1584).

Whitefield, George, *The Eternity of Hell Torments. A Sermon Preached at Savannah in Georgia* (London, 1738).

Satan's Devices: A Sermon Preached at Great St. Helens (London, 1739).

Whitgift, John, *The Works of John Whitgift*, ed. J. Ayre (Cambridge, Parker Society, 3 vols., 1851–3).

The whole workes of W. Tyndall, Iohn Frith, and Doct. Barnes, ed. J. Foxe (London, 1572).

Wilkinson, Henry, *The hope of Glory or Christs Indwelling in true Believers Is an Evident Demonstration of their hope of Glory* (London, 1657).

Counsels and Comforts for Troubled Consciences (London, 1679).

Wilson, Thomas, *Jerichoes Downfall, As it was Presented in a sermon preached at St. Margarets Westminster before the Honourable House of Commons* (London, 1643).

The Witches of Northamptonshire. Agnes Browne Arthur Bill Joane Vaughan Hellen Jenkenson Mary Barber Witches Who were all executed at Northampton the 22. Of July last. 1612 (London, 1612).

The Wonderful Discoverie of the Witchcrafts of Margaret and Philip Flower, daughters of Ioan Flower (London, 1619).

A Wonderfull and Strange Miracle, or Gods Just Vengeance Against the Cavaliers (London, 1642).

A Word for All: or, the Rumps Funerall sermon, held forth by Mr. Feak to a Coventicle of Fanatiques at Bedlam (?London, 1660).

Work for Chimny-sweepers: or a warning for Tobacconists (London, 1602).

The Wretched Miser: or, A brief Account of a covertous Farmer, who bringing a Load of Corn to market, swore the Devil should have it before he should take the honest market price; which accordingly came to pass (London, no date).

W.W., *A true and just Recorde, of the Information, Examination and Confession of all the Witches, taken at S. Oses in the county of Essex* (London, 1582).

The Wyll of the Deuyll, with his detestable commaundements directed to his obedient and accursed chydren, and the rewarde promised to all suche as obediently will endever themselves to fulfill them (London, 1548).

The Zurich Letters, comprising the Correspondence of several English Bishops and others, with some of the Helvetian Reformers, during the Reign of Queen Elizabeth, ed. H. Robinson (Cambridge, Parker Society, 1842).

The Zurich Letters, (second series) comprising the correspondence of several English Bishops and others with some of the Helvetian Reformers, during the reign of Queen Elizabeth, ed. H. Robinson (Cambridge, Parker Society, 1842).

SECONDARY SOURCES

Aarne, A. A. and Thompson, S., *The Types of the Folktale: A Classification and Bibliography* (Helsinki, F. F. Communications CLXXXIV, 1964).
Adams, M. M. and Adams, R. M. (eds.), *The Problem of Evil* (Oxford, 1990).
Anglo, S. (ed.), *The Damned Art: Essays in the Literature of Witchcraft* (London, 1977).
Ankarloo, B. and Henningsen, G. (eds.), *Early Modern European Witchcraft: Centres and Peripheries* (Oxford, 1990).
Archer, I. W., *The Pursuit of Stability: Social Relations in Elizabethan London* (Cambridge, 1991).
Aston, M., *England's Iconoclasts*, vol. I: *Laws against Images* (Oxford, 1988).
Aydelotte, F., *Elizabethan Rogues and Vagabonds* (London, 1913).
Aylmer, G. E. (ed.), *The Interregnum: The Quest for Settlement 1646–1660* (Houndmills, 1972).
Barker, F., *The Tremulous Private Body* (New York, 1984).
Baroja, Julio Caro, 'Witchcraft and Catholic Theology', in B. Ankarloo and G. Henningsen (eds.), *Early Modern European Witchcraft: Centres and Peripheries* (Oxford, 1990), pp. 19–43.
Barry, J., Hester, M. and Roberts, G., (eds.), *Witchcraft in Early Modern Europe: Studies in Culture and Belief* (Cambridge, 1996).
Baskerville, S., 'Blood Guilt during the English Revolution', *Seventeenth Century*, 8 (2) (1993).
Baukham, R., *Tudor Apocalypse: Sixteenth-Century Apocalypticism, Millenarianism and the English Reformation from John Bale to John Foxe and Thomas Brightman* (Abingdon, Oxon., 1978).
Beier, A. L., Cannadine, D. and Rosenheim, J. M. (eds.), *The First Modern Society: Essays in English History in Honour of Lawrence Stone* (Cambridge, 1989).
Bell, I. A., *Literature and Crime in Augustan England* (London, 1991).
Bellany, A., '"Raylinge Rymes and Vaunting Verse": Libellous Politics in Early Stuart England, 1603–1628', in K. Sharpe and P. Lake (eds.), *Culture and Politics in Early Stuart England* (Houndmills, 1994).
Belsey, C., *The Subject of Tragedy: Identity and Difference in Renaissance Drama* (New York, 1985; reprinted London, 1993).
Bennet, M., *The Civil Wars in Britain and Ireland 1638–1651* (Oxford, 1997).
Blench, J. W., *Preaching in England in the Late Fifteenth and Sixteenth Centuries: A Study of English Sermons 1450–c.1600* (Oxford, 1964).
Bossy, J., 'The English Catholic Community 1603–1625', in A. G. R. Smith (ed.), *The Reign of James VI and I* (London and Basingstoke, 1973).
The English Catholic Community, 1570–1850 (London, 1975).
'Moral Arithmetic: Seven Sins into Ten Commandments', in E. Leites (ed.), *Conscience and Casuistry in Early Modern Europe* (Cambridge, 1988).
Bostridge, I., 'Witchcraft Repealed', in J. Barry, M. Hester and G. Roberts (eds.), *Witchcraft in Early Modern Europe* (Cambridge, 1996), pp. 309–34.
Boyd, J. W., *Satan and Mara: Christian and Buddhist Symbols of Evil* (Leiden, 1975).
Brailsford, H. N., *The Levellers and the English Revolution*, ed. C. Hill (Stanford, Calif., 1961).

Brigden, S., *London and the Reformation* (corrected edition, Oxford, 1991).
Briggs, K., *Pale Hecate's Team: An Examination of the Beliefs on Witchcraft and Magic among Shakespeare's Contemporaries and his Immediate Successors* (London, 1962).
A Dictionary of British Folklore in the English Language, Part B: *Folk Legends* (London, 2 vols., 1971).
Briggs, R., *Early Modern France 1560–1715* (Oxford, 1977).
Witches and Neighbours: The Social and Cultural Context of European Witchcraft (London, 1996).
Bruyn, L. de, *Women and the Devil in Sixteenth-Century Literature* (Tisbury, 1979).
Burgess, G., *The Politics of the Ancient Constitution: An Introduction to English Political Thought 1603–1642* (University Park, Penn., 1992).
Burke, P., *Popular Culture in Early Modern Europe* (London, 1978).
Caciola, N., 'Wraiths, Revenants and Ritual in Medieval Culture', *Past and Present*, 152 (1996), pp. 3–45.
Capp, Bernard, 'The Political Dimension of Apocalyptic Thought', in C. A. Patrides and J. Wittrech (eds.), *The Apocalypse in English Renaissance Thought and Literature: Patterns, Antecedents and Repercussions* (Manchester, 1984).
Carmichael, J., *The Satanizing of the Jews: Origin and Development of Mystical Anti-Semitism* (New York, 1992).
Cavendish, R., *The Powers of Evil in Western Religion, Magic and Folk Belief* (London, 1975).
Cervantes, F., *The Devil in the New World: The Impact of Diabolism in New Spain* (New Haven, 1994).
'The Devil's Encounter with America', in J. Barry, M. Hester and G. Roberts (eds.), *Witchcraft in Early Modern Europe* (Cambridge, 1996).
Clark, S., 'Inversion, Misrule and the Meaning of Witchcraft', *Past and Present*, 87 (1980).
Thinking with Demons: The Idea of Witchcraft in Early Modern Europe (Oxford, 1997).
(ed.), *Languages of Witchcraft: Narrative, Ideology and Meaning in Early Modern Culture* (Houndmills, 2001).
Clark, Sandra, *The Elizabethan Pamphleteers: Popular Moralistic Pamphlets 1580–1640* (London, 1983).
Clark, Stuart, 'Protestant Demonology: Sin, Superstition and Society (*c.* 1520–*c.* 1630)', in B. Ankarloo and G. Henningsen (eds.), *Early Modern European Witchcraft: Centres and Peripheries* (Oxford, 1990), pp. 45–81.
'The Rational Witchfinder: Conscience, Demonologcal Naturalism and Popular Superstitions', in S. Pumfrey, P. L. Rossi and M. Slawinski (eds.), *Science, Culture and Popular Belief in Renaissance Europe* (Manchester, 1991), pp. 227–35.
Clifton, R., 'The Popular Fear of Catholics during the English Revolution', *Past and Present*, 52 (1971).
'Fear of Popery', in C. Russell (ed.), *The Origins of the English Civil War* (London, 1973).
Cockburn, J. S., *Calendar of Assize Records: Home Circuit Indictments: Elizabeth I and James I. Introduction* (London, 1975).
Cogswell, T., 'The Politics of Propaganda: Charles I and the People in the 1620s', *Journal of British Studies*, 29 (1990).

Cohn, N., *Europe's Inner Demons: An Enquiry Inspired by the Great Witch-Hunt* (London, 1975).
Cosmos, Chaos and the World to Come: The Ancient Roots of Apocalyptic Faith (New Haven and London, 1993).
Collinson, P., *The Elizabethan Puritan Movement* (Oxford, 1967).
The Religion of Protestants: The Church in English Society 1559–1625 (Oxford, 1982).
The Birthpangs of Protestant England: Religious and Cultural Change in the Sixteenth and Seventeenth Centuries (Houndmills, 1988; reprinted 1991).
'Elizabethan and Jacobean Puritanism as forms of Popular Religious Culture', in C. Durston and J. Eales (eds.), *The Culture of English Puritanism, 1560–1700* (Houndmills, 1996), pp. 32–57.
Cope, Esther S., *Politics without Parliaments 1629–1640* (London, 1987).
Crawford, Patricia, '"Charles Stuart, That Man of Blood"', *Journal of British Studies* (Spring, 1977).
Crawford, P., *Women and Religion in England* (London, 1996).
Cressy, D., *Bonfires and Bells: National Memory and the Protestant Calendar in Elizabethan and Stuart England* (London, 1989).
Birth, Marriage and Death: Ritual, Religion, and the Life-Cycle in Tudor and Stuart England (Oxford, 1997).
Travesties and Transgressions in Tudor and Stuart England: Tales of Discord and Dissension (Oxford, 2000).
Cumming, G. S., *A History of the Anglican Liturgy* (second edn, Houndmills, 1982).
Cushman, L. W., *The Devil and the Vice in English Dramatic Literature before Shakespeare* (London, 1900; reprinted 1970).
Cust, R., 'News and Politics in Early Seventeenth Century England', *Past and Present*, 112 (1986).
The Forced Loan and English Politics 1626–1628 (Oxford, 1987).
Cust, R. and Hughes, Ann (eds.), *Conflict in Early Stuart England: Studies in Religion and Politics, 1603–1642* (London, 1989).
Davies, O., 'Methodism, the Clergy, and the Popular Belief in Witchcraft and Magic', *History*, 82 (266) (1997).
Davis, J. C., *Fear, Myth and History: The Ranters and the Historians* (Cambridge, 1986).
Davison, P., *Popular Appeal in English Drama to 1850* (Totowa, N.J., 1982).
Dawson, A. B., 'Witchcraft/Bigamy: Cultural Conflict in *The Witch of Edmonton*', *Renaissance Drama*, new series, 20 (1989).
Dean, D. M. and Jones, N. L. (eds.), *The Parliaments of Elizabethan England* (London, 1990).
Delany, P., *British Autobiography in the Seventeenth Century* (London, 1969).
Dolan, F. E., *Dangerous Familiars: Representations of Domestic Crime in England 1550–1700* (Ithaca and London, 1994).
Duffy, E., *The Stripping of the Altars: Traditional Religion in England 1400–1580* (New Haven and London, 1992).
Durston, C., '"For the Better Humiliation of the People": Public Days of Fasting and Thanksgiving during the English Revolution', *Seventeenth Century*, 7 (2) (1992).
Durston, C. and Eales, J. (eds.), *The Culture of English Puritanism, 1560–1700* (Houndmills, 1996).
Eales, J., *Puritans and Roundheads: The Harleys of Brampton Bryan and the Outbreak of the English Civil War* (Cambridge, 1990).

'Thomas Pierson and the Transmission of the Moderate Puritan Tradition', *Midland History*, 20 (1995), pp. 75–102.
'A Road to Revolution: The Continuity of Puritanism, 1559–1642', in C. Durston and J. Eales (eds.), *The Culture of English Puritanism* (Houndmills, 1996), pp. 184–209.
Easlea, B., *Witch Hunting, Magic and the New Philosophy: And Introduction to Debates of the Scientific Revolution, 1450–1750* (Brighton, 1980).
Elmer, P., '"Saints or Sorcerers": Quakerism, Demonology and the Decline of Witchcraft in Seventeenth-Century England', in J. Barry, M. Hester and G. Roberts (eds.), *Witchcraft in Early Modern Europe* (Cambridge, 1996).
'Towards a Politics of Witchcraft in Early Modern England', in S. Clark (ed.), *Languages of Witchcraft* (Houndmills, 2001), pp. 101–18.
Emmerson, R. K., *Antichrist in the Middle Ages* (Manchester, 1981).
Erikson, K., *Wayward Puritans: A Study in the Sociology of Deviance* (New York, 1966).
Ewen, C. L'Estrange, *Witch Hunting and Witch Trials: The Indictments for Witchcraft from the Records of 1373 Assizes held for the Home Circuit A.D. 1559–1736* (London, 1929).
Faller, L. B., *Turned to Account: The Forms and Functions of Criminal Biography in Late Seventeenth- and Early Eighteenth-Century England* (Cambridge, 1987).
Ferguson, E., *Demonology of the Early Christian World* (New York and Toronto, Symposium Series XII, 1984).
Fincham, K., *The Early Stuart Church, 1603–1642* (Houndmills, 1993).
Fincham, K. and Lake, P., 'The Ecclesiastical Policies of James I and Charles I', in K. Fincham (ed.), *The Early Stuart Church, 1603–1642* (Houndmills, 1993).
Firth, K. R., *The Apocalyptic Tradition in Reformation Britain, 1530–1645* (Oxford, 1979).
Fisher, J. D. C., *Christian Initiation: Baptism in the Medieval West. A Study of the Disintegration of the Primitive Rite of Initiation* (London, 1965).
Fletcher, A. J., *The Outbreak of the English Civil War* (London, 1981).
Reform in the Provinces: The Government of Stuart England (New Haven and London, 1986).
Fletcher, A. J. and Roberts, P. (eds.), *Religion, Culture and Society in Early Modern Britain* (Cambridge, 1994).
Fletcher, A. J. and Stevenson, J. (eds.), *Order and Disorder in Early Modern England* (Cambridge, 1985).
Flint, V., *The Rise of Magic in Early Medieval Europe* (Oxford, 1991).
Forsyth, N., *The Old Enemy: Satan and the Combat Myth* (Princeton, N.J., 1987).
Foster, Stephen, *Notes from the Caroline Underground: Alexander Leighton, the Puritan Triumvirate, and the Laudian Reaction to Nonconformity* (Hamden, Conn. and Springfield, Ohio, 1978).
French, R. and Wear, A. (eds.), *The Medical Revolution of the Seventeenth Century* (Cambridge, 1989).
Friedman, J., *Miracles and the Pulp Press during the English Revolution: The Battle of the Frogs and Fairford's Flies* (London, 1993).
Gardiner, S. R. (ed.), *The Constitutional Documents of the Puritan Revolution 1625–1660* (3rd edn, Oxford, 1906).
History of England form the Accession of James I to the outbreak of the Civil war 1603–1642 (London, 10 vols., 1884).
Gaskill, M., 'Reporting Murder: Fiction in the Archives in Early Modern England', *Social History*, 23 (1) (1998).

Gattrell, V. A. C., Lenman, B. and Parker, G. (eds.), *Crime and the Law: The Social History of Crime in Western Europe since 1500* (London, 1980).
Gibson, M., *Reading Witchcraft: Stories of Early English Witches* (London, 1999).
Ginzburg, C., *Ecstasies: Deciphering the Witches' Sabbath*, trans. R. Rosenthal (London, 1991).
Godbeer, R., *The Devil's Dominion: Magic and Religion in Early New England* (Cambridge, 1992; reprinted 1994).
Goldhagen, D. J., *Hitler's Willing Executioners: Ordinary Germans and the Holocaust* (London, 1996).
Goodich, M., *Violence and the Miracle in the Fourteenth Century: Private Grief and Public Salvation* (Chicago and London, 1995).
Goring, J., *Godly Exercises or the Devil's Dance? Puritanism and Popular Culture in pre-Civil War England*, Dr Williams Library Lecture (London, 1983).
Gowing, L., *Domestic Dangers: Women, Words, and Sex in Early Modern London* (Oxford, 1996).
Green, I., *The Christian's ABC: Catechisms and Catechising in England c. 1530–1740* (Oxford, 1996).
Greenblatt, S., *Renaissance Self-Fashioning: From More to Shakespeare* (Chicago, 1980).
Griffiths, P., 'The Structure of Prostitution in Elizabethan London', *Continuity and Change* 8 (1993), pp. 39–63.
Gurevich, A., *Medieval Popular Culture: Problems of Belief and Perception*, trans. J. M. Bak and P. A. Hollingsworth (Cambridge, 1988).
Haigh, C. (ed.), *The Reign of Elizabeth* (Houndmills, 1984).
English Reformations: Religion, Politics, and Society under the Tudors (Oxford, 1993).
Haller, William, *The Rise of Puritanism* (London, 1957; first edn, 1938).
Harley, D., 'Mental Illness, Magical Medicine and the Devil in Northern England, 1650–1700', in R. French and A. Wear (eds.), *The Medical Revolution of the Seventeenth Century* (Cambridge, 1989).
'Historians as Demonologists: The Myth of the Midwife-Witch', *Social History of Medicine*, 3 (1990).
Harris, A., *Night's Black Agents: Witchcraft and Magic in Seventeenth-Century English Drama* (Manchester, 1980).
Harris, T., 'Problematising Popular Culture', in T. Harris (ed.), *Popular Culture in England, c.1500–1850* (Houndmills, 1995).
Haydon, C., '"I Love my King and my Country, but a Roman Catholic I Hate": Anti-Catholicism, Xenophobia and National Identity in Eighteenth-Century England', in T. Claydon and I. McBride, *Protestantism and National Identity: Britian and Ireland, c. 1650–c. 1850* (Cambridge, 1998).
Henningsen, G., *The Witches' Advocate: Basque Witchcraft and the Spanish Inquisition* (Reno, 1980).
Henningsen, Gustav, '"The Ladies from Outside": An Archaic Pattern of the Witches' Sabbath', in B. Ankarloo and G. Henningsen (eds.), *Early Modern European Witchcraft: Centres and Peripheries* (Oxford, 1990).
Herr, A. F., *The Elizabethan Sermon: A Survey and Bibliography* (New York, 1969).
Herrup, C., 'Law and Morality in Seventeenth-Century England', *Past and Present* 106 (1985).
The Common Peace: Participation and the Criminal Law in Seventeenth-Century England (Cambridge, 1987).

Hibbard, C. M., *Charles I and the Popish Plot* (Chapel Hill, N.C., 1983).
Hick, John, *Evil and the God of Love* (London, 1968).
Hill, C., *The World Turned Upside Down* (London, 1972; reprinted 1991).
A Turbulent, Seditious, and Factious People: John Bunyan and his Church 1628–1688 (Oxford, 1988).
Antichrist in Seventeenth-Century England (London, 1971; rev. edn, 1990).
The English Bible and the Seventeenth-Century Revolution (London, 1993).
Hillman, R., *Self-Speaking in Medieval and Early Modern English Drama* (Houndmills, 1997).
Holmes, C., 'Popular Culture? Witches, Magistrates, and Divines in Early Modern England', in S. L. Kaplan (ed.), *Understanding Popular Culture* (Berlin, 1984).
'Women, Witnesses and Witches', *Past and Present*, 140 (1993).
Houlbrooke, R. (ed.), *Death, Ritual and Bereavement* (London, 1989).
'The Puritan Death-Bed, *c.* 1560–*c.* 1660', in C. Durston and J. Eales, *The Culture of English Puritanism* (Houndmills, 1996).
Hughes, Anne, '"Popular" Presbyerianism in the 1640s and 1650s?: The Cases of Thomas Edwards and Thomas Hall', in N. Tyacke (ed.), *England's Long Reformation, 1500–1800* (London, 1998).
Hughes, P. E., *Theology of the English Reformers* (London, 1965).
Hutton, R., *The Rise and Fall of Merry England: The Ritual Year 1400–1700* (Oxford, 1994).
Ingram, M., 'Ridings, Rough Music and "the Reform of Popular Culture" in Early Modern England', *Past and Present*, 105 (1984).
'Ridings, Rough Music and Mocking Rhymes', in B. Reay (ed.), *Popular Culture in Seventeenth-Century England* (London, 1988).
de Jesus-Marie, B. (ed.), *Satan* (London, 1951).
Johnstone, Nathan, 'The Protestant Devil: The Experience of Temptation in Early Modern England', *Journal of British Studies*, 43 (2) (2004), pp. 173–205.
Journet, Charles, *The Meaning of Evil* (London, 1963).
Kaplan, S. L. (ed.), *Understanding Popular Culture: Europe from the Middle Ages to the Nineteenth Century* (Berlin, 1984).
Kastan, D. S. and Stallybrass, P. (eds.), *Staging the Renaissance: Reinterpretations of Elizabethan and Jacobean Drama* (London, 1991).
Kelly, H. A., *Towards the Death of Satan* (Garden City, N.Y., 1971).
The Devil, Demonology and Witchcraft (Garden City, N.Y., 1974).
The Devil at Baptism: The Demonic Dramaturgy of Christian Initiation (Ithaca and London, 1985).
Kenyon, J. P., *The Stuart Constitution* (second edn, Cambridge, 1986).
Kermode, J. and Walker, G. (eds.), *Women, Crime and the Courts in Early Modern England* (London, 1994).
Kibbey, A., 'Mutations of the Supernatural: Witchcraft, Remarkable Providences, and the Power of Puritan Men', *American Quarterly*, 34 (1982).
Kieckhefer, R., *European Witch Trials: Their Foundations in Popular and Learned Culture, 1300–1500* (London, 1976).
Magic in the Middle Ages (Cambridge, 1989).
Kinsman, R. S. (ed.), *The Darker Vision of the Renaissance: Beyond the Fields of Reason* (Berkeley, 1974).
Klaits, J., *Servants of Satan: The Age of the Witch Hunts* (Bloomington, Ind., 1985).
Lake, P., 'The Significance of the Elizabethan Identification of the Pope as Antichrist', *Journal of Ecclesiastical History*, 31 (2) (1980).

'Anti-Popery: The Structure of a Prejudice', in R. Cust and A. Hughes, *Conflict in Early Stuart England* (London, 1989), pp. 72–106.
'Puritanism, Arminianism and a Shropshire Axe-Murder', *Midland History*, 15 (1990).
'Deeds against Nature: Cheap Print, Protestantism and Murder in Seventeenth-Century England', in K. Sharpe and P. Lake (eds.), *Culture and Politics in Early Stuart England* (Houndmills, 1994).
'Popular Form, Puritan Content? Two Puritan Appropriations of the Murder Pamphlet from Mid-Seventeenth-Century London', in A. J. Fletcher and P. Roberts (eds.), *Religion, Culture and Society in Early Modern Britain* (Cambridge, 1994).
The Boxmaker's Revenge: 'Orthodoxy', 'Heterodoxy' and the Politics of the Parish in Early Stuart London (Manchester, 2001).
Lake, P. and Dowling, M. (eds.), *Protestantism and the National Church in Sixteenth Century England* (London, 1987).
Lake, P. with Questier, M., *Antichrist's Lewd Hat: Protestants, Papists and Players in Post-Reformation England* (New Haven and London, 2002).
Lamont, W., *Marginal Prynne 1600–1669* (London, 1963).
Godly Rule: Politics and Religion, 1603–1660 (London, 1969).
'Pamphleteering, the Protestant Consensus and the English Revolution', in R. C. Richardson and G. M. Ridden (eds.), *Freedom and the English Revolution* (Manchester, 1986).
Puritanism and Historical Controversy (London, 1996).
Larner, C., *Enemies of God: The Witch-Hunt in Scotland* (London, 1981).
Witchcraft and Religion: The Politics of Popular Belief, ed. A. Macfarlane (Oxford, 1984).
Lea, H. C., *Materials Toward a History of Witchcraft*, ed. A. C. Howland (London, 3 vols., 1957).
Leites, E. (ed.), *Conscience and Casuistry in Early Modern Europe* (Cambridge, 1988).
Levack, B. P., 'The Great Scottish Witch Hunt of 1661–1662', *Journal of British Studies* 20 (1980–1), pp. 90–108.
The Witch-Hunt in Early Modern Europe (London, 1987).
Levine, L., *Men in Women's Clothing: Anti-Theatricality and Effeminization 1579–1642* (Cambridge, 1996).
Lindley, David, *The Trials of Frances Howard: Fact and Fiction at the Court of King James* (London and New York, 1993).
Link, L., *The Devil: A Mask without a Face* (London, 1995).
Loach, J., *Parliament Under the Tudors* (Oxford, 1991).
Luttmer, F., 'Persecutors, Tempters and Vassals of the Devil: The Unregenerate in Puritan Practical Divinity', *Journal of Ecclesiastical History*, 51 (1) (2000), pp. 37–68.
MacCulloch, Diarmaid, 'England', in A. Pettegree (ed.), *The Early Reformation in Europe* (Cambridge, 1992).
MacDonald, M., *Mystical Bedlam: Madness, Anxiety, and Healing in Seventeenth-Century England* (Cambridge, 1981).
'Religion, Social Change and Psychological Healing in England, 1600–1800', in W. J. Sheils (ed.), *The Church and Healing* (Oxford, 1982), pp. 101–25.
(ed.), *Witchcraft and Hysteria in Elizabethan London: Edward Jorden and the Mary Glover Case* (London, 1991).

'The Fearefull Estate of Francis Spira: Narrative, Identity and Emotion in Early Modern England', *Journal of British Studies* 31 (January 1992).
MacDonald, M. and Murphy, T., *Sleepless Souls: Suicide in Early Modern England* (Oxford, 1990).
Macfarlane, A., *The Family Life of Ralph Josselin, a Seventeenth-Century Clergyman* (Cambridge, 1970).
Witchcraft in Tudor and Stuart England: A Regional and Comparative Study (London, 1970).
'The Root of All Evil', in D. Parkin (ed.) *The Anthropology of Evil* (Oxford, 1985).
Maclure, M., *The Paul's Cross Sermons 1534–1642* (Toronto, 1958).
McGrath, A. E., *Reformation Thought: An Introduction* (second edn, Oxford, 1993).
McGrath, P., *Papists and Puritans under Elizabeth I* (London, 1967).
McGregor, J. F. and Reay, B. (eds.), *Radical Religion in the English Revolution* (Oxford, 1984).
Maguire, N. K., *Regicide and Restoration: English Tragicomedy, 1660–1671* (Cambridge, 1992).
Malcolm, J. L., *Caesar's Due: Loyalty and King Charles 1642–1646* (London, 1983).
Maltby, W. S., *The Black Legend in England: The Development of Anti-Spanish Sentiment 1558–1660* (Durham, N.C., 1971).
Mann, D., *The Elizabethan Player: Contemporary Stage Representation* (London, 1991).
Manning, B., *The English People and the English Revolution* (second edn, London, 1991).
Marsh, C., *Popular Religion in Sixteenth-Century England* (Houndmills, 1998).
Marshburn, Joseph, *Murder and Witchcraft in England* (Norman, Okla., 1974).
Marx, C. W., *The Devil's Rights and the Redemption in the Literature of Medieval England* (Cambridge, 1995).
Maus, K. E., *Inwardness and the Theatre in the English Renaissance* (Chicago, 1995).
Messadié, G., *The History of the Devil*, trans. M. Romano (London, 1996).
Midelfort, H. C. E., *Witch Hunting in Southwestern Germany, 1562–1684* (Stanford, Calif., 1972).
Miller, E. H., *The Professional Writer in Elizabethan England: A Study in Nondramatic Literature* (Cambridge, Mass., 1959).
Milward, P., *Religious Controversies of the Elizabethan Age: A Survey of Printed Sources* (London, 1977).
Religious Controversies of the Jacobean Age: A Survey of Printed Sources (London, 1978).
Monter, E. W., *Witchcraft in France and Switzerland: The Borderlands during the Reformation* (London, 1976).
Montrose, Louis, *The Purpose of Playing: Shakespeare and the Cultural Politics of the Elizabethan Theatre* (Chicago and London, 1996).
Moore, R. I., *The Origins of European Dissent* (London, 1977).
The Formation of a Persecuting Society: Power and Deviance in Western Europe 950–1250 (Oxford, 1987).
Morgan, J., *Godly Learning: Puritan Attitudes towards Reason, Learning and Education 1560–1640* (Cambridge, 1988).
Morgan, N. (ed.), *A Survey of Manuscripts Illuminated in the British Isles*, Vol. IV (I): *Early Gothic Manuscripts 1190–1250* (Oxford, 1982).
Morrill, J., *Revolt in the Provinces: Conservatives and Radicals in the English Civil War* (London, 1980).

(ed.), *Reactions to the English Civil War, 1642–1649* (Houndmills, 1982).
(ed.), *Oliver Cromwell and the English Revolution* (London, 1990).
'Cromwell and his Contemporaries', in J. Morrill (ed.), *Oliver Cromwell and the English Revolution* (London, 1990).
The Nature of the English Revolution (London, 1993).
Morrill, J., Slack, P. and Woolf, D. (eds.), *Public Duty and Private Conscience in Seventeenth-Century England: Essays Presented to G. E. Aylmer* (Oxford, 1993).
Muchembled, R., 'Satanic Myths and Cultural Reality', in B. Ankarloo and G. Henningsen (eds.), *Early Modern European Witchcraft* (Oxford, 1990).
Notestein, W., *A History of Witchcraft in England* (New York, 1965; first edn, 1909).
Nicholls, M., *Investigating Gunpowder Plot* (Manchester, 1991).
Nightingale, B., *The Ejected of 1662 in Cumberland and Westmorland: Their Predecessors and Successors* (Manchester, 1911).
Nirenburg, D., *Communities of Violence: Persecution of Minorities in the Middle Ages* (Princeton, N.J., 1996).
Nishan, B., 'The Exorcism Controversy and Baptism in the Late Reformation', *Sixteenth Century Journal*, 18 (1) (1987).
O'Day, R. and Heal, F. (eds.), *Continuity and Change: Personnel and Administration of the Church of England 1500–1642* (Leicester, 1976).
Oldridge, D., *Religion and Society in Early Modern England* (Aldershot, 1998).
The Devil in Early Modern England (Stroud, 2000).
Openshaw, K. M., 'Weapons in the Daily Battle: Images of the Conquest of Evil in the Early Modern Psalter', *Art Bulletin*, 75 (1) (March 1993), pp. 17–38.
Owst, G. R., *Literature and the Pulpit in Medieval England* (Cambridge, 1933; republished Oxford, 1961).
Pagels, E., *The Origin of Satan* (London, 1995).
Papini, G., *The Devil: Notes for a Future Diabology*, trans. A. Foulke (London, 1955).
Parkin, D. (ed.), *The Anthropology of Evil* (Oxford, 1985).
Patrides, C. A. and Wittreich, J. (eds.), *The Apocalypse in English Renaissance Thought and Literature: Patterns, Antecedents and Repercussions* (Manchester, 1984).
Peck, Linda Levy, *Court Patronage and Corruption in Early Stuart England* (London, 1990).
Peters, E., *The Magician, the Witch and the Law* (Philadelphia, 1978).
Poliakov, Leon, *The History of Anti-Semitism* (London, 1965).
Porter, H. C., *Reformation and Reaction in Tudor Cambridge* (Cambridge, 1958).
Porter, R., *The Social History of Madness: Stories of the Insane* (London, 1987).
Purkiss, D., *The Witch in History: Early Modern and Twentieth-Century Representations* (London, 1996).
Quaife, G. R., *Godly Zeal and Furious Rage: The Witch in Early Modern Europe* (London, 1987).
Raymond, Joad, *Making the News: An Anthology of the Newsbooks of Revolutionary England 1641–1660* (Moreton-in-Marsh, 1993).
Reay, B., *The Quakers and the English Revolution* (New York, 1985).
(ed.), *Popular Culture in Seventeenth-Century England* (London, 1988).
Remnant, G. L., *Catalogue of Misericords in Great Britain* (Oxford, 1969).
Rhodes, N., *Elizabethan Grotesque* (London, 1980).
Richardson, R. C. and Ridden, G. M. (eds.), *Freedom and the English Revolution: Essays in History and Literature* (Manchester, 1986).
Ricoeur, Paul, 'Evil, a Challenge to Philosophy and Theology', *Journal of the American Academy of Religion*, 53 (3) (1985).

Roper, L., *Oedipus and the Devil: Witchcraft, Sexuality and Religion in Early Modern Europe* (London, 1994).
Rosen, B., *Witchcraft* (London, 1969).
Roots, I., *The Great Rebellion 1642–1660* (London, 1966).
Rowland, Robert, '"Fantasticall and Devilishe Persons": European Witch-Beliefs in Comparative Perspective', in B. Ankarloo and G. Henningsen (eds.), *Early Modern European Witchcraft: Centres and Peripheries* (Oxford, 1990).
Rubenstein, L. and Roth, J. K., *Approaches to Auschwitz: The Holocaust and its Legacy* (Atlanta, 1987).
Rudwin, M., *The Devil in Legend and Literature* (La Salle, Ill., 1931).
Rushton, P., 'Women, Witchcraft, and Slander in Early Modern England: Cases from the Church Courts of Durham, 1560–1675', *Northern History*, 18 (1982), pp. 116–32.
Russell, C., *The Crisis of Parliaments: English History 1509–1660* (Oxford, 1971).
(ed.), *The Origins of the English Civil War* (London, 1973).
Parliaments and English Politics 1621–1629 (Oxford, 1979).
The Causes of the English Civil War: The Ford Lectures Delivered in the University of Oxford 1987–1988 (Oxford, 1990).
The Fall of the British Monarchies 1637–1642 (Oxford, 1991).
'Divine Rights in the Early Seventeenth Century', in J. Morrill, P. Slack and D. Woolf (eds.), *Public Duty and Private Conscience in Seventeenth-Century England* (Oxford, 1993).
Russell, J. B., *The Devil: Perceptions of Evil from Antiquity to Primitive Christianity* (Ithaca and London, 1977).
Satan: The Early Christian Tradition (Ithaca and London, 1981).
Lucifer: The Devil in the Middle Ages (Ithaca and London, 1984).
Mephistopheles: The Devil in the Modern World (Ithaca and London, 1986).
Samaha, J., *Law and Order in Historical Perspective: The Case of Elizabethan Essex* (New York and London, 1974).
Sawyer, R. C., '"Strangely handled in all her Lyms": Witchcraft and Healing in Jacobean England', *Journal of Social History*, 22 (3) (1989).
Schwarz, H., *Evil: An Historical and Theological Perspective* (Minneapolis, 1995).
Scribner, R. W., *For the Sake of Simple Folk: Popular Propaganda for the German Reformation* (Oxford, 1981).
'The Reformation, Popular Magic, and the "Disenchantment of the World"', *Journal of Interdisciplinary History*, 23 (3) (1993).
Seaver, P. S., *Wallington's World: A Puritan Artisan in Seventeenth-Century London* (Stanford, Calif., 1985).
Shakespeare, J., 'Plague and Punishment', in P. Lake and M. Dowling (eds.), *Protestantism and the National Church in Sixteenth Century England* (London, 1987), pp. 103–23.
Sharpe, K., *The Personal Rule of Charles I* (New Haven, 1992).
Sharpe, K. and Lake, P. (eds.), *Culture and Politics in Early Stuart England* (Houndmills, 1994).
Sharpe, J. A., *Crime in Early Modern England: A County Study* (Cambridge, 1983).
'"Last Dying Speeches": Religion Ideology and Public Execution in Seventeenth-Century England', *Past and Present*, 107 (1985).
'Witchcraft and Women in Seventeenth-Century England: Some Northern Evidence', *Continuity and Change*, 6 (2) (1991).
Witchcraft in Seventeenth-Century Yorkshire: Accusations and Counter Measures, University of York, Borthwick Paper, No. 81 (York, 1992).

'Women, Witchcraft and the Legal Process', in J. Kermode and G. Walker (eds.), *Women, Crime and the Courts in Early Modern England* (London, 1994).
Instruments of Darkness: Witchcraft in England 1550–1750 (London, 1996).
Sharpe, J. A. and Stone, L., 'Debate: The History of Violence in England: Some Observations', *Past and Present*, 108 (1985).
Smith, A. G. R. (ed.), *The Reign of James VI and I* (London and Basingstoke, 1973).
Smith, N., *Literature and Revolution in England, 1640–1660* (New Haven and London, 1994).
Sommerville, J., *Politics and Ideology in England 1603–1640* (London, 1986).
Spufford, M., *Small Books and Pleasant Histories: Popular Fiction and its Readership in Seventeenth-Century England* (London, 1981).
Stachniewski, J., *The Persecutory Imagination: English Puritanism and the Literature of Religious Despair* (Oxford, 1991).
Stannard, D. E., *The Puritan Way of Death: A Study in Religion, Culture, and Social Change* (New York, 1977).
Stephens, F. G., *Catalogue of Political and Personal Satires preserved in the Department of Prints and Drawings in the British Museum*, vol. I: *1320–1689* (London, 1978).
Stone, L., 'Interpersonal Violence in English Society 1300–1980', *Past and Present*, 101 (1983).
Swanson, R. N., *Religion and Devotion in Europe, c. 1215–c. 1515* (Cambridge, 1995).
Thomas, K., *Religion and the Decline of Magic: Studies in Popular Beliefs in Sixteenth- and Seventeenth-Century England* (London, 1971; reprinted 1991).
Man and the Natural World: Changing Attitudes in England 1500–1800 (London, 1983).
Tomlinson, H. (ed.), *Before the English Civil War: Essays on Early Stuart Politics and Government* (Houndmills, 1983).
Trachtenburg, J., *The Devil and the Jews: The Medieval Conception of the Jew in Relation to Modern Anti-Semitism* (Philidelphia and Jerusalem, 1943; reprinted 1993).
Trevor-Roper, H., *Religion, Reformation and Social Change* (London, 1967).
The European Witch-Craze of the Sixteenth and Seventeenth Centuries (London, 1969; reprinted 1988).
Tubach, F. C., *Index Exemplorum: A Handbook of Medieval Religious Tales* (Helsinki, F. F. Communications No. CCIV, 1969).
Tyacke, N., 'Puritanism, Arminianism and Counter-Revolution', in C. Russell (ed.), *The Origins of the English Civil War* (London, 1973).
Underdown, D., *Revel, Riot and Rebellion: Popular Politics and Culture in England 1603–1660* (Oxford, 1985).
'The Taming of the Scold: The Enforcement of Patriarchal Authority in Early Modern England', in A. J. Fletcher and J. Stevenson (eds.), *Order and Disorder in Early Modern England* (Cambridge, 1985).
A Freeborn People: Politics and the Nation in Seventeenth-Century England (Oxford, 1996).
Walker, D. P., *Unclean Spirits: Possession and Exorcism in France and England in the Late Sixteenth and Early Seventeenth Centuries* (London, 1981).
Walsham, A., '"The Fatall Vesper": Providentialism and Anti-Popery in Late Jacobean London', *Past and Present*, 144 (1994).
Providence in Early Modern England (Oxford, 1999).
Watkins, O. C., *The Puritan Experience* (London, 1972).

Watt, T., *Cheap Print and Popular Piety, 1550–1640* (Cambridge, 1991).
Watts, M., *The Dissenters* (Oxford, 2 vols., 1978).
Wear, A., French, R. K. and Lonie, I. M. (eds.), *The Medical Renaissance of the Sixteenth Century* (Cambridge, 1985).
Webster, T., 'Writing to Redundancy: Approaches to Spiritual Journals and Early Modern Spirituality', *Historical Journal*, 39 (1) (1996).
Godly Clergy in Early Stuart England: The Caroline Puritan Movement, c.1620–1643 (Cambridge, 1997).
Wiener, C. Z., 'The Beleaguered Isle. A Study of Elizabethan and Early Jacobean Anti-Catholicism', *Past and Present*, 51 (1971).
Whitacker, E. C. (ed.), *Martin Bucer and the Book of Common Prayer* (Great Wakering, 1974).
White, L., 'Death and the Devil', in R. S. Kinsman (ed.), *The Darker Vision of the Renaissance* (Berkeley, 1974), pp. 25–46.
Williams, P., *The Later Tudors: England 1547–1603* (Oxford, 1995).
Wilks, M. (ed.), *Prophesy and Eschatology*, Studies in Church History, Subsidia X (Oxford, 1994).
Willis, D., *Malevolent Nurture: Witch-Hunting and Maternal Power in Early Modern England* (Ithaca and London, 1995).
Wiltenburg, J., *Disorderly Women and Female Power in the Street Literature of Early Modern England and Germany* (Charlottesville, Va., and London, 1992).
Wymer, R., *Suicide and Despair in Jacobean Drama* (Brighton, 1986).
Yates, F., *The Occult Philosophy in the Elizabethan Age* (London, 1979).

INDEX

absolutism, 197
Adam, 71, 192
  fall of, 2, 5, 44, 67, 69, 70, 109, 186, 190
  temptation of, 51, 61
Ainsworth, Henry, 255
alcohol, 77, 81
alehouses, diabolism of, 39, 56, 80
Allen, Hannah, 120, 125, 126, 129, 130
altar policy, 184
Anabaptists, 261, 265, 266, 267
angels, 91, 93, 94
Anthony, St, 83
anti-Catholicism, 28, 41, 59, 216
Antichrist, 27, 38, 42, 48, 55, 219
antinomianism, 261, 266, 269, 278
apocalypticism, 49, 50, 218, 230
apostasy, 29, 32, 41, 44, 52, 127, 177, 198, 204, 245
  felonious, 14, 19, 76, 149
Apprehension and confession of three notorious Witches, The, 148
Aquinas, Thomas, 73, 74
Armada, Spanish, 40, 218
Arminianism, 5, 6, 199, 233
ars moriendi, 64, 74, 137
Aspinwall, Edward, 100
assurance, 110, 114, 128, 131, 138, 165, 267, 273
atheism, 132, 151
Atkinson, Christopher, 279, 280–1, 282
Augustine, St, 9, 29, 73
autobiography, 107

Babington, Anthony, 187
Bale, John, 33, 49, 52, 55, 58
ballads, 144, 172
Balsom, Robert, 105
Bancroft, Richard, 103, 104, 195
baptism, 34, 47, 60, 87, 204, 206
  godparents' promise in, 60, 63, 64, 85
  diabolic inversion of, 154
  possession of the unbaptised child, 60
  reform of, 2, 63–6
Baptists, 135
Bargrave, Isaac, 198
Barker, Francis, 291
Barnes, Robert, 31, 33, 41, 46, 47, 49, 53
Baroja, J. C., 74
Barrow, Henry, 182
Bastwick, John, 204, 209, 233
Baudelaire, Charles, 1
Bauthumley, Jacob, 268–9
Baxter, Richard, 69, 124, 125, 138
Bayly, Lewis, *The Practice of Piety*, 86, 97, 108, 118, 131, 165
Beard, Thomas, *Theatre of Gods judgements*, 205
Becon, Thomas, 29, 33, 37, 42, 45, 46, 48, 58, 63, 70, 77, 78, 90, 97, 137
  Christen Knight, The, 96, 98, 104
  New Catechism, A, 68, 78
Bellarmine, Robert, 82, 83
Belsey, Catherine, 291
Bennet, Thomas, 32
Bible, 37, 84, 97, 130, 133, 135, 138, 236, 267, 281
  1 Samuel 15: 23, rebellion characterised by, 176, 177, 198, 201, 212, 236
  2 Corinthians 6: 14–15, diabolic subversion characterised by, 43, 177, 179, 181, 189, 210, 221, 250, 253, 263, 265, 268, 269, 271, 276
  2 Corinthians, 11: 14, diabolic subversion characterised by, 43
  1 Peter 5: 8, Devil characterised by, 35–6, 37, 91, 93, 230–1

scriptural archetypes, 30, 45, 67, 69
see also Book of Revelation
bishops, 179, 183; *see also* episcopacy
blasphemy, 123, 276
Blome, Richard, 282
Bolton, Robert, 99, 101, 124
Bossy, J., 87
Bradford, John, 96
Bradshaw, William, 121
Brailsford, H. N., 210
Brandon, Richard, 244
Brettergh, Katherine, 99, 100, 101, 123, 130, 138
Bridges, John, 181
Briggs, R., 10, 13, 14, 74
Bucer, Martin, 35, 63, 65
Bullinger, Heinrich, 34, 36, 38, 103, 186
Bunyan, John, 18, 118, 122, 125, 126, 133, 136, 139–40
Burcher, John, 34
Burges, Cornelius, 218
Burton, Henry, 204, 209, 233, 253–4, 255, 260, 262
Burton, Thomas, 276

Cain, 51
Caldwell, Elizabeth, 145, 152, 157, 166
Calfhill, James, 44, 47, 48, 49
Calvin, John, 34, 35, 36, 44
Institutes of Christian Religion, 30, 31, 108, 132
Calvinism, 44, 107, 255
Candlemas, 2, 74, 84
cannibalism, 154
Capel, Richard, 98, 99, 129
Carter, William, 217, 218, 222–3
Cartwright, Thomas, 178, 180, 181
catechisms, 67–8, 237
inverted, 97–8
Catherine of Siena, 83
Catholic church, 4, 23, 27, 53, 206
anti-demonic practices in, 93–5
clerical abuses, supposed, 27
experience of, Protestant understanding of, 27
false doctrine of, 4, 45, 46, 267
false piety of, 47, 81
good works, 69
hidden diabolism of, 1, 27, 51
image worship, 47, 51, 69
missions, 87
sedition, 38, 191
see also Anti-Catholicism, priesthood
Catholicism, 168, 177, 186–7, 191, 199, 259, 292
Catholics, 28, 87, 89, 157, 177, 185, 189, 193, 197, 198, 203, 204, 205, 208, 209, 224, 227, 257, 265; *see also* recusants
Cavaliers, 213
diabolism of, 214, 229, 231
Cecil, Robert, 195
ceremonial, 47, 60, 62, 67, 83–4, 85, 206, 239, 253, 254
artefacts, use of, 60, 66, 83, 91
chaos, Devil as bringer of, 167, 191
Charles I, 6, 54, 197, 198, 199, 205, 208, 211, 212, 213, 214, 216, 217, 224, 225, 226, 230, 231, 236, 240, 241, 244, 246
diabolic temptation of, 201, 202, 208, 233–6
diabolism of, 234
enemy of Satan, 203
execution of, 214, 234, 235, 241–2, 243
personal rule, 203
Charles II, 245, 247
Chidley, Daniel, 253
Chidley, Katherine, 253, 254, 255, 262
children, 115
Christ
exorcisms of, 219
Passion of, 69, 95, 257, 275
temptation of, 47, 54, 65, 67, 69, 73, 92, 126, 273
see also deicide
church,
history of, 50
pre-Reformation, 91–3
primitive, 52, 54, 178
Church Fathers, 73
Church of England, 257
Civil War, 16, 105, 175, 212, 213, 214, 265, 292
explanatory devices employed during, 216
Clark, S., 15, 19, 176, 286
Clarke, Katherine, 109, 119, 122, 124, 135
Clarke, Samuel, 3, 121
godly lives, 99, 100, 105, 119
Clarkson, Laurence, 269, 271
clergy, *see* ministry, priesthood
Coachman, Robert, 255
Cohn, N., 13
Coke, Edward, 189, 200
Coleman Street, 264
Collinson, P., 57
communion, 271
community, 84
temptation and, 22
complaint literature, 77, 80
conduct books, 3
confession, 88–90
focus of diabolic activity, 89

conformists, 178, 180, 183
conformity, 265
congregations, mixed, 250, 254
conscience,
  afflicted, 96–101, 128
  vigilance over, necessity of, 154, 158, 280
consecration, diabolic, 198
contrariety, 20, 27, 41, 69, 176, 291
Cooper, Thomas, 183
Cook, John, 234
Cope, Esther, 204
Corbet, Margaret, 99, 139
Cosin, 70
Cotton, John, 98
Counter-Reformation, 87
Coverdale, Miles, 47, 53
Cranmer, Thomas, 31, 32, 34, 35, 36, 68, 72, 78, 90, 185
Crawford, P., 234
creed, 85
criminality, 142
  diabolism as an explanation of, 4, 150–3, 154
criminals, mediators of diabolic agency, 150; *see also* sin
Cromwell, Oliver, 245, 246
  diabolism of, 243, 244, 246, 247–8
Crouch, John, 242

dancing, diabolism of, 4, 39, 56, 80
Darcy, Brian, 148, 152
Darrell, John, 102, 103, 104
Davis, J. C., 214, 266, 268
Davy, Sarah, 118, 128, 130, 132, 135
death-bed, 3, 60, 97, 99, 100, 123, 137–8
Decalogue, 52, 85
deicide, 52, 54
Dekker, Thomas, *The Witch of Edmonton*, 170
demonism, 290, 292
  as language of negotiation, 17
  definition of, 19–20, 24
  eclecticism of, 110
  Protestant, characteristics of, 1–2
demonisation, 214, 217, 223
demonology, 286
  as distinct from demonism, 19, 24
  works of, 29
demons, 75
  fallen angels, 71
  familiars, 14, 75, 143, 148
Dering, Edward, 178–80
despair, religious, 12, 17, 22, 97, 107, 114, 292
Detection of damnable drifts practiced by three Witches arraigned at Chelmisford, A, 151
D'Ewes, Simonds, 110, 112, 135
Devil,
  as opportunist, 155
  Christianity, Devil's agency disguised within, 41, 43
  commonwealth, Devil as subverter of, 4–6
  conscience, Devil experienced within, 2, 61, 65, 293
  contingent reality of, 15
  danger of, 1
  de facto power of, 30, 61, 177, 178, 179, 180, 191, 204, 254
  experience of, engagement with, 23, 61, 62, 114, 129, 174, 217, 290, 291
  false doctrine and, 43, 56, 210, 217, 223, 224, 225, 226, 251, 257, 259, 265, 266, 267, 268, 276, 279, 282
  God's ape, 43, 291
  God's hangman, 61, 70–1, 74, 76, 125, 213, 215, 244
  hidden agency of, 1, 23, 41, 44, 49, 56, 61, 76–7
  human life as constant struggle with, 63, 64
  illusion, Devil's power of, 286
  index of significance for belief in, 12
  invasive power of, 28, 65, 72–83, 159, 164, 170, 186, 291
  kingdom of, 150–3
  nomenclature of power, 31, 35–6, 109, 117
  pact with, 55
  patronage of, 224, 228, 237–8
  physical manifestations of, 18, 19, 73, 74–5, 82–3, 112, 121, 125, 143, 148, 170–3, 215
  popular concepts of, 15
  Protestant conception of, 19
  psychology and, 23
  rejection of belief in, 268
  resistance to, 61, 85, 97
  servants of, 4, 164
  subversion, as agency of, 2, 41, 56, 89, 176, 178, 182, 201, 204, 217, 218, 226, 227, 228, 252, 257, 260, 263, 265, 268, 281, 292, 293
  symbol, 20
  vicarious experience of, 143, 153, 164
  victimisation and, 12, 18, 130
  vigilance against, importance of, 138, 139–40, 292
  world, flesh and the, 77–9, 93
  worship of, 43
  see also Bible, consecration, diabolic affliction, inversion, Lucifer, murder, synagogue of Satan, theatre
diabolic affliction, experience of, 60

Directory for the Public Worship of God, 66, 239
disorder, 41, 270
Dod, John, 98, 99, 100, 138
Dolan, F., 167
Drake, Francis, 40
Drake, Joan, 99
Dudley, John, duke of Northumberland, 36
Duffy, E., 62, 66, 91
Dugdale, Gilbert, 152, 157, 166

Eales, J., 100, 184
Earls Colne, 25
Eden, 50, 200
Edgehill, Battle of, 215
Edward VI, 35
Edwards, Thomas, 257–61, 262, 264
  Gangræna, 258–62, 264
election, 61, 110, 116, 140, 292
Eliot, John, 203
Elizabeth I, 5, 38, 40, 181, 183, 184, 187, 188–9, 212
  religious controversies under, 177–84
  religious settlement of, 5, 38, 176, 178
  succession, 184
Elmer, P., 16, 175, 212, 252, 270
empathy, in narratives of diabolic agency, 142, 153–70
Enlightenment, 1, 10, 286, 290, 292, 293
Engagement Oath, 245, 247
England, Reformation in, 1, 34, 37, 38
episcopacy, 5, 204, 208, 209–11
  diabolism of, 177, 179–80, 182, 224, 231
Eucharist, 1, 34, 84, 94
  real presence in, 34, 84, 192
  transubstantiation, 34, 82
Evan, Enoch ap, 209
Eve, temptation of, 51, 61, 67, 70, 73, 164
evil, 8–9, 290, 292
  experiential approach among Protestants, 29
  functional symbols of, 8
  theodicy, 9, 11
Examination and Confession of Certain Wytches at Chensford, The, 148
execution, 166
Exhortation to the Bishops and the Clergie, An, 179
exorcism, 5, 8, 60, 63–5, 66, 91, 102, 113–14, 116, 200, 234, 240
  prayer and fasting, by, 102, 103–4
experimentation in religion, 263

Faller, L., 143, 153
Fairfax, Thomas, 243, 244, 245
fasting, 69
fast sermons, 217–18
  pastoral role of, 220
Faustus, John, 241
Fawkes, Guy, 190–1
Field, John, 179
  Admonition to the Parliament, An, 179
Finch, John, 203
Five Knights case, 198, 200
Fletcher, A., 214, 216
Flower, Joan, 149, 156, 160
folk-tales, 172, 215
forced loan, 197–8, 199, 201
Ford, John, 170
Fox, George, 119, 271, 272–5
Foxe, John, 51, 105
  Acts and monuments, 32, 232
Friedman, J., 216
Frith, John, 42, 46, 49

Galis, Richard, 120, 153
Gardiner, Stephen, 33, 34, 36
  A Detection of the Deuils Sophistrie, 33
Gataker, Thomas, 121
genocide, 9
Geree, John, 257
Gifford, George, 57, 96
Gilpin, John, 129, 252, 278–81
Glover, Mary, 103, 104, 111, 112
Godbeer, R., 17, 20, 110, 129
godly, 86, 107, 293
  biographies, 99
  community, 133, 135
  marginalisation within, 119, 135
  reaction to the Devil, 117
  soldiers against the Devil, 20, 61, 62
  see also temptation
Goldsmiths Hall Committee, 238
good works, doctrine of, 1
Goodcole, Henry, 150
Goodwin, John, 229–30, 233, 255, 260, 263–5
Gosson, Stephen, 39, 56, 80, 86, 204
Green, I., 67
Greenham, Richard, 98
Gregory the Great, 73
Grey, Jane, 36
Gunpowder Plot, 5, 189–93, 196, 208, 211, 212, 218
Gunter, Mary, 119, 124
Gurevich, A., 75

Harley, Brilliana, 108, 109, 113, 116–17, 118, 120
Harris, Robert, 98, 99, 100, 101, 109, 122, 136, 137, 220

Harrison, James, 101
Harrison, William, 101
Hall, Joseph, 256
Hell, 18, 50, 126, 131, 151, 189, 191, 228, 229, 237, 239, 248
Henrietta Maria, 6, 205
Henry IV, king of France, 195
Henry VIII, 32, 33, 34
heresy, 32, 74, 82, 261, 263, 265
heretics, 9, 13, 29, 142, 154, 261
  Marian, 37
Herring, Julines, 138
Hill, C., 218, 223, 234, 235, 252, 272
Hill, Thomas, 221, 230
Hoby, Margaret, 127–8
Holmes, C., 14
Hopkins, Matthew, 213
Houlbrooke, Ralph, 137
Homilies, Book of, 65, 68–9, 80, 85, 185–6
Hooper, John, 32, 36, 44, 45, 71, 72
Hopkins, Matthew, 14
household manuals, 116
Howard, Frances, 197
Hubberthorne, Richard, 271, 283, 284
humankind, 292
  alienation from God, 44
  nature after the fall, 45, 71–2, 79, 87, 114, 153, 154, 176, 186, 274
Hunne, Richard, 32
Hutchinson, Roger, 30, 35, 71

idolatry, 45, 50, 51, 52, 69, 180, 191, 204, 229
  self-idolatry, 198, 235
Independents, 251, 254, 260, 262
  diabolism of, 257
infanticide, 154, 167, 168
intercession, 60, 84, 91, 94
interiority, 24, 291, 292
Interregnum, 242, 265, 267
intolerance, 257
introspection, 107
  political, 221
  protective against the Devil, 86, 113, 114
inversion, 15, 28
  diabolic, 154, 243
  see also baptism

Jackson, Elizabeth, 104
James I, 5, 52, 109, 112, 185, 189, 190, 191, 193, 194, 197, 202, 212, 219
Jessey, Henry, 77
Jesuits, 38, 192, 199, 200, 203, 213, 219, 224, 225, 233
Jewel, John, 38, 44, 45, 48, 52, 55–6, 72
Jews, 9, 51, 52, 142, 154
Job, 30
Joscelin, Elizabeth, 113, 114–15, 116, 117, 120
Judaism, 29
Judas, 53
Judgement Day, 50, 72

Kiffin, William, 254
Kilby, Richard, 118
King, Henry, 70, 71, 73
kingship, divine, 176, 177, 185, 215, 237
Knox, John, 138

Lake, P., 28, 41, 59, 146, 252, 287
Lamb, John, 197
Lamont, William, 205
Latimer, Hugh, 30, 46, 76, 79, 83, 85, 87, 90
Laud, William, 6, 197, 210, 227, 228, 235
Laudianism, 197, 204, 208, 218, 259
  diabolism of, 214, 224, 229, 231, 233, 260, 262
Lawrence, Henry, 69, 73, 86
Leigh, Dorothy, 113–14, 116, 118, 120
Lever, Thomas, 35
Lilburne, John, 6, 204, 209–11
Link, L., 174
liturgy, 62–7, 253, 254
  reform of, 2
Lollardy, 29
London, 238–9
Lord's Prayer, 67, 74, 76, 78, 79, 82, 85
Lucifer, 30, 68, 69, 70, 185, 235, 247; *see also* Devil, parliament
Luther, Martin, 11
Lutheranism, 31
Luttmer, F., 19, 20–1, 100
Lyford, William, 283

MacDonald, M., 17
Macfarlane, A., 25
magic, 91
  disenchantment of Europe, 10
  Protestant rejection of, 10
Mainwaring, Roger, 198, 201, 212
Malcolm, J. L., 236
maleficium, 12, 14, 77
Man in the Moon, 243, 245
Manningham, 108, 110
Marprelate, Martin, 181–2
Marshall, Stephen, 218, 219
Marten, Anthony, 40
Marten, Henry, 243, 244
Martyr, Peter, 34, 35
martyrdom, 232–3, 241
Mary I, 42, 84
  persecution of Protestants under, 36–8, 178

Mary, Queen of Scots, 40, 186
Mass, 43, 62, 77
Mercurius Aulicus, 236
Mercurius Pragmaticus, 243
Mildmay, Grace, 109
Mildmay, Walter, 38
millenarianism, 28, 230, 234
Milton, John, 235
ministry, Protestant, 1, 3–4, 61, 95, 124, 177, 183, 269, 270
  anti-demonic role of, 96, 98–102, 105, 121, 136, 260
  diabolism of, 270
  marriage, 43
  mediation by, 2, 3, 65, 95
  networks, 98–100
  Quaker attacks on, 271, 272–3, 274, 275, 277, 279, 281
  wives of ministers, 100
miracle, 286
Mirk, John, 74
monarchy, magical, 16
monsters, 174
More, Thomas, 42
Morrill, J., 214, 246
Munday, Anthony, 39, 57, 58, 144, 156
murder, 4, 51, 121
  Devil in narratives of, 146–7
  familiar, 145
  narratives of, 144, 232
  premeditation, 145, 161
  violence in, not directly demonised, 162
  see also infanticide, Petty Treason, suicide, uxoricide
Muslims, 154
mystery plays, 74

narrativity, 26
Naylor, James, 275, 276–7
  temptation of, 276
Nedham, Marchemont, 242, 245, 267
Nero, 205, 207
New Model Army, 251
Newcome, Henry, 102
Newcomen, Matthew, 231, 233
newsbooks, 242, 246
nonconformists, 5, 177, 178, 179
Northbrooke, John, 56, 57, 80, 81, 204
Norwood, Richard, 18, 120, 122, 125, 126, 129, 135
Nowell, Alexander, 68, 71, 79

oath of allegiance, 193–5
Oldridge, D., 19, 20, 22–4, 129, 216
Origen, 9

othering, 154, 217, 251, 266
others, 17, 23, 292; *see also* witches

pamphlets, 142, 147
Parkhurst, John, 103
parliament, 176, 184, 187, 188, 190, 191, 192, 197, 198, 203, 204, 257, 276
  anti-demonic role of, 223–32
  House of Commons, 217
  House of Lords, 195, 214
  Long Parliament, 214, 226, 259
  Lucifer, parliament as, 236, 237, 238, 241, 242
  Nominated Assembly, 246
  potential for temptation of, 220
  Rump Parliament, 236, 245
  Short Parliament, 225
parliamentarians, 5, 213, 216, 217, 253
Parnell, James, 271, 275
Parris, Samuel, 20
pastoral culture, 260
patriarchy, 166
Peacock, Thomas, 98, 99, 101, 124
Peck, L. L., 176, 224
Pemble, William, 98, 99
penance, protective against the Devil, 87–90
Penry, John, 182
perception, human, 174
  diabolic agency of, 211, 212, 216, 217
  diabolic crime and, 150–1, 154, 171
  claims to a monopoly of insight into diabolic agency, 29, 49, 77, 189, 197, 202, 290
  protective against the Devil, 49, 51, 86
  spiritual blindness, 85, 266, 268, 274
  spiritual progress and, 250
  weakness of, 1, 67, 265
Perkins, William, 2, 39, 45, 47, 51, 53, 69, 72, 73, 76, 79, 80, 81, 86, 87, 97, 108, 135, 137, 165
  Cases of Conscience, 116, 117, 126
persecution, 54, 142, 231, 263
  experience of, 31
  identity and, 32
  persecutory society, 9, 12–13
Peter, Hugh, 244, 247
Petto, Samuel, 122
Petty Treason, 167
philosophes, 292
Pickering, Thomas, 45
Pierson, Thomas, 76
pluralism, 252
Pole, Reginald, 33, 34
polemic, 251

politics, 16
  consensus, 5, 16, 175, 198, 201, 252
  corruption, 224, 228
  demonism as means to engagement with, 218
  identification of diabolic subversion, contested, 188
  negotiation, discourses of, 252
  oppositional, 202
  resistance, 5–6, 202, 218, 234
  revisionist history, 16
  theocracy, 5
Ponet, John, 68, 70
Pope, 27, 32, 33, 34, 39, 42, 49, 50, 54, 55, 69, 177, 179, 186, 191, 193, 220, 224, 227, 259
Popish Plot, 292
popular culture, 75
possession, 3, 63, 102–5, 112, 269, 276
  debates with the Devil in cases of, 104–5
  physical locations of, 76, 126
  temptation as, 102, 104
Potts, Thomas, *The Wonderfvll discoveries of Witches in the Countie of Lancaster*, 148
Powell, Vavasor, 136
prayer, as weapon against the Devil, 3, 90–1, 92
prayer book, 60, 62–7
  first Edwardian, 63, 64, 66
  second Edwardian, 2, 63, 64, 66
preaching, 178, 220, 259
predestination, 116
Prentice, Joan, 148
Presbyterianism, 178–80, 255
  diabolism of, 180–1, 183, 251, 262
Presbyterians, 180, 239, 251, 260
Preston, John, 98, 99
priesthood, Catholic, 1, 60, 85, 102
  clerical celibacy, 48
  diabolism of, 46–7, 48
propaganda, 214, 217
prostitutes, 163
protestation, 253
Protestantism, 17, 27, 38, 40, 41, 56, 75–7, 84–5, 174, 290
providence, 38, 75, 112, 121, 123, 128, 132, 134, 135, 140, 165, 173, 205, 213, 215, 225, 232, 245
Prynne, William, 6, 204–8, 209, 212, 232, 237, 239, 262
  Histrio-mastix, 204–8
pulp press, 142, 144–5, 215, 217, 223
Puritanism, 12, 20, 103, 107, 184, 204, 240, 243, 274
  'darkness of', 17, 20, 21, 107, 110, 135, 272
  and the family, 18, 116
Puritans, 5, 25, 184, 186, 204, 209, 239, 251
  disputes between, 252
Pym, John, 201, 216, 226, 238

Quakers, 102, 129, 246, 251, 252, 265, 270
  books, 282, 283
  demonism, 270
  diabolism of, 278
  ecstastic symptoms, 276, 278
  false doctrine, 284
  inner light, 269, 272, 274, 279
  perfectibility, 271, 273
  polemic, 275
  popular responses to, 283
  witchcraft, 282–4

radicalism, 246
  attraction of, 258
Raleigh, Walter, 189
Rankins, William, 58
Ranters, 133–5, 246, 251, 265, 266, 267–9
rationalism, 287, 290, 292, 293
Raymond of Capua, 83
Reay, B., 270, 272
rebellion, 69, 175, 212, 218, 236, 241, 252; *see also* Bible
recusants, 5, 38, 178, 191–2, 193, 194, 195, 199, 200
reform,
  anti-demonic role, 250
  diabolic threat to, 217, 262
Reformation, 27, 57, 62, 74
regicide, 177, 192, 241–2, 244
Renaissance, 291
repentance, 246
reprobation, 20–1, 51, 84, 87, 88, 125, 131, 135, 137, 139, 165, 222, 255, 256, 262, 280, 292
resistance theory, 191
Restoration, 246
revelation, 267, 273
Revelation, Book of, 29, 49, 52, 53, 55
  dragon of, 50
Reynolds, Edward, 220
Reynolds, John, *Triumphs of Gods revenge against . . . murther*, 151, 155, 161, 168
Ridley, Nicholas, 32, 37
Ridolfi plot, 186, 189
Roberts, Henry, 39, 56
Rogationtide, 2, 74, 84
Rogers, John, 42, 99, 126
Rogers, Richard, 135
Rothwell, Richard, 105
Roundheads, 126
  diabolism of, 214

Rous, John, 203
Royalists, 5, 217, 218, 229
Rowley, William, 170
Russell, C., 214, 216
Russell, J. B., 8, 10, 84, 286, 292, 293

sabbat, 12, 13, 41, 43, 206
sabbath-breaking, 163
sacraments, 62, 88, 178, 192
saints, 43, 51, 62, 74, 94, 95
  lives of, 64, 73, 83
Sandys, Edwin, 38, 44, 65, 90, 186
Sarum Missal, 2, 62–4, 66
Satan, *see* Devil
satire, 223, 224
Savage, Thomas, 163
Sawyer, Elizabeth, 150
scapegoating, 28
Scientific Revolution, 10
Scotland, 224
Scudder, Henry, 108, 132
Seaver, P., 17, 288
sectarians, 214, 265
Sedgwick, William, 219
self-speaking, 291
senses, physical, 44, 86
  inability to perceive the Devil, 1, 44, 56, 86
separatism, 183, 250
sequestration, 245
  diabolism of, 238
sermons, 3, 67, 68–9, 108, 111, 112, 135, 185
Seymour, Edward, duke of Somerset, 35
Seymour, Thomas, 35
Sharpe, J. A., 14, 143, 148
signing of the cross, 60, 64
sin, 4, 69, 78, 86, 88, 107, 114, 116, 120, 145, 147, 270, 271, 274, 275, 278, 291
  crime as, 151
  cumulative, 149, 153, 159
  diabolic amplification of, 155, 161, 164
sola scriptura, 28, 259
Sommerville, J., 176, 211
soteriology, 116, 119, 126, 143; *see also* temptation
spiritual insight, 44, 52, 110, 114, 151, 210
Sports, Book of, 184, 204
Stachniewski, J., 17, 18, 84, 107, 116, 123, 134, 135, 136, 137, 139, 288
Star Chamber, 6, 182, 205, 207–8
Staunton, Edmund, 99, 101, 124
Stilman, John, 32
Stokesley, John, 33
Stubbes, Katherine, 131, 138
Stubbes, Philip, 57, 58, 131
suicide, 18, 168, 169, 278
Sutcliffe, Alice, 109
Swan, John, 103, 104
synagogue of Satan, 4, 29, 43, 50, 54, 56, 61, 177, 178, 179, 190, 191, 192, 204, 232, 271

Taylor, John, 156, 169
temptation,
  adolescent, 119–20, 147
  body politic, of the, 176, 186, 200, 205, 211, 217, 239, 259, 260
  catalyst to political subversion, 176
  Catholic and Protestant differences on, 90, 94
  childhood, 118–19
  diabolic, 2, 19, 61, 62, 66, 69, 85, 92, 170, 231, 233
  edification from, 110, 136
  enveloping power of, 166
  expectation of, 110, 116
  experience of, 118–35, 270, 272
  experienced as dialogue, 3, 128
  human corruption and, 3
  human mediators of, 157–9
  identification with the experience of, 26, 254
  internal, 23, 28, 73–4, 82–3, 87, 107, 290, 291, 293
  lack of temptation as a sign of reprobation, 87
  long-term, 120
  psychological explanation of, 129
  spiritual progression and, 131
  symptoms of, 86, 120–5, 164, 277
  soteriology and, 3, 85, 110, 114, 131, 138
  test of faith, 3, 61, 85, 97
  vulnerability to amongst the godly, 258, 261, 264, 266
  witchcraft narratives in, 149
  see also Charles I
theatre,
  Catholicism linked to, 39
  diabolism of, 4, 39, 56, 80–1, 204, 206, 212, 293
  representations of the Devil on stage, 170
theocracy, 198, 199, 201, 212, 217, 224, 235, 243
theodicy, 30, 68, 292
Thomas, K., 14, 17, 84, 286, 292
Thomason, George, 234
tobacco, 77, 81
Toldervy, John, 278
toleration, 177, 178, 199, 204, 252, 257
  anti-demonic role of, 263
  diabolism of, 258, 260
treason, diabolism of, 184, 187

Trevor-Roper, H., 218, 223
Tunstall, Cuthbert, 33, 34
Turner, William, 34, 48, 178
two churches, 29, 42
Tyndale, William, 29, 31, 32, 42, 46, 49, 54, 70, 71, 78
An Exposition of the Fyrste Epistle of Seynte Jhon, 32
An Exposition uppon the V. VI. VII. Chapters of Mathew, 32
A pathway into the Holy Scripture, 29, 30, 32
The Practyse of Prelates, 32

Underdown, D., 28, 197, 201, 204, 231, 242, 245, 266
uxoricide, 167

Villiers, George, duke of Buckingham, 112, 197, 202, 235
violence, diabolism of, 231–2
Virgin Mary, 48, 62, 95

Walker, Mary, 119
Wallington, Nehemiah, 119, 120, 125, 127
Ward, Samuel, 81
Watson, Thomas, 84
Webster, T., 98
Wentworth, Peter, 188–9, 205
Wentworth, Thomas, earl of Strafford, 227, 228, 229, 235
Wesley, John, 10
Westminster Assembly, 66, 251, 256
Wheathill, Anne, 109, 122
Whitgift, John, 103, 180, 181
Wigglesworth Michael, 20
Wight, Sarah, 120, 123, 137
Wilcox, Thomas, 179
Wilkinson, Elizabeth, 99, 108, 118, 122, 124, 131, 135, 136–7
Wilkinson, Henry, 99–100
Willard, Samuel, 20
Willis, D., 14
witchcraft, 18–20, 29, 74, 75, 120, 126, 173, 213, 246, 252, 286, 292
importance of in narratives of physical temptation, 173
marginalisation within history, 17
narratives of, 143–4, 147–50
politics and, 175
statutes, 14
see also demons, Devil, *maleficium*, temptation, Quakers
witches, 12–17, 28, 77, 126, 142, 198, 245, 269, 286
malevolent nurture, 14
mark, 14
other, witches as the, 143
pact, 13, 143, 148
swimming test, 14
women, susceptibility to temptation, 159
wonders, 286
Worden, B., 17

Cambridge Studies in Early Modern British History

Titles in the Series

*The Common Peace: Participation and the Criminal Law in Seventeenth-Century England**
CYNTHIA B. HERRUP

*Politics, Society and Civil War in Warwickshire, 1620–1660**
ANN HUGHES

*London Crowds in the Reign of Charles II: Propaganda and Politics from the Restoration to the Exclusion Crisis**
TIM HARRIS

*Criticism and Compliment: The Politics of Literature in the England of Charles I**
KEVIN SHARPE

*Central Government and the Localities: Hampshire, 1649–1689**
ANDREW COLEBY

*John Skelton and the Politics of the 1520s**
GREG WALKER

*Algernon Sidney and the English Republic, 1623–1677**
JONATHAN SCOTT

*Thomas Starkey and the Commonweal: Humanist Politics and Religion in the Reign of Henry VIII**
THOMAS F. MAYER

*The Blind Devotion of the People: Popular Religion and the English Reformation**
ROBERT WHITING

*The Cavalier Parliament and the Reconstruction of the Old Regime, 1661–1667**
PAUL SEAWARD

*The Blessed Revolution: English Politics and the Coming of War, 1621–1624**
THOMAS COGSWELL

*Charles I and the Road to Personal Rule**
L. J. REEVE

*George Lawson's 'Politica' and the English Revolution**
CONAL CONDREN

Puritans and Roundheads: The Harleys of Brampton Bryan and the Outbreak of the Civil War
JACQUELINE EALES

*An Uncounselled King: Charles I and the Scottish Troubles, 1637–1641**
PETER DONALD

*Cheap Print and Popular Piety, 1550–1640**
TESSA WATT

*The Pursuit of Stability: Social Relations in Elizabethan London**
IAN W. ARCHER

Prosecution and Punishment: Petty Crime and the Law in London and Rural Middlesex, c. 1660–1725
ROBERT B. SHOEMAKER

*Algernon Sidney and the Restoration Crisis, 1677–1683**
JONATHAN SCOTT

*Exile and Kingdom: History and Apocalypse in the Puritan Migration to America**
AVIHU ZAKAI

The Pillars of Priestcraft Shaken: The Church of England and its Enemies, 1660–1730
J. A. I. CHAMPION

Steward, Lords and People: The Estate Steward and his World in Later Stuart England
D. R. HAINSWORTH

Civil War and Restoration in the Three Stuart Kingdoms: The Career of Randal MacDonnell, Marquis of Antrim, 1609–1683
JANE H. OHLMEYER

*The Family of Love in English Society, 1550–1630**
CHRISTOPHER W. MARSH

*The Bishops' Wars: Charles I's Campaigns against Scotland, 1638–1640**
MARK FISSEL

*John Locke: Resistance, Religion and Responsibility**
JOHN MARSHALL

*Constitutional Royalism and the Search for Settlement, c. 1640–1649**
DAVID L. SMITH

*Intelligence and Espionage in the Reign of Charles II, 1660–1685**
ALAN MARSHALL

*The Chief Governors: The Rise and Fall of Reform Government in Tudor Ireland, 1536–1588**
CIARAN BRADY

*Politics and Opinion in Crisis, 1678–1681**
MARK KNIGHTS

*Catholic and Reformed: The Roman and Protestant Churches in English Protestant Thought, 1600–1640**
ANTHONY MILTON

*Sir Matthew Hale, 1609–1676: Law, Religion and Natural Philosophy**
ALAN CROMARTIE

*Henry Parker and the English Civil War: The Political Thought of the Public's 'Privado'**
MICHAEL MENDLE

*Protestantism and Patriotism: Ideologies and the Making of English Foreign Policy, 1650–1668**
STEVEN C. A. PINCUS

*Gender in Mystical and Occult Thought: Behmenism and its Development in England**
B. J. GIBBONS

*William III and the Godly Revolution**
TONY CLAYDON

*Law-Making and Society in Late Elizabethan England: The Parliament of England, 1584–1601**
DAVID DEAN

*The House of Lords in the Reign of Charles II**
ANDREW SWATLAND

Conversion, Politics and Religion in England, 1580–1625
MICHAEL C. QUESTIER

*Politics, Religion and the British Revolutions: The Mind of Samuel Rutherford**
JOHN COFFEY

*King James VI and I and the Reunion of Christendom**
W. B. PATTERSON

*The English Reformation and the Laity: Gloucestershire, 1540–1580**
CAROLINE LITZENBERGER

*Godly Clergy in Early Stuart England: The Caroline Puritan Movement, c. 1620–1643**
TOM WEBSTER

*Prayer Book and People in Elizabethan and Early Stuart England**
JUDITH MALTBY

*Sermons at Court, 1559–1629: Religion and Politics in Elizabethan and Jacobean Preaching**
PETER E. MCCULLOUGH

*Dismembering the Body Politic: Partisan Politics in England's Towns, 1650–1730**
PAUL D. HALLIDAY

Women Waging Law in Elizabethan England
TIMOTHY STRETTON

*The Early Elizabethan Polity: William Cecil and the British Succession Crisis, 1558–1569**
STEPHEN ALFORD

The Polarisation of Elizabethan Politics: The Political Career of Robert Devereux, 2nd Earl of Essex
PAUL J. HAMMER

The Politics of Social Conflict: The Peak Country, 1520–1770
ANDY WOOD

*Crime and Mentalities in Early Modern England**
MALCOLM GASKILL

*The Church in an Age of Danger: Parsons and Parishioners, 1660–1740**
DONALD A. SPAETH

*Reading History in Early Modern England**
D. R. WOOLF

The Politics of Court Scandal in Early Modern England: News Culture and the Overbury Affair, 1603–1660
ALASTAIR BELLANY

The Politics of Religion in the Age of Mary, Queen of Scots: The Earl of Argyll and the Struggle for Britain and Ireland
JANE E. A. DAWSON

Treason and the State: Law, Politics and Ideology in the English Civil War
D. ALAN ORR

Pamphlets and Pamphleteering in Early Modern Britain
JOAD RAYMOND

Preaching during the English Reformation
SUSAN WABUDA

Patterns of Piety: Women, Gender and Religion in Late Medieval and Reformation England
CHRISTINE PETERS

*Popular Politics and the English Reformation**
ETHAN H. SHAGAN

Mercy and Authority in the Tudor State
K. J. KESSELRING

Unquiet Lives: Marriage and Marriage Breakdown in England, 1660–1800
JOANNE BAILEY

The Gospel and Henry VIII: Evangelicals in the Early English Reformation
ALEC RYRIE

Images and Cultures of Law in Early Modern England: Justice and Political Power, 1558–1660
PAUL RAFFIELD

Sir Matthew Hale, 1609–1676: Law, Religion and Natural Philosophy
ALAN CROMARTIE

Crime, Gender and Social Order in Early Modern England
GARTHINE WALKER

William III and the Godly Revolution
TONY CLAYDON

Print Culture and the Early Quakers
KATE PETERS

Ireland and the English Reformation: State Reform and Clerical Resistance in the Diocese of Dublin, 1534–1590
JAMES MURRAY

London and the Restoration, 1659–1683
GARY S. DE KREY

Defining the Jacobean Church: The Politics of Religious Controversy, 1603–1625
CHARLES W. A. PRIOR

Queenship and Political Discourse in the Elizabethan Realms
NATALIE MEARS

John Locke, Toleration and Early Enlightenment Culture
JOHN MARSHALL

**Also published as a paperback*

Lightning Source UK Ltd.
Milton Keynes UK

178423UK00001B/110/P

9 780521 120548